Books in the Series

Redefining European Economic Integration
Dariusz Adamski

Human Rights in the Council of Europe and the European Union
Steven Greer, Janneke Gerards and Rosie Slowe

Core Socio-Economic Rights and the European Court of Human Rights
Ingrid Leijten

Free Trade, Fair Trade, and Green Trade in and with the EU: Process-based Measures within the EU Legal Order
Laurens Ankersmit

New Labour Laws in Old Member States
Rebecca Zahn

The Governance of EU Fundamental Rights
Mark Dawson

The International Responsibility of the European Union: From Competence to Normative Control
Andrés Delgado Casteleiro

Frontex and Non-Refoulement: The International Responsibility of the EU
Roberta Mungianu

Gendering European Working Time Regimes: The Working Time Directive and the Case of Poland
Ania Zbyszewska

EU Renewable Electricity Law and Policy: From National Targets to a Common Market
Tim Maxian Rusche

European Constitutionalism
Kaarlo Tuori

Brokering Europe: Euro-Lawyers and the Making of a Transnational Polity
Antoine Vauchez

Services Liberalization in the EU and the WTO: Concepts, Standards and Regulatory Approaches
Marcus Klamert

Referendums and the European Union: A Comparative Enquiry
Fernando Mendez, Mario Mendez and Vasiliki Triga

The Allocation of Regulatory Competence in the EU Emissions Trading Scheme
Jospehine Van Zeben

The Eurozone Crisis
Kaarlo Tuori and Klaus Tuori

International Trade Disputes and EU Liability
Anne Thies

The Limits of Legal Reasoning and the European Court of Justice
Gerard Conway

New Governance and the Transformation of European Law: Coordinating EU Social Law and Policy
Mark Dawson

The Lisbon Treaty: A Legal and Political Analysis
Jean-Claude Piris

The European Union's Fight Against Corruption: The Evolving Policy Towards Member States and Candidate Countries
Patrycja Szarek-Mason

The Ethos of Europe: Values, Law and Justice in the EU
Andrew Williams

State and Market in European Union Law: The Public and Private Spheres of the Internal Market before the EU Courts
Wolf Sauter and Harm Schepel

The European Civil Code: The Way Forward
Hugh Collins

Ethical Dimensions of the Foreign Policy of the European Union: A Legal Appraisal
Urfan Khaliq

Implementing EU Pollution Control: Law and Integration
Bettina Lange

European Broadcasting Law and Policy
Jackie Harrison and Lorna Woods

The Transformation of Citizenship in the European Union: Electoral Rights and the Restructuring of Political Space
Jo Shaw

The Constitution for Europe: A Legal Analysis
Jean-Claude Piris

The European Convention on Human Rights: Achievements, Problems and Prospects
Steven Greer

Social Rights and Market Freedom in the European Constitution: A Labour Law Perspective
Stefano Giubboni

EU Enlargement and the Constitutions of Central and Eastern Europe
Anneli Albi

Redefining European Economic Integration

Dariusz Adamski
University of Wrocław

CAMBRIDGE
UNIVERSITY PRESS

CAMBRIDGE
UNIVERSITY PRESS

University Printing House, Cambridge CB2 8BS, United Kingdom

One Liberty Plaza, 20th Floor, New York, NY 10006, USA

477 Williamstown Road, Port Melbourne, VIC 3207, Australia

314–321, 3rd Floor, Plot 3, Splendor Forum, Jasola District Centre, New Delhi – 110025, India

79 Anson Road, #06-04/06, Singapore 079906

Cambridge University Press is part of the University of Cambridge.

It furthers the University's mission by disseminating knowledge in the pursuit of education, learning, and research at the highest international levels of excellence.

www.cambridge.org
Information on this title: www.cambridge.org/9781108421423
DOI: 10.1017/9781108368643

First published 2018

Printed in the United Kingdom by Clays, St Ives plc

A catalogue record for this publication is available from the British Library.

Library of Congress Cataloging-in-Publication Data
Names: Adamski, Dariusz, 1975– author.
Title: Redefining European economic integration / Dariusz Adamski, University of Wrocław.
Description: Cambridge, United Kingdom; New York, NY: Cambridge University Press, 2018. | Series: Cambridge studies in european law and policy | Includes bibliographical references and index.
Identifiers: LCCN 2017057580 | ISBN 9781108421423 (hardback)
Subjects: LCSH: European Union. | European Union countries – Economic policy. | European Union countries – Politics and government.
Classification: LCC HC241.A33 2018 | DDC 337.1/42–dc23
LC record available at https://lccn.loc.gov/2017057580

ISBN 978-1-108-42142-3 Hardback

Redefining European Economic Integration

European economic integration has relied on policies intended to make the European Union strong and resilient economically, socially and politically. The Eurozone crisis and Brexit have demonstrated, however, how fragile this hope was and how contested reforms to the major European economic policies have become. Dariusz Adamski explains the evolution of these policies – from the Economic and Monetary Union to the internal market, international trade and the EU's climate policy as well as its redistributive policies – and demonstrates how this evolution has made European economic integration increasingly frail. He shows how erroneous economic and political assumptions regarding the direction of the European integration project have interplayed with the EU's constitutional context. Arguing that flaws in individual policies contributing to European economic integration can be remedied in compliance with the existing constitutional setup, he explains why such solutions would be economically beneficial and politically feasible.

Dariusz Adamski is Associate Professor of Law, Vice-Dean for Research and International Cooperation and Head of the Centre for European Economic Law and Governance at the Faculty of Law, Administration and Economics, University of Wrocław, Poland. He is also a Research Associate at the European Research Centre for Economic and Financial Governance in Rotterdam and a member of the leading Polish economic think-tank Civic Development Forum (Forum Obywatelskiego Rozwoju).

Cambridge Studies in European Law and Policy

This series aims to produce original works which contain a critical analysis of the state of the law in particular areas of European law and set out different perspectives and suggestions for its future development. It also aims to encourage a range of work on law, legal institutions and legal phenomena in Europe, including 'law in context' approaches. The titles in the series will be of interest to academics; policy makers; policy formers who are interested in European legal, commercial and political affairs; practising lawyers, including the judiciary; and advanced law students and researchers.

Contents

Series Editors' Preface

At the core of our preoccupations, as Series Editors of Cambridge Studies in European Law and Policy, is the role that law has played, is playing and will play in the context of the process of economic integration that has underpinned the European Union since its inception (in the form of the European Communities) in the 1950s. Historically, engineering instruments of economic integration in order to foster growth (and to indirectly promote additional political elements of integration) has been at the heart of the success of the European integration project. Without that sense of the cake getting bigger across the board as a result of removing the barriers to internal trade, whilst promoting trade with the rest of the world as an increasingly significant global player, the European Union has struggled to maintain the consent of citizens for its incursions into the field of national regulatory and economic sovereignty.

In this book, Dariusz Adamski makes a reappraisal of where we are now and where we should be going, writing in a manner that explicitly attempts to bridge the gap that sometimes exists between what academics write and what policy makers and other stakeholders in the policy making process such as 'think-tankers' will read. His writing is informed by a thorough understanding of both the law and economics of the challenges that stand before us: relating to the single currency and the single market, and relating to redistribution in the context of 'crisis'. The starting point is re-narrating the crisis of the Eurozone and attempts to fix it, but the book goes beyond this, highlighting that fixing problems of the Eurozone will not alone relieve Europe's ongoing economic (and, of course, social) problems. The author points out the tendency of policy makers to proceed by stealth rather than transparently, and emphasises that this does not make sense in the long term, when there needs to be a thorough rethinking of the values and interests that underpin the economic and regulatory choices we make as societies, whilst ensuring that citizens more generally have a say in how these choices are made.

As the reality of the UK's departure from the European Union comes ever closer, the opportunity for the EU27 to rethink in constructive ways their 'living and growing together' becomes clearer. Whether policy makers will decide to grasp the hard choices and make European economic integration work for the long term is not assured, but they could do worse than start by reading this lucid and strongly argued book.

Jo Shaw
Laurence Gormley

Acknowledgments

Four years ago, at the outset of the project leading me up to this point, the goal of ever completing a book on how to fix European economic integration was as elusive as its main idea. I was also unsure whether, even if I were able to accomplish this first stage, anyone would publish this book, and whether anyone would read it. After all, for decades the book's main question had been left for politicians to answer. The thought that scholars should make forays into their domain, instead of pursuing their standard academic debates, could seem both bizarre and practically futile.

But now, in autumn 2017, when the last words of this book are being put down, I am more confident than ever that the European project desperately needs serious readjustments, if it is to avoid future crises endangering its very foundations. The vast body of diligent scientific work in various fields has laid stable foundations for our collective wisdom on what has gone wrong in the past decades of this extraordinary integrationist experiment. This foundation is incomplete, no doubt about it, but much more reliable and more telling than is often admitted. Genuine European integration meeting needs and expectations of Europeans is possible, if only politicians are not allowed to ignore this collective wisdom.

I would never have been able to put together the multitude of puzzles comprising my contribution to it without the extraordinary people I have met. Some of them taught me how to write and how to think creatively. They taught me that science without passion is superfluous and unconvincing. In this respect I am particularly grateful to Charlie Nesson from Harvard, to my old friend from the New York Law School,

Mike Botein, who regrettably passed away last year, and to Wolfgang Kilian from Hannover University. Editors of leading European law journals – especially Stefaan Van den Bogaert and Alison McDonnell (*Common Market Law Review*) as well as Agustín Menéndez (*European Law Journal*) – have also been extremely encouraging for my thinking about the topic of this book. Several of its arguments were previously published in their journals.

Contrary to my original concerns, the vast majority of those who have become familiar with my research have found its constant zigzagging through various fields and the tendency to go against prevailing conventions to be an asset. It has helped build various productive ties; those with Fabian Amtenbrink and René Repasi from Rotterdam University have become particularly strong and friendly.

My acquaintance with Leszek Balcerowicz, who is one of the most extraordinary people I have ever met, the best known contemporary Polish economist and the architect of the Polish transformation in 1989, has also been extremely stimulating. He taught me that in politics – the area on which the future of European integration critically hinges – far-sightedness based on scientific excellence, devotion to the common good and personal integrity are not as infrequent as I would otherwise think. He may disagree with some of this book's arguments on their merits, but his scientific curiosity and excellence have profoundly determined my approach.

I am also grateful to Cambridge University Press for its receptive acceptance of the book proposal. Fortunately, the fact that it is not on law and policy only was no impediment for the series editors and reviewers. The Polish National Science Centre, which supported my research with two grants (UMO-2013/09/B/HS5/04179 and UMO-2015/18/M/HS5/00252), was also helpful in pushing me through the moments of creative despair.

My editors at Cambridge University Press, Kim Hughes, Sharon McCann and Gemma Smith, have helped bring the project to this point. Katarzyna Parchimowicz provided diligent research assistance and Daniel Ross chiselled my English. Dima Zverev kindly agreed to put his beautiful and metaphoric picture on the cover of the book. Witek Wójtowicz and Yulia Ladyzhenko made it happen. I appreciate it all.

The idea of writing this book was born soon before my youngest daughter – Mila – joined us. So she does not know her father as anyone other than a routinely abstracted and intellectually exhausted person. I am extremely happy she will learn another me now. And more than anything, I am grateful to my wife, Agnieszka, and our two older daughters, Iga and Pola, for their love, smiles and patience throughout these years.

Abbreviations

ABSPP	Asset-Backed Securities Purchase Programme
APP	Asset Purchase Programme
CAC	Collective Action Clause
CAP	Common Agricultural Policy
CBPP	Covered Bonds Purchase Programme
CEPS	Centre for European Policy Studies
CJEU	Court of Justice of the European Union
CMU	Capital Markets Union
CSPP	Corporate Sector Purchase Programme
DBP	Draft Budgetary Plan
DIF	Deposit Insurance Fund
EBA	'Everything But Arms' trade preferences scheme
EC	European Commission
ECB	European Central Bank
EEC	European Economic Community
EFSF	European Financial Stability Facility
EFSI	European Fund for Strategic Investments
EFSM	European Financial Stabilisation Mechanism
EFTA	European Free Trade Association
ELA	Emergency Liquidity Assistance
EMFF	European Maritime and Fisheries Fund
EMU	European and Monetary Union
ERDF	European Regional Development Fund
ESCB	European System of Central Banks
ESF	European Social Fund
ESIFs	European Structural and Investment Funds
ESM	European Stability Mechanism

ETS	Emissions Trading System
EUBS	European Unemployment Benefits Scheme
FDIC	Federal Deposit Insurance Corporation
GATT	General Agreement on Tariffs and Trade
GDP	Gross Domestic Product
GHG	Greenhouse Gases
GNP	Gross National Product
GSP	Generalised Scheme of Preferences
GSP+	Generalised Scheme of Preferences, special incentive arrangement for sustainable development and good governance
HICP	Harmonised Index of Consumer Prices
ICTs	Information and Communication Technologies
IMF	International Monetary Fund
ISDS	Investor-State Dispute Settlement
LoLR	Lender of Last Resort
LTROs	Long-Term Refinancing Operations
MoU	Memorandum of Understanding
NCB	National Central Bank
NEET	Not in Education, Employment or Training
NGOs	Non-Governmental Organisations
OECD	Organisation for Economic Cooperation and Development
OMC	Open Method of Coordination
OMT	Outright Monetary Transactions
PSI	Private-Sector Involvement
PSPP	Public Sector Purchase Programme
R&D	Research and Development
SGP	Stability and Growth Pact
SMEs	Small and Medium Enterprises
SMP	Securities Markets Programme
SRF	Single Resolution Fund
SRM	Single Resolution Mechanism
TARGET	Trans-European Automated Real-time Gross Settlement Express Transfer
TEC	Treaty establishing the European Community
TEU	Treaty on European Union
TFEU	Treaty on the Functioning of the European Union
TFGR	Task Force for Greece
TLTROs	Targeted Long-Term Refinancing Operations

TPP	Trans-Pacific Partnership
TTIP	Transatlantic Trade and Investment Partnership
VAT	Value Added Tax
VLTROs	Very Long-Term Refinancing Operations
WEF	World Economic Forum
WTO	World Trade Organization

Table of Treaties, Instruments and Legislation

Agreement on the Transfer and Mutualisation of Contributions to the Single Resolution Fund, available at http://register.consilium.europa.eu/doc/srv?l=EN&f=ST%208457%202014%20INIT.

Charter of Fundamental Rights of the European Union.

Commission Decision of 30.8.2016 on state aid SA.38373 (2014/C) (ex 2014/NN) (ex 2014/CP) implemented by Ireland to Apple, C(2016) 5605.

Commission Regulation 176/2014 of 25 February 2014 amending Regulation 1031/2010 in particular to determine the volumes of greenhouse gas emission allowances to be auctioned in 2013–2020, OJ 2014 No. L 56, 26 February 2014, pp. 11–13.

Commission Regulation 651/2014 of 17 June 2014 declaring certain categories of aid compatible with the internal market in application of Articles 107 and 108 of the Treaty, OJ 2014 No. L 187, 26 June 2014, pp. 1–78.

Council Decision 2003/89/EC of 21 January 2003 on the existence of an excessive deficit in Germany – Application of Article 104(6) of the Treaty establishing the European Community, OJ No. L 34, 11 February 2003, pp. 16–17.

Council Directive 2006/112/EC of 28 November 2006 on the common system of value added tax, OJ 2006 No. L 347, 11 December 2006, pp. 1–118.

Council Directive 2011/85/EU of 8 November 2011 on requirements for budgetary frameworks of the Member States, OJ 2011 No. L 306, 23 November 2011, pp. 41–47.

Council Recommendation of 12 February 2001 with a view to ending the inconsistency with the broad guidelines of the economic policies in Ireland, OJ 2001 No. L 69, 10 March 2001, pp. 22–23.

Council Recommendation of 22 April 2013 on establishing a Youth Guarantee OJ 2013 No. C 120, 26 April 2013, pp. 1–6.

Council Recommendation of 12 July 2016 on the 2016 National Reform Programme of Poland and delivering a Council opinion on the 2016 Convergence Programme of Poland (2016/C 299/04).

Council Regulation 407/2010 of 11 May 2010 establishing a European financial stabilisation mechanism, OJ 2010 No. L 118, 12 May 2010, pp. 1–4.

Council Regulation 1055/2005 of 27 June 2005 amending Regulation 1466/97 on the strengthening of the surveillance of budgetary positions and the surveillance and coordination of economic policies, OJ 2005 No. L 174, 7 July 2005, pp. 1–4.

Council Regulation 1056/2005 of 27 June 2005 amending Regulation 1467/97 on speeding up and clarifying the implementation of the excessive deficit procedure, OJ 2005 No. L 174, 7 July 2005, pp. 5–9.

Council Regulation 1225/2009 of 30 November 2009 on protection against dumped imports from countries not members of the European Community, OJ 2009 No. L 343, 22 December 2009, pp. 51–73.

Council Regulation 1177/2011 of 8 November 2011 amending Regulation 1467/97 on speeding up and clarifying the implementation of the excessive deficit procedure, OJ 2011 No. L 306, 23 November 2011, pp. 33–40.

Council Regulation 1024/2013 of 15 October 2013 conferring specific tasks on the European Central Bank concerning policies relating to the prudential supervision of credit institutions, OJ 2013 No. L 287, 29 October 2013, pp. 63–89.

Decision 406/2009/EC of the European Parliament and of the Council of 23 April 2009 on the effort of Member States to reduce their greenhouse gas emissions to meet the Community's greenhouse gas emission reduction commitments up to 2020, OJ 2009 No. L 140, 5 June 2009, pp. 136–148.

Decision 2015/300 of the European Central Bank of 10 February 2015 on the eligibility of marketable debt instruments issued or fully guaranteed by the Hellenic Republic (ECB/2015/6), OJ 2015 No. L 53, 25 February 2015, pp. 29–30.

Decision 2015/774 of the ECB of 4 March 2015 on a secondary markets public-sector asset purchase programme (ECB/2015/10), OJ 2015 No. L 121, 14 May 2015, pp. 20–24.

Decision 2017/899 of the European Parliament and of the Council of 17 May 2017 on the use of the 470–790 MHz frequency band in the Union, OJ 2017 No. L 138, 25 May 2017, pp. 131–137.

Directive 96/71/EC of the European Parliament and of the Council of 16 December 1996 concerning the posting of workers in the framework of the provision of services, OJ 1997 No. L 18, 21 January 1997, pp. 1-6.

Directive 98/48/EC of the European Parliament and of the Council of 20 July 1998 amending Directive 98/34/EC laying down a procedure for the provision of information in the field of technical standards and regulations, OJ 1998 No. L 217, 5 August 1998, pp. 18–26.

Directive 2000/31/EC of the European Parliament and of the Council of 8 June 2000 on certain legal aspects of information society services, in particular electronic commerce, in the Internal Market, OJ 2000 No. L 178, 17 July 2000, pp. 1–16.

Directive 2003/30/EC of the European Parliament and of the Council of 8 May 2003 on the promotion of the use of biofuels or other renewable fuels for transport, OJ 2003 No. L 123, 17 May 2003, pp. 42–46.

Directive 2003/87/EC of the European Parliament and of the Council of 13 October 2003 establishing a scheme for greenhouse gas emission allowance trading within the Community and amending Council Directive 96/61/EC, OJ 2003 No. L 275, 25 October 2003, pp. 32–46.

Directive 2006/123/EC of the European Parliament and of the Council of 12 December 2006 on services in the internal market, OJ 2006 No. L 376, 27 December 2006, pp. 36–68.

Directive 2009/28/EC of the European Parliament and of the Council of 23 April 2009 on the promotion of the use of energy from renewable sources and amending and subsequently repealing Directives 2001/77/EC and 2003/30/EC, OJ 2009 No. L 140, 5 June 2009, pp. 16–62.

Directive 2010/18 implementing the revised Framework Agreement on parental leave concluded by BUSINESSEUROPE, UEAPME, CEEP and ETUC and repealing Directive 96/34, OJ 2010 No. L 68, 18 March 2010, pp. 13–20.

Directive 2011/24/EU of the European Parliament and of the Council of 9 March 2011 on the application of patients' rights in cross-border healthcare, OJ 2011 No. L 88, 4 April 2011, pp. 45–65.

Directive 2012/27/EU of the European Parliament and of the Council of 25 October 2012 on energy efficiency, amending Directives 2009/125/EC and 2010/30/EU and repealing Directives 2004/8/EC and 2006/32/EC, OJ 2012 No. L 315, 14 November 2012, pp. 1–56.

Directive 2014/26/EU of the European Parliament and of the Council of 26 February 2014 on collective management of copyright and related rights and multi-territorial licensing of rights in musical works for online use in the internal market, OJ 2014 No. L 84, 20 March 2014, pp. 72–98.

Directive 2014/59/EU of the European Parliament and of the Council of 15 May 2014 establishing a framework for the recovery and resolution of credit institutions and investment firms and amending Council Directive 82/891/EEC, and Directives 2001/24/EC, 2002/47/EC, 2004/25/EC, 2005/56/EC, 2007/36/EC, 2011/35/EU, 2012/30/EU and 2013/36/EU, and Regulations 1093/2010 and 648/2012, of the European Parliament and of the Council, OJ 2014 No. L 173, 12 June 2014, pp. 190–348.

Directive 2014/61/EU of the European Parliament and of the Council of 15 May 2014 on measures to reduce the cost of deploying high-speed electronic communications networks, OJ 2014 No. L 155, 23 May 2014, pp. 1–14.

Directive 2015/1513 of the European Parliament and of the Council of 9 September 2015 amending Directive 98/70/EC relating to the quality of petrol and diesel fuels and amending Directive 2009/28/EC on the promotion of the use of energy from renewable sources, OJ 2015 No. L 239, 15 September 2015, pp. 1–29.

Directive 2016/680 of the European Parliament and of the Council of 27 April 2016 on the protection of natural persons with regard to the processing of personal data by competent authorities for the purposes of the prevention, investigation, detection or prosecution of criminal offences or the execution of criminal penalties, and on the free movement of such data, and repealing Council Framework Decision 2008/977/JHA, OJ 2016 No. L 119, 4 May 2016, pp. 89–131.

Economic Adjustment Programme for Greece of May 2010, available at http://ec.europa.eu/economy_finance/publications/occasional_paper/2010/pdf/ocp61_en.pdf.

Economic Adjustment Programme for Greece of March 2012, available at http://ec.europa.eu/economy_finance/publications/occasional_paper/2012/pdf/ocp94_en.pdf.

European Council Decision 2011/199/EU of 25 March 2011 amending Article 136 of the Treaty on the Functioning of the European Union with regard to a stability mechanism for Member States whose currency is the euro, OJ 2011 No. L 91, 6 April 2011, pp. 1–2.

General Agreement on Tariffs and Trade (GATT).

Guideline of the European Central Bank of 20 September 2011 on monetary policy instruments and procedures of the Eurosystem (recast) (ECB/2011/14, 2011/817/EU), OJ 2011 No. L 331, 14 December 2011, pp. 1–95.

Guidelines on certain State aid measures in the context of the greenhouse gas emission allowance trading scheme post-2012, OJ 2012 No. C 158, 5 June 2012, pp. 4–22.

Guidelines on sound remuneration policies under Articles 74(3) and 75(2) of Directive 2013/36/EU and disclosures under Article 450 of Regulation 575/2013, 27 June 2016, available at www.eba.europa.eu/documents/10180/1314839/EBA-GL-2015-22+Guidelines+on+Sound+Remuneration+Policies_EN.pdf.

Guidelines on State aid for environmental protection and energy 2014–2020, OJ 2014 No. C 200, 28 June 2014, pp. 1–55.

International Labour Organization, Recommendation No. 202 concerning National Floors of Social Protection, adopted 14 June 2012.

Memorandum of Understanding between the European Commission, the Hellenic Republic and the Bank of Greece, of August 2015, available at https://ec.europa.eu/info/sites/info/files/01_mou_20150811_en_2.pdf.

Proposal for a Council Regulation on the exercise of the right to take collective action within the context of the freedom of establishment and the freedom to provide services, COM(2012)130.

Proposal for a Directive of the European Parliament and of the Council on services in the internal market, COM(2004)2.

Proposal for a Directive amending Directive 2003/87/EC to enhance cost-effective emission reductions and low-carbon investments, COM(2015)337.

Proposal for a Regulation of the European Parliament and of the Council amending Regulation 806/2014 in order to establish a European Deposit Insurance Scheme, COM(2015)586.

Proposal for a Directive of the European Parliament and of the Council amending Directive 96/71/EC of the European Parliament and of the Council of 16 December 1996 concerning the posting of workers in the framework of the provision of services, COM(2016)128.

Proposal for a directive of the European Parliament and of the Council on preventive restructuring frameworks, second chance and measures to increase the efficiency of restructuring, insolvency and discharge procedures and amending Directive 2012/30/EU, COM(2016)723.

Proposal for a regulation amending Regulation 883/2004 on the coordination of social security systems and regulation 987/2009 laying down the procedure for implementing Regulation 883/200, COM(2016)815.

Proposal for a directive amending Directive 2006/22/EC as regards enforcement requirements and laying down specific rules with respect to Directive 96/71/EC and Directive 2014/67/EU for posting drivers in the road transport sector, COM(2017)278.

Regulation 1408/71 of the Council of 14 June 1971 on the application of social security schemes to employed persons and their families moving within the Community, O.J. 1971 L 149, 5 July 1971, pp. 2–50.

Regulation 883/2004 of the European Parliament and of Council of 29 April 2004 on the coordination of social security systems, OJ 2004 No. L 166, 30 April 2004, pp. 1–123.

Regulation 1173/2011 of the European Parliament and of the Council of 16 November 2011 on the effective enforcement of budgetary surveillance in the euro area, OJ 2011 No. L 306, 23 November 2011, pp. 1–7.

Regulation 1174/2011 of the European Parliament and of the Council of 16 November 2011 on enforcement measures to correct excessive macroeconomic imbalances in the euro area, OJ 2011 No. L 306, 23 November 2011, pp. 8–11.

Regulation 1175/2011 of the European Parliament and of the Council of 16 November 2011 amending Council Regulation 1466/97 on the strengthening of the surveillance of budgetary positions and the surveillance and coordination of economic policies, OJ 2011 No. L 306, 23 November 2011, pp. 12–24.

Regulation 1176/2011 of the European Parliament and of the Council of 16 November 2011 on the prevention and correction of macroeconomic imbalances, OJ 2011 No. L 306, 23 November 2011, pp. 25–32.

Regulation 531/2012 of the European Parliament and of the Council of 13 June 2012 on roaming on public mobile communications networks within the Union, OJ 2012 No. L 172, 30 June 2012, pp. 10–35.

Regulation 966/2012 of the European Parliament and of the Council of 25 October 2012 on the financial rules applicable to the general budget of the Union and repealing Council Regulation 1605/2002, OJ 2012 No. L 298, 26 October 2012, pp. 1–96.

Regulation 978/2012 of the European Parliament and of the Council of 25 October 2012 applying a scheme of generalised tariff preferences and repealing Council Regulation 732/2008, OJ 2012 No. L 303, 31 October 2012, pp. 1–82.

Regulation 345/2013 of the European Parliament and of the Council of 17 April 2013 on European venture capital funds, OJ No. L 115, 25 April 2013, pp. 1–17.

Regulation 472/2013 of the European Parliament and of the Council of 21 May 2013 on the strengthening of economic and budgetary surveillance of Member States in the euro area experiencing or threatened with serious difficulties with respect to their financial stability, OJ No. L 140, 27 May 2013, pp. 1–10.

Regulation 473/2013 of the European Parliament and of the Council of 21 May 2013 on common provisions for monitoring and assessing draft budgetary plans and ensuring the correction of excessive deficit of the Member States in the euro area, OJ No. L 140, 27 May 2013, pp. 11–23.

Regulation 1022/2013 of the European Parliament and of the Council of 22 October 2013 amending Regulation 1093/2010 establishing a European Supervisory Authority (European Banking Authority) as regards the conferral of specific tasks on the European Central Bank pursuant to Council Regulation 1024/2013, OJ 2013 No. L 287, 29 October 2013, pp. 5–14.

Regulation 1194/2013 imposing a definitive anti-dumping duty and collecting definitively the provisional duty imposed on imports of biodiesel originating in Argentina and Indonesia, OJ 2013 No. L 315, 26 November 2013, pp. 2–26.

Regulation 1303/2013 of the European Parliament and of the Council of 17 December 2013 laying down common provisions on the European Regional Development Fund, the European Social Fund, the Cohesion Fund, the European Agricultural Fund for Rural Development and the European Maritime and Fisheries Fund, and laying down general provisions on the European Regional Development Fund, the European Social Fund, the Cohesion Fund and the European Maritime and Fisheries Fund and repealing Council Regulation 1083/2006, OJ 2013 No. L 347, 20 December 2013, pp. 320–469.

Regulation 1304/2013 of the European Parliament and of the Council of 17 December 2013 on the European Social Fund and repealing Council Regulation 1081/2006, OJ 2013 No. L 347, 20 December 2013, pp. 470–486.

Regulation 1307/2013 of the European Parliament and of the Council of 17 December 2013 establishing rules for direct payments to farmers under support schemes within the framework of the Common Agricultural Policy and repealing Council Regulation 637/2008 and Council Regulation 73/2009, OJ 2013 No. L 347/608, 20 December 2013, pp. 608–670.

Regulation 1309/2013 of the European Parliament and of the Council of 17 December 2013 on the European Globalisation Adjustment Fund (2014–2020) and repealing Regulation 1927/2006, OJ 2013 No. L 347, 20 December 2013, pp. 855–864.

Regulation 806/2014 of the European Parliament and of the Council of 15 July 2014 establishing uniform rules and a uniform procedure for the resolution of credit institutions and certain investment firms in the framework of a Single Resolution Mechanism and a Single Resolution Fund and amending Regulation 1093/2010, OJ 2014 No. L 225, 30 July 2014, pp. 1–90.

Regulation 2015/779 of the European Parliament and of the Council of 20 May 2015 amending Regulation 1304/2013, as regards an additional initial prefinancing amount paid to operational programmes supported by the Youth Employment Initiative, OJ 2015 No. L 126, 21 May 2015, pp. 1–2.

Regulation 2015/1017 of the European Parliament and of the Council of 25 June 2015 on the European Fund for Strategic Investments, the European Investment Advisory Hub and the European Investment Project Portal and amending Regulations 1291/2013 and No. 1316/2013 – the European Fund for Strategic Investments, OJ 2015 No. L 169, 1 July 2015, pp. 1–38.

Regulation 2015/2120 of the European Parliament and of the Council of 25 November 2015 laying down measures concerning open Internet access and amending Directive 2002/22/EC on universal service and users' rights relating to electronic communications networks and services and Regulation 531/2012 on roaming on public mobile communications networks within the Union, OJ 2015 No. L 310, 26 November 2015, pp. 1–18.

Regulation 2016/679 of the European Parliament and of the Council of 27 April 2016 on the protection of natural persons with regard to the processing of personal data and on the free movement of such data, and repealing Directive 95/46/EC, OJ 2016 No. L 119, 4 May 2016, pp. 1–88.

Regulation 2016/1036 of the European Parliament and of the Council of 8 June 2016 on protection against dumped imports from countries not members of the European Union, OJ 2016 No. L 176, 30 June 2016, pp. 21–54.

Regulation 2017/920 of the European Parliament and of the Council of 17 May 2017 amending Regulation 531/2012 as regards rules for wholesale roaming markets, OJ 2017 No. L 147, 9 June 2017, pp. 1–8.

Regulation 2017/1128 of the European Parliament and of the Council of 14 June 2017 on cross-border portability of online content services in the internal market, OJ 2017 No. L 168, 30 June 2017, pp. 1–11.

Regulation 2017/1129 of the European Parliament and of the Council of 14 June 2017 on the prospectus to be published when securities are offered to the public or admitted to trading on a regulated market, and repealing Directive 2003/71/EC, OJ 2017 No. L 168, 30 June 2017, pp. 12–82.

Regulation 2017/2321 of the European Parliament and of the Council of 12 December 2017 amending Regulation (EU) 2016/1036 on protection against dumped imports from countries not members of the European Union and Regulation (EU) 2016/1037 on protection against subsidised imports from countries not members of the European Union, OJ 2017 No. L 338, 19 December 2017, pp. 1–7.

Statute of the European System of Central Banks and of the European Central Bank.

Supplemental Memorandum of Understanding between the European Commission, the Hellenic Republic and the Bank of Greece, June 2016, available at http://ec.europa.eu/info/sites/info/files/ecfin_smou_en.pdf.

Treaty establishing the European Community, OJ C 325, 24 December 2002, pp. 33–184.

Treaty on European Union, OJ C 326, 26 October 2012, pp. 13–390.

Treaty on the Functioning of the European Union, OJ C 326, 26 October 2012, pp. 47–390.

Treaty on Stability, Coordination and Governance in the Economic and Monetary Union, signed on 2 March 2012, available at www.consilium.europa.eu/media/20399/st00tscg26_en12.pdf.

US Federal Deposit Insurance Act, available at www.fdic.gov/regulations/laws/rules/1000-1600.html.

World Trade Organization (WTO) Anti-Dumping Agreement.

Table of Cases

Åklagaren, (Case C-617/10) ECLI:EU:C:2013:105
Bundesdruckerei, (Case C-549/13) ECLI:EU:C:2014:2235
Case 2 BvR 2728/13 et al. order of 14 January 2014, available at www.bundesverfassungsgericht.de/SharedDocs/Entscheidungen/EN/2014/01/rs20140114_2bvr272813en.html
Cases 2 BvR 2728/13, 2 BvR 2729/13, 2 BvR 2730/13, 2 BvR 2731/13, 2 BvE 13/13, Judgment of 21 June 2016
Commission v. *France*, (C-381/93) ECLI:EU:C:1994:370
Commission v. *France*, (Cases C-512/08) ECLI:EU:C:2010:579
Commission v. *Germany*, (Case C-562/10) ECLI:EU:C:2012:442
Commission v. *Luxemburg*, (Case C-490/09) ECLI:EU:C:2011:34
Commission v. *Portugal*, (Case C-255/09) ECLI:EU:C:2011:695
Commission v. *Spain*, (Case C-211/08) ECLI:EU:C:2010:340
Corpul Naţional al Poliţiştilor – Biroul Executive Central v. *MAI and Others*, (Case C-369/12) ECLI:EU:C:2012:725
Corpul Naţional al Poliţiştilor – Biroul Executive Central v. *MAI and Others*, (Case C-134/12) ECLI:EU:C:2012:288
Corpul Naţional al Poliţiştilor v. *MAI and Others*, (Case C-434/11) ECLI:EU:C:2011:830
Dassonville, (Case 8–74) ECLI:EU:C:1974:82
EFTA Surveillance Authority v. *Iceland*, (Case E-16/11) judgment of 28 January 2013
Elchinov, (Case C-173/09) ECLI:EU:C:2010:581
Eleftheriou, (Case T-291/13) EU:T:2014:978
Elite Taxi, (Case C-434/15) ECLI:EU:C:2017:364

ESM case, 2 BvR 1390/12, 12 September 2012, available at www.bundesverfassungsgericht.de/SharedDocs/Entscheidungen/EN/2012/09/rs20120912_2bvr139012en.html
Estado Português, (Case C-667/13) ECLI:EU:C:2015:151
European Union – Anti-Dumping Measures on Biodiesel from Argentina, WTO case WT/DS473/AB/R of 6 October 2016
Florescu and Others v. *Casa Județeană de Pensii Sibiu and Others*, (Case C-258/14) ECLI:EU:C:2017:448
Gauweiler, (Case C-62/14) ECLI:EU:C:2015:400
Gebhard, (Case C-55/94) ECLI:EU:C:1995:411
Google, (Joined Cases C-236/08 to C-238/08) ECLI:EU:C:2008:389
Greek rescue package case, 2 BvR 987/10, 7 September 2011, available at www.bundesverfassungsgericht.de/SharedDocs/Entscheidungen/EN/2011/09/rs20110907_2bvr098710en.html
Hünermund, (Case C-292/92) ECLI:EU:C:1993:932
Koufaki, EctHR case (appl. no. 57665/12 and 57657/12), of 7 May 2013
Laval, (Case C-341/05) ECLI:EU:C:2007:809
Ledra Advertising, (Cases C-8/15 P to C-10/15 P) ECLI:EU:C:2016:701
Ledra Advertising, (Cases T-289/13) EU:T:2014:981
Leur-Bloem, (Case C-28/95) ECLI:EU:C:1997:369
L'Oréal, (Case C-324/09) ECLI:EU:C:2011:474
Ognyanov, (Case C-614/14) ECLI:EU:C:2016:514
Opinion 2/15 of the Court of 16 May 2017, ECLI:EU:C:2017:376
Petersen, (Case C-341/08) ECLI:EU:C:2010:4
Petru, (Case C-268/13) ECLI:EU:C:2014:2271
Pistre, (Case C-321/94) ECLI:EU:C:1997:229
Poland v. *Parliament and Council*, (Case C-358/14) ECLI:EU:C:2016:323
PreussenElektra, (Case C-379/98) ECLI:EU:C:2001:160
Pringle, (Case C-370/12) ECLI:EU:C:2012:756
RegioPost, (Case C-115/14) ECLI:EU:C:2015:760
Rüffert, (Case C-346/06) ECLI:EU:C:2008:189
Sanz de Lera, (Joined cases C-163/94, C-165/94 and C-250/94) ECLI:EU:C:1995:451
Sindicato dos Bancários do Norte and Others v. *BPN*, (Case C-128/12) ECLI:EU:C:2013:149
Sindicato Nacional dos Profissionais de Seguros e Afins v. *Fidelidade Mundial – Companhia de Seguros SA*, (Case C-264/12) ECLI:EU:C:2014:2036
Sindicato Nacional dos Profissionais de Seguros e Afins v. *Via Directa – Companhia de Seguros SA*, (Case C-665/13) ECLI:EU:C:2014:2327
Theophilou, (Case T-293/13) EU:T:2014:97

Uber Belgium, (Case C-526/15) ECLI:EU:C:2016:830
UK v. *Parliament and Council*, (Case C-270/12) ECLI:EU:C:2014:18
United States – Import Prohibition of Certain Shrimp and Shrimp Products, WTO case WT/DS58/AB/R of 12 October 1998
Viking, (Case C-438/05) ECLI:EU:C:2007:772
Walrave, (Case 36/74) ECLI:EU:C:1974:140
Watts, (Case C-372/04) ECLI:EU:C:2006:325
Yellow Cab Verkehrsbetrieb (Case C-338/09) ECLI:EU:C:2010:814

Introduction

In mid-2003, a High Level Group convened by the then-President of the European Commission (EC), Romano Prodi, published a report entitled 'Agenda for a Growing Europe'. The report praised the advancements of Europe's economic integration in its various policies, from the Economic and Monetary Union to the internal market and the commercial (international trade) policy. As it highlighted, 'judged by the progress made in the integration process, there is no doubt that the period of the last 15 years has been a tremendous success'.[1]

Simultaneously, the Convention on the Future of Europe was presenting its draft Treaty Establishing a Constitution for Europe. A year earlier, twelve out of the then fifteen EU Member States started to use coins and banknotes bearing European symbols. Economic convergence between the poorer and the richer Member States seemed to be advancing. The Lisbon Agenda, launched in 2000, promised to make the EU 'the most competitive and dynamic knowledge-based economy in the world' by 2010.[2] The 'Big-Bang' enlargement of 2004 would happen in less than a year, elevating the European project to an entirely new level. Romania and Bulgaria were waiting next in the accession pipeline.

All of these unprecedented events appeared to corroborate that Europe's political processes were profoundly robust. The way the 1999 Santer Commission debacle was resolved implied that the EU's

[1] André Sapir et al., 'An Agenda for a Growing Europe. Making the EU Economic System Deliver', July 2003, 1, available at cejm.univ-rennes.eu/digitalAssets/24/24407_sapirreport.pdf.

[2] Lisbon European Council 23 and 24 March 2000 Presidency Conclusions, Sec. A.5., available at www.europarl.europa.eu/summits/lis1_en.htm.

governance system was adaptive and open to improvements,[3] while the simultaneous German economic reforms under the Schröder government suggested that ailing Member States were capable of overcoming on their own the economic crises they were encountering. Only the most obdurate naysayers could fail to appreciate both the speed with which the continent was being united and the soundness of the foundations on which the unification process was based.

Then, however, the foundations started cracking. The Constitution for Europe was foiled in the French and Dutch referenda. The attempts to push the limits of the internal market in the fast-growing service sector with the Bolkestein directive petered out soon after.[4] The sovereign debt crisis revealed the excessively optimistic assumptions behind the Economic and Monetary Union. Unemployment skyrocketed in some European countries and receded to very low levels in others. European policies, previously hailed for paving the way to economic convergence, suddenly either amplified the instability or became patently ineffective in mitigating it. From a breathtaking phenomenon a decade earlier, the economic integration became a serious headache for policymakers at various levels of the European governance system. The ideology of the economic integration driving it since the mid-1980s was unravelling fast.

Some could see it as part of a bigger plan. After all, it was Jean Monnet, one of European integration's founding fathers, who claimed that 'Europe will be forged in crises, and will be the sum of the solutions adopted for those crises'.[5] According to a cognate neo-functionalist perspective,[6] incomplete initial political and economic choices should not be particularly disturbing. In fact they could be conceived of as the main driver of the European project, because successors of those who create incomplete or incompatible policies would be forced to push the integration further, rectifying the flaws once the original incompleteness turns its head.

[3] More broadly on the related developments, see Christian Joerges, Renaud Dehousse, eds, *Good Governance in Europe's Integrated Market* (Oxford: Oxford University Press, 2002).

[4] Proposal for a Directive of the European Parliament and of the Council on Services in the Internal Market, COM(2004)2.

[5] Jean Monnet, *Mémoires* (Paris: Fayard 1976): 488.

[6] For a concise yet rich introduction to the concept, see esp. Carsten Strøby Jensen, 'Neofunctionalism', in: *European Union Politics*, eds. Michelle Cini and Nieves Pérez-Solórzano Borragán (Oxford: Oxford University Press, 2016): 53–64.

The recent economic recovery throughout the EU, largely engineered by bold actions of the European Central Bank (ECB), could seem to corroborate this very point. In the last full year before this book went to press (2016) the EU's real gross domestic product (GDP) growth outperformed the USA's (1.9 per cent against 1.6 per cent).[7] Unemployment in the Eurozone is diminishing. Market confidence largely returned.

This book will argue, however, that the recent economic recovery in the EU (and in the Eurozone in particular) does not stem from any serious improvements in the foundations on which the economic prosperity relies. Persistently low inflation allowed the central banks of the Eurozone to monetise a pile of public debt and to replace it with a pile of central bank money, injected into the banking system without deteriorating the value of the euro. As far as the effects of this alchemic transmutation last, neo-functionalists can maintain the prescience of their theory.

Their perspective misses an important point, though: in peaceful times persistently high public debts are caused by malfunctioning public policies and institutions. It is easy to forget about this relationship when one more – and very big – compartment for stacking up the public debt has been found. But this feat does not make the public policies and institutions responsible for the debt any sounder. All it does is to treat the symptoms of an ailment without addressing its real causes.

In other words, and contrary to the sanguine view prevailing as this book goes to press, the way the Eurozone crisis has been overcome largely corroborates a much less optimistic point: when encountering policy failures caused by their predecessors' mistakes, economic policymakers have largely been entrapped by time-inconsistent incentives. They are tempted to prioritise temporary solutions producing short-term gains at minimum short-term cost, even if in the longer perspective the relationship between the costs and the benefits of the same policy choices is quite certain to reverse. These time inconsistencies are clearly discernible both in the original design of major European economic policies and in responses to their subsequent crises. While scholars can gnash their teeth at it, the time-inconsistent character of the contemporary policymaking (not only at the EU level) is hard to resist for elected politicians, whose thinking is naturally dominated by voting calculations scarcely ever transcending the next

[7] Organisation for Economic Cooperation and Development (OECD) data for the USA, Eurostat data for the EU 28.

elections. When confronted with a policy failure, they are under very serious pressure to extend and pretend, unless fixing the failed policy entails no serious political costs. The ex–Prime Minister of Finland, Alexander Stubb, made the same point when he opined that 'the EU is constant crisis management. You move from one crisis to the other and, at the end of the day, it's just a question of the size of the crisis and who gets hit the hardest. I have always believed the EU advances in three-phases: Phase no. 1 is crisis, phase no. 2 is chaos and phase no. 3 is sub-optimal solution, and that's very much the nature of the beast.'[8]

The sub-optimality may easily be judged as fair enough when economies grow and unemployment decreases. But, instead of inducing policymakers to rebuild the many precarious linchpins sustaining European economic integration, it has lulled them into what Robert Feldman once described (in the context of the ultimately quite similar Japanese economic travails) as the CRIC cycle: crisis, response, improvement and complacency.[9]

The time-inconsistent nature of the responses to side-effects of the major European economic policies can be attributed not only to policymakers' time-inconsistent incentives, but also to the fact that a policy flaw is often relative. A certain socioeconomic choice at the European level may provoke a crisis in one society, while making other societies wealthier and more stable. Solidarity is extremely difficult to achieve in such a setup, as those on the upside of this distributional process can easily find ample pretexts to avoid policy adjustments. One particularly popular and salient excuse has to do with the EU's constitutional system. According to it, because the way the EU exercises its powers is defined by the Treaties,[10] substantial alterations to European policies require Treaty changes. In their turn, more moderate alterations can easily end up in half-baked policy reforms, considering that European decision-making is extremely convoluted and bristled with veto points at each level.

[8] Quoted in David M. Herszenhorn, 'Alexander Stubb: Europe's Endangered Liberal Future', *Politico*, 26 December 2016, available at www.politico.eu/article/alexander-stubb-europes-endangered-liberal-future-populism-finnish-party/.

[9] Robert Feldman, 'Cobwebs and CRICs', *Morgan Stanley Dean Witter's Japan Economics*, 4 April 2001, 1–4, available at www.yumpu.com/en/document/view/4429905/cobwebs-and-crics-japan-economics.

[10] The Treaty on European Union (TEU) and the Treaty on the Functioning of the European Union (TFEU), subsequently referred to as 'the Treaties' or 'the Treaty'.

Most importantly of all, profound policy shifts are hardly conceivable without deep alterations in underlying worldviews, values, beliefs and ideological paradigms. Advancements in European economic integration since the mid-1980s have stemmed from some very powerful and broadly espoused beliefs. One was that the economic integration should be founded on the internal market first and foremost and that its freedoms inevitably induce an efficiency-enhancing win-win situation for all EU societies. Another is that the same applies to international trade. It has also been paradigmatic that the way the EU redistributes its resources must be extremely path-dependent. And last but not least, the Eurozone has been construed as an irreversible political process driven by capital flows and a certain attitude towards the role of markets and governments.

These beliefs, as I will argue throughout this book, are all quite intuitive and plausible. And yet, they have been responsible for various economic crises and political vortex effects driving various subsurface processes of creeping economic disintegration.

Entrapped by the time-inconsistent incentives and confronted with visibly collapsing paradigms on which the European economic integration was founded, policymakers have tended to deploy denial tactics justifying their extend-and-pretend actions. This strategy has so far been good enough to keep the Eurozone and other main linchpins of the economic integration whole. Yet, it has been engraining among many European societies the feeling that the EU is unable to come up with viable solutions to the collective problems and challenges Europe faces. This feeling was easily discernible in the UK before the Brexit referendum. It has also been confirmed by more recent opinion polls. In a survey conducted in mid-2017 by Pew Research, majorities of Greeks (86 per cent), Italians (65 per cent), French (63 per cent) and Spanish (52 per cent) disapproved of the way the EU was dealing with economic issues.[11] Even in the country spared by economic hardships in recent years – Sweden – respondents were dubious about the EU's economic policies.[12] Of the societies surveyed then, the Dutch, Hungarians,

[11] Approving minorities in these five countries were 11 per cent in Greece, 24 per cent in Italy, 35 per cent in France, 38 per cent in Spain; see Bruce Stokes, Richard Wike and Dorothy Manevich, 'Post-Brexit, Europeans More Favorable Toward EU', Pew Research, 15 June 2017, 10, available at assets.pewresearch.org/wp-content/uploads/sites/2/2017/06/06160636/Pew-Research-Center-EU-Brexit-Report-UPDATED-June-15-2017.pdf.

[12] Forty-six per cent disapprove – 42 per cent approve: ibid.

Germans and Poles perceived the EU as properly dealing with economics.[13] Perplexingly enough, however, in two of the four countries openly xenophobic parties with cynical approaches to European integration and with authoritarian proclivities are in power. And the prosperity of Germany as well as the Netherlands is partly enabled by significant economic imbalances in the Eurozone, to which the economic models of the two countries contribute.

While, therefore, political constraints may explain why clandestine tinkering with European economic policies have prevailed whenever the policies needed proper overhauls, this political tactic has produced a profoundly paradoxical situation, in which Europhiles are either unable to come up with viable reforms to failing policy paradigms, or they are unwilling to admit failures of European policies in the first place. They perpetuate schematic thinking, ignoring Einstein's famous insight that one cannot solve problems by using the same kind of thinking used when creating them. Even if the Eurosceptic thinking is self-defeating, as it builds on a craving for disconnection in an ever more interconnected world, it is alluring to many who sense that the paradigms on which European integration was based have failed and that mainstream politicians do not remedy the flaws properly. Unless those to whom European integration is dear wake up to this reality, European integration will be extremely prone to crises that at some point may tear Europe apart politically and economically.

A comfortable majority of Europeans in the EU 27 currently prefers to stay together. Yet, in some countries afflicted by the various negative economic and political processes described in this book the support for leaving the EU has swelled. In mid-2017, one in three Greeks and Italians wanted their country to leave the EU.[14] European institutions and governments of the countries on the upside of the distributional effects propelled by European integration may hope they would be able to stifle Eurosceptic movements there. In Italy in particular – the country disadvantaged both by its dysfunctional domestic politics and by European policies playing out unfavourably – a Eurosceptic government could have its arm twisted, as Syriza was in Greece back in

[13] The Netherlands: 38 per cent disapprove – 54 per cent approve; Hungary: 36 per cent disapprove – 47 per cent approve; Germany: 28 per cent disapprove – 61 per cent approve; Poland: 25 per cent disapprove – 28 per cent approve: ibid.

[14] Bruce Stokes, Richard Wike and Dorothy Manevich, 'Post-Brexit, Europeans More Favorable Toward EU', 4.

2015. But this will not make the Italian society more prosperous, nor the European integration any more stable.

As I will argue throughout this book, to strengthen the economic integration the flaws in the current paradigms behind European policies must be understood first and a convincing narrative on how to remedy them ought to follow in the second step. Both should confront the prevailing intellectual habits, beliefs and ideological oversimplifications head-on, at the same time discerning viable arguments on the left and on the right, in the Europhile and the Eurosceptic camps. Unless the understanding and the narrative stem from an accurate perception of how law, economics and politics interact in the European setup, the European project will remain fragile and contestable, while European leaders fiddle with ambiguous reports on whether there should be more Europe or less of it, more discipline or less discipline, whether a new institution should be added or not, whether a multi-speed Europe is a good thing or bad, or what 'Social Europe' actually means.

Entrapped by time-inconsistent incentives, by distributional effects amplifying conflicts, by the institutional minefield and by their intellectual habits, politicians can hardly be expected to develop this understanding and this narrative on their own. Unfortunately this is not what most scholars specialising in European integration have traditionally excelled in either. For decades, when policymakers seemed to be leading Europeans to an ever brighter future, academics could satisfy themselves with debating causes of this historically unprecedented miracle. They could compare it with developments in other places and in other times. They could develop abstract theories, or simply systematise the growing *acquis communautaire*.

Now, however, none of this is either sufficient or adequate to buttress the integration process. The decades of research on the nature of integration may only serve historians, unless scholars do their part in reassessing the paradigms of European integration, unless they follow Einstein's precept and unless they develop convincing narratives justifying necessary reforms.

This conviction defines both the content and the structure of this book. A large proportion of it is devoted to the Economic and Monetary Union. The fact that the EMU remains very far from anything resembling the optimum currency area is easily forgotten when the unemployment goes down and the GDP is on the rise. But it will resurface when the next crisis occurs, and certainly it will occur. This is why Chapter 1 retells the story of the Eurozone crisis, to demonstrate how naïve its original assumptions were. Chapter 2 then explains how and why the economic coordination in the Eurozone has not worked, either before or after the sovereign debt crisis. Chapter 3 elucidates on the distributional effects (both economic and political) of adjustment processes propelled by the sovereign debt crisis, while Chapter 4 demonstrates how all of this has put an excessively heavy burden on the ECB. Chapter 5 discusses the possibility of establishing viable economic shock absorbers capable of stabilising the monetary union when its countries are hit by so-called asymmetric shocks, while Chapter 6 makes an argument why a partial disintegration of the Eurozone would actually strengthen economic integration more broadly.

The remaining four chapters explain why fixing the Eurozone will not secure Europe's prosperity. I first argue in this part that European economic integration critically hinges on national socioeconomic policies, which in many countries have been failing conspicuously. Politicians are understandably reluctant to admit this, but Europeans see it quite clearly. As unveiled by a recent survey of the European Commission, 'almost eight in ten [survey participants] agree there is a need for significant reforms to improve the performance of their economy (78%), while 76% agree governments need to save more today to prepare public finances for the ageing population ... More than nine in ten think the health system (92%) and the labour market (91%) in their country need reforms, 89% say this about the pension and education systems and 87% about the social security system. Almost eight in ten (79%) say this about taxation and 66% say this about market reforms.'[15]

Although this survey was restricted to Eurozone countries only, the results can hardly be predicted to differ much outside of it. For reasons elucidated in Chapter 7, the potential of the European project to improve Europeans' lives has lain unexploited by barring the EU from making a meaningful difference in all of these areas. As Chapter 8 will explain in more detail, it does not take new Treaties or a bigger EU budget to make up for this crucial loophole.

To complete the picture, the last two chapters investigate why both the internal market (Chapter 9) and the paradigm of maximum liberalisation of international trade (Chapter 10) require alterations mitigating their deleterious side effects. While the reforms involve some

[15] European Commission, Flash Eurobarometer 446 'The Euro Area', December 2016, 5, available at http://ec.europa.eu/COMMFrontOffice/publicopinion/index.cfm/ResultDoc/download/DocumentKy/76001.

hard choices, they are politically more feasible and justifiable than is routinely admitted.

None of the reforms putting European economic integration back on track is riskless. None is costless. Each is made more difficult by the fact that European democracies have become increasingly thin[16] and that national politicians guard the gates of EU policymaking. Each entails distributional effects likely to attract heavy resistance, enticing policymakers to continue with their time-inconsistent muddling-through. If this prevents the European Union from reforming its economic policies, the system may collapse, ushering in a painful resetting process. If this is what happens, the project born to relieve national political orders from their suicidal proclivities[17] will return to the point of departure.

Ultimately, therefore, if the integration project is to be relieved of the wasteful self-destruction gene, it must be based on robust foundations responding to what Europeans need and care about. Otherwise Europe will be entrapped between an unviable integration and a self-defeating disintegration. This is the ultimate reason why the paradigms behind European economic policies should be reassessed and recalibrated. This reason agitates every single thought in this book.

[16] I.e., institutionally and politically insufficiently robust to viably pursue policies improving the socioeconomic foundations of a society's prosperity and stability.

[17] Alan Milward, *The European Rescue of the Nation-State* (London: Routledge, 1992).

1 The Eurozone's Original Sins

1.1 Incomplete Political Vision

Politics and key economic advancements are often two sides of the same coin. The exceptional confluence of political interests and priorities prevailing in France and Germany in the 1980s, on the one hand, and the idea of the Economic and Monetary Union, on the other, is a testimony to this finding. The French President François Mitterrand famously wanted the single currency as a way of elevating the culture of monetary stability and economic prosperity associated with the Bundesbank to the European level. He reckoned that this fundamental yet simple institutional alteration would channel enhanced German economic prowess, expected only to grow after German reunification, for the good of the other Community nations – the French in particular.[1] He wanted, therefore, what German Chancellor Helmut Kohl also yearned for, and what the European project had codified in its genes since its very beginning: to harness German economic ambitions and potential for the benefit of a united Europe.

Kohl, in turn, was aware that the single currency would lock in exchange rates. By the same token, it would make it easier for German exporters to compete on international markets with producers from the other Community countries, in which recurring devaluations had previously boosted price competitiveness (while the Deutsche Mark was

[1] See esp. Karl Kaltenthaler, *Germany and the Politics of Europe's Money* (Durham, NC: Duke University Press, 1998); Kenneth H. F. Dyson and Kevin Featherstone, *The Road to Maastricht: Negotiating Economic and Monetary Union* (Oxford: Oxford University Press, 1999); Harold James, *Making the European Monetary Union* (Cambridge, MA: Harvard University Press, 2012), Markus K. Brunnermeier, Harold James and Jean-Pierre Landau, *The Euro and the Battle of Ideas* (Princeton, NJ: Princeton University Press, 2016).

under the opposite pressure).[2] Now, this particular feature of the euro is rightly considered a continuous source of its long-term instability. Yet, in the run-up to the European Monetary Union (EMU) devaluations, even competitive devaluations were universally associated with economic weakness.[3] The stability to be achieved by modelling the monetary union on the German template was conceived of as a much more reliable foundation of economic prosperity. It could have seemed, back then, that the only economy potentially standing to lose from this paradigm shift was Germany, because in the monetary union it would share its monetary credibility with less prosperous countries. To Kohl, however, this danger was sidelined by the idea encapsulated in what he said to Mitterrand in 1982: 'I may be the last Chancellor with whom you can build Europe.'[4]

By 'Europe', Kohl meant a political union; German policymakers in particular were quite aware that introducing a single currency between incongruent economic systems would be tantamount to establishing a flawed currency peg.[5] Maastricht was supposed to come up with such a political union, but it delivered only pretences of it. At this point, the Economic and Monetary Union became a ticking time-bomb for European integration, rather than its keystone. Many economists were perfectly aware of this. Milton Friedman, for instance, famously argued in 1997 that the Eurozone's Maastricht design 'would exacerbate political tensions by converting divergent shocks that could have been readily accommodated by exchange rate changes into divisive political issues ... Monetary unity imposed under unfavorable conditions will prove a barrier to the achievement of political unity.'[6]

[2] Devaluation – the lowering of the exchange rate by a fiat decision – makes foreign currencies more expensive compared to the domestic currency. Hence it renders exports cheaper (in the domestic currency) and imports correspondingly more expensive.

[3] After a devaluation, prices for imported goods inevitably rise, which translates into growing inflation and diminishes the original cost advantage. While, therefore, devaluations are a powerful method of boosting cost competitiveness of an economy in the short term, in the longer term they can easily spur a feedback loop between weakening exchange rates and inflation, disrupting investment incentives and economic productivity.

[4] Quoted in Dyson and Featherstone, *Road to Maastricht*, 309.

[5] The basic fact that no currency union ever managed to survive in the long term without this type of political integration is particularly telling in this respect. For an extension of the argument see Kathleen R. McNamara, 'The Forgotten Problem of Embeddedness. History Lessons for the Euro', in: *The Future of the Euro*, eds. Matthias Matthijs and Mark Blyth (Oxford: Oxford University Press, 2015), 21–43.

[6] Milton Friedman, 'The Euro: Monetary Unity to Political Disunity?', *Project Syndicate*, 28 August 1997, available at www.project-syndicate.org/commentary/the-euro–monetary-unity-to-political-disunity (accessed 6 December 2017).

I will argue in the subsequent chapters (Chapter 5 in particular) that anything resembling a full economic and political union is nowhere on the Eurozone's horizon. First, however, we should pause at why Friedman's judgment was ignored, despite him being the most vocal advocate of the economic ideology otherwise dominating policymaking at the time of the euro's inception, and what this means for the future of this pivotal European economic policy.

1.2 Volatility and the German Anchorage

This story starts two decades before the German Foreign Minister Hans-Dietrich Genscher came forth with his February 1988 Memorandum unequivocally supporting the creation of the EMU with a central bank modelled on the Bundesbank, which practically initiated the process that ended with the signing of the Maastricht Treaty four years later. Until the late 1960s, the case for a European single currency was very tenuous from an economic perspective, primarily because the Bretton Woods (fixed exchange rate) system delivered one of the main advantages of the single currency – it eliminated the exchange rate risk.[7] However, the unravelling of the Bretton Woods setup in the second half of the 1960s was paving the way for the idea that Europeans should replace it with a more ambitious system of their own making.

It first turned out that currency fluctuations were complicating the Common Agricultural Policy (CAP) ever since its main principle – common agricultural prices – was introduced in the second half of the 1960s.[8] Because agricultural prices were quoted in a common currency (units of account),[9] a downward currency adjustment, as experienced for instance by the French franc in the summer of 1969, would have depressed the prices of agricultural products in France. French farmers would receive comparably lower subsidies. On the other hand, their products would become more competitive on the common market. Upward currency adjustments would play out in the opposite direction. To mitigate these processes, in the summer of 1969, Agriculture

[7] For a comprehensive analysis see, for example, Michael D. Bordo and Barry Eichengreen, eds., *A Retrospective on the Bretton Woods System: Lessons for International Monetary Reform* (Chicago, IL: The University of Chicago Press, 1993).

[8] See also Robert Ackrill, *Common Agricultural Policy* (Sheffield: Sheffield Academic Press, 2000), 37–38; William Mitchell, *Eurozone Dystopia* (Cheltenham: Edward Elgar Publishing, 2015), 65–66.

[9] The unit of account was set in terms of the US dollar gold parity.

Ministers of the six Member States introduced a complicated system of subsidies and levies (called monetary compensatory amounts) aimed to preserve the effects of pre-existing common prices. The system was contentious, because it entailed regular discussions about politically sensitive financial adjustments. In addition, by introducing import and export levies it was hindering the circulation of agricultural products on the common market in ways irreconcilable with its main principles.

The idea of a single currency required, though a much more important catalyst than the practical requisites of the CAP. In certain ways this catalyst, too, was engendered by the collapse of the Bretton Woods monetary management system in the early 1970s. The demise of this system and the first oil shock in 1973 triggered unprecedented exchange rate volatility. Policies prevailing throughout this decade, which pivoted on foreign exchange controls and international arrangements aimed to limit currency fluctuations, proved conspicuously unable to remedy this instability. Soon, therefore, an opposite policy of market-oriented financial deregulation gained traction in the European Economic Community (EEC). It aimed to remove financial constraints for the real economy, which chimed nicely with economic liberalisation being the main driver behind the nascent idea of an internal market for all factors of production, including capital and payments.

Exchange rate volatility did not cease in the 1980s, however, despite the establishment of the European Monetary System in 1979 and regardless of all the efforts towards a new, more liberal, direction. The Deutsche Mark and the Bundesbank dominated monetary relations, putting the authorities behind weaker currencies in an awkward position. German interest rates (established by the Bundesbank) were – just like the Deutsche Mark's exchange rate – under a constant upward pressure. Had the peripheral EEC countries maintained lower interest rates, they would have experienced outflows of funds (seeking higher yields) to Germany. Yet, were they to emulate German policy – to maintain the parity within the European Monetary System – they would have depressed domestic economic activity in another way: by making interest rates on loans offered by domestic banks more expensive than was justified by the economic situation. In consequence, as Robert Raymond summed it up, 'arbitrages between the dollar and the Deutsche Mark added to national imbalances, triggered huge and unstable distortions, in countries other than Germany ... Given the size of the intra-zone exchanges, these countries had no better choice than becoming good followers of the Deutsche Mark instead of pursuing independent monetary policies.'[10] The stability of the strong Deutsche Mark worked very well for the German economy. Yet, when other EEC countries emulated the anti-inflation policy of the Bundesbank – which was important to demonstrate their stability – their economies struggled hard to adjust.

1.3 So Many Benefits

The governments of the countries under this pressure (France in particular) were thus undoubtedly rational when they tried to put an end to the resultant distortions by resuscitating the bold idea of a monetary union governed by a common accord. Its framing on the German model promised price stability and eliminated exchange rate fluctuations, because this is what a single currency ineluctably entails. The single European currency could even aspire to become the global reserve currency, undermining the American 'exorbitant privilege'.[11]

The full liberalisation of capital movements in 1990 – a direct consequence of the Single Market Programme – caused additional frictions to national monetary policies by encouraging the Bundesbank to abandon its lender-of-last-resort (LoLR) role on foreign exchange markets, which in turn ultimately paved the way for a serious crisis in the European Monetary System in 1992–93. This effect was congruent with predictions of the famous financial trilemma: free capital movements (integrated financial markets) and fixed parities left no room for a monetary sovereignty.[12] Accordingly, the single currency was necessary if the allocation of resources was to benefit from free capital movements and if an end was to be put to competitive devaluations by the irreversible fixing of parities (currency stability).

[10] Robert Raymond, 'From the Maastricht Treaty to the Euro: The Role of the EMI', in: *Progress through Crisis? Proceedings of the Conference for the 20th Anniversary of the Establishment of the European Monetary Institute*, eds. Ivo Maes and Frank Moss (Frankfurt am Main: ECB, 2014), 71.

[11] I.e., the economic benefits for the US economy stemming from the status of the US dollar as the main reserve currency. For a comprehensive analysis see esp. Barry Eichengreen, *Exorbitant Privilege: The Rise and Fall of the Dollar and the Future of the International Monetary System* (Oxford: Oxford University Press, 2011).

[12] See Maurice Obstfeld, Jay C. Shambaugh and Alan M. Taylor, 'The Trilemma in History: Tradeoffs among Exchange Rates, Monetary Policies, and Capital Mobility', *The Review of Economics and Statistics* 87 (2005): 423–438.

But the single currency promised many more benefits.

Fixed exchange rates would constrain central banks in their attempts to contribute to macroeconomic stabilisation. When the sovereign debt crisis burst in 2010, this trait proved particularly deleterious. But in the nascent period of the Eurozone, the detachment of the central bank from the function seemed beneficial, because then macroeconomic stabilisation had to depend entirely on the macroeconomic and fiscal policies of a particular government. The very awareness of this fact should – the argument went – act as an external restraint preventing governments and parliaments from pursuing irresponsible, destabilising (read: demand-led) economic and social policies.

This economic intuition with far-reaching political consequences was well-conceptualised under the original theory of optimum currency area. For Robert Mundell, the father of this theory, a fundamental advantage of a currency union was that it 'puts monetary policy out of the reach of politicians … without fiscal policy, the only way nations can keep jobs is by the competitive reduction of rules on business.'[13] In other words, it was hoped that the single currency would force elected politicians to concentrate on economic fundamentals as an economic engine, rather than having recourse to Keynesian fiscal and monetary policies, so conspicuously unable to overcome the stagflation of the 1970s.[14]

In the second half of the 1980s – when monetarist thinking started to dominate policy debates – this argument fell on particularly fertile intellectual ground. Accordingly, the original architecture of the EMU saw an optimal fiscal policy as neutral towards the real economy and conceived of the monetary policy as strictly rule-based and targeted on inflation.[15] The insight was therefore simple and plausible, as long,

[13] Cited by Greg Palast, 'Robert Mundell, Evil Genius of the Euro', *Guardian*, 26 June 2012, available at www.theguardian.com/commentisfree/2012/jun/26/robert-mundell-evil-genius-euro.

[14] For a sample of particularly influential contemporary critique of Keynesian economics see, for example, James M. Buchanan and Richard E. Wagner, *Democracy in Deficit. The Political Legacy of Lord Keynes* (New York: Academic Press, 1977); James M. Buchanan et al., 'The Political Biases of Keynesian Economics', in: *Fiscal Responsibility in Constitutional Democracy*, eds. James M. Buchanan and Richard E. Wagner (Leiden, The Netherlands: Martinus Nijhoff, 1978), 79–100.

[15] This, again, was well-ensconced in a neoclassical insight that the monetary policy should be concerned with maintaining the external macroeconomic balance (zero balance-of-payments position) and the fiscal policy should only maximise output and employment: Brian Snowdon and Howard R. Vane, *Modern Macroeconomics: Its Origins, Development and Current State* (Cheltenham; Northampton, MA: Edward Elgar Publishing, 2005).

at least, as the policy mix is reduced to fiscal and monetary policies only. If low inflation is the guiding principle for monetary authorities and if fiscal dominance (supremacy of the – most often inflationary – public debt management strategies over the monetary policy targeted at low inflation) is precluded by the adherence to sound, prudent and coordinated fiscal policies, then monetary dominance (the prevalence of a policy concentrated on low inflation over priorities of public debt management) would force politicians to act responsibly in the economic domain. In addition, the central bank of a single currency area should not find it difficult to run monetary policy, because its mission would be attuned to the passive, stable and predictable fiscal policy by default. Additionally, instead of quixotically striving to stimulate economic growth with expansionary fiscal and monetary policies, national governments would have no other choice than to animate performance of the economy by concentrating on its supply side: the business environment, competition, innovation and labour flexibility.

It was also hoped that the single currency would amplify all of the beneficial effects that the internal market was intended to produce. By definition, it would betoken lower borrowing and transaction costs, stimulating economic exchange. As one of the leading economists described the underlying belief, 'adopting the euro would eliminate the erratic monetary policies that had been an obstacle to catch-up growth in the past. Lower transaction costs and less policy uncertainty would attract foreign investment, boosting capital formation and hastening technology transfer. Lower transactions costs Europe-wide would enable local firms to better exploit economies of scale and scope. The incentive to invest in structural reforms would be sharpened since countries that failed to reform would lose out in the competition for footloose factors of production.'[16] Seen through this prism, 'EMU was believed to be a logical step in the context of economic spillover from the Single European Act, as a single market with the continued existence of national currencies was considered suboptimal.'[17] The message was clear, sharp and intellectually compelling. Against its crystallisation in the second part of the 1980s, the willingness to bundle German

[16] Barry Eichengreen, 'European Monetary Integration with Benefit of Hindsight', *Journal of Common Market Studies* 50 (2012): 126.

[17] Jonathan Yiangou, Mícheál O'Keeffe and Gabriel Glöckler, '"Tough Love": How the ECB's Monetary Financing Prohibition Pushes Deeper Euro Area Integration', *Journal of European Integration* 35 (2013): 226.

unification in with the establishment of the Economic and Monetary Union could appear both logical and mutually beneficial.[18]

1.4 ... And the Periphery Should Enjoy Them, Too

The decision to set up the EMU moved the agenda to the thorny question of which EEC countries should join it and which ought to remain outside. Soon, however, the dominant economic thinking helped to overcome this question, too. With the benefit of hindsight it is easy to blame the framers of the Eurozone for the flexible (nominal) convergence criteria and for admitting countries ill-suited to adopt one and the same currency as the so-called core countries (Germany, the Benelux countries, Austria, Finland, France). But from the viewpoint of financial allocative efficiency, these countries should have been admitted to the Eurozone *precisely* to improve its performance. It was believed that – in searching for allocative efficiency – financial resources would tend to be invested in the most efficient firms in the regions with the highest future potential for growth. These beliefs conformed to the neo-classical theory of intertemporal utility maximisation, which offered a plausible general explanation. Accordingly, a system characterised by different levels of capital endowment should attract foreign investments – due to higher expected rates of return on capital – to economies characterised by higher productivity growth and lower per capita income. The utility of capital would thus be maximised. Because peripheral countries were economically less advanced (in the sense of lower average per capita levels of income and output), they were particularly predestined to benefit from this process. If true, it would improve welfare both in the economies of the owners of the financial resources and in the recipient economies, at the same time reducing the probability of crises stemming from mispriced investment risks.[19] Furthermore, greater financial integration should lead to reduced growth volatility, because it would strengthen financial risk-sharing.[20]

[18] For more on Kohl's motives see esp. Dyson and Featherstone, *Road to Maastricht*, 307–313.

[19] Mariassunta Giannetti and Steven Ongena, 'Financial Integration and Firm Performance: Evidence from Foreign Bank Entry in Emerging Markets', *Review of Finance* 13 (2009): 181–223.

[20] Geert Bekaert, Campbell R. Harvey and Christian Lundblad, 'Growth Volatility and Financial Liberalization', *Journal of International Money and Finance* 25 (2006): 370–403; Yuliya Demyanyk, Charlotte Ostergaard and Bent E. Sørensen, 'Risk Sharing and Portfolio Allocation in EMU', *Economic Papers* 334 (2008), European Commission.

In a paper published in 1997, when the decision on the final group of the countries to comprise the Eurozone was still hanging in the balance, two American economists – Jeffrey Frankel and Andrew Rose – provided scientific evidence for this very intuition. As they argued, 'some countries may appear, on the basis of historical data, to be poor candidates for EMU entry. But EMU entry per se, for whatever reason, may provide a substantial impetus for trade expansion; this in turn may result in more highly correlated business cycles. That is, a country is more likely to satisfy the criteria for entry into a currency union *ex post* than *ex ante*.'[21] This conclusion dealt a serious blow to the traditional coronation theory, based on the assumption that the single currency should be restricted to a small group of stability-oriented countries characterised by naturally converging economic performances. The coronation theory – for years championed by the German Bundesbank in particular – claimed that the single currency may be introduced only when individual economies are appropriately synchronised throughout an arduous process of domestic reforms and adjustments. Frankel and Rose upended it, conjecturing that economic synchronisation could simply stem from innate (endogenous) processes set in motion by the internal market.[22] By reinforcing the processes, the single currency would facilitate convergence!

According to this argument, economic integration driven by the internal market and spurred on by the single currency would lead to a higher degree of business-cycle harmonisation and hence the more accurate operation of the monetary transmission mechanism. While Frankel and Rose were uninterested in the political effects of this process, these effects could be easily inferred from their economic arguments: politics should also synchronise, following economic convergence.

[21] Jeffrey A. Frankel and Andrew K. Rose, 'The Endogeneity of the Optimum Currency Area Criteria', *NBER Working Paper* No 5700, 22 August 1996, available at www.nber.org/papers/w5700.pdf.

[22] The coronation theory was traditionally espoused in the strong-currency countries (by the group bunched together under the rubric of 'economists'), while the idea that criteria of establishing an optimal currency union are endogenous prevailed in the weak-currency countries (by the so-called monetarists). See, for example, Elena Danescu, 'Economists v. Monetarists – Agreements and Clashes in the Drafting of the Werner Report', *Centre virtuel de la connaissance sur l'Europe* 2012, available at www.cvce.eu/content/publication/2012/4/3/875a85f1-e099-4013-acbf-68b2c50a6879/publishable_en.pdf.

The endogeneity of the optimum currency area espoused by Frankel and Rose solved all of the (otherwise unsolvable) puzzles stemming from divergent economic and political structures of the societies to comprise the single currency area. The elimination of exchange and interest rate uncertainties – i.e., the unavoidable flipside of the single currency – would lubricate the cogs and gears of the internal market. As an upshot, the economies previously prone to asymmetric shocks would become more resilient. They would converge upwards, aligning their performance with the core countries. This belief dovetailed perfectly with the political worldviews and wishes prevailing at the time. Policymakers therefore enthusiastically embraced the idea that 'the EMU is likely to foster intra-industry trade in Europe, leading to more symmetric shocks between member states. The monetary union will endogenously create the conditions of its success.'[23]

This mechanism – largely corroborated by basic economic indicators during the Eurozone's first couple of years[24] – was anticipated to do wonders for the economic prosperity of the Union, assuming that just enough capital could flow from the richer countries to cover the investment needs of the poorer economies without hindering investments in the exporting economies. No unemployment was expected to kick in as a side-effect, because the richer economies would export excess capital only. In poorer ones, the inflowing capital would propel economic growth, pushing unemployment downwards and discouraging emigration. The single market with a single currency could be expected to mitigate the shortcomings of very limited labour mobility; much more limited than what was required, according to the theory of optimal currency area, to secure the proper functioning of the single currency.

1.5 The Legal Tissue of the EMU as an Incentive-Compatible Setup

These arguments may explain why the 'achievement of a high degree of sustainable convergence by reference to' the nominal convergence

[23] Lionel Fontagné and Michael Freudenberg, 'Endogenous Symmetry of Shocks in a Monetary Union', *Open Economies Review* 10 (1999): 281.

[24] European Commission, 'EMU after Five Years', *European Economy*, Special Report No 1/2004, available at docentes.fe.unl.pt/~jamador/Textos/eesp104en.pdf.

criteria established by the Treaty (Art. 140(1) TFEU) was treated so generously in the 1990s. Even when actual economic convergence seemed precarious and superficial, it was still hoped that centripetal forces unleashed by the internal market and the single currency would ultimately reinforce it to a sufficient degree.

As I mentioned earlier, fiscal policies constrained by monetary dominance were expected to become structurally oriented towards passivity, rationality and frugality. But some expected an opposite scenario – one of rampant fiscal recklessness. Under the monetary sovereignty, exchange rate risk premia and interest rate risk premia halt the tendency of politicians to cajole their voters by running irresponsible fiscal policies and macroeconomic mismanagement. But in a monetary union, both of the two powerful factors restraining government spending would disappear. Worse still, some governments could try to offload the consequences of their overspending on taxpayers of other Member States.

To remedy this fundamental (political) flaw, the founding fathers of the Eurozone – under the strong insistence of German central bankers – turned to (constitutional) law. They knew that – contrary to the opinion ascribed to the first President of the Commission, Walter Hallstein – the Communities were not solely a creation and source of law, a contingent legal order. They knew that neither the excessive deficit procedure introduced to the Maastricht Treaty (now Art. 126 TFEU) nor the Stability and Growth Pact (SGP) enacted to enable it by means of secondary law was particularly rigid. The politicians negotiating the Eurozone's constitution must have sensed that politicians in the Council enforcing the SGP could not be trusted in their resolve to remedy the political flaw of insufficient fiscal restraint. But why should they care so much about it, if – according to the constitutional setup of the Eurozone – national governments could not be bailed out, either by central banks, through monetary financing (forbidden by Art. 123 TFEU), or by other governments (precluded by Art. 125 TFEU)? The predecessors of the subsequent creditor governments must have held two related beliefs in this respect – both spurious, as it turned out in 2010. First, no fiscal negative externalities could occur. In other words, macroeconomic or fiscal mistakes of some Eurozone governments could not be shifted onto the societies of the other Eurozone countries. Second, knowing this, (by default, rational) markets would nip misguided national economic and fiscal policies in the bud, demanding higher premiums on sovereign debt whenever a national government acts irresponsibly.[25]

In fact, under the assumption that financial markets and governments (when pressured by the markets) act rationally – the assumption universally espoused at the time of the drafting of the Maastricht Treaty – no excessive deficit procedure should be necessary at all. This is because 'financial markets, in theory, had a clear rationale to enforce discipline. As creditors were exposed to potential losses, they would respond to a deteriorating outlook of public finances by demanding higher risk premia, which in turn would ensure that governments did not pursue profligate fiscal policies.'[26] Under the efficient market hypothesis, so close to the German thinking, no intrusive policy coordination at the European level was therefore indispensable. For this reason it should not come as a surprise that the French officials engaging with Kohl, Genscher and Weigel in the late 1980s to turn them on to the idea of the single currency found it relatively easy to convince their German counterparts that no stiff, automatic sanctions for excessive government deficits would be necessary to provide a linchpin for the single currency.

The underlying logic was simple: if there is nowhere to hide in an environment exposing you to various dangers, you should be very careful to remain fit, vigilant and strong. That is a basic rule of nature. Anticipating it, national governments should correct their policies in order to assuage the markets and retain macroeconomic stability. As Pisani-Ferry recounted back in 2006, the majority of academics and financial market pundits 'argued that, provided the no bail-out clause is credible, there was no reason to expect governments to behave in an irresponsible way'.[27] This constitutional

[25] A 1992 Working Paper of the International Monetary Fund (IMF) argued, for instance, that market forces can prevent unsustainable borrowing if capital markets are open, if information on the existing liabilities are readily available, if no bailout is anticipated and if the borrower responds to market signals: Timothy Lane, 'Market Discipline', *IMF Working Paper* No. 92/42, June 1992, available at papers.ssrn.com/sol3/papers.cfm?abstract_id=884774. The original architecture of the Eurozone seemed to fulfil all these conditions.

[26] Yiangou, O'Keeffe and Glöckler, '"Tough Love": How the ECB's Monetary Financing', 227.

[27] Jean Pisani-Ferry, 'Only One Bed for Two Dreams: A Critical Retrospective on the Debate over the Economic Governance of the Euro Area', *Journal of Common Market Studies* 44 (2006): 830.

argument reinforced the intuitions behind the endogeneity of the optimum currency area. Recall that the monetary integration was expected to particularly improve the output (the economic growth) in its poorer, peripheral countries, whose public finances had been prone to pernicious instincts of politicians. These tendencies should be very significantly mitigated – or reversed – by the hefty economic growth rates this group of countries hoped to experience in the monetary union.

1.6 Asymmetric Shocks

Already before the Great Recession, two American economists – Barro and Tenreyro – had challenged the main argument underpinning the endogeneity of the optimum currency area.[28] Their research suggested that a monetary union may intensify trade between constituent economies, but it does not synchronise their propensity to economic shocks. This finding is important, because monetary policy plays a very important stabilising role when an economy is hit by an economic disruption.[29] In a currency union, a centralised monetary policy can fulfil this stabilisation function if the shock is symmetric, because then the policy has a similar impact on the constitutive economies. If, however, the propensity to asymmetric crises grows in a single-currency area, as Barro and Tenreyro found out, a single monetary policy will gradually become more ineffective in its stabilisation function. Striving to caution an economic slump in one country, it might destabilise other regions, rendering the whole system ultimately less convergent.

Barro and Tenreyro were unsure why intensified trade may lead to less symmetry in the propensity to economic shocks. They conjectured, however, that it is caused by economic specialisation, implied by the Nobel laureate Paul Krugman. In a paper written in 1993, Krugman famously argued that 'both theory and evidence suggest that … a more integrated market leads to divergence in the economic structure and

[28] Robert Barro and Silvana Tenreyro, 'Economic Effects of Currency Unions', *Economic Inquiry* 45 (2007): 1–23.

[29] For economists, shocks are any abrupt changes in an economy caused by forces external to market forces. Economic shocks, therefore, can be positive as well – think of a new export market established when its seclusive government is ousted, or of a devaluation when an economy loses price competitiveness.

the growth rates of regions'.[30] At the time when the drafters of the EMU saw the US economy as an emblem of an optimum currency area, precisely because of the very deep market integration enabled by the flows of factors of production, Krugman alleged that the process was in fact fuelling regional specialisation and significant asymmetries.[31] His argument was pointed and forceful: the asymmetries were massive in the United States, entailing region-specific shocks and hence substantially pushing apart the long-term growth paths of American regions. If this process was noticeable in a politically integrated nation state, characterised by high labour mobility and substantial fiscal transfers, how could one expect a single-currency area in a fiscally fragmented European Union to end up as anything but a seriously disintegrative vortex?

In fact, the thrust of Krugman's argument was pointed at the very heart of the internal market. He asserted 'first, that high mobility of capital in particular tends to magnify regional economic fluctuations; and second, that high mobility of both capital and labour tends to produce divergent economic growth over time'.[32] Think about it for a while. The internal market is 'an area without internal frontiers in which the free movement of goods, persons, services and capital' (now Art. 26(2) TFEU). When Krugman was writing his paper, the free movement of goods was by and large already accomplished in the EEC. The picture looked different when it came to persons, services and capital. Until now, Member States have maintained many of the main restrictions to the free movement of services. Lifting them has proven to be a long process, bristling with hardly surmountable difficulties, as I will explain in Chapter 9. But Krugman was not concerned on how either the free movement of goods or services would influence economic performance. He was wary of how the free movement of labour (a subcategory of the free movement of persons) and capital

30 Paul Krugman, 'Lessons of Massachusetts for EMU', in: *Adjustment and Growth in the European Monetary Union*, eds. Francesco Giavazzi and Francisco Torres (Cambridge: Cambridge University Press, 1993), 241–261.

31 This basic intuition became a part of a more comprehensive new economic geography theory. See, for example, Paul Krugman, *Geography and Trade* (Cambridge, MA: MIT Press, 1991), Marius Brülhart and Johan Torstensson 'Regional Integration, Scale Economies and Industry Location in the European Union', *CEPR Discussion Paper* 1435 (London: Centre for Economic Policy Research, 1996) or Masahisa Fujita, Paul Krugman and Anthony J. Venables, *The Spatial Economy: Cities, Regions and International Trade* (Cambridge, MA: MIT Press, 1999).

32 Krugman, 'Lessons', 247.

would impact on the economic growth in a fiscally fragmented and monetarily integrated area.

Free movements of capital and labour – Krugman warned – may be very handy in improving overall allocative efficiency. But 'the penalty is that regional economies, being less diversified, are more subject to technology and demand shocks'.[33] Most strikingly, some regions might be structurally more susceptible to the shocks than are others, and that susceptibility may intensify over time. The single currency propels the underlying processes, because it disables monetary channels of post-shock macroeconomic adjustments.[34]

One question remained: which regions would become more prone to the asymmetric shocks propelled by the internal market and the single currency? Or, to put the same question differently, what makes some regions particularly susceptible to the shocks? Krugman explained his theoretical arguments using the example of New England. This region was thriving economically in the 1980s but suffered from a serious economic slump in early 1990s. Just as a decade later many predicted that Germany would slide into a long-term gradual economic decline, Krugman was foretelling a similar fate for New England, because markets for its products were evaporating when he was putting forward his theory.

New England, however, like Germany some time later, recovered quite swiftly, despite the tight monetary straitjacket it wore when undergoing its macroeconomic adjustment. Favourable international conditions and fiscal stabilisation (breaching the government deficit Treaty obligations in the German case – a point I will return to in the next chapter) certainly played a role in the process. But there could have been yet another factor at play – a feature economists find more difficult to comprehend (and measure): the quality of public policies and institutions.

Economic shocks are always produced by an action (or inaction) of a government – its public institutions and policies.[35] Both New England

[33] Ibid.

[34] Recent research by leading economists is telling in this context. It concluded that the Eurozone countries experienced real economic convergence until about 1992, and divergence since approximately 1998: Bergljot Barkbu, Barry Eichengreen and Ashoka Mody, 'The Euro's Twin Challenges. Experience and Lessons', in: *The Political and Economic Dynamics of the Eurozone Crisis*, eds. James A. Caporaso and Martin Rhodes, (Oxford: Oxford University Press, 2016), 48–78.

[35] Mattias Kumm put the same point trenchantly when he argued that 'asymmetric shocks are not inevitable. They are the result of aggregate human actions. Institutions and policies can be designed in such a way as to make it highly unlikely

and Germany have traditionally vaunted efficient social and economic policies and political processes sufficiently robust to steadily improve performance of the policies. In this respect, both resemble a much more recent example: Finland. Since 2008, Finland has experienced an array of asymmetric shocks. As the IMF described their origins, 'weak external demand and the parallel declines of Nokia and the paper industry have reduced exports, compounded by ill-timed wage increases in 2008–10 that damaged competitiveness. More recently, the recession in Russia has taken a further toll on exports. Rapid population aging has also started to add to the growth challenge.'[36] Yet, the core tissue of the Finish social and economic policies, as well as their enforcement, have not been seriously undermined by the cyclical (demand) and structural (supply) shocks, while its political processes have remained profoundly robust. In consequence, its stagnant economy piled on other Eurozone's woes during the sovereign debt crisis. But it has never become a serious concern for European policymakers.

Southern Eurozone countries have fared much worse on this account, with Italy for instance experiencing a protracted economic decline – of the type Krugman was foretelling for New England – for more than a quarter of a century now. Since the continuous Italian stagnation began, New England has recovered from its economic malaise to become one of the most competitive regions in the world; Germany was dubbed the sick man of Europe, only to become its powerhouse just a few years later; while Finland emerged from the early 1990s recession as one of the most competitive countries in the world, and then sank into another recession. All in all, therefore, the three regions with strong public institutions (New England, Germany and Finland) might have suffered from asymmetric shocks, but they have also greatly benefited from agglomeration effects, while a region with deteriorating public institutions (Italy) has been gradually losing its ability to withstand shocks over which its government has had no direct influence and to avoid those which have directly stemmed from the national governance system. This may explain why economists have never managed to come up with a consistent theoretical argument on whether a currency

that they will happen (asymmetric shocks are not natural phenomena like volcano eruptions or asteroid strikes)': Mattias Kumm, 'What Kind of a Constitutional Crisis Is Europe in and What Should Be Done About It?', WZB Discussion Paper, February 2013, 7, available at bibliothek.wzb.eu/pdf/2013/iv13-801.pdf.

[36] Finland – Concluding Statement for the 2015 Article IV Consultation, 15 September 2015, available at www.imf.org/external/np/ms/2015/091515.htm.

union mitigates or amplifies the propensity of individual economies to undergo asymmetric shocks, nor on how permanent such shocks would be. The reason may simply be that it all depends on local political, institutional and socioeconomic circumstances.[37]

This may also explain why Krugman underestimated the economic resilience of New England. But this does not belie his main argument: that economic integration should be expected to amplify the asymmetricality of economic shocks. The history of the Eurozone demonstrated it clearly, and painfully.[38]

1.7 Inflation Differentials

In this respect, the argument put forward by Krugman interplayed, in a rather surprising way, with the message of the so-called Walters' critique.[39] Walters, famously discouraging Thatcher from introducing the United Kingdom to the Exchange Rate Mechanism in the late 1980s, focused his attention on the destabilising effects of the real interest rate (nominal interest rates minus inflation) differentials that must occur in a monetary union comprised of economies with varying demand levels.[40] Because in a monetary union the central bank establishes one

[37] Economists have sensed, however, that non-economic factors may play an important role in this respect. In his leading handbook, for instance, De Grauwe cautiously espouses the endogeneity of the optimum currency area: Paul De Grauwe, *Economics of the Monetary Union* (Oxford: Oxford University Press, 2012), esp. 23–27. Yet, he admits that 'while economic integration is likely to produce economic structures that can lead to more convergence, the continued existence of the nation-states can set in motion a macroeconomic dynamics in monetary unions that leads to strong divergence': 33.

[38] It is also remarkable in this context that the business cycle synchronisation between the core and the periphery of the Eurozone has decreased since 2008 and that national amplitudes of business cycles differ significantly, as both of the factors influence the propensity for asymmetric shocks. See Ansgar Belke, Clemens Domnick and Daniel Gros, 'Business Cycle Synchronization in the EMU: Core vs. Periphery', *CEPS Working Document*, No. 427, 14 November 2016, available at www.ceps.eu/publications/business-cycle-synchronization-emu-core-vs-periphery.

[39] Alan Walters, *Sterling in Danger: The Economic Consequences of Pegged Exchange Rates* (London: Fontana/Collins, 1990).

[40] For instance, in 2006 – the last year before global financial markets anxieties leading to the Great Recession – the annual HICP inflation varied from 1.23 per cent in Finland and 1.38 per cent in Germany to 2.50 per cent in Portugal, 2.72 per cent in Spain, 2.98 per cent in Ireland and 3.20 per cent in Greece (data available at www.inflation.eu/inflation-rates/hicp-inflation-2006.aspx). Approaching the same issue more systematically, Van Poeck (André Van Poeck, 'One Money and Sixteen Needs: Has the ECB's Monetary Policy Become More Balanced Towards the Needs of the Member States?', *De Economist* 158 (2010): 43–60) used the so-called Taylor rule to find out that the interest rates prior to the crisis were too low, particularly for Ireland

interest rate for all of the participating countries, the real interest rate would vary. In some countries it would be too low, overheating their economies. In others it would be too high, propelling recessionary tendencies.

For this very reason not only could real interest rates differ significantly in a monetary union, but the differentials should escalate, according to the Walters critique, because the processes driving them are pro-cyclical. In other words, a uniform monetary policy is transmitted to each economy differently and the difference should deepen over time. The economies experiencing particularly low real interest rates would be additionally boosted, while those with particularly high real interest rates should be additionally dampened by the monetary channel.

The Walters critique was a nuisance for the drafters of the Eurozone. Walters dominated Thatcher's thinking about monetary policy and hence was indirectly responsible for her putting spanners in the works on monetary integration. Had other leaders followed her, the Eurozone would not have been created. Germans in particular should have pulled out of the process, because Germany was the main potential culprit of the processes Walters foretold.[41] With its high real interest rates when parities were locked in, Germany would experience an immediate economic drag once it joined the single currency (which, indeed, happened). And, according to Walters' predictions, it would find it only more difficult to adjust economically by its inability to calibrate the monetary policy to the necessities of its macroeconomic adjustment.

Now we know that peripheral countries – experiencing higher inflation and thus lower real interest rates – should have understood his argument as an even more serious warning. For them, the single currency would entail a growing spiral of borrowing (as their real interest rates were sub-optimally low), undermining their financial stability in the longer term. This could have been predicted to breed asymmetric shocks, which would in turn entail macroeconomic adjustments, bringing down inflation levels below the average. At this point economic tables would turn, rebounding on the growth in the peripheral countries. None of these issues was tackled when the Eurozone was

and Greece, and – to a lesser degree – for Portugal and Spain. They were too high for Germany and close to optimal only for France and Italy.

41 Which is why, in the 1990s, leading German economists advocated at least slowing down the process of establishing the single currency, so that the German economy would not enter it overheated by the reunification process.

devised. The Kohl government accepted the headwind effects of the real interest rate differentials for the German economy as a price to pay for an overall more convergent Eurozone, while policymakers in the peripheral countries were rubbing their hands in glee as to how the very same differential would boost their economies. Only British policymakers tended to take Walters' arguments seriously. Others espoused different economic theories, defying the Walters' critique. According to one such theory, the 'effects predicted by Walters only arise when the credibility of the peg differs as between the labour and financial markets: but even if such a difference exists, the system is stable in the long run'.[42]

In hindsight it may be tempting to condemn policymakers for believing so gullibly that the euro system could be 'stable in the long run'. But when the Eurozone was drafted, it was impossible to say which side of the economic debate would prove right, while only one of them fitted into the mainstream political thinking of the day. Because it was optimistic, it played neatly with the prevailing mood of reuniting the continent and undertaking bold historical schemes together. Walters' critique could simply sound too cynical, too parochial, too insular and too much related to the belligerent Thatcherism to be treated seriously. In the reality of overwhelming uncertainties, these gut feelings of policymakers could – and did – serve as no worse policy recommendations than (mutually contradictory) sophisticated economic analyses.

1.8 Troubling Non-Tradables

Walters' misgivings regarding possible long-term effects of a single nominal interest rate for the economies characterised by above-average inflation dovetailed ominously with the so-called Balassa–Samuelson effect. The latter predicts that inter-country differences in the relative productivity of tradable (manufacturing, sea and air transports) and non-tradable sectors (construction, private services, non-market services) lead to varying consumer price levels in the two sectors. A version of the effect instantiated in the first decade of the euro provoked prices for non-tradables to grow fastest when the economy was boosted by the

[42] Marcus Miller and Alan Sutherland, 'The "Walters" Critique of the EMS: A Case of Inconsistent Expectations', *CEPR Discussion Paper* No. 480, November 1990, available at cepr.org/active/publications/discussion_papers/dp.php?dpno=480#.

real exchange rate differential with which Walters was so preoccupied. This attracted a particularly pronounced share of foreign investments to these relatively less-productive sectors of the Eurozone's periphery.

The mutually reinforcing process between capital inflows and inflation in non-tradable sectors could be expected to create serious market distortions, instead of underpinning sustainable economic catch-up effects based on gradually improving productivity. The now-cheaper credit would both induce bubbles in non-tradable sectors and – as the flipside of the same process – deteriorate savings ratios if (predictably) the boom was credit-driven. An inflationary pressure on unit labour costs in non-tradable sectors would soon follow, gradually spilling over to other sectors and undermining their price competitiveness by inflating real effective exchange rates. Rather than stimulating non-price competitiveness (productivity) improvements in tradable sectors, this process would lead to even more distorted economic growth by rendering investments in tradables gradually less attractive in the booming peripheral countries, compared with investments in non-tradable sectors. Created by the capital influx, it would concoct a very poisonous mixture of unsustainable bubbles in non-tradable sectors, deteriorating savings ratios and seriously undermined competitiveness in tradables.[43]

The singleness of the monetary policy could not suppress inflation in the countries experiencing these processes without hampering growth in the Eurozone's core, an outcome the ECB wholeheartedly wanted to avoid. Both in the 1990s and in the following decade, this problem was rejected on the premise of rational markets eager to prevent patent exchange-rate appreciations.[44] This counterargument had proved entirely wrong, though, since the very inception of the Eurozone: already by 2002 there were clear signs of real exchange rate overvaluation in the Eurozone's periphery.[45]

43 Jose L. Dias Sanchez and Aristomene Varoudakis, 'Tracking the Causes of Eurozone External Imbalances: New Evidence', *VOX CEPR's Policy Portal*, 6 February 2014, available at www.voxeu.org/article/causes-eurozone-external-imbalances.

44 Michael Emerson et al., *One Market, One Money. An Evaluation of the Potential Benefits and Costs of Forming an Economic and Monetary Union* (New York: Oxford University Press, 1992); Miller and Sutherland, 'The "Walters" Critique of the EMS'; Boris Hofmann and Hermann Remsperger, 'Inflation Differentials among the Euro Area Countries: Potential Causes and Consequences', *Journal of Asian Economics* 16 (2005): 403–419.

45 Barry Eichengreen, 'Imbalances in the Euro Area', University of California, Berkeley, November 2010, 3, available at eml.berkeley.edu/~eichengr/Imbalances_Euro_Area_5-23-11.pdf.

We now know that the markets were not far-seeing enough even to recognise that the scenario described in Walters' critique was materialising, fuelling macroeconomic divergences that almost tore the EMU apart in the aftermath of the global financial crisis. The single monetary constraint was not internalized, despite some alarm bells ringing early on. For instance, in a paper published in 2006, Pisani-Ferry argued that 'the focus on the Maastricht nominal deficit criterion led to the fact being overlooked that the benefits from the reduction in risk premia on bond rates had been passed on to the private sector in the form of higher spending and lower taxes. Those policies contributed to triggering price increases in the non-traded goods sector that would eventually translate into an excessive real appreciation.'[46]

All in all, therefore, the storm devastating the economies of the peripheral Eurozone countries, its societies and political systems during the sovereign debt crisis did not come out of the blue. It did not approach from across the ocean. It was caused by financial flows funnelled to wrong sectors in wrong locations. The single currency was not a precondition of this process.[47] But the very architecture of the euro proved very conducive to it.[48] Those who were profiting from the flows, seeking steeper yield curves, found themselves in the line of fire when policymakers and the media ultimately started looking for scapegoats. But, in fact, they only acted according to the incentives carved in the edifice of the Eurozone. Some, like Barro and Tenreyro, or Pisani-Ferry, saw the incentive structure early on. Some, like Krugman or Walters, anticipated it even earlier. But others simply believed that the reality would ultimately prove different.

1.9 Impossible Imbalances That Materialised

The majority of pundits also believed that, in a monetary union between advanced economies with integrated financial markets, current account deficits (imports exceeding exports) should always be

[46] Pisani-Ferry, 'One Bed for Two Dreams', 837.

[47] Outside the Eurozone it was experienced painfully in Romania, Hungary and the Baltic states in particular.

[48] For a broader argument on how the single currency fostered cross-border financial activity much more than trade (the integration of the real economy), see Daniel Gros, 'One Market, One Money – A Mistaken Argument (post factum)?', *CEPS Policy Insight* No. 2017/05, 16 February 2017, available at www.ceps.eu/system/files/DG_OneMarketOneMoney_0.pdf.

balanced by corresponding capital account surpluses. Because current account deficits were believed to never translate into a balance-of-payments crisis in such a system, the underlying macroeconomic imbalances were perceived as entirely innocuous. The dogma held it that 'a major effect of EMU is that balance-of-payments constraints will disappear ... Private markets will finance all viable borrowers, and savings and investment balances will no longer be constraints at the national level.'[49] This very dogma was grafted onto the structure of the euro: while non-Eurozone countries (the countries with derogation) could well fall into a balance-of-payments crisis – precisely because their financial markets were not sufficiently integrated with the rest of the internal market – a separate provision establishing a mechanism for assisting them financially was retained by the Treaty.[50] But, as it turned out, exactly because these countries controlled their own monetary policies, they found it easier to avoid or remedy balance-of-payments crises. The Eurozone's periphery was in an entirely different situation. Bini Smaghi recounted tellingly in this context that 'between 1999 and 2008, Italy's competiveness relative to Germany fell more than 30% in terms of average unit labour costs. Spain lost about 40%, and Ireland and Portugal about 20%. With the loss of competitiveness and the growth of domestic demand outstripping GDP, external deficits increased. In 2007, before the outbreak of the crisis, Greece recorded an external deficit of 15% of GDP, Spain and Portugal 10% and Ireland by 5%.'[51] Instead of preventing balance-of-payments crises from occurring, the financial integration of the Eurozone was nurturing imbalances that induced a systemic explosion in 2010.

[49] European Commission, 'One Market, One Money. An Evaluation of the Potential Benefits and Costs of Forming an Economic and Monetary Union', *European Economy*, Report No 44/1990, 24, available at ec.europa.eu/economy_finance/publications/pages/publication7454_en.pdf.

[50] According to Art. 143 TFEU mutual assistance can be granted – but only to a country with a derogation – by the Council, when the country 'is in difficulties or is seriously threatened with difficulties as regards its balance of payments either as a result of an overall disequilibrium in its balance of payments, or as a result of the type of currency at its disposal, and where such difficulties are liable in particular to jeopardise the functioning of the internal market or the implementation of the common commercial policy'. Additionally, the Maastricht Treaty made it clear that the possibility of receiving such a balance-of-payments assistance 'shall cease to apply from the beginning of the third stage' (i.e., from the introduction of the euro; Art. 119(4) TEC) for the Member States joining the euro.

[51] Lorenzo Bini Smaghi, *Austerity: European Democracies against the Wall* (Brussels: CEPS Paperback, July 2013), 45, available at aei.pitt.edu/47681/1/LBS_Austerity.pdf.

Furthermore, it was – again wrongly – hoped that national governments of the peripheral Eurozone countries would overcome the fallouts of the Balassa–Samuelson effect propelled by diminishing real interest rates, introducing policies preventing bubbles on non-tradable markets (especially by constraining credit for residential purposes). Aware of its potentially devastating consequences, those governments should have known that, unless properly countenanced, excessive real appreciations would set in, undermining the convergence process so much yearned for by the very same governments.

The Eurozone setup failed on the first of the two points (balance-of-payments crises should not happen in the Eurozone) because it failed on the second (national policymakers and financial markets would prevent them). But could national policymakers really be expected to prevent the imbalances from occurring? Booming asset markets translated directly and impressively into falling unemployment and growing fiscal revenues. A countercyclical policy aimed at restraining excessive real exchange rate appreciations becomes politically impossible in such a situation, simply because 'when all banks are delivering great profits, all managers look competent; when all countries are delivering the public goods demanded by voters, all governments look efficient (this mechanism applies both to real estate bubbles, as in Ireland and Spain, and to sovereign debt bubbles, as in Portugal and Greece)'.[52] So, certainly, lower average interest rates on mortgages paid by borrowers in Ireland or Spain relative to Germany (a consequence of floating rates on mortgage credit used in the first two countries, as opposed to Germany, where fixed rates prevailed) and higher loan-to-value ratios available in the Eurozone's periphery seriously contributed to the property market boom. But confronting the local governments would have upset local societies expecting more jobs and higher economic growth.

For all these reasons, preventing the growing macroeconomic imbalances – e.g., by enforcing very conservative practices on mortgage lending – would be both largely requisite in the long term and impossible to achieve for short-term considerations. This outcome should be all the more expected when one considers that only after the event can we be sure what, in the past, was requisite in the longer perspective. In the shorter perspective, too many uncertainties occlude the picture to follow

[52] Jésus Fernández-Villaverde, Luis Garicano and Tano Santos, 'Political Credit Cycles: The Case of the Euro Zone', *NBER Working Paper No. 18899*, 15 March 2013, 2, available at economics.sas.upenn.edu/~jesusfv/Political_Credit_Cycles.pdf.

anything but short-term incentives. When a system produces such time-inconsistencies, no actor can be blamed for rising to the immediate bait.

Market players face an ultimately similar dilemma, with their field of view constrained by their shareholders' pressure to deliver immediate profits rather than waiting for them for three or five years. Of course, there are some methods to mitigate the problems. Bonuses paid to staff of financial institutions may be capped, as the European Banking Authority recommended in a document issued in mid-2016.[53] Certain economic policies may be taken out of the hands of politicians and bestowed on independent - counter-majoritarian - institutions. The independence of central banks, in charge of monetary policy, is a prime example of this pattern.[54] The methods are imperfect, but for my argument another aspect is more important. Maybe politicians and financial markets should have done more to avoid the pernicious effects described earlier. And certainly by not doing so they did put fire under the Eurozone during the first decade of the single currency. But they did not act irrationally. Rather, their rationality was different to the rationality expected from them by the Eurozone's arrangement.

1.10 Stupefying the Banking System

Financial flows - originally hoped to propel economic convergence - finally turned out to fuel a tremendous systemic crisis, not only due to their role in the billowing of macroeconomic imbalances, but also because of how they played out with banking systems. As a quirk of the original Eurozone setup, interbank markets of the single currency area were almost completely integrated when the sovereign debt crisis burst in 2010, while retail banking remained divided across national

53 Guidelines on sound remuneration policies under Arts. 74(3) and 75(2) of Directive 2013/36/EU and disclosures under Art. 450 of Regulation 575/2013, 27 June 2016, available at www.eba.europa.eu/documents/10180/1314839/EBA-GL-2015-22+Guidelines+on+Sound+Remuneration+Policies_EN.pdf.

54 The independence of central banks in the EU - enshrined in Art. 130 and Art. 282(3) TFEU and Art. 7 of the Statute of the European System of Central Banks (ESCB) and the ECB - has been motivated by the finding that (democratically elected) decision-makers in charge of economic policy have a tendency to maximise economic growth by all means, even if it ensues very serious side-effects, like high inflation. The independence of central banks (i.e., their counter-majoritarian status) is to protect society against negative consequences of such policies. For a comprehensive discussion see, for example, Johannes M. Groeneveld, *Inflation Patterns and Monetary Policy: Lessons for the European Central Bank* (Cheltenham; Northampton, MA: Edward Elgar, 1998).

borders.[55] This discrepancy caused devastating consequences for the banking systems of the engulfed countries.[56]

In the good times the short-term liabilities that had integrated the Eurozone's interbank market provided ample liquidity. It lulled banks into petrifying their business models, whether sustainable in an adverse scenario or not. When the good times ended, the liquidity immediately dried up, amplifying vulnerabilities of the previously most fragile financial institutions. Furthermore, because foreign creditor banks did not hold equity stakes in the distressed banks, they did not have a sufficiently strong motive to sustain funding to the affected banking systems, rendering banks in the Eurozone's periphery vulnerable both to macroeconomic instability (deteriorating solvency of their retail clients) and financial instability (limited confidence on the wholesale markets).

Instead of enhanced risk-sharing, therefore, the integrated interbank market amplified risks of illiquidity in the countries undergoing asymmetric shocks, of domestic (e.g., asset price bubbles) or international (e.g., fallouts of international financial crises) making. When the risks materialised in 2010, policymakers faced a particularly difficult dilemma: who should bear the brunt of the asymmetric shock? One answer is: burn foreign depositors and foreign financial institutions. Another is: burn domestic financial institutions and their equity holders. And yet another is: burn domestic taxpayers. The original Eurozone setup did not even attempt to direct the process of loss distribution, optimistically assuming that systemically important banking crises would not occur in the single currency area.

1.11 The Accident Waiting to Happen

The architecture of the Eurozone produced effects opposite to what Frankel, Rose and their like predicted: the economic integration brought by the single currency to a brand new level rendered the peripheral countries more susceptible both to asymmetric shocks and to

[55] 'Financial Integration in Europe', European Central Bank, April 2015, available at www.ecb.europa.eu/pub/pdf/other/financialintegrationineurope201504.en.pdf?ec20b5e9b09b9003ce3e08ab27a6acb8.

[56] Mario Draghi, 'Financial Integration and Banking Union', in *Progress through Crisis? Proceedings of the Conference for the 20th Anniversary of the Establishment of the European Monetary Institut*, eds. Ivo Maes and Frank Moss (Frankfurt am Main: ECB, 2014), 153.

financial instability. National political processes and their economic outcomes not only unencumbered, but largely propelled by the architecture of the single currency and of the internal market, fuelled disequilibria only waiting for an external ignition to flare fully fledged balance-of-payments crises. The fact that financial stability – contrary to the (aggregate) price stability – was of no concern to the drafters of the EMU helped the processes grow unnoticed until all the ingredients of the perfect storm were in place and the close financial connections propelling the imbalances were ready to transmit its devastating consequences from one country to the next. In consequence, 'instead of producing sustainable real convergence between the core and periphery, the single currency had resulted in imbalances and was ill-prepared to deal with them'.[57]

The free flow of capital, the main linchpin of the hoped-for economic convergence, triggered balance-of-payments crises when its direction reversed. The crises deprived banking systems first, and the real economy soon after, of the liquidity necessary to sustain economic activity. Sovereigns stepped in and soon were themselves brought to their knees by the fact that they did not control the currency in which the mounting pile of private and public debts was denominated.[58] Capital flights from the financially engulfed periphery to the core contributed further to imbalances and undermined debt sustainability of certain sovereigns to the extent that the scenario of a major financial implosion became very realistic.

As I will argue more broadly in Chapter 4, this scenario has been staved off largely by the alchemy of the ECB under Mario Draghi. Before we delve into this, however, we should first examine more comprehensively how the political and economic dynamics of the Eurozone has interacted with the rules defining the economic coordination established by the Treaty both prior to and after the sovereign debt crisis. This is the story to which we will now turn.

[57] André Sapir and Guntram B. Wolff, 'Euro-area Governance: What to Reform and How to Do It', *Bruegel Policy Brief* No. 2015/01, February 2015, available at bruegel.org/2015/02/euro-area-governance-what-to-reform-and-how-to-do-it/.

[58] Paul De Grauwe, 'The Governance of a Fragile Eurozone', *CEPS Working Document* No. 346, May 2011, available at www.ceps.eu/system/files/book/2011/05/WD%20346%20De%20Grauwe%20on%20Eurozone%20Governance.pdf.

2 Dead Rules Walking

2.1 High Hopes for Disciplining Institutions

The drafters of the Eurozone wanted economic convergence – the prerequisite and the goal of monetary integration – to be achieved not only by the salutary effects of the internal market and financial integration (the rickety assumptions discussed more thoroughly in the previous chapter), but also by more advanced institutional developments. Those developments would be aimed at securing what the President of the Eurogroup, Jeroen Dijsselbloem, characterised much more recently in the following manner: 'We are a monetary union that is rule-based, and requires the strong commitment from the members.'[1]

As I explained in the previous chapter, the Eurozone was framed on the belief that the Treaty – precluding bailouts of national governments by other governments and central banks – would force national politicians to act rationally in socioeconomic policies, because it would expose them to the pressure of other agents, who were also hoped to act rationally: market players. The Delors Report was aware, however, that 'uncoordinated and divergent national budgetary policies would undermine monetary stability and generate imbalances in the real and financial sectors of the Community'.[2] As its authors also heeded, 'evidence suggests that market perceptions do not necessarily provide strong and compelling signals ... market views about the creditworthiness of

[1] 'We Are a Rule-Based Monetary Union: Dijsselbloem', *Sigmalive*, 13 July 2015, available at www.sigmalive.com/en/news/greece/132105/we-are-a-rulebased-monetary-union-dijsselbloem.

[2] Committee for the study of economic and monetary union, 'Report on Economic and Monetary Union in the European Community', April 1989, 19, available at aei.pitt.edu/1007/1/monetary_delors.pdf.

official borrowers tend to change abruptly and result in the closure of access to market financing. The constraints imposed by market forces might either be too slow and weak or too sudden and disruptive.'[3] Coordinating procedures devised by the Treaties, in fiscal area peppered with potential financial sanctions imposed on defecting governments, were therefore hoped to correct what market pressure might fail to achieve and hence to precipitate the economic convergence necessary for the sustainability of the monetary union.

The belief in the rationality of governments when exposed to the pressure of unassailably rational markets sprang up quite late, gaining prominence with the rise of neo-liberalism in the 1980s. But the other tenet of the plan for the single currency - the disciplining institutional infrastructure - was devised much earlier. The Werner Report of 1970 in particular advocated a two-pronged approach to the monetary union. On the one hand, it recognised the need for a centralised, and seriously enlarged, Community budget. On the other, it admitted that, because any such a budget 'will still be weak compared with that of the national budgets, the harmonised management ... will be an essential feature of cohesion in the union'.[4] For this reason, the very same report recommended that 'the margins within which the main budget aggregates must be held both for the annual budget and the multi-year projections will be decided at the community level, taking account of the economic situation and the particular features of each country ... In order to be able to influence the short-term economic trend rapidly and effectively it will be useful to have at the national level budgetary and fiscal instruments that can be handled in accordance with Community directives.'[5] I will argue in Chapter 5 that it is quite uncertain if even a significantly bigger Union budget and decisions on 'the annual budget and the multi-year projections' elevated to the community level would provide for sufficient convergence in a monetary union as socioeconomically divergent as the Eurozone has been. First, however, we should understand the nature and practical effects of the disciplining institutional infrastructure agreed two decades after the Werner Report.

[3] Committee for the study of economic and monetary union, 'Report on Economic and Monetary Union', 20.

[4] Pierre Werner et al., 'Report to the Council and the Commission on the Realisation of Economic and Monetary Union in the Community', 1970, 11, available at ec.europa.eu/economy_finance/publications/publication6142_en.pdf.

[5] Ibid.

2.2 The Stability and Growth Pact: Disabled at Birth, Incurably

The setup established in Maastricht provided for a bifurcated coordination pattern: fiscal policy coordination (Art. 126 TFEU) as well as macroeconomic and employment policy coordination (Arts. 121 and 148 TFEU). Macroeconomic and employment policy coordination could not go further than the issuing of (by design, non-binding) recommendations to national governments by European institutions. In this respect, market pressure was hoped to produce the disciplining effects European institutions could not themselves exert. However, governments running excessive deficits and disrespecting fiscal policy recommendations could be sanctioned financially by the Council. But, as is well known, the latter option was practically aborted when the European institutions backtracked from levelling-up the excessive deficit procedure against Germany and France in 2003.

This particular story is worth retelling because it demonstrates all of the weaknesses of a rules-based Eurozone attainable by the European Union; weaknesses too big to be remedied without very deep constitutional adaptations.

The prevailing storyline of what happened in 2003 has it that the original setup of the Eurozone, encapsulated in the 1997 version of the SGP, was correctly based on orthodox monetarist thinking (that fiscal policy should avoid high budget deficits). But soon the Schröder government ran an excessive government deficit and blocked (complicitly with France, where monetarism has never gained traction) the excessive deficit procedure in the Council. As soon as the Commission raised the issue in 2003,[6] Germany and France responded by championing the process of watering down the original rules of fiscal discipline (which

[6] Germany and France disrespected the 3 per cent Treaty limit on government deficit in 2002. In early 2003, both were addressed with decisions on the existence of an excessive deficit and specific recommendations on how to remedy it. A few months later the Commission recommended that the Council should – first – acknowledge that 'there has been no effective action in response to its recommendations' (Art. 126(8) TFEU). Simultaneously, the Commission recommended that both countries 'persist in failing to put into practice the recommendations', with the inevitable Treaty consequence of giving 'notice to the Member State to take, within a specified time limit, measures for the deficit reduction which is judged necessary by the Council in order to remedy the situation' (Art. 126(9) TFEU). In late November 2003, however, it turned out that the two countries managed to form a sufficiently strong minority in the Council (with Italy, Ireland, Luxembourg, Portugal and the United Kingdom) to block further actions.

indeed happened in 2005),[7] opening the gates for fiscal irresponsibility and the Eurozone crisis that burst in 2010. As one contemporary commentator argued, 'the Eurozone's Stability and Growth Pact was effectively killed off ... when EU finance ministers refused to enforce treaty law against France and Germany for persistently breaching the spending rules'.[8]

More specifically, the German mistake – according to this storyline – was that 'in the late 1990s, when Germany enjoyed relatively strong economic growth, progress in fiscal consolidation was limited, with the general government deficit remaining at around 1.5% of GDP. Thus, there had been little budgetary leeway to accommodate for the effects of a cyclical slowdown or for any unexpected revenue shortfalls from a tax reform implemented in 2001.'[9] In short, when raising its flag (only to put it down a few months later) in January 2003, the Council wanted the second Schröder government to pay for the mistakes of the first Schröder government. It acted according to the original constitutional belief espoused by the founders of the Eurozone: that sinners should pay for their mistakes; otherwise the credibility of the whole system would be compromised.

But Schröder was expected to pay for his earlier mistakes two years before Germany's next general election. In addition, the European institutions demanded government spending cuts precisely when he struggled to mitigate the political costs of his socially disruptive Agenda 2010. The original setup of the Eurozone did not recognise such nuances. Or, in fact, it was programmed to ignore them. But Schröder – as a politician – can hardly be blamed for paying critical attention to them. Nor can he be blamed for using all the political possibilities he had to avoid squandering his re-election chances by simultaneously pursuing the painful (and – in hindsight – effective) structural reforms

[7] Council Regulation 1055/2005 of 27 June 2005 amending Regulation 1466/97 on the strengthening of the surveillance of budgetary positions and the surveillance and coordination of economic policies, OJ 2005 No. L 174, 7 July 2005, pp. 1–4 and Council Regulation 1056/2005 of 27 June 2005 amending Regulation 1467/97 on speeding up and clarifying the implementation of the excessive deficit procedure, OJ 2005 No. L 174, 7 July 2005, pp. 5–9.

[8] Ambrose Evans-Pritchard, 'France and Germany Smash Euro Pact', *The Telegraph*, 26 November 2003, available at www.telegraph.co.uk/finance/2870055/France-and-Germany-smash-Euro-pact.html.

[9] Council Decision 2003/89/EC of 21 January 2003 on the existence of an excessive deficit in Germany – Application of Article 104(6) of the Treaty establishing the European Community, OJ No. L 34, 11 February 2003, pp. 16–17, preamble, Sec. 7.

and slashing government spending at the same time. A decade later, the next generation of national politicians, pursuing (or pretending to pursue) similar macroeconomic adjustments in other Eurozone countries used precisely the same argument to escape the ostensibly reinforced reincarnation of the coordination procedures. In both instances they have been perfectly successful.

In 2003 the Commission was very reticent to pursue a case against Germany, unofficially sharing the reservations of the Schröder government that the original rules of the SGP were too unreflective. They did not pay any attention to the reasons underlying government deficits. Romano Prodi, then the President of the Commission, famously admitted with disarming frankness: 'I know very well that the stability pact is stupid, like all decisions which are rigid.'[10] Well-known economists confirmed this assessment in more diplomatic and sophisticated terms. Eichengreen, for instance, argued that 'the case for rigid ceilings on budget deficits was never particularly compelling. The idea that the ECB would run an inflationary monetary policy if Germany's budget deficit was 4 per cent rather than 3 per cent was never plausible. And now that there are no national monetary policies to be tailored to French or German economic conditions, the importance of a flexible fiscal policy that can respond to the state of demand is greater still.'[11] By underestimating the scope of cyclical fluctuations and the dynamics of macroeconomic adjustments in a monetary union, the strenuousness of structural reforms in particular – the argument went – the original SGP setup was eating its own tail.

The 2005 reform of the SGP was precisely to address this dysfunctionality. Now structural reforms would weigh in, and government deficits were to be measured in cyclically adjusted, structural, terms (net of one-off and temporary measures). To customise the Pact further, the reform introduced the concept of country-specific 'medium-term objectives'. They were aimed at heeding characteristics of each country, especially its potential growth and the debt-to-GDP ratio. Adjustment efforts were individualised accordingly, depending on the phase of the economic cycle. Furthermore, not only

[10] Andrew Osborn, 'Prodi Disowns "Stupid" Stability Pact', *Guardian*, 18 October 2002, available at www.theguardian.com/business/2002/oct/18/theeuro.europeanunion.

[11] Barry Eichengreen, 'After the Stability Pact', University of California, Berkeley, 19 November 2003, available from eml.berkeley.edu/~eichengr/reviews/die-zeitnov20-03.pdf.

the countries experiencing an annual fall of real GDP of at least 2 per cent could claim 'severe economic downturn' circumstances absolving them – according to the 1997 version of the SGP – of the obligation to run excessive government deficit. Since 2005 any negative growth rate, or even a period of positive but very low growth compared to the trend, was bringing about the same effect. Even when the excessive deficit procedure could not be avoided on this ground, the national government could still expect extended correction deadlines, as also authorised by the 2005 reform.

But compliance did not improve in subsequent years, despite the reformed SGP going far in customising the rules of fiscal coordination and making it easier for the Member States to meet its requirements.[12] Research papers published about the same time warned that the budgetary stabilisation efforts of Eurozone governments became lower than in the rest of the OECD[13] and more flexible rules could hardly be predicted to achieve any more synchronisation. To make it even worse, deficit figures especially in Greece, Italy, Spain, Ireland and Portugal were so much misreported that the Eurostat had to revise the deficit numbers these governments were submitting to the Commission.[14] Instead of using the boom period of the cycle preceding the 2008 financial meltdown to run budgetary surpluses and to undertake structural reforms, the majority of Eurozone Member States went for procyclical fiscal stimuli and amplified the upcoming shock, with European institutions standing idle on the sidelines.

[12] According to calculations of the CESifo, up until 2010 the deficit-to-GDP ratios had exceeded the 3 per cent mark ninety-seven times since the establishment of the Euro area. The excesses could not be justified pursuant to Art. 2 Regulation 1467/97 in sixty-eight cases: CESifo, 'EEAG Report on the European Economy 2011', 79, available at www.cesifo-group.de. It is even more striking that Germany, France and Italy – the three biggest Euro Area economies – had altogether breached the Stability and Growth pact rules twelve times between 2000 and 2007.

[13] Charles Wyplosz, 'European Monetary Union: The Dark Sides of a Major Success', *Economic Policy* 21 (2006): 207–261; Barry Eichengreen, 'Europe, the Euro and the ECB: Monetary Success, Fiscal Failure', *Journal of Policy Modeling* 27 (2005): 427–439.

[14] Jeffrey Frankel and Jesse Schreger, 'Over-Optimistic Official Forecasts in the Eurozone and Fiscal Rules', *NBER Working Paper* No. 18283, August 2012; Victor Ngai, 'Appendix. Introduction to the Stability and Growth Pact', in: *Governance for the Eurozone: Integration or Disintegration?*, eds. Allen Franklin, Elena Carletti and Saverio Simonelli, 2012, 219, available at www.eui.eu/DepartmentsAndCentres/Economics/SeminarsEvents/Conferences/GovernancefortheEurozoneIntegrationorDisintegration.aspx.

All in all, therefore, the original version of the Pact was arguably obtusely rigid. But the more flexible one, established in 2005, did not prove any smarter. In theory this could be surprising, because the SGP, as reformed in 2005, takes into account a broad set of factors influencing the economic cycle. It still pivots on the questionable 3 per cent GDP deficit criterion, famously devised in response to a political necessity and deprived of any deeper economic justification.[15] Economists have argued, however, that 'if the fiscal stabilisation coefficient (which measures the response of the overall fiscal deficit to changes in the output gap) is 0.7, then a 3.6 percent of GDP negative output gap is compatible with the 3 percent deficit criterion'.[16] For advanced economies this coefficient and these negative output gaps should theoretically be enough (most of the time) to meet the Pact's deficit criterion. But only theoretically. Why?

2.3 Impossible Rules and Concepts

The basic principle of sustainable public finances seems very simple: if private demand contracts by, say, 3 per cent, then public demand should expand in a similar fashion to cancel it out. Subsequently (or previously), public demand ought to decrease by a corresponding figure when private demand grows, to keep the public debt at a constant level.[17] But even when the Treaties are attached with solemn declarations of running countercyclical fiscal policies,[18] only very few societies expect

[15] One of its original authors – an official at the French Ministry of Finance – confessed that the criterion was put up in less than an hour at the demand of French President Mitterrand back in 1981. The group of economists who invented appreciated, in particular, its affinity to the Trinity [*sic*]. See William Mitchell, *Eurozone Dystopia* (Cheltenham: Edward Elgar Publishing, 2015): 123–125.

[16] Grégory Claeys, Zsolt Darvas and Alvaro Leandro, 'A Proposal to Revive the European Fiscal Framework', *Bruegel Policy Contribution* No. 2016/07, 29 March 2016, 4, available at bruegel.org/wp-content/uploads/2016/03/pc_2016_07.pdf.

[17] It is often argued that the provision of public infrastructure is always a good investment, as, by default, investments pay for themselves in the long term. While theoretically plausible (depending on the local specifics of individual infrastructure projects), in practice this argument has been routinely used as an excuse for deficit spending more generally.

[18] According to the Declaration on Article 126 of the TFEU, annexed to the TEU: 'the Conference agrees that Member States should use periods of economic recovery actively to consolidate public finances and improve their budgetary positions. The objective is to gradually achieve a budgetary surplus in good times which creates the necessary room to accommodate economic downturns and thus contribute to the long-term sustainability of public finances.'

their governments to run government surpluses in economic good times. They would do so even less were they to realise that government surpluses exchange long-term macroeconomic stability for less economic activity – and less jobs! – in the short term. So most societies are deceived by time-inconsistent incentives. They choose the shorter perspective over the longer one. They want more jobs and higher salaries promised by additional public demand (government deficits) when the economy is at full swing. They reward the politicians who deliver it and punish those who do not. In consequence, the simple arithmetical calculation underpinning sustainable public finances in practice often morphs into a political Millennium Prize Problem.

The concept of financial sanctions imposed on the states stubbornly disrespecting Council recommendations issued during the excessive deficit procedure is another idea theoretically congruent but practically impossible to achieve. Governments of monetarily independent countries pursuing policies considered irresponsible by financial markets pay higher premia on their borrowing. The process was predicted to be muted in the Eurozone (in practice it disappeared altogether since its inception, until it reignited in the aftermath of the Great Recession), because the single currency was originally believed to absolve even the traditionally least effective national governments of serious economic troubles. But if the market penalty would disappear, an institutionalised penalty should take its place. And if national governments of monetarily independent states care so much about the market penalty they are exposed to, why would they react differently to a functionally similar mechanism administered by the Council?

There is, of course, a huge (political) loophole in this thinking. Those who devised financial sanctions as a method of enforcing the SGP entirely ignored another European experience. According to the Treaty (Art. 258 et seq. TFEU) a Member State allegedly disrespecting Treaty obligations may be brought before the Court of Justice on a motion of either the Commission or another Member State. But national governments have not sued each other, for fear of the related publicity and international tensions, or in order to demonstrate good political intentions. The underlying political calculus is both irresistible and predictable, as some warned in respect to the SGP very soon after it was set up.[19] For the very same reasons, prime

[19] Barry Eichengreen and Charles Wyplosz 'The Stability Pact: More Than a Minor Nuisance?', *Economic Policy* 13 (1998): 65–114.

ministers or finance ministers cannot be expected to press for financial sanctions on other (economically diverging) governments, even in economic good times, when the sanctions would not trigger financial illiquidity of the punished government. And imposing the sanctions when an action is most expected – when the national economy slides into an economic crisis – would only exacerbate its calamities by additionally undermining confidence in the economy. At this point there are no rational reasons for imposing the sanctions, either economic, political or social. In all of these respects the incentive structure of national politicians to put peer pressure on other governments is entirely different to what financial markets care about. And the rules-based union was doomed, from its very beginning, for disregarding this very difference.

It was also doomed for being unable to provide mechanisms to prevent macroeconomic imbalances from ballooning. As I mentioned in the previous chapter, one reason for this huge institutional rift was the trust in the converging effects of the internal market and fiscal rectitude. Another was the belief that balance-of-payments crises – the effect of excessive macroeconomic imbalances – would not occur in the Eurozone. Had its drafters realised that all of these assumptions were spurious, they would have faced yet more serious practical problems. What level of a current account deficit should spur European institutions to action? What level of inflation? What type of tax policy, social security policy, labour market policy etc.? And how legitimate could any actions of European institutions be when responding to any of the questions, considering that the transferring of any serious powers in any of the areas to the European level was not part of the original Eurozone's setup?

As it later turned out, while ignoring all the questions and concentrating the institutional tissue on the fiscal matters was a fatal mistake, tackling macroeconomic imbalances in a monetary union would be an absolutely heroic task. The experiences of Ireland and Spain before the crisis demonstrate the point vividly. In both countries consecutive national governments ran conservative fiscal policies throughout the Eurozone's first decade. In consequence, Ireland halved its public debt between 1999 and 2007, from 46.7 per cent down to 23.9 per cent. Spain also managed to reduce its public debt by a quarter of the GDP in the same period, from 60.9 per cent of GDP in 1999 to 35.5 percent in 2007. Five years later – in 2012 – the public debt of Ireland peaked at 120.2

per cent of GDP, however, while Spain's stood at 85.4 per cent, and was rising fast.[20] Why? The two countries may have looked fiscally sound in 2007, but their economies were heavily unbalanced; extremely susceptible to asymmetric shocks and financial instability. No fiscal policy could countenance them. As Martin Wolf of the *Financial Times* argued, '[I]n retrospect, the only way the Spanish authorities could have prepared themselves for the shock would have been to run fiscal surpluses of 10 per cent of GDP over the five or six years before the crisis, so generating a positive net asset position of at least 20 per cent of GDP. That might have been enough (though even that is uncertain). There is no chance whatsoever that a democracy would run such surpluses.'[21]

The Irish example is telling also in another respect: whether the institutional tissue of the rules-based union could remedy the imbalances by any viable alternative to the (otherwise defunct) SGP. According to the original concept, the macroeconomic coordination was very flexible both within the Eurozone and outside of it: it was based on non-binding recommendations only. This setup had no chance of withstanding the pressure of diverging economic processes (discussed in the previous chapter) as powerful as those set in motion by the single currency.

In 2001 – i.e., even before Europeans started using euro coins and banknotes – a booming Ireland introduced tax cuts, despite the Council's warning that the cuts would 'aggravate overheating and inflationary pressures and widen the positive output gap'.[22] The Irish government ignored the recommendation, exposing one obvious vulnerability of the new procedure: its flexibility rendered the positions of the Commission and the Council impossible to enforce. But, while a decade later European legislators were at pains to devise more rigid procedures to remedy this ostensibly excessive flexibility, they missed the other lesson from the Irish debacle a decade earlier. Back in 2001 many economists disagreed with the European institutions' assessment of Irish policies, arguing that its economic growth was actually in line with the (fast-improving) macroeconomic fundamentals. Hence, tax cuts would not excessively widen the output gap. Nor would they

[20] All statistical data based on Eurostat.

[21] Martin Wolf, 'What Was Spain Supposed to Have Done?', *Martin Wolf's Exchange*, *Financial Times Blogs*, 25 June 2012.

[22] Council Recommendation of 12 February 2001 with a view to ending the inconsistency with the broad guidelines of the economic policies in Ireland, OJ 2001 No. L 69, 10 March 2001, pp. 22–23.

lead to excessive inflation.[23] What, therefore, looked like the headstrong behaviour of a national government irresponsibly ignoring admonitions of European institutions could very have been an economically accurate policy to follow.

This, of course, raises a fundamental question. How could it be that the government of a small country could prevail on merits in confrontation with European institutions, despite all the analytical advantages they should have over each individual government and despite their more pronounced insulation from short-sighted political calculations so often blinding national politicians in their economic choices?

2.4 Incentivised to Procrastinate

The reason is as simple as it is disturbing: macroeconomists like to see their discipline as a science in which individual aggregates interact with each other in a predictable and quantifiable manner. But in practice macroeconomics is much closer to politics, with all its unpredictable causalities. It should not be surprising, therefore, that even (or particularly) very sophisticated macroeconomic calculations err so often, and so conspicuously.

This point is particularly crucial from the institutional perspective, both in respect to macroeconomic, fiscal and any other economic coordination. Policymakers populating the institutions in charge of the coordination must avail themselves of macroeconomic indicators if they want to mitigate political pressures from individual capitals, if they want to render the coordination reliable and if they want to neutrally compare the performance of individual economies. But they fight an uphill battle in any squabble with national policymakers whenever the latter argue that the coordinating institution misunderstands the economic (and social, and political) situation on the ground. For not only can economic indicators, formulae and Excel calculations not faithfully render the whole picture; they may be entirely wrong even in the part they are supposed to depict correctly. Those who populate the economic departments of the Commission, the IMF, or the OECD know it well. And they are aware that in a democratic system national politicians both have a mandate to pursue the policies they think are most appropriate and pay the electoral price if they err in

[23] Olivier Blanchard, 'Country Adjustment within Euroland: Lessons after Two Years', *Monitoring the European Central Bank*, annual CEPR report, March, 2001.

their calculations. Any type of supranational economic coordination compares very poorly in all these respects. For this very reason any (rules-based) system lacks both the legitimacy and predictability necessary for its sustainability.

This argument is both far-reaching and quite abstract. But one example should suffice to demonstrate its practical meaning. Take the Spanish case again. In spring 2007 both the Commission and the IMF estimated the so-called cyclically adjusted structural fiscal balance of this country in 2006 at 1.8 per cent.[24] This means that – according to contemporary calculations – its fiscal policy was sound not only in nominal terms, but also when adjusted to the economic cycle. But, four years later, the IMF realised that the Spanish structural fiscal balance for 2006 must be revised downwards by the whole 3.0 per cent, to −1.2 per cent.[25] So, as it turned out in 2011, this country was fiscally underperforming five years earlier, nurturing vulnerabilities, back then invisible to any of the world's expert institutions, which were soon to turn their head. Why was it so? Because the analytical underpinnings of the whole system on which the institutional tissue of macroeconomic and fiscal monitoring and surveillance relies is very hypothetical and impossible to estimate correctly in real time.

To be more specific: in one way or another, all the underpinnings – fiscal, macroeconomic and monetary – use the output gap as their conceptual anchorage. The output gap envisages the difference between actual output (actual GDP) and potential output, i.e., the GDP achievable if production factors are utilised at their long-term sustainable levels. When it is positive (actual GDP is bigger than the potential GDP), the gap indicates inflationary tendencies. When it is negative, recessionary tendencies prevail.[26] So much for the theory. In practice, however, as Chris Giles of the *Financial Times* phrased it, the output gap 'creates the appearance of precision when the reality is ignorance'.[27] Writing in 2015, some other economists put its disadvantages differently, but

[24] European Commission, 'Economic Assessment of the Stability Programme of Spain', 20 March 2007, ECFIN/50968/07-EN and IMF, 'Spain: 2007 Article IV Consultation – Staff Report', IMF Country Report No. 07/175, May 2007.

[25] IMF, 'Spain–Staff Report for the 2011 Article IV Consultation', IMF Country Report No. 11/215, July 2011.

[26] See, for example, Richard Lipsey and Alec Chrystal, *Economics* (Oxford: Oxford University Press, 2015): 710.

[27] Chris Giles, 'Ditch This Daft Concept and Expose Economists to Reality', *Financial Times*, 13 June 2012.

equally vividly: 'The estimation of the output gap is a tricky matter. The revisions made by the European Commission are an illustration of this difficulty: whereas it estimated that the Eurozone economy was close to its potential in 2007, its latest estimates show that it was in fact substantially above.'[28]

Central bankers have been struggling with this limitation for decades (any version of the so-called Taylor rule, which defines the monetary policy, is largely built upon the output gap).[29] So have national governments, when trying to base their fiscal policy upon it. But each of them must make decisions. Neither fiscal policy, nor monetary policy, nor any economic policy can run on autopilot. Policymakers may make good or bad choices, but at some point they are bound to choose.

In this respect, inter- or supranational officials in charge of coordinating national policies may take yet another stance: knowing their legitimacy is very thin compared to national governments, and being aware of the unreliability of economic data, they are exposed to the almighty incentive of compliance and acquiescence to national policymakers. This argument cuts the same way no matter whether the institution in charge of economic coordination is required to use unsophisticated or refined analytical concepts and formulae in underlying its policy stance. In the first of the two situations its officials must know that their stance is economically 'stupid' – to paraphrase Prodi again – for it is too crude. But when they are required not to be 'stupid' by using sophisticated economic concepts – like the output gap – they may err even more badly in their prescriptions.

As I mentioned earlier, the 2005 reform of the SGP aimed to tackle the problem of insufficiently sophisticated economic principles behind the rules-based union. But then it fell into the second trap (and, as I will explain soon, it has not escaped it since the 'rules-based union' was overhauled in the aftermath of the sovereign debt crisis). All in all, therefore, the concept of a rules-based monetary union in which national fiscal and macroeconomic policies are coordinated upon some quasi-scientific knowledge derived from economic formulae places European officials in an impossible situation. They can hardly ever

[28] Anton Brender, Florence Pisani and Emile Gagna, *Money, Finance and the Real Economy: What Went Wrong?* (CEPS Paperback, 17 March 2015), available at www.ceps.eu/publications/money-finance-and-real-economy-what-went-wrong.

[29] Athanasios Orphanides, 'Taylor Rules', *Finance and Economics Discussion Series, Board of the Federal Reserve System*, January 2007, available at www.federalreserve.gov/pubs/feds/2007/200718/200718pap.pdf.

be sure they are right, and, even then, they are poorly equipped to confront national politicians when the latter want to pursue another agenda. No doubt, therefore, that 'the first nine years of the euro – from 1999 to 2007 – can, in retrospect, probably be best characterised as "wasted good times" during which the foundations were laid for the ... crisis in EMU'.[30] But how can one expect it to be any different when the whole coordination system was contestably based on very unreliable economic assumptions (and worse – no more reliable alternatives existed) and when no policymaker, either in Brussels or in a national capital, had an incentive to swim against the tide pursuing particularly hawkish policies? When they knew that the elected politicians in charge of fiscal or macroeconomic policies would be busted if their procyclical policies backfired, but busted even more predictably if they raised unemployment by running countercyclical policies in economically good times?

2.5 Bound to Blunder

At the onset of the Great Recession, economic coordination within the EU was clearly a bogus exercise. In 2008, Caroline de la Porte concluded that the processes comprising social policy coordination 'due to their soft character, do not embody sufficient "European pressure" to engender change, no matter what the domestic landscape looks like and no matter where the respective policies are located among governmental priorities'.[31] National fiscal and macroeconomic policies went similarly uncoordinated. International economic institutions were, however, perfectly content with this very treacherous setup. In 2008 – the same year when de la Porte complained about insufficient 'European pressure' – the IMF argued that 'there is general satisfaction with the operation of the SGP... The broadly shared view is that a policy approach cast within the SGP serves countries best.'[32] It is worth

[30] Ludger Schuknecht et al., 'The Stability and Growth Pact: Crisis and Reform', *ECB Occasional Paper Series* No. 129, September 2011, 10, available at pdfs.semanticscholar.org/3975/f02101490ea78caec8cffbaaf8b3017a7a59.pdf.

[31] Caroline de la Porte, 'The European Level Development and National Level Influence of the Open Method of Coordination: The Cases of Employment and Social Inclusion', (PhD diss., European University Institute, 2008), 249, available at cadmus.eui.eu//handle/1814/10463.

[32] IMF, 'Euro Area Policies: 2008 Article IV Consultation', IMF Country Report No. 08/262, August 2008, 3, available at www.imf.org/external/pubs/ft/scr/2008/cr08262.pdf.

noting in this context that one of the declarations annexed to the TEU by the Lisbon Treaty insisted 'that a rule-based system is the best guarantee for commitments to be enforced and for all Member States to be treated equally'.[33] Yet, while the coordination framework 'treated all Member States equally'– it was equally tolerant for transgressors – it had nothing to do with any 'enforceable commitments'.

In 2010, all of the institutions suddenly came round. The mood of the day was that 'the onset of the financial crisis in the Eurozone has seen the emergence of a new paradigm for economic governance, under which stabilisation of the single currency requires the imposition of stricter controls over national economic and social policy'.[34] Policymakers rushed to redesign the loose procedures to make them more comprehensive, streamlined and painful for rogue national governments. Doing so they persisted in their belief in the rules-based monetary union. The Commission argued, in May 2010, when the sovereign debt crisis erupted for the first time, that

> the rules and principles of the Stability and Growth Pact are relevant and valid. But, despite the Pact, Member States failed to build up adequate buffers in good times. Reinforcing the preventive dimension of budgetary surveillance must be an integral part of closer coordination of fiscal policy. Also, compliance with the rules needs to be improved and more focus needs to be given to sustainability of public finances.[35]

This line of thinking, universally espoused by policymakers at the time, assumed that sovereign national governments running very diverging socioeconomic policies and exposed to very different political forces could nonetheless stick to the same set of demanding rules in respect to both their fiscal and macroeconomic performance. Yet, it does not require a fortune-teller to predict that nothing of this type could actually happen, leaving the Eurozone more sundered and divergent.

Before turning to this point yet another should be made clear first: irrespective of how ridiculous the path chosen by European

[33] Declaration No. 30 on Article 126 of the TFEU.

[34] Samuel Dahan, 'The EU/IMF Financial Stabilisation Process in Latvia and Its Implications for Labour Law and Social Policy', *Industrial Law Journal* 41 (2012): 323.

[35] European Commission, 'Communication: Reinforcing Economic Policy Coordination' COM(2010)250, 12 May 2010, 4, available at ec.europa.eu/economy_finance/articles/euro/documents/2010-05-12-com(2010)250_final.pdf.

policymakers in the aftermath of the sovereign debt crisis may seem, they were bound to make the mistakes they did.

The rules-based union was the default option enshrined by primary European law ever since the Maastricht Treaty laid the foundations for the single currency. Granted, its original version proved ineffective. But the Lisbon Treaty, which entered into force just a few months before the sovereign debt crisis burst in the spring of 2010, opened up new possibilities for enhanced surveillance and discipline.[36] So why try anything other than the (strengthened) version of the original coordination, if any other method of pursuing economic and institutional convergence could be hard to square with European law?

Furthermore, without a serious common budget, the single currency does not offer much space for discretionary fiscal policies, while the community method of decision-making in the EU, quite successful prior to 2010, does not fit neatly with (or clearly precludes) any discretionary programmes, especially any devised for the Eurozone only. The constitutional framework of the EU thus allows for new benchmarks, as well as the refining of monitoring and surveillance procedures. But it was not devised with their alternatives in mind.

Finally, sheer politics also drew policymakers to opt for a 'revamped' rules-based union. In 2010, the governments of the creditor countries knew they had to somehow explain to their taxpayers why their money was committed to bail out the governments of other countries; the countries that had made serious policy mistakes in the previous decade. Imagine they would admit the point I was making in the previous chapter: that the single currency was based on entirely flawed economic assumptions and a spurious institutional setup. How could one expect Chancellor Merkel to admit in 2010 that German policymakers had been entirely wrong two decades earlier, when they hoped that the single currency would usher in economic convergence while the rules-based union would be a bedrock of responsible economic governance, and that the flaws are irrectifiable unless the Eurozone was to be profoundly overhauled? It does not require an exceptionally far-seeing politician to realise that, after the 2005 failures of the Treaty referenda

[36] Art. 136(1) TFEU – added by the Treaty of Lisbon – authorises the Council, first, 'to strengthen the coordination and surveillance of their budgetary discipline' and, second, 'to set out economic policy guidelines for them, while ensuring that they are compatible with those adopted for the whole of the Union and are kept under surveillance'.

in France and the Netherlands, any significant Treaty revision would be very difficult to accomplish even in economic good times. And playing with a fully-fledged Treaty renegotiation in the middle of 'the deepest existential crisis of the European Union'[37] since the beginning of European integration could very well end up as fatal for the whole European project. No responsible politician wants to go down in history as the one who lit this fuse.

Actually, once they realised, in 2010, that the original setup had failed, top Eurozone policymakers should have returned to the coronation theory. According to the main tenet of it, 'monetary union would be the final moment of a process of economic and political union'.[38] For political, social and economic reasons no such a union is conceivable among societies as divergent as these comprising the Eurozone. So, on the flipside of the same argument, the Eurozone should be reduced to a limited group of ('stability oriented') societies that traditionally share the same political and socioeconomic priorities. Because any such a setup would be much less susceptible to the pernicious economic processes described in Chapter 1, the need for external institutions pressing for convergence from the outside would then be seriously reduced, compared to the current situation.

I will argue in next chapters that, sooner or later, this is indeed what will have to happen. The sooner, the lower the concomitant costs and higher the chances for a truly prosperous Europe. But it is natural that, like in medicine, a doctor tries all less-invasive treatments before she decides to undertake extremely complicated and untested brain surgery.

2.6 An Ostensibly Deep Constitutional Transformation

While betting on the rules-based union again in the midst of the sovereign debt crisis was a gamble, policymakers could at least hope that they would be able to stick to the original Eurozone's setup, while at the same time mitigating the risks involved. On the other hand, they clearly opined that the Eurozone crisis which followed the global financial crisis of 2008

[37] Agustín José Menéndez, 'The Existential Crisis of the European Union', *German Law Journal* 14 (2013): 511.

[38] Kenneth Dyson, 'Germany and the Euro: Redefining EMU, Handling Paradox and Managing Uncertainty and Contingency', in: *European States and the Euro: Europeanization, Variation, and Convergence*, ed. Kenneth Dyson (New York: Oxford University Press, 2002): 178.

had something to do with the very loose original patterns of the macroeconomic policy coordination. In 2010, when they painfully discovered that balance-of-payments crises could – and do – occur in a monetary union, new procedures preventing Member States from nurturing excessive macroeconomic imbalances seemed to be the right remedy to probably the most significant original sin behind the sovereign debt crisis.

The Eurozone's first decade demonstrated that sanctioning otherwise-sovereign governments is an immense task, if at all manageable, so no automatic sanctions would be politically viable. Nonetheless, the policymakers redrafting the rules-based Eurozone cared more about something that would not necessarily be different but would at least look different to national politicians of the debtor countries, to societies of the creditor countries and to financial markets: a perception that sanctions might really be triggered now. The reformed system of fiscal and macroeconomic surveillance established between 2010 and 2013 aimed at rendering this very perception more credible, rather than actually enforcing European policymakers to punish national governments politically or financially. What followed were eight pieces of secondary EU law – the Six-Pack, enacted in 2011,[39] and the Two-Pack, adopted two years later[40] – plus an international

[39] Regulation 1173/2011 of the European Parliament and of the Council of 16 November 2011 on the Effective Enforcement of Budgetary Surveillance in the Euro Area, OJ 2011 No. L 306, 23 November 2011, pp. 1–7; Regulation 1174/2011 of the European Parliament and of the Council of 16 November 2011 on Enforcement Measures to Correct Excessive Macroeconomic Imbalances in the Euro Area, OJ 2011 No. L 306, 23 November 2011, pp. 8–11; Regulation 1175/2011 of the European Parliament and of the Council of 16 November 2011 Amending Council Regulation 1466/97 on the Strengthening of the Surveillance of Budgetary Positions and the Surveillance and Coordination of Economic Policies, OJ 2011 No. L 306, 23 November 2011, pp. 12–24; Regulation 1176/2011 of the European Parliament and of the Council of 16 November 2011 on the Prevention and Correction of Macroeconomic Imbalances, OJ 2011 No. L 306, 23 November 2011, pp. 25–32; Council Regulation 1177/2011 of 8 November 2011 Amending Regulation 1467/97 on Speeding Up and Clarifying the Implementation of the Excessive Deficit Procedure, OJ 2011 No. L 306, 23 November 2011, pp. 33–40; Council Directive 2011/85/EU of 8 November 2011 on Requirements for Budgetary Frameworks of the Member States, OJ 2011 No. L 306, 23 November 2011, pp. 41–47.

[40] Regulation 472/2013 of the European Parliament and of the Council of 21 May 2013 on the Strengthening of Economic and Budgetary Surveillance of Member States in the Euro Area Experiencing or Threatened with Serious Difficulties with Respect to Their Financial Stability, OJ No. L 140, 27 May 2013, pp. 1–10; Regulation 473/2013 of the European Parliament and of the Council of 21 May 2013 on Common Provisions for Monitoring and Assessing Draft Budgetary Plans and Ensuring the Correction of Excessive Deficit of the Member States in the Euro Area, OJ No. L 140, 27 May 2013, pp. 11–23.

agreement Loïc Azoulai once called a monster:[41] the Fiscal Compact.[42] Together, they formed a basic rules-based system, supplemented by a specific institutional framework of the schemes offering rescue financing to crisis-stricken countries in exchange for strict macroeconomic conditionality (a qualified rules-based system). While the rest of this chapter is devoted to the basic rules-based system, the next chapter focuses exclusively on the qualified one.

Those who see the European Union as a Law Empire (quite predictably, these are mainly lawyers and legal academics) found the overhaul resulting from the haze of new rules breathtaking. The President of the Court of Justice, Judge Lenaerts, for instance, believed they 'altered the constitutional balance on which the European Union is founded'.[43] Many other legal scholars, who naturally assumed that if new powers are established, they will be used, and if new procedures are devised, they will be followed, have been of a similar opinion. As they argued, the modifications to the rules-based union introduced since 2010 have marked 'a process of mutation of European constitutional law',[44] 'a deep transformation of the European constitutional constellation'[45] and a 'new constitutional balance'.[46] All of them echoed the Commission President Barroso, who claimed that 'what is going on is a silent revolution – a silent revolution in terms of stronger economic governance by small steps'.[47]

Indeed, looking at the new rules it is hard to escape a similar impression. Paths leading to sanctions were straightened and shortened. While previously Member States could be censured only during the excessive deficit procedure (the so-called corrective arm of the SGP), now

[41] Loïc Azoulai et al., 'Another Legal Monster? An EUI Debate on the Fiscal Compact Treaty', ed. Anna Kocharov, *EUI Working Papers LAW* 09 (2012), available at cadmus.eui.eu/handle/1814/21496.

[42] Treaty on Stability, Coordination and Governance in the Economic and Monetary Union, signed on 2 March 2012, available at www.consilium.europa.eu/media/20399/st00tscg26_en12.pdf.

[43] Koen Lenaerts, 'EMU and the European Union's Constitutional Framework', *European Law Review* 39 (2014): 753.

[44] Menéndez, 'Existential Crisis', 511.

[45] Christian Joerges, 'Europe's Economic Constitution in Crisis and the Emergence of a New Constitutional Constellation', *ZENTRA Working Papers In Transnational Studies* 06 (2012), available at papers.ssrn.com/sol3/papers.cfm?abstract_id=2179595##.

[46] Mark Dawson and Floris De Witte, 'Constitutional Balance in the EU after the Euro-Crisis', *The Modern Law Review* 76 (2013): 824.

[47] Quoted in Leigh Phillips, 'EU Ushers in "Silent Revolution" in Control of National Economic Policies', *EUObserver*, 16 March 2011, available at euobserver.com/institutional/31993.

a sanction of an interest-bearing deposit amounting to 0.2 per cent of GDP in the preceding year could be imposed in respect to an Eurozone country also at an earlier (monitoring) stage of the so-called preventive arm of the SGP.[48] Sanctioning decision-making in the corrective arm was expedited[49] and both in the preventive and corrective arm of the SGP it was rendered semi-automatic by the requirement that a decision imposing sanctions 'shall be deemed to be adopted by the Council unless it decides by a qualified majority to reject the Commission's recommendation' (reverse qualified majority-voting).[50] Furthermore, a new expenditure benchmark complementing structural budgetary balance targets and an operationalisation of the Treaty's debt criterion (the debt to GDP ratio of 60 per cent) were introduced in the SGP, to render the procedures more consistent with Treaty requirements.[51] To avoid repetitions of previous fiscal misreporting, requirements for national budgetary frameworks – with regard to accounting, statistics, macroeconomic and budgetary forecasts, numerical fiscal rules, budgetary frameworks and coordination across sub-sectors of general government – were imposed on Member States.[52]

With the aim of controlling the propensity of individual countries to macroeconomic shocks, new procedures aimed at controlling macroeconomic imbalances were set up.[53] They are based on the logic borrowed from the SGP: the preventive arm is to gauge national performance,[54] flexing the corrective arm, up to the point of financial sanctions, if the country experiencing excessive macroeconomic imbalances repeatedly ignores specific recommendations it is addressed by European institutions.[55]

So much for the Six-Pack. Then comes the Two-Pack – two additional regulations, enacted in 2013 – with its procedures of monitoring and assessing draft budgetary plans (DBP) of the Eurozone countries[56] and

[48] Art. 4 Regulation 1173/2011.
[49] Arts. 5–6 Regulation 1173/2011.
[50] Arts. 4–6 Regulation 1173/2011.
[51] New Art. 5.1 of Regulation 1466/97, as amended by Regulation 1175/2011 and the new Art. 2.1a of Regulation 1467/97, as amended by Regulation 1177/2011.
[52] Arts. 3 to 14 of Directive 2011/85/EU.
[53] For a comprehensive analysis of the economic indicators used to determine whether imbalances exist, see Armin Steinbach, *Economic Policy Coordination in the Euro Area* (London and New York: Routledge, 2014): 106–122.
[54] Regulation 1176/2011.
[55] Regulation 1174/2011.
[56] Arts. 5 to 8 of Regulation 473/2013.

with a Commission's 'semi-voting' power over national budgetary plans when it 'identifies a particularly serious non-compliance with the obligations stemming from the SGP'.[57] Pursuant to the Two-Pack, European institutions also gained additional monitoring powers in respect to a broad set of Eurozone countries: those under the Excessive Deficit Procedure, those experiencing 'serious difficulties with respect to' their 'financial stability which are likely to have adverse spill-over effects on other Member States in the euro area', those having their macro-economic adjustment programmes pending, and those undergoing post-programme surveillance.[58]

On top of all of this, the Fiscal Compact requires governments of the countries that have signed up to its fiscal provisions[59] to introduce a fiscal golden rule ('budgetary position of the general government of a Contracting Party shall be balanced or in surplus')[60] to national 'provisions of binding force and permanent character, preferably constitutional, or otherwise guaranteed to be fully respected and adhered to throughout the national budgetary processes'.[61] It also puts on them an obligation to liaise with the Commission in order to sue before the Court of Justice any of the countries failing to introduce the Compact's fiscal golden rule, while the Court can impose a fine (up to 0.1 per cent of GDP) on obdurate laggards.[62]

2.7 Paper Cannons

Law scholars, quite naturally for their profession, took the rules seriously. Some of them argued that the reverse majority voting, on which the most important new procedures relied, 'contravenes the legal framework of the Treaties'.[63] Others added that 'some of the

[57] Art. 7.2 Regulation 473/2013.

[58] Arts. 9 to 13 of Regulation 473/2013 and Arts. 3 to 14 of Regulation 472/2013. The post-programme surveillance lasts until at least 75 per cent of the financial assistance received has been repaid (Art. 14.1 of Regulation 472/2013).

[59] Czechia and the UK refused to sign the Treaty. Croatia has never joined it since its accession in mid-2013. Hungary, Poland and Sweden excluded their participation in the fiscal provisions of the Treaty when signing it.

[60] Art. 3.1.a Treaty on Stability, Coordination and Governance in the Economic and Monetary Union.

[61] Art. 3.2 Treaty on Stability, Coordination and Governance in the Economic and Monetary Union.

[62] Art. 8 Treaty on Stability, Coordination and Governance in the Economic and Monetary Union.

[63] Rainer Palmstorfer, 'The Reverse Majority Voting under the "Six-Pack": A Bad Turn for the Union?', *European Law Journal* 20 (2014): 203. This argument becomes graver if

measures to achieve convergence and budgetary control are highly doubted in EU legal terms'.[64] There were also voices claiming that the Fiscal Compact – as a separate international agreement formally outside EU law but actually inherently related to it – does not 'fit within the existing EU legal framework'.[65] Still others, who also treated the rules seriously and grew concerned with their actual impact, complained that the reformed rules-based system transferred decisions on what is best for the economic prospects of European societies, at least within the Eurozone, from national parliaments and governments to a compound system driven partly by the European Council, partly by the Council of Ministers, partly by the Commission, and partly by the ECB.[66] And this would mean the end of national democracy as we know it in the Eurozone, a deep foray into inherently redistributive areas the EU has traditionally shunned from interfering with. This 'will only render ordinary people more powerless', some warned.[67] To those who espoused this approach, the revamped rules-based union constituted a 'trend towards increasingly detailed and enforceable prescriptions from the centre'[68] and 'a kind of economic managerialism with an authoritarian flavour'.[69] As Päivi Leino

one agrees that 'reverse majority voting has significantly extended the Commission's discretion, providing it with an almost autonomous executive decision-making competence in the area of economic and fiscal policies': Daniel Seikel, 'Flexible Austerity and Supranational Autonomy. The Reformed Excessive Deficit Procedure and the Asymmetry between Liberalization and Social Regulation in the EU', *Journal of Common Market Studies* 54 (2016): 1410.

64 Matthias Ruffert, 'The European Debt Crisis and European Union Law', *Common Market Law Review* 48 (2011): 1800–1801.

65 Angelos Dimopoulos, 'The Use of International Law as a Tool for Enhancing Governance in the Eurozone and Its Impact on EU Institutional Integrity', in: *The Constitutionalization of European Budgetary Constraints*, eds Maurice Adams, Federico Fabbrini and Pierre Larouche (Oxford: Hart Publishing, 2014): 43.

66 See, e.g., Sonja Puntscher Riekmann and Doris Wydra, 'Representation in the European State of Emergency: Parliaments against Governments?', *Journal of European Integration* 35 (2013): 565–582; Michael W. Bauer and Stefan Becker, 'The Unexpected Winner of the Crisis: The European Commission's Strengthened Role in Economic Governance', *Journal of European Integration* 36 (2014): 213–229.

67 Janet Daley, 'This Was the Week That European Democracy Died', *The Telegraph*, 29 October 2011, available at www.telegraph.co.uk/finance/financialcrisis/8857533/This-was-the-week-that-European-democracy-died.html.

68 Alicia Hinarejos, 'Fiscal Federalism in the European Union: Evolution and Future Choices for EMU', *Common Market Law Review* 50 (2013): 1635.

69 Christian Joerges, 'Law and Politics in Europe's Crisis: On the History of the Impact of an Unfortunate Configuration', *EUI Working Papers LAW* 9 (2013): 8. See also Dawson and De Witte, 'Constitutional Balance', 817–844.

put it, 'the result is a maze of alternative or even conflicting rules, which few understand. Owing to its complexity, the application of the fiscal framework has, in practice, become an exercise of nearly unlimited discretion.'[70]

Some of the acerbic comments referred only to bailout programmes (on which I will concentrate in the next chapter). Yet the basic model of the rules-based union described in this chapter was seen as essentially the same type of ill-conceived approach, an extension and generalisation of the socially and politically disruptive austerity prescribed for the Eurozone's periphery.

I will soon try to demonstrate that all of the grievances have essentially proven irrelevant in the basic model of the rules-based union, for the very simple reason that 'by adding complexity and intrusiveness, the technical advances in governance have deepened the traditional incentives for delays and half-measures; but, without political legitimacy, the enforcement and disciplining challenge remains unchanged'.[71] Or, as Lannoo put it more precisely, using any of the new powers would violate a basic political commandment that 'the adoption of national budgets is a unique responsibility of national parliaments, which cannot be overruled by an unelected administration'.[72] This commandment must be followed, because no system violating it would enjoy the legitimacy necessary to secure its sustainability.[73] So

[70] Päivi Leino and Tuomas Saarenheimo, 'Sovereignty and Subordination: On the Limits of EU Economic Policy Co-ordination', *European Law Review* 42 (2017): 174. Leino also notes, however, that the discretion has not been exercised in practice, pointing at insufficient legitimacy of potential European actions towards otherwise economically sovereign Member States as the main reason.

[71] Ashoka Mody, 'A Schuman Compact for the Euro Area', *Bruegel Essay and Lecture Series*, 20 November 2013, 29, available at bruegel.org/2013/11/a-schuman-compact-for-the-euro-area/. For an accurate broader critique of the incentive incompatibility inherent in the European economic policy coordination, see Steinbach, *Economic Policy Coordination*, 62 et seq.

[72] Karel Lannoo, 'EU Federalism in Crisis', *CEPS Policy Brief* No. 259, October 2011, available at www.ceps.eu/publications/eu-federalism-crisis.

[73] Jukka Snell argued that sovereignty, mass politics and economic and monetary union are entrapped in a trilemma: only two of the three can be pursued: see Jukka Snell, 'The Trilemma of European Economic and Monetary Integration, and Its Consequences', *European Law Journal* 22 (2016): 157–179. While this trilemma can be reduced to the choice between sovereignty and the EMU (because dismantling mass politics is unimaginable), in Europe sovereignty has consistently prevailed and can hardly be predicted to give in anytime soon. See also Dariusz Adamski, 'Economic Policy Coordination as a Game Involving Economic Stability and National Sovereignty', *European Law Journal* 22 (2016): 180–203.

supranational or international institutions may be granted new powers. The powers may be far-reaching. But the officials supposed to actually execute them are not politically empowered to do so. If they do not realise this, embracing the formal new authority, the gun will backfire in their hands: national elected politicians will not hesitate to use the allegiances they enjoy among national societies to fight back. And if they do realise this, as they actually have done, the credibility of the rules-based system is damaged.

Therefore, all the monitoring, surveillance and disciplining procedures and powers have been stillborn for fundamental political reasons. To see this we must now turn from what lawyers like the most, words comprising rules, to what really matters: rules comprising policy in action.

2.8 New-Old Fiscal Coordination

Among the new rules to coordinate fiscal policies, one is particularly important. It is the procedure for 'monitoring and assessment of Member States draft budgetary plans', instituted in respect to the Euro Area by one of the 'Two-Pack' Regulations. According to Art. 6(1) Regulation 473/2013: 'Member States shall submit annually to the Commission and to the Eurogroup a draft budgetary plan for the forthcoming year by 15 October'. The Commission issues its opinion on the draft budgets by the end of November. If 'in exceptional cases' it 'identifies particularly serious non-compliance with the budgetary policy obligations' of the SGP, it 'shall request that a revised draft budgetary plan be submitted as soon as possible and in any event within three weeks of the date of its opinion' (Art. 7(2)).

The first year the Commission had a chance to use the procedure was 2013. It then singled out five Eurozone countries (Spain, Italy, Luxembourg, Malta and Finland) as posing a risk of non-compliance. It emphasised that 'for Italy there is a risk that on current plans the debt reduction rule would be breached in 2014. For Luxembourg and Finland there is a risk of significant deviation from the adjustment path towards the medium-term budgetary objective.'[74] Yet, no DBP was vetoed. The next year (2014), even though six

[74] European Commission, 'Communication: 2014 Draft Budgetary Plans of the Euro Area: Overall Assessment of the Budgetary Situation and Prospects', COM(2013)900, 15 November 2013.

more EU countries exited the excessive deficit procedure,[75] the list of Eurozone countries ascertained by the Commission as posing a risk of non-compliance with the SGP grew to seven (Belgium, Spain, France, Italy, Malta, Austria and Portugal). The institution even asserted that 'for France in particular, the information available indicates that the country has not taken effective action in 2014 at this stage and is at risk of non-compliance in 2015'.[76] Yet, again, it did not use its (semi)veto powers in respect to any of the budgetary plans. The Commission's President Juncker even admitted that the fiscal coordination scheme, so meticulously restructured since 2010, 'has never been applied in a more flexible way'.[77] This statement is particularly remarkable when you realise that the regulation governing the procedure just mentioned (No 473/2013) provides in its title that it is 'on common provisions for monitoring and assessing draft budgetary plans and *ensuring the correction* of excessive deficit of the Member States in the euro area' (my emphasis).

Only one month later, in January 2015, the Commission endorsed a Communication entitled 'Making the Best Use of the Flexibility within the Existing Rules of the Stability and Growth Pact'.[78] As its title heralds, this Communication does not have much to do with strengthening fiscal rules. Conversely, its goal is to relax them. First, the Commission pledged to be (even) more responsive to the economic cycles of Member States when performing its functions under the preventive arm of the SGP. Second, it averred that it would accept temporary deviations from fiscal adjustment paths, if the deviations stemmed from public investments and certain additional conditions were met.[79] Also, Member State contributions to the European Fund

[75] Austria, Denmark, Netherlands, Belgium, Slovakia, Czechia.

[76] European Commission, 'Communication: 2015 Draft Budgetary Plans. Overall Assessment', COM(2014)907, 28 November 2014, 3.

[77] 'Juncker Says Italy "Can't Complain"', *ANSA*, 11 December 2014, available at www.ansa.it/english/news/2014/12/11/juncker-says-italy-cant-complain_2cb65dde-cf3b-4d40-9646-fa97b89293a0.html.

[78] COM(2015)012.

[79] The conditions are: (a) GDP growth negative or the output gap greater than 1.5 per cent of GDP; (b) the deviation does not lead to a breach of the 3 per cent of GDP limit and a safety margin is preserved; (c) investment levels are increased as a result of public investment; (d) EU programmes co-fund them; (e) the deviation should be compensated within the timeframe of the Member State's fiscal (stability/convergence) programme.

for Strategic Investments (more on this in Chapter 8) or national co-financing of the Fund's projects[80] would not count when defining fiscal adjustment under either the preventive or the corrective arm of the SGP (government deficits reported to the Commission for monitoring purposes would be lowered by their values). Third, the Commission opined that both under the preventive and corrective arms of the SGP Member States should be treated more flexibly if they introduce major structural reforms with verifiable long-term budgetary benefits. The structural reforms concession would be granted to national governments under the condition that they 'present a medium-term structural reform plan which is comprehensive and detailed ... and includes well-specified measures and credible timelines for their adoption and delivery'.

The ECB – the fiscally most hawkish European institution – could be expected to lambast the Commission for softening what was supposed to be strengthened. Its officials in particular detested the structural reforms flexibility clause. A few months after the Communication was issued they argued that 'the possibility to apply the flexibility provisions also to ex-ante reform plans (as opposed to effectively implemented reforms) risks being counterproductive. Ensuring that ex-ante plans are effectively implemented requires continuous monitoring of reform implementation ... otherwise countries may have an incentive to delay or even backtrack on their plans once the fiscal flexibility has been granted.'[81]

Indeed, politicians in power are strongly incentivised to backtrack on any electorally costly reforms and do not hesitate to act accordingly when otherwise their political careers would suffer. This is perfectly clear, not only to the ECB or the Commission, but also – or especially – to the officials in national capitals. So much so that the spin the Commission gave to the notion of a strengthened economic governance alarmed even the institution comprising the very group of national officials particularly benefitting from the enhanced flexibility: national finance ministers (the Council). First, the Council's Legal Service opinion, leaked to press, argued that 'a plan announcing upcoming reforms, as a simple manifestation of political intentions or

[80] During the European Council of 18 December 2015, the Commission also agreed that national contributions to the Turkey Refugee Facility would be subtracted from government deficits for the purposes of the SGP.

[81] ECB, Economic Bulletin, Issue 7/2015, November 2015, 56.

of wishes, would … not fulfil the application of' the SGP requirements.[82] And, as Euractiv reported a few months later (in December 2015), 'EU member states believe the European Commission is giving too much breathing space to struggling national economies when applying the Stability and Growth Pact, and decided to adopt a more restrictive view of EU fiscal rules'.[83]

Simultaneously (November 2015), the Commission, like in the two previous years, reached the point in the annual economic monitoring and surveillance process, called European Semester,[84] when it is empowered to block the budgetary plans of Eurozone countries if it concludes that they violate budgetary obligations under the reformed SGP seriously enough. In 2015, Spain was closest to this point. The Commission argued in respect to this country that 'neither the recommended fiscal effort nor the headline deficit target for 2016 is forecast to be achieved'.[85] But, nonetheless, it concluded that 'No DBP (draft budgetary plan: DA) for 2016 has been found in particularly serious non-compliance with the requirements of the SGP', albeit 'in several cases … the Commission finds that the planned fiscal adjustments fall short, or risk doing so, of what is required by the SGP'.[86] So what non-compliance would be 'particularly serious'? If a deficit of 1 per cent too high does not trigger the procedure, why would 2 per cent? If 2 per cent would not, why would 3 per cent? If 3 per cent would not, why would 4 per cent? And so on. The procedure is still the same, but – because it is particularly prone to the salami-slicing argument – it is dead when the aggregate comes up.

Because by 2015 the ostensibly reinforced SGP was visibly defunct, nuanced excuses were replaced with cruder political actions soon after. During 2016, the Commission President Juncker did his utmost

[82] Council of the European Union, 'Opinion of the Legal Service', Ref. 7739/15, 7 April 2015.

[83] Jorge Valero, 'Member States Limit New Flexibility Clauses in EU Fiscal Pact', *EurActiv*, 9 December 2015, available at www.euractiv.com/section/euro-finance/news/member-states-limit-new-flexibility-clauses-in-eu-fiscal-pact/.

[84] For an overview of the European Semester see Steinbach, *Economic Policy Coordination*, 124–126.

[85] European Commission, 'Communication: 2016 Draft Budgetary Plans. Overall Assessment', COM(2015)800, 16 November 2015, 4, available at eur-lex.europa.eu/resource.html?uri=cellar:5d0db65c-8d14-11e5-b8b7-01aa75ed71a1.0002.02/DOC_1&format=PDF.

[86] European Commission, 'Communication: 2016 Draft Budgetary Plans. Overall Assessment', 3.

to turn a blind eye on the fiscal indicators of France, which missed the goals established one year earlier. He admitted with a disarming frankness that he did so 'because it is France'.[87] Weeks after, he nonetheless pushed for sanctions against Spain and Portugal for their fiscal deficits (after all, none of them is France). And then the German Finance Minister Schäuble disoriented bystanders by phoning Commissioners and lobbying for their forgiveness towards the Iberian countries.[88] He succeeded, causing an astute observer to herald 'the silent death of Eurozone governance'.[89]

In fact at that point the SGP was not only dead, but also buried, and the funeral was quite spectacular. The IMF wrote an obituary to it half a year later. In a paper published in early 2017, it evidenced the Eurozone's fiscal procyclicality, distorted budget composition and poor compliance with any version of a rules-based union.[90] European policymakers turned a deaf ear to it, however, exuberantly rejoicing higher-than-expected economic growth in the Eurozone.

2.9 Macroeconomic Imbalances and Non-Credible Procedures

Anyone who hopes that fiscal coordination – defunct prior to 2010 and then reformed only to become as much lifeless again – is a basket case and that the brand new rules, non-existent before 2010, on the monitoring and correction of macroeconomic imbalances could fare better, will also be disappointed. They too were derailed immediately after EU legislators put them on the tracks.

In April 2013 – the first year the macroeconomic imbalance procedure was applied – the Commission announced that eleven Member States were 'experiencing macroeconomic imbalances, which deserve

[87] Francesco Guarascio, 'EU Gives Budget Leeway to France "Because It Is France" – Juncker', *Reuters*, 31 May 2016, available at uk.reuters.com/article/uk-eu-deficit-france-idUKKCN0YM1N0.

[88] Bjarke Smith-Meyer, 'Commission Decides against Fining Portugal, Spain for Budget Breaches', *Politico*, 27 July 2016, available at www.politico.eu/pro/commission-decides-against-fining-portugal-spain-for-budget-breaches/.

[89] Daniel Gros, 'The Silent Death of Eurozone Governance', *Project Syndicate*, 10 August 2016, available at www.project-syndicate.org/commentary/eu-fiscal-rules-not-enforced-spain-portugal-by-daniel-gros-2016-08?barrier=accessreg.

[90] Luc Eyraud, Vitor Gaspar and Tigran Poghosyan, 'Fiscal Politics in the Euro Area', *IMF Working Paper* No. 17/18, 30 January 2017, available at www.imf.org/en/Publications/WP/Issues/2017/01/30/Fiscal-Politics-in-the-Euro-Area-44601.

monitoring and policy action' (countries on fully fledged international financial rescue programmes at this point in time, i.e., Greece, Ireland, Portugal and Cyprus, were excluded from the review). Two others – Slovenia and Spain – were, according to the Commission's assessment, experiencing excessive macroeconomic imbalances. If the Commission considers that a Member State is affected by excessive macroeconomic imbalances, the Council may issue 'a recommendation establishing the existence of an excessive imbalance and recommending that the Member State concerned take corrective action' (Art. 7(2) Regulation 1176/2011). This recommendation starts a procedure that may ultimately lead to imposing financial sanctions on the country with an 'excessively imbalanced' economy. Neither in 2013 nor later, however, did the Council decide to do so.

From the next year (2014) on, the Commission made it easier for the Council to be so reticent, by concluding that there should be two types of excessive macroeconomic imbalances. One (so-called Stage 5) requires 'specific monitoring and continuing strong (or decisive) policy action'. The other (Stage 6) implies 'decisive policy action and the activation of the Excessive Imbalance Procedure'. Politically, this bifurcation is quite convenient both for the Commission and the Council, because the first of the two institutions may admit what would be otherwise hard to question: some Eurozone economies suffer from very serious macroeconomic imbalances. But it can both admit it and avoid recommending to the Council that it should start the procedure leading towards sanctions by putting the given country in the Stage 5 basket. And the Stage 5 procedure goes nowhere.

This point reveals fundamental paradoxes behind the concept of the revamped rules-based union better than any other aspect of the overhauled system established during the sovereign debt crisis. The ostensibly revamped enforcement, both within the SGP and the new excessive macroeconomic imbalance procedure, does, as I mentioned earlier, rely on the perception of immediate sanctions. The sanctions are financial. Imposing them would deplete the fiscal resources the villain country otherwise needs to balance its fiscal position and the economy more generally. Also, such an action could easily scare off financial markets and would certainly undermine the allegiance of the domestic population to the EU. Politically, therefore, the sanctions would certainly be understood as an attempt to devastate the national economy. From this perspective no stiffer rules could be viable alternatives to the otherwise-unviable original setup for economic coordination in the Eurozone. The sanctions devised in the aftermath of the 2010 shock are therefore non-credible – a rationally acting actor (the Commission, for that matter) should not impose them, because they would make everyone involved worse off.

On the other hand, laws in books that are unenforceable in practice compromise the whole underlying system. If the rules are supposed to prevent macroeconomic divergences from mounting, and if they are not credible, there is nothing to prevent the system from collapsing in the longer term. The new macroeconomic imbalance procedure is particularly telling in this respect. While since 2013, not a single state been put in the Stage 6 situation, the number of macroeconomically excessively imbalanced countries was growing. I mentioned earlier that, in 2013, the Commission pinpointed two (Spain and Slovenia). The next year (2014), there were three (Italy, Croatia and Slovenia). In 2015, there were already five (Bulgaria, France, Italy, Croatia and Portugal). In both 2016 and 2017, there were six (the same countries in both years: Bulgaria, Croatia, Cyprus, France, Portugal and Italy).

In other words, the new coordination rules intended to prevent macroeconomic imbalances were also quietly dying, making it clear that they would not bring about any serious economic convergence. By late 2015, it was so conspicuous that Bruegel – the think-tank previously publishing quite optimistic prognoses on whether the new procedures would work – released an analysis concluding that 'despite huge efforts by European institutions to coordinate economic policies within the European Semester, the rate of implementation of these [fiscal and macroeconomic] recommendations is not higher than the rate of implementation of the OECD's unilateral recommendations'.[91] And, even more perplexingly, 'euro-area countries, for which policy coordination should be stronger in principle, implemented their recommendations only somewhat more than non-Euro Area countries (31 percent versus 23 percent for the 2014 recommendations), while the implementation rate fell steadily in both country groups from 2011–14'.[92] All in all, therefore, the adoption of merely consultative

[91] Zsolt Darvas and Álvaro Leandro, 'The Limitations of Policy Coordination in the Euro Area under the European Semester', *Bruegel Policy Contribution* No. 2015/19, 12 November 2015, 2.

[92] Ibid.

OECD recommendations has proven higher than the enforcement of the revamped rules-based union within the Eurozone.

2.10 The Fiscal Compact: Why Numerical Fiscal Rules Are Bound to Fail

The Fiscal Compact has not fared any better when it comes to its enforcement. In fact it has fared worse, despite various European policymakers having repeated time and again that 'in the unfolding of the recent debt crisis we first saw a confirmation of a key intuition underlying the Maastricht architecture – namely, that excessive public indebtedness does pose a serious threat to the stability of the monetary union'.[93]

According to the Compact's wording, the Commission was 'invited to present in due time to the Contracting Parties a report' (Art. 8.1) on how the golden (balanced budget) rule it enshrines has been incorporated into national legal systems. The report, published in early 2017,[94] follows the familiar pattern of a far-reaching ingenuity in excusing national deviations from the agreed rules. It admits that in some countries national provisions implementing the golden rule to the national law have not been, contrary to Art. 3(2) of the Fiscal Compact, 'guaranteed to be fully respected and adhered to throughout the national budgetary processes'. Yet it also opines that such aberrations can be excused by 'formal and public commitments given by Contracting Parties that the national legal framework will be applied in line with the requirements' of the Fiscal Compact, by 'the presence of strong national independent institutions monitoring compliance with the rules' and by specific additional measures 'announced ... [and] needed to bring national law into line with the Fiscal Compact' (p. 4). In other words, the Commission endorsed all national transpositions of the golden rule, whether they complied with the Compact's letter or not. As a corollary, it spared the German government the dilemma whether to accept transgressions of the Treaty it had pushed for a few years earlier, or to infuriate the European public opinion and the governments of the economically

[93] Marco Buti and Nicolas Carnot, 'The EMU Debt Crisis: Early Lessons and Reforms', *Journal of Common Market Studies* 50 (2012): 901.

[94] European Commission, 'Report from the Commission presented under Article 8 of the Treaty on Stability, Coordination and Governance in the Economic and Monetary Union', C(2017)1201, 22 February 2017.

less-auspicious states by waging against them a legal battle over their fiscal indicators.

This, too, has demonstrated the smoke-and-mirrors nature of the underlying rules-based system. The golden fiscal rule of the Fiscal Compact is essentially the same as what the SGP requires from EU Member States. German officials who pressed for signing the former during the sovereign debt crisis apparently realised that the SGP, even if reformed, may not deliver the results for which they aimed (fiscal stabilisation in the countries engulfed by the crisis), precisely because it introduced only a perception of immediate sanctions. So they wanted to achieve the same goal by forcing the governments of other states to pledge that the rules would become part and parcel of their domestic regimes.[95] The same policymakers certainly believed that 'incorporation of the said rules in national constitutional law might significantly enhance the legitimacy of the budgetary limitations by emphasising that they are self-imposed'.[96]

Their action was mistimed, though. It happened precisely when the majority of Eurozone societies and leading economists started associating fiscal discipline with economic asphyxiation (more on this in the next chapter). But it was also politically very naive. Two observers, coming from a country whose governments traditionally support rules imposing external constraints (It. *vincolo esterno*) on their economic and fiscal policies only to disobey them afterwards,[97] highlighted a very important point, corroborated amply by historic precedents:

> If a Member State already possesses a rather strong 'stability culture' (Stabilitätskultur) ... there is no need to rack one's brain in order to find out the best rule to tighten up public finance management. If a Member State does not possess such a culture, a structurally balanced budget rule will serve as a placebo for calming down financial markets, but, because of the many loopholes with which the rule will inevitably be filled, it won't per se change

[95] The original version of the Fiscal Compact required that the golden rule becomes a part of national constitutions, while its final version consents also to any other 'provisions of binding force and permanent character ... guaranteed to be fully respected and adhered to throughout the national budgetary processes'.

[96] Leonard Besselink and Jan-Herman Reestman (Editorial), 'The Fiscal Compact and the European Constitutions: "Europe Speaking German"', *European Constitutional Law Review* 8 (2012): 6.

[97] Kenneth H. F. Dyson and Kevin Featherstone, *The Road to Maastricht: Negotiating Economic and Monetary Union* (Oxford: Oxford University Press, 1999): 462 et seq.

or straighten out the attitude of a political class, which will make every effort to procrastinate regarding budgetary consolidation.[98]

Also, previous experiences demonstrated that introducing fiscal rules into domestic systems could not be a game changer in this respect. One cautionary tale came from Reagan-era USA. In 1985, a law known as the Gramm–Rudman–Hollings Act imposed year-by-year reductions of deficits and a return to budget equilibrium in 1991. In case the reductions would not have been achieved, most federal programs would have faced automatic cuts ('sequestration'). The reductions, however, would have depended on growth assumptions, which became notoriously overoptimistic under the new fiscal rules, in order to avoid the brake. All in all, during the five years of its existence (in 1990 the Gramm–Rudman–Hollings Act was replaced by its softer version – the 1990 Budget Enforcement Act) the federal deficit barely declined. In 1990, it reached 3.9 per cent of GDP, despite the initial target being 0.6 per cent.[99]

Fiscal rules of the UK, adopted in 1997 by the incoming Labour government, were similarly doomed. Conceptually, they embodied an impeccable version of the golden rule: government borrowing over the economic cycle may fund investments only; but it should not be used to fund current spending. In the auspicious years between 1997 and 2001 this rule worked brilliantly, bringing government debt:GDP ratio down by 4.5 per cent of GDP. And then it perished, for similar reasons as its American counterpart. Dupont and Kwarteng explained in this context that 'in each new budget the government promised their books would balance tomorrow – but tomorrow never seemed to arrive'.[100] In 2008, when the global financial crisis wrought havoc on the UK economy, all the pretences were dropped. The government of Gordon Brown – the man who championed the introduction of the rule a decade earlier – abandoned it altogether when the UK's deficit went through the roof.

[98] Giovanni Boggero and Pasquale Annicchino, '"Who Will Ever Kick Us Out?": Italy, the Balanced Budget Rule and the Implementation of the Fiscal Compact', *European Public Law* 20 (2014): 247–261.

[99] Anton Brender, Florence Pisani and Emile Gagna, *The Sovereign Debt Crisis. Placing a Curb on Growth* (CEPS, 2012), 64, available at www.ceps.eu/publications/sovereign-debt-crisis-placing-curb-growth.

[100] Jonathan Dupont and Kwasi Kwarteng, 'Binding the Hands of Government – A Credible Fiscal Rule for the UK', *The Institute of Economic Affairs Current Controversies Paper* No. 36, 13 May 2012, available at iea.org.uk/wp-content/uploads/2016/07/Binding%20the%20hands%20of%20government-1.pdf.

The experiences under the Fiscal Compact are even more telling. For instance, in 2015, only the exotic set of Germany, Greece and Luxembourg followed its fiscal prescriptions. All sixteen other Eurozone countries (as well as all seven non-Eurozone countries that signed the Fiscal Compact) ran deficits higher than prescribed by the Fiscal Compact. Its provision, according to which 'in the event of significant observed deviations from the medium-term objective or the adjustment path towards it, a correction mechanism shall be triggered automatically' (Art. 3(1)(e)), was hapless. From the political perspective there is nothing surprising in it at all. Fiscal and macroeconomic policies are social phenomena that no algorithm can effectively control. On this, the Greek ex-Minister of Finance Yanis Varoufakis brought the point home when he argued that 'when economics clashes with an institution's rules, policymakers must either find creative ways to amend the rules or watch their creation collapse'.[101] During the sovereign debt crisis the coordination rules were stiffened in hope to reign in economics (and politics). But this only precipitated their clash with the reality. In effect, policymakers – and the general public[102] – could only watch the 'rules-based union' fading away.

[101] Yanis Varoufakis, 'A New Approach to Eurozone Sovereign Debt', *Project Syndicate*, 17 August 2015, available at www.project-syndicate.org/commentary/eurozone-sovereign-debt-solution-by-yanis-varoufakis-2015-08?barrier=accessreg.

[102] A survey conducted for the EC in October 2016 revealed that 'less than one in five respondents (18%) think EU economic policy coordination amongst euro area countries in recent years has been strengthened: 46% say it has been weakened, and 22% that it has not changed … Since 2015 there has been an eight-point increase in the proportion who say coordination has been weakened', European Commission, Flash Eurobarometer 446, The Euro Area, 2016, 4.

3 Thirty Pieces of Silver in Exchange for Sovereignty?

3.1 Enter the New Kings

In the previous chapter I made a distinction between the basic rules-based union – the Six-Pack, the Two-Pack, the Fiscal Compact – and a qualified one. The main thrust of that chapter was that the first of them is defunct. The qualified rules-based union, instantiated when a debtor country applies for international financial assistance and signs a memorandum of understanding (MoU) establishing conditions on which the assistance is granted,[1] seems to be very different. The creditors are not as eager as in the basic setup to wink at transgressions of the agreed rules by the debtors. So the qualified rules-based union is not a paper tiger. It is not just another futile exercise of Brussels bureaucracy.

First of all, though, it is very tempting to claim that the relationship between the creditors and the debtors does not make up for any union (as the phrase 'rules-based union' would imply), only a very unequal commercial relationship that does not have anything to do with solidarity on which any actual union must rely. An Irish newspaper neatly captured the general feeling about the inequality between the creditors and the debtors within the qualified rules-based system. In December 2013, the month the Irish Economic Adjustment Programme expired,[2]

[1] With the European Stability Mechanism (ESM), in operation since late 2012, or with any of its predecessors: the European Financial Stability Facility (EFSF) and the European Financial Stabilisation Mechanism (EFSM) – in operation since 2010 to 2012.

[2] The Irish Economic Adjustment Programme started in November 2010 and ended in December 2013; the Portuguese programme was launched in May 2011 and completed in June 2014; the programme for Cyprus was agreed in March 2013 and ended in March 2016; Spain completed its programme – requested in July 2012 – for the recapitalisation of its financial institutions in January 2014; Greece's first Economic Adjustment Programme started in May 2010, while the second expired in June 2015 and has been followed by the third, devised to end in 2018.

it asserted that the Troika – the Commission, the IMF and the ECB, in charge of monitoring the programme – had been 'our new government now – unelected, unwanted and absolutely indispensable. Three Kings bearing a bitter gift of €85bn for a broken nation teetering on the edge of the precipice. Thirty pieces of silver in exchange for our hard-won, precious sovereignty.'[3]

Indeed, the rules imposed by international creditors on the societies engulfed by the Eurozone crisis could seem to have scarcely left any space for a democratic self-government. They were invasive and offensive for the basic notion of sovereignty, placing the debtor societies 'under a form of "receivership"'.[4] This is what most people in the countries that went through an adjustment programme ordeal will tell you. Allegedly, only some officials in the Troika and in capitals of the creditor countries would disagree that '*de facto* the countries under adjustment programmes lost part of their sovereignty when they lost their solvency and parliaments had no other choice than to accept the measures imposed by the Troika'.[5] To add insult to injury, the new Kings, the argument goes, have curtailed the national sovereignty of their subjects for a very wrong cause: they have asphyxiated the engulfed societies fiscally through austerity policies and devastated their social contracts through so-called structural reforms.

What is particularly important is that all these arguments are partly right and partly wrong. And, arguably, the Eurozone will not be really cured unless this ambivalent nature of financial assistance programmes is understood properly and unless this understanding translates properly into policy actions.

3.2 Austerity: Between Ricardo and Multipliers

Fiscal austerity championed by the Troika throughout the Eurozone crisis – the requirement that government accounts of debtor countries

[3] Lise Hand, 'The Week Ireland Gave Up Its Sovereignty', *Irish Independent*, 1 December 2013, available at www.independent.ie/lifestyle/the-week-ireland-gave-up-its-sovereignty-29796376.html.

[4] Fritz Scharpf, 'Monetary Union, Fiscal Crisis and the Preemption of Democracy', *MPIfG Discussion Paper* No. 11/11, July 2011, 29, available at www.mpifg.de/pu/mpifg_dp/dp11-11.pdf.

[5] Cinzia Alcidi, Alessandro Giovannini and Sonia Piedrafita, 'Enhancing the Legitimacy of EMU Governance', *CEPS Special Report* No. 98, 18 December 2014, 22, available at www.ceps.eu/publications/enhancing-legitimacy-emu-governance.

post surpluses – has suffocated entrepreneurs and consumption (when austerity has entailed higher taxes) and/or betokened various income protection reductions, from cuts in pensions and disability entitlements to restrictions in out-of-work income maintenance and curtailments of minimum wages. It shrivelled funding for labour market policies, from labour market services to training to supported employment and rehabilitation. Healthcare and education funding also routinely suffered from it.

In other words, austerity affected the most sanctified premises of the welfare state. But, more importantly, it suppressed economic activity, it dealt a heavy blow to employment and it contributed to legions of people deprived of jobs or precariously employed. In a 2011 manifesto, signed in Athens, the European Trade Union Confederation ominously warned that 'the austerity measures imposed, for example in Greece, Portugal and Ireland, have made the situation worse, and the countries concerned face a long period of continued recession, rising debt burdens, pressure on labour standards and labour rights and unemployment. There is a real risk of countries and their populations becoming even more strongly indebted, with huge dangers for Europe and its Member States.'[6]

Back in 2010 or 2011, economic pundits behind bailout programmes spurned such reservations. Their logic was very simple: at the very minimum public debt is sustainable when the government can demonstrate its ability to service it. In other words, public debt should be sustainable when the primary budget balance (the difference between government revenue and expenditure in the budget, excluding interest) is higher than the total interest due in the same period. Drafters of the assistance programmes for the Eurozone countries drew a direct conclusion from this simple relationship: the bigger the primary budget balance, the more private creditors would become convinced of a country's debt sustainability. This conviction should arrest interest hikes, it was hoped, augmenting primary surpluses and bringing the levels of public debts further down the path to safe areas.

The economic theory was on their side. In the 1970s, economists discovered that in the face of a negative supply shock (structural ailments of a longer-lasting nature, like artificially inflated product or labour prices) the fiscal multiplier – the measurement of growth

[6] The Athens Manifesto, signed 19 May 2011, available at www.etuc.org/athens-manifesto-0.

contraction due to austerity – is close to zero. Neither a fiscal stimulus nor government spending cuts can, positively or negatively, influence growth in such a situation, as it is inhibited by non-fiscal factors. Because peripheral Eurozone countries were diagnosed in 2010 to have suffered from a negative supply shock, proponents of austerity policies claimed that fiscal multipliers should not be any bigger than they had been earlier on. In addition, it was argued that expenditure cuts today reduce economic distortions by reducing taxes tomorrow. Economic agents should see it and, in line with the so-called Ricardian Equivalence[7] (a very non-Keynesian theory), they would expect higher incomes after the rebalancing process. Hence economic activity should be sustained by private demand also in the shorter perspective, even under stringent austerity conditions. All in all, therefore, fiscal contraction was predicted to be expansionary: it ought to support GDP growth.[8] In a way, the logic here is similar to force a glutton to put away his marshmallows and start jogging to get fit. As Pisani-Ferry put it,

> constraining the deficit is a powerful way to ... signal to all domestic stakeholders that growth is not going to come from more public spending. Rather, the only way to foster it is to improve supply-side conditions and deliver better, cheaper products that find demand on world markets. Seen from this angle, budgetary consolidation – especially when it takes the form of spending cuts – is merely an instrument at the service of the goal of shaking up the economy.[9]

Soon, though, the Greek debacle had them reconsidering what they thought they knew. When an economy is in recession, when private spending is low because households strive to reduce their indebtedness (deleverage) – in other words, when a 'balance sheet recession' (a major financial-cycle bust following a boom and accompanied by low

[7] When public debt grows, the society should save its excess money (depress private demand) in order to garnish resources for future tax increases initiated to pay off the debt. The process should work in the opposite direction in the case of lowering the public debt.

[8] Alberto F. Alesina and Silvia Ardagna, 'Large Changes in Fiscal Policy: Taxes versus Spending', *NBER Working Paper* No. 15438, October 2009; Alberto Alesina, Carlo Favero and Francesco Giavazzi, 'The Output Effect of Fiscal Consolidations', *NBER Working Paper* No. 18336, August 2012. For a broader account on the theory, and for its critique, see Rafael Muñoz de Bustillo, 'Questioning the Myth of Expansionary Austerity: European Macroeconomic Policy during the Crisis and Its Aftermath', in: *The Economic Crisis and Governance in the European Union: A Critical Assessment*, ed. Javier Bilbao-Ubillos (London: Routledge, 2014): 114–133.

[9] Jean Pisani-Ferry, *The Euro Crisis and Its Aftermath* (New York: Oxford University Press, 2014): 113.

inflation)[10] sets in – austerity can easily make things worse on all accounts. Because government spending translates into someone's income, its reduction depresses consumption. Both tax increases and government spending cuts – two conceivable faces of austerity – dump private demand (much more directly in the first of the two options and less so in the second), while government spending cuts additionally reduce public demand. Collapsing demand makes tax revenues fall further. Such an environment is extremely hostile to economic growth, while growth is a necessary precondition of debt sustainability. This is because debt sustainability is correlated with the debt:GDP ratio rather than with nominal debt levels. So when the GDP grows faster than debt (no matter how big it is), the latter becomes relatively less problematic, due to the falling ratio between the two. But by that token public debt reductions jeopardise debt sustainability when output (GDP) falls more pronouncedly than does the public debt. Fiscal austerity, therefore, becomes self-defeating when fiscal rebalancing contributes to economic contraction. When households desperately try to reduce their debt levels, while interest rates of the central bank are reduced to zero and unresolved banking crises drag down credit supply, there is nothing to stimulate economic growth if the fiscal policy is also contractionary. In this environment, austerity sets in motion a pernicious debt-deflation dynamic: it increases the very government debt ratios it is intended to suppress.

In 2012, Blanchard and Leigh made precisely this argument on three influential pages of an IMF report.[11] The two claimed that, since 2009, fiscal multipliers in advanced economies were up to three times higher than in the previous three decades. They calculated, and other economists soon confirmed, that 1 per cent of GDP increase in austerity (reduction of public debt) would not entail an output decline by about 0.5 per cent, as the Commission had maintained as late as in the autumn of 2012.[12] Rather, the economic activity would contract by a

[10] Mathias Drehmann, Claudio Borio and Kostas Tsatsaronis, 'Characterising the Financial Cycle: Don't Lose Sight of the Medium-Term!', *BIS Working Paper* No. 380, June 2012; Richard C. Koo 'The World in Balance Sheet Recession: Causes, Cure, and Politics', *Real-World Economics Review* 58 (2011): 19–37; Luc Eyraud and Anke Weber, 'The Challenge of Debt Reduction during Fiscal Consolidation', *IMF Working Paper* No. 13/67, March 2013.

[11] IMF, 'World Economic Outlook. Coping with High Debt and Sluggish Growth', October 2012, 42–44.

[12] It wrote in its 'European Economic Forecast Autumn 2012', *European Economy* No. 7/2012, 'Forecast Errors and Multiplier Uncertainty', Box 1.5, page 41, available at ec.europa.eu/economy_finance/publications/european_economy/2012/pdf/ee-2012-7_

figure much closer to 1.5 per cent of GDP.[13] When this is the case, austerity becomes entirely self-defeating, because economic growth never gets a chance to reduce the debt burden.

More recently, it turned out that the picture may be even more perverse: some economists argued that the results of Blanchard and Leigh are entirely convincing for the period of 2009–2011, less so for the two years 2012 and 2013, and unconvincing afterwards.[14] Paradoxically, the pressure on fiscal austerity in the programme countries let up in 2013 – partly because this is when economists made up their minds about fiscal multipliers and partly because the pressure on regaining market confidence through austerity lapsed then due to the effectiveness of the ECB's declaration that it would 'do whatever it takes' in arresting previous spikes in government debt premia. In other words, austerity was prioritised when it was particularly damaging to economic activity, receding when in fact it made more economic sense.

3.3 The Ugly Face of Structural Reforms

Fiscal austerity is just one side to the conditionality coin. Adjustments under the notion of structural reforms is the other, equally disruptive side.

In a narrow sense, structural reforms are intrinsically related to balance-of-payments crises, which are always currency crises occurring when a nation runs out of the currency it needs to service its debt repayments and pay for essential imports. To reverse the course, real exchange rates of the local currency, which routinely grow in the years preceding the currency crisis, must be readjusted. One strategy is to do it fast, by nominal exchange (external) depreciation or devaluation. Because in this scenario foreign currencies become suddenly more expensive in the local currency, import prices grow by fiat and debt

en.pdf, that: 'The multiplier for a permanent consolidation for the EU aggregate in normal circumstances lies, depending on the instrument, between 0.2–0.8, and is on average for a balanced composition consolidation around 0.4. However, when interest rates are constrained by the zero rate floor, and in an environment of global fiscal retrenchment, as in the current environment, the average multiplier can rise to 0.5–0.7.'

[13] Paul De Grauwe and Yuemei Ji, 'The Legacy of Austerity in the Eurozone', *CEPS Commentary*, 4 October 2013, available at www.ceps.eu/publications/legacy-austerity-eurozone.

[14] Jan Mohlmann and Wim Suyker, 'An Update of Blanchard's and Leigh's Estimates in "Growth Forecast Errors and Fiscal Multipliers"', *CEPR Policy Portal*, 1 December 2015, available at www.voxeu.org/article/blanchard-and-leigh-s-fiscal-multipliers-revisited.

denominated in foreign currencies becomes (sometimes much) more onerous. At the same time, though, the economy is stimulated by exports abruptly becoming more competitive. The adjustment is automatic and inevitable, even if growing costs of imported goods push up inflation, mitigating competitiveness effects of the process. In a monetary union, however, in which an individual government cannot adjust nominal exchange rates, this option is precluded. The only way left to perform the macroeconomic adjustment, and in consequence the only exit path from the balance-of-payments crisis, is to devalue internally.

In practice, this can only mean relative deflation: unit labour costs must decline (labour productivity must improve and/or nominal wages must fall), just as must prices on product markets. Both of the processes should facilitate exports and inward direct investments in the country undergoing the adjustment, while at the same time discouraging imports.

Deregulation is the main vehicle to accomplish the feat on product markets. Product and service markets are liberalised, to let competition exert a downward pressure on prices. Public enterprises are privatised, again to allow competition to operate more freely in the sectors where public control previously produced distortions in wages and productivity.[15]

On labour markets the internal devaluation strategy is twofold. First, it tackles terms of employment in the public sector. And second, it softens the influence of employees on terms of employment throughout the whole economy, so that wage reductions necessary for internal devaluation can proceed more smoothly.

In the first of the two strands, public-sector employees experience salary reductions, direct redundancies and sweeping civil service reforms. The argument behind this is that public-sector adjustments

[15] There is a long way, however, between finding out what is to be done and how it is to be achieved. In Greece in particular the adjustment programmes disregarded the latter aspect. Loopholes in tax reforms allowed the rich to escape them and product market reforms tended to focus on trivialities, while no reforms seriously tackled the oligarchic and crony nature of Greek capitalism and the weaknesses in the policies determining macroeconomic foundations (from education to technology and the financial sector). It is also paradigmatic that privatisation in a political and institutional system conducive to cronyism may easily eliminate all its possible efficiency gains altogether. For an insightful critique of the Greek programmes from this perspective, see esp. Joseph Stiglitz, *The Euro: How a Common Currency Threatens the Future of Europe* (New York: W. W. Norton, 2016): 190–196, 216–230.

must be particularly pronounced, because this is where the government determines terms of employment directly and because unit labour cost declines applied to the public sector would transmit to the rest of the economy. While there are serious arguments against this causality,[16] the strand of structural reforms now discussed becomes more reasonable where the public sector is particularly outsized and unproductive. In this scenario both the possible transmission to the rest of the economy and the structural gains of reduced bureaucratic burdens to entrepreneurship enabled by civil service reforms may be largest. In addition, lower payroll expenditures in the public sector betoken lower government expenditures, going hand-in-hand with the goal of fiscal consolidation.

The second strand – the overhaul of labour law – concentrates on collective bargaining arrangements (wage indexation schemes in particular), labour market institutions and employment protection. All of these are trimmed down or dismantled altogether. The goal all around is to 'decentralise' collective agreements: replace industry-level agreements with company-level arrangements as the latter are less rigid and therefore more accommodative to wage suppressions.[17] Overhauling collective relations is just one way of lifting employment protections, however, out of many methods deployed under the rubric of structural reforms. Researchers of the European Trade Union Institute aptly noted that during the Eurozone crisis the repertoire of alterations to basic premises of labour law was concentrated on eliminating 'redundancy avoidance measures, avoiding recourse to the courts in the event of disputes, increasing the length of service required before redundancy rules apply, reducing the level of compensatory sanctions, calling into question the principle of reinstatement as a penalty for unfair dismissals, increasing the thresholds used to define specific obligations in the area of redundancy, etc.'[18]

[16] See Ana Lamo, Javier Pérez and Ludger Schuknecht, 'Public and Private Sector Wages: Co-Movement and Causality', *ECB Working Paper Series* No. 963, November 2008, available at www.ecb.europa.eu/pub/pdf/scpwps/ecbwp963.pdf.

[17] Ana Rute Cardoso and Miguel Portela, 'Micro Foundations for Wage Flexibility: Wage Insurance at the Firm Level', *The Scandinavian Journal of Economics* 111 (2009): 29–50; Juan Jimeno and Carlos Thomas, 'Collective Bargaining, Firm Heterogeneity, and Unemployment', *European Economic Review* 59 (2013): 63–79; Giuseppe Bertola et al., 'Price, Wage and Employment Response to Shocks: Evidence from the WDN Survey', *ECB Working Paper Series* No. 1164, March 2010, available at www.ecb.europa.eu/pub/pdf/scpwps/ecbwp1164.pdf.

[18] Sylvaine Laulom et al., 'How Has the Crisis Affected Social Legislation in Europe?', *ETUI Policy Brief. European Economic, Employment and Social Policy* No. 2/2012, 3, available

None of the alterations is politically palatable. Altogether they are politically fiery, because the structural changes they entail require the societies undergoing them to 'effectively renegotiate their basic social contracts'.[19] The protections originally calibrated to alleviate social risks are replaced by 'an almost full commodification of labour'[20] and 'the explosive growth of inequalities and insecurity'.[21] The structural changes to the public sector and employment relations undercut fundamental social rights, while – in light of the tradition so prevalent throughout Europe – 'fundamental rights, whether social or otherwise, should not be subject to economic and technocratic considerations. On the contrary it is the economy that must be placed at the service of fundamental rights.'[22]

In fact, proponents of structural reforms have only one strategy to tackle the charges: the society must be persuaded that the reforms are necessary to regain economic prosperity and that the pain will end soon. For two basic reasons, however, this strategy may turn out an uphill battle.

First, unit labour cost moderations are very slow and painful, because wages are sticky-down: they find it difficult to deflate. And, second, even when, under the pressure of the very high unemployment, wages do go down pronouncedly, they may not translate into cheaper export products and higher foreign direct investments if other factors (e.g., the general profile of the economy, state deficiencies – corruption, distortive taxes, ineffective law enforcement – and regulatory requirements, etc.) discourage economic activity or exports.[23]

In consequence, unemployment may stabilise at very high levels. For instance, the Greek unemployment rate was estimated in 2010 to be

at www.etui.org/Publications2/Policy-Briefs/European-Economic-Employment-and-Social-Policy/How-has-the-crisis-affected-social-legislation-in-Europe.

[19] Jan-Werner Müller, 'Beyond Militant Democracy?', *New Left Review* 73 (2012): 44.

[20] Aristea Koukiadaki and Lefteris Kretsos, 'Opening Pandora's Box: The Sovereign Debt Crisis and Labour Market Regulation in Greece', *Industrial Law Journal* 41 (2012): 277.

[21] Laulom et al., 'Social Legislation in Europe', 1.

[22] Nicola Countouris and Mark Freedland, 'Epilogue: Resocialising Europe – Looking Back and Thinking Forward', in: *Resocialising Europe in a Time of Crisis*, eds. Nicola Countouris and Mark Freedland (Cambridge: Cambridge University Press, 2013): 496.

[23] It has been argued that changes in relative unit labour costs have actually no bearing on changes in the current account balance: Hubert Gabrisch and Karsten Staehr, 'The Euro Plus Pact: Competitiveness and External Capital Flows in the EU Countries', *ECB Working Paper Series* No. 1650, March 2014, available at www.ecb.europa.eu/pub/pdf/scpwps/ecbwp1650.pdf?b634be5ae6e3564a096c8dc2cf9e3203.

standing at 15 per cent by the end of 2013, while it had actually reached 27 per cent by then. This in turn deepens the recession, precipitates social fatigue and puts an additional burden on government accounts, through unemployment and other social benefits. And, due to the so-called hysteresis effects, it cuts even more deeply through social tissue. A protracted recession erodes human capital and inflicts damage on companies through credit constraints.[24] In short, therefore, structural reforms can easily hinder longer-term growth of economic productivity and efficiency if they are only partly successful, e.g., when labour market reforms proceed much faster than product market or business environment reforms.

Now, if financial assistance is granted in exchange for what is called in the official parlance 'strict conditionality', if the strict conditionality boils down to a mixture of austerity and structural reforms, and if both policies feel like pulling teeth, then financial assistance itself is endangered. As the argument goes, any institution in charge of its enforcement becomes a public enemy, and deservedly so. By pursuing brutal policies the strict conditionality deprives the society on the ground of the economic prospects necessary to regain its economic independence. According to this storyline, the Troika should not be named the Quadriga, as the Commission President Juncker has preferred, after the ESM joined the three institutions for the third Greek bailout programme. Other names, prevailing on the Internet - like JUNTA (Joint Umbrella for Neutral Technical Advice) or the Four Horsemen of the Apocalypse - would more properly epitomise the flawed policies administered by foreign governments and their unelected agents, whose only achievable result is to keep the local society on its knees. Many observers could agree in this respect with those who have argued that 'anything goes, it seems, to satisfy the fervour of national and supranational policymakers eager to use the economic crisis as a further opportunity to demolish the frail social pillars of labour and social rights on which the very notion of "Social Europe" rests'.[25]

24 John Van Reenen, 'Fiscal Consolidation: Too Much of a Good Thing?', *CEPR's Policy Portal*, 27 April 2012, available at www.voxeu.org/article/fiscal-consolidation-too-much-good-thing; J. Bradford DeLong and Lawrence H. Summers, 'Fiscal Policy in a Depressed Economy', *Brookings Paper on Economic Activity*, Spring 2012, available at www.brookings.edu/bpea-articles/fiscal-policy-in-a-depressed-economy/.

25 Nicola Countouris and Mark Freedland, 'Preface', in: *Resocialising Europe in a Time of Crisis*, eds. Nicola Countouris and Mark Freedland (Cambridge: Cambridge University Press, 2013): ix.

One additional factor reinforcing this very narrative is the role of two supranational institutions – the ECB and the Court of Justice – throughout the Eurozone crisis. Both should arguably stay away from economic and fiscal choices, because each of the two areas involves political decisions neither of the two institutions can legitimately make. But, instead, they have sided with creditor countries and institutions, largely amplifying the stranglehold of the economic conditionality.

3.4 Frankfurt Commands

The original justification for the ECB's participation in the Troika (together with the IMF and the Commission) was to have an eye on the performance of banking systems in countries undergoing macroeconomic adjustments. The Frankfurt bank, though, has also been very active in the fiscal side of the programmes, representing a more hawkish approach than has the Commission and the IMF.[26] And it has not been removed from the Troika despite the overwhelming influence it has received upon national financial systems of the Eurozone since a new channel of its pressure on national banking systems – the Single Supervisory Mechanism[27] – was created in November 2014.

In fact, however, the influence of an independent central bank beyond the banking system is virtually unavoidable when a banking crisis is conflated with a balance-of-payments crisis and a sovereign debt crisis, first because commercial banks use sovereign debt as collateral when accessing central bank liquidity. Second, and more generally, if a sovereign becomes unviable, its banking system is certain to follow suit, due to the effects of this eventuality on the assets side of the balance sheet and because of the economic implications any such event would have on the non-financial sector: the original

[26] Jean Pisani-Ferry, André Sapir and Guntram Wolff, 'EU-IMF Assistance to Euro Area Countries: An Early Assessment', *Bruegel Blueprint Series* No. 19/2013, 16 June 2013, 111, available at bruegel.org/2013/06/eu-imf-assistance-to-euro-area-countries-an-early-assessment/.

[27] Council Regulation 1024/2013 of 15 October 2013 Conferring Specific Tasks on the European Central Bank Concerning Policies Relating to the Prudential Supervision of Credit Institutions, OJ 2013 No. L 287, 29 October 2013, pp. 63–89 and Regulation 1022/2013 of the European Parliament and of the Council of 22 October 2013 Amending Regulation 1093/2010 Establishing a European Supervisory Authority (European Banking Authority) as Regards the Conferral of Specific Tasks on the European Central Bank Pursuant to Council Regulation 1024/2013, OJ 2013, No. L 287, 29 October 2013, pp. 5–14.

target of financial intermediation. So even if financial stability is not enumerated among the main tasks of a central bank (which is the case for the ECB), it is natural that the central bank tries to prevent such a scenario, stretching its original mandate if necessary and trying to pressure sovereigns to pursue policies, which, as it sees them, would render the banking system more secure and stable. In other words, the inherent role of central banks – buttressing the banking system when a financial crisis upsets its liquidity (the lender of last resort function) – encourages them to extend their leverage to the realm of economic and fiscal policies, particularly when they consider that the fate of their interventions towards the banking system depends on certain actions of the national government.

The examples of the Irish package, to which I will return in a while, and (especially) the third Greek package have demonstrated vividly that the very intimation of the ECB's readiness to block the influx of central bank Emergency Liquidity Assistance (ELA)[28] to the national financial system gives it the upper hand in any negotiations with a debtor government. This is why the ECB could easily force unwilling national governments of Ireland in 2010, Cyprus in 2013 and Greece in 2015 to apply for bailout packages, which, to many, corroborated that technocratic unelected officials prevail over democratic choices in the Eurozone.

In the particular case of the ELA, such a concern is not well-placed, because by default this emergency liquidity can be provided to solvent banks only.[29] Without a bailout each of the countries just mentioned would have become insolvent, pulling the banking systems, stuffed with government bonds, down with it. Providing emergency liquidity

[28] National central banks of the Eurozone are authorised to provide ELA to solvent financial institutions facing temporary liquidity problems. According to Art. 14.4 of the Statute of the ESCB and the ECB, the Governing Council of the ECB is authorised to restrict ELA operations if it considers that such operations interfere with the objectives and tasks of the Eurosystem. Such decisions require a majority of two-thirds of the votes cast.

[29] While this tenet stems explicitly from the Statute of the ESCB and the ECB, there have been voices claiming that, according to the interpretation of EU primary law by the Court of Justice of the European Union (CJEU), even insolvent financial institutions should receive access to ELA funding when this option is considered necessary for financial stability purposes: Armin Steinbach, 'The Lender of Last Resort in the Eurozone', *Common Market Law Review* 53 (2016): esp. 373–374. The fact that in practice access to ELA funding has not been based on any rigid analysis of whether financial institutions to benefit from it are actually solvent or not suggests that the actual policy may have gone precisely in this direction.

to a banking system of an insolvent sovereign would therefore both violate EU law and would be economically irrational (emergency liquidity should flow to illiquid but solvent institutions; insolvent ones should be restructured). No matter, however, how understandable the stance of the ECB is from the legal or economic point of view, politically it is very difficult. Without the financial lifeline controlled by the ECB, banking systems of the distressed countries would implode precisely when the sovereign becomes insolvent. The national economic, political and social systems would tank immediately. Because, therefore, the central bank is the only source of financing for commercial banks in times of a financial stress, national governments of Eurozone countries engulfed by a financial crisis must pay utmost attention to the policy the ECB pursues towards them. In particular, when the Frankfurt institution opines that a Eurozone country should apply for international financial assistance, the government of the latter has no choice but to follow it through.

3.5 Rubberstamping Luxembourg

The stance of the Court of Justice, siding with creditor institutions and governments each time it has had a chance to speak up, has also been politically (and legally) contestable.

Take the following examples.

The no-bailout clause was devised to be an indispensable keystone of fiscal discipline in the Eurozone, as I mentioned in Chapter 2. It was a part of the original Maastricht EMU architecture. From the very beginning of the Eurozone it was to set a basic constitutional principle, while one of the basic rules of legal interpretation has it that general legal principles should be interpreted extensively. For these (legalistic) reasons the German government required a Treaty amendment making an explicit exception to this principle as a precondition for establishing the ESM, i.e., the permanent bailout scheme.[30] But the ESM started its operations in October 2012, while the Treaty amendment anchoring it in EU primary law entered into force only in May 2013.

[30] Art. 136(3) TFEU provides that 'the Member States whose currency is the euro may establish a stability mechanism to be activated if indispensable to safeguard the stability of the Eurozone as a whole. The granting of any required financial assistance under the mechanism will be made subject to strict conditionality.' This

The question of whether all of this was legally acceptable finally reached the Court of Justice.[31] It answered it in the affirmative, which – however, required exceptional legal ingenuity and made some leading European lawyers profoundly aghast.[32] In the case now discussed, *Pringle,*[33] the Court simply predicated that financial assistance programmes are not really bailouts, because they assume that, due to the economic conditionality they entail, debtor countries will be able to regain economically and fiscally. At that point they will pay back whatever financial assistance they have received. In consequence, precisely because of the conditionality sewn into assistance programmes, no permanent bailouts will be necessary, while the Treaty prohibition deals with this type of a bailout only.

There is clear logic in this argument. The basic principle of international financial assistance is that the assistance should go to fiscally sustainable countries only, those capable of paying back the outlays received (and the fact, discussed more broadly in Chapter 6, that some rescue packages were different undermines their legality according to the *Pringle* standard). For now, however, something else is more important: pursuant to *Pringle* no temporary bailout in the Eurozone is legally problematic, as long as it works and the assistance is paid back. The Eurozone states are free to set up such assistance schemes and no Treaty amendment is necessary to vindicate them.

provision was added to TFEU by Art. 1 European Council Decision 2011/199/EU of 25 March 2011 amending Article 136 of the TFEU with regard to a stability mechanism for Member States whose currency is the euro, OJ 2011 No. L 91, 6 April 2011, pp. 1–2.

[31] As Vestert Borger noted aptly in this context, 'if the Court would rule that Article 136(3) TFEU clears the way for the ESM this would have as a consequence that the euro area member states would have contravened Article 125 TFEU by concluding and ratifying the ESM Treaty before the entry into force of Decision 2011/199. Indirectly, it would also have meant that euro area member states would have violated Article 125 TFEU by granting assistance via the temporary fund EFSF which, like the ESM, also does not have its legal basis in Union law': Vestert Borger, 'How the Debt Crisis Exposes the Development of Solidarity in the Euro Area', *European Constitutional Law Review* 9 (2013): 23–24.

[32] Paul Craig, 'Guest Editorial. Pringle: Legal Reasoning, Text, Purpose and Teleology', *Maastricht Journal of European Law* 20 (2013): 3–11.

[33] Case C-370/12, *Thomas Pringle* v. *Government of Ireland and Others*, ECLI:EU:C:2012:756. For a comprehensive discussion thereof see Etienne De Lhoneux and Christos Vassilopoulos, *The European Stability Mechanism before the Court of Justice of the European Union. Comments on the Pringle Case* (Cham: Springer, 2014).

This reading of EU primary law did not only save the ESM's actions undertaken before the Treaty amendment authorising them entered into force. It also emphasised the role of the economic conditionality of the assistance programmes and of the institutions, the ECB in particular, exerting pressure on national governments to respect it.

The Court adhered to the same approach when in 2015 it opined in another landmark decision, *Gauweiler*,[34] that the ECB would not violate its monetary policy mandate were it to purchase government bonds within its Outright Monetary Transactions (OMT) programme (to which I will return in the next chapter), while supervising, as a member of the Troika, economic conditionality programmes offered to the very same government. The CJEU imposed no conditions, limitations or reservations on how the ECB – a monetary policy institution – can oversee the intrinsically economic and fiscal conditions of the assistance programmes in such a situation, despite the Advocate General was quite assertive that we are talking about a legally unacceptable conflict of interests here.[35]

In consequence, the message of *Pringle* is only reinforced: the original Maastricht design – the limits of the ECB's mandate in this particular case – can be creatively readjusted by European institutions to allow for undisrupted enforcement of the strict conditionality paradigm.

[34] Case C-62/14, *Peter Gauweiler and Others* v. *Deutscher Bundestag*, ECLI:EU:C:2015:400.

[35] The Advocate General argued that 'under no circumstances would it be possible for the ECB, in a situation in which a programme such as OMT is under way, to continue to take part in the monitoring of the financial assistance programme to which the Member State is subject when, at the same time, that State is the recipient of substantial assistance from the ECB on the secondary government bond market': opinion of Advocate General Cruz Villalón in case C-62/14, *Peter Gauweiler and Others* v. *Deutscher Bundestag*, delivered on 14 January 2015, ECLI:EU:C:2015:7, § 150. More broadly on the conflicts of interests in this situation, see also Karl Whelan, 'The ECB's Role in Financial Assistance Programmes', June 2012, available at www.europarl.europa.eu/document/activities/cont/201207/20120705ATT48408/20120705ATT48408EN.pdf; Silvia Merler, Jean Pisani-Ferry and Guntram Wolff, 'The Role of the ECB in Financial Assistance: Some Early Observations', June 2012, available at www.europarl.europa.eu/document/activities/cont/201207/20120702ATT48160/20120702ATT48160EN.pdf; Daniel Gros, 'Countries under Adjustment Programmes: What Role for the ECB?', *CEPS Special Report* No. 124, 10 December 2015, available at www.ceps.eu/publications/countries-under-adjustment-programmes-what-role-ecb; Zsolt Darvas 'Regional and Global Financial Safety Nets: The Recent European Experience and Its Implications for Regional Cooperation in Asia', *Bruegel Working Paper* No. 6/2017, 20 April 2017, esp. 14–15, available at bruegel.org/2017/04/regional-and-global-financial-safety-nets-the-recent-european-experience-and-its-implications-for-regional-cooperation-in-asia/.

The same approach comes from a different strand of the cases decided by the CJEU, in which it was confronted with claims that some aspects of the strict conditionality imposed on debtor countries violated rights enshrined in the EU's Charter of Fundamental Rights.

There was a whole slew of such cases flowing to the CJEU during the sovereign debt crisis. One strand challenged public-sector salary and welfare benefit reductions in the countries on financial assistance programmes. In these cases plaintiffs argued that such reductions violated the fundamental right to property (Art. 17(1) Charter), equality before the law (Art. 20 Charter) and the non-discrimination principle (Art. 21(1) Charter), as well as the right to fair and just working conditions (Art. 31(1) Charter).[36] In the other strand plaintiffs questioned the 37.5 per cent levy imposed on uninsured (above €100,000) deposits in the Bank of Cyprus, agreed as a part of the 2013 Cypriot adjustment programme.[37] They claimed that this policy flagrantly breached their right to property.

When the constitutional system is pre-programmed to affirm socialist values – which is the case of Portugal[38] – the constitutional court dealing with such cases may be expected to be quite amenable to such claims.[39]

[36] E.g., Cases C-434/11, *Corpul Naţional al Poliţiştilor* v. *MAI and Others*, ECLI:EU:C:2011:830; C-134/12, *Corpul Naţional al Poliţiştilor – Biroul Executiv Central* v. *MAI and Others*, ECLI:EU:C:2012:288; and C-369/12, *Corpul Naţional al Poliţiştilor – Biroul Executiv Central* v. *MAI and Others*, ECLI:EU:C:2012:725, Case C-128/12, *Sindicato dos Bancários do Norte and Others* v. *BPN* ECLI:EU:C:2013:149, Case C-264/12, *Sindicato Nacional dos Profissionais de Seguros e Afins* v. *Fidelidade Mundial – Companhia de Seguros SA*, ECLI:EU:C:2014:2036, Case C-665/13, *Sindicato Nacional dos Profissionais de Seguros e Afins* v. *Via Directa – Companhia de Seguros SA*, ECLI:EU:C:2014:2327.

[37] Cases C-8/15 P to C-10/15 P, *Ledra Advertising and Others* v. *Commission and ECB*, ECLI:EU:C:2016:701.

[38] The preamble to the Portugal's 1976 Constitution states that 'The Constituent Assembly affirms the Portuguese people's decision to ... open the way to socialist society.'

[39] In its judgments laid down since 2012 to 2014, the Portuguese Constitutional Court struck down several provisions introducing to Portuguese law requirements enclosed in this country's MoU with the international creditors: Claire Kilpatrick, 'Constitutions, Social Rights and Sovereign Debt States in Europe: A Challenging New Area of Constitutional Inquiry', *EUI Working Papers LAW* 34 (2015): 8. For a broader overview of the case law, see Mariana Canotilho, Teresa Violante and Rui Lanceiro, 'Austerity Measures under Judicial Scrutiny: The Portuguese Constitutional Case-law: Portuguese Constitutional Court Decision 399/2010 (Surtax on Personal Income Tax 2010) Decision 396/2011 (State Budget 2011) Decision 353/2012 (State Budget 2012) Decision 187/2013 (State Budget 2013) Decision 474/2013 (Public Workers Requalification) Decision 602/2013 (Labour Code) Decision 794/2013 (40-Hour Work Week) Decision 862/2013 (Pensions Convergence) Decision 413/2014 (State Budget 2014) Decision 572/2014 (Special Solidarity Contribution 2014) Decision 574/2014

The EU Treaties are quite different on this account, though. They are more neutral in the sense of being more accommodative to economic ideologies currently prevailing in European institutions, whatever the ideologies are.

Of course, it would be hard to argue that the right to property is not restricted by a sequestration of more than a third of one's bank deposit, or by a 25 per cent pay cut applied to the public sector. The individuals in the line of fire of these measures stand to lose financially. But, as I mentioned in Chapter 1, when a bank goes bust someone has to be burnt: either equity holders, or creditors, or depositors, or taxpayers. The logic is even more straightforward during an internal devaluation. It has no chance to succeed unless those whose living is funded by the state take its brunt first. The situation may get more complicated, of course, when the economy does not visibly recover despite these painful treatments. The question of whether crisis measures restricting fundamental rights are adequate and necessary to achieve their objective (economic recovery), i.e., whether they fulfil the crucial precondition of proportionality,[40] is less clear-cut in such a situation. But as long as the restrictions belong to the standard toolbox used by policymakers in banking or balance-of-payment crises, a court of law should hardly be expected to second-guess economic policymakers on what is necessary to achieve economic adjustment.

For a few years the Court of Justice did not want to tackle the problem head-on, claiming instead that it manifestly lacked jurisdiction, because national courts referring to it in those cases ostensibly did not provide sufficient evidence that national laws introducing austerity measures were implementing any EU law. This tactics was devastating

(Pay cuts 2014–2018) Decision 575/2014 (Special Sustainability Contribution)', *European Constitutional Law Review* 11 (2015): 155–183. See also three contributions to Claire Kilpatrick and Bruno De Witte, eds, 'Social Rights in Times of Crisis in the Eurozone: The Role of Fundamental Rights' Challenges', *EUI Working Papers LAW* 5 (2014), available at cadmus.eui.eu/handle/1814/31247: Miguel Nogueira de Brito, 'Putting Social Rights in Brackets? The Portuguese Experience with Welfare Challenges in Times of Crisis', 67–77; Júlio Gomes, 'Social Rights in Crisis in the Eurozone. Work Rights in Portugal', 78–84; Roberto Cisotta and Daniel Gallo, 'The Portuguese Constitutional Court Case Law on Austerity Measures: A Reappraisal', 85–94.

40 According to Art. 52(1) of the Charter of Fundamental Rights of the European Union, 'subject to the principle of proportionality, limitations may be made only if they are necessary and genuinely meet objectives of general interest recognised by the Union or the need to protect the rights and freedoms of others'.

for the Court's credibility, because it was conspicuously altering the reality. The CJEU was pursuing this approach even when the preliminary questions themselves highlighted the causality between the austerity measures and the conditions of international financial assistance well-anchored in EU law. A provision of the 2012 Portuguese finance law challenged in one of the cases explicitly indicated, for instance, that '*during the period of application of the Economic and Financial Assistance Programme (PAEF)*, payment of holiday and Christmas allowances or of any sums corresponding to the thirteenth and/or fourteenth months ... shall be suspended as an exceptional measure to secure budgetary stability' (my emphasis).[41] The relation between EU law and the Portuguese assistance programme was quite direct: the European Union financed one-third of it under the EFSM, which in turn was based on Art. 122(2) TFEU.[42] The regulation establishing the EFSM makes it clear that installments of the assistance can be disbursed only after the Commission "verifies" whether the agreed general economic policy conditions are complied with.[43] This is quite important, because the very same Court of Justice preordained that EU Member States act 'in the scope of Union law', which entails 'the requirement to respect fundamental rights defined in the context of the Union', whenever national measures at stake 'are connected in part' at least with EU law.[44] This connection was all too clear to see in each case challenging austerity measures.

The Court reversed its stance in the 2016 *Ledra Advertising*[45] appeal decision, delivered by its Grand Chamber. In this case, the plaintiffs, whose deposits in Cypriot banks were converted into bank shares, which in turn lost value, argued that the ECB, negotiating the MoU with the Cypriot government in spring 2013, and the Commission,

[41] Case C-264/12, *Sindicato Nacional dos Profissionais de Seguros e Afins* v. *Fidelidade Mundial*, § 4.

[42] Art. 122(2) TFEU justifies financial assistance to a Eurozone country 'in difficulties or is seriously threatened with severe difficulties caused by natural disasters or exceptional occurrences beyond its control' and with bravado reinterpreted back in 2010 as vindicating balance-of-payments assistance for Eurozone countries.

[43] Art. 4 Council Regulation 407/2010 of 11 May 2010 establishing a European financial stabilisation mechanism, OJ 2010 No. L 118, 12 May 2010, pp. 1–4.

[44] Case C-617/10, *Åklagaren*, ECLI:EU:C:2013:105, § 20 and 24.

[45] Cases C-8/15 P to C-10/15 P, *Ledra Advertising and Others* v. *Commission and ECB*, ECLI:EU:C:2016:701.

which also signed it, violated the fundamental right to property of the account holders and therefore should compensate them for the diminution in value of their deposits.

Considering the previous case law, their chances to have the Court come down on the merits of the case were very slim. In Cyprus both EU institutions were acting as agents of the ESM; an entity established outside of the EU legal system. In fact, for this very reason the General Court, which decided in the first instance, dismissed the case.[46] But in the appeal the Court of Justice first emphasised that the EU institutions are bound to respect EU law (including the fundamental rights it enshrines) even when they act as agents of organisations established outside the EU legal regime.[47] And then, in the second step, it asserted that

> in view of the objective of ensuring the stability of the banking system in the euro area, and having regard to the imminent risk of financial losses to which depositors with the two banks concerned would have been exposed if the latter had failed, such measures do not constitute a disproportionate and intolerable interference impairing the very substance of the appellants' right to property. Consequently, they cannot be regarded as unjustified restrictions on that right. (§ 74)

In short, the Cypriot bail-in did not violate any fundamental right.[48]

[46] Cases T289/13, *Ledra Advertising* v. *Commission and ECB*, EU:T:2014:981, T-291/13, *Eleftheriou and Papachristofi* v. *Commission and ECB*, EU:T:2014:978 and T-293/13, *Theophilou* v. *Commission and ECB*, EU:T:2014:979.

[47] The Court put it that 'the tasks conferred on the Commission and the ECB within the ESM Treaty do not alter the essential character of the powers conferred on those institutions by the EU and FEU Treaties' (§ 56). The Commission, in particular, retains its role of guardian of the Treaties in these situations (§ 59).

[48] Similarly, in another case – C-258/14, *Eugenia Florescu and Others* v. *Casa Judeţ eană de Pensii Sibiu and Others*, ECLI:EU:C:2017:448 – the Court of Justice was asked by a Romanian court how to interpret the Romanian MoU, signed in 2009. The national law leading to the dispute prohibited, in certain cases, the combining of a pension in the public sector with income from other activities in public institutions. Plaintiffs alleged that this law was implementing the MoU, and that it violated the fundamental right to property. In its June 2017 judgment the Court concluded first that the MoU remained entirely within the EU legal system, which made it amenable to scrutiny from the perspective of the fundamental rights enshrined in the Charter and that, second, this conclusion is not undermined by the fact that the particular legal provision of the domestic law questioned by the plaintiffs was not specifically indicated in the MoU. Then it argued (esp. § 50–60) that the restriction did not breach the fundamental right to property.

As I will argue in the next chapter, the Court of Justice should not be expected to interfere any more deeply with assessments of economic policymakers in cases entailing serious distributive effects. After *Ledra Advertising* its stance is also congruent with the analogous case law of the European Court of Human Rights.[49] Nonetheless, it will not reassure those inclined to opine that 'once again, the social constitution has proven to be the underdog among the many constitutions of Europe'.[50]

3.6 Hard Choices in Macroeconomic Adjustments

The hardline rhetoric of the Commission and the ECB, as well as the dismissive attitude of the Court of Justice, all contributed to the general feeling that 'the European crisis management ... disregards the European order of competences, disempowers national institutions, and burdens, in particular, Southern Europe with austerity measures'.[51] For those who espouse this approach, economic crisis management mechanisms available at the European level have amounted to 'authoritarian liberalism', which 'is content with a weak, deracinated public, one that can be better managed and controlled by the technocratic and political elites at national and supranational level'.[52] And even

[49] In the EctHR case *Koufaki and Adedy* v. *Greece* (appl. no. 57665/12 and 57657/12), 7 May 2013, plaintiffs claimed that Greek austerity measures violated the right to property (protected by Art. 1 of Protocol No. 1 to the European Convention on Human Rights). The EctHR found this claim manifestly ill-founded, though. It highlighted that Greek authorities had a wide margin of appreciation in defining tools necessary to overcome the fiscal crisis, while austerity measures, intended to re-impose budgetary discipline and to preserve the stability of the Eurozone, served a legitimate general interest, justifying restrictions of the fundamental right.

[50] Kaarlo Tuori, 'The European Financial Crisis – Constitutional Aspects and Implications', *EUI Working Papers LAW* 28 (2012), 49, available at cadmus.eui.eu/handle/1814/24301; Margot E. Salomon, 'Of Austerity, Human Rights and International Institutions', *European Law Journal* 21 (2015): 521–545, gave short shrift to the EctHR decision in *Koufaki and Adedy* v. *Greece*, indicated in the previous note, arguing 'that the governance of the crises in the European Union has led to massive violations of human rights' (p. 522).

[51] Christian Joerges, 'Europe's Economic Constitution in Crisis and the Emergence of a New Constitutional Constellation', *ZENTRA Working Papers in Transnational Studies* 6 (2012): 2, available at papers.ssrn.com/sol3/papers.cfm?abstract_id=2179595##.

[52] Michael A. Wilkinson, 'The Specter of Authoritarian Liberalism: Reflections on the Constitutional Crisis of the European Union', *German Law Journal* 14 (2013): 527–560, at 552. See also the collection of articles published in *European Law Journal* 21 (2015).

those standing behind the adjustment programmes had to agree that voters in the Eurozone's periphery 'cannot be blamed for concluding that the economic, social, and personal pain that they suffer – and that many of our colleagues in economics seem to ignore or belittle – is not delivering or is even backfiring'.[53]

But, nonetheless, the anti-austerity narrative I have presented so far in this chapter is very incomplete. The role of austerity and structural reforms has been largely misjudged and the influence of the bailout programmes on national sovereignty of the debtor countries has remained more complicated than is routinely admitted.

Let's start with the economic side. Governments of countries undergoing balance-of-payments crises, as long as they run independent monetary policies, can choose any macroeconomic adjustment strategy between two extremes mentioned earlier.[54] One is pure nominal (external) adjustment, undertaken merely by correcting the exchange rate, i.e., by depreciating or devaluing the national currency. The other extreme is internal adjustment: deflation of domestic prices by monetary and fiscal tightening (the hated austerity) and (equally hated) structural reforms. Governments of countries in a monetary union have no choice but to adjust internally, unless of course they decide to return to their national currencies. So they must exert a downward pressure on prices as well as wages and allow for relocation of productive resources across firms and industries, none of which is possible unless unemployment goes up and aggregate demand seriously retracts. It is, therefore, certainly true that national governments of the countries in the Eurozone facing a balance-of-payments crisis 'have lost any meaningful ability to choose among alternative policy options and [had to], as a result, implement everywhere pretty much the same, deeply unpopular austerity package'.[55] Yet these dramatic outcomes are intrinsically related to the very logic of a macroeconomic adjustment in a 'naked' monetary union, where the union level offers hardly any facilitation of the macroeconomic adjustment.

[53] Charles Wyplosz, 'The Impossible Hope of an End to Austerity', *CEPR's Policy Portal*, 14 May 2012, available at voxeu.org/article/impossible-hope-end-austerity.

[54] For an exquisite (comparative) analysis of the thesis and its policy implications, see esp. Stefanie Walter, *Financial Crises and the Politics of Macroeconomic Adjustments* (New York: Cambridge University Press, 2013).

[55] Klaus Armingeon and Lucio Baccaro, 'Political Economy of the Sovereign Debt Crisis: The Limits of Internal Devaluation', *Industrial Law Journal* 41 (2012): 254.

3.7 The Baltics as Unmatchable Role Models

In addition, in 2010, when the first Eurozone assistance programmes were devised, policymakers were encouraged by how the mixture of austerity and structural reforms panned out in the three Baltic states hit very hard in 2008 by deep balance-of-payments crises. In none of the countries did the governments take recourse to external devaluations. They did not do so partly because each of the three wanted to join the Eurozone as soon as possible (Estonia did so in 2011, Latvia in 2014 and Lithuania in 2015). Also, because the vast majority of household loans there were denominated in foreign currencies,[56] an external devaluation would badly exacerbate the situation both in the banking sector and among the population at large. In consequence, all the three Baltic countries performed tough internal devaluations. They did voluntarily what they would be forced to do had they been in the Eurozone already. In 2009, the GDP of each collapsed by more than 14 per cent – a plight no other Eurozone country has experienced in one year.[57] Between 2007 and 2010, the GDP of Latvia shrunk by 20 per cent – twice the figure envisaged in the country's December 2008 assistance programme assumptions. Additionally, in 2010 the unemployment rate went through the roof in all the three countries, reaching 16.7 per cent in Estonia, 17.8 per cent in Lithuania and 19.5 per cent in Latvia.[58] But by 2011 the Lithuanian and Latvian economies were growing by 6.0 and 6.4 per cent, respectively, while the Estonian posted 7.6 per cent of real GDP growth.[59]

The recession in the Baltic states was therefore deeper than expected. But also, the subsequent recovery based on strenuous austerity and structural reforms surprised everyone, including the Commission and the IMF.[60] Symptoms of the recovery were clear to see in mid-2010, when the sovereign debt crisis hit the Eurozone. So policymakers of

[56] Samuel Dahan, 'The EU/IMF Financial Stabilisation Process in Latvia and Its Implications for Labour Law and Social Policy', *Industrial Law Journal* 41 (2012): 305–327.

[57] Eurostat, Real GDP growth rate – volume.

[58] Eurostat, Unemployment by sex and age – annual average.

[59] Eurostat, Real GDP growth rate – volume.

[60] In spring 2011, the Commission predicted that the Estonian GDP growth for that year would be 4.9 per cent, Latvian 3.3 per cent and Lithuanian 5 per cent: European Commission, 'European Economic Forecast – Spring 2011', *European Economy* No. 1/2011, 204, available at ec.europa.eu/economy_finance/publications/european_economy/2011/pdf/ee-2011-1_en.pdf.

the creditor countries and institutions can be excused for prescribing very similar remedies for the Eurozone's periphery. Nor should they be condemned for trying to make the reform efforts very intense, because the intensity of the adjustment in the Baltic states went hand-in-hand with their pace. Macroeconomic adjustments there were completed before social and political fatigue set in and before it managed to put its stick in the spokes of the reforms. Also, because the economies bounced back sooner than expected, unemployment levels went down to acceptable levels faster; as low as 7.4 per cent in Estonia already in 2014. Hence, the speed of the adjustment mitigated the erosion of human capital (long-term unemployment) in particular.[61]

It is tempting to think that the Baltic states benefitted from global fiscal stimuli in 2009 and 2010, while the Eurozone's periphery was facing a much more difficult task simply because it was adjusting when the stimuli ended. For this very reason the adjustment in the Eurozone's periphery was inevitably much more difficult than it was in the Baltic states. Hence, allegedly, it should have been spread over a longer period of time.

Much more important than any external factors, however, are domestic differences between the states successfully completing the economic transformation and the less-fortunate ones. In 2008, at the beginning of its adjustment process, Estonian exports comprised 67 per cent of the country's GDP, rising further by an additional 20 per cent of GDP three years later. Latvia's exports amounted to 40 per cent of GDP in 2008, to reach 58 per cent of GDP in 2011, and Lithuania's started with 57 per cent of GDP in 2008, and, again, were 18 per cent of GDP higher three years later.[62] In other words, all the three were fairly open, export-oriented economies at the beginning of the adjustment, and became seriously more so in the process. What is probably even more important, in the globally less-auspicious three years between 2010 and 2013, Estonian exports gained another 12 per cent of GDP, Latvian 7 per cent of GDP, and Lithuanian a whopping additional 19 per cent of GDP growth. All in all, the three economies could succeed in their

[61] It is sometimes argued in this context that in the Baltic states the effects of austerity measures were muted by intensified emigration of their youth. While, however, depopulation in these countries is a fact, yearly numbers of population shrinkages have not varied significantly during 2008–2010, comparing to the trend since 2004. See Eurostat, Population on 1 January by Age and Sex.

[62] Eurostat, Exports of Goods and Services in % of GDP.

macroeconomic adjustment efforts because of the hefty improvements in their export performance.

This aspect is theoretically obvious, considering that a country can escape a balance-of-payments crisis only when it seriously improves its accounts with the rest of the world. This goal may be achieved, for instance, by very substantial financial transfers through fiscal burden-sharing and a banking union. However, if the transfers are small or negative (due, for example, to a capital flight) and the country wants to avoid a protracted depression, improvements in balance-of-payment accounts must be achieved by a coupled strategy of attracting foreign investments and boosting exports. It is telling in this respect that Ireland's exports grew by 22 per cent of GDP between 2008 and 2013, starting from the already very high 84 per cent of GDP. Spain's and Portugal's gained only 7 and 8 per cent in the same period, starting from seriously lower levels of 25 per cent of GDP and 31 per cent of GDP, respectively. Greek exports reached only 30.5 per cent in 2013 (7 per cent more than five years earlier) and stagnated thereafter. In 2016 they decreased to 30.2 per cent of GDP. In consequence, the engine driving the Baltic states and Ireland through their adjustment process spluttered in Spain and Portugal and throttled down in Greece.

One of the most prominent reasons behind these varying outcomes was the difference in the pace of structural reforms in the Baltic states and in the Eurozone's south (as I mentioned earlier, this factor also determines the levels and the durability of the unemployment). On this account, too, the Baltic states stood out favourably when the shock hit them. All the three of them shared a similar broadly neo-liberal social contract.[63] It comprised relatively weak trade unions, low employment protections and civil service unfamiliar with any superior protection standards.[64] Furthermore, Baltic societies had fresh memories of a successful but harsh post-Soviet transformation achieved by forceful structural reforms and spending cuts performed in the face of falling

[63] For a comprehensive and balanced analysis of the neo-liberal socioeconomic model of the Baltic states, see Jeffrey Sommers and Charles Woolfson, eds., *The Contradictions of Austerity: The Socio-Economic Costs of the Neoliberal Baltic Model* (Abingdon: Routledge, 2014).

[64] Heribert Kohl and Hans Platzer, eds., *Industrial Relations in Central and Eastern Europe: Transformation and Integration: A Comparison of the Eight New EU Member States* (Brussels: European Trade Union Institute, 2004); Epp Kallaste and Charles Woolfson,

government revenues.[65] These experiences differed conspicuously from the history of Greece in particular; the country spending half of the time between 1800 and 2010 either in default or restructuring.[66]

And there have been many more differences between the two extremes of successful adjustments in the Baltic states and Greece in particular.

First, the Baltic states were still in the Eurozone's anteroom when the asymmetric shock hit them. Yearning for the benefits universally associated at that time with Eurozone membership – macroeconomic and geopolitical stability – their societies were very much determined to respect the Maastricht criteria.[67] No similar motivation could agitate the resolve of the Eurozone's periphery.

Second, in all of the Baltic countries, public debt levels in 2008 – when the three started their forceful adjustment programmes – stood below 20 per cent of GDP (it was 4.5 per cent of GDP in Estonia!). The three countries could thus double or triple their public debt levels (as Latvia and Lithuania in fact did) without triggering debt sustainability concerns. Conversely, Greece was up against the wall, with its public debt standing at approximately 130 per cent of GDP when it applied for financial assistance in 2010, and with the government deficit for that year reaching a whopping 10 per cent.

Third, private-sector deleveraging proceeded swiftly in the Baltic states and procrastinated in the engulfed Eurozone's periphery. This difference was particularly crucial, because it allowed the Baltic banking systems to quickly redirect credit from non-tradable sectors to tradables. And this redirection process was key for boosting exports. The fact that Estonia and Lithuania did not receive any international financial assistance and that Latvia's programme was rather modest forced them to perform a front-loaded deleveraging of the private non-bank sector. Receiving much more generous financial assistance, the Eurozone's periphery could deleverage more slowly, debilitating the adjustment process.[68]

'The Paradox of Post-communist Trade Unionism: You Can't Want What You Can't Imagine', *The Economic and Labour Relations Review* 20 (2009): 93–109.

65 Anders Åslund, *The Last Shall Be the First: The East European Financial Crisis* (Washington, DC: Peterson Institute for International Economics, 2010).

66 Carmen M. Reinhart and Kenneth S. Rogoff, *This Time Is Different – Eight Centuries of Financial Folly* (Princeton, NJ: Princeton University Press, 2010).

67 Ringa Raudla and Rainer Kattel, 'Why Did Estonia Choose Fiscal Retrenchment after the 2008 Crisis?', *Journal of Public Policy* 31 (2011): 163–186.

68 Michael Biggs and Thomas Mayer, 'Latvia and Greece: Less Is More', *CEPS High-Level Brief*, 12 February 2014, available at www.ceps.eu/publications/latvia-and-greece-less-more.

3.8 A Grinder for the Unfit

All of these reasons make it quite clear that the Baltic states were well-poised to perform a macroeconomic adjustment based on internal devaluation without major social or political disruptions. For the very same reason, Greece in particular has been disappointing. Of course, the inauspicious global economic outlook contributed to the Greek misery. But it was just one of many factors. What could have mattered much more is that it was particularly ill-suited to accomplishing an internal devaluation in the first place.

In other words, the fact that this country – or, to a lesser extent, Italy, Spain or Portugal, and even France – was a poor candidate for a macroeconomic adjustment performed without an external devaluation does not mean that the strategy based on austerity and structural reforms is necessarily self-defeating. It only means that the countries unfit for internal devaluation should not join a monetary union, because by doing so they deprive themselves of adjustment methods available to the states with relatively less resilient economic, social and political tissue.[69] So Gros was only partly right when he noted that 'it is disingenuous to claim that the troika forced Greece into excessive austerity. Had Greece not received financial support in 2010, it would have had to cut its fiscal deficit from more than 10% of GDP to zero immediately. By financing continued deficits … the troika actually enabled Greece to delay austerity.'[70] Surely, without international financial assistance the Greek economy would have immediately imploded in 2010. But, nonetheless, Greece forced itself into the fate of excessive austerity when it joined a naked monetary union with its political, social and economic systems unfit for the only macroeconomic adjustment available there. With unsustainable debt, an autarchic and sclerotic economy, obsolete socioeconomic relations and a dysfunctional political system (more

[69] When disregarding the fundamental socioeconomic and political differences between countries like Ireland and Latvia (on the one hand) and Greece and Cyprus (on the other), leading economists could come up with opposite assessments of austerity. While Stiglitz, for instance, was asking 'Why we should not have expected internal devaluation to work', drawing his conclusion from the Greek experience (Joseph E. Stiglitz, *The Euro*, 100) Sinn claimed that 'The Baltics: Austerity Works' (Hans-Werner Sinn, *The Euro Trap: On Bursting Bubbles, Budgets, and Beliefs* (New York: Oxford University Press, 2014): 130. Depending on the example one chooses, each of the theses may be either right or wrong.

[70] Daniel Gros, 'The Greek Austerity Myth', *CEPS Commentary*, 10 February 2015, 2, available at www.ceps.eu/system/files/COMDGGreekAusterityMyth.pdf.

on this in Chapter 7), the Greek macroeconomic adjustment based on internal devaluation was doomed from day one. So claiming that the first Greek bailout package did not pay enough attention to structural reforms necessary 'to reorient Greece swiftly towards a new growth model based on the private sector' and that the second suffered from poor reform resolve on the ground in Athens[71] does not explain the whole story. It is simply disputable whether any policy mix based on internal devaluation could succeed in this particular case.

It is this context, rather than austerity demands of the creditors, which explains the economic plight of Greece. For, indeed, fiscal consolidation was particularly destructive for economic growth there. But the reason was not so much that the consolidation was so pronounced. Rather, the pervasively autarchic character of the Greek economy prevented exports from cushioning the effects of falling private and public demand. This is because 'the final effect of fiscal consolidation on output is influenced by two factors: the (marginal) propensity to save and the degree of openness to trade. The multiplier is large when the savings rate is low and/or when the degree of trade openness is low. A low degree of trade openness also means that exports cannot provide a strong offset to low domestic demand – adding to the political difficulties of maintaining a tight fiscal stance.'[72]

The argument behind it is very simple: if public demand decreases as a result of fiscal adjustments and private demand collapses due to relative deflation, exports are the only conceivable method of achieving economic growth necessary to improve the economic situation. From this perspective the difference between Spain and Portugal, on the one hand, and Greece (as well as Italy), on the other, is very significant. In the first of the two groups investment demand has grown, as have exports. Their growth was not as impressive as in the Baltic states (or in Ireland), which at least partly explains the political backlash the governing coalitions faced there in 2015–2016 elections. But it nonetheless allowed the economies to get reignited again.

More generally, growing exports are a sign of a resilient, flexible economic system, one which will suffer less from a fiscal contraction

[71] Alessio Terzi, 'Reform Momentum and Its Impact on Greek Growth', *Bruegel Policy Contribution* No. 12/2015, 29 July 2015, 10, available at bruegel.org/2015/07/reform-momentum-and-its-impact-on-greek-growth/.

[72] Daniel Gros et al., *Implementation of the Macroeconomic Adjustment Programmes in the Euro Area. State-of-play* (CEPS E-BOOK, 2014), 11, available at www.ceps.eu/system/files/Macroeconomic%20Adjustment%20Programmes%20in%20Euro%20Area%20e-book.pdf.

than will an ossified economy. No doubt, therefore, 'austerity without growth is a recipe for depression, despair and growing social and political dissonance'.[73] But again, this only means that any highly indebted country is doomed if it is unable to devise other growth engines than fiscal stimulation. And its fate is particularly sinister if it is unable to do so while being a member of a currency area.

3.9 Conundrums of More Symmetric Adjustments

It is often argued that this does not exempt creditor countries in a monetary union from the obligation to adjust their own domestic policies. If some countries (debtors) in a monetary union run contractionary policies, others (creditors) should not. If the debtors strive to post current account surpluses, creditors should stimulate domestic demand, instead of trying to export even more. Otherwise contractionary policies will become asphyxiating on the debtor side and the whole system will dwindle away. In addition, as I explained in Chapter 1, the very architecture of the Eurozone hindered processes preventing creditor countries from amassing current account surpluses. To be more specific: when countries like Germany or the Netherlands were monetarily independent, their growing current account surpluses were leading to currency appreciations, in turn reducing their external economic competitiveness and putting downward pressure on the surpluses. But in a monetary union with competitively weaker countries, no similar mechanism exists. Current account surpluses of the creditor countries can reach levels they would never attain outside of it. For the sake of its sustainability, the competitiveness valve inherent in an independently run monetary policy should therefore arguably be replaced with its 'artificial' version of a deliberate political decision of the creditor countries.

While such a 'more symmetric adjustment' – a stimulation of public and private demand in creditor countries to encourage imports from the debtor countries – is theoretically compelling,[74] it has certain serious loopholes undermining its practical usefulness.

[73] Charles Goodhart, 'The United Kingdom and the Eurozone: How to Co-exist', in: *Governance for the Eurozone: Integration or Disintegration?*, ed. Franklin Allen, Elena Carletti and Saverio Simonelli (Florence; Philadephia: European University Institute and Wharton Financial Institutions Center, 2012): 161.

[74] Paul De Grauwe, 'How to Avoid a Double-Dip Recession in the Eurozone', *CEPS Commentary*, 15 November 2012, available at www.ceps.eu/publications/how-avoid-double-dip-recession-eurozone; De Grauwe and Ji, 'Legacy of Austerity'.

First of all: at what level of current account surpluses should a country alter its macroeconomic policy: 4 per cent of GDP, 6 per cent of GDP, 8 per cent of GDP or any other; and what should a 'more symmetric adjustment' mean at each of the levels? One of eleven indicators in the Commission's 'Scoreboard for the Surveillance of Macroeconomic Imbalances'[75] is 'three-year backward moving average of the current account balance as a percent of GDP, with a threshold of +6% and −4%'. Results below or above suggest that the national economy may be imbalanced. Some observers have soberly questioned this methodology, noting that it should rather gauge balances relative to the Eurozone, and that it should be forward, not backward, looking.[76] But what is more important for my argument here is that the 6 per cent current account surplus threshold only means that, above it, the maturity and composition of net foreign assets ought to be more closely investigated, because they may lead to certain pernicious effects for the financial system, and asset markets in particular.[77] And that is all. By the same token, crossing the threshold does not entail any clear and incontestable 'adjustment' policy.

Even, however, if one accepts that all of these complications should not occlude the main argument – that the countries posting surpluses above the 6 per cent threshold ought to do something to help rebalance the Eurozone – there are further, and more serious, barriers to overcome.

In 2016, Germany posted a very high 8.1 per cent three-year backward current account surplus, while the Netherlands reached 8.7 per cent.[78] But Denmark (not a Eurozone country) posted exactly the same current account surplus as did the Netherlands (8.7 per cent of GDP). In other words, Eurozone membership may facilitate amassing serious current account surpluses. But it is entirely possible for the countries outside of it to do the same, which hollows the compensation argument.

[75] European Commission, 'Scoreboard for the Surveillance of Macroeconomic Imbalances', *European Economy*, Occasional Paper 92, February 2012, available at ec.europa.eu/economy_finance/publications/occasional_paper/2012/pdf/ocp92_en.pdf.

[76] Daniel Gros and Alessandro Giovannini, 'The "Relative" Importance of EMU Macroeconomic Imbalances in the Macroeconomic Imbalance Procedure', *CEPS Portal*, 25 March 2014, available at www.ceps.eu/publications/%E2%80%98relative%E2%80%99-importance-emu-macroeconomic-imbalances-macroeconomic-imbalance-procedure.

[77] Angelique Herzberg, *Sustainability of External Imbalances: A Critical Appraisal* (Cham: Springer, 2014): 282.

[78] Eurostat, Current Account Balance: Three-year Average.

Furthermore, hypothetically, the German government could have introduced its national minimum wage in 2011, instead of 2015,[79] and invested more in its public infrastructure or education since the eve of the Eurozone crisis. A part of this additional redistribution stream would certainly finance purchases of Portuguese goods, Spanish properties or Greek holidays in the spirit of a 'more symmetric adjustment'. But it could well be that a disproportionally big share of such a stimulus would land in the pockets of Finnish, Irish, Dutch or Swedish producers.[80] Gros put this point vividly when he remarked back in 2013 that 'the peripheral Eurozone countries account for only about 10% of German imports, compared to almost 40% for the other surplus countries in northern Europe. Stronger domestic demand in Germany would thus benefit these other surplus countries (with low unemployment) four times more than the peripheral countries, where unemployment is so much higher.'[81]

In consequence, any unilateral rebalancing by Germany or the Netherlands could well primarily stimulate exports from otherwise competitive economies. Overall, therefore, unless performed simultaneously by all creditor countries in Europe – a political impossibility – any attempt to stimulate domestic demand by creditor countries could easily contribute to economic imbalances in the Eurozone. Additionally, a serious fiscal stimulus performed by the German government when its economy was expanding would amplify the economic cycle in Germany, with rather inevitable fiscal tensions when the cyclical tables turn.

In that way or another, therefore, creditor countries could hardly have contributed much more to the adjustment process than by funding assistance programmes. The outcome, however, was indeed bizarre. The creditors provided financing facilitating macroeconomic adjustment in debtor countries, while at home running policies making the adjustment more difficult. This effect was devastating for the debtor countries, as it further depressed their economies and amplified hysteresis

[79] For a broader explanation of the political factors behind this development, see Deborah Mabbett, 'The Minimum Wage in Germany: What Brought the State In?', *Journal of European Public Policy* 23 (2016): 1240–1258.

[80] See also Ansgar Belke and Thomas Osowski, 'Measuring Fiscal Spillovers in EMU and Beyond: A Global VAR Approach', *CEPS Working Document* No. 428, December 2016, available at www.ceps.eu/system/files/WD428%20Fiscal%20spillover.pdf.

[81] Daniel Gros, 'Germany as Scapegoat', *CEPS Commentary*, 10 December 2013, available at www.ceps.eu/system/files/Germany%20as%20Scapegoat.pdf.

effects, by the same token making future repayments of the assistance funding less probable.

This finding corroborates the basic message of this chapter: a premature accession to a monetary union maintaining economic and fiscal sovereignty is very dangerous economically, socially and politically. In such a system soft currency regimes find it particularly difficult to complete their macroeconomic adjustment and there is not much the creditors can do to facilitate the rebalancing process, making it even more torturous.

3.10 Rescue People, Not Banks?

There are, however, some other grounds on which it is often argued that the creditors could do, and should have done, more to facilitate adjustment among the countries on the other side of the spectrum.

First, the international creditors demanded in 2010 that the Irish government would bail out private creditors of the Irish banks. The government yielded, straining its accounts and making the already-difficult adjustment even more so. And private creditors, many of them banks from creditor countries, escaped scot-free.

Most of the Irish would probably say that this was exactly what happened. But the story behind it was a bit different, and the difference is quite telling. In fact, it did not start in autumn 2010, when Ireland applied for international assistance, but two years earlier, in September 2008, when this country unilaterally provided a blanket guarantee for virtually all liabilities of its six major banks. This huge pledge – worth €440 billion – enacted by the Irish Parliament was not forced by any foreign agent. Quite to the contrary, policymakers in Brussels and in other EU capitals went ballistic because the pledge rendered the Irish banking system more attractive than the systems of the countries that did not offer a similar safe harbour.

It is fairly probable that without the assurance the Irish banking system would have melted away, as did the Icelandic – where no similar guarantee was issued – at the same time. In hindsight, however, it is quite clear that, in the long term, Irish society would be better off going through the financial crash Iceland experienced. For it is true that the Icelandic banking system literally dissipated in 2008. But there was a plan behind it: Iceland let its banks fail, introduced strict capital controls and burnt foreign depositors, primarily from Germany, the UK and the Netherlands, while redeeming domestic depositors, in addition to heavily devaluing its currency. Back in 2008 or 2009 it could have seemed that this policy both excessively devastated Iceland's economy and gravely violated EU laws by which Iceland was bound as a member of the European Free Trade Association (EFTA). But it soon turned out that Iceland recovered much faster and more convincingly than did Ireland or Latvia – two comparable economies in a similar starting position.[82] By 2012, it was perfectly clear that in Iceland 'the unemployment rate [had] fallen ... The economy [was] growing.'[83] In addition, the country won a dispute before the EFTA court (the so-called Icesave case) brought before it by an EFTA equivalent of the EC for refusing to pay foreign depositors the insurance (then up to €20,000) stipulated by EU law. The Court decided that Iceland was not obliged to stick to these obligations, which were unbearable for its economy and its public policy.[84]

Ireland could not have followed Iceland's path without leaving the Eurozone. Nor could Latvia without dropping its euro-peg. It is, furthermore, quite certain that an Irish dropout from the Eurozone would have triggered chain reactions jettisoning some other Eurozone countries as well and destabilising the financial systems of the creditor countries. But arguably this would have made the adjustment process much faster, at the same time eliminating the main source of the single currency's future instability.

As I mentioned earlier, instead of following Iceland, back in 2008 the Irish government made the fatal mistake of providing a blanket liability guarantee: a promise of a comprehensive bank bailout. By the time the Irish Economic Adjustment Programme was negotiated in late 2010, the bailout had cost Irish taxpayers €46.3 billion already (30 per cent of

[82] Zsolt Darvas, 'A Tale of Three Countries: Recovery after Banking Crises', *Bruegel Policy Contribution* No. 2011/19, 29 December 2011, available at bruegel.org/2011/12/a-tale-of-three-countries-recovery-after-banking-crises/.

[83] Brady Dennis, 'Iceland Makes Fledgling Recovery from Its Economic Meltdown', *The Washington Post*, 16 January 2012, available at www.washingtonpost.com/business/economy/iceland-makes-fledgling-recovery-from-its-economic-meltdown/2012/01/12/gIQAW1q83P_story.html?utm_term=.3783fbaf817f.

[84] As the EFTA Court argued in Case E-16/11, *EFTA Surveillance Authority* v. *Iceland*, judgment of 28 January 2013: 'Article 7 of the Directive does not lay down an obligation on the State and its authorities to ensure compensation if a deposit guarantee scheme is unable to cope with its obligations in the event of a systemic crisis' (§ 144). Furthermore, 'consumer protection under the Directive does not entail full protection ... since increasing consumer protection may reach a point where the costs outweigh the benefits' (§ 170).

the 2010 Irish GDP).[85] When negotiations with international creditors started in October 2010 the outstanding senior unsecured bank bondholder exposure amounted to €16.4 billion (10 per cent of the 2010 Irish GDP).[86] Assuming a haircut of 50 per cent, the Irish public purse could have saved up to €8 billion by burning these bondholders (5 per cent of the Irish 2010 GDP).[87] The IMF was for it, because – as its officials argued in 2015 – the bondholders expected the losses, so the risk of a financial contagion (the main reason for the bailout) was low, while it could have been muted even further by limited recapitalisations in the exposed jurisdictions and by additional liquidity assistance from the ECB.[88] Furthermore, even an uneducated policymaker should have known that the main Irish bank whose creditors were exposed to a potential haircut – Anglo Irish – could have been by no means compared to Lehman Brothers, either by its size or its systemic significance. In other words, it was not too big to fail. And yet, as an Irish official attending the Irish negotiations with the Troika admitted, there was 'a strong negative reaction from the ECB and others … that … the EU-IMF programme would not go ahead if senior bondholder burden sharing was contemplated'.[89]

In hindsight, it is quite clear that the IMF and the Irish government were right to oppose further bailouts of banks' creditors in Ireland, and the ECB was wrong in pressing hard for it. This mistake cost the Irish population additional international loans worth €1,500 per capita. The ECB's president at that time, Jean-Claude Trichet, added insult to injury by constantly denying the role the institution played in the process. Yet, the ECB's mistake in assessment was in fact produced by the very difficult role it was not designed to play but it suddenly had to assume: it was the last man standing to sustain financial stability against massive

[85] John FitzGerald and Ide Kearney, 'Irish Government Debt and Implied Debt Dynamics: 2011–2015', *The Economic and Social Research Institute Quarterly Economic Commentary*, 6 September 2011, available at www.esri.ie/publications/irish-government-debt-and-implied-debt-dynamics-2011–2015/.

[86] Finfacts, 'Irish bank Senior Debt and Subordinated Debt Outstanding February 2011', 2 March 2011, available at www.finfacts.ie/irishfinancenews/article_1021762.shtml.

[87] Pisani-Ferry, Sapir and Wolff estimate the figure to be €5–10 billion (Pisani-Ferry, Sapir and Wolff, 'EU-IMF Assistance', 89).

[88] International Monetary Fund Finance Department, 'Ireland: Ex Post Evaluation of Exceptional Access under the 2010 Extended Arrangement', International Monetary Fund, 29 January 2015, 27–29, available at www.imf.org/external/pubs/cat/longres.aspx?sk=42656.0.

[89] 'Ireland "Pushed into Bailout"', *The Telegraph*, 18 June 2015, available at www.telegraph.co.uk/finance/economics/11683995/Ireland-pushed-into-bailout.html.

financial withdrawals from the Eurozone's periphery, against the panic on sovereign debt markets, and against political restraints to reform its mandate. Apparently, the ECB's decision-makers concluded that from the perspective of the Irish debt sustainability it did not really make a big difference if the ultimate bank bailout ticket would be 35 or 40 per cent of GDP. And, which seems particularly important, any concomitant risks were rather predictable, while the risks related to reversing the bailout strategy were not.

So, while this particular story does demonstrate that governments of the countries on assistance programmes must yield to the pressure of particularly mighty creditor institutions, its ultimate point is not that Ireland – or, for that matter, any other country on an assistance programme – has been deprived of its sovereignty by the Troika pursuing its excruciating policies. In fact, the stance of the ECB on Ireland in late 2010 was perfectly consistent with the previous stance of the Irish government: bailing out all creditors of the banking sector. This policy was originally enacted two years earlier by Irish policymakers against external pressure. The bill of the bank bailouts that Irish society has had to foot under this unilateral pledge was seven times higher than the costs of continuing the policy under the ECB's insistence. And, more fundamentally, it was the original approach of the Irish government, which ultimately, against all expectations of local policymakers,[90] forced the country to apply for international financial assistance.

The same is true for Cyprus. Its banks have suffered blows both from very high levels of non-performing loans and from the Private Sector Involvement: the 2012 restructuring of Greece's sovereign bonds (to which Cypriot banks were heavily exposed)[91] held by private investors. The previously unquestioned EU policy of bank bailouts was reversed in respect to this country when in March 2013 official creditors forced,

[90] As late as in October 2010 the Bank of Ireland claimed that deficit needs of the government were 'fully funded well into 2011' (Bank of Ireland Economic Research Unit, 'The Outlook. A Quarterly Analysis of Trends in the Irish Economy', October 2010, available at www.bankofireland.com/fs/doc/wysiwyg/outlook_oct10.pdf). In fact, though, the pace of deterioration on sovereign debt markets forced the Irish government to apply for an assistance programme the next month (November 2010).

[91] Cypriot commercial banks held €5 billion in Greek government bonds in 2011, on which the Greek PSI imposed €3.6 billion losses (20 per cent of GDP): International Monetary Fund, 'Cyprus: Staff Report for the 2011 Article IV Consultation', *IMF Country Report* No. 11/331, 3 November 2011, available at www.imf.org/external/pubs/ft/scr/2011/cr11331.pdf.

as a condition for an international rescue scheme, the Cypriot government to wipe out both junior and senior bondholders of Cyprus' two biggest banks (the Bank of Cyprus and the Cyprus Popular Bank). They also demanded that deposits above €100,000 in the two banks incur a 37.5 per cent haircut.

The claims in the *Ledra Advertising* case before the Court of Justice, discussed earlier, corroborate that the transition from the bail-out to the bail-in paradigm was highly unpopular in Cyprus. But, in fact, the harshness of the macroeconomic adjustment there was caused first and foremost by the policies undertaken by previous Cypriot governments, by the very dynamics of macroeconomic adjustment in a monetary union and, ultimately, by the premature accession of this country to the Eurozone. As in Ireland, for economic and political reasons Cyprus could hardly perform a different adjustment programme when remaining a member of the Eurozone. And the exit was not on the table.

The same was true for Greece. In this case, however, the anti-austerity criticism could invoke one more argument important in the present context. Namely, it may be pointed out that back in 2010 the official creditors actually bailed out their financial institutions with future Greek tax revenues. According to this argument, 'contrary to widely held beliefs, less than €10 bn or a fraction of less than 5% of the overall programme went to the Greek fiscal budget. In contrast, the vast majority of the money went to existing creditors in the form of debt repayments and interest payments.'[92] While, however, private creditors had been benefiting from crediting the Greek governments prior to 2010, ultimately their interest payments comprised only a small part of the official Greek debt owed to private creditors in spring 2010. The vast majority of it were sums previously borrowed by the Greek governments and then spent through the state budget, just like taxes collected in this period had been. In this part it is therefore very misleading to talk about northern official creditors bailing out northern private creditors back in 2010.

3.11 The Greek Fiscal Paradox

Even if you agree with this point, you can still argue that throughout the sovereign debt crisis the creditors should have been more generous (or more realistic). This is what their self-serving instincts should have

[92] Jörg Rocholl and Axel Stahmer, 'Where Did the Greek Bailout Money Go?', ESMT White Paper No. WP-16-02, 2016, 19.

told them. Adjustment programmes have demanded forceful austerity, with devastating consequences for the economic growth and repayment prospects. According to this argument, pursuing adjustment programmes based on harsh austerity is self-defeating for both sides. Take, for example, the following passage from the third Greek bailout MoU, the agreement between the ESM and Greece, on which financial assistance is premised, concluded in August 2015: 'Greece will target a medium-term primary surplus of 3.5% of GDP to be achieved through a combination of upfront parametric fiscal reforms, including to its VAT and pension system, supported by an ambitious programme to strengthen tax compliance and public financial management, and fight tax evasion, while ensuring adequate protection of vulnerable groups'. Some may try to defend the emphasis on achieving a very high primary surplus in Greece by the (also very high) Greek debt overhang. But a medium-term primary surplus as high as required by the third Greek bailout is simply unachievable in Greece, where fiscal multipliers have proven particularly pronounced. It will further damage the economy, contributing to the very debt overhang it was intended to remedy. The IMF Managing Director, Christine Lagarde, has been very clear about it. In spring 2016, for instance, she noted that 'in short term, the Primary Surplus 3.5% of GDP might be achievable with heroic efforts by the Greek people, but it is highly unrealistic that it can by maintained on long term'.[93]

The point to be taken from the Greek calamity is not, however, that the third Greek bailout would become any more realistic if the creditors put a different digit of the government surplus into the MoU – say 2.5 per cent instead of 3.5 per cent, or 1.5 per cent. This is simply because international creditors made a very serious mistake back in 2010, when they signed up to an assistance programme based on the spurious assumption that Greek public debt, and the Greek economic model more generally, were sustainable (more on this in Chapter 6). By depriving Greece of a fresh start, the IMF, European institutions and European governments, including the Greek government itself, have locked the Greek economy into a situation in which the wheels are rolling, but the engine barely works. Yet, the situation could hardly

[93] 'Lagarde: 3.5% Primary Surplus Might Be Achievable in Short-Term with Heroic Efforts by Greek People', KeepTalkingGreece, 14 April 2016, available at www.keeptalkinggreece.com/2016/04/14/lagarde-3-5-primary-surplus-might-be-achievable-in-short-term-with-heroic-efforts-by-greek-people/.

have been expected to look different had they been any more generous. Instead, it simply shows the plight of a Eurozone country, on the one hand unable, for structural, social and political reasons, to effectively pursue internal devaluation and, on the other, unable (and unwilling) to return to its national currency.

In fact, it can be argued that the international creditors have been too generous to Greece, and that it was the price to pay for the initial mistake of treating this country as if it were merely illiquid, instead of admitting that fiscally and economically it went bankrupt in 2010. The financial assistance committed to Greece has amounted to almost €300 billion by 2015 (€80 billion in the first programme, plus an additional €130 billion in the second programme and almost €90 billion in the third programme). In addition, as soon as July 2011, Greece, Ireland and Portugal received various financial concessions alleviating the burden of the international financial assistance: very long grace periods (payment delays; up to thirty years in respect to Greece), back-loaded amortisation and low interest rates. Greece has even seen profits the ECB made purchasing Greek bonds during the sovereign debt crisis entirely returned to this country, instead of being distributed to the Eurozone Member States according to its basic rules (proportionally to the equity share of each country in the ECB). This essentially means that the Greek, the Irish and the Portuguese programmes have been much less onerous than it might seem at first glance.

3.12 Good Cops and Bad

Yet another potential argument against economic conditionalities of the assistance programmes is that the creditors should offer the debtors some means to shield the most vulnerable groups. The 2009–2012 Latvian programme may be invoked as a role model here. During this programme the World Bank launched a multi-million-dollar scheme named the Safety Net and Social Sector Reform Programme, which, according to the then-country director for Latvia in this institution, was to ensure 'that society's most vulnerable groups are shielded from the worst effects of the downturn until the growth momentum can restore employment opportunities in the economy'[94] (the Romanian bailout

[94] The World Bank, 'World Bank Lending Helps Latvia Improve Social Safety Nets', 26 May 2011, www.worldbank.org/en/news/press-release/2011/05/26/world-bank-lending-helps-latvia-improve-social-safety-nets.

programme, launched half year after the Latvian, included a similar component).[95] In addition, in Latvia, officials of the Commission, supporting the government on the ground in its resolve to avoid external devaluation, seemed to have acted inconsistently with their policies towards Greece, when they insisted that the Latvian government should avoid too-deep intrusions into (otherwise thin) social protections, to preclude civil unrest.[96] In consequence, in Latvia 'the lenders ended up putting pressure on the government to ensure that the cuts did not go too far in endangering social stability and prospects for longer-term growth'.[97]

Does not the fact that the creditors acted differently in the Eurozone's south make it clear that they privilege poster-children, sharing with them neo-liberal beliefs, and do not hesitate to exert pain on the societies more eager to withstand what one observer called 'economic imperialism'?[98] Granted, scientific evidence suggests that international creditors are more lenient on debtors espousing the same policy prescriptions and economic beliefs.[99] But, what seems by far more important in this context, in Latvia, the creditors could play 'the good cop' because the government on the ground was sufficiently eager to play 'the bad cop'. Altogether, this division of roles played out well for Latvian society (economic growth soon resumed), for the international creditors (macroeconomic adjustment was shorter than originally anticipated, hence the creditors could commit less resources than they had planned, and their reputation did not suffer in the process), and for national politicians (the way the then-Latvian Prime Minister Dombrovskis handled the crisis catapulted him to the role of EC vice-president a few years later).

All of this was possible because the Latvian government adamantly stuck to the rules of macroeconomic adjustment exclusively based on internal devaluation and because Latvian society withstood concomitant hardships. The Greek assistance programmes have been the

95 Luana Pop, 'The Decoupling of Social Policy Reforms in Romania', *Social Policy & Administration* 47 (2013): 161–181.

96 Dahan, 'EU/IMF Financial Stabilisation Process', 318.

97 Ibid., 316.

98 Mattias Kumm, 'What Kind of a Constitutional Crisis Is Europe in and What Should Be Done about It?', WZB Discussion Paper, February 2013, 9, available at bibliothek.wzb.eu/pdf/2013/iv13-801.pdf.

99 Stephen C. Nelson, 'Playing Favorites: How Shared Beliefs Shape the IMF's Lending Decisions', *International Organization* 68 (2014): 297–328.

other extreme. There, 'the activation of external stakeholders enables leaders to "pass the buck", credibly arguing that the terms are dictated by creditors. Accountability is diffused, highlighting responses driven by short-term electoral incentives over long-term reform.'[100] In other words, the political strategy prevailing among Greek governments has taken away from the international creditors the chance to play the good cop. Instead, the creditors have been forced to play the really bad one, pressing for painful policies, pursuing increasingly detailed adjustment programmes and intensifying the intrusiveness of programme evaluation.[101]

This leads to the final point on what is exchanged for what by debtors and creditors during a bailout. The creditors are aware that their outlays will be paid back if the assisted economy recovers. They also know that every surgery, this one too, should be as short as possible, which in turn depends on the resolve of the governments and the societies on the ground. The more strenuous the reform process, however, the sooner the political capital enjoyed by the national government pursuing the macroeconomic adjustment runs out. For this reason, national governments are strongly incentivised to procrastinate, especially when it comes to structural reforms – the particularly crucial element of internal devaluation. The very institutional design of assistance programmes, with the hawkish ECB and the unequivocal CJEU, can be read as an attempt to offset the incentive. Even then internal devaluation in societies whose models have traditionally gravitated towards soft currency regimes is an epic, ungrateful and torturous task, however. But ultimately it is a logical consequence of joining a monetary union by countries unsuited to its dynamics in the first place.

[100] Nikolaos Zahariadis, 'Leading Reform Amidst Transboundary Crises: Lessons from Greece', *Public Administration* 91 (2013): 658.

[101] Pisani-Ferry, Sapir and Wolff, 'EU-IMF Assistance', 74–75.

4 The Frankfurt Alchemist

4.1 From the Shadows to the Limelight

The former Governor of the Bank of England, Mervyn King, used to say that a successful central bank should be boring. And for a long time central banks all over the EU were both quite boring and quite successful. Since the 2008 financial crisis, though, non-standard actions of central banks all over the world have become increasingly intriguing. For some time the ECB wanted to remain as dull as ever before, which, however, did not make it any more successful in combating the Eurozone's disarray. Then, in mid-2012, the Frankfurt institution removed the gloves, immediately catching the attention of media, politicians and even the most influential constitutional courts. With a few words it ended the sovereign debt crisis.

Then, however, the Eurozone's monetary policy kindled a fundamental rift between two very different ideological stances on what the central bank of the single currency should – and should not – do. One of the stances asserted that the Eurozone's chain of central banks (the Eurosystem) has a serious role to play in engineering economic growth, while the other alleged this would be irreconcilable with its price stability mandate and might seriously backfire. The spat reached a point at which the ECB's President Mario Draghi was characterised by the former Greek finance minister Yanis Varoufakis as 'an exquisite central banker who is ... in an iron cage of constraints and rules that he has to work within',[1] only to be accused by the German Finance Minister

[1] CNBC, 'An Interview for the CNBC', 3 September 2015, available at video.cnbc.com/gallery/?video=3000417089.

Schäuble half a year later of giving ammunition to far-right political forces in Germany.[2]

What is arguably more momentous is that in the last few years the Eurozone's central bank has hardly had a chance to be any more boring. First, during the previous decade the constitutional paradox of the Eurozone – which Yanis Varoufakis characterised as 'the central bank without a state to back it up and states without their central banks'[3] – did not have any serious practical repercussions. But throughout the crisis the ECB has found it increasingly difficult to apply one monetary policy to structurally very different economies. Second, even national central banks of the advanced economies relieved of these constraints – such as the USA to the UK, Switzerland, Sweden, Japan and so on – have struggled with the 'zero lower bound'.[4] There, too, central bankers have had to drop their dull mask and generate media headlines with their unprecedented and unconventional new policies. And third, the ECB has been confronted with largely undecided or feigned reactions of the Eurozone's elected politicians to the crisis engulfing some Eurozone states and boosting others. If it threw in the towel against the growing divergences in the economic foundations of the Eurozone, the Frankfurt institution would soon see the EMU unravelling.

Maintaining unity against the divergences has been possible through the economic effects of a quantitative easing programme. As I will argue later in this chapter, the programme has been justified by the persistently low inflation prevailing in recent years. As a crucial corollary, it entailed a miraculous transmutation of the public debt purchased by the ECB into (appreciating) central bank money. This debt management effect has not removed the original causes of the huge pile of debt in the Eurozone's south, however, and as such it has hardly been a proper foundation of a durable economic rejuvenation or convergence in the single-currency area. While, therefore, the monetary miracle performed by the ECB has ushered in strong economic growth in the Eurozone, it has also sown seeds of a significant political conflict when the economic recovery ends and structural divergences between

[2] Stefan Wagstyl and Claire Jones, 'Germany Blames Mario Draghi for Rise of Rightwing AfD Party', *Financial Times*, 10 April 2016.

[3] CNBC, 'An Interview for the CNBC'.

[4] The zero lower bound is a situation in which nominal short-term interest rates in the economy become very close to zero. On the role of the zero lower bound as a constraint on monetary policy, see, for example, William Scarth, *Macroeconomics: The Development of Modern Methods for Policy Analysis* (Cheltenham: Edward Elgar Publishing, 2014): 167–172.

Eurozone countries force the weakest of them to come to ECB to plea for (inevitably heavily contingent) further aids.

The ECB has therefore become entrapped. Trying to prevent the Eurozone's disintegration by squashing yields on sovereign bonds and ceaselessly stimulating credit creation, it has challenged the intuition, inherent in the very constitutional design of the Eurozone, that monetary policy is not the right tool to engineer economic growth and cannot sustain it on a lasting basis. The fact that the ECB has been enticed to take a different monetary stance, while time and again admitting publicly that it can do nothing more than buy elected politicians more time to fix economic fundamentals, has put this institution in an impossible situation. In order to give the Eurozone a financial boost, it has embarked on an alchomic experiment of turning stones into gold. This temporary relief comes, however, with the price of potential serious problems down the road.

4.2 Stage No. 1: Securities Markets Programme

Draghi has been confronted with this fundamental paradox since he took over the helm at the ECB in November 2011. The ups and downs in his endeavours to contain the risks and minimise the fallout effects illustrate the situation in which the ECB has been playing a role that goes far beyond the traditional monetary policy, involving into very substantial debt (as well as risk) management operations and gaining in political clout along the way.

From May 2010 – the beginning of the sovereign debt crisis – to November 2011 – when Draghi arrived in Frankfurt – European leaders managed to establish the temporary multi-billion financial assistance (bailout) scheme, i.e., the EFSF, and then they authorised it to purchase sovereign bonds both on primary (directly from the issuer) and secondary (from financial institutions) markets.[5] Later on, they agreed to replace the temporary vehicle with the permanent ESM.

[5] On 11 March 2011, the Euro Area summit authorised the EFSF (and subsequently the ESM) to intervene in the primary markets 'on an exceptional basis'. Then, on 21 July 2011, the assistance funds were authorised to act on the basis of a precautionary programme, to finance the recapitalisation of financial institutions through loans to governments including, in non-programme countries, and to intervene in the secondary markets (on the basis of an ECB analysis that financial stability is at risk). On 26 October 2011, the Euro Area summit allowed the EFSF to provide credit enhancement to primary sovereign bonds and to create co-investment funds.

Yet, none of this impressed financial markets. The pressure on Spanish and Italian sovereigns grew incessantly throughout 2011. In October, the three major rating agencies downgraded the ratings of both countries, sending additional jitters to the bond markets. With a 6.2 per cent yield on ten-year Spanish paper in November 2011, and especially with a 7.1 per cent yield on its Italian counterpart, it was very clear that, unless a serious drug was dispensed in both cases, the two would soon become illiquid. And each was too big to be bailed out by any available financial assistance scheme.

The room to dispense such heavy drugs was restrained by the no-monetary financing clause of Art. 123 TFEU.[6] Since the very beginning of the Eurozone this clause was read as precluding ECB interventions to rescue national governments unable to service their debt at market prices. As I mentioned in Chapter 1, the underlying logic had it that the governments were to run responsible economic and fiscal policies, which the financial markets were expected to appreciate by pricing their bonds high (demanding low yields), in which case no emergency bond purchases by the central bank would be indispensable to sustain the liquidity of national governments. However, when in 2010 it turned out that none of these premises was correct anymore, the ECB, despite growing German resistance, became 'lender of last resort (LoLR) for the sovereigns of the eurozone since it first started its outright purchases of eurozone periphery sovereign debt under the Securities Markets Programme (SMP) in May 2010'.[7]

Within the SMP the ECB was buying, on secondary markets, government paper of the engulfed sovereigns. The basic goal of the programme was clear and straightforward: it was to mitigate the pressure on government bond markets and to prevent the commotion taking place there from escalating into an uncontrollable pandemonium. Yet it was the type of intervention the drafters of the Eurozone wanted to avoid. And its German detractors asserted that the central bank should not replace politicians either in determining the composition of the Eurozone, or in debt management.

[6] Art. 123(1) TFEU: 'Overdraft facilities or any other type of credit facility with the European Central Bank or with the central banks of the Member States ... in favour of ... central governments, regional, local or other public authorities, other bodies governed by public law, or public undertakings of Member States shall be prohibited'.

[7] Willem Buiter and Ebrahim Rahbari, 'The European Central Bank as Lender of Last Resort for Sovereigns in the Eurozone', *Journal of Common Market Studies* 50 (2012) Annual Review: 6–35.

So the ECB came up with a different justification of its interventions, namely the need to 'address the malfunctioning of securities markets and restore an appropriate monetary policy transmission mechanism'.[8] The argument behind it was that during the first decade of the Eurozone sovereign bond markets underestimated economic and fiscal risks in the Eurozone's periphery. In spring 2010, they suddenly rebounded, precipitating a vicious, mutually reinforcing circle of panicking bond markets, shivering banking systems and suppressed activity in the real economy. This process, according to the ECB, was hindering the monetary policy transmission mechanism, i.e., the uniform transmission of central bank policy rates into local loan rates. To restore it, the ECB should have departed from its previous thinking that the single monetary policy required a single policy being applied indiscriminately to all Eurozone Member States. Because the monetary transmission was clogged up in some jurisdictions only, actions of the central bank aimed to restore it must be equally selective to remain adequate, the argument went.

While Draghi clearly subscribed to this thinking since the very beginning of his tenure, the arguments supporting interventions on government bond markets could not obviate the crux of the criticisms seeing the SMP as a fiscal policy instrument. Hans-Werner Sinn, one of the most eloquent detractors of the SMP, put the crux of the counterargument as follows: 'the government bond purchases made in the framework of the ECB's SMP ... constitute purely fiscal credit with no direct influence on the regional distribution of the money supply. This credit is granted in this way by the Community via the ECB to certain states just as it grants these states such credit via the ESM bail-out fund.'[9] From this perspective, the monetary transmission argument was just a smokescreen for an equivalent of an overdraft facility for national governments, prohibited by the no-monetary financing clause. By the same token the programme was deeply flawed in economic terms. While the mainstream thinking of the ECB held that since 2010 sovereign bond markets did not

[8] European Central Bank, 'ECB Decides on Measures to Address Severe Tensions in Financial Markets', 10 May 2010, available at www.ecb.europa.eu/press/pr/date/2010/html/pr100510.en.html.

[9] Hans-Werner Sinn, 'Responsibility of States and Central Banks in the Euro Crisis', Expert report commissioned by the German Constitutional Court, Second Senate, Session of 11 and 12 June 2013: 24, available at www.cesifo-group.de/portal/page/portal/DocBase_Content/ZS/ZS-CESifo_Forum/zs-for-2014/zs-for-2014-1/forum1-14-1.pdf.

price sovereign risks appropriately, the mainstream German central bankers who opposed the SMP maintained that financial markets reacted quite accurately to the situation in the engulfed Eurozone's periphery. It was clear to them that Italy would not manage servicing its debt for a long time had its bonds traded at 7 per cent+, as they did in 2011. Yet, they argued that this country had been losing competitive edges for many years before, that it suffered from an inept political class, from outgrown, often corrupt administration, from ballooning labour costs and from rigid product markets. Between 2008 and 2011 its public debt rose by 15 per cent, reaching almost 120 per cent of GDP. Government debt of Spain was much lower, but Spanish deficits were twice as large as the Italian, as was Spain's unemployment rate, while the banking system hovered at the edge of a precipice in late 2011.

If financial markets were pricing all of these factors in, the mainstream German thinking contended, the monetary transmission mechanism was malfunctioning for reasons independent of the monetary policy. Without 'reinventing themselves' economically, socially and politically the Eurozone peripheral countries could not properly function within the monetary union. The pressure by financial markets should not be debilitated by interventions of the ECB, their argument was, because this very pressure was prodding national governments to do what was necessary (ousting – as in the Italian case – inept incumbent politicians and enthroning reformists).[10] Alleviating the pressure by massive government bond purchases the ECB would do disservice to the resolve of local policymakers to put through the reforms bolstering economic fundamentals.

The vicissitudes of the SMP, when relaunched in summer 2011 (the programme was discontinued a year earlier, after only two months of bond purchases), seemed to have corroborated the merits of this very concern. The then-President of the ECB, Jean-Claude Trichet, and the incoming President, Mario Draghi, rendered the Italian and Spanish bond purchases dependent on whether the governments of the two countries would accept specific economic conditions. The conditions, both when it came to requested structural and fiscal reforms, were laid

[10] Just a few days after Draghi became the president of the ECB on 1 November 2011, Berlusconi quit as prime minister, under the combined pressure of domestic opposition, European politicians and sovereign debt markets, and was replaced by Mario Monti.

down in two separate letters the ECB duet wrote to the prime ministers of Spain and Italy in August 2011.[11] And while both senior national politicians acquiesced to the terms of the bond market intervention, the Berlusconi government defected soon after, leaving the ECB confronted with a hard choice: whether to discontinue the programme, propelling the sovereign debt crisis, or to sustain it, undermining further the resolve of national politicians to do their part. At the same time the very fact that bond purchases were contingent on economic and fiscal adjustments demanded by the ECB was driving home the point of the German critics. The ECB was clearly pushing the string of its (narrow) monetary policy mandate by actively pursuing economic and fiscal goals.

Worst of all, its interventions were patently ineffective. By the time Draghi assumed his office in November 2011, SMP purchases totalled more than €230 billion.[12] And yet they had no impact whatsoever on credit or liquidity risks in the Eurozone. Government bond yields soared, while the monetary transmission mechanism was as choked up in Spain and Italy as it had been before.

4.3 Stage No. 2: VLTROs

So the ECB under Draghi changed tacks. First, very soon after the new president assumed his office, the ECB withdrew two earlier – quite unfortunate, indeed – decisions to raise benchmark refinancing rates (from 1.0 to 1.5 percent). And soon after it flooded the Eurozone's financial system with two large injections of central bank money, one in December 2011 and the other in February 2012, amounting together to more than €1 trillion.[13]

Technically there was nothing very special about the injections. They were performed as Long-Term Refinancing Operations (LTROs) – one of

[11] The Italian letter was leaked to *Corriera della Sera*: 'Trichet e Draghi: Un'azione Pressante per Ristabilire la Fiducia Degli Investitori', 5 August 2011, available at www.corriere.it/economia/11_settembre_29/trichet_draghi_inglese_304a5f1e-ea59-11e0-ae06-4da866778017.shtml.

[12] European Central Bank, 'Consolidated Financial Statement of the Eurosystem as at 28 October 2011', 1 November 2011, available at www.ecb.europa.eu/press/pr/wfs/2011/html/fs111101.en.html.

[13] European Central Bank, 'ECB Announces Measures to Support Bank Lending and Money Market Activity', 8 December 2011, available at www.ecb.europa.eu/press/pr/date/2011/html/pr111208_1.en.html.

four main types of open market operations at the ECB's disposal.[14] In short, the ECB offered commercial banks funding (liquidity) for a given period, in exchange for assets (securities) posted to the ECB as collateral. Similarly to the most standard repo operations, with the LTROs the ECB aimed to expand money supply and to ease refinancing concerns on the interbank market. The money supply would be reabsorbed by the central bank when it was no longer needed to achieve its objectives.

After the collapse of Lehman Brothers, when banking liquidity evaporated together with market confidence, LTROs became indispensable to stymie money market interest rates hikes and to avert a credit crunch. The ECB extended the maturities of the LTROs it was deploying (from three months in 2008 to one year in October 2011) and dramatically softened its collateral requirements.[15] The two LTROs executed shortly after Draghi took his office pushed these limits further. First, their maturity was lengthened to three years (hence, they have often been referred to as Very Long-Term Refinancing Operations – VLTROs). Second, the ECB accepted a yet-broader list of assets eligible as collateral.[16] And third, the interest rate on which the liquidity would be provided (1 per cent) was particularly attractive.

For a while it seemed that the two VLTROs sufficed to do the trick: conditions on interbank markets improved and yields on Italian and Spanish government bonds diminished. The observers, therefore, had grounds to argue that the injections 'supported liquidity, ensured stable long-term … financing of banks, subsidised the banking system and helped to restore its profitability, and temporarily supported distressed government bond markets … Considering the alternative of a potentially escalating financial crisis, these developments were beneficial.'[17]

But there was a price to pay for it. Banks of the strained South engaged in what Acharya and Steffen called 'great interest rate carry

[14] For details, see Sec. 1.3.1 of Guideline of the European Central Bank of 20 September 2011 on monetary policy instruments and procedures of the Eurosystem (recast) (ECB/2011/14, 2011/817/EU), OJ 2011 No. L 331, 14 December 2011, pp. 1–95, as subsequently amended.

[15] John Whittaker aptly noted that 'The ECB's collateral rules are effectively being driven by the financing needs of the weakest banks': 'Intra-Eurosystem Debts', Lancaster University Management School, 30 March 2011: 3, available at papers.ssrn.com/sol3/papers.cfm?abstract_id=1836470.

[16] For details, see Hans-Werner Sinn, *The Euro Trap: On Bursting Bubbles, Budgets, and Beliefs* (Oxford: Oxford University Press, 2014): esp. 153–175.

[17] Gregory Claeys, 'The (Not So) Unconventional Monetary Policy of the European Central Bank since 2008', Bruegel External Publication for the European Parliament's Montary Dialogue with the President of the European Central Bank Mario Draghi,

trade'.[18] They exchanged government securities in their possession for central bank liquidity, to then buy more government bonds and again use it as collateral for more funds from the ECB. Because credit risk premia on Spanish or Italian bonds were high and the cost of borrowing from the ECB within the LTRO low, the carry trade entailed serious profits for the banks involved. The higher demand for government paper used as collateral inevitably exerted a downward pressure on Spanish and Italian government bond yields, soothing the sovereign debt crisis. But while the ECB's economists defended this artificial drug as a countermeasure to the previous unnatural cascade effects caused by the panic on sovereign debt markets, the 'carry trade' had some perverse side effects.

To start with, it propelled the fragmentation of the Eurozone's banking system,[19] because the northern banks were happy to use the VLTROs to reduce their exposures to southern banks and sovereigns, hoarding the cheap central bank funding at the deposit facility of the ECB. At the same time, their southern counterparts augmented their exposure to government securities, which the ECB was so willing to accept as collateral. In consequence, southern banks (and French banks, which were also massively involved in the carry trade) became all the more dependent on their sovereigns. They were more liquid, but ultimately weaker than before. It should not come as a surprise, therefore, that the banks in the Eurozone's periphery were not any more willing to provide credit to the private sector after the VLTROs than they had been under the previous one-year LTROs.[20] Furthermore, the arbitrage profits of the banks involved in the carry trade essentially amounted to a massive subsidy from southern governments to their ailing banking systems. In the longer term, the subsidy only postponed (and amplified) problems in the exposed financial systems, because it kept otherwise non-viable banks afloat and delayed the momentum for restructuring them.[21] As one observer put it, the VTLROs were 'most important for

June 2014: 8, available at bruegel.org/2014/07/the-not-so-unconventional-monetary-policy-of-the-european-central-bank-since-2008/.

[18] Viral V. Acharya and Sascha Steffen, 'The "Greatest" Carry Trade Ever? Understanding Eurozone Bank Risks', *Journal of Financial Economics* 115 (2015): 215–236.

[19] Diego Valiante, 'Banking Union in a Single Currency Area: Evidence on Financial Fragmentation', *Journal of Financial Economic Policy* 7 (2015): 251–274.

[20] Jean Pisani-Ferry and Guntram Wolff, 'Propping up Europe?', *Bruegel Policy Contribution* No. 2012/07, 23 April 2012, available at bruegel.org/2013/06/eu-imf-assistance-to-euro-area-countries-an-early-assessment/.

[21] Ansgar Belke, '3-year LTROs – A First Assessment of a Non-Standard Policy Measure', Briefing paper prepared for the April 2012 Monetary Dialogue at the European

those banks that had the weakest equity positions and the greatest difficulties in obtaining market funding'.[22]

The division was further broadened by the losses southern (mainly Greek and Cypriot) banks incurred in consequence of the Private-Sector Involvement. Instituted in February 2012, this government debt swap entailed a write-off of approximately €100 billion, i.e., 53.5 per cent of the face value of Greek governmental bonds possessed by private financial institutions.[23] Soon after banks in other 'suspicious' jurisdictions faced growing refinancing costs, when other financial institutions perceived them to be potential victims of future PSIs. The banks exposed to government bonds of the engulfed Eurozone's periphery found it more difficult again to get funding on the interbank market and their appetite for sovereign debt dwindled. As a result, since April 2012 yields on sovereign paper of Spain and Italy went up steeply again and in July 2012 Spanish government bonds were trading at interest rates higher even than in November 2011.

The sovereign debt crisis was at its apex.

4.4 Stage No. 3: OMT

At that point the ECB found itself in a corner. Limited bond purchases under the SMP failed, as did the liquidity injections within the VLTROs. Draghi had to demonstrate that he was ready to go for broke. And he did, famously stepping forward and saying: 'We think the euro is irreversible … Within our mandate, the ECB is ready to do whatever it takes to preserve the euro. And believe me, it will be enough.'[24] By this pledge, he declared the ECB's willingness to take over sovereign debt risks from the banking systems had the market situation not calmed down. He

Parliament, available at www.europarl.europa.eu/document/activities/cont/201204/20120423ATT43715/20120423ATT43715EN.pdf, Huw Pill, 'The ECB Can't Substitute for Periphery Financial Reform', *The Economist Free Exchange*, 20 May 2013, available at www.economist.com/blogs/freeexchange/2013/05/european-central-bank-5.

22 Martin Hellwig, 'Financial Stability, Monetary Policy, Banking Supervision, and Central Banking', *Preprints of the Max Planck Institute for Research on Collective Goods*, Bonn 2014/9: 4, available at www.mpp-rdg.mpg.de/pdf_dat/2014_09online.pdf.

23 The eligible bonds totalled €206 billion, out of €356 billion of Greek government debt outstanding prior to the bond swap.

24 Speech by Mario Draghi at the Global Investment Conference in London, 26 July 2012, available at www.ecb.europa.eu/press/key/date/2012/html/sp120726.en.html.

implicitly admitted that the Eurosystem's printing press would provide the necessary financial assistance, if needed.

The OMT programme, announced in September 2012,[25] operationalised this pledge and introduced further conditions. Some of them were meant to placate the markets, while others were to appease the critics of the previous bond-purchasing SMP.

Because the Treaty precludes purchases of debt instruments 'directly from them [Member States] by the European Central Bank or national central banks' (Art. 123(1) TFEU), the OMT would only involve secondary market interventions. While this particular feature did not differentiate it from the SMP, the critics of the latter received another pledge: the ECB would buy only government bonds of the countries on an official bailout programme and only 'as long as programme conditionality is fully respected, and terminate them [the purchases] … when there is noncompliance with the macroeconomic adjustment or precautionary programme'. The SMP, which did not provide for any similar conditionality, relying instead on informal, and unreliable, letter demands and promises, would be terminated for good. The ECB also maintained it would respect certain blackout periods, i.e., embargo durations between the bond issuances and purchasing them by the Eurosystem. Finally, the institution pledged to sterilise the purchases by conducting liquidity-absorbing operations of the corresponding amount, to counter any effects on money supply and thus on inflation.

While the features were calibrated to placate German critics, none of them could reassure the markets. But the programme's other traits could. And they did. Two of those were of particular importance. First, the ECB set 'no ex ante quantitative limits' on the size of the transactions it was willing to undertake. Second, it accepted the *pari passu* status (no preferential treatment comparing to other creditors in case of a credit event). These were precisely what the markets wanted to see. Suddenly, the banks previously exposed to sovereign risks became credible again, because everyone knew that they would primarily profit from the OMT. The demand for sovereign paper of the distressed governments recovered.

[25] European Central Bank, 'Technical Features of Outright Monetary Transactions', 6 September 2012, available at www.ecb.europa.eu/press/pr/date/2012/html/pr120906_1.en.html.

Following precisely the stance previously maintained in respect to the SMP, the ECB consistently repeated that the OMT had purely monetary purposes.[26] Supported by leading European economists,[27] its top officials argued that in 2012 the Eurozone found itself in a state of a 'bad equilibrium', in which growing doubts of debt sustainability were negatively bouncing back on bond prices and again on doubts of market participants, moving the situation towards the point when this mutually reinforcing mechanism levers interest rates of distressed sovereigns up to the point of fiscal unsustainability. Because bank ratings are closely associated with sovereign ratings, a deterioration of the latter inevitably leads to a worsening of banks' borrowing positions and in consequence constrains their lending to each other, as well as to households and non-financial companies. By compressing sovereign bond spreads the OMT was to improve borrowing conditions of banks and stimulate their credit action in the countries where the monetary transmission mechanism had been choked up.

The logic was not new, and the counterarguments were also the same. This time, however, the critics could not use their crowning argument: that bond purchases were patently ineffective. Granted, the OMT did not unclog the monetary transmission mechanism. But it averted a systemic collapse of the Eurozone.

The detractors had two options in such a situation: they could turn a blind eye to the debt management logic of the interventions, accepting the fact that without them the Eurozone would die, as no less-radical tool had been capable of soothing the sovereign debt crisis. Or they could simply repeat that this was not what the single currency had been meant to entail.

[26] See, for example, 'Introductory Statement to the Press Conference (with Q&A). Mario Draghi, President of the ECB, Vítor Constâncio, Vice-President of the ECB', 6 September 2012, available at www.ecb.europa.eu/press/pressconf/2012/html/is120906.en.html; or 'Outright Monetary Transactions, One Year On' (speech by Benoît Cœuré, Member of the Executive Board of the ECB, at the conference 'The ECB and Its OMT Programme', organised by the Centre for Economic Policy Research, German Institute for Economic Research and KfW Bankengruppe), 2 September 2013, available at www.ecb.europa.eu/press/key/date/2013/html/sp130902.en.html.

[27] For example, Paul De Grauwe and Yuemei Ji, 'Self-Fulfilling Crises in the Eurozone: An Empirical Test', *CEPS Working Document* No. 367, June 2012, available at www.ceps.eu/system/files/WD%20No%20367%20Empirical%20Test%20Fragility%20Eurozone.pdf; Daniel Gros, 'On the Stability of Public Debt in a Monetary Union', *Journal of Common Market Studies* 50 (2012) Annual Review: 36–48.

4.5 The Clash of the Titan Courts

The dilemma became all the more serious when the German Constitutional Court, which in an earlier case endorsed the SMP without blinking (despite this earlier bond-buying programme providing no institutional safeguards comparable to the OMT[28]), implied in early 2014 that the OMT could be *ultra vires*, instantiating a manifest and structurally significant transgression of the ECB's mandate.[29] In addition, it could, according to the Karlsruhe judges, upset the core of the German constitutional identity, failing the so-called identity review (*Identitätskontrolle*).[30]

Public lawyers, who could previously still be lulled into a false sense that central banking was not only boring, but also remote from basic conflicts in their natural habitat - the distribution and exercise of powers - were suddenly vivified. The Court of Justice additionally electrified them (and many others) when, in response to the preliminary reference of the German Constitutional Court, it entirely disagreed with the German judges on their assessment of what the EU law authorised and what it precluded.[31]

Contrary to what the German court surmised, the Court of Justice preordained that the OMT safely falls into the ECB's mandate. The Luxembourg court eagerly accepted the monetary transmission justification averred by the ECB. And it stated that the no monetary financing clause is not breached as long as the ECB uses one of the instruments in its toolbox to purchase the bonds (technically, the OMT falls into the broad group of monetary policy instruments called 'outright open market transactions')[32] and if the programme has some features (like blackout periods, or keeping the purchasing strategy secret to deter

[28] Greek rescue package case, 2 BvR 987/10, 7 September 2011, § 116, available at www.bundesverfassungsgericht.de/SharedDocs/Entscheidungen/EN/2011/09/rs20110907_2bvr098710en.html.

[29] Case 2 BvR 2728/13 et al., order of 14 January 2014, available at www.bundesverfassungsgericht.de/SharedDocs/Entscheidungen/EN/2014/01/rs20140114_2bvr272813en.html.

[30] Ibid.

[31] Case C-62/14, *Peter Gauweiler and Others* v. *Deutscher Bundestag*, ECLI:EU:C:2015:400.

[32] According to Sec. 3.2.1 of Guideline of the European Central Bank of 20 September 2011 on Monetary Policy Instruments and Procedures of the Eurosystem (Recast) (ECB/2011/14, 2011/817/EU), OJ 2011 No. L 331/1, 14 December 2011, 'outright open market transactions refer to operations where the Eurosystem buys or sells eligible assets outright on the market'.

speculation) differentiating it from the prohibited interventions on the primary market.

In addition to those, the Court of Justice sided with the Frankfurt institution in two other important respects. First, it vindicated the bad-equilibrium theory, pinpointing that the OMT paved the way for 'dispelling unjustified fears about the break-up of the euro area' (§ 76). What better evidence, the Luxembourg judges implicitly asked, could the ECB come up with to prove the bad-equilibrium argument than the fact that the market sentiment changed so rapidly after the OMT announcement without there being any OMT bond intervention, no single euro of German taxpayers put at risk? And second, it is settled case law of the Court of Justice that European institutions enjoy 'a discretion, the exercise of which involves complex assessments of an economic and social nature … Thus, the Court, in reviewing whether that discretion was lawfully exercised, cannot substitute its own assessment.'[33] This finding has one important consequence for the judicial review: judges should not try to demonstrate superior expertise in non-legal areas, like central banking, on which the proper experts, in this case central bankers, hold very diverging opinions. This might apply in particular to emergency measures with profound systemic consequences. As an upshot of this 'wide margin of appreciation' doctrine, the Court can quash a decision of a specialised institution only when its irregularity is so grave that it is evident even for non-specialists. Quite paradoxically, the German Constitutional Court followed the very same standard of prudence in an earlier case on the economic crisis management, arguing in addition that it would also take practical consequences of the vetted act into account.[34] Yet in the OMT case it used a very different yardstick, putting its findings at odds with universal standards of judicial review.

[33] Case C-667/13, *Estado Português* v. *Banco Privado Português*, ECLI:EU:C:2015:151, § 67 and the case law cited therein. See also Case C-62/14, *Peter Gauweiler and Others* v. *Deutscher Bundestag*, ECLI:EU:C:2015:400, § 68, and the case law cited.

[34] As it argued in the so-called *ESM case*, 2 BvR 1390/12, 12 September 2012, § 271: 'the risks involved with making available the German shares in the European Stability Mechanism were manageable, while without the granting of financial facilities by the European Stability Mechanism the entire economic and social system was under the threat of unforeseeable, serious consequences. Even though these assumptions are the subject of great controversy among economic experts, they are at any rate not evidently erroneous. Therefore the Federal Constitutional Court may not replace the legislature's assessment by its own.' Available at www.bundesverfassungsgericht.de/SharedDocs/Entscheidungen/EN/2012/09/rs20120912_2bvr139012en.html.

Even if the legal arguments of the German Constitutional Court were extremely tortuous and inconsistent, they conveyed, however, some very apt misgivings on the evolving role of the ECB.

According to the first one, already mentioned in Chapter 1, central banks' independence springs from a very specific finding that (democratically elected) decision-makers in charge of economic and fiscal policies tend to maximise economic output by all means, even if it might entail very serious side effects, like high inflation. Central banks should thus be independent in a deep sense: they ought to be counter-majoritarian, actively defying elected politicians whenever they try to indulge their basic instincts. Only then can central bankers protect society from time-inconsistent consequences of short-sighted political decisions. This founding assumption of the central banks' independence is upended when the guardians of price stability, instead of confronting spending habits of elected politicians, pledge they will not hesitate to erect an insurmountable wall of digital money to defend the sovereigns from the financial markets. According to the flipside of the same argument a democratically elected body, like the Bundestag, might assume even very serious financial risks if it considers them an indispensable remedy to a systemic crisis, simply because of its democratic mandate. But the ECB is not a democratically elected body. It is the opposite: an insulated institution of politically unaccountable technocrats. Should a properly functioning system allow them to influence national economic and fiscal policies, or to determine debt management strategies, financial risk allocation and the very composition of the Eurozone?

Second, even stalwart supporters of the ECB's very active stance had to admit that 'since 2010 the markets were first gripped by negative sentiments and tended to exaggerate the default risks of individual countries, i.e., they pushed the spreads way above the fundamental risks. Since the announcement of OMT, the reverse has happened: the spreads went down spectacularly, mostly driven by positive market sentiments unrelated to the improvements (if any) in the fundamentals.'[35] The OMT, therefore, dazed the markets. According to the OMT's very basic feature, the market pressure was to be replaced with conditionalities accompanying official bailouts. Otherwise OMT bond purchases could not be effectuated. But bailout conditions, as well

[35] Paul De Grauwe and Yuemei Ji, 'Disappearing Government Bond Spreads in the Eurozone – Back to Normal?', *CEPS Working Document* No. 396, 14 May 2014: 4.

as their implementation, are always subject to political haggling and backlash. What is even more important, nothing in the OMT's design can prevent individual Eurozone countries from gradually deteriorating their economic fundamentals without any perceivable effects on bond spreads. Experiences in the previous decade demonstrate that when the alarm sounds in this situation, it may be too late to contain the systemic damage.

Third, the OMT, just like the SMP, was deployed 'to preserve the singleness of our monetary policy and to ensure the proper transmission of our policy stance to the real economy throughout the area'.[36] Yet, as its predecessor SMP, it did not deliver on this promise.

4.6 Unclogging the Real Economy?

After September 2012, the monetary transmission mechanism was as much handicapped in the Eurozone's periphery as before. In other words, credit conditions for households and non-financial companies did not improve in reaction to the OMT announcement, in stark contrast to the refinancing situation of the Eurozone governments. The stock of loans to non-financial corporations, which in principle should grow when the monetary policy is eased, rose slightly in the two years before President Draghi made his 'whatever it takes' statement in July 2012, only to slide down during the next two years.[37] Another indicator of the monetary transmission – costs of new loans to non-financial corporations – corroborates the very same conclusion.[38] In July 2010 these costs were marginally higher in Germany than in Spain or Italy (0.2 per cent higher in Germany than in Spain and 0.1 per cent higher in Germany than in Italy). In July 2012, Spanish entrepreneurs were paying approximately 0.6 per cent more for their loans than their German counterparts, and the Italians approximately 1.2 per cent more. In July 2014 the difference between the German and the Italian cost of borrowing stayed roughly the same, while the difference between the German and Spanish costs grew to 1.0 per cent. If anything, therefore,

[36] Draghi, 'Introductory Statement to the Press Conference (with Q&A)'.

[37] The figure was €4,302,541 million in July 2010, €4,706,019 million in July 2012 and €4,680,807 million in July 2014: 'Loans vis-a-vis Euro Area NFC Reported by MFI Excluding ESCB in the Euro Area (Stock)', available from sdw.ecb.europa.eu.

[38] Euro area statistics, Bank interest rates – Loans, available at www.euro-area-statistics.org/bank-interest-rates-loans?cr=eur&lg=en&page=2.

the divergences in monetary transmission widened in the aftermath of the OMT.

From the perspective of the efforts to rescue the Eurozone's periphery this situation was deeply perplexing. But it is very questionable if it could be deemed irrational, stemming from yet another 'bad equilibrium'. Different lending conditions in Germany or Austria than in Italy or Spain could be justified by the fact that entrepreneurs of the Eurozone's periphery were much more leveraged before 2010 and that macroeconomic fundamentals there, just like the broader system of public governance, were incomparably frailer and more ineffective. On top of these differences, banking systems of the core did not struggle with huge piles of non-performing loans or exposures to unstable governments. The same credit conditions in very divergent economies could therefore simply be read as mispricing the credit risks involved.

The ECB has always been perfectly aware of all the factors behind the diverging monetary transmissions. But for the majority of its Governing Council something else was far more concerning: no matter how economically rational divergences in the monetary transmission might have been, the credit rationing they entailed contributed to the asphyxiation of the southern economies and magnified their relative competitive disadvantages. Economically natural processes were therefore undermining the financial stability of the Eurozone. The ECB felt obliged to act, even if its actions would confront natural behaviour of economic agents.

In January 2013 it allowed the banks to repay their VLTRO loans before the three-year maturity period. In consequence, within the next few months the currency previously absorbed by Eurozone's commercial banks evaporated almost entirely. And as the two VLTROs entailed no visible improvements in lending to the private sector throughout the periphery, the ECB switched to yet more drastic measures. In June 2014, it first announced new LTROs, this time called Targeted Long-Term Refinancing Operations (TLTROs): cheap funding offered in eight auctions between September 2014 and June 2016, in volumes depending on net lending of individual banks to the private sector. And, soon after, it suppressed its deposit rate on reserves held by commercial banks with the ECB to negative territories (then −0.1 per cent). The purpose of these measures was obvious and straightforward: banks lending to the private sector would obtain very cheap credit; these hoarding funds with the ECB instead would be punished with negative deposit rates.

4.7 Stage No. 4: The APP

In summer 2014, when the ECB came about with the TLTRO and negative interest rates, yet another issue emerged on the horizon: the ostensible threat of deflation. While falling prices might be a positive phenomenon for consumers, economists worry about the so-called deflationary spiral, which may set in if decreasing prices are a byproduct of a weakening economy. When it happens, price decreases lead to lower production, which then leads to lower wages and demand, further decreasing prices. The economy enters a tailspin.

While in September 2012, when the ECB officially announced the OMT programme, the benchmark (HICP) Eurozone's inflation stood at 2.6 per cent, two years later, in September 2014, it had collapsed to 0.3 per cent. The slide rang all of the alarm bells in Frankfurt, because price stability – defined as a year-on-year increase in the Harmonised Index of Consumer Prices (HICP) for the Euroarea of below but close to 2 per cent over the medium term[39] – is the primary objective of the ESCB.[40]

These new developments encouraged the ECB to do what other major central banks had done before: it embarked on (unsterilised) asset purchases. Because this quantitative easing was an anathema to many German central bankers, the ECB first resuscitated purchases of covered bonds, i.e., of the debt instruments issued by credit institutions, which are secured by a pool of mortgage loans or public-sector debt. In 2009, the ECB had already intervened on this market, which suffered badly from the 2008 financial crisis, with its first Covered Bonds Purchase Programme (CBPP1). While CBPP2 was discontinued in October 2012, two years later the ECB launched CBPP3, coupled with purchases of debt securities collateralised by a pool of assets other than mortgages (the so-called Asset-Backed Securities Purchase Programme – ABSPP).

Neither covered bonds, however, nor asset-backed securities were available in quantities necessary to achieve the monetary policy goals of the quantitative easing. So in January 2015, when the HICP inflation plummeted to −0.6 per cent, even Germans, previously staunchly opposing any purchases of government debt by the Eurosystem,

[39] A slightly narrower version of this definition was announced by the Governing Council of the ECB in October 1998. It was subsequently refined in May 2003. See also European Central Bank, 'The Definition of Price Stability', available at www.ecb.europa.eu/mopo/strategy/pricestab/html/index.en.html.

[40] Arts. 119(2), 127(1), 282(2) TFEU.

succumbed. The ECB announced it would soon launch what it called the Public Sector Purchase Programme (PSPP).[41] Since then all the interventions have been lumped together into one programme called the Asset Purchase Programme (APP).

Originally, the ECB pledged that the Eurosystem would buy €50 billion of public-sector bonds a month (plus €10 billion in private bonds within the CBPP3 and the ABSPP) until interest rates reached the statutory target of almost 2 per cent 'over the medium term'. Out of the public-sector bonds, €6 billion (12 per cent) would comprise securities of European institutions, while €44 billion would involve government bonds and bonds issued by national public agencies, in proportions reflecting the weighing of individual countries in the ECB's capital key. Out of the national public-sector pool, national central banks would buy €40 billion in bonds issued by their home countries and the ECB would purchase €4 billion a month (8 per cent). Only the ECB's part – 20 per cent of all purchases[42] – would be subject to loss-sharing (which entails direct losses of the ECB in case of a default). All in all, therefore, national public-sector bonds directly exposing other nations to sovereign credit risk comprise a small fraction of the quantitative easing programme. According to the original design, the risks were to be additionally mitigated by the fact that the national structure of the purchases corresponded with the ECB's capital key. To simplify a bit, economically weaker Eurozone countries would therefore have less of their government bonds purchased than the stronger ones. And the most risky sovereign paper – Greek – has been excluded from the PSPP from its very beginning.[43]

[41] European Central Bank, 'ECB Announces Expanded Asset Purchase Programme', 22 January 2015, available at www.ecb.europa.eu/press/pr/date/2015/html/pr150122_1.en.html. Formalised as decision 2015/774 of the ECB of 4 March 2015 on a secondary markets public sector asset purchase programme (ECB/2015/10), OJ 2015 No. L 121, 14 May 2015, pp. 20–24.

[42] In March 2016, the Governing Council of the ECB decreased the share of EU supranational bonds within monthly PSPP purchases from 12 to 10 per cent and raised the share of other bonds purchased by the ECB from 8 to 10 per cent, so the ultimate level of risk sharing has remained the same.

[43] In February 2015, shortly after Syriza came to power in Greece, the ECB withdrew its 2010 decision to accept – for monetary policy purposes – Greek marketable debt securities below the Eurosystem's credit quality threshold (Decision 2015/300 of the European Central Bank of 10 February 2015 on the Eligibility of Marketable Debt Instruments Issued or Fully Guaranteed by the Hellenic Republic OJ 2015 No. L 53, 25 February 2015, pp. 29–30). This disqualified Greek public-sector bonds from the PSPP.

But, nonetheless, when making its decisions on the PSPP in early 2015, the Governing Council introduced two types of limits on the purchases of the public-sector bonds. The Eurosystem could amass neither more than 25 per cent of any bond issue (the so-called issue limit), nor more than 33 per cent of all the bonds (of maturities longer than two years) issued by any individual issuer (the so-called issuer limit).[44] The two conditions were clearly aimed to appease potential critics of the programme, who alleged that the PSPP was excessively exposing the Eurosystem to credit risks.

The first of the two limits was imposed 'in order to avoid obtaining a blocking minority in a debt restructuring involving collective action clauses'[45] introduced to all Eurozone government securities issued since January 2013. According to the collective action clauses, holders of more than 25 per cent of a single issue are able to block debt restructuring. As some observers conjectured, 'the ECB does not want to be in a position in which it has the power to block a potential vote on the restructuring of ECB-held debt of a euro-area country, because not blocking such a restructuring could be interpreted as monetary financing of a member state'.[46] The rub, though, is that the Treaty ban on monetary financing says nothing about collective action clauses, nor about either voluntary or forced participation in a debt restructuring. And in the OMT decision the Court of Justice highlighted that Art. 123 TFEU does not preclude any possibility of ECB's losses. Dealing with the ultimately similar question of whether the ECB could accept the *pari passu* status as a government bondholder, the Luxembourg Court

While the decision to waive standard requirements for Greek debt was reinstated in mid-2016 (ECB press release of 22 June 2016, 'ECB Reinstates Waiver Affecting the Eligibility of Greek Bonds Used as Collateral in Eurosystem Monetary Policy Operations', available at www.ecb.europa.eu/press/pr/date/2016/html/pr160622_1.en.html), the ECB has not decided to include Greek public-sector bonds into PSPP purchases, possibly expecting another debt restructuring.

[44] The issue limit was extended to 33 per cent in September 2015, under the condition that an increase in the Eurosystem's holdings would not permit a blocking minority for the purpose of collective action clauses.

[45] European Central Bank, 'Account of the Monetary Policy Meeting of the Governing Council of the European Central Bank Held in Frankfurt am Main on Wednesday and Thursday, 21–22 January 2015', available at www.ecb.europa.eu/press/accounts/2015/html/mg150219.en.html.

[46] Grégory Claeys, Álvaro Leandro and Allison Mandra, 'European Central Bank Quantitative Easing: The Detailed Manual', *Bruegel Policy Contribution* No. 2015/02, 11 March 2015: 4, available at bruegel.org/2015/03/european-central-bank-quantitative-easing-the-detailed-manual/.

preordained that the risk of losses is inherent in any monetary policy action. The Statute of the ESCB and the ECB accepts it by providing for a method of allocating consequent losses, which, according to the Court, means that the ECB does not have to be shielded from the risk by the privileged creditor status.[47] The very same legal argument could be extended to the loss-sharing within the PSPP.

The 33 per cent cap on the exposure to an individual issuer was introduced to the PSPP programme 'as a means to safeguard market functioning and price formation as well as to mitigate the risk of the ECB becoming a dominant creditor of euro area governments'.[48] The first of the two functions has never been particularly convincing, because from the perspective of the 'market functioning and price formation' it really does not matter if the Eurosystem garners 33 or 43 per cent of bonds issued by an individual government. And, as radically falling interest rates on sovereign debt after the activation of the PSPP have demonstrated, the programme has profoundly manipulated the price formation process of Eurozone government bonds even with this issuer cap engrafted on it. The fact, however, that this goal has been inherent in the process since its very beginning does not diminish the other function of the issuer limit. The bigger the share of sovereign bonds the Eurosystem amasses, the higher its leverage over national governments (not necessarily what the ECB would dislike) and the higher the losses the Eurosystem would incur in case of a default. In a sense, the issuer limit was therefore installed as a hedging device, which is only corroborated by the fact that, when the APP purchases were stepped up from €60 billion a month to €80 billion in spring 2016, the issuer and issue limits for securities of international organisations and multilateral development banks (very trustworthy issuers) were increased to 50 per cent.

4.8 Unruly Inflation

Originally the limitations did not seem perplexing. It was hoped that the programme would achieve its goals in the eighteen months (i.e., until September 2016) for which it was originally designed. It is because the logic behind it seemed theoretically compelling. In

[47] Case C-62/14, *Peter Gauweiler and Others* v. *Deutscher Bundestag*, ECLI:EU:C:2015:400, § 125 and 126.

[48] European Central Bank, 'Account of the Monetary Policy Meeting'.

exchange for the bonds it had been purchasing, the Eurosystem had been releasing to the banking system its reserve currency and was therefore hoped to bring about moderate inflation. In addition, as President Draghi put it when he announced the programme, 'banks basically substitute bonds with cash, and therefore banks, at that point, will have more incentive to lend to the private sector, households and companies'.[49] Furthermore, because financial assets – like stocks and bonds – would become scarcer due to the purchases, their prices should go up. On the one hand, therefore, their issuers would benefit from wealth effects. They are expected to spend and invest more when becoming richer in result of the assets becoming more valuable. On the other hand, holders of the assets would earn comparably less (interest rates should go down), which is expected to force them to look for other profit opportunities. They therefore ought to become more interested in debt and equity of businesses in the real economy. Another possible strategy of theirs is to invest outside the Eurozone, which would in turn lead to capital outflows from the single currency area, lowering demand for the euro. Depreciation is expected to follow, boosting exports. All these factors together should contribute to growing investments, consumption and exports, rejuvenating demand and, in consequence, pushing up inflation also through that channel.

The first harbingers corroborated all these intuitions. In the first four months of the programme, inflation in the Eurozone jumped from the lows of −0.6 per cent in January 2015 to 0.3 per cent in May 2015. Interest rates on both government and corporate bonds dropped further, just as did interest rates on the interbank market. The costs of new loans to non-financial corporations converged throughout the Eurozone.[50] Other credit constraints for the private sector also abated in the periphery, while banks reported improvements in their financial situation (except for profitability).[51] One commentator even argued that 'the enormous program of quantitative easing that Draghi pushed through,

[49] Mario Draghi, 'Introductory Statement to the Press Conference (with Q&A), Frankfurt am Main', 22 January 2015, available at www.ecb.europa.eu/press/pressconf/2015/html/is150122.en.html.

[50] For instance, twelve months after the PSPP was launched, in January 2016, the long-term cost of borrowing to both households and non-financial corporations was 2 per cent in Germany, 2.32 per cent in Spain and 2.81 per cent in Italy: see www.euro-area-statistics.org/bank-interest-rates-loans?cr=eur&lg=en&page=2.

[51] See 'Euro Area Bank Lending Survey', available at www.ecb.europa.eu/stats/money/surveys/lend/html/index.en.html. Whether profitability of Eurozone banks

against German opposition, has saved the euro by circumventing the Maastricht Treaty's rules against monetizing or mutualizing government debts', which allegedly demonstrated 'the transformation of the ECB into the world's most creative and proactive central bank'.[52] The only flaw seemed to have related to timing: introducing the quantitative easing earlier would have saved the national governments some of the refinancing costs which spiked when the sovereign debt crisis burst in spring 2010.[53]

Since May 2015, however, headline inflation slackened off again, plummeting to below 0 per cent soon after. The economic activity in the months following January 2015 was as anaemic as it had been before. When in addition global markets shivered in early 2016, the ECB had to up the ante, pressing interest rates yet lower, raising monthly asset purchases of the monetary easing by yet another €20 billion and extending the APP to include 'investment-grade euro-denominated bonds issued by nonbank corporations established in the euro area' (the so-called Corporate Sector Purchase Programme: CSPP).[54] Furthermore, it launched a series of four new TLTROs (TLTRO II), which allowed banks to receive funds on particularly favourable terms, under the condition that they lend it out to private businesses.[55]

With all those heavy drugs injected, the Eurozone economy was coming to life again. Simultaneously, energy prices, falling in 2015, started climbing up, boosting headline inflation (from 0.6 per cent in November 2016 to 2 per cent in February 2017). This, however, did not change the ECB's course. In March 2017 – pointing out that the growth of inflation was primarily

suffered as an effect of the quantitative easing has been questioned, however: see Maria Demertzis and Guntram Wolff, 'What Impact Does the ECB's Quantitative Easing Policy Have on Bank profitability?', *Bruegel Policy Contribution* No. 20/2016, 30 November 2016, available at bruegel.org/2016/11/what-impact-does-the-ecbs-quantitative-easing-policy-have-on-bank-profitability/.

52 Anatole Kaletsky, 'Roman Europe?', *Project Syndicate*, 26 April 2016, available at www.project-syndicate.org/commentary/italy-not-germany-leads-europe-by-anatole-kaletsky-2016-04?barrier=accessreg.

53 Grégory Claeys, Álvaro Leandro and Allison Mandra, 'European Central Bank Quantitative Easing: The Detailed Manual', *Bruegel Policy Contribution* No. 2015/02, 11 March 2015: 12, available at bruegel.org/2015/03/european-central-bank-quantitative-easing-the-detailed-manual/.

54 European Central Bank, 'ECB Adds Corporate Sector Purchase Programme (CSPP) to the Asset Purchase Programme (APP) and Announces Changes to APP', 10 March 2016, available at www.ecb.europa.eu/press/pr/date/2016/html/pr160310_2.en.html.

55 European Central Bank, 'ECB Announces New Series of Targeted Longer-Term Refinancing Operations (TLTRO II)', 10 March 2016, available at www.ecb.europa.eu/press/pr/date/2016/html/pr160310_1.en.html.

driven by growing prices of volatile items[56] – the ECB announced that the APP would be limited to €60 billion a month, but, at the same time, that it would last 'until the Governing Council sees a sustained adjustment in the path of inflation consistent with its inflation aim'.[57]

Making this decision the ECB relied more on the so-called 'core inflation'[58] than the HICP inflation, despite its official definition of price stability referring to the latter only. Economically this alteration was fully justified, because core inflation, stripped of the most volatile items, measures durable price movements more accurately than HICP inflation does.

Core inflation was standing at 0.6 per cent in the Eurozone in March 2015, when the first purchases within the sovereign bond component of the APP started. Five months later it reached 1 per cent, to fall below this level until the summer of 2017, when it temporarily jumped to 1.3 per cent. Any possible relationship between core inflation and the APP has therefore been very tortuous. Still, Benoît Cœuré, Member of the Executive Board of the ECB, might have been right when insisting that 'not acting would have meant failing in our mandate. Without our measures, current inflation would be much lower and the inflation outlook would be much worse. Moreover, economic activity would be subdued, there would be fewer jobs, and a sound public budget would be more difficult to achieve, even in Germany.'[59] The question which remains, however, is for how long the extraordinary monetary policy can rejuvenate the economies with unstable economic, social and political foundations and what this implies for the ECB and the Eurozone.

4.9 The Lessons of the Abenomics

From this perspective, a different point emphasised by another senior official of the ECB seems more important than the remark of Benoît

[56] European Central Bank, 'Monetary Policy Decisions', 9 March 2017, available at www.ecb.europa.eu/press/pr/date/2017/html/pr170309.en.html. In October 2017 the ECB announced the purchases would be further downscaled, to €30 billion a month, "until the end of September 2018, or beyond, if necessary, and in any case until the Governing Council sees a sustained adjustment in the path of inflation consistent with its inflation aim": 'Monetary Policy Decisions', 26 October 2017, available at www.ecb.europa.eu/press/pr/date/2017/html/ecb.mp171026.en.html.

[57] Ibid.

[58] That is, HICP all-items inflation excluding energy and unprocessed food.

[59] Benoît Cœuré, 'People Are Not Only Savers', opinion piece from Benoît Cœuré, Member of the Executive Board of the ECB, for the *Frankfurter Allgemeine Sonntagszeitung*, 1 May 2016, available at www.ecb.europa.eu/press/key/date/2016/html/sp160501.en.html.

Cœuré. President Draghi has often averred that to succeed in producing sustainable economic growth and undistorted monetary transmission, the ECB's quantitative easing must be a part of a broader strategy, accompanied by structural reforms in the Eurozone's periphery and by fiscal easing in the countries (read: Germany) that have leeway to do so.[60]

Monetary policy accommodation, structural reforms and targeted fiscal expansion – the three main tenets of the ECB's preferred strategy to kick-start the economy in the Eurozone – resemble the three arrows of the recent Japanese experiment called Abenomics. Its experiences are worth mentioning here, for Japan found itself in what Krugman called 'the dreaded "liquidity trap", in which monetary policy becomes ineffective because you can't push interest rates below zero'[61] several years before the rest of the developed world faced the same challenge. And Abenomics, launched in late 2012 by the government of Prime Minister Shinzō Abe, aimed to remedy the very similar problems which also plague the Eurozone: deflation tendencies, low growth and rising public debt. The goal was also similar: to induce investments and domestic demand.

A few years after it was instituted, however, Abenomics has produced mixed effects. First and foremost, the arrow of structural reforms has not flown far. The OECD highlighted it in its 2017 report on Japan:

> [L]abour productivity remains around a quarter below the top half of OECD countries. Obstacles to entry and exit of firms limit the number of innovative new firms and trap labour and capital in low productivity activities. The productivity gap between the service sector and manufacturing and between leading and lagging firms has widened, contributing to wage and income inequality. Labour market dualism is becoming even more entrenched ... driving up the relative poverty rate. Dualism, which especially affects women, drives up inequality and holds back productivity growth, as nonregular workers are paid low wages and receive little training.[62]

Many of the same admonitions have been repeated regarding Eurozone countries as well. President Draghi was certainly correct

[60] See, for example, Draghi, 'Introductory Statement to the Press Conference (with Q&A)', 21 April 2016, available at www.ecb.europa.eu/press/pressconf/2016/html/is160421.en.html.

[61] Paul Krugman, 'Japan's Trap', May 1998, available at web.mit.edu/krugman/www/japtrap.html.

[62] OECD, *The 2017 OECD Economic Surveys: Japan 2017* (Paris: OECD Publishing, 2017): 2.

when he argued that 'structural policies are essential, given continued high structural unemployment and low potential output growth in the euro area. In particular, actions to raise productivity and improve the business environment, including the provision of an adequate public infrastructure, are vital to increase investment and boost job creation.'[63] But, like in Japan, there has been a lot of talk on such reforms, yet much less action. This leg of the ECB's preferred strategy has been much too short to hold the balance for a longer period of time.

Another lesson of Abenomics is that fiscal stimulation, as a method of reinforcing the effects of monetary easing on aggregate demand and output, comes with a price. No doubt with public debt at 215 per cent of GDP and with government deficit at 8 per cent in 2012, when Abenomics was launched, the Japanese fiscal arrow could not be particularly promising. And Japan, similarly to many European countries, has been ageing fast, which puts an upward pressure on pension and healthcare fiscal transfers. Prioritising public investments becomes a very tricky goal in such an environment, because stimulating public consumption is expected and directly rewarded by the (ageing) constituents. Public investments can hardly compete with these transfers from the electoral perspective.

In an environment so much skewing the fiscal arrow, where the debt overhang is otherwise unprecedented, any growth strategy based on fiscal stimulation can easily backfire, forcing future governments to tighten the belt, with a negative impact on the economic growth. The OECD put this emphatically in 2017, when it highlighted that without serious fiscal consolidation the gross government debt ratio of Japan would surpass 600 per cent of GDP by 2060.[64] Of course, the Eurozone is not in this situation, at least not yet. But its public finances experience very similar tensions limiting the space for devoting more public resources to investments. In addition, as I argued in the previous chapter, more fiscal stimulation in those countries where the scope for fiscal flexibility does exist would not necessarily translate into a superior economic activity in the Eurozone's south.

This leaves the central bank the only archer in the field. President Draghi conceded this when he confessed in April 2016 that: 'I should say with rare exceptions our monetary policy has been the only policy

[63] Draghi, 'Introductory Statement to the Press Conference (with Q&A)', see note 61.

[64] OECD, *The 2017 OECD Economic Surveys*, 39.

in the last four years to support growth.'[65] Of course, President Draghi, or any other member of the ECB's Governing Council, should not be blamed for this situation. It is also hardly contestable that monetary policy has become 'the only game in town' all over industrialised countries recently; the only consistently applied growth accelerator.[66] This is particularly true for the Eurozone, where, according to the standard monetary policy toolbox, the monetary policy has been excessively expansionary since 2015,[67] producing various perverse side effects.

4.10 The Janus-Faced Anti-Deflation Crusade

Since the inception of the APP there has been a clear relationship between massive purchases of debt instruments and growing prices of these instruments (falling yields).[68] As it was hoped when the programme was activated, investments and consumption have been on the rise and borrowing costs have declined. The relationship between these effects and the APP has been complicated, however.

When the ECB was announcing the PSPP in January 2015, the unemployment rate in the Eurozone was 0.8 per cent lower than at its peak of 12.1 per cent almost two years earlier, gradually diminishing

[65] Draghi, 'Introductory Statement to the Press Conference (with Q&A)', see note 61.

[66] Mohamed A. El-Erian, *The Only Game in Town: Central Banks, Instability, and Avoiding the Next Collapse* (New York: Random House, 2016).

[67] Cinzia Alcidi, Matthias Busse and Daniel Gros, 'Is There a Need for Additional Monetary Stimulus? Insights from the Original Taylor Rule', *CEPS Policy Brief* No. 342, April 2016, available at www.ceps.eu/system/files/PB342TaylorRule.pdf.

[68] Decreasing long-term interest rates is a phenomenon witnessed in the last thirty-five years and driven by complicated causalities. For a broader analysis, see, for example, Daniel Gros, 'Ultra-low or Negative Yields on Euro-Area Long-Term Bonds: Causes and Implications for Monetary Policy', *CEPS Working Document* No. 426, September 2016, available at www.ceps.eu/publications/ultra-low-or-negative-yields-euro-area-long-term-bonds-causes-and-implications-monetary; Grégory Claeys, 'Low Long-Term Rates: Bond Bubble or Symptom of Secular Stagnation?', *Bruegel Policy Contribution* No. 15/2016, 26 September 2016, available at bruegel.org/2016/09/low-long-term-rates-bond-bubble-or-symptom-of-secular-stagnation/. Yet, under the APP interest rates on some government bonds deemed safest have fallen below the ECB's deposit facility rate, which itself turned negative in June 2014. Governments actually make profits on issuing debt in this situation. In December 2016, the ECB made a decision to purchase bonds even at such negative rates (European Central Bank, 'ECB Adjusts Parameters of Its Asset Purchase Programme (APP)', 8 December 2016, available at www.ecb.europa.eu/press/pr/date/2016/html/pr161208_1.en.html), which means it has been making losses accumulating them, at the same time further diminishing their interest rates.

from quarter to quarter.[69] Gross disposable incomes of households per capita were also growing in the Eurozone stably since 2012.[70] The APP programme might have reinforced these trends (in the two years since its announcement in January 2015, Eurozone unemployment was falling twice as fast as earlier), but it was hardly a game changer of the recovery. In addition, low inflation, as I was emphasising in the previous chapter, is also a crucial element of an asymmetric macroeconomic adjustment in a single monetary system. It is quite telling in this respect that throughout 2015 and 2016 headline inflation in Ireland tended to stay below the Eurozone's trend. It remained at rock bottom of only 0.3 per cent when the Eurozone's inflation hit 2 per cent in February 2017 (and when it simultaneously soared to 3 per cent in Spain), contributing to the Irish price competitiveness. And yet, instead of showing any symptoms of a deflation trap, the economy there grew by a staggering 25.6 per cent in 2015 and by 5.1 per cent in 2016.[71] Deflation certainly did not disrupt the process.

This leads to the crux of the paradox behind the ECB's monetary policy. A long trend of falling inflation rates, to which the global competition, technological progress and ageing have all greatly contributed, has upended the mandates of all the world's major central banks. Together with falling rates of economic growth and growing public debt levels, the deflationary tendencies have forced these banks to exchange a big share – in the summer of 2017 equal to several percentage points of the 2016 Eurozone's GDP, or a figure corresponding to the 2016 Italian GDP – of government bonds for freshly printed central bank money. The recycling of the stifling burden of public debt (government liabilities) into the needed economic propulsion of money (central bank liabilities) injected into the banking system has brought about miraculous effects. It has diminished the costs of servicing public debt throughout the Eurozone. The increased liquidity resulting from banks' sales of marketable (yet in some Eurozone's jurisdictions quite toxic) government bonds has improved the condition of the banking systems. First and foremost, it has

[69] Eurostat, Unemployment Rate by Sex and Age – Monthly Average.

[70] Eurostat, Real Adjusted Gross Disposable Income of Households Per Capita.

[71] Eurostat, Real GDP Growth Rate – Volume. The astonishing economic growth in 2015 was driven mainly by foreign companies switching their tax domicile to Ireland to take advantage of its very low corporate tax rates. See Phillip Inman, 'Irish Economy Surges 26% as Revised Figures Take in Foreign Investment', *Guardian*, 12 July 2016, available at www.theguardian.com/business/2016/jul/12/irish-economic-growth-revised-figures-foreign-investment-aircraft.

changed the sentiment in the so-called real economy. Optimism returned and the end of the lost decade could be trumpeted. Politicians could return to their favourite mode of mutual congratulations championed throughout the first decade of the euro experiment.

The picture beneath this surface is less rosy, however. The Eurozone's periphery remains fragile for reasons independent of the contemporary monetary policy, so the ECB cannot make it any stronger on a sustainable basis. National politicians – the only decision-makers controlling the policies producing economic, social and political vulnerabilities of the Eurozone's periphery – have too often proven unable to come up with viable solutions as to how to uproot the fragilities when they obtained the additional fiscal breathing space of unnaturally low interest rates. This has entrapped the ECB, otherwise certainly aware that, as the Bank of International Settlements put it, 'unless the underlying problems are addressed head-on, short-term gain may be purchased at the price of long-term pain: debt does not come down sufficiently, the policy room for manoeuvre shrinks further and the seeds are sown for the next financial bust. None of this, however, means higher inflation. Paradoxically, an easing bias in the short term may end up being contractionary longer-term.'[72]

4.11 Non-Performing Loans at the Eurozone's Periphery

One obvious 'underlying problem' is a huge pile of non-performing loans (the loans overdue for more than ninety days, considered unlikely to be repaid in full) in the Eurozone's periphery. Non-performing loans are an outcome of excessive borrowing in comparison to the actual economic situation of households, companies and the whole economies. For this reason, levels of non-performing loans inevitably grow during crises and, if unresolved, drag down the economic recovery. This point is particularly important because, when levels of non-performing loans remain high, credit supply (forced out by the monetary policy of the ECB) can easily lead to evergreening of non-performing loans.[73] Then, instead of stimulating an economically productive allocation

[72] Bank of International Settlements, 85th Annual Report, 28 June 2015, 15, available at www.bis.org/publ/arpdf/ar2015_ec.pdf.

[73] Silvia Merler and Guntram Wolff, 'Ending Uncertainty: Recapitalisation under European Central Bank Supervision', *Bruegel Policy Contribution* No. 2013/18, 17 December 2013, available at bruegel.org/2013/12/ending-uncertainty-recapitalisation-under-european-central-bank-supervision/.

of resources, the credit supply supports 'zombie lending' to unviable borrowers.

For years levels of non-performing loans have remained at alarmingly high levels in some of the economically most vulnerable Eurozone countries. By mid-2017, for instance, they stood at 15.5 per cent in Portugal, 16.4 per cent in Italy, 36.4 per cent in Greece and 45.3 per cent in Cyprus.[74] As a comparison, at the peak of the subprime crisis in the USA, when almost one in four American homeowners with mortgages had a negative equity, i.e. owed more on their mortgage than the mortgaged house was worth, the ratio of non-performing loans was 5 per cent, to subsequently slide down to only 1.1 per cent seven years later (at the end of June 2017).

In Europe, high levels of non-performing loans are not restricted to the Eurozone only.[75] Furthermore, there are exceptions to the rule that high levels of non-performing loans inevitably inhibit economic growth.[76] But the negative experiences of Japan, where delays in redeeming the problem in the 1990s dragged down the economy,[77] and the positive example of Spain, where the problem was resolutely addressed in 2012/2013, boosting economic growth,[78] highlight the significance of this legacy problem.

There is a broad consensus that addressing it is both possible and necessary.[79] This matters a great deal, because no economist would now

[74] International Monetary Fund, Nonperforming Loans to Total Gross Loans, Financial Soundness Indicators, available from data.imf.org.

[75] In Bulgaria and Croatia, for instance, non-performing loans also stand at high levels: 12.4 per cent and 13.0 per cent (2017, Q2).

[76] In Ireland non-performing loans were at 11.9 per cent in Q2 of 2017, despite the economy growing fast.

[77] Yoichi Matsubayashi, 'The Effort to Stabilise the Financial System in Japan: An Outline and the Characteristics of the Programme for Financial Revival', *Bruegel Working Paper* No. 2015/02, 18 March 2015, available at bruegel.org/2015/03/the-effort-to-stabilise-the-financial-system-in-japan-an-outline-and-the-characteristics-of-the-programme-for-financial-revival/; Christopher Gandrud and Mark Hallerberg, 'How Not to Create Zombie Banks: Lessons for Italy from Japan', *Bruegel Policy Contribution* No. 6/2017, 8 March 2017, available at bruegel.org/2017/03/how-not-to-create-zombie-banks-lessons-for-italy-from-japan/.

[78] Alexander Lehmann, 'Credit Recovery in Spain: NPL Resolution Was Essential, but Success Depended on Broader Sector Reform', *Bruegel Blog Post*, 21 November 2016, available at bruegel.org/2016/11/credit-recovery-in-spain-npl-resolution-was-essential-but-success-depended-on-broader-sector-reform/ sets it against a broader context.

[79] For recent broader analyses, including methods of dealing with legacy assets – such as non-performing loans – under the resolution framework now in place see: Daniel Gros and Willem Pieter de Groen, 'A Radical Cure for Italy's Banking Problems: A

challenge the finding that early and resolute bank recapitalisations substantially shorten recoveries after financial crises and render them more durable.[80] Yet the process is also politically unpalatable, because it entails costs both for borrowers and, especially, for lenders.

Under higher official interest rates non-performing loans would be more difficult to hide: zombie borrowers would find it less easy to pay even the interest necessary to roll over their loans. But it is much easier to do so when credit is extremely cheap. The TLTROs and the negative interest rates in fact encouraged banks to perpetuate this dysfunctionality. Researchers of a Brussels think tank concluded that the 'cash for loans' subsidy inherent in the TLTROs announced in March 2016 can cost the ECB as much as €24 billion, and that it is likely to be counterproductive.[81] First, it would go largely to the banks expected to enhance lending anyway. And second, as with the extraordinary profits derived by financial institutions from the carry trade enabled by the VLTROs in the first half of 2012, this subsidy, too, helps otherwise non-viable institutions stay afloat, delaying their restructuring.

On the other hand, the restructuring of banking sectors in countries with precarious economic fundamentals and treacherous fiscal outlook is very difficult. This fact remains much more important in practice than the European legislation allowing for an orderly

Combination of Good Banks and Soft Bail-In', *CEPS Policy Brief* No. 351, December 2016, available at www.ceps.eu/publications/radical-cure-italy's-banking-problems-combination-good-banks-and-soft-bail; 'Resolving Europe's NPL Burden: Challenges and Benefits', keynote speech by Vítor Constâncio, Vice-President of the ECB, at Bruegel event: 'Tackling Europe's Nonperforming Loans Crisis: Restructuring Debt, Reviving Growth', Brussels, 3 February 2017, available at bruegel.org/2017/02/resolving-europes-npl-burden-challenges-and-benefits/; Willem Pieter de Groen, 'Carving Out Legacy Assets: A Successful Tool for Bank Restructuring?', *In-Depth Analysis for the European Parliament*, March 2017, available at www.europarl.europa.eu/RegData/etudes/IDAN/2017/587398/IPOL_IDA(2017)587398_EN.pdf or Alexander Lehmann, 'Carving Out Legacy Assets: A Successful Tool for Bank Restructuring?', *Bruegel Policy Contribution* No. 9/2017, available at bruegel.org/wp-content/uploads/2017/03/PC-09-2017-NPL-29317.pdf; Maria Demertzis and Alex Lehmann, 'Tackling Europe's Crisis Legacy: A Comprehensive Strategy for Bad Loans and Debt Restructuring', *Bruegel Policy Contribution* No. 11/2017, 21 April 2017, available at bruegel.org/2017/04/tackling-europes-crisis-legacy-a-comprehensive-strategy-for-bad-loans-and-debt-restructuring/.

[80] Timotej Homar and Sweder van Wijnbergen, 'Bank Recapitalisation and Economic Recovery after Financial Crises', *VOX CEPR's Policy Portal*, 13 February 2016, available at voxeu.org/article/bank-recapitalisation-and-economic-recovery-after-financial-crises.

[81] Daniel Gros, Diego Valiante and Willem Pieter de Groen, 'The ECB's Latest Gimmick. Cash for Loans', *CEPS Policy Brief* No. 341, March 2016, available at www.ceps.eu/system/files/ECBLoanSubsidies.pdf.

resolution of financial institutions[82] (or new legal frameworks of insolvency[83]). The standard official storyline has it that this legislation should protect taxpayers from public bailouts of financial institutions, akin to the Irish scheme introduced in the aftermath of the 2008 financial crisis, because now the restructuring would follow the bail-in principle, with equity-holders and uninsured bank creditors taking the brunt of the costs.[84] And the Single Resolution Board, established at the heart of the new institutional setup for bank resolution, would make sure the process is efficient and unbiased.

The reality, however, has not necessarily corroborated this picture. Italy in particular is a case in point. Throughout the sovereign debt crisis the pile of non-performing loans grew unrecognised in the Italian banking system, corroding its profitability and contributing to the misallocation of credit. Italian banks performed poorly in stress tests undertaken by the ECB in the run-up to its taking control of prudential supervision in the Eurozone in late 2014.[85] Because the situation hardly improved in the following months, in early 2016 the ECB, acting in its supervisory function,[86] announced a capital call, which in turn prompted the government to negotiate with some of its strongest banks a private backstop fund, worth €5 billion, to bail

[82] Directive 2014/59/EU of the European Parliament and of the Council of 15 May 2014 establishing a framework for the recovery and resolution of credit institutions and investment firms and amending Council Directive 82/891/EEC, and Directives 2001/24/EC, 2002/47/EC, 2004/25/EC, 2005/56/EC, 2007/36/EC, 2011/35/EU, 2012/30/EU and 2013/36/EU, and Regulations No. 1093/2010 and No. 648/2012, of the European Parliament and of the Council, OJ 2014 No. L 173, 12 June 2014, pp. 190–348.

[83] Proposal for a directive of the European Parliament and of the Council on preventive restructuring frameworks, second chance and measures to increase the efficiency of restructuring, insolvency and discharge procedures and amending Directive 2012/30/EU, COM(2016)723.

[84] For an insightful analysis of the complexities involved see Stefano Micossi, Ginevra Bruzzone and Miriam Cassella, 'Fine-tuning the Use of Bail-in to Promote a Stronger EU Financial System', *CEPS Special Report* No. 136, 21 April 2016, available at www.ceps.eu/publications/fine-tuning-use-bail-promote-stronger-eu-financial-system.

[85] There were nine Italian banks among the Eurozone banks that failed the stress tests: European Central Bank, 'Aggregate Report on the Comprehensive Assessment', October 2014, available at www.ecb.europa.eu/pub/pdf/other/aggregatereportonthecomprehensiveassessment201410.en.pdf.

[86] Art. 16(2)(a) Council Regulation 1024/2013 of 15 October 2013 conferring specific tasks on the European Central Bank concerning policies relating to the prudential supervision of credit institutions, OJ 2013 No. L 287/63 29 October 2013, empowers the ECB to require banks to hold own funds (so-called Pillar 2 capital) in excess of basic capital requirements (i.e., the Common Equity Tier 1 ratio).

out the weakest Italian lenders. The fund, Atlante, was set up in April 2016. When the deal was struck, the markets heaved a sigh of relief. But, soon after, market jitters returned, forcing the Italian government to set up, in December 2016, an additional €20 billion fund to buttress the troubled banks.[87] A few months later almost all of its resources were depleted to facilitate the liquidation of two Veneto banks.[88] This happened without causing the Single Resolution Board to contemplate a resolution scheme, because, according to the rules now in place, the board does not act, even if a bank 'is failing or is likely to fail', as long as there is 'reasonable prospect that any alternative private sector measures ... would prevent its failure within a reasonable timeframe' and/or a resolution action is not 'necessary in the public interest'.[89]

Since this point in time it has been perfectly clear that the banking resolution rules designed in the aftermath of the sovereign debt crisis and intended to avoid the socialisation of the banking losses are very easy to flout. It has been also clear that the Italian banking sector is yet another serious drag on the Italian public finances.

4.12 TARGET 2 and the Search for a Monetary Equilibrium

Arguably nothing in the debate on the Eurozone's monetary policy has stirred more emotions on the side of both supporters of the ECB's stance and its detractors than the devilishly obscure TARGET balances.

[87] Giovanni Legorano, 'Italy Sets Up Fund to Help Troubled Banks', *Wall Street Journal*, 23 December 2016, available at www.wsj.com/articles/italy-sets-up-fund-to-help-troubled-banks-1482458087.

[88] Sonia Sirletti and Alexander Weber, 'Italy Commits $19 Billion for Veneto Banks in Biggest Rescue', 25 June 2017, available at www.bloomberg.com/news/articles/2017-06-25/italy-mobilizes-up-to-19-billion-to-keep-veneto-banks-afloat.

[89] Art. 18(1)(b) and (c) Regulation 806/2014 of the European Parliament and of the Council of 15 July 2014 establishing uniform rules and a uniform procedure for the resolution of credit institutions and certain investment firms in the framework of a Single Resolution Mechanism and a Single Resolution Fund and amending Regulation 1093/2010, OJ 2014 No. L 225, 30 July 2014, pp. 1–90. In response to the Italian decision to use public resources in the process of liquidating the Veneto banks in June 2017, the SRB stated that 'following today's decision taken by the European Central Bank to declare Banca Popolare di Vicenza S.p.A. and Veneto Banca S.p.A. as "failing or likely to fail" ... the SRB has today concluded that for these two banks, resolution action is not warranted in the public interest': Single Resolution Board, 'The SRB Will Not Take Resolution Action in Relation to Banca Popolare di Vicenza and Veneto Banca', 23 June 2017, available at srb.europa.eu/en/node/341.

The acronym TARGET stands for Trans-European Automated Real-Time Gross settlement Express Transfer. It is a settlement tool owned and operated by the Eurosystem (since 2007 the second generation of it – TARGET2 – has been in use) for cross-border payments; a technical backbone allowing a financial institution in one country to execute money transfers with a financial institution in another country that uses the TARGET system. Because payment systems are inherently neutral from the economic perspective, for a long time payment balances envisaged by TARGET accounts remained below the radar of monetary policymakers. During the sovereign debt crisis, however, the situation changed, because when payments between financial institutions transacting through the system become systemically skewed – in particular due to lopsided current account payments (payments for imported/exported goods or services), or as a result of a capital flight to safety – this device may induce systemic consequences far beyond its original technical function.

These consequences are as counterintuitive as the nature of the fiat money. When, for whatever reason and on the basis of whatever legal title, holders of accounts in a commercial credit institution (a sending bank) want to exact a money transfer to a bank account in another Eurozone country (a receiving bank), no actual movement of money is induced. Instead, the paying bank requests its central bank to execute the payment order with the central bank of the receiving bank. The latter then credits the receiving bank to the amount of the money transferred. The whole process occurs automatically. As its flipside, the receiving bank (say, in Germany) obtains a claim towards its central bank, which acquires a claim on the Eurosystem. Simultaneously, the Eurosystem obtains a claim on the central bank of the sending bank and by the same token this central bank now has a claim on the sending bank. The payment is settled merely by shifting claims and liabilities in the banking payments system.

The participation of central banks in this chain is important, because they generate claims and corresponding liabilities towards the Eurosystem mirroring the transactions recorded in accounting books of the respective commercial banks. It is also understandable, considering that the money transfer occurs in the currency generated by the Eurosystem. In some federal monetary regimes, the United States in particular, in which the equivalent of the Eurosystem comprises private banks, accounts between the equivalents of the Eurozone's central banks are settled annually: the banks with liabilities transfer ownership of certain assets to creditor banks.[90] In the Eurozone, arguably in order to achieve the Treaty objective of promoting 'the smooth operation of payment systems',[91] no similar periodical settlement process has been designed. After all, under the assumption that the monetary policy is separate from fiscal and economic policies, central banks should not be preoccupied with preventing economic imbalances from occurring, even when the imbalances trigger a systemic outflow of money from one jurisdiction to another.

In addition, as long as the Eurozone's composition is intact, even serious TARGET liabilities of some central banks towards the Eurosystem should not be particularly disturbing, because payment orders triggering capital outflows to other Eurozone countries cannot cause any shortage of liquidity in the jurisdiction of the sending bank. Its central bank makes sure of it, providing the national banking system with corresponding refinancing credit (freshly created central bank money). On the other hand, in the jurisdiction of the receiving bank the fact that TARGET balances are not settled regularly allows for an influx of payments that otherwise would be prevented by the inability of sending banks in other jurisdictions to receive necessary credit from their central banks.

Without, however, periodic settlements in the Eurosystem, TARGET imbalances between the central banks raise the question of whether those among them which amass particularly high amounts of liabilities are still viable. If the assets they possess (securities or foreign exchange reserves) do not match in quality the liabilities, then, in the event that their country leaves the Eurozone, they might find it impossible to redeem the TARGET liabilities, which would immediately come due in this scenario. Countries of the central banks previously amassing corresponding claims towards the Eurosystem would go empty-handed,

[90] The US equivalent of TARGET2 is called Interdistrict Settlement Account of the Federal Reserve. For a broader comparison with the TARGET2 system, see esp. Hans-Werner Sinn, *The Euro Trap: On Bursting Bubbles, Budgets, and Beliefs* (Oxford: Oxford University Press, 2014): esp. 246–251. In the aftermath of the Great Recession, ISA settlements have been disrupted, however, leading to mounting imbalances resembling those in the TARGET2 system. See Michiel Bijlsma and Jasper Lukkezen, 'TARGET 2 of the ECB vs. Interdistrict Settlement Account of the Federal Reserve', *Bruegel Blog Post*, 6 March 2012, available at bruegel.org/2012/03/target-2-of-the-ecb-vs-interdistrict-settlement-account-of-the-federal-reserve/.

[91] Art. 127(2) TFEU and Art. 3(1) of the Statute of the ESCB and the ECB.

in the proportion in which the liabilities of the central banks leaving the Eurozone remain unsettled.

When TARGET imbalances surge because the systemic outflow of deposits from a country is a reaction to a materialising danger that the country would leave the Eurozone, policymakers can tackle them by convincing markets that the disintegration scenario will be prevented. This is what President Draghi did with his 'whatever it takes' pledge, and what the ECB echoed in the statements like this one: 'The size of the TARGET balances does not pose additional risk to the Eurosystem or the NCBs given the irreversibility of the euro and the integrity of the Eurosystem.'[92]

To succeed, however, this strategy requires a unison action of national politicians in charge of economic policies in the countries experiencing payment outflows. They ought to goad the money back to bank accounts in their jurisdictions by convincing economic agents that the national economy can manage the participation in the monetary union. Only then can the TARGET rebalancing process be sustainable on a lasting basis.

In mid-2012, the ECB succeeded in accomplishing its part of the task. With the government of Mariano Rajoy in Spain committed to internal devaluation and to cleaning up its banking system, as well as with the technocratic Monti government in Italy, the second prong of the strategy seemed to have been sufficiently reliable as well. The simultaneously emerging banking union was promising a healthy financial foundation of the economic recovery in the crisis-stricken countries. In consequence, TARGET imbalances gradually went down during the next two years. At their apex (August 2012), TARGET claims of the German Bundesbank stood at €751.4 billion, while those of the Dutch central bank equalled €125.0 billion.[93] Liabilities of the Spanish and Italian central banks amounted to €434.4 billion and €289.3 billion, respectively. Two years later (July 2014) the balances dwindled to €443.5 billion of Bundesbank claims, €1.7 billion of De Nederlandsche Bank claims, €216.4 billion of Banco de España liabilities and €130.3 billion of Banca d'Italia liabilities.

Then, however, shortly before the ECB activated the first two elements of the APP (CBPP3 in October 2014 and ABSPP a month later), the

92 European Central Bank, Monthly Bulletin May 2013, 112, available at www.ecb.europa.eu/pub/pdf/mobu/mb201305en.pdf.

93 All data of Statistical Data Warehouse, TARGET balances, available from sdw.ecb.europa.eu.

imbalances started growing again. The process has accelerated since May 2015 – two months after the ECB launched the PSPP. In April 2015, Spanish TARGET liabilities were at their low ebb of €207.4 billion and next month Portuguese liabilities reached their lowest level of €55.7 billion. Then they rebounded and gradually deteriorated again. In consequence, by September 2017 (the last month for which data was available when these words were put down) Germany and Luxembourg stockpiled a daunting €878.9 billion and €190.3 billion of TARGET claims, respectively, while Italy, Spain and Portugal garnered €432.5 billion, €373.4 billion and €76.8 billion of liabilities, respectively. At the same time, TARGET liabilities of the ECB itself towards the Eurosystem gradually rose to €215.3 billion, contributing to the huge imbalances.

Causalities behind this trend are unobvious. Certainly, however, the direction of the flows gauges the credibility of individual economies and the magnitude of the imbalances depicts the credibility of the Eurozone as a whole. The relationship between the timing of APP purchases and TARGET imbalances also does not seem to be random: the liquidity released due to the PSPP greatly facilitated the imbalances. The specific Greek example confirms this point. Because Greece has not participated in the PSPP since its inception, its banking system has not benefitted from the corresponding additional refinancing credit. And, although its bank account holders have had strong incentives to transfer money out of the country, TARGET balances have in fact followed the opposite trend, with liabilities of the Bank of Greece diminishing gradually since their apex in summer 2015.

Regardless of the exact causalities, TARGET imbalances reflect fundamental divergences between Eurozone countries, to which economic agents respond. On the one hand, the APP conceals the imbalances: massive purchases of sovereign debt stave off the danger of yet another sovereign debt crisis, while the mechanics of the Eurozone payment system camouflages the balance-of-payments crisis continuously experienced by much of the Eurozone's south. On the other, the quantitative easing programme amplifies the divergences, because it allows to redirect the credit pumped into the banking systems of the crisis-stricken countries towards other jurisdictions, especially Germany and Luxembourg, where it additionally stimulates the real economy, contributing to the overall macroeconomic imbalances.

None of it, however, has made the Eurozone more stable. As I mentioned earlier, the monetary painkiller can give national policymakers time to uproot the soft currency syndrome traditionally prevailing in certain Eurozone economies, societies and political systems. But when its roots reach very deeply in the collective consciousness of the local societies, the painkiller can only delay the inevitable. It cannot prevent future bouts of the mismatch between the monetary system and the nature of the local societies, economies and politics. Smart money knows that as the mismatch grows, the bouts will be all the more painful for the patient. And one of them may be terminal.

This finding reaffirms the point made earlier. When political discrepancies at national levels propel economic divergences, it becomes all too clear that the ECB can only provide quick fixes preventing the Eurozone from an immediate collapse. But it cannot guarantee irreversibility of the euro. It cannot force the traditional soft currency regimes to become economically, socially and politically fit for the necessities of a hard currency regime, nor can it change the nature of the export-driven, strong currency economies. Most perplexingly, its fixes allow national economies (and their politicians) to deny this and delay systemic adjustments. When in the 1970s Italy and Portugal received loans from the Bundesbank, they had to put up their gold reserves as collateral.[94] This, of course, had serious disciplining consequences. But when the Italian, Spanish and Portuguese central banks, on the one hand, draw in very significant amounts of sovereign bonds, making their burden much less onerous for the governments, and, on the other, redeem the economies of the consequences of a capital flight, the pressure on national politicians to take any resolute actions seriously flattens. The politicians also have a motive to cater for moral hazard, because any ultimate failure in preventing the divergences from getting out of hand would be (at least partly) socialised within the Eurosystem.

The monetary policy of the ECB, intended to reset the Eurozone into a good equilibrium, becomes self-defeating in this setup. The Bank for International Settlements saw through it in a 2013 report, warning that 'continued low interest rates and unconventional policies have made it easy for the private sector to postpone deleveraging, easy for the government to finance deficits, and easy for the authorities to delay

[94] Ansgar Belke, 'Gold-Backed Sovereign Bonds: An Effective Alternative to OMTs', in: *Financial Crises, Sovereign Risk and the Role of Institutions*, eds. Dominik Maltritz and Michael Berlemann (Cham: Springer, 2014): 11.

needed reforms in the real economy and in the financial system. After all, cheap money makes it easier to borrow than to save, easier to spend than to tax, easier to remain the same than to change.'[95]

Ultimately, therefore, the quick fixes have perpetuated the imbalanced nature of the Eurozone, contributing to its centrifugal processes while at the same time concealing them. Economic agents in the countries on the downside of the process, sensing that unconventional policies of the ECB cannot secure irreversibility of the euro, rationally flee for safety in such a situation, no matter how much their actions amplify financial imbalances. The clearer the process becomes to market players, the higher the imbalances and the more incredible assertions of the ECB alleging the singleness of the Eurozone. The panic may be delayed by policymakers and pundits arguing that the current equilibrium is good and stable. It can be deferred by elections bringing to power politicians committed to do 'whatever it takes' to maintain the Eurozone for its symbolic significance. But, in fact, mounting TARGET imbalances should instead be understood as a subcutaneous process of pushing the Eurozone economies away from the current equilibrium, in which a large proportion of Eurozone economies live in a system that is too rigid, too daunting for their social and political tissue. Without the TARGET system the search for a new equilibrium would soon translate into a currency crisis. With this system it manifests itself by growing TARGET imbalances. Because, however, the causes of the imbalances have not been eradicated and because they reach much deeper than the ECB could hope, the current equilibrium is unstable. In the longer perspective, therefore, the one economic arrow the institutionally lonely[96] ECB can use mounts the costs accompanying the ultimate shift towards a new economic equilibrium. In this equilibrium, traditionally hard currency societies and economies use a strong currency and those unaccustomed to its straightjacket adopt currencies more congruent with the nature of their economic, social and political realities.

[95] Bank for International Settlements, '83rd Annual Report', 23 June 2013, 5, available at www.bis.org/publ/arpdf/ar2013e.pdf.

[96] Back in 2000, Tommaso Padoa-Schioppa, then a member of the Executive Board of the European Central Bank, argued that 'since the strength of a currency – and the public's confidence in it – is closely related to the political structure that supports it, the current imbalance and the Eurosystem's "institutional loneliness" will need to be addressed': Tommaso Padoa-Schioppa, 'An Institutional Glossary of the Eurosystem', prepared for the conference on 'The Constitution of the Eurosystem: The Views of

4.13 Who Pays the Piper Calls the Tune

The alternative equilibrium of a redomination in the Eurozone countries most unaccustomed to the various constraints imposed by the monetary union has been perceived by European and national policymakers as the worst-case scenario for the European integrity. The transmutation of government debt into economic propulsion of central bank money can stave off this scenario for some time. With interest rates at the zero lower bound the ECB can continue its monetary alchemy even when inflation exceeds its stated goal. Instead of ending the programme, the Franfurt bank could raise interest rates while maintaining bond purchases within the PSPP. It may be all the more tempted to do so by the fact that if the miraculous propulsion of the quantitative easing stops, unsound foundations of economic prosperity in some Eurozone countries will be much more difficult to hide.

At some point, however, the programme will have to end simply because the debt of more reliable sovereigns will become increasingly scarce. If financial markets factor it in their decisions, capital flight for safety from the periphery is likely to intensify, triggering yet another confluence of balance-of-payments and banking crises.

It can be argued that now the ECB is largely prepared for this scenario. Acting in liaison with the ESM (or its future reincarnation), it is authorized to pacify financial markets by actvating the OMT programme. Then the Eurosystem would soak up toxic government debt, replacing it again with an adrenaline shot of central bank liquidity released to the banking system of the beleaguered country. Because, however, the OMT programme can only be activated in exchange for strict conditionality, and because it ought to be funded by the digital printing presses of the ECB, the Franfurt institution would inevitably become the dominating member of any Troika or Quadriga convened to oversee the reforms imposed on the society on the ground. The key political role of the Eurozone's central bank throughout an OMT programme would only be amplified by its LoLR status for each Eurozone national domestic banking system. Some European nations will then be required to accept macroeconomic and social recipes administered by a technocratic, countermajoritarian institution operating from Frankfurt, Germany, which by then may be governed by a

the EP and the ECB', 8 March 2000, available at www.ecb.europa.eu/press/key/date/2000/html/sp000308_1.en.html.

German central banker. It is naïve to believe that in any such a situation a macroeconomic adjustment, whether properly designed by international technocrats or not, would enjoy legitimacy necessary to make the preordained reforms sustainable. And by pursuing the alternative route of issuing blanque cheques to governments failing to adjust national economies to high competitive demands of a monetary union, the ECB would gradually undermine its credibility. At some point it is therefore most likely to be squeezed between its pledge to do whatever it takes to preserve the euro and the necessity to maintain its monetary credibility. That way or another, however, the time of miracles is bound to end at some point.

5 Shock Absorbers

5.1 Naked and Barefoot

My argument in the previous chapters has time and again returned to the point that to some Eurozone countries the single currency has become too heavy a burden and that various preventive and rescue actions of European institutions have not been able to reduce serious economic, political and social divergences undermining the stability of the euro-experiment. A critic of this narrative may retort, however, that it misses a very important aspect of the Eurozone's imbalances, ostensibly vitiating my whole argument. Namely, successful monetary unions do not prosper because their components preach to any unavoidable economic model of a well-performing economy (say Germany or the Netherlands in Europe, or New England in the USA, or Alberta in Canada) towards which the remaining parts converge, or from which they secede if they are unable to achieve the necessary convergence. Just like in the Eurozone, there is a lot of specialisation and competition between regions and states in any contemporary federal structure sharing the same currency. As an upshot, in any federal state some regions boom when others struggle with recessions. In none can a single region smooth its cyclical swings by automatic monetary (nominal exchange-rate) adjustments, because this privilege is reserved for monetary sovereigns only.[1] And yet regions are not expelled from federal states when they face an economic downside. Instead, fully fledged federations have developed various methods of buffering asymmetric (region-specific) shocks by central governments and by the financial system.

[1] For a classical account, see Milton Friedman, 'The Case for Flexible Exchange Rates', in: *Essays in Positive Economics* (Chicago: University of Chicago Press, 1953): 157–203.

The Eurozone has had none of these buffers, which proved fatal when the introduction of the euro first ushered in a period of extraordinary, and unsustainable, boom in the Eurozone's periphery, which then turned into an extraordinary bust. The Eurozone's periphery has therefore suffered from excessively amplified business cycle fluctuations, which have gone unaddressed at the central level.[2]

It can be argued further that, more ominously still, European policymakers actively encouraged procyclical policies in the downturn. When the Eurozone's periphery experienced demand shocks, first due to the global financial crisis in 2008 and then as a consequence of financial sudden stops in 2010–2011,[3] fiscal automatic stabilisers – unemployment benefits and social assistance in particular – were set in motion. In other words, when its economies faced negative shocks to gross incomes back in 2008, government transfers to the unemployed accelerated and tax revenues decreased, cushioning declines in disposable incomes. But when the sovereign debt crisis billowed out, the reverse gear of fiscal austerity was taken in an attempt to soothe financial markets and facilitate internal devaluation. In consequence, national fiscal policies have striven to cushion and amplify the swing in the business cycle at the same time. The only clear exception to this rule was Germany, where a contractionary fiscal policy (shunning budget deficits in an expansion) during the sovereign debt crisis was well justified by the basic logic of macroeconomic stabilisation, for its economy was booming.[4] The situation in which all but one country of a monetary union ran quite schizophrenic, largely procyclical, policies was fiscally and socially damaging especially in the Member States where the crisis was caused by business cycle fluctuations (Spain and Ireland in particular). While the magnitude of the upswing in the pre-crisis period brought public finances of these countries to very comfortable areas, the free fall that followed questioned their very debt sustainability. The cyclical rollercoaster experienced by other peripheral states (Greece, Italy and Portugal) might not have been comparably neck-breaking.

[2] Céline Allard et al., 'Toward a Fiscal Union for the Euro Area', *IMF Staff Discussion Note*, September 2013, available at www.imf.org/external/pubs/ft/sdn/2013/sdn1309.pdf; Paul De Grauwe and Yuemei Ji, 'Flexibility versus Stability. A Difficult Trade-Off in the Eurozone', *CEPS Working Document* No. 422, 29 April 2016, available at www.ceps.eu/publications/flexibility-versus-stability-difficult-trade-eurozone.

[3] Silvia Merler and Jean Pisani-Ferry, 'Sudden Stops in the Euro Area', *Bruegel Policy Contribution* No. 2012/06, 29 March 2012, available at bruegel.org/2012/03/sudden-stops-in-the-euro-area-2/.

[4] De Grauwe and Ji, 'Flexibility versus Stability'.

But fiscally they were in a much worse situation at the beginning of the adjustment process, which also pressurised their governments to implement procyclical policies in the downturn. This in turn prevented stabilisers from achieving what they were designed for.

All in all, according to this argument the Eurozone's plight does not really stem from its current composition. Rather, it has been bred by its original incomplete design, which deprived it of the basic features every successful monetary union possesses to cushion idiosyncratic shocks.

Many – especially outside the Eurozone – saw it early on. The British economist (and notorious pessimist) Wynne Godley wrote as early as 1992:

> [I]f a country or region has no power to devalue, and if it is not the beneficiary of a system of fiscal equalisation, then there is nothing to stop it suffering a process of cumulative and terminal decline leading, in the end, to emigration as the only alternative to poverty or starvation. I sympathise with the position of those (like Margaret Thatcher) who, faced with the loss of sovereignty, wish to get off the EMU train altogether. I also sympathise with those who seek integration under the jurisdiction of some kind of federal constitution with a federal budget very much larger than that of the Community budget.[5]

Simultaneously, senior experts of the Commission were making (even if much more cautiously) a case for some insurance scheme which would work as a financial buffer to be activated when a Eurozone country is hit by an asymmetric shock.[6] Even the Commission, in its landmark 1990 study, stated (more cautiously still) that 'if the role of central public finance is enhanced, the structural Funds may improve the adjustment capacity of regions, while – possibly conditional – shock-absorption mechanisms could provide insurance against the remaining burden of shocks'.[7]

[5] Wynne Godley, 'Maastricht and All That', *London Review of Books* 14 (1992): 3–4, available at www.lrb.co.uk/v14/n19/wynne-godley/maastricht-and-all-that.

[6] Alexander Italianer and Jean Pisani-Ferry, 'Systèmes budgétaires et amortissement des chocs régionaux: implications pour l'Union économique et monétaire', *Économie de Prospective Internationale*, n° 51, CEPII, Paris, 3e trimestre 1992; Alexander Italianer and Marc Vanheukelen, 'Proposals for Community Stabilization Mechanisms: Some Historical Applications', in: *The Economics of Community Public Finance*, European Economy No. 5, 1993: 493–510.

[7] European Commission, 'One Market, One Money. An Evaluation of the Potential Benefits and Costs of Forming an Economic and Monetary Union', *European Economy* No. 44, October 1990, 169, available at ec.europa.eu/economy_finance/publications/pages/publication7454_en.pdf.

The underlying argument is simple: in economic bad times, when private spending contracts, the government should stimulate the economy, to avoid a protracted recession. In economic good times the process should be reversed. A reasonable fiscal policy, in other words, ought to go against the current phase of the business cycle all the time, to stabilise the economy when in the opposite phase. To achieve this goal, it must be properly coordinated with monetary policy, which, too, ought to be countercyclical. In consequence, when the monetary function is alleviated to the supranational level, it is also logical that at least some fiscal stabilisation follows there. In economic good times individual regions of the monetary union should thus allocate some of their fiscal resources to a supranational fund, to draw from it on rainy days.

5.2 The Precepts of Fiscal Federalism Against the Lacking Sense of National Solidarity

This very intuitive logic is scientifically anchored in the classical theory of fiscal federalism. This theory is preoccupied with the questions of how to allocate responsibilities for public policies in a multilevel political system and how to adjust fiscal instruments accordingly.[8] It predicts that fiscal responsibilities should be centralised if there are cost savings from the centralisation and if inter-country externalities are present.[9] Macroeconomic stabilisation is one of three most obvious candidate functions for such a centralisation.[10] Wallace Oates, the theory's best-known promoter, explained that 'in the absence of monetary and exchange-rate prerogatives and with highly open economies that cannot contain much of the expansionary impact of fiscal stimuli, provincial, state, and local governments simply have very limited means for traditional macroeconomic control'.[11] This observation dovetails with the arguments stemming from the theory of optimum currency areas, especially in the form developed by Peter Kenen half a century

[8] Richard Musgrave, *The Theory of Public Finance: A Study in Public Economy* (New York: McGraw Hill, 1959); Wallace E. Oates, *Fiscal Federalism* (New York: Harcourt Brace Jovanovich, 1972).

[9] Oates, *Fiscal Federalism*; Wallace E. Oates, 'An Essay on Fiscal Federalism', *Journal of Economic Literature* 37 (1999): 1120–1149; Wallace E. Oates, 'On the Theory and Practice of Fiscal Decentralization', *IFIR Working Paper* No. 2006-05, May 2006.

[10] The other two are assistance to the poor, i.e., income redistribution, and provision of certain common public goods – national defence most obviously.

[11] Oates, 'An Essay on Fiscal Federalism', 1121.

ago.[12] According to it, a single currency area will not function properly without some form of fiscal equalisation, even if other basic conditions for labelling it 'optimum' (factor mobility, labour mobility, economic openness)[13] are fulfilled.

Experiences of successful monetary unions have corroborated these theoretical predictions. Barry Eichengreen wrote in a paper published in 1991 that 'a popular explanation for the tolerance in currency areas like the U.S. and Canada of region-specific shocks is that their federal fiscal systems provide regional insurance. If incomes in a U.S. state decline by $1, federal tax payments by residents of that state decline by 30 cents, while transfers from Washington, D.C., mostly in the form of federally-funded unemployment benefits, rise by 10 cents … Insofar as the locus of regional shocks shifts over time, all regions are rendered better off by risk sharing achieved via the federal fiscal system.'[14] This remains in stark contrast with the situation in the Eurozone. Writing more than twenty years later IMF economists emphasised that 'while almost 70 percent of shocks to GDP is not smoothed in euro area countries, the share of unsmoothed shocks is only about 25 percent for the U.S. and 20 percent for Germany'.[15]

Why, therefore, was a monetary union without necessary stabilisation functions introduced in Europe in the first place and what does the answer tell us about its destiny? It is worth quoting the Delors Report again to grasp the main reason. It famously highlighted that 'in all federations the different combinations of federal budgetary mechanisms have powerful "shock-absorber" effects dampening the amplitude either of economic difficulties or of surges in prosperity of individual states. This is both *the product of and the source of the sense of national solidarity* which all relevant economic and monetary unions share' (my emphasis).[16] In 1989, as well as in subsequent decades, this

[12] Peter Kenen, 'The Theory of Optimum Currency Areas: An Eclectic View', in: *Monetary Problems of the International Economy*, eds. Robert Mundell and Alexander Swoboda (Chicago: University of Chicago Press, 1969): 41–60.

[13] Robert Mundell, 'A Theory of Optimum Currency Areas', *American Economic Review* 51 (1961): 509–517, Ronald McKinnon, 'Optimum Currency Areas', *American Economic Review* 53 (1963): 717–724.

[14] Barry Eichengreen, 'Is Europe an Optimum Currency Area?', *NBER Working Paper* No. 3579, January 1991, 16–17.

[15] Davide Furceri and Aleksandra Zdzienicka, 'The Euro Area Crisis: Need for a Supranational Fiscal Risk Sharing Mechanism?', *IMF Working Paper* No. WP/13/198, September 2013, 9, available at www.imf.org/external/pubs/ft/wp/2013/wp13198.pdf.

[16] Jacques Delors, 'Regional Implications of Economic and Monetary Integration', in: *Report on Economic and Monetary Union in the European Community. Collection of Papers Submitted to the Committee for the Study of Economic and Monetary Union*, ed. Committee for

'sense of national solidarity' necessary to set up shock absorbers at the European level was absent. In 2010, the consequences of this systemic incompleteness have become painfully clear. Yet, simultaneously, the 'senses of national solidarity' started colliding with one another in a mutually reinforcing process, in which the more it was clear that the shock absorbers were needed, the more improbable their development was becoming.

5.3 From High Hopes to Reflection

Earlier on – throughout the 1970s and during most of the 1980s – the lacking European 'sense of national solidarity' swayed mainstream economic thinking against the feasibility of any actual monetary union in Europe. It was reckoned that without non-trivial supranational fiscal equalisation, entirely precluded both then and now, some of basic conditions for a successful monetary union would be absent. But the neo-liberal thinking, maturing in the years preceding the Maastricht process, questioned the role of fiscal shock absorption, eliminating the conceptual constraints previously deterring European leaders from pursuing a 'naked' monetary union.

First, the backfiring attempts to stabilise the down-sliding economies in the 1970s by fiscal stimulation made many economists suspicious of active fiscal policies. Already in the 1970s the so-called MacDougall Report paid attention to this shift, arguing that 'member states have in recent years experienced difficulties in keeping Keynesian deficit financing under control; it would seem inopportune to propose that a new tier of government be given by design an unprecedently wide potential margin of contra-cyclical budgetary imbalance.'[17] As I mentioned in Chapter 3, growing literature published at the time suggested that fiscal multipliers in industrial economies are small. By the same token, attempts to stimulate the economy fiscally in downturns of the business cycle would certainly push up inflation and public debt.

the Study of Economic and Monetary Union, 1989, 89, available at aei.pitt.edu/1008/1/monetary_delors_collected_papers.pdf.

[17] Commission of the European Communities, 'Report of the Study Group on the Role of Public Finance in European Integration', 1 (1977), April 1977, 58, available at ec.europa.eu/archives/emu_history/documentation/chapter8/19770401en73macdougallrepvol1.pdf. On the other hand, only one page earlier the Report indicated that 'Community fiscal stabilisation policy is a key element in any programme for European monetary integration' (p. 57).

But the maturing theory and practical experiences had it that positive effects of such attempts for output would be very illusory.[18] Rather than trying to smooth the downturns through fiscal equalisation, the thinking reigning the day implied that governments should avoid cyclical downturns by performing conservative fiscal policies during economic good times and by improving structural resilience and robustness (flexibility) of the economy. Furthermore, as I discussed more broadly in Chapter 1, the EMU was believed to propel macroeconomic convergence. It was therefore hoped that asymmetric shocks – the events otherwise justifying fiscal equalisation – would gradually wane. All in all, the drafters of the Eurozone reckoned that in a system in which the monetary policy is calibrated towards price stability and the fiscal policy is passive, the cycle should not fluctuate more than the fiscal leeway within the SGP allows for.

Furthermore, the theory of fiscal federalism, as the earlier quote from Oates corroborates, was preoccupied with 'highly open economies'. Also, Kenen's work referred to the specific situation in which basic conditions for an optimum currency area (labour mobility and flexibility of prices and wages in particular) were fulfilled. None of this fit the EEC of the late 1980s. Already in 1977, the MacDougall report stressed it, in the context of permanent fiscal equalisation (supranational transfers going beyond temporary shock absorption), in the following manner: 'The case … for discharging the … function at the "top" level of government depends essentially on a high level of geographic mobility of the individual, which is not at present the Community situation.'[19] In other words, because national economies were less interlinked than in theoretical models, spillover effects debilitating national shock absorbers could be less significant than in fully integrated federations. If this had been the case, national fiscal stabilisation should be sufficiently effective, especially as it always

[18] As Palier noted, referring to France, 'at the turn of the 1980s, two French governments – Jacques Chirac's in 1974–1976 and Pierre Mauroy's in 1981–1982 – learned the hard way that the traditional Keynesian chain was broken. In both cases, these governments raised social benefits in order to boost private consumption and economic activity, and both gained only larger public deficits, a negative trade balance, inflation and increases in unemployment and taxation. Henceforth the Keynesian use of social benefits was delegitimized for governments of both Left and Right': Bruno Palier, 'The Dualizations of the French Welfare System', in: *A Long Goodbye to Bismarck?*, ed. B. Palier (Amsterdam: Amsterdam University Press, 2010): 78.

[19] Commission of the European Communities, 'Report of the Study Group', 59.

operates through welfare state policies – the offspring of the national solidarity – in Europe traditionally pursued (and jealously guarded) by national governments.

Finally, the Commission's 1990 'One Market, One Money' report argued that 'in order to minimize the costs of EMU, either the role of central public finance in EMU has to be strengthened or Member States/ regions need to be left with a very high degree of fiscal autonomy'.[20] Formally the SGP, with its stiff budgetary rules and potential sanctions for breaching them, had gone in the other direction. But, as I argued in Chapter 2, in practice it has never seriously limited national fiscal autonomy.[21] The unspoken feature of the original Eurozone's setup provided therefore that, had a major economic crisis occurred, national governments would break the fiscal rules and provide the necessary stabilisation on their own.

All the beliefs collapsed when the sudden stops of international financial flows during the Great Recession made it clear that spillover effects were very strong in the Eurozone, when fiscal multipliers proved to be much higher than previously expected and when national fiscal spaces to buffer these two processes were insufficient to prevent the system from sliding into a sovereign debt crisis. Instead of cushioning any of the processes, the naked monetary union, with its interest rates too low for the booming economies and too high for the countries on the other side of the spectrum, additionally destabilised the currency union.[22] Theories have followed these empirical phenomena, returning to the insight that in an open economy with incomplete markets (imperfectly operating capital markets, low factor mobility, sticky prices and wages), some mechanisms of smoothing private consumption must be introduced to cushion business cycles and to provide demand externalities (social benefits of risk sharing greater than what is appreciated by private economic agents).[23]

[20] European Commission, 'One Market, One Money'.

[21] See also Dariusz Adamski, 'Economic Policy Coordination as a Game Involving Economic Stability and National Sovereignty', *European Law Journal* 22 (2016): 180–203.

[22] See also Paul De Grauwe, 'Design Failures in the Eurozone: Can They Be Fixed?', *LSE Europe in Question Paper Series* No. 57/2013, February 2013, available at www.lse.ac.uk/ europeanInstitute/LEQS%20Discussion%20Paper%20Series/LEQSPaper57.pdf.

[23] Philipp Engler and Simon Voigts, 'A Transfer Mechanism for a Monetary Union', *SFB 649 Discussion Paper* No. 2013-013, 5 March 2013, available at sfb649.wiwi.hu-berlin.de/ papers/pdf/SFB649DP2013-013.pdf; Emmanuel Farhi and Iván Werning, 'Fiscal Unions', July 2014, available at scholar.harvard.edu/files/farhi/files/fiscal-unions_july_2014_0.pdf.

European politicians lurched in the same direction, at least in their declarations, right at the point when they finished overhauling the SGP (otherwise doomed, as explained in Chapter 2). Like their predecessors two decades earlier, decision-makers populating European institutions in 2012 were very aware of the poignant European solidarity problem. They knew that, as long as it persists, the shock-absorption capacity through a mature fiscal equalisation scheme would inevitably require redistribution rejected for political reasons by the societies exposed to its costs. But they were also aware that the Eurozone desperately needed robust shock-absorption mechanisms lest it be exposed to continuous paroxysms of idiosyncratic shocks.

In its communication, published in November 2012, the Commission reiterated the idea expressed in the 1990 'One market, one money' report, arguing that 'a common instrument dedicated to macroeconomic stabilisation could provide an insurance system whereby risks of economic shocks are pooled across member states, thereby reducing the fluctuations in national incomes'.[24] Subsequently, both the Four Presidents' Report (2012) and the Five Presidents' Report (2015) also endorsed the idea, introducing some additional 'guiding principles'.[25] First, the shock-absorption scheme should not, according to these documents, lead to permanent transfers (income equalisation) from some countries to others. It would, therefore, operate as a self-financed insurance, in which payments correspond to ex-ante premiums. Second, and relatedly, it is to avoid moral hazard produced by the awareness that, in the event that risky fiscal and economic policies expose an economy to a shock, external resources will buffer it, rendering national governments less risk-averse and more prone to gaming the system. Third, it ought to be anchored in EU law. In other words, it should not follow the example of major ex post stabilisation mechanisms, like the EFSF and the ESM, based on separate

[24] European Commission, 'Communication: A Blueprint for a Deep and Genuine Economic and Monetary Union. Launching a European Debate', COM(2012)777, 28 November 2012, Sec. 3.3.2, available at http://eur-lex.europa.eu/Lex-UriServ/LexUriServ.do?uri=COM:2012:0777:FIN:EN:PDF.

[25] Herman Van Rompuy, José Manuel Barroso, Jean-Claude Juncker and Mario Draghi, 'Towards a Genuine Economic and Monetary Union', 5 December 2012, 12, available at www.consilium.europa.eu/uedocs/cms_Data/docs/pressdata/en/ec/134069.pdf; Jean-Claude Juncker, Donald Tusk, Jeroen Dijsselbloem, Mario Draghi and Martin Schulz, 'The Five Presidents' Report: Completing Europe's Economic and Monetary Union', 22 June 2015, 15, available at ec.europa.eu/priorities/publications/five-presidents-report-completing-europes-economic-and-monetary-union_en.

international treaties. Fourth, the mechanism was considered to be 'the culmination of a process of convergence and further pooling of decision-making on national budgets'.[26]

The motivations behind the idea of macroeconomic shock absorption and all the above-mentioned conditions are quite obvious and logical, considering that, on the one hand, fully fledged federations have developed shock-absorption tools and, on the other, a lack in national solidarity has led to allergic reactions in Germany to anything resembling a 'transfer union'. A lively and multifaceted debate followed on how to strike the delicate balance between what might be necessary and what is politically feasible.[27]

5.4 Cyclical Shock Insurance

Some economists have called for a supranational fund based on national contributions paid in economic good times, enabling national governments to draw from it for anti-cyclical purposes when in an economic downturn.[28] Advocates of this approach have named it 'cyclical shock insurance'. They have proposed that the contributions and payouts be based on output gap (the difference between the actual GDP and the highest level of output sustainable in the longer term) relative to the aggregate Eurozone's output gap. Each Eurozone country would contribute to the scheme when its cyclical position is stronger than the Eurozone average and would draw from it in the opposite situation. Because the output gap determines the position of the economy in the business cycle, this indicator is conceptually the most obvious candidate for determining the magnitude and direction of transfers. The authors of this proposal surmised that in the first fifteen years of the single currency this mechanism would have prevented any serious inter-country transfers, and with payments of about 0.2 per cent of GDP

[26] Juncker, Tusk, Dijsselbloem, Draghi and Schulz, 'The Five Presidents' Report', 14.

[27] For a recent summary of it, see, for example, Gilles Thirion, 'European Fiscal Union: Economic Rationale and Design Challenges', *CEPS Working Document* No. 2017/01, 20 January 2017, available at www.ceps.eu/publications/european-fiscal-union-economic-rationale-and-design-challenges.

[28] Henrik Enderlein, Lucas Guttenberg and Jann Spiess, 'Blueprint for a Cyclical Shock Insurance in the Euro Area', *Notre Europe-Jacques Delors Institute Studies and Reports*, September 2013, available at www.institutdelors.eu/media/blueprintforacyclicalshockinsurancene-jdisept2013.pdf?pdf=ok.

it could have reduced standard deviations from average output gap by at least 20 to 25 per cent.

Nonetheless, the idea of cyclical shock insurance has two very serious downsides.

First, I mentioned in Chapter 2 that the output gap is an unobserved variable partly dependent on estimated future economic outlook. It is therefore subject to serious revisions over time. The proponents of 'cyclical shock insurance' argue that the problem is not profoundly significant because both the output gaps of individual countries and the aggregate Eurozone's output gap are subject to similar biases.[29] Hence choosing the relative output gap as a policy indicator should in most cases partly nullify the impact of the bias on policy decisions. Remarkably, however, the scope of the revisions differs from one country to another, and some countries – France and Greece in particular – have happened to go against the bias trend.[30] In the scheme now discussed national governments may be incentivised to minimise further the reported output gap in economic good times (this would minimise their contributions to the scheme) and to do the opposite in recessions. They would therefore be motivated to reinforce the current bias in cyclical upswings and counteract it in downswings. Furthermore, because in various countries recessions and expansions have different amplitudes and durations, national contributions should logically lead to non-trivial inter-country transfers.[31]

Second, different types of fiscal spending have very different macroeconomic effects. Unemployment benefits in recessions have strong consumption smoothing properties. Investment spending in recession fares much worse on this account. But investment spending serves as a structural launch pad for the subsequent expansion. In other words, in recessions national governments might face conflicting motivations as to how to spend public resources. Proponents of cyclical

[29] Other researchers, relying on 2002–2014 data for the EU 15, found that both the estimated output gaps in real time and their revisions are downward-biased during expansions and upward-biased during economic recessions: Pablo Hernández de Cos, Aitor Lacuesta and Enrique Moral-Benito, 'An Exploration of Real-Time Revisions of Output Gap Estimates across European Countries', *Banco de Espana Occasional Paper* No. 1605, 28 July 2016.

[30] Hernández de Cos, Lacuesta and Moral-Benito, 'An Exploration of Real-Time Revisions'.

[31] Lars P. Feld and Steffen Osterloh, 'Is a Fiscal Capacity Really Necessary to Complete EMU?', *Freiburger Diskussionspapiere zur Ordnungsökonomik* No. 13/5, October 2013, available at www.econstor.eu/bitstream/10419/88113/1/77216021X.pdf.

shock insurance argue that the leeway left for national governments in this respect should be restrained by 'a common rulebook for macroeconomic stabilization policies' establishing some standards of social security systems and labour market institutions.[32] They also argue that 'there has to be a procedure to make sure that countries comply with the common rulebook. This could be set up akin to the Excessive deficit procedure or like the system under the Fiscal compact for non-compliance with its debt-break provision.'[33] However, the lesson stemming from the 'revamped' rules-based union (see Chapter 2) is precisely that any such a rulebook would be subject to political haggling, posturing and bickering. There could be good or bad reasons for it. But in any case they would vitiate its effectiveness. This basic deficiency would be further exacerbated by the fact that some revisions of output gap – to adjust national contributions, which in turn is necessary to eliminate inter-country transfers – could often entail the same effects as financial fines prescribed by the SGP (magnifying contributions or limiting payouts in recessions). This too would fuel political conflicts, most probably paving the way for rotten compromises killing the effectiveness of the cyclical shock insurance.

5.5 The Stabilisation Effects of a European Unemployment Benefits Scheme

Sensing these complications, most proponents of Eurozone shock absorbers point at unemployment benefits instead. These benefits yield the largest welfare gains by stabilising the disposable income (improving consumption capacity) of households directly exposed to the effects of macroeconomic shocks. Thus, they immediately alleviate local downswings in business activity.[34] In addition, recorded unemployment is a much less volatile and contestable variable than

[32] Enderlein, Guttenberg and Spiess, 'Blueprint', 33.

[33] Ibid., 33–34.

[34] Xavier Debrun and Radhicka Kapoor, 'Fiscal Policy and Macroeconomic Stability: Automatic Stabilizers Work, Always and Everywhere', *IMF Working Paper* No. 10/111, 1 May 2010, available at www.imf.org/en/Publications/WP/Issues/2016/12/31/Fiscal-Policy-and-Macroeconomic-Stability-Automatic-Stabilizers-Work-Always-and-Everywhere-23818; Mathias Dolls, Clemens Fuest and Andreas Peichl, 'Automatic Stabilizers and Economic Crisis: US vs Europe', *Journal of Public Economics* 96 (2012): 279–294; Michael P. Evers, 'Federal Fiscal Transfer Rules in Monetary Unions', *European Economic Review* 56 (2012): 507–525.

the output gap. Finally, this mechanism has been championed by supranational policymakers for political reasons. In fully fledged federations, unemployment benefits received from the federal system stimulate allegiance to the federal state. European federalists therefore argue that 'pooling a part of unemployment insurance within the euro area would provide a new instrument for solidarity that would in turn be a concrete incarnation of the social dimension of EMU'.[35] Or, as Giles Merritt puts it, what he calls Euro-dole 'would be a high-profile sign that the EU is recovering the spirit of solidarity between member states that is currently in full retreat. Another reason – more complicated, but fundamentally more important still – is that it would move social policy back near the top of the EU's agenda.'[36]

Proposals for a countercyclical European unemployment benefits scheme (EUBS) coalesce around its two generic types.[37] The system could be operational irrespective (non-contingent) of the cyclical position of each country. Payouts from such a common basic unemployment benefit scheme would grow in recessions and dry up during expansions. As an alternative, the payouts could be activated only during particularly pronounced surges in short-term unemployment. In this 'catastrophic insurance' (contingent) variant the scheme would be set in motion during major recessions only.

In the non-contingent version of the EUBS the common basic unemployment benefit scheme would partly replace national unemployment insurance systems. It would therefore be funded directly either from labour or corporate taxation.[38] In the contingent version the insurance would be funded by country contributions.

[35] Thomas Lellouch and Arthur Sode, 'An Unemployment Insurance Scheme for the Euro Area', *Trésor-Economics* No. 132, June 2014, 1, available at www.tresor.economie.gouv.fr/File/403124.

[36] Giles Merritt, 'Euro-dole: A German Initiative That Berlin Doesn't Welcome', *Friends of Europe*, 23 November 2016, available at www.friendsofeurope.org/publication/euro-dole-german-initiative-berlin-doesnt-welcome.

[37] Anne Epaulard, 'Contingent vs. Non-Contingent Unemployment Benefit Scheme for the EMU', paper for conference 'Economic Shock Absorbers for the Eurozone' in Brussels, 20 June 2014, available at ec.europa.eu/social/BlobServlet?docId=11889&langId=en.

[38] 'Because direct labour taxation raises labour costs (tax wedge), some authors propose that the EUBS be funded from EU-wide corporate taxation (with a rate estimated at 12.6%) to partly replace national corporate taxes'; Jean Pisani-Ferry, Erkki Vihriälä and Guntram Wolff, 'Options for a Euro-area Fiscal Capacity', *Bruegel Policy Contribution* No. 2013/01, 10 January 2013, available at bruegel.org/2013/01/options-for-a-euro-area-fiscal-capacity/.

Protagonists of the EUBS tend to agree that the scheme should cover short-term unemployment (its first six to twelve months),[39] with a 50 per cent replacement rate (i.e., 50 per cent of the previous wage) according to most of the proposals.[40] Each country could top it up, by increasing the replacement rate, by extending the duration of the benefits, or by broadening the coverage (the share of unemployed receiving their benefits from the EUBS). To avoid the situation in which transfers are systemically skewed towards some of the Member States, most authors propose various methods of experience rating (fiscal rules) requiring that contributions be cyclically adjusted according to labour market performance in individual countries. The contingent version of the scheme ought to be additionally equipped with a system of triggers activating payouts only during more serious idiosyncratic output shocks, i.e., when the upsurge of unemployment is particularly pronounced.[41]

[39] Epaulard, 'Contingent vs. Non-Contingent', proposes that the scheme cover the period between the third and twelfth month of unemployment. Lellouch and Sode, 'An Unemployment Insurance Scheme', and Sebastian Dullien, 'The Macroeconomic Stabilisation Impact of a European Basic Unemployment Insurance Scheme', *Intereconomics* 49 (2014): 189–193, support a scheme covering the first twelve months of unemployment. Andrea Brandolini, Francesca Carta and Francesco D'Amuri, 'A Feasible Unemployment-Based Shock Absorber for the Euro Area', *Banca D'Italia, Questioni di Economia e Finanza* (Occasional papers) No. 254, November 2014, available at www.bancaditalia.it/pubblicazioni/qef/2014-0254/QEF_254.pdf suggests the first eight months of unemployment and László Andor, in 'Basic European Unemployment Insurance – The Best Way Forward in Strengthening the EMU's Resilience and Europe's Recovery', *Intereconomics* 49 (2014): 184–189, proposes that the EUBS covers the first six months of unemployment.

[40] Andor, 'Basic European Unemployment Insurance', and Miroslav Beblavý et al., 'Common Unemployment Insurance Scheme for the Euro Area', Annex I to 'Common unemployment insurance scheme for the euro area. Cost of Non-Europe Report', European Parliamentary Research Service, September 2014, available at www.europarl.europa.eu/RegData/etudes/STUD/2014/510984/EPRS_STU(2014)510984_REV1_EN.pdf, propose a 40 per cent replacement rate.

[41] For example, when the three- to twelve-month unemployment rate exceeds its five-year moving average plus 1 per cent, with sunset at the point in time when the three- to twelve-month unemployment rate returns to the five-year average (Epaulard, 'Contingent vs. Non-Contingent'), when short-term unemployment rate exceeds its ten-year average plus a fraction between one and two standard deviations of the rate across EU countries (Miroslav Beblavý, Daniel Gros and Ilaria Maselli, 'Reinsurance of National Unemployment Benefit Schemes', *CEPS Working Document* No. 401, January 2015, available at www.ceps.eu/system/files/wd401.pdf), or when the national unemployment rate exceeds the non-accelerating rate of unemployment (NAWRU; structural unemployment) by 2 per cent (Beblavý et al., 'Common Unemployment Insurance Scheme').

What difference would the EUBS schemes make to the Eurozone's economic stability during idiosyncratic downturns? Income stabilisation effects (and their impact on the economy more generally) depend on assumptions regarding contribution rates paid in good times, on the coverage, on the generosity of the scheme, as well as on the very uncertain assessment of the fiscal multiplier of unemployment benefits for the economic growth. While, depending on those assumptions, various authors have come up with different calculations, they all have demonstrated that an EUBS would somewhat stabilise Eurozone economies, as long as their instability is caused by business cycle fluctuations. By the same token, however, it would not be useful if the economic hardship is bred by deeper – structural – reasons.

Dolls et al. came to the conclusion that under a uniform contribution rate (1.57 per cent) across the Member States a common basic unemployment benefits scheme would have absorbed 36 per cent of the overall Eurozone unemployment shocks between 2000 and 2013, with Austria and the Netherlands contributing to the scheme slightly more than they benefitted from it in the 2000–2013 period, and France, Latvia and Spain being net recipients throughout the same period.[42] The income stabilisation of the scheme would have been around 50 per cent in Greece, Ireland and Portugal in 2009, as well as in Italy in 2012.[43] The authors admit, however, that the macroeconomic output would not have been seriously altered as a result, with the biggest GDP improvements in Estonia, Ireland and Spain (1.9 per cent, 0.8 per cent and 0.6 per cent, respectively) in 2009.[44] Dullien suggested that the stabilisation effects of an EUBS on disposable income would only sporadically exceed 10 per cent if the coverage ratio were 50 per cent.[45] In two episodes, the effect could have exceeded 50 per cent, however, had the

[42] Mathias Dolls et al., 'An Unemployment Insurance Scheme for the Euro Area? A Comparison of Different Alternatives Using Micro Data', *Centre for European Economic Research-ZEW Discussion Paper* No. 14–084, 28 October 2014, available at ftp.zew.de/pub/zew-docs/dp/dp14095.pdf.

[43] Study by Mathias Dolls et al., Annex II to 'Common Unemployment Insurance Scheme for the Euro Area. Cost of Non-Europe Report', European Parliamentary Research Service, September 2014, II-49, available at www.europarl.europa.eu/RegData/etudes/STUD/2014/510984/EPRS_STU(2014)510984_REV1_EN.pdf.

[44] Dolls et al., 'Common Unemployment Insurance Scheme', II-51.

[45] Spain 2007–2009 (17.8 per cent) and 2011–2012 (31.5 per cent), Ireland 2008–2009 (11.5 per cent), Netherlands 2002–2004 (17.2 per cent), Austria 2001–2002 (31.7 per cent), Portugal 2010–2012 (13.7 per cent): Dullien, 'The Macroeconomic Stabilisation Impact', 193.

coverage ratio been higher.[46] Beblavý et al. surmised that had Eurozone countries been able to draw from the fund (under the assumption of 75 per cent coverage, 40 per cent replacement rate, fiscal rules preventing inter-country redistribution and 1.5 per cent fiscal multiplier), the inflow would have generated an additional output of 6.08 per cent of GDP for Spain, 2.19 per cent of GDP for Ireland and 1.60 per cent of GDP for Greece between 2008 and 2013.[47]

According to the same authors, in the contingent (catastrophic recessions only) scenario payouts from the fund in the 1999–2012 period would have amounted to 1.3 per cent of GDP annually in Spain in some of the years, cumulatively reaching 4.75 per cent of GDP throughout the whole period.[48] Also for Lithuania and Latvia the cumulative payouts would have been nontrivial (3.66 per cent of GDP and 2.43 per cent of GDP, respectively). Yet, among other EU countries only Estonia, Ireland and Greece would have also received payouts exceeding 1 per cent of GDP (1.46 per cent of GDP, 1.76 per cent of GDP and 1.94 per cent of GDP, respectively).

What do all those figures mean for the usefulness (or the necessity) of establishing an EUBS? They make it clear that in Spain and (to a lesser degree) in Ireland as well as in the Baltic states – the Eurozone countries that experienced the most pronounced cyclical downturns in the previous decade – the scheme would have visibly cushioned the effects of the recession. On the other hand, however, the calculations also make it quite clear that no EUBS can provide any systemic convergence to economies imbalanced not for temporary – cyclical – reasons (demand shocks), but due to their more structural incongruities (supply shocks).

5.6 Legal Facilitators of a EUBS

Supporters of an EUBS might be encouraged not only by its smoothing effects during asymmetric demand shocks, but also by the fact that neither serious divergences in the current national unemployment policies nor the Treaty setup pose insurmountable obstacles to the idea, as long at least as it is indeed necessary for the stability of the Eurozone.

46 Austria 2001–2002 (75.3 per cent) and Spain 2011–2012 (62.9 per cent): Dullien, 'The Macroeconomic Stabilisation Impact', 193.

47 Beblavý et al., 'Common Unemployment Insurance Scheme', I-88.

48 Ibid., I-69.

Differences in employment protection and unemployment policies across the Eurozone are bigger than in fully fledged federations.[49] For instance, in 2012 the maximum duration of unemployment benefits was six months in Malta, Cyprus and Slovakia, thirty-six months in France and forty-eight months in Belgium.[50] Also, unemployment benefits per inhabitant differ significantly in the Eurozone. In 2014, unemployment expenditures per inhabitant in the Eurozone stood at €42 in Lithuania, €73 in Slovakia, €178 in Greece, €631 in Austria, €1,207 in Belgium and €1,288 in Luxembourg.[51] Varying unemployment rates do not explain these differences at all.[52] Such significant discrepancies regarding the generosity of unemployment benefits are important, because 'higher replacement rates, longer duration of unemployment benefits, higher employment protection, a higher tax wage, higher union contract coverage and density, lead to a larger effect of shocks on unemployment'.[53]

Also in fiscal federations, however, serious differences between regions persist. In the USA, for instance, unemployment benefits can vary from $133 (Puerto Rico) to $1,011 (Massachusetts) per week, without undermining shock-absorbing functions of unemployment benefits there.[54] Any version of an EUBS accepts the fact that different

[49] For an overview, see, for example, Jörg Paetzold and Olaf van Vliet, 'EU Co-Ordination and the Convergence of Domestic Unemployment Protection Scheme', *Journal of Common Market Studies* 52 (2014): 1070–1089; Ingrid Esser et al., 'Unemployment Benefits in EU Member States', paper prepared for the European Commission, Directorate-General for Employment, Social Affairs and Inclusion, 2013; Danielle Venn, 'Eligibility Criteria for Unemployment Benefits: Quantitative Indicators for OECD and EU Countries', *OECD Social, Employment and Migration Working Papers* 131, 9 January 2012, available at www.oecd-ilibrary.org/social-issues-migration-health/eligibility-criteria-for-unemployment-benefits_5k9h43kgkvr4-en.

[50] Grégory Claeys, Zsolt Darvas and Guntram Wolff, 'Benefits and Drawbacks of European Unemployment Insurance', *Bruegel Policy Brief* No. 2014/06, 12 September 2014, available at bruegel.org/2014/09/benefits-and-drawbacks-of-european-unemployment-insurance/.

[51] Eurostat, Expenditure: Main Results, Euro Per Inhabitant, Unemployment.

[52] At the end of 2014 unemployment rates in these countries were: 10 per cent in Lithuania, 12 per cent in Slovakia, 26 per cent in Greece, 6 per cent in Austria and Luxembourg and 8 per cent in Belgium: Eurostat, Unemployment by Sex and Age – Monthly Average.

[53] Olivier Blanchard and Justin Wolfers, 'The Role of Shocks and Institutions in the Rise of European Unemployment: The Aggregate Evidence', *NBER Working Paper* No. 7282, August 1999, available at www.nber.org/papers/w7282.pdf.

[54] Julie M. Whittaker and Katelin P. Isaacs, 'Extending Unemployment Compensation Benefits during Recessions', *Congressional Research Service* No. RL34340, 2 May 2013, available at www.fas.org/sgp/crs/misc/RL34340.pdf.

systems of unemployment benefits have different shock-absorption capacities. None aims to eliminate them, but, instead, each requires a minimum floor only.[55] To achieve this, it suffices to harmonise national systems in two aspects: eligibility conditions and minimum replacement rates. The two should be necessarily harmonised to avoid the situation in which an EUBS is irreconcilable with national legislation requiring shorter protection durations or setting up eligibility conditions resulting in a more limited unemployment coverage. Such a minimum harmonisation would not affect most of the Eurozone's Member States, however, because they tend to offer long durations, reasonably high coverage stemming from rather generous eligibility conditions and replacement rates most often above 50 per cent.

If necessary for the Eurozone's stability, an EUBS would be also reconcilable with the Treaty framework. In this respect, however, a distinction should be made between, on the one hand, a Treaty basis for harmonising unemployment schemes in individual countries, so that they meet minimum conditions (of eligibility and replacement rates) necessary for an EUBS to function in the same way across the Eurozone, and, on the other hand, a legal basis for establishing its financial resources and redistribution flows.

For the first of the two aspects it is important to note that the Treaty (Art. 153(2)(b) TFEU) authorises the European Parliament and the Council to adopt 'by means of directives, minimum requirements for gradual implementation' of social security harmonisation, 'having regard to the conditions and technical rules obtaining in each of the Member States'.[56] While this provision refers to all EU countries, the case for extending an EUBS to non-Eurozone countries is very thin, considering that in the latter group the monetary channel (nominal exchange rate adjustments) compensate for the lack of fiscal shock-absorption mechanisms at the European level. In other words, it would

[55] In addition, the floor may differ greatly as to how it is construed, where it is located and for whom. For an economic, legal and organisational analysis of several basic variants in this respect see Miroslav Beblavý, Karolien Lenaerts and Ilaria Maselli, 'Design of a European Unemployment Benefit Scheme', *CEPS Research Report* No. 2017/04, February 2017, available at www.ceps.eu/system/files/Design%20of%20EUBS%20RRpt%20No%202017-04.pdf.

[56] Unemployment benefits are a branch of social security, as confirmed by Art. 3(1) Regulation 883/2004 of the European Parliament and of Council of 29 April 2004 on the coordination of social security systems, OJ 2004 No. L 166, 30 April 2004, pp. 1–123, with amendments.

be hard to claim that an EUBS complies with the general principles of subsidiarity and proportionality in the non-Eurozone countries.[57]

The flip side of the same argument leads to the conclusion that minimum harmonisation based on Art. 153(2)(b) TFEU and limited in practice to the Eurozone countries should be justifiable by general principles of EU law. In addition, such a geographical limitation has a recent precedent, of the regulation setting up the Single Resolution Mechanism (SRM).[58] The SRM is a pillar of the European banking union. It is based on Art. 114 TFEU: the legal basis for harmonisation in the internal market. Despite the internal market by definition covering the whole EU, it was clear from the very beginning of the legislative process on the SRM Regulation that at least some of the non-Eurozone countries would not join it. And yet no one has questioned the legal basis of the SRM. If this legislative strategy could go unchallenged in respect to the sanctified unity of the internal market, it would be all the more rational regarding the minimum harmonisation of social security, especially if it were necessary to fix the Eurozone problems and if the scheme remains open for accession by the non-Eurozone countries, no matter how improbable it is that they may be inclined to do so.

One additional point to be made in this respect is that Art. 153(4) TFEU introduces certain restrictions on the harmonisation of social security systems. The directives adopted upon it 'shall not affect the right of Member States to define the fundamental principles of their social security systems and must not significantly affect the financial equilibrium thereof' and 'shall not prevent any Member State from maintaining or introducing more stringent protective measures compatible with the Treaties'. These conditions, too, would be fulfilled, however, whenever an EUBS simply replaces some part of a national unemployment benefits scheme and whenever it allows national governments to top them up with more generous benefits. And in any case the question of whether the general clauses of Art. 153(4) TFEU are respected or not would be answered by a political decision in the

[57] 'The Union shall act only if and in so far as the objectives of the proposed action cannot be sufficiently achieved by the Member States' and 'the content and form of Union action shall not exceed what is necessary to achieve the objectives of the Treaties': Arts. 5(3) and (4) TEU.

[58] Regulation 806/2014 establishing uniform rules and a uniform procedure for the resolution of credit institutions and certain investment firms in the framework of a Single Resolution Mechanism and a Single Resolution Fund and amending Regulation 1093/2010, OJ 2014 No. L 225/1, 30 July 2014.

legislative process. Because the Treaty requires unanimous decisions in the harmonisation of social security and social protection of workers (Art. 153(2) TFEU), any government could express its objection in this respect – vetoing the draft legislation.

It is one thing, however, to prejudge that the harmonisation of national unemployment benefits schemes necessary to avoid their incongruities with basic prerequisites of an EUBS is possible under EU law.[59] Yet, it is another to determine if any fiscal shock absorber redirecting national resources to the European level in good times to redistribute them back in bad times is compatible with EU law.[60]

One particularly promising legal basis for this redistribution is Art. 175(3) TFEU. This provision, located in the part of the Treaty entitled 'Economic, Social and Territorial Cohesion', empowers the Council to act 'if specific actions prove necessary outside' the regional policy funds 'and without prejudice to the measures decided upon within the framework of the other Union policies'. The 'specific actions' may in particular stand for establishing financial vehicles pursuing social cohesion, as corroborated by the fact that, in the past, this article was used to set up the European Globalisation Adjustment Fund.[61] Another possible Treaty basis is Art. 352 TFEU – the so-called flexibility clause. In its most important part, the clause reads: 'if action by the Union should prove necessary, within the framework of the policies defined in the Treaties, to attain one of the objectives set out in the Treaties, and the Treaties have not provided the necessary powers, the Council, acting

[59] To avoid delving into excessive complexities I leave legal and operational hurdles at the national level aside. However, as Michael Coucheir, Grega Strban and Harald Hauben, 'The Legal and Operational Feasibility of a European Unemployment Benefits Scheme at the National Level', *CEPS Special Report* No. 145, 26 September 2016, available at www.ceps.eu/publications/legal-and-operational-feasibility-european-unemployment-benefits-scheme-national-level noted, an EUBS might require a constitutional amendment in Finland and a five-sixths parliamentary majority or a referendum in Denmark. It would also undermine the role of social partners in designing unemployment insurance schemes in France and it would cause frictions with the liberal, least generous national unemployment benefits schemes (the Anglo-Saxon and the Eastern European countries).

[60] It should be added that fiscal-equalisation mechanisms mimicking those operating in fully fledged federations could be seen as falling foul of the no-bailout clause (Art. 125 TFEU) because they would entail inter-country transfers. As long, however, as the transfers are precluded – which is the reality of the Eurozone now – political constraints keep this counterargument at bay. In other words, if fiscal equalisation is prevented, the no-bailout clause could not kick in.

[61] For an extension of the argument see René Repasi, 'Legal Options and Limits for the Establishment of a European Unemployment Benefit Scheme', January 2017, 20–31, available at ec.europa.eu/social/BlobServlet?docId=16886&langId=en.

unanimously on a proposal from the Commission and after obtaining the consent of the European Parliament, shall adopt the appropriate measures.' Social security is one of 'the policies defined in the Treaties', and it seems most obvious that 'the Treaties have not provided the necessary powers' to set up any anti-cyclical shock absorber (it was considered unnecessary when the Treaty was drafted). One last condition for activating this clause is the necessity to attain one of the Treaty objectives (the condition of necessity is also inscribed in Art. 175(3) TFEU). So when an EUBS can be deemed necessary from the perspective of social cohesion (Art. 175(3) TFEU) and/or for the proper functioning of the EU more generally and the stability of the Eurozone in particular (Art. 352 TFEU), one or both of the Treaty bases could anchor the entailing redistribution in primary law.

The conclusion that an EUBS would be necessary to achieve any of the goals should not be taken for granted, however, because any European shock absorber entails serious side effects. It can even be argued that its very ability to achieve any of the abovementioned goals remains very dubious, undermining the case for its adequacy.

5.7 The Dark Side of Fiscal Shock Absorbers

It is often argued that an EUBS could be played by national politicians, unemployment administrations and individual recipients of benefits, because it would skew their incentive structure. This in turn leads to moral hazard problems and the tendency to demand oversupply of the risk-sharing on the side of potential financial winners, as well as the tendency to undersupply on the side of potential financial losers.[62] Accordingly, 'a Member State may be tempted to reduce activation efforts or loosen supervision of eligibility conditions when it receives central funding'.[63] National unemployment administrations may be interested in reclassifying the long-term unemployed as short-term unemployed, because under any version of an EUBS only the latter group would receive Union benefits. They might also be insufficiently incentivised to 'put the same effort into placing the unemployed into new jobs as they would if they had to bear all costs for unemployment. This is a problem that has been observed empirically in some federal

[62] Torsten Persson and Guido Tabellini, 'Federal Fiscal Constitutions: Risk Sharing and Moral Hazard', *Econometrica* 64 (1996): 623–646.

[63] European Commission, 'Paper on Automatic Stabilisers', 4 October 2013, 5.

systems of unemployment insurance, for example in Belgium.'[64] Finally, some are also concerned that 'a generous unemployment benefit might induce individuals to stay longer in the unemployment status and reduce their effort in looking for a job'.[65]

No doubt any insurance against the consequences of risky behaviour entails a danger of more risky behaviour. In addition, when 'the sense of national solidarity' is missing in the Eurozone and when some of its governments are against the wall of the public debt overhang, serious political and moral hazard problems are unavoidable.

The causality here is quite complicated, however. On the one hand, if an EUBS is to replace a part of national unemployment benefits schemes, individuals would not be more motivated to abuse it than they are now. In addition, an EUBS preventing permanent inter-country transfers reduces both the policy and the bureaucratic moral hazards mentioned earlier, for attempts to play it would lead to higher national adjustment contributions to the scheme. The common-pool problem of public finances, which arises when those who enjoy the marginal benefit of additional spending do not bear the costs of funding it,[66] should therefore be precluded. On the other hand, with the no-bailout clause seriously weakened, which is now the case, national governments running risky economic and fiscal policies would know that if these policies fail, bringing about fiscal stress and an economic

[64] Dullien, 'The Macroeconomic Stabilisation Impact', 193. See also Frank Vandenbroucke et al., 'Institutional Moral Hazard in the Multi-Tiered Regulation of Unemployment and Social Assistance Benefits', *CEPS Special Report* No. 137, 27 April 2016, available at www.ceps.eu/publications/institutional-moral-hazard-multi-tiered-regulation-unemployment-and-social-assistance.

[65] Andrea Brandolini, Francesca Carta and Francesco D'Amuri, 'A Feasible Unemployment-Based Shock Absorber for the Euro Area', *Banca D'Italia, Questioni di Economia e Finanza* (Occasional papers) No. 254, November 2014, 8, available at www.bancaditalia.it/pubblicazioni/qef/2014-0254/QEF_254.pdf.

[66] For a discussion in the current context see for example Jürgen von Hagen, 'Common Pools – Why a European Fiscal Union Will Make Things Worse', *Bonn Journal of Economics* 1 (2012): 65–73. As Steffen Osterloh, Friedrich Heinemann and Philipp Mohl, 'EU Budget Reform Options and the Common Pool Problem', *Centre for European Economic Research ZEW*, August 2008, 2, available at aei.pitt.edu/33114/1/osterloh._steffen.pdf, characterised it, 'the common pool problem is at the heart of inefficiencies in centralised decision-making, as locally elected representatives decide on the allocation of spending at the central level, which is financed out of a common pool, so that it is largely borne by other jurisdictions. As a consequence, local representatives face incentives to use their influence in central decision processes for promoting those transfers with an advantageous distributive effect from their country's position.'

downturn, the other countries would rush in with a bailout, instead of expecting any additional adjustment contribution to a common shock-absorption mechanism from the country in trouble. In various forms this problem has reared its head even in the countries sharing 'the sense of national solidarity', like Argentina, or Brazil, or – to a lesser degree – Spain or Germany.[67] With an enfeebled no-bailout clause in lieu of 'the sense of national solidarity' at the European level, the positive economic effects of fiscal stabilisation could thus easily be dwarfed by political and economic expectations, resentments and accusations. Leszek Balcerowicz, a leading Polish macroeconomist and one of the most important political figures of the Polish transformation, grasped this economic and political debacle when he argued that 'fiscal union ... can only follow the process of the gradual build-up of a common identity. If fiscal transfers are rushed ahead of this process, they will undermine it. This is especially true in the case of fiscal transfers to countries affected by the crises caused by their own policies.'[68]

Furthermore, the previous overview of the research simulating potential effects of an EUBS in the Eurozone (had it been introduced together with the single currency) leads to the conclusion that in a sudden and deep recession, like the one that hit Spain in 2010, or the Baltic states and Ireland two years earlier, European fiscal capacity could reduce the impact of the recession by anything up to 2 per cent of GDP altogether. But in a system in which the European shock-absorption capacity replaces a part of national shock absorbers and the inter-country permanent transfers are precluded, the added value of such a scheme would be much smaller. Essentially, every additional 1 per cent of the fiscal capacity offered by the European level would require that the same fiscal capacity cannot be used for the same purpose at the national level. In other words, it would exchange national insurance for a European insurance, of comparable shock-absorption faculties.

A supporter of European fiscal shock absorbers may retort at this point that they make sense, nonetheless, due to the so-called inter-temporal budget constraint. In short, if, acting counter-cyclically, a

[67] Michael D. Bordo, Agnieszka Markiewicz and Lars Jonung, 'A Fiscal Union for the Euro: Some Lessons from History', *NBER Working Paper* No. 17380, September 2011, available at www.nber.org/papers/w17380.

[68] Leszek Balcerowicz, 'On the Prevention of Crises in the Eurozone', in: *Governance for the Eurozone: Integration or Disintegration?*, eds. Allen Franklin, Elena Carletti and Saverio Simonelli, 2012, 78, available at www.eui.eu/DepartmentsAndCentres/Economics/SeminarsEvents/Conferences/GovernancefortheEurozoneIntegrationorDisintegration.aspx.

country puts aside some resources on sunny days, it can more easily avoid liquidity problems on rainy days. It can economise on the costs of borrowing on unfavourable market conditions during recession. This observation, however, is a double-edged sword. For no doubt had the Eurozone been born with a countercyclical mechanism at the European level, its national governments would have been spared some of the headaches they had during the sovereign debt crisis. But a contrary argument is true now, when some of the Eurozone's countries are still mired in high unemployment (especially Greece, Spain and Italy). It is hard to expect that the governments of these countries would save up for future rainy days, when for many of them the rainy days could be just around the corner.

More generally, by definition a shock absorber is particularly useful in fending off a sudden turn of the economic tide. Yet, by the same token, it cannot provide any substantial relief if a country suffers from a protracted slowdown, for instance in consequence of its limited ability to perform macroeconomic adjustment without an external devaluation. Then the short-term unemployment is replaced by long-term unemployment, and the latter situation would remain unaffected by any shock absorber.

5.8 Looking Closer at the American Example

The basic intuition behind the idea of Eurozone's fiscal shock absorbers – that in order to address various asymmetries the currency area should emulate one of the components of a fully fledged federal fiscal system – is also too quick to make. To substantiate this point it is enough to look at how the unemployment benefits system works in the USA. The US Unemployment Compensation (UC) programme, which dates back to New Deal legislation,[69] allows individual American states to determine benefit amounts, duration (typically twenty-six weeks)[70] and other eligibility criteria of basic unemployment insurance. Each state also funnels a share of unemployment insurance premiums, covered by employer taxes there, to its account with the federal unemployment trust fund. In recessions each draws from the account, going into deficit if necessary. The states are obliged to repay (with interest) the resultant loans, however. If the

[69] It was first introduced by the Social Security Act of 1935.

[70] In eight states the maximum duration is shorter than twenty-six weeks, in Montana it is twenty-eight weeks and in Massachusetts thirty weeks.

loans are not repaid voluntarily, the federal payroll tax rate for the state concerned is automatically raised until the balance is cleared.

All of these features are particularly attractive in the European reality precluding any actual transfer union. Yet, in the USA, the UC programme is not a tool to stabilise the economy during a downturn. This task has been performed by two other types of schemes. The first is a permanent Extended Benefits (EB) programme, which has been in place for almost fifty years now.[71] If a given state uses it, the unemployed person receives up to thirteen or twenty additional weeks of unemployment benefits (depending on fluctuations of the insured unemployment and the total unemployment). The states participating in the programme have half of the additional costs covered by the federal government on a non-refundable basis, irrespective of individual states' experience ratings. The system thus redistributes federal taxes from the states experiencing less severe business cycle fluctuations to those more exposed to cyclical booms and busts.

The picture changes further in more significant demand shocks. The Great Recession is a remarkable example. At its beginning, many American states partly or entirely opted out of the EB programme, returning to it only after Congress agreed to cover all of its costs.[72] Simultaneously, another, discretionary federal stabilisation scheme – the Emergency Unemployment Compensation (EUC08) programme, in operation until the end of 2013[73] – was introduced, to cover up to fifty-three additional weeks of benefits, depending on the unemployment rate in individual states. None of the earlier American discretionary unemployment benefits schemes had provided for similarly extended coverage. But, nonetheless, discretionary unemployment programmes had provided the bulk of macroeconomic stabilisation through unemployment benefits in every recession since World War II.[74]

[71] Introduced by the Federal-State Extended Unemployment Compensation Act of 1970.

[72] Marcus Hagedorn et al., 'Unemployment Benefits and Unemployment in the Great Recession: The Role of Macro Effects', *Federal Reserve Bank of New York Staff Reports* No. 646, October 2013, revised February 2015, 12, available at pdfs.semanticscholar.org/c726/0118ccd96e3ad6e7eb6f966584b3b18ee228.pdf.

[73] The Emergency Unemployment Compensation Act of 2008, as modified and expanded by subsequent legislation.

[74] Previous discretionary schemes were activated in 1958–1959, 1961–1962, 1972–1973, 1975–1978, 1982–1985, 1991–1994 and 2002–2003: see Ben Gitis, 'Primer: Unemployment Compensation and Labor Market Recovery', *American Action Forum*, 9 January 2015, available at www.americanactionforum.org/research/primer-unemployment-compensation-and-labor-market-recovery/#_ftnref6.

No preprogrammed EUBS could act similarly, especially if it were to prevent inter-country redistribution, because any redistributive vehicle comparable to the US pattern requires a swiftly achieved political compromise and incurs significant unexpected costs at the federal level. This in turn involves two prerequisites. The first is expedited decision-making, which remains a distant dream in the Eurozone, especially when fiscal transfers would be involved. The second is additional fiscal capacity allowing for the covering of fiscal deficits produced by such discretionary programmes. While many recent proposals have suggested methods of creating such a capacity (e.g., tax on financial transactions, tax on cross-border pollution, a European corporate tax, a modified VAT, or a tax on corporate shareholders[75]), none of them is particularly credible in the situation where taxation is already high in most Eurozone societies.[76] In this situation IMF economists might be right that a countercyclical budget of 4.5 per cent of GNP could 'fully insure euro area countries against very severe, persistent and unanticipated downturns'.[77] But it is a safe guess that no European society would be willing to foot the bill for this type of insurance.[78] It is equally hard to imagine that national governments would give up a share of their current tax revenues to feed a federal discretionary unemployment

[75] Ben Crum, 'Saving the Euro at the Cost of Democracy?', *Journal of Common Market Studies* 51 (2013): 614–630; Miguel Poiares Maduro, 'A New Governance for the European Union and the Euro: Democracy and Justice', *RSCAS Policy Paper* No. 2012/11, 30 August 2012.

[76] In 2016, total receipts from taxes and social contributions averaged 41.3 per cent in the Eurozone (EU 19). They were 1.3 per cent higher than in 2007: Eurostat, Main National Accounts Tax Aggregates, Total Receipts from Taxes and Social Contributions (Including Imputed Social Contributions) After Deduction of Amounts Assessed but Unlikely to Be Collected. While in some Eurozone countries the burden is clearly lighter (e.g., Portugal: 36.9 per cent; Spain: 34.1 per cent; Slovakia: 32.4 per cent; Ireland: 23.8 per cent), and while some others "creditor countries" (esp. Germany: 40.4 per cent; the Netherlands: 39.3 per cent) are also below the average, in other very important Eurozone countries the burden of taxation is above average (France: 47.6 per cent; Belgium: 46.8 per cent; Finland: 44.3 per cent; Austria and Italy: 42.9 per cent). Raising corporate taxes could be conceived as an alternative from this perspective, because then a different group of economic agents takes the financial brunt. But this strategy is hardly viable in the reality of tax competition propelled by globalisation.

[77] Furceri and Zdzienicka, 'The Euro Area Crisis', 4.

[78] Mathias Trabandt and Harald Uhlig, 'How Do Laffer Curves Differ across Countries?', *NBER Working Paper* No. 17862, February 2012, available at www.nber.org/papers/w17862, demonstrate that many European societies are close to realistically measured Laffer curves. New taxes would thus lead to low additional tax revenues and could prove recessionary, through basic supply- and demand-side channels.

benefits programme, particularly that emulating the US example would inevitably lead to what is otherwise politically impossible to achieve in the Eurozone: a fiscal union.

It is also important in this context that back in 2011 or 2012 the relationship between the lacking shock absorbers and fiscal stress was obvious and painful. But since the ECB pacified financial markets and since European policymakers demonstrated that they would not constrain automatic stabilisers by dutifully enforcing the SGP, the problem of the intertemporal budget constraint has receded. Now, therefore, the Eurozone Member States are essentially unrestrained in their macroeconomic stabilisation fiscal policy efforts, while the ESM and the ECB are ready to provide financial assistance in case this leads to fiscal stress. In other words, practical necessities have led to the establishment of a peculiar system of macroeconomic stabilisation in the Eurozone, which respects the political reality in which 'the sense of national solidarity', highlighted in the Delors Report, is missing.

A proponent of European shock absorption could still retort that this European workaround violates the basic lesson stemming from the theory of fiscal federalism: macroeconomic stabilisation in a federation should be elevated to the central level. While this point indeed marks a fundamental paradox casting a wide shadow on the Eurozone's future, it is equally true that fully fledged fiscal federations have developed a much broader shock-absorption and capacity-building toolbox than unemployment benefits.

First of all, federal income taxes provide for significant shock absorption there, for revenues rise in expansions and dwindle away in recessions. Second, in fully fledged federations broader fiscal equalisation schemes, from anti-poverty programmes to allocating federal public procurement to ailing regions, are used to ameliorate the effects of recessions on disposable incomes. In other words, unemployment benefits are only one of many channels through which the fiscal policy cushions macroeconomic shocks there. Comparisons with the US federal system in particular are difficult also for the reason that the American states tend to act procyclically in recessions,[79] which correlates with effective no-bailout clauses determining their fiscal

[79] Joshua Aizenman and Gurnain K. Pasricha, 'Net Fiscal Stimulus during the Great Recession', *NBER Working Papers* No. 16779, February 2011, available at www.nber.org/papers/w16779; Annika Kasparek, 'Fiscal Policy in US States', *Deutsche Bank Research Current Issues*, December 2011.

policies. Against this background the federal system must have assumed the stabilisation role, because otherwise its very existence would be severely jeopardised. The Eurozone has been very different in this respect. Because the supranational system has not developed the stabilisation function, economic stabilisers have remained firmly with the Member States. The European level has both tolerated it, regardless of what the SGP may imply, and alleviated the inter-temporal budget constraint by ex post assistance and the ECB's quantitative easing.

Most importantly of all, however, combined effects of all the various fiscal transfers available in fully fledged federations are moderate. Most researchers have concluded that, in the USA, the whole fiscal channel absorbs no more than 15 per cent of output shocks (the stabilisation effects are so limited there, despite federal spending amounting to 21 per cent of GDP,[80] while in the EU it stands at just 1 per cent of GDP) and that in other federations its effects are comparable.[81]

In the USA the vast majority of macroeconomic shocks are absorbed by capital markets (almost 40 per cent) and by credit markets (almost 25 per cent).[82] How is this possible?

Think of a capital – equity and corporate debt – market first. If residents of one region invest in the equity or debt of companies located in other regions, or in a national or a global company, an idiosyncratic (asymmetric) shock hitting the former region does not corrode the income earned by its residents on this equity or debt, because it pertains to companies located somewhere else. As a flipside, however, residents of the non-crisis region may experience losses if they have invested in a company located in the state undergoing an asymmetric shock. In fully fledged federations the banking system, the backbone of credit markets – operates in a similar fashion. If a bank is active on a federal level, the losses incurred in some regions can be offset against

[80] Center on Budget and Policy Priorities, 'Policy Basics: Where Do Our Federal Tax Dollars Go?', 4 March 2016.

[81] Pierfederico Asdrubali, Bent E. Sorensen and Oved Yosha, 'Channels of Interstate Risk Sharing: United States 1963–1990', *Quarterly Journal of Economics* 111 (1996): 1081–1110; Jacques Melitz and Frederic Zumer, 'Regional Redistribution and Stabilization by the Center in Canada, France, the UK and the US: A Reassessment and New Tests', *Journal of Public Economics* 86 (2002): 263–286; Stefano Athanasoulis and Eric van Wincoop, 'Risk Sharing within the United States: What Do Financial Markets and Fiscal Federalism Accomplish?', *The Review of Economics and Statistics* 83 (2001): 688–698.

[82] Asdrubali, Sorensen and Yosha, 'Channels of Interstate Risk Sharing', 1081–1110.

profits generated somewhere else. Of course, this does not address the problem of local banks going bankrupt as a consequence of their exposure to a local shock. However, even in this situation there are various risk-absorbing options still available to the banks. Their creditors (presumably from various locations) may be forced to foot the losses. Local banks can also be taken over by other banks, either from the same or another region. Finally, in fully fledged federations a federal entity, like the Federal Deposit Insurance Corporation (FDIC) in the USA, can step in as yet another scenario, to contain the entailing losses.

None of the above-mentioned mechanisms implies that the regional shock is prevented. They all only mean that capital markets and the banking system can diffuse the entailing costs by spreading them across the other regions of the federation, either through entirely private mechanisms or, as is the case with FDIC interventions, by a federal agency.

Early on the role of financial integration as a source of consumption smoothing and risk sharing was highlighted by the theory of optimum currency areas.[83] Yet, as I emphasised in Chapter 1, the financial integration in the EMU has taken a very narrow, and seriously disruptive, path of interbank markets integrated primarily by short-term liabilities. Instead of providing any shock absorption, this pattern fuelled bubbles leading up to shocks during the first decade of the Eurozone, only to prick them when the interbank market dried up. Soon after the banks still exposed to the countries experiencing the shocks were sheltered from the losses by assistance programmes. In consequence, the governments of the crisis countries redeemed banking sectors of the creditor countries from the shock-absorption role. Ultimately, therefore, the most important private methods of mitigating idiosyncratic shocks, automatically triggered in mature federations, were either non-existing in the Eurozone, or they were disabled by a political fiat when they actually should have borne the brunt.

But is this depiction not outdated now, when the Capital Markets Union (CMU) has become one of the most ambitious goals of the Commission and when developing the banking union has preoccupied European policymakers? When answering this question, the two

[83] Robert Mundell, 'Uncommon Arguments for Common Currencies', in: *The Economics of Common Currencies*, eds. Harry Johnson and Alexander Swoboda (London: Allen & Unwin, 1973): 114–132. See also Ronald I. McKinnon, 'Optimum Currency Areas and Key Currencies: Mundell I versus Mundell II', *Journal of Common Market Studies* 42 (2004): 689–715.

and from ossified socioeconomic policies, all of which have been amplified, but not created, by the basic architecture of the Eurozone. The Greek ex-Minister of Finance Varoufakis may have therefore been right when he argued that 'the problem with currency unions, as Argentina was to discover in the late 1990s and Europe in the aftermath of the Crash of 2008, is the simple fact of life that trade and capital flows can remain systematically unbalanced for decades, if not centuries'.[118] But instead of remedying the source of this conundrum, a countercyclical fiscal union in particular could only maintain the standard of living of the societies exposed to it, despite their crumbling economic fundamentals. It would thus lead to sclerotic solidification of the source problems, as the fate of Italy's south suggests conspicuously. It is particularly telling in this context that Puglia, Campania, Calabria and Sicilia, the Italian *Mezzogiorno*, have been receiving fiscal transfers from the country's north and from the European community for many decades.[119] And, instead of offering shock absorption to other Italian or European regions now, the plight of the Mezzogiorno has caused many in Italy to ask 'what if the South dies?'[120]

All in all, therefore, it is natural that policymakers and opinion leaders are seeking methods of responding to the famous call of Harvey Milk: 'You got to give 'em hope.' Yet, as I tried to explain in this chapter, demand management will not usher in this hope for the Eurozone's south, while attempts to establish a capital markets union or a banking union will not do much good either if the economies which need them most badly suffer from quashed profit opportunities by their innate systemic problems, by the straightjacket of fixed exchange rates and, in consequence, by the economy caving in under the pressure of the mounting pile of debt.

Hope can sustainably return there only when, in the first step, the problem of indebtedness in the Eurozone's south and its inability to

[118] Yanis Varoufakis, *The Global Minotaur: America, Europe and the Future of the Global Economy* (London; New York: Zed Books, 2011): 61.

[119] For an insightful analysis in a broader European context, see Wolfgang Streeck and Lea Elsässer, 'Monetary Disunion: The Domestic Politics of Euroland', *Journal of European Public Policy* 23 (2016): 1–24.

[120] Gian Antonio Stella and Sergio Rizzo, *Se Muore il Sud* (Milano: Feltrinelli, 2013). For a pointed and balanced summary of what the *Mezzogiorno* debacle entails for the idea of a Eurozone fiscal union see Alberto Mingardi, 'What Europe Can Learn from Italy', *Politico*, 2 March 2017, available at www.politico.eu/article/what-europe-can-learn-from-italy-economics-budget-monetary-union/.

function in the monetary harness of the single currency is tackled head-on and, in the second step, when European policies are recalibrated to counter the socioeconomic and institutional problems of the periphery. The next chapter deals with the first of the two issues. Chapters 7 and 8 concentrate on the second.

6 Redenomination

6.1 The Crumbling Original Constitutional Setup

According to the understanding of the Eurozone's constitutional script championed in particular by German policymakers during the nascent stage of the single curency, the politically contingent rules for maintaining fiscal responsibility, epitomised by the SGP (discussed more broadly in Chapter 2), differed conspicuously from the unforgiving and automatic scenario for what should follow when a Member State is priced out of international sovereign debt markets. Before the Maastricht setup was given another meaning during the sovereign debt crisis, the constitutional accord implied that the government allowing its fiscal policy to deteriorate to the point at which financial markets no longer roll over its debt ought to find itself in the ninth circle of hell. Due to the no-bailout clause, governments of the other EU countries would not come to its rescue. Nor should the ECB or the national central bank cushion the collision with the ground, due to the prohibition on monetary financing.[1]

The reasons for the worsening of the fiscal stance should not matter. The wording of the Treaty makes it clear in particular that the countries sharing the single currency should not receive financial assistance either from the EU or its individual Member States once in a balance-of-payments crisis. The Treaty (Art. 143 TFEU) admits

[1] Matthias Ruffert, 'The European Debt Crisis and European Union Law', *Common Market Law Review* 48 (2011): 1777–1806; Stefan Korioth, 'Das Rechtsregime für die Unterstützung notleidender Staaten des Euro-Raums – Analyse nach Maßgabe des nationalen und des Unionsrechts', in: *Grundlagen, aktuelle Entwicklungen und Perspektiven der Europäischen Währungsunion*, eds. Eckhard Pache and Kyrill-A. Schwarz (Baden-Baden: Nomos, 2012), 61–97.

that the countries outside the Eurozone could experience 'a sudden crisis in the balance of payments', in which case they are allowed to receive mutual financial assistance from the other Member States. Yet, because the euro club was thought to be immune to balance-of-payments crises (more on this in Chapter 1), its members were explicitly excluded from the Treaty provisions authorising the EU to rescue the countries in 'a sudden crisis in the balance of payments'. Granted, the Treaty provides (Art. 122(2) TFEU) that if a Eurozone country 'is in difficulties or is seriously threatened with severe difficulties caused by natural disasters or exceptional occurrences beyond its control, the Council, on a proposal from the Commission, may grant, under certain conditions, Union financial assistance to the Member State concerned'. This Treaty basis was used in 2010 to set up the €60 billion EFSM – the bailout vehicle for Ireland and Portugal in operation during the first phase of the sovereign debt crisis. But, while no challenge to the EFSM's legality has ever reached any court, it requires a particularly ignorant observer to argue that the Irish, or the Portuguese, or any other balance-of-payments crisis plaguing the Eurozone in the last decade was caused either by a natural disaster or by any other calamity beyond the control of the national government. Quite to the contrary: both the Irish and the Portuguese macroeconomic imbalances were an outcome of a certain fiscal, economic and social policy design pursued at the national level.

According to this stringent reading of the Eurozone's constitution, neither the smaller bailout schemes (the EFSM, just mentioned, and the Greek Loan Facility – the almost €80 billion bilateral loans scheme pooled by the Commission in May 2010 to bail out Greece the first time) – nor the bigger EFSF and the ESM, set up later, should ever have come into existence.

In addition, a Eurozone country – again, according to the original constitutional script – would be agonised further, because external devaluation (more on this in Chapter 3) would not ameliorate its macroeconomic adjustment. The IMF could hardly be expected to significantly assuage the entailing pains of the inevitable internal devaluation either, because its resources are too limited to offer a meaningful cushion to any advanced economy.

Restructuring public debt is the main shock absorption option available in this situation. Defaulting sovereigns ought to negotiate their debt restructuring with their creditors, which – according to the original Eurozone's design – were supposed to be all private. No Treaty provision whatsoever has ever precluded this scenario. Contrary to the no-bailout clause, stating that 'assuming the commitments of another Member State' by EU countries or its institutions is precluded, the Treaty has not prevented financial institutions from incurring losses on sovereign paper. Of course, this scenario could force national governments of the financial institutions' home countries to step in and use the public purse to recapitalise the banks burnt by an insolvency of a Eurozone sovereign, in order to prevent a credit crunch stemming from domino effects. But this particular fallout would also be entirely compliant with the Maastricht design, because state aid granted to make good the damage caused by exceptional occurrences is always compatible with the Treaty (Art. 107(2)(b) TFEU).

All in all, while the drafters of the Maastricht accord certainly believed that the worst-case scenario would never materialise, the stringently interpreted Treaty script provided for a system in which every villain would pay for its own sins in such a scenario: the debtor countries for their extravagances, the financial institutions for their reckless investments and the governments of their countries for their mistakes in financial supervision.

The credibility of this pattern was already questioned in the early 1990s.[2] Nonetheless, historical records of the country whose experiences the Eurozone's drafters wanted to emulate – the USA – suggested that it should be viable. More importantly still, some American experiences implied that following it could be the best possible way of solidifying the single currency's political underpinnings.

When, after a few years of excessive borrowing, eight US states and one territory (Arkansas, Illinois, Indiana, Louisiana, Maryland, Michigan, Mississippi, Pennsylvania and Florida) defaulted on their debts in the 1840s, the remaining twelve did not come to their rescue.[3] Instead,

[2] E.g., Clemens Fuest, 'Stabile fiskalpolitische Institutionen für die Europäische Währungsunion', *Wirtschaftsdienst* 10 (1993): 539–545.

[3] See Erik Wibbels, 'Bailouts, Budget Constraints, and Leviathans: Comparative Federalism and Lessons from the Early United States', *Comparative Political Studies* 36 (2003): 475–508, William English, 'Understanding the Costs of Sovereign Default: American State Debts in the 1840s', *American Economic Review* 86 (1996): 259–275; Alasdair Roberts, '"An Ungovernable Anarchy": The United States' Response to Depression and Default, 1837–1848', *Intereconomics* 45 (2010): 196–202; John Joseph Wallis, Richard E. Sylla and Arthur Grinath, 'Sovereign Debt and Repudiation: The Emerging-Market Debt Crisis in the US States, 1839–1843', *NBER Working Paper* No. 10753, September 2004, available at www.nber.org/papers/w10753.

however, of unleashing its disintegration, the crisis strengthened the young republic. As Frieden summarised it, 'the eventual result was twofold. On the one hand, once the debts were restructured and the states resumed normal operations, they were substantially more careful about their own financial and fiscal policies. On the other hand, pressure grew for a more effective centralisation of monetary and financial policies.'[4] The American Union became healthier and more resilient as a result.

The outlays on the European balance-of-payments assistance have been many times higher, which suggests that the same path should be chosen all the more so here as well.[5] Unfortunately, the American episode differs from the European crisis in one fundamental respect: in the USA, the states that avoided the spending spree knew they would avoid losses if they had not bailed out the defaulting ones, because their banking systems were not particularly exposed to the debts of the states in trouble. The debt was either owned by the residents of the defaulting states or by foreigners. The Eurozone's creditor countries could not be spared in a similar manner, because 'in 1994 roughly 85 per cent of Greek public debt was held by domestic investors (banks, insurance and pension funds, and others) ... By 2009 debt holdings completely reversed with almost 82.5 per cent held by foreign investors, 93.5 per cent of which were claims by European banks.'[6] Thus a debt restructuring following the Greek default in 2010 would have entailed serious losses for financial institutions located in the creditor countries, France and Germany in particular.

Again, these institutions should have been burnt according to the understanding of the rules of the game championed in particular by the German governments before the sovereign debt crisis. But in 2010 the script confronted national leaders of the creditor countries with a task extremely dangerous for their political careers: they would have to admit to the taxpayers that public funds ought to be used to pay both

[4] Jeffry Frieden, 'Lessons for the Euro from Early American Monetary and Financial History', *Bruegel Essay and Lecture Series*, May 2016, 29, available at bruegel.org/wp-content/uploads/2016/05/essay_frieden_may16.pdf.

[5] According to Robert Inman, 'Managing Country Debts in the European Monetary Union: Stronger Rules or Stronger Union?', in: *Political, Fiscal and Banking Union in the Eurozone?*, eds. Franklin Allen, Elena Carletti and Joanna Gray (Philadelphia: FIC Press 2013), 83: 'the costs of the bailout [during the US debt crisis of the 1840s] would have been $200 million or approximately $6.2 bn in today's dollars'. This figure is comparable to the actual payouts within the 2008–2012 balance-of-payments assistance programme to the tiny Latvia (€4.5 billion).

[6] Nikolaos Zahariadis, 'The Politics of Risk-sharing: Fiscal Federalism and the Greek Debt Crisis', *Journal of European Integration* 35 (2013): 277.

for the profligacy and frauds of the consecutive Greek governments in the preceding years and for the recklessness of the northern banks feeding it up. And all this should happen shortly after the public purse had been used to bail out financial institutions gambling on the US subprime market. The chances that a political career could survive any such a communication were extremely thin. Hence another tack was chosen: of defying the constitutional script, denying that the Greek debt was unsustainable and rejecting that some of the Greek syndromes were symptomatic for other peripheral Eurozone countries.

6.2 The Gamble for Resurrection

Claiming that the Greek debt remained sustainable was problematic, however, simply because the figures did not add up. The Greek fiscal and economic outlook was making it very clear that Greece was insolvent rather than illiquid. And because an insolvent debtor is by definition unable to settle its debts, lending more money to it without restructuring its debts first only predicted higher losses to its creditors down the road.[7]

Back in 2010, European creditors were not much concerned about debt sustainability analyses demonstrating that an upfront Greek debt restructuring was necessary. In 2013 the IMF admitted that 'an upfront restructuring would have been better for Greece although this was not acceptable to the euro partners. A delayed debt restructuring ... provided a window for private creditors to reduce exposures and shift debt into official hands ... leaving taxpayers and the official sector on the hook.'[8] Put more concisely, 'by the time the IMF was invited to provide its expertise and financing in late March 2010, the option of debt restructuring at the programme's outset was off the table'.[9]

Instead of insisting on Greek debt restructuring, the IMF succumbed to the European leaders' inability to admit the truth. To do so, the Fund altered its policy on the so-called exceptional access to its funding, i.e.,

[7] For a more nuanced analysis see Philip R. Wood, *Principles of International Insolvency* (London: Sweet & Maxwell, 2007).

[8] International Monetary Fund, 'Greece: Ex Post Evaluation of Exceptional Access under the 2010 Stand-By Arrangement', *IMF Country Report* No. 13/156, June 2013, 28, available at www.imf.org/external/pubs/ft/scr/2013/cr13156.pdf.

[9] Independent Evaluation Office of the IMF, 'The IMF and the Crises in Greece, Ireland, and Portugal: An Evaluation by the Independent Evaluation Office', 8 July 2016, 15, available at www.ieo-imf.org/ieo/files/completedevaluations/EAC__REPORT%20v5.PDF.

financing above normal lending limits. Its rules at that time rendered the exceptional access contingent on four conditions, one of which was 'a high probability that debt will remain sustainable, based on rigorous and systematic analysis'.[10] Because the IMF's 'rigorous and systematic analysis' did not point to any such a high probability in the case of Greece, a loophole was introduced to the policy, to allow the institution to join the bandwagon of Greek creditors. As the amended policy would have now provided, 'in instances where there are significant uncertainties that make it difficult to state categorically that there is a high probability that the debt is sustainable ... exceptional access would be justified if there is a high risk of international systemic spillovers'.[11]

The IMF explained that 'while risks regarding debt sustainability are undeniably high, the Fund's support is nevertheless justified given the new government's strong initiatives and the substantial cofinancing by the eurozone countries, coupled with the systemic concerns arising from spillover effects if Greece were not given an opportunity to improve its economic policies'.[12] When read carefully, this one sentence shows that the IMF, just like its European creditor peers, was ready to play a gamble for resurrection in Greece. It implies that rescue financing with no previous debt restructuring should have happened in Greece back in 2010, first, because the new government was determined to fix the economy; second, because other Eurozone countries were willing to pour billions into its rescue; and, third, because banking systems of

[10] International Monetary Fund, 'Access Policy in Capital Account Crises' (SM/02/246; 7/30/02), 29 July 2002, 13, available at www.imf.org/external/np/tre/access/2003/pdf/072902.pdf.

[11] International Monetary Fund, 'Access Policy and Limits in the Credit Tranches and under the Extended Fund Facility and on Overall Access to the Fund's General Resources, and Exceptional Access Policy – Review and Modification', prepared by the Legal Department of the IMF, as updated as of 31 December 2013. Later on this requirement was altered again. According to the policy updated as of 29 February 2016: 'Where the member's debt is assessed to be unsustainable ex ante, exceptional access will only be made available where the financing being provided from sources other than the Fund restores debt sustainability with a high probability. Where the member's debt is considered sustainable but not with a high probability, exceptional access would be justified if financing provided from sources other than the Fund, although it may not restore sustainability with high probability, improves debt sustainability and sufficiently enhances the safeguards for Fund resources', available at www.imf.org/external/pubs/ft/sd/index.asp?decision=14064-(08/18).

[12] International Monetary Fund, 'Greece: Staff Report on Request for Stand-By Arrangement', *IMF Country Report* No. 10/110, May 2010, 25, available at www.imf.org/external/pubs/ft/scr/2010/cr10110.pdf.

other Eurozone countries were highly exposed to the Greek sovereign debt. Symptomatically, however, none of the arguments supporting the bailout was based on an implication that the Greek debt was sustainable. And in the event of a Greek insolvency none of the other three premises of intervention could provide much of a consolation.

On the other hand, as any game for resurrection, this one too had some chances to succeed. When the first Greek bailout programme was agreed in 2010, the Greek public debt stood at 115 per cent of GDP. The decision-makers could thus hope that with a (substantial) dose of good luck, if the Greek economy would only grow briskly again, the debt level could be reduced gradually towards the Maastricht target of 60 per cent of GDP. While they were clearly wrong, assuming that fiscal consolidation can be expansionary (more on it in Chapter 3), they were correct in believing that, when it comes to debt sustainability, macroeconomic fundamentals and prevailing political attitudes matter much more than econometric formulae. If Ireland managed to miraculously reduce its debt level from 119 per cent of GDP in 2013 to 75 per cent three years later – the hope of the gamblers could have been – so could other highly indebted countries, like Portugal, Italy, Cyprus or even Greece. The only condition was that sufficiently strong economic growth be engineered (it reached a whopping 25.6 per cent of GDP in Ireland in 2015).[13]

Furthermore, because debt sustainability depends on macroeconomic variables, an insolvent debtor may only become illiquid on paper if sufficiently optimistic future variables are taken into calculation. Back in 2010, the creditors, after putting the Greek macroeconomic data together, figured out that Greece needed budget surpluses of at least 6 per cent of GDP since 2014, economic growth of 2.75 per cent since 2015 and inflation only moderately below EU average for the bailout gamble to pan out.[14] Such an effort would be historically

[13] See also Chapter 4 on causes of this spectacular achievement. High (even if lower) growth levels are typical for Ireland throughout earlier decades as well: 'Ireland previously (from 1988–2000) had a 4.6 percent of GDP average primary surplus, but during that time, the primary surplus was supported by 7.0 percent per year real (and 10.8 percent nominal) growth': Zsolt Darvas, André Sapir and Guntram Wolff, 'The Long Haul: Managing Exit from Financial Assistance', *Bruegel Policy Contribution*, 20 February 2014, 4–5, available at bruegel.org/2014/02/the-long-haul-managing-exit-from-financial-assistance/.

[14] Published as 'The Economic Adjustment Programme for Greece', *European Economy Occasional Paper* No. 61, May 2010, 35, available at ec.europa.eu/economy_finance/publications/occasional_paper/2010/pdf/ocp61_en.pdf.

unprecedented.[15] And it was entirely improbable in a closed, inefficient economy at the beginning of a painful internal devaluation. The mere scale of the public sector in Greece was making it clear that the fiscal contraction of the size implicated in its programme would wreck the Greek economy, in turn suppressing inflation and making the fiscal goals more difficult to achieve.

In other words, the Greek programme relied on entirely improbable macroeconomic assumptions. The country was insolvent and lending any more to it should have been preceded by debt restructuring. Yet, again, these misgivings were pushed aside by the unassailable political calculus of the politicians in the creditor countries unwilling to risk their political careers by admitting the basic facts. Instead, they chose the strategy heralded in the Introduction: of extending and pretending, or what many commentators have called the 'muddle-through model'.[16]

The muddling through was dressed up with the rhetoric of solidarity and compassion, devised to appeal to the electorates on both sides of the creditor–debtor divide. Chancellor Merkel's famous statement that 'nobody in Europe will be abandoned. Nobody in Europe will be excluded. Europe only succeeds if we work together'[17] epitomises this model better than anything else. In the short term this approach may save political careers and prevent a scenario in which the politicians in charge would go down in history as those who undermined the European project. Its only broader consequence, however, is shifting European fiscal problems between sectors, countries and in time. The 'inclusion' and the 'working together' simply entailed lending to an unviable borrower, expecting it to do the impossible and augmenting the ultimate losses.

[15] Cinzia Alcidi and Daniel Gros, 'Adjustment Difficulties and Debt Overhangs in the Eurozone Periphery', *CEPS Working Document* No. 347, 4 May 2011, available at www.ceps.eu/publications/adjustment-difficulties-and-debt-overhangs-eurozone-periphery.

[16] Josef Janning, 'The Ultimate Test for Merkel's "Muddle-through" Model', *European Council on Foreign Relations*, 10 July 2015, available at www.ecfr.eu/article/commentary_the_ultimate_test_for_merkels_muddle_through_model3066.

[17] Quoted in Quentin Peel, 'German MPs Clash on Future of Eurozone', *Financial Times*, 15 December 2010, available at www.ft.com/content/bb9bea42-085f-11e0-8527-00144feabdc0?mhq5j=e2.

6.3 The IMF Flip-Flops

All of this became painfully clear soon after. Greece did not post anything close to brisk economic growth (in fact, anything close to any economic growth at all), the reformatory zeal of its government evaporated fast, the fiscal consolidation proved very recessionary and unemployment went through the roof.

It is most striking from the perspective of its fiscal travails that even at this stage the creditors were able to come up with debt sustainability models demonstrating that Greece was fiscally viable. Some ambiguities behind the concept of the debt sustainability made it easier. Over a shorter term, debt remains sustainable when the government can demonstrate its ability to service it. This can be done when the primary budget balance, i.e., the difference between government revenue and expenditure, excluding interest, is equal to or higher than the total interest due in the same period. In this case the nominal budget balance is positive, evincing that the government is able to service its debt. In other words, even if a debtor is insolvent under market interest rates, the creditors can still pretend it is only illiquid if they offer it sufficiently low official rates. As Bruegel economists put it: 'Greek public debt does not look sustainable if the country has to return to market borrowing at the end of the third bail-out programme, but could be sustainable if preferential ESM funding continues in the long-term.'[18] This is why some argued that (in this artificial environment) the Greek debt was sustainable.[19]

Maintaining the illusion of Greek fiscal sustainability required, however, something more than tinkering with the concept of debt sustainability or with the underlying macroeconomic assumptions. As I discussed more broadly in Chapter 3, when it turned out in 2011 that Greek public debt kept spiralling out of control, public lenders accepted debt rescheduling and the private lenders who did not manage to withdraw from Greece incurred serious losses in the 2012 PSI.

For the next three years the creditors believed this debt relief would be enough. As late as in mid-2014 the IMF was praising the Greek

[18] Zsolt Darvas and Pia Hüttl, 'Is Greek Public Debt Unsustainable?', *Bruegel Blog Post*, 7 May 2016, available at bruegel.org/2016/05/is-greek-public-debt-unsustainable/.

[19] Ferdinando Giugliano, 'Greece's Debt Pile: Is it Really Unsustainable?', *Financial Times*, 25 January 2015.

government for achieving 'substantial progress on restoring fiscal and external sustainability'.[20] It woke up – suddenly – a year later, a few months into Syriza's government. In mid-2015, conspicuously abandoning its previous stance, the Washington institution publicly asserted that 'significant changes in policies ... not least, lower primary surpluses and a weak reform effort that will weigh on growth and privatization – are leading to substantial new financing needs. Coming on top of the very high existing debt, these new financing needs render the debt dynamics unsustainable.'[21] Only two weeks later, the Greek government succumbed to tough new conditionality demands. Yet, the IMF remained unmoved. It had not signed up to the third Greek bailout.[22]

The important question posed by this turnaround is why it happened when it did. Certainly, the first encounters with the Syriza government made the IMF realise that the gamble for resurrection ultimately failed, or, to put it differently, that Greece went bankrupt in 2010 and that the original macroeconomic assumptions necessary to save its solvency were spurious. Internal devaluation, no matter how inevitable economically to pursue macroeconomic adjustment in a monetary union, and the extend and pretend strategy, no matter how unavoidable politically, only precipitated the failure of the approach chosen in 2010. They paved the way for political forces hostile to the economic adjustment, again no matter how necessary the adjustment was. The Fund's defection – its enraging European leaders by admitting that the Greek government was insolvent precisely when European governments were about to issue it a huge new cheque – should therefore be conceived of as an attempt to rectify the political and economic mistake made in 2010, when the creditors chose the strategy of lending to an unviable borrower.

[20] International Monetary Fund, 'Greece: Grounds for Cautious Optimism', *IMF Survey*, 10 June 2014, available at www.imf.org/external/pubs/ft/survey/so/2014/car060914a.htm.

[21] International Monetary Fund, 'Greece: Preliminary Draft Debt Sustainability Analysis', *IMF Country Report* No. 15/165, 26 June 2015, available at www.imf.org/external/pubs/ft/scr/2015/cr15165.pdf.

[22] The IMF joined it 'in principle' in June 2017, offering a small (less than $2 billion) precautionary programme only after a future debt relief agreement between Greece and its European creditors: Francesco Guarascio, 'IMF to Join Greece Bailout, but No Funds Until Debt Relief Deal: Lagarde', *Reuters*, 15 June 2017, available at www.reuters.com/article/us-eurozone-greece-imf-idUSKBN1962PX.

In a calculation produced in mid-2016 (bearing the cachet of strict confidentiality, yet immediately leaked to the press),[23] the IMF computed the dynamics of the Greek debt under an auspicious 'baseline scenario' of moderate but stable growth rates of 1.25 per cent and of budgetary primary surpluses of 1.5 per cent run for several decades, of reasonable financial market interest rates and model inflation of 2 per cent. Privatisation and bank restructuring also progress stably in this scenario. Even then, however, the level of Greek debt would rocket up to 294 per cent of GDP in 2060 (from almost 180 per cent of GDP at the point of making the projection). So even if the Greek state was run the way it has not been run so far – predictably, reasonably and fairly efficiently – if it overcomes its major fragilities and if exogenous shocks spare it for the next fifty years, the country still ends up with an unprecedented mountain of debt. The message the IMF was sending with such a calculation is loud and clear: lending any longer to Greece without restructuring the public debt held by its official creditors is not a viable option either for the Greeks or for their creditors.

6.4 Bright New... Dead End

After almost a year of bickering with the Washington institution, the Eurozone creditors finally (partly) conceded, admitting that 'the possible debt relief will be delivered at the end of the programme in mid-2018'.[24] Yet they also insisted 'that nominal haircuts are excluded'.[25] Future debt rescheduling and interest rebates were therefore implied, and debt restructuring covering partial cancellation of the principal on the debt (notional haircuts) was precluded. Adjusting again to these political constraints, the IMF recommended, in the first place, longer grace periods, i.e., a moratorium, lasting at least until 2040, on repayments of the Greek loans held by official creditors (as well as longer deferrals of interest payments).[26] Second, and what logically stems from the

[23] International Monetary Fund, 'Greece: Debt Sustainability Summary Note', available at www.documentcloud.org/documents/2840552-IMF-Greece.html.

[24] Eurogroup Statement on Greece, 25 May 2016, available at www.esm.europa.eu/press-releases/eurogroup-statement-greece-25-may-2016.

[25] Eurogroup Statement on Greece, 9 May 2016, available at www.consilium.europa.eu/en/press/press-releases/2016/05/09-eg-statement-greece/.

[26] This uniform grace period for all the loans owed to EFSF, ESM and Member States would be up to six years longer than what is now envisaged in the ESM repayment schedule and up to twenty years longer than the grace periods within the Greek loan facility.

longer grace periods, also maturities (end dates of the loans) should be extended by twenty to forty years. Third, the IMF endorsed the replacement of the floating rates on the Greek debt possessed by official creditors with a single fixed rate of 1.5 per cent at least until 2045. Finally, it underwrote the idea – wholeheartedly supported by the Greek ex-Finance Minister Yanis Varoufakis, among others – of 'GDP-linked bonds'[27] under the additional condition that the third bailout to expire in 2018 is successfully completed.

And yet, despite all these efforts and under the very auspicious baseline scenario described earlier, the rescheduling outlined by the IMF in 2016 would only bring down the Greek debt to 106 per cent in 2060. In other words, thanks to this debt rescheduling in 2060 Greece returns to the public debt level it posted immediately before the outbreak of the sovereign debt crisis, assuming it can pursue very responsible fiscal policies for more than forty years, that it can achieve optimal inflation (the goal on which it has limited influence) and positive average growth rates. It needs fifty years of struggles only to return to the point of departure.

In addition, one of the lessons to be learnt from the sovereign debt crisis is that optimistic baseline scenarios do not materialise in Greece. This tendency can only be expected to fortify in the future. The very high unemployment recorded for years now has produced devastating hysteresis effects (erosion of human capital) and massive human haemorrhages. As Constantinos Michalos, the President of the Athens Chamber of Commerce and Industry, put it in mid-2015: 'The most dynamic part of Greece's human resources is leaving … Brain drain is one of the biggest problems.'[28] The country has been gradually depopulating since 2010, with serious economic and fiscal consequences of ageing yet to materialise. Its banking system has been in shambles, with more than one in three of all bank loans seriously overdue. Add

[27] GDP-linked bonds tie repayments to the country's economic performance; the repayments are higher when the economic growth accelerates, and go down in the opposite scenario. See also Zsolt Darvas, 'The Greek Debt Trap: An Escape Plan', *Bruegel Policy Contribution* No. 2012/19, 9 November 2012, available at bruegel.org/2012/11/the-greek-debt-trap-an-escape-plan/; Charles Goodhart, 'GDP Bonds Are Answer to Greek Debt Problem', *Financial Times*, 5 August 2015, Olivier Blanchard, Paolo Mauro and Julien Acalin, 'The Case for Growth-Indexed Bonds in Advanced Economies Today', *Peterson Institute for International Economics Policy Brief* No. 16-2, February 2016, available at piie.com/publications/policy-briefs/case-growth-indexed-bonds-advanced-economies-today.

[28] Helen Popper, 'The Erosion of Greece's Future', *Politico*, 13 July 2015, available at www.politico.eu/article/greece-future-youth-unemployment-grexit-crisis-eurozone/.

to this deflationary tendencies accompanying any internal devaluation, which in turn do their part in augmenting the debt overhang, and devastated institutional and socioeconomic tissue (more on the last point in the next chapter).

These are all symptoms of a very serious social, economic and political plight. Worst of all, the crucial ingredient of any successful political and economic transformation – hope – has largely evaporated from the lands between the Ionian and the Aegean seas. If anything, this country is poised for major social and political upheavals when the next economic slowdown occurs, not for decades of economic growth and stability under responsible and thrifty governments. This is why the debt relief contemplated when this book hits bookstores is yet another exercise in unrealistic forecasting which, if anything, will feed a sense of despair and hopelessness. So, while admitting that the extend-and-pretend strategy of the creditors has backfired would indeed be tantamount to admitting that Europe has failed in Greece (which only the IMF has dared to imply so far), it is equally certain that otherwise neither Greece nor the euro can be fixed.

6.5 How to Disarm the Ticking Bomb?

Since 2010, Greece has been in need of a new engine of economic growth, a new social contract and a new political class. Confronting its insolvency head-on is a necessary, even if insufficient in itself, prerequisite for this. Five decades of sacrifices for the mistakes committed by their fathers and grandfathers at the turn of the twenty-first century, only to return to the brink of the precipice in 2060, is not really what Greek society may consider a fresh start. It is merely the next stage of the muddle-through strategy. A network of forty-six non-governmental organisations (NGOs) from twenty European countries shrewdly put it in an open letter to the Eurogroup published soon after the plans for the post-2018 debt relief endorsed by the Eurogroup were announced in mid-2016: 'The evidence from developing countries' debt crises since the 1980s is that attempts to address debt overhangs through debt reprofiling have left countries burdened with unsustainable debts and have led to lost decades for development. Only actual haircuts managed to resolve the debt overhangs and restore growth. It is fair to conclude that the situation will not be different when it comes to Greece.'[29]

[29] Available at www.eurodad.org/files/pdf/573db8530e0bc.pdf.

In addition, while politicians have been at pains to argue that Greece is a basket case, in fact it is the most extreme example of a malaise plaguing the Eurozone's south more generally.

By the end of 2016, government debt reached more than 130 per cent of GDP in Italy and Portugal, and was heading towards 110 per cent of GDP in Cyprus. Certainly, the figures themselves do not mean that these public debts are unsustainable. What really matters is whether the countries are able to generate growth higher than their deficits. If so, their debt compared to the GDP will diminish. Economists may come up with their formulae, claiming that above certain levels of debt – say 90 per cent of GDP,[30] or 107 per cent of GDP,[31] or any other – the economy is irreparably damaged. But the example of Ireland, mentioned earlier, undermines all of their calculations, providing ammunition to those who argue that 'there is little evidence for a negative long-run effect of sovereign debt on economic growth'.[32]

On the other hand, engineering the economic growth necessary to follow Ireland out of the macroeconomic and fiscal shock is very difficult when political processes are ineffective, when governance standards deteriorate, when the social tissue is compromised, when economic policies throttle down, when the demographic situation is adverse, and when the financial system is a minefield. In all these respects Italy, Cyprus (and – to a lesser degree – Spain and Portugal) resemble Greece and differ from Ireland. As long as the monetary policy suppresses interest rates to unprecedentedly low levels, these ailments are not very pernicious, because then even low economic growth prevents public debt from going off the tracks, unless the government runs a spectacularly irresponsible fiscal policy. But the public debt of the Eurozone's south is a ticking bomb, an accident waiting to happen when inflation and interest rates go up. The longer the rates remain low, the longer the moment of the explosion can

[30] Carmen M. Reinhart and Kenneth S. Rogoff, 'Growth in a Time of Debt', *American Economic Review*, 100 (2010): 573–578.

[31] Pier Carlo Padoan, Urban Sila and Paul van den Noord, 'Avoiding Debt Traps: Fiscal Consolidation, Financial Backstops and Structural Reforms', *OECD Journal: Economic Studies* 2012, available at www.oecd.org/eco/public-finance/AvoidingdebttrapsFiscalconsolidationfinancialbackstopsandfinancialreforms.pdf.

[32] Matthijs Lof and Tuomas Malinen, 'Determinants of the Growth and Sovereign Debt Correlation', *VOX CEPR's Policy Portal*, 25 May 2014, available at voxeu.org/article/growth-and-sovereign-debt-correlation.

be postponed, but by the same token the bigger its striking power will become – the higher the ultimate costs of debt restructuring as well as the more arbitrary and inequitable their final distribution will be. Economists do not hold much doubt about this causality.[33] As they also argue, while the relationship between the scope of the debt cancellation and the effects for subsequent borrowing conditions is complicated, larger haircuts (which, as I just indicated, will grow the longer the extend-and-pretend strategy lasts) are associated with higher subsequent spreads on bond yield and longer periods of exclusion from capital markets.[34]

This leads to the question of how to dismantle the bomb.

Unexpectedly, a viable blueprint should start with a proposal uttered by the German Finance Minister, Wolfgang Schäuble, at the apex of the psychological war with Greek Prime Minister Tsipras over the fate of Greece and its creditors after the fruitless expiry of the second bailout package. On 10 July 2015, the German Finance Minister sent a one-page memo to a few other top European officials. This short non-paper argued that, as an alternative to the third bailout, Greece could 'be offered swift negotiations on a time-out from the Eurozone, with possible debt restructuring, if necessary, in a Paris Club-like format over at least the next 5 years … The time-out solution should be accompanied by supporting Greece as an EU member and the Greek people with growth enhancing, humanitarian and technical assistance over the next years.'[35]

The very moment the proposal was aired, its form and the author gave the idea an offensive spin. Even some Germans perceived it as 'a German diktat and nothing other than blackmail'.[36] Schäuble's stub concept was greeted with hostility both in Brussels and in the

[33] Ugo Panizza, 'Do We Need a Mechanism for Solving Sovereign Debt Crises? A Rule-Based Discussion', *Graduate Institute of International and Development Studies Working Paper* No. 03/2013, February 2013, available at www.econstor.eu/bitstream/10419/77428/1/736082816.pdf.

[34] Juan J. Cruces and Christoph Trebesch, 'Sovereign Defaults: The Price of Haircuts', *American Economic Journal: Macroeconomics* 5 (2013), July 2013, 85–117, available at www.aeaweb.org/articles?id=10.1257/mac.5.3.85.

[35] 'Comments on the Latest Greek Proposals', 10 July 2015, available at www.sven-giegold.de/wp-content/uploads/2015/07/grexit_bundesregierung_non_paper_10_juli_2015.pdf.

[36] Dietmar Bartsch, a prominent figure of the German Die Linke party, quoted in Simon Shuster, 'Germany Finds Itself Cast as the Villain in Greek Drama', *The Time*, 15 July 2015, available at time.com/3959164/germany-greece-bailout-deal-athens-merkel/.

Eurozone's south. A senior Brussels diplomat was reported as saying 'A lot of people were really scandalised. It was incredible. No country could have accepted this.'[37] The then-Italian Prime Minister Renzi immediately retorted that 'Italy does not want Greece to exit the euro and to Germany I say: enough is enough … humiliating a European partner after Greece has given up on just about everything is unthinkable'.[38] Ultimately, therefore, the memo was perceived as an attempt to mount pressure on the Greeks to accept the third bailout programme rejected in a national referendum only a few days earlier. It paved the way for yet another round of the extend-and-pretend game, earning the German Finance Minister even more foes in the Eurozone's south.

While, however, the idea was aired in probably the worst possible moment and in the worst possible form, in fact it depicted the essence of the only durable way out of the Eurozone's fiscal trap. European leaders clearly sensed it back in July 2015. While the Italian Prime Minister was ranting and raving, he was not in the majority back then, even if others were much more reticent about expressing their opinions. As Schäuble averred a few months later, at the European Council meeting taking place the day after the memo was circulated, only Greek, French, Italian and Cypriot delegations opposed the plan.[39] Some others, like the Slovakian Finance Minister, who said: 'I appreciate the courageous Wolfgang Schäuble proposals on timeout Grexit … He told us the truth about the situation,'[40] had very different feelings about the idea. It was unacceptable not because it was wrong, but because it was aired in the wrong situation.

This leads to some major questions. Why was it right in substance? What specific steps would it require and what price would it entail? Would it ever be politically acceptable? And, finally, is it legally possible within the existing Treaty framework? In the remainder of this chapter I will deal with each of these questions in turn.

[37] 'Three Days That Saved the Euro', *Guardian*, 22 October 2015, available at www.theguardian.com/world/2015/oct/22/three-days-to-save-the-euro-greece.

[38] 'Italy's Renzi to Tell Germany to Accept Greece Deal', *Reuters*, 12 July 2015, available at www.reuters.com/article/us-eurozone-greece-renzi-idUSKCN0PM08320150712.

[39] Jack Duffy, 'Schaeuble: Plan for Greece "Timeout" Was Widely Backed', 20 October 2015, available at www.marketnews.com/content/schaeuble-plan-greece-timeout-was-widely-backed-press.

[40] Gabriele Steinhauser, 'Schäuble's Timeout Plan for Greece Was "Courageous", Says Slovak Minister', *The Wall Street Journal*, 15 July 2015, available at http://blogs.wsj.com/brussels/2015/07/15/schaubles-timeout-plan-for-greece-was-courageous-says-slovak-minister/.

6.6 The Three Tenets

The Schäuble plan relied on three presumptions. The first was debt relief going beyond debt rescheduling, i.e., also covering principal cancellations. The second was the Eurozone time-out: an euphemism for Grexit. The third was an assistance programme funded by the creditors to finance reforms necessary for the longer-term debt sustainability of Greece.

The three tenets will be discussed in reverse order, to reveal the background before turning to the fulcrum.

The last of the elements, especially when proposed by the hawkish Finance Minister in the government of Chancellor Merkel, smells of more austerity and despised structural reforms administered by some new reincarnation of the despised Troika. But, as I will argue in the next two chapters, Greece, as well as other countries of the Eurozone's south, badly needs investments and reforms of its institutional and socioeconomic systems. Greece has no expertise or resources to pursue the reforms necessary to be pulled out of the meagre position in which it has found itself recently. While explaining this point takes two chapters, it is necessary to point out here that no debt restructuring of the Eurozone's south can succeed without significantly redesigning the European approach to structural reforms, to the role of the EU in the socioeconomic realm and to the redistribution at EU level.

Grexit – and the secession from the Eurozone of other traditionally soft-currency countries – is another indispensable tenet of a proper debt relief. There are two main reasons for this. One of them refers to the countries to benefit from it. The other is necessary from the perspective of the creditor countries.

Eurozone exits of soft-currency nations (a byword for a social, economic and political system, rather than a currency system used therein) are justified because, as explained in Chapter 3, a country in a single-currency area finding itself in a balance-of-payments crisis cannot perform macroeconomic adjustment other than through internal devaluation – another expression for austerity. When the country is monetarily sovereign the adjustment can rely on external devaluation, i.e., on downward realignments of its nominal exchange rate (combined, in that way or another, with internal devaluation to mitigate the effects of the adjustment on the costs of imports and on debt denominated in foreign currencies).[41] The more the external

[41] Stefanie Walter, *Financial Crises and the Politics of Macroeconomic Adjustments* (New York: Cambridge University Press, 2013).

devaluation drives the process, the less the internal devaluation (austerity) is needed to achieve the macroeconomic adjustment.

The very division between the hard-currency nations, cyclically and structurally compatible with the dominating German economy, and the soft-currency nations, which was derailing the attempts to harmonise exchange rates between the 1970s and 1990s, showed, furthermore, that some societies are well-positioned to adjust through internal devaluation, while others find it very tortuous and ineffective. The experience of the Eurozone's south since the onset of the sovereign debt crisis affirms that the difference has persisted in most of the cases, rendering the EMU too disparate to function properly.

In a shorter term the disparity makes the single currency cheaper for the creditor economies, compared to a situation when the traditionally soft-currency countries leave the system. The participation of the soft-currency nations puts downward pressure on the euro's exchange rate, boosting exports of the traditionally strong-currency states – an advantage their industries and government budgets would not enjoy in a different scenario. At the same time it acts as a *vincolo esterno* (external tie), without which the Eurozone's south would face serious political, economic and social instability.[42] Sharing currency with the strong-currency regimes mitigates risks in the banking systems of the south, prevents the danger that inflation could spiral out of control, that the debts denominated in euros could make debtors insolvent and that society becomes impoverished in consequence of recurring external devaluations. The then-Greek Minister of Finance, Yannis Varoufakis, confessed in summer 2015 in a conference call, which then leaked to the press, that: 'Once you are inside the grasps of a monetary union, it is ever so hard to create the kind of public dialogue which is necessary in order to prepare people for what comes, for the process of disengagement from the currency union, while at the same time not precipitating a collapse. It's a little bit like, imagine if you had to prepare a population, an electorate, for a devaluation, a very large devaluation,

[42] Mainly this motivation was driving the Eurozone's south to join the single currency back in the 1990s. Discussing Italy, Kenneth Dyson and Kevin Featherstone wrote: 'A greater fiscal and monetary discipline was necessary for two reasons: to contain the "part-state" (*partitocrazia*); and to secure Italy's chief foreign-policy interest, its European role. EMU provided the means to achieve both objectives: it would be a new *vincolo esterno* (external tie) to encourage domestic discipline and at the same time tie Italy to a deepening European integration process': *The Road to Maastricht: Negotiating Economic and Monetary Union* (Oxford: Oxford University Press, 1999): 452.

12 months before it takes place, through a dialogue. You can understand that this is an impossibility.'[43] And, last but not least, the financial system of the outcast would immediately implode were it cut off from the Eurosystem's liquidity, blasting the whole economy out of existence. No prime minister, either in the country to leave or in the ones to stay, wants to witness the social and political convulsions that would follow.

The costs – uncertain, but no doubt far from insignificant – of leaving the Eurozone may justify why in Greece, Portugal, Italy, Cyprus and Spain there are about twice as many supporters of the euro than there are objectors, regardless of all the pains their societies and economies have suffered when deprived of the external devaluation channel of macroeconomic adjustment.[44] It may also explain why in the creditor countries the share of the population accepting the euro is even higher: for every one detractor you find about four supporters of the EMU there.[45]

But at the same time the situation in which the Eurozone's south is entrapped in a monetary system it has never been fit for inhibits its economic revival (which only means this: a durable economic revival is not guaranteed by secession from the Eurozone, but it will be hindered unless the most indebted countries return to their national currencies). The entrapment breeds social despair, further undercutting, otherwise traditionally fragile, political processes and the state capacity: 'the ability of a government to administer its territory effectively',[46] forcing at the same time the creditors to commit very significant resources to multifaceted financial rescue operations. The secession would give the southern countries the competitive advantage on export markets they so desperately need in order to generate economic growth. It

[43] Peter Spiegel, 'Varoufakis Unplugged: The London Call Transcript', *Financial Times*, 27 July 2015, available at blogs.ft.com/brusselsblog/2015/07/27/varoufakis-unplugged-the-london-call-transcript/.

[44] Greece: 68–30 per cent, Portugal: 69–26 per cent, Italy: 53–37 per cent, Cyprus: 52–43 per cent, Spain: 71–25 per cent: Standard Eurobarometer 85, Autumn 2016, Annex, T86.

[45] Germany: 81–15 per cent, Luxembourg: 87–11 per cent, Netherlands: 77–22 per cent, Austria: 62–34 per cent, Finland: 78–20 per cent: Standard Eurobarometer 85, Autumn 2016, Annex, T86.

[46] See, for example, Shaoguang Wang, 'The Rise of the Regions: Fiscal Reform and the Decline of Central State Capacity in China', in: *The Waning of the Communist State: Economic Origins of Political Decline in China and Hungary*, ed. Andrew Walder (Berkeley; Los Angeles; Oxford: University of California Press, 1995) 89; Daron Acemoglu, Camilo García-Jimeno and James A. Robinson, 'The Role of State Capacity in Economic Development', *The Political Economist* XI (1) (2015): 7–9.

would also force restructuring of their debts, because, when leaving the Eurozone, its highly indebted countries would become unable to service their debts denominated in euros with their depreciating national currency. It would also help the countries inflate a part of their remaining debt away.

Politicians, both in the south and in the north, have viewed the economic and political costs of this scenario as greater than the costs of the extend-and-pretend strategy. Acting according to the preferences of their electorates, overwhelmingly supporting the euro, the decision-makers have confirmed a broader conclusion, drawn when the Eurozone was at its nascent stage: 'Rather than reflecting the benefits of institutionalized exchange, continuing integration could easily reflect the rising costs of non-Europe.'[47] But at some point the cost–benefit analysis will most probably point to the exit option, because the Eurozone system is irreparably, as argued in the previous chapter, deprived of any other serious shock absorption mechanisms. The exits may happen in a controlled way, as a part of a debt redemption and a reinvention of the European project, or abruptly, propelling European disintegration. In that way or another, though, they are quite inevitable.

6.7 Moral Hazard

Another reason why the debt redemption of the Eurozone's soft-currency nations is impossible without the latter group exiting the single monetary system stems from an insurmountable moral hazard problem. The Eurozone countries facing debt overhangs manifest some (or many) traits of the 'soft budget constraint' syndrome. This term, coined by the Hungarian economist Janos Kornai a few decades ago, describes a situation in which economic agents rely on state subsidies, which undermines market efficiency and ultimately leads to wasteful allocation of resources, both private and public.[48] The soft budget constraint may stem in particular from overly closed links between publically owned companies and public officials, supported by an ideological

[47] Paul Pierson, 'The Path to European Integration: A Historical Institutionalist Analysis', *Comparative Political Studies* 29 (1996): 145.

[48] Eric S. Maskin, 'Theories of the Soft Budget-Constraint', *Japan and the World Economy* 8 (1996): 125–133; János Kornai, Eric Maskin and Gérard Roland, 'Understanding the Soft Budget Constraint', available at www.sss.ias.edu/files/papers/econpaper19.pdf.

justification of the links,[49] or from crony capitalism. In that way or another, the societies of the Eurozone's south are familiar with this problem, as they are with ossified and inefficient welfare states (more on this in the next chapter). Each of these factors drives up public debt in the Eurozone's south and each is hard to extirpate, due to collective action problems.[50] Inflation and devaluations were the most conspicuous side effects of the ailments in the Eurozone's south prior to the the EMU. However, while hindering economic activity and entailing wealth corrosion, they were helpful in regaining external competitiveness and in doing away with excessive public debt. The drafters of the Eurozone feared that in the single-currency regime these correcting mechanisms may be replaced by an alternative in which the costs of malfunctioning domestic political, economic and social systems are shifted onto other societies. The no-bailout clause was designed precisely to make it impossible.

Defying it in 2010, top European politicians made the fears all the more justified. The ostensibly reinforced system of economic governance, introduced in the aftermath of the sovereign debt crisis, was to address this problem. But, as discussed in Chapter 2, the Eurozone's 'rules-based system' has been patently incentive-incompatible and is doomed to fail as a consequence.

Remaining in the Eurozone, its south, even after a substantial debt restructuring, would still find itself in a system depressing economic growth, putting upward pressure on public debt and inducing recurring expectations of further debt reliefs. Those in Germany who reacted to the third Greek package by saying 'however much water you put into a bottomless barrel, it will never fill up'[51] quite accurately conceived of the resultant bigger problem. For the very same reason

[49] Kornai, who studied the soft budget constraint in the communist system of Eastern Europe, was particularly interested in this group.

[50] Mancur Olson, who coined the term 'collective action', put it famously: 'the most important single point about small groups … is that they may very well be able to provide themselves with a collective good simply because of the attraction of the collective good to the individual members. In this, small groups differ from larger ones. The larger a group is, the farther it will fall short of obtaining an optimal supply of any collective good, and the less likely that it will act to obtain even a minimum amount of such a good. In short, the larger the group, the less it will further its common interests': Mancur Olson, *The Logic of Collective Action: Public Goods and the Theory of Groups* (Cambridge, MA; London: Harvard University Press, 1965): 36.

[51] Klaus Peter Willsch of the German CDU, quoted by Kate Connolly on Twitter, 17 July 2015.

the German resistance to the idea, epitomised by various concepts of Eurobonds,[52] of debt mutualisation has been similarly excusable.

All in all, because the no-bailout clause is compromised and meaningful shock absorption at the European level remains a very distant dream, there has been no viable alternative to Eurozone exits as a durable remedy to the entailing moral hazard problem. No one who has advocated systemic debt relief and at the same time maintaining the Eurozone in its current composition has come up with a convincing remedy to this problem. Pâris and Wyplosz, for instance, proposed that a supranational agency swaps government paper for its bonds and, as a flipside, that two mechanisms are put in place to eliminate the moral hazard stemming from a national debt relief.[53] First, they argued that the supranational agency should be obliged to execute a reverse swap of the debt in the event that a country benefitting from the relief accumulates public debt again or acts against fiscal discipline (e.g., voting in the Council against sanctions for breaching the rules of the SGP). Second, according to the very same proposal, the Fiscal Compact should be implemented in full. These remedies, however, run against the lesson to be drawn both from the original SGP and its ostensibly reinforced version (discussed in Chapter 2): any version of the rules-based union, to which both of the remedies boil down, will either be bypassed, altered or openly violated, due to the time-inconsistent nature of the political incentives experienced by those who are to execute them.

For the very same reason, the idea of the European Redemption Pact, proposed by the German Council of Economic Experts in late 2011, was stillborn.[54] It assumed that a portion of the Eurozone's sovereign

[52] For an overview see Stijn Claessens, Ashoka Mody and Shahin Vallée, 'Paths to Eurobonds', *IMF Working Paper* No. WP/12/172, 1 July 2012, available at www.imf.org/en/Publications/WP/Issues/2016/12/31/Paths-to-Eurobonds-26034 and Alexandra Hild, Bernhard Herz and Christian Bauer, 'Structured Eurobonds: Limiting Liability and Distributing Profits', *Journal of Common Market Studies* 52 (2014): 250–267.

[53] Pierre Pâris and Charles Wyplosz, 'PADRE. Politically Acceptable Debt Restructuring in the Eurozone', *Geneva Reports on the World Economy Special Report* No. 3, CEPR, January 2014, available at www.cepr.org/sites/default/files/geneva_reports/GenevaP252.pdf and Pierre Pâris and Charles Wyplosz, 'PADRE 2.0:Politically Acceptable Debt Restructuring in the Eurozone', May 2014, available at graduateinstitute.ch/files/live/sites/iheid/files/sites/international_economics/shared/international_economics/prof_websites/wyplosz/Papers/PADRE%202.pdf/.

[54] See the website of the German Council of Economic Experts dedicated to The European Redemption Pact: www.sachverstaendigenrat-wirtschaft.de/schuldentilgungspakt.html?&L=1. For a succinct overview see Armin Steinbach, *Economic Policy Coordination in the Euro Area* (London; New York: Routledge, 2014): 96–98.

debt be (temporarily) transferred to a fund covered by a joint and several liability of the Eurozone countries. The authors highlighted that this would take place 'in exchange for the commitment that they [the Member States] will be using this advantage exclusively to facilitate the reduction of their sovereign debt overhang. Specifically, all participant countries would have to accept the obligation to individually redeem their own transferred debt.'[55] Again, such conditions require a fully viable 'rules-based union', while the Eurozone's is defunct, and, for political reasons, it is impossible to resuscitate it. Chancellor Merkel was therefore on point when she gave the idea short shrift, describing it as 'totally impossible'.[56]

Other experts, sensing that the rules-based union is not a viable remedy, have proposed valves to the moral hazard, based entirely on market mechanisms.[57] Mody and colleagues, for instance, came forth with the idea of 'contingent convertible' bonds providing for automatic restructuring whenever a country's debt-to-GDP ratio crosses an agreed threshold.[58] This forward-looking proposal[59] is based on the premise that purchasers of the bonds ought to have a clear yardstick for sovereign risk incorporated in any bond tranche, which should make it easier for them to enforce fiscal discipline by pricing the bonds accordingly. Yet the whole idea topples down in a system in which the no-bailout clause is compromised, which is the Eurozone's case now. In a

[55] Peter Bofinger et al., 'A Redemption Pact for Europe: Time to Act Now', *VOX CEPR's Policy Portal*, 25 July 2012, available at http://voxeu.org/article/redemption-pact-europe-time-act-now.

[56] Ambrose Evans-Pritchard, 'Debt Crisis: Germany Signals Shift on €2.3 Trillion Redemption Fund for Europe', *The Telegraph*, 13 June 2012, available at www.telegraph.co.uk/finance/financialcrisis/9330398/Debt-crisis-Germany-signals-shift-on-2.3-trillion-redemption-fund-for-Europe.html.

[57] This does not mean that redemption mechanisms based on transferring government bonds to the supranational level do not appeal to market mechanisms. For instance, the blue bond proposal of Bruegel (Jacques Delpla and Jakob von Weizsäcker, 'The Blue Bond Proposal', *Bruegel Policy Brief* No. 2010/03, 5 May 2010, available at www.bruegel.org/publications/publication-detail/publication/403-the-blue-bond-proposal) and the 2011 proposal of the German Council of Economic Experts on the European Redemption Pact both assumed that the safety of borrowing diminishes as the debt-to-GDP ratio grows, which was intended to deter the governments from amassing public debt.

[58] Bergljot Barkbu, Barry Eichengreen and Ashoka Mody, 'Financial Crises and the Multilateral Response: What the Historical Record Shows', *Journal of International Economics* 88 (2012): 422–435; Ashoka Mody, 'Sovereign Debt and Its Restructuring Framework in the Eurozone', *Oxford Review of Economic Policy* 29 (2013): 715–744.

[59] Because no bond contracts now in place provide for such a contingent convertibility, the concept cannot be applied to the legacy debt.

setup implying that fiscally strained sovereigns are bailed out, pricing decisions of bond purchasers would be guided by past experiences of official creditors stepping in and replacing private creditors to suppress the cost of servicing public debt. This invites even more moral hazard, instead of preventing it.

6.8 The Case for Redenomination

Again, therefore: in a single-currency system deprived of a credible no-bailout rule and lacking viable shock absorption mechanisms it is not enough to alleviate the debt burden, as has been the case with Greece. Such a solution would turn back the clock without addressing the underlying problem of the monetary harness unfit for the needs of the local society. This latter problem could be addressed only by what one commentator called a 'resizing solution'[60]: a redenomination, i.e., returning to national currencies, in the Eurozone's countries unfit for the harsh logic of a strong currency regime.

The very idea of some Eurozone countries returning, for example, to drachmas, liras, escudos or pesetas has been an anathema to those who argue that if the euro fails, Europe fails. On the other hand it has been abused by Eurosceptics, who, despising the euro for symbolic reasons, would like to see it unravelled on ideological grounds. Yet, while withdrawals from the Eurozone would indeed have strong symbolic consequences,[61] they are actually a precondition for a stronger, more robust, more effective and healthier union. As Hall remarked shrewdly in this context a few years ago, 'the continued insistence on all countries remaining in the euro, with the continued support this entails from the ECB and other Member States, will lead to an unsustainable spiral of debt and demands for support that may ultimately wreck the European Union itself'.[62]

Averting this fate faces many challenges.

[60] Nazaré da Costa Cabral, 'Which Budgetary Union for the E(M)U?', *Journal of Common Market Studies* 54 (2016): 1280–1295.

[61] President Draghi put it neatly once: 'The banknotes that we issue bear the European flag and are a powerful symbol of European identity': Mario Draghi, 'The Future of the Euro: Stability through Change', *Die Zeit*, 29 August 2012, available at www.ecb.europa.eu/press/key/date/2012/html/sp120829.en.html.

[62] Hal S. Scott, 'When the Euro Falls Apart – A Sequel', *Harvard Public Law Working Paper* No. 12-16, 31 January 2012, 3, available at papers.ssrn.com/sol3/papers.cfm?abstract_id=1998356.

The prime one is that no Eurozone country can return to its national currency against the will of the ECB, which, at each stage, can twist the arms of national governments by depriving domestic financial systems of their access to refinancing credit (more on this in Chapter 3). So, as long as the ECB sticks to its flipside of the 'whatever it takes' pledge – which reads: 'we think the euro is irreversible'[63] – no Eurozone exit can happen.

At some point, however, the ECB will no longer be able to stymie, using its monetary alchemy, the consequences of growing divergences within the Eurozone. Then the option of a consensual withdrawal from the Eurozone will resurface again. And when this happens, policymakers should not repeat the previous mistake of pretending that insolvent debtors face only transitory payment problems. Instead, they ought to get ready for redenomination in the most vulnerable countries of the Eurozone's south.

The process would be difficult, but arguably much more manageable and less painful than is routinely thought.

Preparations for the redenomination ought to be kept secret, which essentially requires that only a very limited number of creditors can know anything about them. Otherwise a major capital flight would set in, sending TARGET imbalances through the roof, demolishing the banking system of the country intending to return to its national currency and tremendously complicating the exit operation. For the same reason, negotiations ought to be 'swift', as Wolfgang Schäuble correctly indicated in his 2015 memo.

The negotiations would have to tackle many issues. Even less redistributive aspects, like choosing the exchange rate applicable at the point of redenomination, organising the process of establishing the new currency (and especially exchanging banknotes and coins), introducing new local payment systems, or imposing capital controls and bank closures,[64] are challenging. The more redistributive points would become even thornier, because any Eurozone country exiting the single currency inevitably faces a steep depreciation of its nominal exchange rate.

[63] Speech by Mario Draghi, President of the European Central Bank at the Global Investment Conference in London, 26 July 2012, available at www.ecb.europa.eu/press/key/date/2012/html/sp120726.en.html.

[64] For organisation and legal issues involved in capital controls see 'Eurozone Bulletin: Capital and Exchange Controls', Linklaters, April 2013, available at www.linklaters.com/pdfs/mkt/london/Eurozone-Bulletin-Capital-Exchange-Controls.pdf.

In the Eurozone's context, depreciation would be the main purpose of redenomination. It allows for the lowering of effective exchange rates where more difficult methods of achieving the same goal, i.e., internal devaluation, have been too ineffective. But it also entails some painful (even if, when redenomination is performed properly, short-lived) economic side effects. Depreciation unavoidably leads to a sudden initial impoverishment of the seceding society. It also hits back on creditors, forcing them to incur a large share of depreciation losses. In consequence, the banking system of a seceding country, the main creditor of households and companies, inevitably goes deeply under in this scenario.

Depreciation expected in any southern country exiting the Eurozone would certainly be deep. Back in 2012, Capital Economics conjectured it could reach as much as 70 per cent.[65] It would also require painful structural reforms, because rigidities in the economy – especially wage indexation or product market regulations inhibiting competition – seriously deteriorate competitiveness gains produced by falling nominal exchange rates, as they boost inflation.[66]

None of this is palatable either for local societies or politicians. Each spurs protracted squabbles between creditors and debtors on how to share the burden of losses. Nonetheless, these effects could be mollified. The scope of depreciation might be mitigated by pegging the exchange rate at a certain margin. In particular, swap lines from the ECB would be useful in backing up the peg.[67] On the other hand, however, while deeper depreciations entail larger upfront losses, they can also be expected to precipitate a stronger economic revival, because then the cost competitiveness of the economy experiencing it is boosted more pronouncedly. This in turn justifies caution in interfering with exchange rate adjustments by establishing pegs at insufficiently discounted rates.

Whenever euro-denominated obligations are governed by laws of the exiting country, its government can manage the debt resolution process along the so-called *Lex Monetae* principle. Accordingly, the national legislator redenominates amounts specified in the contracts at exchange

[65] Roger Bootle, 'Leaving the Euro: A Practical Guide', *Capital Economics*, 4 June 2012, a revised submission for the Wolfson Economics Prize MMXII by Capital Economics, 50 and 162–163, available at www.capitaleconomics.com/wp-content/uploads/2016/11/wolfson-prize-submission.pdf.

[66] See also Bootle, 'Leaving the Euro', 53–54.

[67] Scott, 'When the Euro Falls Apart'.

rates it chooses. It can do the same with assets and liabilities on balance sheets of banks domiciled in the same country. In each of the scenarios loans and assets depreciate, shifting losses towards creditors.

The distribution of losses flows in the opposite direction, towards debtors, when euro-denominated obligations are established under a foreign law, when banks, operating through branches in the redenominating country, are domiciled in other countries, or when redenomination of certain contracts is undesirable, e.g., when a share of bank deposits is to be spared in order to shield the purchasing power of deposit holders. In each of the latter situations, liabilities become more onerous because they cannot be redenominated. In consequence the debt burden grows, contrary to the goal of debt redemption. Even in this situation, however, the government of the exiting country – especially if supported by governments of other EU countries and by European institutions – could pressurise creditors to participate in the burden-sharing, e.g., through its tax policy.

Regardless of these modalities, in any scenario domestic financial institutions, and foreign financial institutions exposed to them, would take a particularly painful hit. The banking sector would have to be seriously restructured. While this process would be unachievable unless the ECB takes a lead in it, it should proceed rather smoothly if the Frankfurt institution puts its hands on board. As the ultimate prudential supervisor of Eurozone banks, it could easily obtain all the necessary information to assess the distribution of the likely losses, liaising with the SRM on the parameters of necessary restructuring actions.[68]

Furthermore, while the restructuring of sovereign debt held by official creditors would also be painfully redistributive and hence politically contestable, under sufficient political will the process is perfectly manageable within the so-called Paris Club format, extended, if necessary, by creditor European bailout institutions.[69] And when it comes to

[68] According to Art. 30(2) Regulation 806/2014 'in the exercise of their respective responsibilities under this Regulation, the Board, the Council, the Commission, the ECB and the national resolution authorities and national competent authorities shall cooperate closely, in particular in the resolution planning, early intervention and resolution phases … They shall provide each other with all information necessary for the performance of their tasks.' This generic cooperation obligation is developed in more specific provisions of the Regulation.

[69] The Paris Club is an informal group of the world's twenty-two major creditor countries, aimed to address payment difficulties of debtor countries.

restructuring sovereign debt held by private bond-holders, the perennial problem of debt 'holdouts' (creditors who refuse to accept reduced payments)[70] could in turn be mitigated by the fact that the ESM Treaty[71] (Art. 12(3)) mandated an introduction of the most important contractual provision aimed to alleviate it, a collective action clause,[72] into 'all new euro-area government securities, with maturity above one year' issued since 1 January 2013. A secondary EU act recognising the redenomination by other EU countries would further strengthen the case for its government in possible holdout litigations before foreign courts.

6.8.1 Dealing with Losses of Central Banks

Eliminating the obstacles to successfully restructuring debts of nonfinancial agents, banks and sovereigns would in no way address the particularly serious problem of central banks' losses incurred due to their exposures to sovereign bonds of redenominating sovereigns and due to TARGET imbalances.

Within the PSPP (more thoroughly discussed in Chapter 4) the Eurosystem has been purchasing very large amounts of public-sector securities issued in the countries most obviously predestined to exit the Eurozone, with the notable exception of Greece, whose public-sector bonds have been excluded from the programme since its very beginning. To give a picture of potential losses it should be enough to mention that at the end of September 2017 the book value of the Italian public-sector bonds purchased within the PSPP amounted to approximately €301 billion[73] and TARGET liabilities of Banca d'Italia totaled additional €433 billion.[74]

70 Robert W. Kolb, *Sovereign Debt: From Safety to Default* (Hoboken, NJ: John Wiley & Sons, 2011); Lee C. Buchheit, G. Mitu Gulati and Ignacio Tirado, 'The Problem of Holdout Creditors in Eurozone Sovereign Debt Restructurings', Draft, 22 January 2013, available at https://pdfs.semanticscholar.org/bbb9/94b33376f0352cbe9dd6f1e1c27155b24a59.pdf.

71 Treaty Establishing European Stability Mechanism, signed in Brussels on 2 February 2012.

72 Collective action clauses (CACs) authorise a supermajority of bondholders to agree on changes to bond payment terms with binding effects for all bondholders. The Euro Area Model CAC 2012 was approved by the Economic and Financial Committee (EFC) on 18 November 2011. It is available, with ancillary documents, at europa.eu/efc/euro-area-model-cac-2012_en.

73 European Central Bank, asset purchase programmes, available at www.ecb.europa.eu/mopo/implement/omt/html/index.en.html.

74 Statistical Data Warehouse, TARGET balances, available at sdw.ecb.europa.eu/browse.do?node=bbn4859.

Because Italian bonds are mainly issued under Italian law, in the case of an Italian Eurozone exit the value of the securities would depreciate sharply, in line with the Italian currency, reducing the market value of assets in the books of their holders. TARGET liabilities, on the other hand, would become correspondingly more onerous for Banca d'Italia, because its liabilities would not similarly depreciate.

This may be a sufficiently scary perspective to dissuade policymakers from ever contemplating the redenomination option. Yet it is also a very superfluous depiction of what would happen in the redenomination scenario.

To start with, I argued in Chapter 4 that high TARGET imbalances largely stem from a capital flight towards the Eurozone's financial 'safe heavens'. Or, to put it differently, large and persistent TARGET imbalances betoken a credit risk transfer from financial institutions to central banks in some jurisdictions, and then from these central banks to the rest of the Eurosystem.[75] The process is not irreversible, though. The redenomination should halt it first, and reverse soon after, because then the reason for the capital flight ceases to exist. Capital owners would benefit from the process, because 'German/Luxembourgish' euros previously exchanged for 'Italian' or 'Spanish' euros would inevitably appreciate. This result may be condemned on ethical grounds, but for my point here something else is more important. When the current speculators considered that a new lira has reached its new low ebb and started appreciating, their incentives would reverse. Now they will be strongly motivated to move the financial assets back to the countries from which they have fled. Were the countries allowed to remain in the TARGET2 system after seceding from the Eurozone,[76] the reversal flows would, potentially significantly, reduce the current TARGET imbalances.

At this stage the ECB should negotiate with central banks of the seceding countries how to redistribute the remaining TARGET losses and possibly also the losses incurred by the Eurosystem due to the depreciation of public-sector bonds amassed by the Eurosystem under

[75] Marcello Minenna, Giovanna Maria Boi and Paulo Verzella, *The Incomplete Currency: The Future of the Euro and Solutions for the Eurozone* (Chichester, West Sussex: John Wiley & Sons, 2016): 84–89.

[76] What makes it easier is that TARGET2 is available for non-Eurozone countries. Bulgaria, Denmark, Poland and Romania also participate in it.

the risk-sharing principle.[77] The value of the losses will depend on many aspects, from the number of succeeding countries, to the depth of depreciation their new currencies would incur, the scale of TARGET imbalances at the point of the split-up, the book value of depreciating securities purchased within the quantitative easing, etc. Even, however, when the losses of central banks are serious, neither unmanageable costs for taxpayers nor hyperinflation should follow if some basic rules are abided.

6.9 The Conundrums of Central Banks' Negative Equity

It is necessary first to explain why a central bank's losses incurred as a result of its purchases of its own country's government bonds are not particularly problematic. Within the PSPP, the Eurosystem has been exchanging public-sector debt for central bank debt (money supply). Due to the nature of seigniorage – the right of the central bank to issue money – the central bank debt in the form of money supply is always issued at 0 per cent interest: central banks do not pay interest on the money base. The government debt the Eurosystem has purchased within the PSPP is different in this respect. It should entail a yield. In other words, other than in the case of safest government bonds traded at negative yields, the Eurosystem makes profit on the debt it has purchased within the quantitative easing programme. It does not retain this profit, though. Instead, according to the Treaty rules,[78] it rebates its profits to the Eurozone governments.

Furthermore, because public debt is not really repaid but rolled over in most of the cases, the debt amassed during quantitative easing is functionally frozen. It features in the books of the Eurozone's central banks (as assets) and in the books of the individual states (as liabilities). Yet, as de Grauwe and Ji noted, 'at the moment of the purchase, the

[77] As indicated in Chapter 4, 80 per cent of public-sector bonds within the PSPP are purchased by national central banks of the issuing sovereign and the remaining 20 per cent by the ECB under the principle of risk sharing.

[78] This is explicitly expressed in the case of the profits made by the ECB: according to art. 33(1)(b) of the Statute of the ESCB and the ECB, 'net profit shall be distributed to the shareholders of the ECB in proportion to their paid-up shares'. The Statute also provides that 'the amount of each national central bank's monetary income shall be equal to its annual income derived from its assets held against notes in circulation and deposit liabilities to credit institutions' (Art. 32(2)), leaving it up to individual Member States to determine how the income accruing to the share of PSPP bond purchases is to be allocated.

government bonds cease to exist from an economic point of view. All that is left of the bonds is a monetary liability of the central bank.'[79]

There is one reservation to be made about this description: in principle, the bonds subject to the PSPP do not cease to exist, either economically, or legally, or in accountancy terms. Their economic consequences are merely suspended. In theory, the Eurosystem should sell them in monetary operations reverse to the 'quantitative easing' at a point in time when inflation goes beyond its intended goal. But, nonetheless, De Grauwe and Ji are very accurate about what has been happening to government debt during quantitative easing. In any scenario the ECB can hardly be expected to perform any 'quantitative hardening', because this would directly lead to higher interest rates on government bonds, which in turn could easily shove the most indebted Eurozone countries into a liquidity crisis. Instead, it is easy to predict that the ECB will use its more standard monetary policy instruments, short-term interest rates and reserve requirements in particular, to limit the money supply when inflation goes beyond its stated goal. By the same token, the more financially imbalanced the Eurozone is, the more the Eurosystem becomes inclined to purchase government bonds. Yet the more it succumbs to this inclination, the more exposed central banks are to even higher losses when the mechanism breaks down and redenomination becomes the only viable method of correcting the imbalances.

It may be tempting to argue that, just as the bonds purchased within the PSPP should be sold one day, losses of central banks incurred in the case of redenomination should be covered by a government recapitalisation. This logic is envisaged in the prevailing accounting convention, according to which liabilities exceeding assets betoken legal (balance sheet) insolvency. Normally, unless this situation is only transitory, legal insolvency translates into equitable insolvency, i.e., the failure to pay debts as they come due. This picture, however, becomes more complicated when it comes to central banks, due to the nature of fiat money. Erstwhile currency – liabilities on the central bank's balance sheet – had a fixed value in terms of gold or other similar assets.

[79] Paul De Grauwe and Yuemei Ji, 'Why the ECB Should Not Insist on Repayment of Its Greek Bonds', *VOX CEPR's Policy Portal*, 16 July 2015, available at voxeu.org/article/why-ecb-should-not-insist-repayment-its-greek-bonds. See also Paul De Grauwe et al., 'The Future of Europe's Economy: Disaster or Deliverance?', *Centre for European Reform Report*, 18 September 2013, esp. 19–22, available at www.cer.org.uk/publications/archive/report/2013/future-europes-economy-disaster-or-deliverance.

Currency was then a liability for central banks, because it entailed an obligation to exchange it for assets the banks possessed. But this setup passed into history with the gold standard decades ago. And under fiat money, 'the only claim a private holder of fiat base money has on the issuer is the right to exchange X units of fiat base money for X units of fiat base money'.[80] In other words, the fact that money base features as a liability on balance sheets of a central bank entails no actual obligation on the side of the bank other than to exchange its liabilities for the same quantity of the same type of liabilities.

This does not mean that there is no relationship between the value of the liabilities and the value of the assets possessed by the central bank. The relationship is much more complicated than the accounting convention suggests, though.

The mainstream German insight has it that the quality of the assets possessed by a central bank determines the quality of its liabilities. This is important, because the quality of the central bank's liability is another expression for the level of inflation. The relationship is intuitively obvious. It is rebuffed, however, by the German history on which it ostensibly builds. The German hyperinflation of 1923, in particular, was not caused by any assets possessed by the German central bank or missing on its balance sheet. Instead, it stemmed from the deadly mix of the money base created by private banks and German liabilities (not assets) engendered by the Treaty of Versailles reparations, payable in gold or foreign currencies only.[81] In other words, this episode confirms the otherwise incontestable finding that substantial government liabilities denominated in foreign currencies may indeed lead a central bank to insolvency if the economy weakens, which in turn undermines the value of the national currency.[82]

Another German experience – much less known than the hyperinflation of the early 1920s – also makes it clear that the relationship between the quality of the central bank's liabilities and the assets on its balance sheet is tricky. In the mid-1930s the Third Reich's national public works programme was entirely financed by Labour Treasury

[80] Willem H. Buiter, 'Helicopter Money: Irredeemable Fiat Money and the Liquidity Trap', *NBER Working Paper* No. 10163, December 2003, 2, available at www.nber.org/papers/w10163.pdf.

[81] Adam Fergusson, *When Money Dies: The Nightmare of Deficit Spending, Devaluation, and Hyperinflation in Weimar Germany* (New York: PublicAffairs, 2010).

[82] Ansgar Belke and Thorsten Polleit, 'How Much Fiscal Backing Must the ECB Have? The Euro Area Is Not (yet) the Philippines', *International Economics* 124 (2010): 5–30.

Certificates, with no corresponding assets purchased in return.[83] The basic idea was simple: the public works funded by the Certificates would produce actual value, underpinning the growth of the German economy. By the same token, the value of the public works fulfilled the function of a balance sheet asset, even if formally it was not recorded as such. As a result, the central bank's balance sheet recorded losses. Instead of leading to equitable insolvency, however, the situation had no negative effects on the German economy. Quite to the contrary, it was vital for producing tangible assets and reducing unemployment, as well as bolstering economic growth.

Conclusions stemming from the two episodes are telling. Depreciation of assets accumulated during quantitative easing would not be problematic from the perspective of inflation. It would deprive future governments of seigniorage profits, because central banks would retain future profits to gradually work out the losses. But otherwise it would not cause economic tensions. For the same reason, however, any outstanding liabilities denominated in euros – TARGET liabilities in particular – are much more treacherous and a sufficiently long moratorium on repaying them must become an inherent part of the redenomination process.

Ultimately, therefore, as the ECB put it itself in its report, 'central banks are protected from insolvency due to their ability to create money and can therefore operate with negative equity',[84] while practical consequences of a hole in a central bank's balance sheet depend on its purpose. Negative equity should be rewarding if it is a price to pay for re-establishing an effective path to a macroeconomic adjustment when the more difficult path of internal devaluation does not do the trick for economic, social and political reasons.

Granted, this finding can in no way address the TARGET problem, because liabilities of central banks, if treated unwisely, could propel hyperinflation in exiting countries. But the magnitude of TARGET imbalances should simply diminish over time, because capital flows can be expected to significantly reverse after local currencies depreciate. It can also be predicted that the economic rejuvenation following

[83] Ellen Brown, 'Thinking Outside the Box: How a Bankrupt Germany Solved Its Infrastructure Problems', *The Web of Debt*, 9 August 2007, available at www.webofdebt.com/articles/bankrupt-germany.php.

[84] Daniela Bunea et al., 'Profit Distribution and Loss Coverage Rules for Central Banks', *ECB's Occasional Paper* No. 169, April 2016, 14, ft. 7.

the initial recession would push up both inflation and seigniorage profits of the central banks in the seceding countries. With time, therefore, the burden of TARGET liabilities would become gradually more manageable.

6.9.1 *Legal Tinderboxes*

It can be argued at this point that whatever the virtues of redenomination and no matter how viable organisationally and economically it may be, the idea remains incongruent with the Eurozone's constitutional setup. In other words, it is untenable simply because it violates EU law. Three main arguments can seem particularly plausible in this respect. The first is that a Eurozone exit requires a Treaty amendment and that is precluded for political reasons. Second, any debt restructuring covering a reduction of the principal on sovereign debt – another plank of the plan – is barred by the no-bailout and the no-monetary financing clauses. And third, the ECB should not accept any losses from either the quantitative easing or TARGET imbalances, or at least the Eurozone's central banks, including the ECB, ought to be immediately recapitalised by national governments when the losses occur.

All three arguments are spurious. To explain why, each will be dealt with in turn.

The legality of a consensual withdrawal from the Eurozone – for practical reasons the only conceivable withdrawal option – has never raised serious concerns of EU lawyers.[85] But, as Proctor noted several years ago, 'the substitution of the euro for the currencies of participating Member States was stated to be "irrevocable", and the process of monetary union was declared to be "irreversible"'.[86] President Draghi said the very same thing much more recently: 'L'euro e' irrevocabile, the euro is irrevocable ... Questo e' il trattato, this is the treaty.'[87]

[85] René Smits, 'The European Constitution and EMU: An Appraisal', *Common Market Law Review* 42 (2005): 425–468; Gilles Thieffry, 'The Not So Unthinkable – The Break-up of the European Monetary Union', *International Financial Law Review*, 1 July 2005, 15–17; Charles Proctor, 'The Future of the Euro – What Happens if a Member State Leaves?', *European Business Law Review* 17 (2006): 909–937; Phoebus Athanassiou, 'Withdrawal and Expulsion from the EU and EMU. Some Reflections', *ECB's Legal Working Paper Series* No. 10, December 2009, available at www.ecb.europa.eu/pub/pdf/scplps/ecblwp10.pdf.

[86] Proctor, 'The Future of the Euro', 924.

[87] Alessandro Speciale, 'Draghi Says Euro Is Irreversible as Le Pen Urges French Exit', *Bloomberg Markets*, 6 February 2017, available at www.bloomberg.com/news/articles/2017-02-06/draghi-says-euro-is-irreversible-as-le-pen-urges-french-exit.

Indeed, the Treaty clearly provides that if a Member State is admitted to the Eurozone, 'the Council shall ... irrevocably fix the rate at which the euro shall be substituted for the currency of the Member State concerned' (Art. 140(3) TFEU). Can the irrevocability ever mean anything but locking the Eurozone Member States together into the monetary union with no exit option admitted?

Actually it can.

The provision on the irrevocable fixing of the exchange rates is located in the chapter of the TFEU entitled 'Transitional Provisions'. It may be argued, therefore, that it exclusively refers to the specific context of admitting new countries to the single currency area. At some point of the transition process the decision as to the parity at which national currency is exchanged for euros must be ultimately – and irrevocably – taken. The context in which the word 'irrevocable' is used in Art. 140 TFEU remains, therefore, narrow and very specific. In this context the Treaty simply requires that after the Council makes its decision on the matter, the exchange rate cannot be altered any longer *during the transition process*.[88] It also confirms one of the basic consequences of a single currency: when in a currency union, its members cannot alter exchange rates of the currency they use domestically towards the currency other Member States use, for it is one and the same currency.

Nonetheless, even if it is assumed that no legal argument bars a return of one or more of the Eurozone's Member States to their national currencies pursuant to a consensual withdrawal, none clearly facilitates it, either. In particular no Treaty provision determines the procedure to be taken in this situation or its consequences. This is an important point, considering that arguably even a partial disintegration of the Eurozone is systemically too important to be dealt with legally at a sub-Treaty level.

This argument is powerful, yet too crude. The EU Treaty provides for a simplified revision procedure to be applied when an amendment refers to union policies and internal actions, as well as when the amendment

[88] Some primary law provisions corroborate this reading of the Treaty. In particular, Art. 49 of the Statute of the ESCB and the ECB states that: 'Following the irrevocable fixing of exchange rates in accordance with Article 140 of the Treaty on the Functioning of the European Union, the Governing Council shall take the necessary measures to ensure that banknotes denominated in currencies with *irrevocably fixed exchange rates are exchanged by the national central banks at their respective par values*' (my emphasis).

does not increase the competences conferred on the Union.[89] Both of the conditions are fulfilled in the case of a Eurozone exit. Yet, even if the European Council, which decides about the amendment in this case, manages to pass it, its members should be informed about the amendment plan weeks before the summit. In addition, according to the TEU 'that decision shall not enter into force until it is approved by the Member States in accordance with their respective constitutional requirements'. Such a requirement additionally stretches the procedure potentially by several months and makes it entirely unfit for the necessarily very fast negotiation process.

All in all, for practical reasons a Eurozone exit cannot hinge on a Treaty amendment. As, however, the Treaty does not preclude it, redenomination could happen simultaneously to starting the amendment process. The goal of the latter would be specific in this setup, because it does not intend to establish an exit procedure, but to recognise and endorse constitutional consequences of the consensual withdrawal.

Establishing this brings us to other questions. What is the relationship between a notional haircut and the no-bailout and the no-monetary financing clauses? In other words, is a serious debt restructuring reconcilable with the Treaty?

According to the stringent interpretation of the Eurozone's constitutional arrangement, explained at the beginning of this chapter, any reason for debt redemption and adjacent measures discussed so far should be shrugged off as constitutionally unacceptable. The no-monetary financing clause, just like the statutory division between the monetary and the fiscal functions, should preclude any burden-sharing within the Eurosystem. The no-bailout clause, in turn, ought to prevent any cancellation of principal amounts of sovereign debt held by financial vehicles created and guaranteed by other Member States. Even debt

[89] According to Art. 48(6) TEU: 'the Government of any Member State, the European Parliament or the Commission may submit to the European Council proposals for revising all or part of the provisions of Part Three of the Treaty on the Functioning of the European Union relating to the internal policies and action of the Union. The European Council may adopt a decision amending all or part of the provisions of Part Three of the Treaty on the Functioning of the European Union. The European Council shall act by unanimity after consulting the European Parliament and the Commission, and the European Central Bank in the case of institutional changes in the monetary area. That decision shall not enter into force until it is approved by the Member States in accordance with their respective constitutional requirements. The decision referred to in the second subparagraph shall not increase the competences conferred on the Union in the Treaties.'

rescheduling becomes legally vulnerable under this interpretation, because it entails opportunity costs, i.e., benefits of an alternative allocation of resources, forgone after the debt reprofiling.[90]

Had European policymakers followed this constitutional thinking, history (and this chapter) would have looked different. Most probably redenomination in the Eurozone's periphery and restructuring of financial institutions exposed to it in what became 'creditor countries' would have been long completed by now. Yet, because by the same token the Eurozone as we know it would shrink substantially, the stringent script has been rejected.[91]

Especially the Court of Justice has manifested far-reaching judicial restraint (performing the so-called 'marginal review'[92]) of anti-crisis measures and has acquiesced to the intrinsically political decisions shaping the Eurozone's constitutional script. Now the question is if the same court – which has reserved solely for itself the role of bindingly interpreting EU law[93] – would ever consider the Treaty no-bailout or no-monetary financing clauses as preventing a restructuring of sovereign debt including notional haircuts when policymakers opine that it is the right way of rejuvenating the economies of the Eurozone's south.

Some legal scholars suggest that this is precisely what should happen, first of all because in the famous *Pringle* decision the CJEU highlighted that financial stability of the monetary union 'is the objective pursued by Article 125 TFEU' and hence 'it must be held that that provision prohibits the Union and the Member States from granting financial assistance as a result of which the incentive of the recipient Member

[90] For a recent, almost nostalgic, restatement of the underlying legal arguments, see Christian Hofmann, 'Greek Debt Relief', *Oxford Journal of Legal Studies* 37 (2017): 1–30.

[91] Even the German Constitutional Court, sticking to the original interpretation of the EU law in its OMT preliminary reference (Case 2 BvR 2728/13 et al., order of 14 January 2014, English translation available at www.bundesverfassungsgericht.de/SharedDocs/Entscheidungen/EN/2014/01/rs20140114_2bvr272813en.html), which led to the CJEU's *Gauweiler* decision, subsequently backtracked (Judgment of 21 June 2016–2 BvR 2728/13, 2 BvR 2729/13, 2 BvR 2730/13, 2 BvR 2731/13, 2 BvE 13/13) when the Court of Justice came up with a very different understanding of the Eurozone's constitution.

[92] For an overview of the concept, in the context of the proportionality analysis undertaken by the CJEU, see esp. Alexander H. Türk, *Judicial Review in EU Law* (Cheltenham; Northamption, MA: Edward Elgar Publishing, 2010), 137–138.

[93] It is settled case law that 'a judgment in which the Court gives a preliminary ruling is binding on the national court, as regards the interpretation or the validity of the acts of the EU institutions in question, for the purposes of the decision to be given in the main proceedings': e.g., Case C614/14, Ognyanov, ECLI:EU:C:2016:514, § 33.

State to conduct a sound budgetary policy is diminished'.[94] According to the argument opposing debt restructuring covering principal amounts, any such a policy would only contribute to moral hazard problems sketched earlier in this chapter. It therefore should be precluded, because it would debilitate the incentives of national authorities to conduct a sound budgetary policy.[95] Others disagree, essentially claiming that a deep restructuring of sovereign debt is congruent with the goal of the no-bailout clause whenever less radical measures have not been able to achieve the stated goals of international financial assistance; when it is an ultimate remedy to a persistent inability of a Member State to return to international debt markets.[96]

If European leaders agree on redenomination, the Court can all but be expected to follow the second of the arguments, not to undermine delicate and systemically crucial decisions of political actors and not to second-guess economic policies on what is best for European societies. The marginal review doctrine would provide the Court with the necessary legal tools. The pronouncement of *Pringle* that 'under ... the ESM Treaty, any financial assistance granted ... must be repaid to the ESM by the recipient Member State and that ... the amount to be repaid is to include an appropriate margin'[97] would most likely be redefined or simply passed over. What, instead, the Luxembourg Court may want to emphasise – when a dispute on any serious restructuring of peripheral countries' debts comes to a head – is that, according to *Pringle*, the defaulting 'ESM Member State remains bound to pay its part of the capital'.[98] This short phrase hints that burden-sharing between ESM Member States is permissible. When the worst-case scenario of a sovereign default materialises, the country previously receiving payouts from the ESM is not to repay them in full. Instead, it ought to pay its

[94] Case C-370/12, *Pringle*, EU:C:2012:756, § 136. Similarly, in *Gauweiler* the Court indicated that 'it is apparent from the preparatory work relating to the Treaty of Maastricht that the aim of Article 123 TFEU *is to encourage the Member States to follow a sound budgetary policy*, not allowing monetary financing of public deficits or privileged access by public authorities to the financial markets to lead to excessively high levels of debt or excessive Member State deficits' (§ 100, my emphasis).

[95] Armin Steinbach, 'The "Haircut" of Public Creditors under EU Law', *European Constitutional Law Review* 12 (2016): 223–239.

[96] Alexander Thiele, '(No) Haircut for Hellas?: A Short and Critical Reply to Armin Steinbach, "The 'Haircut' of Public Creditors under EU Law" EuConst (2016) p. 223', *European Constitutional Law Review* 12 (2016): 520–537.

[97] Case C-370/12, *Pringle*, EU:C:2012:756, § 139.

[98] Case C-370/12, *Pringle*, EU:C:2012:756, § 145.

due premiums only. By the same token, other Member States have to foot the bill for the rest of the unpaid financial assistance received by the defaulting country.

But while the Court of Justice should be expected to find restructuring of sovereign debt held by official creditors as compliant with the no-bailout and no-monetary financing clauses when it is presented as an ultimate remedy, accepting such a debt restructuring without redenomination would doom the past to repeat itself in the future. The moral hazard problems discussed earlier would resurface with a vengeance. Indeed, notional haircuts of sovereign debt in the countries in which political, economic and social tissue makes internal devaluation particularly devastating do not make much sense either from the perspective of the Eurozone's financial stability, or of a sound budgetary policy. A contrary argument can be made, however, in respect to debt cancellations combined with a Eurozone exit. This way, a prime hindrance to sound economic and fiscal policies – the ineffectiveness of internal devaluation as a method of macroeconomic adjustment – would be eliminated.

The last main legal question still to be addressed here is if the Eurosystem banks, and the ECB in particular, can admit losses on their monetary policy transactions. In other words, can Eurozone central banks function with holes in their balance sheets occurring in the case of a Eurozone exit without violating the no-monetary financing clause? Or, to put it differently, does EU law require that national governments recapitalise the central banks when their equity turns deeply negative?

In *Gauweiler* the CJEU admitted that the ECB may incur losses when it performs monetary policy transactions. More specifically, 'a central bank, such as the ECB, is obliged to take decisions which, like open market operations, inevitably expose it to a risk of losses and that Article 33 of the Protocol on the ESCB and the ECB duly provides for the way in which the losses of the ECB *must* be allocated'.[99] The word 'must' used at the end of the phrase implies an obligation to allocate the losses. But, in fact, Art. 33(2) of the Statute of the ESCB and the ECB, in the part relating to losses, does not provide for such an obligation. It only states that 'in the event of a loss incurred by the ECB, the shortfall *may* be offset against the general reserve fund of the ECB and, if necessary, following a decision by the Governing Council monetary income

[99] Case C-62/14, Gauweiler et al., EU:C:2015:400, § 125, my emphasis.

of the relevant financial year' (my emphasis). The Governing Council of the ECB is authorised to cover losses with its current or accrued profits, in which case standard profit distribution to NCBs would be correspondingly limited. But, according to the clear wording of the Statute, it cannot be forced to do so.[100] And certainly national governments cannot be forced to recapitalise the ECB in such a scenario.

The situation is even more remote from the scenario of forced recapitalisation when it comes to losses national central banks can incur either as a result of depreciating government bonds they have purchased, or due to unsettled TARGET liabilities of central banks of the countries departing the Eurozone. In this respect, the Statute of the ESCB and the ECB only states that 'the Governing Council may decide that national central banks shall be indemnified ... in exceptional circumstances for specific losses arising from monetary policy operations undertaken for the ESCB. Indemnification shall be in a form deemed appropriate in the judgment of the Governing Council' (Art. 32(4)). Again, it says nothing about government recapitalisation of national central banks. What is equally important, giving the Governing Council a free hand to decide 'that national central banks shall be indemnified' – some of them or all – the ECB can shift losses between the central banks. In particular, this authorisation allows the Governing Council to prevent or minimise the burden-sharing of losses incurred in effect of purchasing sovereign bonds within the PSPP by relocating all the depreciating government bonds of the exiting countries, even those subject to loss-sharing, according to the original setup, to their central banks. It could also do the opposite, when – as is the case of TARGET2 claims – demanding that central banks of the exiting countries immediately settle their liabilities easily provoke hyperinflation. In this latter situation, central banks of the exiting countries should be at least temporarily indemnified, by receiving sufficiently long grace periods that allow them to start repaying debts only when the shock of redenomination fades away.

[100] Instead, the Eurosystem banks can either carry the losses forward against future seigniorage profits, or they can present them as claims against future profits. The practical effects of the two are identical. Balance sheet effects differ, however, because in the first of the two scenarios the losses are presented as negative equity, while in the other as claims against national governments. See also Daniela Bunea et al., 'Profit Distribution and Loss Coverage Rules for Central Banks', *ECB's Occasional Paper* No. 169, April 2016, 13–14, available at www.ecb.europa.eu/pub/pdf/scpops/ecbop169.en.pdf?f7073b79c2f6f62c79918dc24088dd00.

7 Centrifugal National Institutions and Public Policies

7.1 The Integration Bargain in Socioeconomic Fields

In the previous chapter I argued that Greece is the most extreme case of a very simple – and very fundamental – mistake committed at the beginning of the Eurozone: of bringing together in an inherently hard currency system both the economies well-suited to its demands and those unfit for it for political, economic and social reasons. I also claimed that redenomination and debt redemption are both feasible prerequisites for remedying this flaw and for restoring a sustainable vitality to the Eurozone's south.

To succeed, however, this plan must be accompanied by a set of socioeconomic programmes preventing the monetary adjustment from triggering major social and political upheavals. I will delineate their contours in the next chapter, in the context of the EU's current redistribution policies. Before we can get there, however, we must grapple with two preliminary questions: what role has the EU played in determining national socioeconomic policies so far and what has it meant for European societies and the European project?

Answers to both of the questions may seem straightforward. Ostensibly they spring directly from a political compromise about the allocation of powers between the Union and its Member States in all major socioeconomic public policies – from education to business environment to judicial and tax systems, healthcare, industrial relations, labour market institutions, social security etc. – since the very beginning of European integration. The compromise posits that European integration is to generate additional economic resources to then be redistributed by individual Member States according to their preferences and political arrangements, with no European institutions steering it or interfering with national priorities. In this context Damjanovic and De Witte argued that the EU has been entrusted with the task of 'promoting economic growth stemming from a common and competitive market ... The Member States, from their side, continue to provide specific welfare services within their social policy systems and their health and education systems (the "core" of the welfare state), and also through their public utilities (the "outer ring" of the welfare state), and all these are regarded to be within their primary responsibility.'[1]

Such division of powers can primarily be attributed to the very specific nature of all major socioeconomic policies: each of them has traditionally played an important role in maintaining internal peace within domestic economic systems, at the same time supporting national cohesion.[2] Therefore, national governments instinctively guard them against external incursions. They consider each as a core state power defining the sovereignty of their nation.

Yet these natural mechanics behind the European division of powers in major public policies also reveal some of the most significant constitutional weaknesses of economic integration in Europe. For how can European countries maintain sovereignty in core socioeconomic fields if wealth creation through market transactions largely depends on them? How can the common market be expected to bring about economic prosperity if this prosperity profoundly hinges on the core state powers jealously preserved, for political reasons, at the national level? How could the political compromise keeping the two fields apart stay intact when the original thin integration within the common market morphed during the 1980s into a much more biting internal market and then entered the whole new level of monetary integration? How reasonable was it to assume that the countries sharing one market and one currency could have very different welfare systems, seriously divergent administrative capacities, incompatible income taxation, as well as educational and judicial systems sharply diverging in their performances? Would any such a mismatch be reconcilable with the

[1] Dragana Damjanovic and Bruno De Witte, 'Welfare Integration through EU Law: The Overall Picture in the Light of the Lisbon Treaty', *EUI Working Papers LAW* No. 2008/34, 5–6.

[2] Francesco Costamagna, 'The Internal Market and the Welfare State: Anything New after Lisbon?', in: *The Treaty of Lisbon and the Future of European Law and Policy*, eds. Martin Trybus and Luca Rubini (Cheltenham; Northampton, MA: Edward Elgar Publishing, 2012): 381–397.

Treaty principles of consistency between the Union's policies and activities, as well as of sincere cooperation?[3]

For the last few decades such questions have been dispensed of as irrelevant and spurious.

First and foremost, according to the prevailing view, the mismatches are inevitable because national socioeconomic choices throughout Europe simply vary too much to even think of their effective integration at the European level. So maybe the disconnect between the flowing factors of production at the European level and socioeconomic policies left for national governments to define entails some tensions or inefficiencies. But no other pattern is conceivable in practice. Neither European nor national politicians should be condemned for failing to deliver what is impossible.

The principles of subsidiarity[4] and proportionality,[5] as well as basic requirements of democracy, also seem to preclude an upward devolution of powers towards the EU within core socioeconomic policies of its Member States. Think, for example, of the 'welfare state', defined as an institutional system managed by public authorities to address needy individuals and intended to pursue their social integration. How a 'needy individual' is defined varies from one country to the next, depending on the financial resources available for these purposes and the prevailing beliefs of what society should provide to each of its members. The same applies to what 'social integration' betokens.

Furthermore, market-making as well as market extension processes – the home turf of economic integration – and the core socioeconomic policies should arguably be governed at two different levels of the European project simply because their logic is very different. Welfare

[3] Pursuant to the former, 'the Union shall ensure consistency between its policies and activities, taking all of its objectives into account and in accordance with the principle of conferral of powers' (Art. 7 TFEU). The other requires that 'the Union and the Member States shall, in full mutual respect, assist each other in carrying out tasks which flow from the Treaties … The Member States are required to take any appropriate measure to ensure fulfilment of the obligations arising out of EU law, to facilitate the achievement of the Union's tasks and refrain from any measure which could jeopardise this goal' (Art. 4(3) TEU).

[4] According to which 'in areas which do not fall within its exclusive competence, the Union shall act only if and in so far as the objectives of the proposed action cannot be sufficiently achieved by the Member States, either at central level or at regional and local level, but can rather, by reason of the scale or effects of the proposed action, be better achieved at Union level': Art. 5(3) TEU.

[5] 'Under the principle of proportionality, the content and form of Union action shall not exceed what is necessary to achieve the objectives of the Treaties': Art. 5(4) TEU.

state policies 'are said to "de-commodify": they reduce individuals' reliance on the market – and the need to sell their labour as a commodity – for meeting their welfare needs'.[6] European integration has always been driven by the socially and politically less palatable process of market liberalisation aimed at stimulating human commodification. Putting the two opposite forces to one and the same level would be self-defeating, the argument goes. After all, mixing fire and water does not make any of them more plentiful.

7.2 Capitalist Ecosystems

Social scientists have provided more arguments for the current European distribution of powers in the socioeconomic realm. During the last three decades they have been busy defining similarities and differences between national socioeconomic set-ups and their institutional underpinnings. Esping-Andersen famously identified three such major models in his seminal work published in 1990: liberal (Anglo-Saxon countries), social-democratic (Nordic countries) and conservative (the rest of what then comprised the EEC).[7] The three, as another leading social scientist put it, differ in 'the centrality of the market in the allocation of resources and the residuality of state intervention in the liberal regime; the centrality of equality, social citizenship and "harmonization" of the population in social-democratic welfare regime; and the centrality of security, work, status and occupational identity in Conservative–corporatist social insurance systems'.[8] In all of these fundamental respects the three models were built on significantly different beliefs and priorities. And soon some other researchers figured out that in fact there are more 'worlds of welfare capitalism' in Europe. They concluded that the conservative model espoused by Mediterranean countries differs too much from the German (or French) archetype to put them in one basket,[9] and that the patterns common for

[6] David Lain, Sarah Vickerstaff and Wendy Loretto, 'Reforming State Pension Provision in "Liberal" Anglo-Saxon Countries: Re-Commodification, Cost-Containment or Recalibration?', *Social Policy and Society* 12 (2013): 78.

[7] Gøsta Esping-Andersen, *The Three Worlds of Welfare Capitalism* (Cambridge: Polity Press, 1990).

[8] Bruno Palier, 'Ordering Change: Understanding the "Bismarckian" Welfare Reform Trajectory', in: *A Long Goodbye to Bismarck?*, ed. Bruno Palier (Amsterdam: Amsterdam University Press, 2010): 26.

[9] On characteristics of the latter, see esp. Giuliano Bonoli, 'Classifying Welfare States: A Two-dimension Approach', *Journal of Social Policy* 26 (1997): 351–372; Francis G. Castles and Herbert Obinger, 'Worlds, Families, Regimes: Country Clusters in European and

the Eastern European countries make up for yet another, quite eclectic on the fringes and aggressively liberal in its core 'world of capitalism'.[10]

In addition, in socioeconomic policies, like in physics, everything depends on everything else. Each country's core policies and institutions are heavily interdependent and remain in historically contingent equilibriums. Some societies have traditionally espoused more liberal production regimes, while others have prioritised more coordination between capital owners and workers, as well as more interventionist public authorities.[11] Major ancillary policies – like vocational training,[12] employment protection, or labour market policy – must be attuned to these original choices. If the choices vary significantly at the rudimentary level, and they do, then so should the accompanying policies.

The same applies to redistributive policies.[13] Think of pensions systems. Some of them, those of the Bismarckian mould, traditionally purport to preserve the income status of individuals, while the Anglo-Saxon and the Scandinavian systems intend, instead, to provide minimum income (at various levels) in the form of state pensions, encouraging additional private contributions to funded schemes.[14] More generally, Bismarckian welfare states traditionally aim to avoid income redistribution, instead striving to secure one's income and position on the labour market. This basic idea distinguishes them from the Anglo-Saxon and Scandinavian models. The same applies to

OECD Area Public Policy', *West European Politics* 31 (2008): 321–344; Christos Minas et al., 'Welfare Regime, Welfare Pillar and Southern Europe', *Journal of European Social Policy* 24 (2014): 135–149.

[10] For a broader account on the Eastern European model see Andreas Nölke and Arjan Vliegenthart, 'Enlarging the Varieties of Capitalism: The Emergence of Dependent Market Economies in East Central Europe', *World Politics* 61 (2009): 670–702; Dragos Adascalitei, 'Welfare State Development in Central and Eastern Europe: A State of the Art Literature Review', *Studies of Transition States and Societies* 4 (2012): 59–70, available at www.ssoar.info/ssoar/bitstream/handle/document/36268/ssoar-stss-2012-2-adascalitei-Welfare_State_Development_in_Central.pdf?sequence=1.

[11] Peter A. Hall and David Soskice, *Varieties of Capitalism: The Institutional Foundations of Comparative Advantage* (Oxford: Oxford University Press, 2001).

[12] Marius R. Busemeyer and Raphaela Schlicht-Schmälzle, 'Partisan Power, Economic Coordination and Variations in Vocational Training Systems in Europe', *European Journal of Industrial Relations* 20 (2014): 55–71.

[13] Esping-Andersen, *The Three Worlds*; Benjamin Danforth, 'Worlds of Welfare in Time: A Historical Reassessment of the Three-world Typology', *Journal of European Social Policy* 24 (2014): 164–182.

[14] Martin Kolmar, 'Beveridge versus Bismarck Public-pension Systems in Integrated Markets', *Regional Science and Urban Economics* 37 (2007): 649–669.

healthcare, disability or social assistance schemes: they, too, differ in generosity, coverage and funding patterns depending on their constitutive purposes and principles. Could some European authorities legitimately try to influence policy effects of the choices, superseding them with some alien concepts and goals? Even the most ardent Europhiles could not seemingly purport to answer 'yes'.

Path dependencies kick in even when you think of the features each socioeconomic model should arguably master, regardless of its indigenous preferences and prevailing world views. This applies, for instance, to the appropriate matching between education (and vocational training) systems and market needs, to premises of effective dispute resolution and tax collection systems, to investor-friendly public administration, or to cost-efficient healthcare. Each national system should strive to achieve these goals, but individual paths of reaching them naturally hinge on broader political and economic choices, on idiosyncratic governance traditions and on complex trade-offs and competition for scarce resources between various interest groups. They all rest upon an equilibrium arguably sustainable only under sovereign and democratic decision-making.

Social scientists have argued that this equilibrium is intrinsically stable over time.[15] Reforms to individual policies adjusting the systems on their fringes tend largely to protect the kernel of the model (and hence the underlying preferences and values). In addition, as Hall and Soskice implied in their seminal book,[16] thanks to the path-dependent idiosyncrasies, nations find it easier to specialise and hence to exploit their comparative institutional advantages to the benefit of the whole international community. The underlying intuition is that, as in nature, the diversity of national socioeconomic policies helps maintain the stability of the international economic ecosystem. Coercive isomorphism, like all monocultures, would be destructive in the long run.

[15] See, for example, Gregory Jackson and Richard Deeg, 'The Long-term Trajectories of Institutional Change in European Capitalism', *Journal of European Public Policy* 19 (2012): 1109–1125; Andreas Kammer, Judith Niehues and Andreas Peichl, 'Welfare Regimes and Welfare State Outcomes in Europe', *Journal of European Social Policy* 22 (2012): 455–471; Mehmet Fatih Aysan and Roderic Beaujot, 'Welfare Regimes for Aging Populations: No Single Path for Reform', *Population and Development Review* 35 (2009): 701–720.

[16] Hall and Soskice, *Varieties of Capitalism*. See also Bob Hancké, Martin Rhodes and Mark Thatcher, eds., *Beyond Varieties of Capitalism. Conflict, Contradictions, and Complementarities in the European Economy* (Oxford: Oxford University Press, 2008).

7.3 Unifying Pressures

Yet, somehow the varieties of national institutional and socioeconomic systems throughout the EU have not made it any easier for economic integration to achieve its goals. They have produced a lot of economic negative spillover effects and political conflicts. Why? Among possible answers one is particularly telling for European integration: the varieties of capitalism have been subject to the same pressures, to which, however, they have reacted differently.

In all of the preceding chapters I argued that these effects have largely stemmed from centrifugal effects propelled by the Eurozone. Now this argument should be qualified by how 'a fiscal regime of austerity' – a concept coined by Paul Pierson years before it became a buzzword among European policymakers and a dirty word among a large proportion of the European population – has influenced the major socioeconomic policies of European countries.[17] Pierson paid attention to the downward pressures on the economic activity already clearly visible in the 1990s: tax competition limiting revenues from corporate taxation,[18] economic growth persistently lower than during the previous *trente glorieuses*, the maturation of welfare transfers committed to postwar baby boomers during the previous period of the expanding welfare state and, last but not least, to population ageing caused both by growing longevity of retirees and by falling birth rates in advanced economies.[19] He argued that all of these pressures were multiplying the number of risks societies expected their governments to shield them from.[20] But while

[17] Paul Pierson, 'From Expansion to Austerity. The New Politics of Taxing and Spending', in: *Seeking the Center: Politics and Policymaking at the New Century*, eds. Martin A. Levin, Marc K. Landy and Martin Shapiro (Washington, DC: Georgetown University Press, 2001): 54–80; Paul Pierson, 'Coping with Permanent Austerity: Welfare State Restructuring in Affluent Democracies', in: *The New Politics of the Welfare State*, ed. Paul Pierson (New York: Oxford University Press, 2001): 410–456.

[18] For a more detailed picture, see, for example, Philipp Genschel and Peter Schwarz, 'Tax Competition and Fiscal Democracy', in: *Politics in the Age of Austerity*, eds. Wolfgang Streeck and Armin Schafer (Cambridge: Polity Press, 2013): 59–83.

[19] This list of factors is non-exclusive, of course. In particular, low inflation, achieved by advanced economies in 2000s, makes it more difficult to inflate public debt away, and hence it reinforces austerity pressures.

[20] As some commentators described the resultant picture, 'today's welfare states have taken up some new functions. They are expected to help and/or push non-working people back into employment, to complement work income for the working poor, to help parents reconcile work and family life, to promote gender equality, to support child development, and to provide social services for an ageing society': Giuliano Bonoli and David Natali, 'The Politics of the "New" Welfare States: Analysing Reforms

redistribution expectations were growing, financial resources to meet them languished. National governments struggled under the pressure of scarcity and competing priorities.

Pierson had a foreboding that politicians would not be able to meet these challenges and that socioeconomic stagnation produced by the ossification of essential public policies would follow, putting national systems under an even more painful strain.[21] Others have seen a reformist window of opportunity, and necessity, in the new pressures and challenges.[22] These scholars have highlighted that 'reforms are difficult to achieve, politically risky and easily derailed, yet they happen'.[23] They have argued that the pressures underlined by Pierson force national governments to rationalise their socioeconomic policies and to improve their governance processes, because obsolete systems would not be able to meet the demands of their citizens. Kersbergen and Vis, for instance, have contended that 'such pressures constitute a functional demand for change, because if there is no change, this static condition [the new social risk structure] implies an existential threat. Ill-adaptation and new social risks to which the postwar welfare state does not cater ask for permanent reform.'[24]

In addition, because the new social risks are essentially uniform across countries belonging to different traditions of political economy, the 'rationalisation' it necessitates nudges national politicians towards the same priorities and orientations.

In some areas, the new policies require more funding, and the supporters of the social investment paradigm[25] have gladly welcomed it,

in Western Europe', in: *The Politics of the New Welfare State*, eds. Giuliano Bonoli and David Natali (Oxford: Oxford University Press 2012): 3.

21 Paul Pierson, 'Irresistible Forces, Immovable Objects: Post-Industrial Welfare States Confront Permanent Austerity', *Journal of European Social Policy* 5 (1998): 539–560.

22 Anton Hemerijck, *Changing Welfare States* (Oxford: Oxford University Press, 2013).

23 Anton Hemerijck and Jelle Visser, 'Policy Learning in European Welfare States', *Center for European Studies*, October 2003, 2.

24 Kees van Kersbergen and Barbara Vis, *Comparative Welfare State Politics: Development, Opportunities, and Reform* (New York: Cambridge University Press, 2014): 159.

25 Social investments is public spending intended to improve qualifications of workers, current and future, as well as to improve employability of the groups traditionally less active on the labour market (e.g., older workers, women). 'The policy areas considered under social investment include *inter alia* early childhood education and care (ECEC), active labour market policies (in particular, training and job-search assistance), education, retraining and lifelong education, healthcare, social services, housing support, rehabilitation and healthcare and long-term care services': Denis Bouget et. al., 'Social Investment in Europe. A Study of National Policies', April 2015,

even at the expense of fiscal deficits. They have praised the governments striving to funnel more funds to active labour market policies intended to improve the employability of society[26] and to family policies aimed to stave off the effects of new family and demographic patterns.[27] To boost employment rates, they also encourage governments to obviate traditional barriers to women's participation in labour markets.

The rationality of such adjustments is intuitive, so national governments of many countries have embarked on the reform process. Some observers noted, for instance, that 'while European welfare states differ considerably in their policy mixes as well as in their welfare expenditure levels, one can observe a tendency towards an increase in social investment expenditure on families, active labour market policy and education'.[28] As a result of these adaptations, the traditionally more conservative socioeconomic models of family policy[29] have been moving (at various speeds) closer to the social-democratic type prevailing in the Scandinavian countries. Also, healthcare systems of many continental countries have undergone a similar reorientation

4, available at ec.europa.eu/social/BlobServlet?docId=15131&langId=en. For more extensive discussions of the concept, see, for example, Nathalie Morel, Bruno Palier and Joakim Palme, *Towards a Social Investment Welfare State?: Ideas, Policies and Challenges* (Bristol: Policy Press, 2012); Anton Hemerijck et al., 'Assessing Social Investment Synergies (ASIS)', October 2016, available at ec.europa.eu/social/BlobServlet?docId=16878&langId=en; Anton Hemerijck, ed., *The Uses of Social Investment* (Oxford: Oxford University Press, 2017).

[26] I.e., public employment services (brokerage services, vocational guidance and counselling to the unemployed), as well as employment incentives, training and direct job creation. The scope to which active labour market policies were capable of improving employability is a highly contestable issue. For an overview, see, for example, Eithne Mclaughlin, *Understanding Unemployment: New Perspectives on Active Labour Market Policies* (London, New York: Routledge, 2013).

[27] Priscilla A. Lambert, 'The Comparative Political Economy of Parental Leave and Child Care: Evidence from Twenty OECD Countries', *Social Politics* 15 (2008): 315–344.

[28] Verena Dräbing, 'The Role of the State: Reform Pressures and Welfare Reform Towards Social Investment', in: *Let's Get to Work! The Future of Labour in Europe, Vol. 1*, eds. Miroslav Beblavý, Ilaria Maselli and Marcela Veselková, CEPS 2014, 179, available at www.ceps.eu/system/files/NEUJOBS%20Future%20of%20Labour%20Vol%20I_FINAL_1_0.pdf.

[29] As Esping-Andersen noted, 'the Bismarck countries are indisputably weakening their traditional male breadwinner bias, and we detect a trend towards defamilialization on many fronts. All countries have introduced job security provisions for mothers and have, rather cautiously, begun to encourage fathers to take childcare leaves': Gøsta Esping-Andersen, 'Prologues: What Does It Mean to Break with Bismarck?', in: *A Long Goodbye to Bismarck?* ed. Bruno Palier (Amsterdam: Amsterdam University Press, 2010): 14.

towards the Beveridge (universalist) model (shared by Anglo-Saxon and Scandinavian states).[30] In particular, 'the principle of entitlement based on citizenship rather than employment has found its way into health reforms in many countries, including France, Italy and Spain'.[31]

But even if some areas have been shielded from the permanent austerity paradigm, in others the retrenchment pressure of the world economy played out with a vengeance.[32] Facing the consequences of technological advancements for labour markets, of deindustrialisation produced both by the growing role of services in the GDP and by the industrial relocation to low-cost countries, subordinated to the whims of international financial flows and pressed by demographic change, governments of economically advanced countries embarked on investor- and work-first reorientations of their institutional systems, as well as on cost-containment surgeries to their welfare systems. As was already predicted by some scholars in the 1990s,[33] national variations of both the conservative model and the social-democratic model have undergone various changes towards their (increasingly more) liberal counterpart.[34] Collective bargaining has evolved in the direction of greater flexibility, employment protections have been weakened, social entitlements cut and conditions on access to benefits tightened, striving to accommodate the 'workfarist' approach.[35] Rather than decommodifying, welfare states have been re-commodifying. Various countries have experimented with the marketisation of core welfare

[30] E.g., Fosco Foglietta and Franco Toniolo, *New Models of Governance and Health System Integration* (Milano: FrancoAngeli 2013).

[31] Esping-Andersen, 'Prologues', 14.

[32] 'The novelty of the recent epoch lies in the simultaneous application of both positive incentives of active and investment-oriented labour market policies and negative incentives of retrenched welfare benefits of shorter duration, increased targeting, and sanctioning': Hemerijck, *Changing Welfare States*, 48.

[33] Mary Daly, 'Welfare States under Pressure: Cash Benefits in European Welfare States over the Last Ten Years', *Journal of European Social Policy* 7 (1997): 129–146; Duane Swank, 'Social Democratic Welfare States in a Global Economy: Scandinavia in a Comparative Perspective', in: *Globalization, Europeanization, and the End of Scandinavian Social Democracy?*, ed. Robert Geyer (London: Macmillan, 1998): 85–138.

[34] Lucio Baccaro and Chris Howell, 'A Common Neoliberal Trajectory: The Transformation of Industrial Relations in Advanced Capitalism', *Politics & Society* 39 (2011): 521–563.

[35] Minna van Gerven, 'The Broad Tracks of Path Dependent Benefit Reforms. A Longitudinal Study of Social Benefit Reforms in Three European Countries, 1980–2006', 2008, available at pure.uvt.nl/ws/files/1032352/van_Gerven_tutkimuksia_100.pdf.

state functions, hoping to achieve efficiency gains.[36] Writing back in 2009, some scientists concluded that 'the neoliberalized rule regime of the early 2000s has been more than three decades in the making, and throughout that period, it has been in a perpetual state of contestation and reconstruction. Yet, its central consequence has been to subject otherwise diverse forms of (localized and national) regulatory experimentation to certain common, underlying parameters of marketization and commodification.'[37]

7.3.1 *Different Reactions*

While some governments enthusiastically embraced the paradigm shifts, others have striven to resist them.[38] This might have been because pro-reform coalitions were too weak and/or the economic situation seemed sufficiently good to avoid painful restructurings. Ultimately, the reasons why some countries have resisted changes are less important for my argument in this chapter than what this stance has entailed. Reform-averse governments have not nurtured any institutional competitive advantages, contrary to the basic idea behind the 'varieties of capitalism'. Instead, the reform resistance has proved self-defeating in the longer term, because, as Thelen powerfully argued, 'the successful defense of traditional institutions and policies has often been a recipe for institutional erosion and rising inequality through declining coverage and dualisation'.[39]

The countries striving to maintain the paradigms performing well during the three decades following World War II but failing afterwards have therefore been putting themselves on the losing side of the global economy. This, in turn, has thinned their resources and further undermined their core state powers, rendering their economies and politics more volatile and unstable. Especially in the Eurozone,

[36] Timo Weishaupt, 'A Silent Revolution? New Management Ideas and the Reinvention of European Public Employment Services', *Socio-Economic Review* 8 (2010): 461–486; Matthias Knuth, 'Broken Hierarchies, Quasi-markets and Supported Networks – A Governance Experiment in the Second Tier of Germany's Public Employment Service', *Social Policy &Administration* 48 (2014): 240–261.

[37] Neil Brenner, Jamie Peck and Nik Theodore, 'Variegated Neoliberalization: Geographies, Modalities, Pathways', *Global Networks. A Journal of Transnational Affairs* 10 (2010): 38.

[38] Huw Macartney, *Variegated Neoliberalism: EU Varieties of Capitalism and International Political Economy* (New York; London: Routledge, 2011).

[39] Kathleen Thelen, *Varieties of Liberalization: The New Politics of Social Solidarity* (New York: Cambridge University Press, 2014): xx.

where individual countries are unable to compensate socioeconomic parochialisms by boosting the economy with lower interest and exchange rates, public policy slipups can, and do, catalyse very serious chain reactions undermining the stability of the whole edifice. They do not contribute to any balanced ecosystem based on evenly distributed comparative advantages. Conversely, they render the EU prone to jungle-style dog-eat-dog instincts, because the socioeconomically weaker specimens have become weaker and the stronger ones have become even stronger. This is hardly an environment conducive to sustainable economic or political integration, nor to the goal of achieving 'solidarity between their peoples while respecting their history, their culture and their traditions', as the Preamble of the TEU requires. Rather, it is a recipe for a spectacular economic and political disaster at the heart of the European project.

To see what this point actually implies, we should now look more closely to the trajectory of socioeconomic policies and their institutional underpinnings in Sweden and Germany, on the one hand, and in Italy and Greece, on the other. Both groups of countries are at polar ends of the ability to adjust to the requirements of the global economy. Their socioeconomic and institutional choices have seriously influenced the well-being and the political resilience of their societies. In performing this case study, I do not intend to stigmatise either Italians or Greeks. Instead, I want to demonstrate that under the current division of powers between the EU and the Member States in the socioeconomic realm the centrifugal effects of the variegated national choices can only accelerate in the future, augmenting the divide between the well-off and the worse-off.

7.4 Sweden: The Socioeconomic Laboratory

When the Swedish model broke down in the early 1990s,[40] the country's very active state intervention, redistribution of wealth and rigid labour markets reinforced the case for the then-dominant neo-liberal argument. And yet, while in the following decades consecutive Swedish

[40] In the early 1990s, Sweden suffered from a combination of a banking crisis (see, for example, Peter Englund, 'The Swedish Banking Crisis: Roots and Consequences', *Oxford Review of Economic Policy* 15 [1999]: 80–97) and a broader economic crisis produced by socioeconomic and institutional obsolesces: Assar Lindbeck et al., 'Options for Economic and Political Reform in Sweden', *Economic Policy* 8 (1993): 219–263.

governments experimented with various neo-liberal ideas and policies, the Swedish socioeconomic model (characterised by a very active – and effective – state, as well as by high redistribution) soon regained its vitality without substantially altering any of its traditional defining features.[41]

Steinmo convincingly argued that the source of the model's vitality should be sought in the nature of governance processes prevailing in this country, rather than in the political and economic world views of Swedish policymakers.[42] In other words, Swedish governments have managed to maintain the resilience of Swedish public policies largely because governance processes there have been traditionally less ideologised than in other countries. Socioeconomic policies have been approached there mainly as engineering questions to be answered with expertise targeted at achieving efficiency gains. Less dependent on the immediate pressures of interest groups and more reliant on exceptionally professional, effective and unbiased administration, Sweden's policymakers could more easily concentrate on longer-term goals, rather than striving for immediate endorsements of their actions in opinion polls.

This political pattern has a long tradition in all Scandinavian countries. Sweden provided its exemplar when in the early 1950s two economists of the Swedish Trade Union Confederation – Gösta Rehn and Rudolf Meidner – developed their groundbreaking socioeconomic model, which laid the foundations for Swedish prosperity in the decades to come. The model was exceptional both because it was profoundly scientific, and because, despite being engendered by trade unionists, it served as an intrinsically capitalist vehicle for Schumpeterian economic creative destruction.[43]

[41] Anders Lindbom, 'Dismantling the Social Democratic Welfare Model? Has the Swedish Welfare State Lost Its Defining Characteristics?', *Scandinavian Political Studies* 24 (2001): 171–193. See also Jonas Edlund and Ingemar Johansson Sevä, 'Is Sweden Being Torn Apart? Privatization and Old and New Patterns of Welfare State Support', *Social Policy & Administration* 47 (2013): 542–564. As the authors conclude (545): 'Gradually adapting the welfare state in a more market-friendly direction (e.g., freedom of choice, vouchers and market-inspired competition) has, therefore, secured a continuing strong support among a large middle-class that otherwise would have "abandoned" the Swedish welfare model.'

[42] Sven Steinmo, 'Governing as an Engineering Problem: The Political Economy of Swedish Success', in: *Politics in the Age of Austerity*, eds. Wolfgang Streeck and Armin Schafer (Cambridge: Polity Press, 2013): 84–107.

[43] For broader overviews of the ascent and subsequent demise of the model, see, for example, Peter A. Swenson, *Capitalists against Markets: The Making of Labor Markets*

The scheme was based on the tenet of equal wages across the economy, to be achieved through top-level collective bargaining. Sweden was already, by that point, a very open economy. Rehn and Meidner correctly anticipated that equal wages across the board would pull the whole less profitable (less productive) Swedish industries out of their markets, because growing costs of labour would make them unable to stand up to competitive pressure from outside. To avoid the resulting high and persistent unemployment that could otherwise easily follow, the state had to step in to shepherd the upgrading of workers' skills and their transition from the companies on the downside of the process towards those at the high-productivity end. This transition would not be possible without sufficient unemployment benefits and without carefully calibrated active labour market and educational policies. The activist welfare state in the Rehn–Meidner model was not, therefore, intended to liberate the society (or a part of it) from the shackles of the economy. It was not meant to de-commodify. Quite the contrary. The two economists wanted to make private companies more profitable, workers more productive and this productivity translate into higher real wages. By the same token they wanted to make sure that the productivity gains were not entirely retained by the capitalists. Yet, they also strived to prevent trade unions from excessively bloating the costs of productive companies. By aligning the interests of capitalists and trade unions, the Swedish governments inspired by the Rehn and Meidner model sought to mitigate industrial conflicts, putting employers and trade unions in one boat and encouraging them to row towards a more competitive economy. In consequence, Swedish labour relations generously lubricated the cogs of the capitalist economy. When you add to it that under the Rehn–Meidner model fiscal and monetary policies were inherently countercyclical, you come up with a device that uses socialist concepts to achieve what Margaret Thatcher could only dream of.

Ultimately, the original effectiveness of state interventions and redistribution in achieving the Schumpeterian creative destruction vanished and Sweden entered almost two decades of much more defensive policies, paving the way to economic decline. But, with resilient governance

and Welfare States in the United States and Sweden (New York: Oxford University Press, 2002); Lennart Erixon, 'The Rehn-Meidner Model in Sweden: Its Rise, Challenges and Survival', *Journal of Economic Issues* 44 (2010): 677–715; Mats Benner and Torben Bundgaard Vad, 'Sweden and Denmark Defending the Welfare State', in: *Welfare and Work in the Open Economy Volume II: Diverse Responses to Common Challenges in Twelve Countries*, eds. Fritz Scharpf and Vivien A. Schmidt (Oxford: Oxford University Press, 2000): 399–466; Kathleen Thelen, *Varieties of Liberalization*, 173–192.

processes, efficient administration, intelligent educational and family policies well-calibrated to boost employment,[44] and with the productivity-enhancing ethos deeply entrenched in society, Sweden was well-predisposed to an economic and social resuscitation after the turning point of 1993. When in other economically advanced countries public debt:GDP ratios spiralled upwards, Sweden has managed to cut its public debt from approximately 70 per cent of GDP in 1996 to less than 42 per cent of GDP in 2016.[45] During his tenure, the Swedish Minister of Finance between 2006 and 2014, Anders Borg, championed neo-liberal reforms, preaching to what the WSJ called 'The Swedish Model. It's the free-market reforms, stupid.'[46] The goal, of course, was not to fundamentally reorient the Swedish model of public policies, but to gradually push it towards a mixed welfare state model, where public funding and private provision of various public services could successfully coexist.

One may argue, of course, that Sweden is not heaven on earth. There are countries in Europe with higher educational achievements.[47] Swedish executives complain that high taxes discourage entrepreneurs from working and investing in this country.[48] The country's famous social cohesion is strained[49] and the integration

[44] Universalistic social services, a hallmark of the social-democratic welfare state model, have in Sweden been considered indispensable to boost employment among women and to improve the socialisation of children, while at the same time mitigating risks stemming from family change (like single parenthood). See Linda Haas, 'Family Policy in Sweden', *Journal of Family and Economic Issues* 17 (1996): 47–92; Kimberly Earles, 'Swedish Family Policy – Continuity and Change in the Nordic Welfare State Model', *Social Policy & Administration* 45 (2011): 180–193.

[45] Eurostat, General Government Gross Debt.

[46] Johnny Munkhammar, 'The Swedish Model. It's the Free-market Reforms, Stupid', *The Wall Street Journal Europe*, 26 January 2011, available at www.wsj.com/articles/SB10001424052748704698004576104023432243468. For a more comprehensive account, in the historical context, see Gerhard Schnyder, 'Like a Phoenix from the Ashes? Reassessing the Transformation of the Swedish Political Economy since the 1970s', *Journal of European Public Policy* 19 (2012): 1126–1145.

[47] In the 2015 round of the Programme for International Student Assessment (PISA) tests, its fifteen-year-old students scored precisely at the OECD mean science performance, behind their peers from thirteen other EU countries. See PISA 2015 Results in Focus, available at www.oecd.org/pisa/pisa-2015-results-in-focus.pdf.

[48] In the 2016/2017 Global Competitiveness Report of the World Economic Forum Sweden was classified as the seventy-sixth country in the category of 'effect of taxation on incentives to invest' and 120th in the category 'effect of taxation on incentives to work' (331).

[49] In 2013, eleven other OECD countries (including two Eastern European: Czechia and Slovakia) had more equal income levels than Sweden: data.oecd.org/inequality/income-inequality.htm. For context, see Olof Bäckman and Åke Bergmark, 'Escaping

of third-country immigrants faces great challenges.[50] Its housing market has been overheated.[51] But ultimately, very few societies in the world are happier than the Swedes are[52] and very few live in similarly stable and well-performing economies.[53] Angel Gurría, OECD's Secretary-General, noted in February 2017 that 'with GDP growing at a rate of over 3% in 2016 despite sluggish global demand, Sweden is outpacing major advanced economies, including Germany and the United States, as well as its Nordic neighbours. Bucking the global trend, productivity has picked up. Unemployment is receding, and Sweden has a higher employment rate than any other EU Member State. Moreover, only 5% of total Swedish employment is in low-skilled jobs.'[54]

This country has gotten there because its policymakers have striven to draw lessons from past mistakes and to constantly reorient its socioeconomic policies accordingly. With effective public institutions and resilient governance processes, impressive outputs of its public policies should not be very surprising.

7.5 Germany: Imperfect but Sturdy

The same is essentially true for Germany, even though here certain path dependencies have produced more ambivalent effects. The German socioeconomic model belongs to a different family of welfare capitalism than does the Swedish. As an archetypical continental conservative-corporatist system, its welfare state is traditionally less inclusive, more

Welfare? Social Assistance Dynamics in Sweden', *Journal of European Social Policy* 21 (2011): 486–500 (explaining factors behind growing social assistance recipiency periods in Sweden).

50 OECD, *Working Together: Skills and Labour Market Integration of Immigrants and Their Children in Sweden* (Paris: OECD Publishing, 2016).

51 OECD, *The 2017 OECD Economic Surveys: Sweden 2017* (Paris: OECD Publishing, 2017).

52 Swedes are the tenth-happiest nation in the world, according to John Helliwell, Richard Layard and Jeffrey Sachs, eds., *World Happiness Report 2017*, available at worldhappiness.report/wp-content/uploads/sites/2/2017/03/HR17.pdf.

53 According to the 2016/2017 Global Competitiveness Report of the World Economic Forum, Sweden was the sixth-most competitive economy in the world. It was also the most innovative EU economy in 2016, according to the European Innovation Scoreboard of the European Commission (available at ec.europa.eu/growth/industry/innovation/facts-figures/scoreboards_pl).

54 Speech 'Launch of the 2017 Economic Survey of Sweden', 8 February 2017, available at www.oecd.org/about/secretary-general/launch-of-the-2017-economic-survey-of-sweden.htm.

dual, less concerned with providing public services and less willing to accept changing family relations. But, akin to Sweden, German socio-economic policies have also undergone massive reorienting changes, recalibrations and experiments with neo-liberal concepts in the past few decades.[55] Like in Sweden, in Germany profoundly resilient public institutions and governance processes have facilitated the transitions.

The Hartz reforms introduced in the early 2000s, deeply inspired by the permanent austerity and workfarist paradigms, were all about reorienting the German welfare state from its affixation on guaranteeing achieved living standards towards the more liberal objective of publicly securing one's minimum existence and highlighting individual responsibility for any higher achievements.[56] As such, they have reinforced the pressure towards general labour market flexibility.[57] This pressure helped broaden the labour market and facilitate wage moderations in the industrial core within the traditionally cooperative German collective bargaining system. On the downside, it entrenched labour market duality and amplified social inequalities instantiated by the very broad low-wage sector of atypical workers.[58] Thelen accurately remarks that in Germany 'the two sides of dualization – the stabilization of the core and the flexibilization of the periphery – are not separate stories, but two sides of the same coin because extending employment guarantees to core workers is increasingly "bought" through outsourcing strategies that benefit from liberalization outside the core'.[59]

[55] For an introduction, see, e.g., Wolfgang Streeck, *Re-Forming Capitalism. Institutional Change in the German Political Economy* (Oxford: Oxford University Press, 2010).

[56] Timo Weishaupt, 'Germany after a Decade of Social Democrats in Government: The End of the Continental Model?', *German Politics* 19 (2010): 105–122; Timo Fleckenstein, 'Restructuring Welfare for the Unemployed: The Hartz Legislation in Germany', *Journal of European Social Policy* 18 (2008): 177–188; Jochen Clasen, *Reforming Welfare States – Germany and the UK Compared* (Oxford: Oxford University Press 2005); Wolfram Lamping and Friedbert W. Rüb, 'From the Conservative Welfare State to an "Uncertain Something Else": German Pension Politics in Comparative Perspective', *Policy & Politics* 32 (2004): 169–191; Peter Bleses and Martin Seeleib-Kaiser, *The Dual Transformation of the German Welfare State* (Basingstoke: Palgrave Macmillan, 2004): 92; Karl Hinrichs, 'A Social Insurance State Withers Away. Welfare State Reforms in Germany – Or: Attempts to Turn Around in a Cul-de-Sac', in: *A Long Goodbye to Bismarck?*, ed. Bruno Palier (Amsterdam: Amsterdam University Press, 2010): 45–72.

[57] Werner Eichhorst and Paul Marx, 'Reforming German Labour Market Institutions: A Dual Path to Flexibility', *Journal of European Social Policy* 21 (2011): 73–87.

[58] Gerhard Bosch and Claudia Weinkopf, *Low-Wage Work in Germany* (New York: Russell Sage Foundation 2008).

[59] Thelen, *Varieties of Liberalization*, 151.

This labour market dualisation has rendered jobs in the economically strategic sectors more attractive and nurtured comparative advantages of these sectors in global markets.[60] The advantages of such an approach have been further magnified by well-functioning dual vocational education and training, effectively morphing from the traditional industrial firm-based system towards technologically advanced and hybrid education bringing together higher education and apprenticeships.[61] Successful experiments with firm-level decentralisation of management[62] and strategic incorporation of low-cost Eastern European subcontractors into German global production chains gave the model an additional boost. All of these factors together have allowed for constant incremental innovation in German tradable sectors, going hand-in-hand with cost containment in order to support the economy's stellar export performance in recent years.

From the outset the German reform path was less universalistic and – expectedly in a more conservative society, it was also less inclusive. The dualisation of the German labour market doubled the in-work at-risk-of-poverty rate between 2005 and 2016, a change unparalleled by any other EU country and deeply perplexing in an economy close to full employment.[63] By prioritising countercyclical fiscal policy and striving to put a lid on taxation, the German government has managed to keep public expenditure relatively low in recent years, at the expense, however, of very low public investments.[64] This

[60] Luigi Bonatti and Andrea Fracasso, 'The German Model and the European Crisis', *Journal of Common Market Studies* 51 (2013): 1023–1039; Bernhard Gräf et al., 'Focus Germany: Structural National Improvements Support Exceptional Position', *Research Brief Deutsche Bank*, 1 July 2013.

[61] However, certain features of the German vocational educational and training system – especially an insufficient number of high-quality training slots within firm-based apprenticeship schemes, lacking school-based vocational education and training, as well as underdeveloped continuing (life-long) vocational education – have been adding a fly to this ointment. See Thelen, *Varieties of Liberalization*, 86–98.

[62] Dalia Marin, Jan Schymik and Jan Tscheke, 'Europe's Exports Superstar – It's the Organisation', *Bruegel Working Paper* No. 2015/05, 14 July 2015, available at bruegel.org/2015/07/europes-exports-superstar-its-the-organisation/.

[63] The in-work at-risk-of-poverty rate (share of employed persons of eighteen years or over with a disposable income below 60 per cent of the national median disposable income, after social transfers) grew in Germany from 4.8 to 9.5 per cent, respectively. In crisis-stricken Greece, the rate raised by only 1.2 percentage points in the same period (from 12.9 to 14.1 per cent), in Spain by 2.5 percentage points (from 10.6 to 13.1 per cent) and in Italy by 3.0 points (from 8.7 to 11.7 per cent).

[64] As throughout the previous two decades, in 2016 the German general government gross fixed capital formation, which is a proxy for public investments in tangible assets (land improvements, property and machinery upgrades, infrastructure,

factor – together with the pressures of an ageing population, the influx of unskilled third-country immigrants, sluggish productivity growth and rigid product markets[65] – has been putting a downward pressure on this economy's potential growth as well as on the long-term resilience of its socioeconomic model.

7.5.1 *Worlds Apart*

All in all, therefore, neither the Swedish nor the German model is perfect. But both have been undergoing constant processes of public policy experimentation intended to achieve rational problem-solving within resilient governance processes and public institutions.

Similar transitions have been witnessed in other advanced economies that have withstood the Great Recession and the sovereign debt crisis without serious economic damage.[66] In none of them have policymakers tried to insulate their societies from capitalistic pressures. Instead of trying to stymie capitalism, they have endeavoured to adapt major public policies to its evolving necessities. They have striven to approach glitches and anachronisms of national socioeconomic policies as 'engineering problems' to be solved by experts and effective public servants in the best (long-term) interest of the society. Such governance approaches have kept policymakers constantly busy and the socioeconomic policies in constant flux, rendering, however, the societies undergoing them well-prepared to reap the benefits of globalisation and to avoid its pitfalls.

In all of these aspects, many other EU countries have proven much less successful. Italy and Greece are some of the most extreme

etc.), was much below the EU average (2.1 per cent of GDP in Germany, compared to 2.7 per cent of GDP on average in the EU). It equalled the level of Italian public investments (also 2.1 per cent of GDP). Only Spain (1.9 per cent of GDP), Ireland (1.8 per cent of GDP) and Portugal (1.5 per cent of GDP) spent a lower share of GDP on public investments that year: Eurostat, General government gross fixed capital formation, General government.

65 OECD, *The 2016 OECD Economic Surveys: Germany 2016* (Paris: OECD Publishing, 2016).

66 Take the Netherlands as another example. One observer noted that 'in the Netherlands, from the 1980s onwards, welfare retrenchment and restructuring are not merely rhetorical concepts. On the contrary, the picture that emerges is that of an incremental but systemic and steady process of continuous reform in reaction to various challenges brought about by economic, demographic, social and cultural factors': Wim van Oorschot, 'The Dutch Welfare State: Recent Trends and Challenges in Historical Perspective', *European Journal of Social Security* 8 (2006): 58. See also, for example, Mara Yerkes and Romke van der Veen, 'Crisis and Welfare State in the Netherlands', *Social Policy & Administration* 45 (2011): 430–444; Anton Hemerijck and Ive Marx, 'Continental Welfare at a Crossroads: The Choice between Activation and

examples. In both countries the state has been traditionally 'weak'[67] – its institutions have been throttling back when implementing public policies.[68] In both countries inefficient state institutions have been undermining economic prosperity and social cohesion.[69] As a result, governments there have often been perceived as extracting economic resources produced by society, in exchange for hindering business acumen that could otherwise be deployed more productively.

7.6 Italy: Melting Away

International comparisons revealing the effects of these malfunctions give a comprehensive picture of the Italian ailments.[70] This country's economy still enjoys high innovation potential and business sophistication, which have sustained its competitiveness.[71] Yet, the Italian institutional and socioeconomic performance has been deeply

Minimum Income Protection in Belgium and the Netherlands', in: *A Long Goodbye to Bismarck?*, ed. Bruno Palier (Amsterdam: Amsterdam University Press, 2010): 129–155.

[67] Richard Gunther, P. Nikoros Diamandouros and Dimitri A. Sotiropoulos, eds., *Democracy and the State in the New Southern Europe* (New York: Oxford University Press, 2006).

[68] Some authors described this state malfunction as the 'Mediterranean Syndrome' (Antonio La Spina and Giuseppe Sciortino, 'Common Agenda, Southern Rules: European Integration and Environmental Change in the Mediterranean States', in: *European Integration and Environmental Policy*, eds. Duncan Liefferink, Philip Lowe and Arthur Moll [London: Belhaven Press, 1993]: 217–236), but it could equally well refer to a large proportion of other EU countries as well, especially in its eastern part.

[69] Inefficient institutions and policy flaws at more generic policy levels make an introduction of more progressive policy paradigms virtually impossible and often self-defeating. For a broader argument, see Yuri Kazepov and Costanzo Ranci, 'Is Every Country Fit for Social Investment? Italy as an Adverse Case', *Journal of European Social Policy* 27 (2017): 90–104.

[70] For concise accounts on policy patterns of the Italian welfare state, from a historical perspective, see Matteo Jessoula and Tizziana Alti, 'Italy: An Uncompleted Departure from Bismarck', in: *A Long Goodbye to Bismarck?*, ed. Bruno Palier (Amsterdam: Amsterdam University Press, 2010): 157–181; Franca Maino and Stefano Neri, 'Explaining Welfare Reforms in Italy between Economy and Politics: External Constraints and Endogenous Dynamics', *Social Policy & Administration*, 45 (2011): 445–464. For a more comprehensive discussion, see Ugo Ascoli and Emmanuele Pavolini, *The Italian Welfare State in a European Perspective: A Comparative Analysis* (Bristol: Policy Press, 2016).

[71] In the 2016/2017 edition of the Global Competitiveness Report, Italy was classified as the forty-fourth-most competitive country in the world (out of 138 countries ranked), while Croatia, for instance, was ranked a whole thirty positions lower, available at www3.weforum.org/docs/GCR2016-2017/05FullReport/TheGlobalCompetitivenessReport2016-2017_FINAL.pdf.

disappointing. It has greatly amplified the economic stress caused by the Italian participation in the Eurozone and it would drag economic and social prosperity down even if Italy was to achieve a competitive boost through currency depreciation, as discussed in the previous chapter.

Each year, the Global Economic Forum scrutinises individual national economies under more than 100 indicators measuring their productivity and resilience. The results are then published in annual Global Competitiveness Reports. In the 2016/2017 edition of the report, in which 138 countries (out of 206 sovereign states on the planet that year) were surveyed, Italy was rated 116th when it comes to public trust in politicians. In other words, quite a large proportion of the societies in the developing world were less disaffected with their political classes than were Italians. Other indicators showed why: in 2016 Italy was ranked 120th (remember: out of 138 countries on the list) in the category 'Favoritism in decisions of government officials'. Only two countries on the list (with Italy being ranked 136th) scored worse in the categories 'Burden of government regulation' and 'Efficiency of legal framework in settling disputes'. Only ten fared worse in 'Transparency of government policymaking' and only sixteen in 'Organized crime'. Italian labour market efficiency indicators were equally disappointing. The country was rated 111th in 'Cooperation in labour-employer relations', 131st in 'Flexibility of wage determination', 124th in 'Hiring and firing practices' and 127th in 'Pay and productivity'.

The institutional resilience and reliability of national policymaking remains, therefore, at an alarmingly low level in Italy. Employment relationships are confrontational and, differently to the picture in Sweden or Germany, they constrain productivity improvements and hence undermine Italian economic performance on global markets. Rigid labour markets propel dualisation, in which outsiders (unemployed, youth) find it particularly hard to compete with insiders.[72]

Highly centralised collective bargaining has prevented wages in the Italian south from adjusting downwards, compared to the much more productive north of the country. As Terzi noted, 'clearly, the price the Mezzogiorno pays for this is a higher unemployment rate

[72] For a broader discussion of factors driving the dualisation, see, for example, David Rueda, *Social Democracy Inside Out: Partisanship and Labour Market Policy in Industrialised Democracies* (Oxford: Oxford University Press, 2007).

than the north, as adjustment cannot take place on the basis of wages and happens on quantity'.[73] In addition, rigid product markets make it more difficult to succeed for whoever has developed a competitive new product. This is hardly an environment conducive to any rational socioeconomic reforms or long-term economic stability. The society is hostile to its own future: 'About 60,000 young people are thought to emigrate annually from Italy, over two thirds of them with college degrees. The outflow of the young is driven partly by very high rates of youth unemployment; but also by a sense that society is organised to marginalise them.'[74]

None of the damaging results contribute to an Italian comparative advantage. To see it in yet another dimension, take the following three facts into account. First, in 2016, among EU countries, only in Greece and Bulgaria was the perceived level of public-sector corruption, gauged annually by Transparency International, higher than in Italy (the level of corruption perception in Italy was the same as in Cuba, slightly higher than in Hungary and Romania and lower than in Greece and Bulgaria).[75] Second, in the 2016/2017 edition of the World Competitiveness Report, the World Economic Forum (WEF) rated Italy as 130th in the categories 'Wastefulness of government spending' and 'Effect of taxation on incentives to work' (i.e., only eight countries surveyed in this edition of the report had more wasteful institutions and more work-distortive taxation) and 137th when it came to 'Effect of taxation on incentives to invest'. And, third, the so-called 'VAT gap', i.e., value-added tax (VAT) revenues lost mainly due to tax evasion and fraud, vary significantly in the EU, depending on the effectiveness of tax collection. When assessed most recently (2015), the VAT gap stood at 25.8 per cent in Italy. This essentially means that more than one euro out of every four expected as VAT revenue was not declared or paid. Only Lithuania (26.4 per cent), Greece (28.3 per cent), Slovakia

[73] Alessio Terzi, 'An Italian Job: The Need for Collective Wage Bargaining Reform', *Bruegel Policy Contribution* No. 2016/11, 6 July 2016, available at bruegel.org/2016/07/an-italian-job-the-need-for-collective-wage-bargaining-reform/.

[74] European Economic Advisory Group, 'Intergenerational Fairness', in: *2016 The EEAG Report on the European Economy* (Munich: CESifo, 2016): 59.

[75] Italy was ranked sixtieth, Hungary and Romania (ex aequo) fifty-seventh, Greece sixty-ninth and Bulgaria seventy-fifth (counting from the least corrupt country in the world – Denmark) out of 176 rating levels: www.transparency.org/news/feature/corruption_perceptions_index_2016.

(29.4 per cent) and Romania (37.2 per cent) fared worse, while the EU-wide gap was half of the Italian (12.8 per cent).[76]

These statistics depict a clear pattern. On the financial side, the Italian government loses a large proportion of its potential tax revenues because its tax authorities are inefficient, biased or even corrupt, while consecutive governments have been unable to reform them. In effect, the taxation burden is shifted towards income taxes, stifling incentives to work and invest. To make it worse, the collected taxes are then subject to wasteful spending, again because public institutions are ineffective or even corrupt. This makes the state unable to target redistribution properly. No wonder that even when exposed to the pressure of financial markets and moral suasion of its international partners, Italian governments have not managed to come up with any serious overhauls of the welfare state.[77] As a result of parochial and distortive policies produced by weak and inefficient institutions, Italy, like Greece and several other EU countries, has been crushing its talents and has remained unable to attract new ones.[78]

7.7 The Hellenic Socioeconomic Inferno

The same applies to Greece, where public institutions have traditionally been similarly feeble, where governance patterns were similarly unwieldy and public policies plagued by statism, dualisms, inequalities and distribution of transfers based on patronage, party clientelism and rent-seeking networks.[79] Such policies have been conducive to

[76] Study and Reports on the VAT Gap in the EU-28 Member States: 2017 Final Report, TAXUD/2015/CC/131, 18 September 2017, 19, available at ec.europa.eu/taxation_customs/sites/taxation/files/study_and_reports_on_the_vat_gap_2017.pdf.

[77] Manuela Naldini and Teresa Jurado, 'Family and Welfare State Reorientation in Spain and Inertia in Italy from a European Perspective', *Population Review* 52 (2013): 43–61.

[78] Youth unemployment in Italy is twice the average in the EU 28: for instance, 35.0 per cent against 16.5 per cent in September 2017 (Eurostat, Unemployment by Sex and Age – Monthly Average, less than twenty-five years). The 2016/2017 Global Competitiveness Report classified Italy in 107th place in the category 'Country capacity to retain talent' and 105th in the category 'Country capacity to attract talent'.

[79] Maurizio Ferrera, 'The "Southern Model" of Welfare in Social Europe', *Journal of European Social Policy* 6 (1996): 17–37; Elias Mossialos and Maria Petmesidou, eds., *Social Policy Developments in Greece* (London: Routledge, 2006); Kevin Featherstone and Dimitris Papadimitriou, *The Limits of Europeanization: Reform Capacity and Policy Conflict in Greece* (Basingstoke: Palgrave Macmillan, 2008); Kevin Featherstone, 'The Greek Sovereign Debt Crisis and EMU: A Failing State in a Skewed Regime', *Journal of Common Market Studies* 49 (2011): 193–217; Takis S. Pappas, 'Why Greece Failed',

crony capitalism, corruption, the shadow economy[80] and rampant tax evasion.[81] They could hardly respond to evolving social and economic needs, dooming the country's future.

When the sovereign debt crisis hit Greece, its socioeconomic policies were in disarray. One commentator noted that 'until 2010, the Greek welfare state remained fragmented, uneven in terms of contributions and benefits, inefficient in its function, and patronage ridden in terms of personnel management and allocation of resources. Over the last 30 years, social services continued to be underdeveloped, transfers were primarily monetary, and, above all, the Greek family remained the most reliable institution upon which the unemployed or working poor family members could count for sufficient living conditions.'[82]

The Greek pension system was an ersatz redistributive nostrum in lieu of more effective and efficient social policies. This design was undermining the very foundations of the Greek prosperity. Yet, 'although Greek pensions were clearly inequitable as well as unsustainable, attempts at significant reform had ended in failure. A combination of

Journal of Democracy 24 (2013): 31–45; Constantine Dimoulas, 'Exploring the Impact of Employment Policy Measures in the Context of Crisis: The Case of Greece', *International Social Security Review* 67 (2014): 49–55; Vassilis Fouskas and Constantine Dimoulas, *Greece, Financialization and the EU: The Political Economy of Debt and Destruction* (International Political Economy Series, Basingstoke: Palgrave Macmillan, 2013); Maria Petmesidou and Ana Guillén, '"Southern Style" National Health Services? Recent Reforms and Trends in Spain and Greece', *Social Policy and Administration* 42 (2008); Aris Trantidis, 'Clientelism and Economic Policy: Hybrid Characteristics of Collective Action in Greece', *Journal of European Public Policy* 23 (2016): 1460–1480.

80 Stavros Katsios, 'The Shadow Economy and Corruption in Greece', *South-Eastern Europe Journal of Economics* 1 (2006): 61–80.

81 In the years directly preceding the sovereign debt crisis up to 45 per cent of self-employed income went unreported for tax purposes in Greece: Nikolaos Artavanis, Adair Morse and Margarita Tsoutsoura, 'Measuring Income Tax Evasion Using Bank Credit: Evidence from Greece', 25 September 2015, available at faculty.haas.berkeley.edu/morse/research/papers/ArtavanisMorseTsoutsouraTaxEvasionGreece..pdf.

82 Dimitri Sotiropoulos, 'Usages of "Europe": Welfare Policies in Greece, 1981–2010', in: *The EU and the Domestic Politics of Welfare State Reforms*, eds. Paolo R. Graziano, Sophie Jacquot and Bruno Palier (London: Palgrave Macmillan, 2011): 144–145. See also Platon Tinios, 'International Accounting Standards as Catalysts for Pension Reform: Greek Pensions and the Public/Private Boundary', *Journal of European Social Policy* 21 (2011): 164–177. These features are quite typical for the whole so-called Mediterranean model of the welfare state. According to Ascoli and Pavolini, *The Italian Welfare State*: 'The model is characterised by policies with a negligible redistributive impact and the allocation of social responsibilities to the family … which shares the resources of the retired (male) breadwinner with family members to face emerging needs' (107–108, citations omitted).

fierce opposition on the part of labour unions and other professional associations, and lack of resolve on the part of the political class, led to paralysis.'[83]

This 'world of capitalism', exemplified by the conundrum of the pension system, did not entail any comparative advantage. It did not make either the Greek economy and the society or the European economic integration more resilient, effective or equitable. The then Greek Prime Minister George Papandreou put it candidly when he admitted in early 2010 that 'we developed a lot of corruption at the highest levels and we did not take the structural measures to change our economy, to move our economy, to make it more competitive'.[84] Greek core socioeconomic policies were an accident waiting to happen, a latent giant negative externality, a 'fiscal sclerosis pre-empting what could be called "fiscal democracy"'.[85]

And they have only gotten worse under the rescue packages launched since 2010. Ostensibly, in exchange for the financial assistance Greece has been expected to remedy its various institutional and policy weaknesses.[86] If this country is to regain its ability to service public and private debt, the idea was, it must reform its institutional framework and crucial socioeconomic policies, from the welfare state to the tax system, as otherwise its ability to return what it owed to the creditors would be undermined. If, for instance, its healthcare and pension systems were outgrown and inefficient, structural and organisational

[83] Manos Matsaganis, 'The Welfare State and the Crisis: The Case of Greece', *Journal of European Social Policy* 21 (2011): 504. For further analysis, see the literature cited therein. See also Platon Tinios, 'International Accounting Standards'.

[84] Larry Elliott, 'No EU Bailout for Greece as PM Promises to "Put Our House in Order"', *Guardian*, 28 January 2010, available at www.guardian.co.uk/business/2010/jan/28/greece-papandreou-eurozone.

[85] Wolfgang Streeck and Daniel Mertens, 'Public Finance and the Decline of State Capacity in Democratic Capitalism', in: *Politics in the Age of Austerity*, eds. Wolfgang Streeck and Armin Schafer (Cambridge: Polity Press, 2013): 26–58.

[86] The first Economic Adjustment Programme for Greece (May 2010, available at ec.europa.eu/economy_finance/publications/occasional_paper/2010/pdf/ocp61_en.pdf) generally endorsed healthcare, pension and administrative reforms. The second Programme (of March 2012, available at ec.europa.eu/economy_finance/publications/occasional_paper/2012/pdf/ocp94_en.pdf) was slightly more specific in these areas, and added privatisation, tax collection and expenditure control reforms and public procurement, as well as labour and product market improvements and judicial reform. The third (MoU of August 2015, available at ec.europa.eu/info/sites/info/files/01_mou_20150811_en_2.pdf) added to this list new measures on education and vocational training, as well as on 'social safety nets'.

improvements should take place. If Greek state-owned companies were pervasively inefficient,[87] they should be privatised. Rigid product and labour markets should be overhauled if they had discouraged entrepreneurship and forestalled the access of Greek products to international markets. Its patchy tax collection system should be sealed.

The collapsing economy, accompanied by very strenuous budgetary retrenchment and disappointing exports (more on it in Chapter 3), proved very hostile to a viable institutional and socioeconomic revival, however. As I mentioned earlier, the Greek pension system, generous before the crisis, performs there the similar role to the (more properly tailored) social assistance programmes in economically more advanced countries. This situation was clearly unsustainable in the longer term. But a sudden retrenchment of the pension system in the middle of a very deep economic crisis, without establishing any vehicles to cushion the economic shock for the social strata most exposed to the pains of the adjustment, made the adjustment much more contestable than would otherwise have been the case. Similarly, no doubt without the privatisation of the patently inefficient public companies, the growth potential of the Greek economy would be undermined. But in the midst of a profound economic crisis, privatisation was naturally heavily opposed, first because the valuation of the companies was low, and second because it could be expected that the entailing layoffs would heighten the wave of otherwise very high unemployment.

Unable to ignite its economy through external devaluation, facing very high unemployment and pernicious short-term consequences of reforms, dumped by highly inefficient public institutions and dysfunctional policymaking processes, Greek governments could hardly find any consolation in the conditionality programmes. The creditors could admonish the Greek government, as the IMF did in February 2017, that 'as a result of the sub-optimal policy mix, the pension system remains highly imbalanced (with a deficit four times the euro-area average of 2.5 percent of GDP), discretionary spending is compressed to unsustainable levels, and the tax burden is unevenly distributed due to exceptional exemptions that relieve the middle class from any personal income tax obligation (more than half of wage earners are exempt from paying personal income tax compared to the euro area average of 8 percent)'.[88]

[87] Christos Ioannou, 'Greek Public Service Employment Relations: A Gordian Knot in the Era of Sovereign Default', *European Journal of Industrial Relations* 19 (2013): 295–308.

[88] International Monetary Fund, '2016 Article IV Consultation Country on Greece', Report No. 17/40, 7 February 2017, 8, available at

At the same time, however, the creditors have demanded the same government to achieve very ambitious fiscal targets and did not help it shield any particular category of spending from cutbacks. Driven by perverse political calculations, lacking expertise as well as an overall vision of how to reinvent its socioeconomic policies, and confronted by conflicting demands of the creditors, Greek institutions and core state policies have been drifting.

While the creditors have time and again emphasised that reform ownership is essential, they, too, have lacked an overall plan as to how to fix key Greek social and economic policies. Take the example of healthcare reform. In the first Greek Economic Adjustment Programme (agreed in May 2010) the Greek government declared that by the end of 2010 it would 'complete the programme of hospital computerisation, upgrading hospital budgeting systems, and the reform of management, the accounting (including double-entry accrual accounting) and financing systems'.[89] In the longer term these reforms would unquestionably improve the cost-effectiveness of the Greek healthcare system. More scarce resources could fund healthcare services, instead of being wasted by poor management. But the necessary reforms required time for planning and careful implementation, as well as financial outlays to cover their upfront costs. Greece had none of this. Quite on the contrary: it was expected to simultaneously achieve significant fiscal retrenchment, and this goal overshadowed any other. No wonder, therefore, that the Greek healthcare system, deprived of necessary resources, neither reduced waste nor improved the quality of services. By the time of the second Economic Adjustment Programme (March 2012) it was a decaying source of a very significant stock of arrears, sending wrinkles throughout the whole economy.[90] In summer 2016, six years into the crisis, a new memorandum between the creditors and Greece again envisioned a long list of healthcare system reforms.[91] Yet again, it

www.imf.org/en/Publications/CR/Issues/2017/02/07/Greece-2017-Article-IV-Consultation-Press-Release-Staff-Report-and-Statement-by-the-44630.

[89] The first Economic Adjustment Programme for Greece, 67.

[90] Henriette Jacobsen, 'Private Clinics Deny Patients Treatment as Greece's Health System Collapses', *Euractiv*, 31 October 2013, available at www.euractiv.com/section/health-consumers/news/private-clinics-deny-patients-treatment-as-greece-s-health-system-collapses/.

[91] 'The authorities have committed to continue reforming the health care sector, controlling public expenditure, managing prices of pharmaceuticals, improve hospital management, increase centralized procurement of hospital supplies,

did not respond to the basic question: how would the ineffective and demoralised Greek administration, which was conspicuously lacking resources for necessary investments, accomplish the multitude of adjustments necessary to reform its healthcare system?[92]

More generally, as time went by Greece saw its public policies gradually declining despite the assistance programmes.[93] According to the WEF, the quality of Greek public institutions worsened between 2009 and 2016.[94] The same picture stems from World Bank statistics on governance standards. In every one of the five criteria comprising this institution's Worldwide Governance Indicators,[95] the country fared significantly worse in 2016 than it did ten years earlier.[96]

In 2016, Greek government spending was one of the most wasteful among the 138 countries listed by the WEF, and this country's burden of government regulation was among the most onerous.[97] The

manage demand for pharmaceuticals and health care through evidence-based e-prescription protocols, commission private sector health care providers in a cost effective manner, modernize IT systems, developing a new electronic referral system for primary and secondary care that allows to formulate care pathways for patients': Supplemental Memorandum of Understanding, 16 June 2016, 16, available at ec.europa.eu/info/sites/info/files/ecfin_smou_en.pdf.

92 According to WHO data, the share of healthcare expenditure in government expenditure fell from 13 per cent in 2009 to 10 per cent in 2014 in Greece. Among EU countries the share of healthcare expenditure in government expenditure was lower in 2014 only in Latvia and Cyprus: WHO, Global Health Expenditure Database, available at apps.who.int/nha/database/QuickReports/Index/en.

93 For an insightful discussion of the causalities involved, see, for example, Kevin Featherstone, 'External Conditionality and the Debt Crisis: The "Troika" and Public Administration Reform in Greece', *Journal of European Public Policy*, 22 (2015): 295–314.

94 In the 2009/2010 edition of the Global Competitiveness Report (available at www3.weforum.org/docs/WEF_GlobalCompetitivenessReport_2009-10.pdf) Greek institutions were ranked seventieth out of 133 on the list. Seven years later, Greece slid down to eighty-first in this category (out of 138 countries compared).

95 These are: 1. Voice and Accountability, 2. Political Stability and Absence of Violence/Terrorism, 3. Government Effectiveness, 4. Regulatory Quality, 5. Rule of Law and 6. Control of Corruption.

96 Voice & Accountability: – 9 percentage points (from 78 in 2006 to 69 per cent in 2016); Political Stability and Absence of Violence/Terrorism: –23 points (from 65 to 42 per cent); Government Effectiveness: –9 points (from 72 per cent to 63 per cent); Regulatory Quality: –17 points (from 76 to 59 per cent); Rule of Law: –18 points (from 77 to 59 per cent); Control of Corruption: –11 points (from 68 to 57 per cent): World Bank, Worldwide Governance Indicators, available from info.worldbank.org/governance/wgi/#reports.

97 123rd and 129th, respectively: Global Competitiveness Report 2016–2017, 191, available at www.weforum.org/reports/the-global-competitiveness-report-2016-2017-1.

efficiency of its legal framework in settling disputes and its transparency of government policymaking were some of the lowest, behind a large number of developing countries.[98] After years of painful conditionality programmes, Greece has not managed to improve the efficiency of its goods or labour markets.[99] The country's primary education system deteriorated compared to other countries (ranked eighty-second in 2016, compared to sixty-fifth seven years earlier); the quality of its higher education system, ranked as ninetieth in the world in 2009, worsened further (to 108th), just like the local availability of specialised training services, intended to improve skills of the local population (106th in the world, from eighty-fourth seven years earlier).[100] Greek government expenditures in relation to the GDP and the share of social expenditures in relation to GDP are among the highest in the EU.[101] And yet, in 2016 (the most recent year for which comprehensive data is available), more than one child in three was facing poverty or social exclusion there.[102] Only in Bulgaria and Romania was a larger proportion of the whole population exposed to the same risk.[103] It should not be surprising, therefore, that Greece is now one of the countries least capable of retaining and attracting talents.[104]

[98] 130th and 121st, respectively: Global Competitiveness Report 2016–2017, 191, available at www.weforum.org/reports/the-global-competitiveness-report-2016-2017-1.

[99] Ranked seventy-fifth and 116th, respectively, in the 2009/2010 edition of the Global Competitiveness Report (out of 133 countries assessed). In the 2016/2017 edition of the Global Competitiveness Report Greece was ranked eighty-ninth and 114th, respectively.

[100] The 2016/2017 and 2009/2010 editions of the Global Competitiveness Report.

[101] In 2016 government expenditure represented 49 per cent of GDP for Greece. Within the EU it was higher only in France (56.2 per cent), Finland (56.1 per cent), Denmark (53.6 per cent), Belgium (53.3 per cent), Austria (51.1 per cent), Sweden (50.0 per cent) and Italy (49.6 per cent): Eurostat, Government Revenue, Expenditure and Main Aggregates. In 2016, social expenditure in Greece stood at 27 per cent of GDP. Among OECD countries it was, again, higher only in France (31.5 per cent), Finland (30.8 per cent), Belgium (29.0 per cent), Italy (28.9 per cent), Denmark (28.7 per cent), Austria (27.8 per cent) and Sweden (27.1 per cent): stats.oecd.org/Index.aspx?DataSetCode=SOCX_AGG.

[102] 36.3 per cent of children below sixteen years old: Eurostat, People at Risk of Poverty or Social Exclusion by Age and Sex.

[103] Ibid.

[104] Ranked 124th (capacity to retain talent) and 130th (capacity to attract talent) – out of 138 countries listed – in the 2016/2017 edition of the Global Competitiveness Report.

7.8 The Embarrassing Face of European Politics

From the perspective of my argument in this chapter, yet another point is crucial: the EU bares some responsibility for the Italian and Greek plights. There, as in some other EU countries, 'the EU as a polity has not managed to sustain the kind of domestic change away from clientelism or corruption towards respect for the rule of law which would make membership of the club sustainable'.[105]

In the period between the onset of the single currency and the sovereign debt crisis, the EMU improved the economic performance of the Eurozone's periphery, at the expense, however, of washing away its economic foundations (Chapter 1 explains how) and perpetuating unsustainable public institutions and policies. But the EMU was not the only European policy inadvertently hurting the resilience of the otherwise very fragile Italian or Greek public policies (to mention only two examples). As I will explain more broadly in the next chapter, EU funding reaching these countries, either within the regional policy or the CAP, easily falls victim to ineffective or corrupt institutions. It provides for additional financial resources with which the government can plug fiscal holes produced by malfunctioning public institutions, delaying their necessary reforms. The internal market was making it easier for young Greeks or Italians (again, just to mention two examples) to start afresh in EU countries offering them more prosperity and stability. This, however, was further undermining the prospects of the emigrant countries, while malfunctioning institutions and domestic policies there have been making it more difficult to use internal market freedoms to attract investments to the tradable sectors or otherwise develop long-term comparative advantages. Even when it comes to the VAT gap problem, so debilitating in countries like Greece and Italy, the EU has played a very ambivalent role. This harmonised tax[106] is based on a huge number of market transactions, which are relatively easy to hide. Thus, it is particularly prone to fraud and evasion practices in the countries where, like in Italy or Greece, tax authorities lag behind institutionally, organisationally and technologically.[107] This institutional atrophy pushes the performance of ineffective tax systems further away from

[105] Kalypso Nicolaïdis, 'European Democracy and Its Crisis', *Journal of Common Market Studies* 51 (2013): 361.

[106] Council Directive 2006/112/EC of 28 November 2006 on the common system of value added tax, OJ 2006 No. L 347, 11 December 2006, pp. 1–118.

[107] VAT is especially susceptible to fraud when it is due for cross-border transactions, because then its basic principle, according to which the supplier of goods collects VAT from his customer and settles against the tax it pays itself to the seller as its

the effective ones, amplifying the comparative economic disadvantages of the former.

One can retort at this stage, however, that the EU has possibly not helped its Member States enough in institutional and socioeconomic adaptations, and that some of its policies may indeed have made the process of reforming domestic public institutions and public policies more difficult. But each time it has tried to do some good, it was being held off by national politicians.

This is indeed true. After all, as I mentioned earlier, because core state powers define national sovereignty, governments of sovereign states should be expected to defend these very state powers from external influences. In some countries, like Germany or Sweden, this basic relationship between state powers and self-government has additionally made perfect sense from the perspective of policy outputs, for one could hardly imagine a European institution or a governance process capable of designing better public policies for these countries than their domestic processes. If you accept the pointed, even if provocative, remark of Mario Draghi that 'sovereignty relates to the ability to deliver in practice the essential services people expect from government',[108] then transferring more powers to the European level would undermine this very functional and important understanding of sovereignty both in Germany and in Sweden. Governments of virtually all EU countries, even of the poor group joining this organisation in this century, have acted in the very same way. They have reckoned that European interventions would upset their sovereignty in the most fundamental sense espoused by Draghi.

It should not therefore be surprising that the idea of Jacques Delors, the Commission's president between 1985 and 1995, of 'Social Europe'[109] was nipped in the bud by national governments. National

customer, does not apply. An attempt to establish the definitive VAT system for intra-Union B2B trade, in which cross-border transactions are treated in the same manner as these entirely domestic transactions (proposed by the Commission in its 'Communication on an Action Plan on VAT. Towards a Single EU VAT Area Time to Decide', COM(2016)148, 7 April 2016) necessitates very effective exchange of information between various tax authorities and, more generally, it requires very seamless cooperation in tax collection. This, in turn, is unachievable when institutional capacities differ conspicuously.

108 'Europe's Pursuit of "A More Perfect Union"', Lecture by Mario Draghi, President of the ECB, at Harvard Kennedy School, 9 October 2013, available at www.ecb.europa.eu/press/key/date/2013/html/sp131009_1.en.html.

109 Commission, 'European Social Policy – A Way Forward for the Union. A White Paper', COM(94)333.

politicians have been staunchly defending their powers in the socioeconomic realm of core state powers partly because under conspicuously different production and investor appeasement models it is impossible to agree on one European social model (even at a rudimentary level) and partly because in a club of advanced economies no one could imaginably better exercise core state powers than the states themselves.

The Delors' thinking behind 'Social Europe' managed to pave the way to the so-called social dialogue between the Commission, management and labour (the Protocol and the Agreement on Social Policy annexed to the Treaty of Maastricht; now Arts. 154–155 TFEU).[110] Accordingly, the Commission is to consult Union-level organisations of management and labour on proposals in the field of social policy (Art. 154 TFEU). More importantly from the perspective of the power distribution, the social dialogue authorises the social partners to conclude agreements in this area, and empowers the Council to elevate them to the stage of binding EU law (Art. 155 TFEU). This latter process, however, largely lost traction soon after it was established, leading to only one directive in the twenty-first century.[111] The social dialogue has therefore proved to be yet another episode in 'a saga of high aspirations and modest results' of European forays into the socioeconomic realm.[112]

This early experience did not encourage the Commission to go forward with similar initiatives in other fields traditionally perceived as

[110] See also Gerda Falkner, *EU Social Policy in the 1990s: Towards a Corporatist Policy Community* (London: Routledge, 1998); Janine Goetschy, 'The European Employment Strategy: Genesis and Development', *European Journal of Industrial Relations* 5 (1999): 117–137; Satoshi Nakano, 'Maastricht Social Protocol Revisited: Origins of the European Industrial Relations System', *Journal of Common Market Studies* 52 (2014): 1053–1069. For a broader discussion, see Andreas Bieler, 'European Integration and the Transnational Restructuring of Social Relations: The Emergence of Labour as a Regional Actor', *Journal of Common Market Studies* 43 (2005): 461–484; Thomas Prosser, 'Economic Union without Social Union: The Strange Case of the European Social Dialogue', *Journal of European Social Policy* 26 (2016): 460–472.

[111] Directive 2010/18 implementing the revised Framework Agreement on parental leave concluded by BUSINESSEUROPE, UEAPME, CEEP and ETUC and repealing Directive 96/34, OJ 2010 No. L 68, 18 March 2010, pp. 13–20. For a broader discussion see Elise Muir, *EU Regulation of Access to Labour Markets: A Case Study of EU Constraints on Member State Competences* (Alphen aan den Rijn: Kluwer Law International, 2012); Andreas Bieler, 'European Integration and the Transnational Restructuring of Social Relations: The Emergence of Labour as a Regional Actor?', *Journal of Common Market Studies* 43 (2005): 461–484.

[112] Stephan Leibfried and Paul Pierson, *European Social Policy: Between Fragmentation and Integration* (Washington, DC: Brookings Institution Press, 1995): 46.

socioeconomic core state powers. European policymakers must have been aware that most socioeconomic policies entail some form of redistribution, directly and indirectly, and can therefore easily ignite serious conflicts between potential winners and losers. Policymaking in these areas necessitates difficult value judgments, for instance, between passive traditional (compensating) welfare entitlements and more active, service-oriented and capacitating social investments, which are painful enough to reconcile within individual nations. For this reason, too, European institutions may be excused for not pressing harder to exercise more powers in these areas.[113]

In addition, for the whole previous decade they believed that institutional adaptations and policy reforms in core state powers could be encouraged by means of soft coordination measures of benchmarking, peer reviews, multi-level input and other forms of mutual learning (the so-called Open Method of Coordination [OMC]).[114] To provide for more strategic orientation, the Commission came up with the European Employment Strategy in 1997, and eight years later merged it with the Broad Economic Policy Guidelines (BEPG) into a single set of Integrated Guidelines for Growth and Jobs under the Lisbon Strategy.[115] In 2010, it launched the Europe 2020 Strategy, putting the guidelines under the roof of the European Semester.[116]

Yet, all of them, as one commentator noted aptly, have been 'like nailing blancmange to a wall. There was no obvious way of grasping what was actually required, just a sense that (lots of big) "things have

[113] 'There has been no hard law, no Directives in the "traditional" fields of the welfare state (with the exception of vocational training and other employment subpolicy fields) and in the literature limited empirical evidence for direct EU influence on national welfare reforms can be found': Paolo R. Graziano, Sophie Jacquot and Bruno Palier, 'Introduction: The Usages of Europe in National Employment-friendly Welfare State Reforms', in: *The EU and the Domestic Politics of Welfare State Reforms*, eds. Paolo R. Graziano, Sophie Jacquot and Bruno Palier (London: Palgrave Macmillan, 2011): 6.

[114] See, for example, Charles F. Sabel and Jonathan Zeitlin, eds., *Experimentalist Governance in the European Union* (Oxford: Oxford University Press, 2012); Mark Dawson, *New Governance and the Transformation of European Law: Coordinating EU Social Law and Policy* (Cambridge: Cambridge University Press, 2011); Jörg Paetzold and Olaf Van Vliet, 'EU Co-Ordination and the Convergence of Domestic Unemployment Protection Schemes', *Journal of Common Market Studies* 52 (2014): 1070–1089.

[115] For a broader picture, see Armin Steinbach, *Economic Policy Coordination in the Euro Area* (London and New York: Routledge 2014): 55–60.

[116] Currently broad economic policy guidelines for the EU (e.g., Council Recommendation 2015/1184 of 14 July 2015 on broad guidelines for the economic policies of the Member States and of the European Union, O.J. 2015 L 192/27) are supplemented by EMU specific guidelines (issued on the basis of Art. 121(2) in

got to be done."'[117] European bureaucrats could rationally advise, for instance, more investments in high-quality education or vocational training, in revamping public employment services or in overhauling social security arrangements and labour market policies.[118] They could recommend curbing legacy transfer programmes and replacing them with new ones more properly responding to the emerging socioeconomic needs. But, as they were not put on the frontline of implementing the reforms and as they were not accountable for their advice, European institutions have naturally ignored domestic political contexts. They had no skin in the game, also because no European funding has followed the advice. The political salience of their opinions could not therefore be greater than of the OECD or the IMF. When politically cumbersome, national governments were eager to shrug off their advice.

As I explained in more detail in Chapter 2, national governments have done so en masse. It would be naïve to believe that this has been happening because national politicians in charge have been insufficiently advised by international organisations. Rather, as the then-Prime Minister of Luxembourg, Jean-Claude Juncker, admitted in 2007: 'We all know what to do, but we don't know how to get re-elected once we have done it.'[119] Even when perfectly aware that poor socioeconomic policies and inefficient state institutions have been undermining their future prosperity, many national governments have treated socioeconomic reforms like a political third rail: 'You touch it and you die.'[120]

conjunction with Art. 136 TFEU). See e.g. Council Recommendation of 21 March 2017 on the economic policy of the euro area (2017/C 92/01). Individual Member States report on their progress towards the goals established in the economic policy guidelines each year in National Reform Programmes (NRPs). Each July the Council issues its recommendations on the NRPs of individual Member States.

117 Catherine Barnard, *EU Employment Law* (Oxford: Oxford University Press, 2012): 140.

118 Tim Van Rie and Ive Marx, 'The European Union at Work? The European Employment Strategy from Crisis to Crisis', *Journal of Common Market Studies* 50 (2012): 335–356.

119 Quoted in 'The Quest for Prosperity', *The Economist*, March 15, 2007, available at www.economist.com/node/8808044.

120 A quip ascribed (in the context of the US social security) to a staff counsel to an erstwhile Speaker of the US House of Representatives in the early 1980s, Tip O'Neill: William Safire, 'On Language: Third Rail', *The New York Times*, February 18, 2007, available at www.nytimes.com/2007/02/18/magazine/18wwlnsafire.t.html.

8 European Redistributive Policies: Grass-Sprinkling Instead of Rebuilding the Garden

8.1 The Challenges of Peripherality

A common market bringing together diverse economies can hardly be expected to distribute its benefits equally between regions and sectors. Due to the facilitated interstate movements, skilled workers and entrepreneurs from its 'periphery' would naturally look for ways to relocate to 'core' areas, where living standards are higher. This would amplify agglomeration (location) benefits of the core, making it more difficult for the periphery to catch up economically.[1] Furthermore, facilitated interstate trade makes it easier to replace less efficient production in one country with its more competitive substitutes manufactured in others. This process, otherwise welcomed from the efficiency perspective, additionally strains economically less competitive sectors and regions, facilitating their industrial decline.

These effects have been mitigated by the ultimately modest impact of the internal market on the allocation of production factors throughout the Union. In addition, free movement of capital[2] offers some potential remedies to the disadvantages of peripherality. The economic

[1] Generally on location effects, see, for example, Dennis Swann, *The Economics of Europe: From Common Market to European Union* (London: Penguin, 2000): 268; Richard E. Baldwin and Charles Wyplosz, *The Economics of European Integration* (London: McGraw-Hill Higher Education, 2015): 242–244. Agglomeration effects are beneficial from the efficiency point of view, even if problematic from the equity perspective: Philippe Martin, 'Are European Regional Policies Delivering?', CERAS-ENPC, Paris and CEPR, 1999, available at willmann.com/~gerald/euroecon-04/martin-paper.pdf.

[2] Constitutionalised with the adoption of the Maastricht Treaty, when Treaty provisions on free movement of capital were overhauled to institutionalise an unconditional free movement in the run-up to the EMU. Soon after the CJEU endorsed the direct effect of the key Treaty provision in this respect (now Art. 63 TFEU): Joined cases C-163/94, C-165/94 and C-250/94, *Sanz de Lera*, ECLI:EU:C:1995:451, § 40–43.

headwinds put an upward pressure on unemployment in the periphery and a corresponding downward pressure on wages there. By the same token, however, location disadvantages boost the cost-competitiveness of its labour force, attracting foreign investments and precipitating an economic rebound.

Sectoral distributional effects of the integration should be even more clearly innocuous. According to the logic of the comparative advantage, discussed more broadly in Chapter 10, only some sectors can succeed in international trade; others give in to foreign competitors. In a flexible, open economy investments and employment should concentrate where the comparative advantage is present, propelling the economically beneficial reallocation of resources from the comparatively disadvantaged sectors.

Seen from this perspective, facilitated market exchanges in a diverse economic system could be expected to both propel distributional inequalities and keep them in constant flux, mitigating their long-term negative effects. And, what is particularly important from the policy perspective, the government's role is quite specific in this setup: it ought to keep the various channels of market adjustments open and attune national policies (from labour market to industrial policy) properly calibrated to maximise the benefits of the internal market and to minimise its costs for the local society.

8.2 One Policy Struggling Against Another

This feat requires a very resilient institutional tissue as well as governance processes; a luxury the periphery hardly ever enjoys. So when the accession of the UK and Ireland (together with Denmark) to the Communities in 1973 made regional distributional imbalances more conspicuous, European policymakers decided that less-advantaged regions of the Communities should receive an additional boost: European redistribution. The outcome of this conviction – the regional policy – was aimed to facilitate economic rejuvenation in the areas either declining industrially or economically retarded. It was therefore intended to facilitate the adjustment process otherwise driven by the common market.

With the advancements of the economic integration in the 1980, the picture of EU redistribution as yet another flywheel of economic convergence gained new supporters.[3] The accession of Greece and the

[3] E.g., Iain Begg, 'Cohesion in the European Community: A Key Imperative for the 1990s?', *Regional Science and Urban Economics* 23 (1993): 427–448.

Iberian countries pushed the Community towards the 1988 reform of the European structural funds, adapting them institutionally to the demands of the expanding policy.[4] The single currency – simultaneously reaching the top political agenda – provided additional arguments for a further growth of interstate redistribution. The EMU project required an expedited economic convergence of the poorer EU countries, which in turn necessitated higher public investments.[5] Yet national governments of the poorer countries could arguably not afford them. This is why, first, the Maastricht Treaty rebranded the regional policy into the 'economic and social cohesion',[6] concentrating it strategically on the poorest regions. Second, in 1993, the Structural Funds were reformed again.[7] Third, the resources committed to this policy increased steeply in the period 1994–1999,[8] accounting for approximately 35 per cent of the Community budget by 1999.

[4] Back then the European structural funds comprised the European Regional Development Fund (ERDF; established in 1975), the European Social Fund (ESF; created by the 1957 Treaty of Rome) and the European Agricultural Guidance and Guarantee Fund (set up in 1962). 'The landmark reforms of 1988 doubled the budget for the structural funds and introduced a number of principles for their implementation which remain at the core of cohesion policy: programming (based on strategic, multi-annual plans instead of a project-based approach); concentration (on a limited number of objectives and focused on the least developed regions); additionality (to ensure that EU funding does not substitute for national expenditure); and partnership (the participation of national, sub-national and supranational actors in the design and implementation of programmes)': John Bachtler and Carlos Mendez, 'Who Governs EU Cohesion Policy? Deconstructing the Reforms of the Structural Funds', *Journal of Common Market Studies* 45 (2007): 537. See also Philip Lowe, 'The Reform of the Community's Structural Funds', *Common Market Law Review* 25 (1988): 503–521.

[5] See also John Bachtler and Rona Michie, 'Strengthening Economic and Social Cohesion? The Revision of the Structural Funds', *Regional Studies* 28 (1994): 789–796.

[6] The Maastricht Treaty added 'economic and social cohesion and solidarity among Member States' to the list of main tasks of the European Community and added a separate title (Arts. 130a–130e) on it, as well as a Protocol on cohesion to the Treaty establishing the European Community. Now this policy is covered by Title XVIII TFEU (Arts. 174–178), entitled 'Economic, Social and Territorial Cohesion'. For broader analyses of the policy see John Bachtler, Carlos Mendez and Fiona Wishlade, *EU Cohesion Policy and European Integration: The Dynamics of EU Budget and Regional Policy Reform* (Farnham: Ashgate Publishing, 2014) or Michael Baun and Dan Marek, *Cohesion Policy in the European Union* (New York: Palgrave Macmillan, 2014).

[7] For details of the reforms see Commission of the European Communities, 'Community Structural Funds 1994–1999. Revised Regulations and Comments', August 1993, available at aei.pitt.edu/1750/1/structure_funds_93_commentary.pdf. At that stage two new funds – Financial Instrument for Fisheries Guidance (a predecessor of the current European Maritime and Fisheries Fund [EMFF]) and the Cohesion Fund – were established.

[8] From 43.8 becu for the period 1988–1993 to 141 becu during 1994–1999, at 1992 prices: Rona Michie and Rona Fitzgerald, 'The Evolution of the Structural Funds',

In subsequent years the effectiveness of the cohesion policy was broadly applauded. Some researchers expressed the general sentiment when writing in 2003 that 'EU regional support through the structural funds has a significant and positive impact on the growth performance on European regions and, hence, contributes to greater equality in productivity and income in Europe.'[9]

Then, however, the sovereign debt crisis thwarted the previous decades of the income convergence in the EU 15. It is tempting to contend that the crisis – pulling down in particular the regions like the Greek Attiki, Notio Aigaio or Ionia Nisia (where GDP per capita fell by more than 26 per cent relative to the EU 28 average in the period 2008–2014)[10] – has had nothing to do with the cohesion policy. It can even be argued that this policy has mitigated the worst effects of the Eurozone crisis,[11] performing the role of a macroeconomic shock absorber there, imperfect as it is due to the ultimately small EU budget (about 1 per cent of EU GDP) and its inflexibility.

Commission estimates confirm this view. Accordingly, in the 2007–2014 programming period its five European Structural and Investment Funds[12] (ESIFs) invested €346.5 billion in all EU countries, generating almost €1 trillion of additional GDP (counted for the period up to 2023) and one million new jobs (i.e., one-third of all net job creation between 2007 and 2014).[13] Furthermore, between 2007 and 2014 this policy supported more than 120,000 start-ups, almost 95,000 research projects and about 4,900 km of new roads.[14] Every year about fifteen

in: *The Coherence of EU Regional Policy: Contrasting Perspectives on the Structural Funds*, eds. John Bachtler and Ivan Turok (London: Routledge, 2013), 20.

9 Aadne Cappelen et al., 'The Impact of EU Regional Support on Growth and Convergence in the European Union', *Journal of Common Market Studies* 41 (2003): 640.

10 Eurostat, 'GDP at Regional Level'. Other Greek regions experienced similar economic hardships, as GDP per capita in Purchasing Power Standards fell by 26 percentage points in Greece between 2008 and 2016 (from 93 to 67 per cent of the EU average): Eurostat, GDP Per Capita in PPS.

11 Silvia Merler, 'Income Convergence during the Crisis: Did EU Funds Provide a Buffer?', *Bruegel Working Paper* No. 6/2016, 18 October 2016, available at bruegel.org/2016/10/income-convergence-did-eu-funds-provide-a-buffer/.

12 I.e., the ERDF, the ESF, the Cohesion Fund, the European Agricultural Fund for Rural Development and the EMFF.

13 European Commission, '9 Ways Cohesion Policy Works for Europe – Main Results 2007–2013', 10 July 2016, available at ec.europa.eu/regional_policy/sources/docgener/evaluation/pdf/expost2013/wp1_synthesis_factsheet_en.pdf.

14 European Commission, Key Achievements of Regional Policy, available at ec.europa.eu/regional_policy/en/policy/what/key-achievements/.

million people participated in ESF actions aimed to improve the employability of Europeans, while six million benefitted from modernised water supply systems.[15] In Hungary, Lithuania, Slovakia and Latvia, more than 50 per cent of government capital investments were coming from the EU structural funds and in all of the new Member States (except for Cyprus) the share of EU funds in all government capital investments was well more than 20 per cent.[16] Among the 'older' EU countries, 19 per cent of Greek and 27.5 per cent of Portuguese government capital investments also came from the same source.[17]

In the next programming period (2014–2020) the EU budget allocated to the five ESI Funds[18] has grown to €454 billion. Including national co-financing – estimated at €183 billion – the total investment across the EU due to the cohesion policy will therefore amount to at least €637 billion by 2020.[19] With a bigger policy budget, the bang for the buck can only be expected to grow accordingly.

However, regardless of this vertiginous financial effort cushioning some of the worst effects of the Eurozone crisis and boosting economies in the Eastern countries in particular, no congruous economic convergence has followed. The strongest economic growth has been shared by some of the poorest EU regions and some of the richest, with the vast majority of the locations in between moving either forward or backward. Eurostat confirmed this finding, estimating in 2016 that 'those regions that expanded at a fast pace … (between 2008 and 2014) were principally located in Poland (7 of its 16 regions), Austria (three of its nine regions), Germany (12 of its 38 regions), Lithuania and Luxembourg (both single regions at this level of detail), while – as a percentage of the EU-28 average – GDP per capita also increased by more than 10.0 percentage points in Nyugat-Dunántúl (Hungary), Sud-Est (Romania), Bratislavský kraj (Slovakia), and Inner London – East'.[20]

[15] Ibid.

[16] European Commission, '9 Ways Cohesion Policy Works for Europe'.

[17] Ibid.

[18] I.e., the ERDF, the ESF, the Cohesion Fund, the European Agricultural Fund for Rural Development (EAFRD) and the EMFF.

[19] European Commission, 'Contribution of the European Structural and Investment Funds to jobs and growth, the Investment Plan and the Commission's priorities', available at ec.europa.eu/regional_policy/en/policy/what/investment-policy/esif-contribution/.

[20] Eurostat, 'GDP at Regional Level'.

In consequence of the economic expansion, disposable private incomes increased in many Eastern European regions.[21] At the same time, however, nominal disposable incomes grew more in nominal terms in several richest EU regions.[22] In other words, the gap in wealth between the richest regions and the Eastern 'tigers' often increased. What is even more discomfiting is that the economic growth has not gone hand-in-hand with more economic inclusion in the new Member States. Quite to the contrary: in many of the countries it has been accompanied by growing poverty levels.[23]

In the EU 15 the situation was more straightforward, and more grim. Many of the regions of the 'old' EU have been conspicuously diverging economically since 2008, regardless of hundreds of billions of euros in financial support flowing there in the previous decades. Disposable incomes retracted due to the sovereign debt crisis.[24] Neither modern transport infrastructure, nor research support, nor labour market institutions subsidised by EU funds could facilitate their macroeconomic adjustment. The goods produced thanks to the cohesion support often remained underutilised. Most of their advantages were obliterated by high unemployment, public and private debt and

[21] E.g., by €1,000 per inhabitant in Slovakia (from €6,700 to €7,700) and €600 in Poland (from €5,700 to €6,300) between 2008 and 2014: Eurostat, Income of Households by NUTS 2 Regions, Disposable Income, Euro per Inhabitant.

[22] E.g., by €1,900 per inhabitant (from €21,800 to €23,700) in the richest German region (Stuttgart) or by €5,400 per inhabitant (from €17,700 to €23,100) in the richest Danish region (Hovedstaden) between 2008 and 2014: Eurostat, Income of Households by NUTS 2 Regions, Disposable Income, Euro per Inhabitant.

[23] The at-risk-of-poverty (60 per cent of median equalised income after social transfers) proportion of the European population grew by 0.8 per cent in the EU 28 between 2008 and 2016 (from 16.5 to 17.3 per cent). Among EU 12 countries, the poverty ratio actually fell only in Latvia in this period (by – 4.1 percentage points of population, from the very high initial level of 25.9 per cent in 2008) and grew somewhat slower than the EU average in Cyprus (0.2 points), Poland (0.4 points) and Czechia (0.7 points). In the other EU 12 countries, the poverty rate was growing more steeply than the EU average: by 2.2 points in Estonia, 2.1 points in Hungary, 1.8 points in Slovakia, 1.7 points in Romania, 1.6 points in Slovenia, 1.5 points in Bulgaria, 1.2 points in Malta and 1.0 point in Lithuania. Eurostat data, At risk-of-poverty Rate by Poverty Threshold, Age and Sex – EU-SILC survey.

[24] E.g., by −€1,500 per inhabitant (from €20,000 to €18,500) in Ireland, by −€4,300 per inhabitant (from €14,200 to €9,900) in Greece, by –€900 per inhabitant (from €17,600 to €16,700) in Italy, by –€500 per inhabitant (from €10,800 to €10,300) in Portugal and by –€400 per inhabitant (from €13,700 to €13,300) in Spain, in all cases between 2008 and 2014: Eurostat, Income of Households by NUTS 2 Regions.

vulnerable financial systems, all of which at least partly stemmed from the pernicious vortex effects of the single currency.

The conclusion stemming from this finding is straightforward: one European policy (the EMU) was wiping out convergence effects of another (the cohesion policy) in all the countries unfit for the former. Such dynamics have damaged both of the policies, which only corroborates the argument made in Chapter 6: comprehensive debt restructuring and selected Eurozone exits (as a precondition for external devaluation) are among the most significant prerequisites for fixing the European project. They would facilitate economic rejuvenation of the Eurozone's south, at the same time improving the effectiveness of other EU policies; not least the cohesion policy.

8.3 Do Something! Juncker's Investment Plan

This solution to the self-defeating redistribution within the EU entails some very unpalatable consequences: symbolic (acknowledging that the main symbol of European integration has failed), economic (losses incurred by the creditor countries and currency depreciation in the debtor countries) and political (as a fallout of the symbolic and economic consequences).

Because they are all very unsavoury, back in 2014 the incoming Commission's President Juncker had another idea as to how to overcome the nullifying effects of the sovereign debt crisis on the economic convergence in the Eurozone's periphery. What the Eurozone's periphery needed, according to his view, was a Marshall Plan (of sorts) called the 'Investment Plan for Europe'.[25] Announcing it in November 2014, President Juncker claimed bombastically that 'after years of fighting to restore our fiscal credibility and to promote reform, today we are adding the third point of a virtuous triangle: An ambitious, yet realistic "Investment Plan for Europe". Europe needs a kick-start and today the Commission is supplying the jump cables.'[26]

As I was arguing in the previous chapters, the first two tenets of the 'virtuous triangle' have never actually materialised. Now it is time to explain

[25] European Commission, 'Communication: An Investment Plan for Europe', COM(2014)903, 26 November 2014.

[26] Jean-Claude Juncker, speech, 'Investing in Europe: Speech by President Juncker in the European Parliament Plenary Session on the €315 bn Investment Plan', delivered in the European Parliament on 26 November 2014, available at europa.eu/rapid/press-release_SPEECH-14-2160_en.htm.

why the same applies to the third one, and what it means for the cohesion policy more generally.

An economic slump always sends investment indicators falling, because private agents do not have incentives (nor, typically, resources) to invest then.[27] This process is exacerbated when conflated with a sovereign debt crisis, because, by definition, the government does not have much leeway to stimulate investments through deficit spending when potential creditors turn their backs to the sovereign debt. When President Juncker uttered his idea of the Investment Plan, the Eurozone's periphery was a testimony to this finding. A Commission Communication published in autumn 2014 pointed out that by this year investments in the EU dropped by about 15 per cent comparing to 2007, taking a particularly very deep dive in Italy (−25 per cent), Portugal (−36 per cent), Spain (−38 per cent), Ireland (−39 per cent) and, especially, in Greece (−64 per cent).[28] To tackle this problem the new Commission pressed hard 'to mobilise ... additional public and private investment in the real economy over the next three years'.[29]

The Investment Plan was based on a very simple logic. It assumed that the sovereign debt crisis made investors excessively risk-averse. They were reticent to put their money into perfectly profitable projects in what economists call the real economy. Investments languished, in consequence, and unemployment soared. To grow, the argument is, the countries have to overcome this 'market failure in risk-taking which hinders investment in Europe'.[30] Public authorities should pour public

[27] On the negative impact of fiscal austerity on public investment (as opposed to social spending) more generally, see, for example, Wolfgang Streeck and Daniel Mertens, 'Fiscal Austerity and Public Investment: Is the Possible the Enemy of the Necessary?', *MPIfG Discussion Paper* No. 11/12; Christian Breunig and Marius R. Busemeyer, 'Fiscal Austerity and the Trade-off between Public Investment and Social Spending', *Journal of European Public Policy* 19 (2012): 921–938. This is also telling for economic growth, as increases in public social spending (as opposed to government consumption spending and public investment) have significant negative effects on subsequent economic growth: Michael Connolly and Cheng Li, 'Government Spending and Economic Growth in the OECD Countries', *Journal of Economic Policy Reform* 19 (2016): 386–395.

[28] Commission, 'Communication: An Investment Plan for Europe'.

[29] Jean-Claude Juncker, 'A New Start for Europe: My Agenda for Jobs, Growth, Fairness and Democratic Change. Political Guidelines for the next European Commission. Opening Statement in the European Parliament Plenary Session', Strasbourg, 15 July 2014, available at ec.europa.eu/commission/publications/president-junckers-political-guidelines_en.

[30] European Investment Bank, 'What Is the European Fund for Strategic Investments (EFSI)?', available at www.eib.europa.eu/efsi/what-is-efsi/index.htm.

resources into selected projects, in order to goad private investors back to the real economy.

The financial resources the Commission could mobilise were not particularly impressive. The budget of the European Fund for Strategic Investments (EFSI) – the main pillar of the Investment Plan[31] – is only €21 billion,[32] i.e., less than 5 per cent of the ESI Funds allocated to the regional policy in the period 2014–2020. Moreover, this limited funding is spread across the whole Union, including the countries with robust levels of investments. This did not really dishearten the drafters of the Investment Plan, though. They apparently thought that if Mario Draghi managed to put the confidence crisis on the sovereign debt market to an end in summer 2012 with only one pledge, then Jean-Claude Juncker could well end the confidence crisis in the real economy with €21 billion. If he managed it, private investors, as expected, should be eager to put several times more resources than its financial capacity into the projects supported by the EFSI.[33]

For many reasons, however, this logic is flawed. The €21 billion the EFSI was ready to commit could never have a psychological effect similar to the 2012 pledge of Draghi. His 'whatever it takes' statement was credible at least in principle: the Eurosystem could indeed print as much euros as necessary to buy all toxic sovereign bonds. Juncker had no similar tool at his hand to assure would-be investors in the real economies of Cyprus, Greece or Italy. In addition, parallel to the Investment Plan, the ECB offered commercial banks extremely cheap money under the condition that they invest it in the real economy (more on this in Chapter 4). For this reason, the case for 'additionality' – the requirement

[31] The other two parts of the plan are the European Investment Advisory Hub and the European Investment Project Portal. The first of the two is intended 'to build upon existing EIB and Commission advisory services in order to provide advisory support for the identification, preparation and development of investment projects and to act as a single technical advisory hub for project financing within the Union', while the latter was devised as 'a transparent European investment project portal (EIPP) gathering current and future investment projects in the Union' – Arts. 14(1) and 15(1), respectively, of Regulation 2015/1017 of the European Parliament and of the Council of 25 June 2015 on the European Fund for Strategic Investments, the European Investment Advisory Hub and the European Investment Project Portal and amending Regulations 1291/2013 and No. 1316/2013 – the European Fund for Strategic Investments, OJ 2015 No. L 169, 1 July 2015, pp. 1–38.

[32] €16 billion of a EU budget guarantee and €5 billion of the EIB's own capital.

[33] The Commission sought a fifteen-fold leverage – fourteen times more private money attracted to the projects than the outlays and guarantees of the EFSI.

that public funds be deployed through the EFSI only when otherwise viable investment opportunities cannot be funded on commercial terms[34] – has been very tenuous since day one. After all, when credit becomes cheaper, the threshold of profitability necessary to recoup investments funded with it goes down as well.

In June 2017, two years into the three-year period for which the EFSI was originally established, its funding supported fifteen projects (eight in infrastructure and innovation and another seven small and medium enterprise [SME] financing agreements) in Greece, totalling approximately €1.2 billion of EFSI funding and €2.2 billion of private outlays.[35] In Italy – by far the main beneficiary of the scheme – EFSI disbursements were almost five times higher in the same period (€5.5 billion) and other investors were much more eager than in Greece to put their money in the scheme (additional €28 billion).[36] To give a few examples: one particularly big project was Telecom Italia's upgrading of its broadband network (€1.4 billion of total investment, €0.5 billion coming from the EFSI).[37] Another allowed the major Italian train operator, Trenitalia, to purchase forty-nine regional trains (€0.6 billion, half of which would come from the EFSI) and yet another, worth €3.5 billion, bolstered the Italian Guarantee Fund for SMEs.[38] Together the three projects are worth €5.5 billion. Nonetheless, even if the Italian economy receives ten times more

[34] According to Art. 5(1) Regulation 2015/1017 of the European Parliament and of the Council of 25 June 2015 on the European Fund for Strategic Investments, the European Investment Advisory Hub and the European Investment Project Portal and amending Regulations 1291/2013 and No. 1316/2013 – the European Fund for Strategic Investments, OJ 2015 No. L 169, 1 July 2015, pp. 1–38, '"additionality" means the support by the EFSI of operations which address market failures or sub-optimal investment situations and which could not have been carried out in the period during which the EU guarantee can be used, or not to the same extent, by the EIB, the EIF or under existing Union financial instruments without EFSI support. Projects supported by the EFSI shall typically have a higher risk profile than projects supported by EIB normal operations and the EFSI portfolio shall have overall a higher risk profile than the portfolio of investments supported by the EIB under its normal investment policies before the entry into force of this Regulation'.

[35] Country factsheet available at ec.europa.eu/commission/publications/country-factsheets-investment-plan-state-play_en.

[36] Ibid.

[37] European Investment Bank, 'EFSI project list', available at www.eib.org/efsi/efsi-projects/?c=IT&se=.

[38] European Commission, 'Investment Plan for Europe: 55, 000 Small Companies in Italy to Benefit from EUR 3.5 billion', 15 February 2017, available at aec.europa.eu/commission/commissioners/2014–2019/katainen/announcements/investment-plan-europe-55-000-small-companies-italy-benefit-eur-0_en.

similar transactions within the Investment Plan, the deep roots of its meagre investment levels would still prevail. Under the current 'see no evil, hear no evil' strategy of European policymakers towards the deep roots of the Eurozone economic incongruities, the EU's southern periphery would suffer from the headwind effects I was discussing in the previous chapters: the inability to get an economic boost through currency depreciation, the very high ratio of non-performing loans, failing public institutions and public policies making it even more difficult for the societies to compete on the internal market and globally.[39]

8.4 A Gardener's Quandary

The story behind the Investment Plan corroborates the point made earlier: in some of the Eurozone countries investments have been low not because of a market failure (of excessive risk aversion), but due to profound government (policy) failures both at the national and the European level. These failures have produced very serious private risks to which potential investors have been responding quite rationally. In other Member States, Ireland or Spain in particular, the investment fall simply marked a correction after a period of excessive activity, primarily in non-tradeable sectors, before the crisis. In these countries, the adverse process after the asset bubbles burst was both requisite and unavoidable. In Ireland, for instance, investments indeed fell by almost 40 per cent from 2007 to 2014. But they stood at a very high level of 28.67 per cent of GDP in 2007, compared to the EU average of 22.82 per cent of GDP.[40] After the reduction, in 2014, investments in this country were still above the EU average (20.49 per cent of GDP compared to 19.74 per cent of GDP in EU 28).[41] The investment correction in Ireland

[39] As Bruegel researchers put it, 'when regulations inhibit the formation or growth of firms, when it takes them an excessively long time to address administrative requirements, when competition is undermined because of protectionist regulations, when labour market regulations do not encourage workers towards higher performance and make it difficult to reallocate the labour force efficiently, and when public institutions work inefficiently and various kinds of public spending are used wastefully and need to be financed by distorting taxes, it is no surprise that investment and growth is low.': Zsolt Darvas and Guntram Wolff, 'Memos to the New EU leadership. To the Commissioner for Economic and Monetary Affairs', *Bruegel EU to do in 2015–2019*, available at eu2do.bruegel.org/economic-and-monetary-affairs/.

[40] Eurostat, Investment by Institutional Sectors.

[41] Ibid.

was therefore both unavoidable and harmless (or actually beneficial) to the business activity. This is confirmed by the fact that the following year (2015) Irish GDP surged by an astonishing 25.6 percentage points.[42] There was clearly no trace of an excessive risk aversion at any stage of this process.

Granted, the finding that the Investment Plan misdiagnoses the Eurozone's deep investment problems does not bring much consolation to the societies where investments have fallen to particularly low levels, like Greece, Portugal, or Italy.[43] The Commission, it can be argued, should not be condemned for its efforts to entice investors into financing infrastructure, innovation and SMEs. After all, these goals underpin the ESIFs and the cohesion policy more generally.[44] The Investment Plan may therefore be palliative treatment wherever obstacles to investments are caused by government failures. But as infrastructure, entrepreneurship and innovation undoubtedly pursue public goals, this drug may be better than no treatment at all.[45]

While this thinking is politically understandable, it dissipates when lofty intentions are translated into practical actions. Good transport infrastructure, for instance, does something more than pursuing a

[42] Eurostat, Real GDP Growth Rate – Volume.

[43] In 2016, average investment for the total economy (government, business and household sectors) stood at 20.23 per cent for the whole EU (twenty-eight countries), at 11.74 per cent of GDP in Greece, 15.30 per cent of GDP in Portugal, 17.08 per cent of GDP in Italy (it was also relatively low in some other EU countries, especially in the UK – 16.66 per cent – and in Luxembourg – 17.19 per cent). Source: Eurostat, Investment by institutional sectors.

[44] The ESI Funds are designed to advance 'the Union strategy for smart, sustainable and inclusive growth'. The term is used precisely forty-eight times in Regulation 1303/2013 of the European Parliament and of the Council of 17 December 2013 laying down common provisions on the ERDF, the ESF, the Cohesion Fund, the European Agricultural Fund for Rural Development and the EMFF and laying down general provisions on the ERDF, the ESF, the Cohesion Fund and the EMFF and repealing Council Regulation 1083/2006, OJ 2013 No. L 347, 20 December 2013, pp. 320–469.

[45] Especially when one judges the scheme solely on the basis of whether it is in a position to spend all of the resources assigned to it and attain the established private leverage. For a sample of this approach, see David Rinaldi and Jorge Núñez Ferrer, 'The European Fund for Strategic Investments as a New Type of Budgetary Instrument', *CEPS Research Report* No. 2017/07, 5 April 2017, available at www.ceps.eu/publications/european-fund-strategic-investments-new-type-budgetary-instrument.

public interest: it is essentially a (non-rivalrous and non-excludable) public good in the economic sense.[46] And, as Gary Marks noted aptly, 'government exists to provide public goods ... Such goods benefit all, but are not used up by those who consume them.'[47] Recall, however, the Trenitalia trains I just mentioned, or another purchase (worth €0.5 billion) in which the EFSI participated: 'Modernisation and enlargement of Grimaldi Euromed SpA fleet through the acquisition of 10 new Pure Car/truck carrier vessels which are to be employed on their Europe-North-America route.'[48] In these instances public resources are not used to finance public goods. Instead, they are tantamount to a public subsidy to private goods, which can easily distort the market rather than promote a public interest.[49] Similarly, while entrepreneurship is a public good, SME guarantees are basically a private good to be provided by market forces in the countries where economies and financial systems are in a good shape.

This point is important, because to a large extent both the Investment Plan and the cohesion policy more generally convey similar subsidies to private goods excluded from the market only because of government failures, while, as the previous chapter demonstrated, the most important public goods – public policies and institutions[50] – remain underfunded and strained by the merciless paradigm of permanent austerity. Such a European redistribution sprinkles economic lawns

[46] The use of a public good by one individual does not reduce its availability to others (hence it is non-rivalrous) and individuals cannot be effectively excluded from using it (hence it is non-excludable).

[47] Gary Marks, 'JCMS Annual Lecture 2011 Europe and Its Empires: From Rome to the European Union', *Journal of Common Market Studies* 50 (2012): 3.

[48] European Commission, 'Investment Plan for Europe. Country Factsheet: Italy', available at www.eib.org/projects/pipelines/pipeline/20150563.

[49] Even if similar projects fit comfortably into one of the Treaty exemptions to the prohibition of state aids: according to Art. 107(3)(b) the prohibition may not apply to 'aid to promote the execution of an important project of common European interest or to remedy a serious disturbance in the economy of a Member State'.

[50] It has been argued that both public institutions and geography (resources) matter for regional development (Jeffrey D. Sachs, 'Institutions Matter, But Not for Everything', *Finance and Development* 40 (2003): 38–41, available at www.imf.org/external/pubs/ft/fandd/2003/06/). Europe's history of the last few centuries, however, has clearly demonstrated the key role of public institutions, as many of its least prosperous parts have ample natural resources and favourable geography, while the opposite has been true for many of its most successful regions. For a particularly insightful account on the relationship between public institutions (and their outcomes: public policies) and regional development see Andrés Rodríguez-Pose, 'Do Institutions Matter for Regional Development?', *Regional Studies* 47 (2013): 1034–1047.

here and there, rather than planting trees in the shadows of which a vibrant local economic ecosystem could thrive.

8.5 What European Resources Should Fund

When underfunded, proper public goods become rivalrous,[51] but private markets can never provide them in sufficient quantities.

Take the first example: daycare and early education, which should be affordable and universally available to remain a public good. In an ageing society and a knowledge-intensive economy it is particularly important to boost female participation in the labour market and education attainments of children, for which widely available day-care is indispensable.[52] Private markets can offer it only to the more affluent social strata, amplifying inequalities of opportunities and attenuating deeper foundations of future collective prosperity.[53]

[51] Underinvested public goods can lose the status – and become a common good in the economic sense – when they turn rivalrous even if still non-excludable.

[52] As Esping-Andersen put it: 'Universal provision of childcare is doubly Paretian because it can be shown that the initial cost to government is fully reimbursed via mothers' superior life-time earnings and tax payments … It is now well-established that the key foundations for cognitive abilities and learning are laid in the pre-school ages. If the main impulse in these years comes solely from parents (or grandparents) it is to be expected that conditions in the family of origin predict so strongly how children fare later on. High quality early childhood programs have been shown to be extremely effective in evening the playing field – again a strong case for abandoning the familialistic ideology and moving towards a service-intensive welfare state': Gøsta Esping-Andersen, 'Prologues: What Does It Mean to Break with Bismarck?' in: *A Long Goodbye to Bismarck?*, ed. Bruno Palier (Amsterdam: Amsterdam University Press 2010): 16–17. Another leading social policy scholar argued that, when 'greater numbers of disadvantaged children' have 'access to early education and high quality primary and secondary education', then 'overall levels of skill attainment improve, resulting in higher employment and labour productivity and more upward social mobility. Quality childcare and preschool programmes, alongside effective parental leave arrangements and other family benefits and services – and supported by appropriate tax and benefit incentives, active labour market policies, and vocational rehabilitation programmes – enable more parents to engage in gainful employment without lengthy (gendered) career interruptions': Anton C. Hemerijck, 'Making Social Investment Happen for the Eurozone', *Intereconomics* 51 (2016): 342–343. For a more nuanced account see Sneha Elango et al., 'Early Childhood Education', 4 November 2015, available at heckmanequation.org/assets/2017/01/FINALMoffitt-ECE-Paper2015.pdf.

[53] Market failure in this respect is understandable and inevitable, 'since social returns to the expansion of human capabilities are substantially higher than private returns, private markets consistently and perennially underinvest in human capabilities. Instead, markets channel investment to other areas where total returns are lower but private returns appear higher … Early childhood education, where the

Arguably, therefore, Italian society would benefit much more from public investments in affordable pre-school education (a public good in normal circumstances) than from a private company's fleet of carrier vessels (a private good in normal circumstances).

More generally, good education and vocational training are the single most beneficial public good from the economic, social and political perspective.[54] The underlying relationship is quite obvious: more educated societies are more productive, more innovative[55] and more competitive, and hence they are richer. Employment tends to be higher[56] and the social as well as political tissue more resilient, with positive fiscal, social and political consequences. Conversely, societies in which the proportion of the poorly educated group is bigger inevitably face headwind effects in the knowledge-intensive global economy.[57]

The same point refers to life-long learning and re-skilling.[58] The two, however, additionally stymie the effects of ageing, because outdated

capabilities generated will have an impact on production only in the distant future, is the best example': Peter B. Evans, 'In Search of the 21st Century Developmental State', *The Centre for Global Political Economy at the University of Sussex*, Working Paper No. 4, December 2008, 12, available at www.sussex.ac.uk/webteam/gateway/file.php?name=cgpe-wp04-peter-evans.pdf&site=359.

[54] For an overview of policy problems and outcomes in the European perspective see, for example, Torben M. Andersen et al., 'Tuning Secondary Education', *The EEAG Report on the European Economy* (Munich: CESifo 2016): 70–84.

[55] Of course, there is still a long way between a good educational system and a good innovation policy. For an insightful depiction of the latter, against the European context, see Reinhilde Veugelers, 'The European Union's Growing Innovation Divide', *Bruegel Policy Contribution* No. 2016/06, 7 April 2016, available at bruegel.org/2016/04/the-european-unions-growing-innovation-divide/. For empirical evidence that national innovation policy mixes are surprisingly stable and similar across the EU, see Kincsö Izsak, Paresa Markianidou and Slavo Radošević, 'Convergence of National Innovation Policy Mixes in Europe – Has It Gone Too Far? An Analysis of Research and Innovation Policy Measures in the Period 2004–12', *Journal of Common Market Studies* 53 (2015): 786–802.

[56] In 2016, the EU 28 labour force participation rate was 87.9 per cent for the group with tertiary education, against a 72.9 per cent participation rate in the whole population of fifteen- to sixty-four-year-olds and 53.3 per cent in the population with less than primary, primary and lower-secondary education: Eurostat, Activity Rates by Sex, Age and Educational Attainment Level.

[57] In 2016, the share of the population of fifteen- to sixty-four-year-olds with less than primary, primary and lower-secondary education stood at 26.5 per cent in the EU 28. While in some Eastern European countries it was lower than 15 per cent (12.4 per cent in Czechia and Lithuania, 14.3 per cent in Slovakia, 14.6 per cent in Poland, 14.9 per cent in Latvia), it reached the highest levels in Greece (30.0 per cent), Italy (41.6 per cent), Spain (42.6 per cent), Malta (50.6 per cent) and Portugal (52.9 per cent): Eurostat, Population by Educational Attainment level, Sex and Age.

[58] For a valuable comparative sketch of national policies in this respect, see Miroslav Beblavý and Elisa Martellucci, 'Extending Working Lives. A Comparative Analysis of

skills are among the major reasons for early exits from the labour market, while ageing requires the opposite to extend working lives,[59] to economise on fiscal resources and to alleviate the fiscal paradigm of permanent austerity.[60]

Healthcare and long-term care are yet other examples of goods in which markets can only play an ancillary function.[61] While traditionally they have been recognised as public goods in all EU countries, their growing costs – a trend induced both by ageing and by the costs of technological progress – have made them gradually more rivalrous (scarce) goods.[62] To offset this trend, improvements in healthcare

How Governments Influence Lifelong Learning', *CEPS Special Report* No. 111, July 2015, available at www.ceps.eu/system/files/No%20111%20Beblavy%20%26%20Martelucci%20Mopac%20FINAL.pdf.

59 For an insightful analysis of the relationship between ageing and the length of working life in the EU, see Mikkel Barslund and Marten von Werder, 'Measuring Ageing and the Need for Longer Working Lives in the EU', *CEPS Working Document* No. 417, February 2016, available at www.ceps.eu/system/files/WD417%20MB%20%26%20MVW%20Measuring%20ageing%20and%20need%20for%20longer%20working%20lives%20%281%29.pdf.

60 According to 2016 data, participation in education and training in the population of twenty-five- to sixty-four-year-olds (life-long learning) was very high in Sweden (29.6 per cent), Denmark (27.7 per cent) and Finland (26.4 per cent). It was particularly low in Romania (1.2 per cent), Bulgaria (2.2 per cent), Slovakia (2.9 per cent), Croatia (3.0 per cent), Poland (3.7 per cent) and Greece (4.0 per cent): Eurostat, Participation Rate in Education and Training (Last 4 Weeks) by Sex and Age.

61 There are three main reasons for market failure in healthcare (perceived broadly, including long-term care). The first is that the market for health insurance tends to inflate premiums and management costs. The second is that the less well-off are at higher risk of poor health and, according to market logic, they should pay higher premiums, which they cannot afford. Third, when in good health, healthcare consumers are generally disinterested in and unable to choose healthcare protection, as they cannot predict their future healthcare status. With this type of consumer ignorance the market can hardly be expected to function properly. See Cam Donaldson, *Credit Crunch Health Care: How Economics Can Save Our Publicly Funded Health Services* (Bristol: Policy Press, 2011): esp. 9–12.

62 In a 2015 report, the Commission estimated that in the period 2013 to 2060 costs of healthcare would grow by almost 1 per cent of GDP (from 6.9 per cent of EU 28 GDP to 7.7 or 7.8 per cent of EU 28 GDP, depending on the assumptions as to scenarios) and the costs of long-term care would grow by 1.1 per cent of GDP (from 1.6 per cent of EU 28 GDP in 2013 to 2.7 per cent of EU 28 GDP in each scenario): European Commission, 'The 2015 Ageing Report', *European Economy* No. 3/2015, 9–10, available at ec.europa.eu/economy_finance/publications/european_economy/2015/pdf/ee3_en.pdf. It is a continuation of the trend in the past two decades. Among OECD countries, health expenditure (all financing schemes) grew between 2000 and 2015 by less than 1 per cent of GDP only in Latvia (−0.3 per cent), Hungary (0.2 per cent), Slovenia (0.3 per cent) and Portugal (0.5 per cent). In the same period they grew by more than 2 per cent of GDP in Sweden (3.7 per cent), the Netherlands (3.7 per

management and organisation are indispensable, regardless of specific features behind national healthcare systems.[63]

All of the policies are crucial both individually and socially. Euzéby noted correctly that 'investing in health, families and the quality of training and education at all ages offers a threefold positive outcome: for individuals in terms of sustainable labour market integration; for companies in terms of structural competitiveness; and for society in terms of social cohesion and collective well-being'.[64] The list of public policies with tremendous economic, political and social consequences does not end here, however. Some others – like tax collection, law enforcement, administration of justice, business environment – should always remain public goods delivered by the state only. Their non-rivalrous and non-excludable character is a prerequisite for social peace and stability. In respect to all of the policies of the EU's periphery in general, and the Eurozone's south in particular, fare poorly.

For instance, in the previous chapter I mentioned data confirming a very miserable state of tax systems in the EU's periphery. Deeply dysfunctional tax collection has been depriving its societies of the resources necessary to fund the most vital public goods. And this has all happened when technology allows the problem of tax evasion to effectively be eliminated altogether.[65]

cent), Ireland (3.5 per cent), Finland (2.7 per cent), Belgium and Denmark (2.5 per cent) and Spain (2.2 per cent): OECD, Health Expenditure and Financing, available at https://stats.oecd.org/index.aspx?DataSetCode=HEALTH_STAT.

63 Unsurprisingly, a recent WHO report highlights 'the need to explore the nature of the resources available for health systems, and the use to which they are put, rather than focusing solely on estimates of the level of resources ... How public resources are used has a direct impact on both levels of service and financial coverage, as well as how equitably both are distributed': Matthew Jowett et al., 'Spending Targets for Health: No Magic Number', *WHO Health Financing Working Paper* No. 1, 2016, available at apps.who.int/iris/bitstream/10665/250048/1/WHO-HIS-HGF-HFWorkingPaper-16.1-eng.pdf. See also European Commission, 'Report on Public Finances in EMU 2013', *European Economy* No. 4/2013, Part IV, titled: 'Public Expenditure on Health: Its Growing Importance, Drivers and Policy Reforms to Curb Growth', 147–197, available at ec.europa.eu/economy_finance/publications/european_economy/2013/pdf/ee-2013-4.pdf.

64 Chantal Euzéby, 'Social Protection to Achieve Sustainable Inclusion: A European Imperative in the Current Economic Crisis', *International Social Security Review* 65 (2012): 69–88.

65 Joseph Stiglitz argued that the process of redenomination in the countries like Greece could be facilitating if the redenominated currency was issued as electronic money only (Joseph Stiglitz, *The Euro*, 275–276). While applying such a principle across the counter from the outset would certainly be difficult in the countries where payment technologies are less developed, introducing it swiftly in the spheres

Furthermore, it takes, on average, more than two years to settle a simple commercial dispute in the Eurozone's south, twice the time needed to do the same more to the north.[66] Proceedings before administrative courts in Greece to resolve a straightforward dispute last for more than three years and a bankruptcy procedure often takes more than six years.[67] These are effects of deep malfunctions of the national state, rather than of any politically irresolvable redistributive conflict justifying a policy stalemate. They, too, beg for reforms to vital public goods, no matter how deeply the current inefficiencies are embedded in local idiosyncrasies and traditions. One could hardly disagree with Papaioannou, who asserted in this context that 'it is vital to reform the anachronistic, formalistic, and in many cases absurdly slow legal institutions in the South (and also in France and Luxemburg)'.[68]

To be sure, the European structural funds are devised to support some of these public goods financially. Objectives like 'promoting sustainable and quality employment and supporting labour mobility', 'promoting social inclusion, combating poverty and any discrimination', 'investing in education, training and vocational training for skills and lifelong learning' and 'enhancing institutional capacity of public authorities and stakeholders and efficient public administration' are four out of eleven so-called thematic goals of the ESI Funds.[69] One ESI Fund (ESF) is exclusively dedicated to pursuing them.

But, following the grass-sprinkling approach, none of the ESI Funds has striven to eradicate deeper roots of local shortages in the provision of these public goods. In consequence, the ESF can support projects like the one which enables a few hundred Spanish students with disabilities to have access to several weeks of traineeships,[70] or the French programme intended to give a dozen French school dropouts a sense

particularly prone to tax evasion is a no-brainer, of course if tax authorities are simultaneously equipped with the technological tools to screen the transactions.

66 Elias Papaioannou, 'Needed: A European Institutional Union', in: *How to Fix Europe's Monetary Union. Views of Leading Economists*, eds. Richard Baldwin and Francesco Giavazzi (London: CEPR, 2016), 210.

67 Ibid., 210 and 219.

68 Ibid., 219.

69 Art. 9 Regulation 1303/2013.

70 European Social Fund, 'The ESF in the News: Breaking Down Social Barriers in Spain', 10 March 2017, available at ec.europa.eu/esf/main.jsp?catId=67&langId=en&newsId=2760.

'that they are also able to learn'.[71] But no similar projects can durably change the economic situation of the recipients, as long as the Spanish or French economies are caught in the trap of excessively high unemployment, which, on the one hand, accompanies internal devaluation and, on the other, occurs when the internal devaluation in a monetary union is postponed.[72]

8.5.1 The Youth Guarantee

A European scheme intended to soothe the effects of the Eurozone crisis on youth unemployment – dubbed the Youth Guarantee – should make the point yet more vividly.

To start with, youth unemployment refers to the unemployment of the cohort up to twenty-five years old (the share of it outside the education system). The least productive workers – and inexperienced ones by definition belong to this group – are always the first and main victims of upswings in unemployment, while botched beginnings of their vocational careers can easily inflict serious hysteresis effects, undermining employment prospects and earnings throughout the rest of their vocational lives. For all of these reasons high youth unemployment naturally agitates policymakers to action. Yet, high youth unemployment never stems from a simple causality and therefore remedying it is a complex task. It may be a side effect of dysfunctional educational and vocational training systems, where rates of so-called NEETs (not in education, employment or training) are high and where matching between the education and market requirements is low.[73] More perplexingly from the EU perspective, excessively high unemployment more generally, and even

[71] European Social Fund, 'The ESF in the News: Support for Young People in France to Restart Education', 3 March 2017, available at ec.europa.eu/esf/main.jsp?catId=67&langId=en&newsId=2752.

[72] As I argued in Chapter 3, internal devaluation inserts a downward pressure on output, raising unemployment levels. On the other hand, inflated local prices in a single-currency regime are tantamount to loses in the external competitiveness, to falling shares of the local economy on global markets, to a deterioration of its industrial base and – again – to growing unemployment.

[73] The NEETs problem has been perennial in many Eastern European countries and the Eurozone's periphery. In 2016, it stood above the EU 28 average (15.6 per cent of the population fifteen to thirty-four years of age) in Italy (26.0 per cent), Greece (25.6 per cent), Bulgaria (22.8 per cent), Romania (20.8 per cent), Croatia (20.6 per cent), Spain (19.5 per cent), Cyprus (18.8 per cent), Slovakia (18.2 per cent), Ireland (16.3 per cent) and Hungary (15.8 per cent): Eurostat, Young People Neither in Employment nor in Education and Training by Sex, Age and Labour Status (NEET Rates).

higher youth unemployment in particular, are difficult to remedy when economic activity is suppressed by an over-appreciated currency or ineffective internal devaluation within a fixed exchange rate system. From this perspective it should not be very surprising that among the EU countries with youth unemployment above 25 per cent only Croatia is outside the Eurozone.[74] The remaining countries – Spain, Greece, Italy, Cyprus[75] – all simultaneously suffer both from very high youth unemployment and from the unfavourable exchange rate syndrome.

Sometimes, therefore, remedying the problem of youth unemployment requires reforms in the employment policy,[76] sometimes in the educational and vocational training systems[77] and sometimes in the monetary policy (and quite often it necessitates a coordinated action on all these fronts). In the current political setup European institutions can provide none of these remedies. When, however, the Eurozone crisis brought youth unemployment to 60 per cent in Greece and 56 per cent in Spain in the first quarter of 2013, European institutions decided to demonstrate their resolve in fighting the problem. They set up the Youth Guarantee, intended to 'ensure that all young people under the age of 25 years receive a good-quality offer of employment, continued education, an apprenticeship or a traineeship within a period of four months of becoming unemployed or leaving formal education'.[78] The idea received €6.4 billion in financial backing.[79]

[74] 25.3 per cent of youth unemployment in September 2017, against an EU 28 average of 16.6 per cent: Eurostat, Unemployment by Sex and Age – Monthly Average, Less Than Twenty-five Years.

[75] 40.3 per cent in Greece, 37.7 per cent in Spain and 35.0 per cent in Italy in September 2017. Also in some other EU countries, especially in Cyprus (24.9 per cent), Portugal (24.5 per cent) and in France (22.0 per cent) youth unemployment remains at an alarmingly high level: Eurostat, Unemployment by Sex and Age – Monthly Average, Less Than Twenty-five Years, Seasonally Adjusted Data (September 2017).

[76] As school graduates are outsiders of the labour market, higher employment protections make it more difficult for them to replace labour market insiders. By the same token, more flexible employment protection regimes facilitate their access to the labour market.

[77] See also Dennis Tamesberger, Heinz Leitgöb and Johann Bacher, 'How to Combat NEET? Evidence from Austria', *Intereconomics* 49 (2014): 221–227.

[78] Sec. 1 of Council Recommendation of 22 April 2013 on establishing a Youth Guarantee OJ 2013 No. C 120, 26 April 2013, pp. 1–6.

[79] This financial counterpart of the Youth Guarantee (called Youth Employment Initiative) is available in the period 2014–2020 for the regions with youth unemployment rates higher than 25 per cent in 2012 (as a general rule): Art. 16 Regulation 1304/2013 of the European Parliament and of the Council of 17 December 2013 on the European Social Fund and repealing Council Regulation 1081/2006, OJ 2013 No. L 347, 20 December 2013, pp. 470–486.

Three-and-a-half years after the Youth Guarantee was adopted – in autumn 2016 – the Commission touted the scheme, proclaiming that 'more than 14 million young people have entered Youth Guarantee schemes, and an average of nearly two million young people were registered at any one point in time ... Around nine million young people took up an offer of employment, education, traineeship or apprenticeship under the Youth Guarantee.'[80]

The true picture behind the Youth Guarantee is much less rosy, though. The Court of Auditors poured a bucket of cold water over the Commission in its report investigating the effectiveness of the Youth Guarantee in five EU countries with very high levels of youth unemployment.[81] As it found out, 'the contribution of the Youth Employment Initiative to the achievement of the Youth Guarantee objectives ... was very limited' (p. 7). During the year following its announcement not a single euro from its budget was paid out, partly due to demanding pre-financing conditions[82] and partly because local public services in the crisis-stricken regions were not prepared to offer sufficient employment, education or apprenticeships to the eligible youth.[83] However, the uptake of the economic cycle, which simultaneously occurred in the Eurozone's periphery, was reducing the level of youth unemployment there.[84] Youth employment was therefore put on the upward

[80] European Commission, 'Communication: The Youth Guarantee and Youth Employment Initiative Three Years On', COM(2016)646, 4 October 2016.

[81] Court of Auditors, 'Youth Unemployment – Have EU Policies Made a Difference? An Assessment of the Youth Guarantee and the Youth Employment Initiative', *Special Report* No. 5/2017, available at www.eca.europa.eu/Lists/ECADocuments/SR17_5/SR_YOUTH_GUARANTEE_EN.pdf. The five countries were Spain, France, Croatia, Italy and Portugal. The report refers to the period from April 2013 to May 2016.

[82] In 2015, Regulation 2015/779 of the European Parliament and of the Council of 20 May 2015 amending Regulation 1304/2013, as regards an additional initial prefinancing amount paid to operational programmes supported by the Youth Employment Initiative, OJ 2015 No. L 126, 21 May 2015, pp. 1–2, replaced the previous very low level of 1 per cent initial prefinancing disbursed for the activities covered by the Youth Employment Initiative with 30 per cent, making the scheme financially more attractive for national employment agencies.

[83] See Henriette Jacobsen, 'Merkel Admits EU's Youth Unemployment Initiative Has Been a Failure', *Euractiv*, 30 June 2014, available at www.euractiv.com/section/social-europe-jobs/news/merkel-admits-eu-s-youth-unemployment-initiative-has-been-a-failure/.

[84] In April 2013, when the Youth Guarantee Council Recommendation was adopted, youth unemployment in the EU 28 was at 23.9 per cent. Twelve months later it slid to 22.6 per cent, despite no Youth Guarantee funds having yet been mobilised. When the distribution of its funding was facilitated by amending its prefinancing rules in May 2015, youth unemployment receded further to 20.6 per cent: Eurostat, Unemployment by Sex and Age – Monthly Average, Less Than Twenty-five Years.

path exclusively by market forces, no matter how much credit for it politicians subsequently strived to ascribe to themselves.

Still, it can be argued that in the subsequent months, when the levels of youth unemployment were falling further and the main obstacles to the disbursement of the funds overcome, the Youth Guarantee might have (even if very slightly, as the Court of Auditors pinpointed) reinforced the upswing. It offered local businesses and public authorities a subsidy for accepting inexperienced workers. To some extent it also cushioned some of the hysteresis effects stemming from massive idleness. But, nonetheless, instead of grappling with the real causes of youth unemployment, the Youth Guarantee has followed the familiar grass-sprinkling pattern. It offered a temporary dole without giving the youth a chance, and even less a guarantee, of good quality, durable career opportunities in the regions where the share of NEETs is particularly high. It was devised as a crisis mitigation instrument rather than as a tool to prevent crises in the future by putting young people on the path to highly skilled jobs.

8.6 Gesture Redistribution

Neither the Investment Plan nor the Youth Guarantee are exceptional in this respect. More systemically, the institutional vehicles like the venerable ESF, or the much more recently established European Globalisation Adjustment Fund,[85] follow a similar approach. They all epitomise a political setup in which the EU is merely an additional layer in the redistribution process, rather than an originator of meaningful reforms to national socioeconomic systems and institutions. In this setup, all that the European institutions can be expected to achieve is some temporary relief to the ailments they are politically prevented from addressing in a more proper fashion.

[85] According to Art. 2 of Regulation 1309/2013 of the European Parliament and of the Council of 17 December 2013 on the European Globalisation Adjustment Fund (2014–2020) and repealing Regulation 1927/2006, OJ 2013 No. L 347, 20 December 2013, pp. 855–864, this Fund targets 'workers made redundant and self-employed persons whose activity has ceased as a result of major structural changes in world trade patterns due to globalisation' and 'workers made redundant and self-employed persons whose activity has ceased as a result of the continuation of the global financial and economic crisis'. The financial capacity of the fund during the Multiannual Financial Framework 2014–2020 is EUR 150 million annually.

It should not be surprising that the effects produced by such an awkward setup have been deeply discomfiting. A large proportion of EU countries, confronted with the permanent austerity paradigm, have systematically failed to reform and sufficiently fund the most vital public goods; the crucial public policies and institutions mentioned a few pages earlier. Despite grandiose EU plans, like the Lisbon Strategy or the Europe 2020 Strategy, and regardless of the continuous financial streams for decades flowing from the rich countries north of the Alps to Spain, Italy, Portugal and Greece, deep structural differences have persisted. As CEPS researchers aptly noted in this respect,

> all four of these Mediterranean countries suffered and still suffer from the same phenomena: overall employment rates are low due to the fact that the utilization of their female labour force lies idle, and the overall stocks of intangible capital are below the EU average leading among other things to suboptimal investment in the innovation capacities of their firms. To these handicaps one has to add high levels of corruption and inefficient governmental structures, especially in Greece and Italy. These fundamental factors are the underlying cause of the crisis, which is unlikely to abate until deep reforms allow the crisis countries to increase their productivity.[86]

The reality, therefore, has found European institutions in a truly schizophrenic situation. On the one hand, they have regularly admonished the institutionally weaker countries for failing to reform their core socioeconomic policies. On the other, EU redistribution has propelled the ailing systems with European funds.

Take Poland, the main beneficiary country of the cohesion policy, as an example. Its 2016 country-specific Council recommendation issued within the European Semester (more on the latter in Chapter 2) rightly pointed out that this country's government's fiscal policy predictions are excessively optimistic and that – in violation of EU law – Poland is 'the only Member State without a fully-fledged independent fiscal council and with no known plans to create one'.[87] More importantly

[86] Daniel Gros and Felix Roth, 'The Europe 2020 Strategy. Can It Maintain the EU's Competitiveness in the World?', *CEPS* 2012, i–ii, available at www.ceps.eu/system/files/Europe%202020.pdf.

[87] Sec. 5 and 6 Council Recommendation of 12 July 2016 on the 2016 National Reform Programme of Poland and delivering a Council opinion on the 2016 Convergence Programme of Poland (2016/C 299/04). Art. 6(1)(b) Council Directive 2011/85/EU of 8 November 2011 on requirements for budgetary frameworks of the Member States, OJ 2011 No. L 306, 23 November 2011, p. 41–47, which provides that national fiscal rules be monitored 'by independent bodies or bodies endowed with functional autonomy vis-à-vis the fiscal authorities of the Member States'.

from the perspective of the public policies mentioned in this chapter, the recommendation chastened Polish educational (including pre-school) and vocational training systems, as well as various preferential sector-specific social security arrangements.[88] After years of subsidising all major infrastructure projects in Poland with EU structural funds, the Council recommendation hinted also that 'weaknesses in managerial and administrative capacity have a negative effect on the timely implementation of investment projects in the railway sector and other transport, energy and telecommunication infrastructure projects' (Sec. 13).

The ailments pinpointed in the case of Poland can hardly be undermined on merits. In fact, their list could be extended further (the 2016 Polish recommendation, for instance, did not mention faltering rule of law conditions since the 2015 general elections). Similar, and in fact often longer and structurally even more serious, lists of weak spots in national socioeconomic policies and institutions have been repeated time and again by the Council regarding all the other beneficiary countries. Worse still, because corruption and a country's institutional weakness naturally go hand-in-hand, because they both depress GDP levels and because regional funds are concentrated in the regions where the GDP is lower, EU funding often lands where incumbent

[88] The relevant passages (Secs. 9, 10, 12) deserve an extensive quotation: 'Despite recent improvements, the Polish labour market faces significant challenges – an ageing labour force, low productivity and high segmentation of the labour market. These are coupled with shortcomings in the education system. Although the education system has improved significantly in recent years, it still fails to equip pupils sufficiently with the transversal skills needed for the rapidly changing labour market and innovation. The relatively low average standing of Polish higher education and science has a negative effect on the quality of provision. The degree of internationalisation of Polish higher education is very limited, both in terms of the number of foreign students and participation in international scientific collaboration. The financing model of higher education does not promote quality sufficiently, as it largely uses past university standings and quantity variables, such as the number of students and academic staff. According to employers, graduates lack transversal skills such as problem solving, critical thinking, or teamwork. Participation in lifelong learning is low, and vocational education and training do not correspond to market needs. While the availability and take-up of pre-school education has increased significantly in recent years, the availability of early childcare services remains among the lowest in the Union. Raising the obligatory school starting age to the age of seven years, and removing the obligation for five-year-olds to attend pre-school, combined with the new child benefit, may have negative effects on labour market participation, especially of women, and deserves close monitoring ... Preferential sector-specific social security arrangements, in particular the highly subsidised pension systems for farmers and miners, have high budgetary costs and may contribute to reducing labour mobility.'

politicians are particularly inclined to use the funding to enrich themselves as well as the corrupt coteries around them.[89] The grass-sprinkling logic of this policy has mainly helped to perpetuate dysfunctional domestic policies and institutions. At the very minimum, it has helped mitigate their negative effects, reducing political motivation to reform them. Doing so, this policy has traded a real change in everyday life of Europeans for an impression of it.

There are a number of reasons why this may be so.

To start with, the cohesion policy has been hailed as a bedrock of the 'multilevel governance, in which supranational, national, regional and local governments are enmeshed in territorially overarching policy networks'[90] towards the common good of economic advancement in a structurally divergent Europe.[91] In the name of 'Europe, in which decisions are taken as closely as possible to the citizen in accordance with the principle of subsidiarity',[92] Member States have been able to choose how exactly they want to prioritise the main trunk of the regional spending. This assumption has found its way to EU law as the principle of shared management. According to it, 'implementation tasks shall be delegated to Member States',[93] which in practice has left European institutions with quite a limited leverage over the recipient countries.

Furthermore, since the Lisbon Strategy of 2000, the cohesion policy has been driven by a certain understanding of 'smart, sustainable

[89] Pethő András and Zöldi Blanka, 'How EU-funded Projects Secretly Contributed to the Orbán Family's Enrichment', *DIREKT36*, 9 May 2017, available at www.direkt36.hu/en/2017/05/09/rejtett-allami-munkakbol-is-jott-penz-az-orban-csalad-gyorsan-szerzett-milliardjaihoz/.

[90] Gary Marks, 'Structural Policy and Multilevel Governance in the EC', in: *The State of the European Community, Vol. 2: The Maastricht Debates and Beyond*, eds. Alan W. Cafruny and Glenda G. Rosenthal (Boulder, CO: Lynne Rienner Publishers, and Harlow: Longman Group U.K. Ltd., 1993): 401–402.

[91] For another classical tack on the relationship between the cohesion policy and multi-level governance see Liesbet Hooghe, ed., *Cohesion Policy and European Integration: Building Multi-level Governance* (Oxford: Oxford University Press, 1996). As to more comprehensively theoretical leading accounts on multilevel governance, see esp. Liesbet Hooghe and Gary Marks, *Multi-level Governance and European Integration* (Lanham, MD: Rowman & Littlefield, 2001); Simona Piattoni, *The Theory of Multi-level Governance: Conceptual, Empirical, and Normative Challenges* (Oxford: Oxford University Press, 2010).

[92] TEU, preamble.

[93] Art. 59(1) Regulation 966/2012 of the European Parliament and of the Council of 25 October 2012 on the financial rules applicable to the general budget of the Union and repealing Council Regulation 1605/2002, OJ 2012 No. L 298, 26 October 2012, pp. 1–96.

and inclusive growth'. Research, Information and Communications Technologies (ICTs), SMEs, low-carbon economy, climate change adaptations, environment protection or transport and network infrastructure clearly reverberate with it. It is, therefore, understandable that these items have topped the list of the ESI Funds' so-called thematic priorities, mentioned earlier.[94] It should not be surprising that EU institutions are loath to exchange these fashionable goals for politically more divisive alternatives – like family policy, healthcare, employment policies, administration of justice or tax collection – even where the principle of shared management does not tie their hands.[95]

8.7 The Constitutional Bargain

The legal framework behind European integration has additionally discouraged European and national policymakers from rethinking European redistribution. In healthcare, industry policy, research, education, vocational training or youth policies, as well as in administrative cooperation, the Union only has so-called supporting, coordinating and supplementary powers.[96] It has similar (coordinating) powers in economic, employment and social policies.[97] In consequence, in principle each Member State is free to exercise its powers in these areas even when the Union has exercised its own.[98] By the same token, Member States retain an upper hand in policy design; their idiosyncratic choices are not to be overridden by EU institutions. The current grass-sprinkling

[94] Art. 9(1)–(6) Regulation 1303/2013.

[95] According to Art. 59(1) Regulation 966/2012, unless governed by the principle of shared management, the EU budget is managed by the Commission ('direct management') or by other public or private bodies, like the EIB or the EIF ('indirect management'). Both in the direct and indirect schemes all management decisions are retained at the EU level. Some Treaty amendments introduced by the Lisbon Treaty made indirect management more political than before and therefore more prone to the grass-sprinkling syndrome: Giannangelo Marchegiani, 'The European Investment Bank after the Treaty of Lisbon', *European Law Review* 37 (2012): 70–78.

[96] Art. 6 TFEU and, in particular: Art. 168 TFEU (healthcare), Art. 173 TFEU (industry), Arts. 179–188 TFEU (research), Art. 165 TFEU (education), Art. 166 TFEU (vocational training) and Art. 197 TFEU (administrative cooperation).

[97] Arts. 5(1) and 121 TFEU (economic policies), Arts. 5(2) and 145–150 TFEU (employment), Arts. 151–161 TFEU (social policy).

[98] Conversely, in the areas where the EU has shared competences (the internal market being the most important one) the principle of pre-emption applies. According to it, 'The Member States shall exercise their competence to the extent that the Union has not exercised its competence. The Member States shall again exercise their competence to the extent that the Union has decided to cease exercising its competence' (Art. 2(2) TFEU).

approach to the relationship between EU funding and core state powers in the socioeconomic realm accepts this division of powers, forcing the EU to support and supplement national policies with additional funding, even when its other actions (e.g., recommendations) point out their weaknesses. This pattern would be seriously upset if European institutions ventured an attempt to use EU funding to rebuild national gardens of socioeconomic policies.

Politically, they are seriously discouraged from doing so. Each crucial socioeconomic policy and institution falls within core state powers. In order to consolidate their influences, national politicians naturally claim that external influences would undermine these public goods, even if the same politicians (and their predecessors) have been failing to deliver the very same goods through domestic political processes. Achieving the goal is greatly facilitated by tribal instincts resurfacing especially when social, economic and political uncertainties prevail. In their consequence European societies, despite decades of European integration, still preach to the instinct of 'parochial altruism'.[99] It tells them that 'rule by foreigners is the greatest punishment'.[100] Exploiting this instinct, national politicians have been achieving the best of all political worlds in their domestic 'win-set':[101] claiming political credit for whatever positive comes from the integration, channelling cohesion resources where they can most easily win them popular support[102] and shifting blame onto the EU for as many hard choices as they manage to peddle.

But while the political coalition behind the current power equilibrium between the Member States and the European institutions can hardly be expected to change its preferences unless dodging the reality is no longer possible, the current setup is not constitutionally inevitable. Within the existing Treaty framework, the division between shared and coordinating competences is ultimately quite fluid. In particular,

[99] I.e., altruism towards members of one's own group: Helen Bernhard, Urs Fischbacher and Ernst Fehr, 'Parochial Altruism in Humans', *Nature* 442 (2006): 912–915.

[100] Thietmar of Merseburg, *Ottonian Germany: The Chronicon of Thietmar of Merseburg*, trans. and annot. by David A. Warner (Manchester: Manchester University Press, 2001): 81.

[101] For a classical theoretical account explaining the setup, see Robert Putnam, 'Diplomacy and Domestic Politics: The Logic of Two-level Games', *International Organization* 42 (1988): 427–460.

[102] For empirical evidence, see Lisa Maria Dellmuth, Dominik Schraff and Michael F. Stoffel, 'Distributive Politics, Electoral Institutions and European Structural and Investment Funding: Evidence from Italy and France', *Journal of Common Market Studies* 55 (2017): 275–293.

when the EU legislators opine that a certain area within supporting and coordinating EU powers falls simultaneously into the realm of the internal market, they can treat it as a shared competence, exercising far-reaching powers bestowed on the EU in the latter domain.[103] Then they are authorised to issue directives or regulations where under supporting and coordinating competences none of the tools is available to the EU.[104] They can also delegate far-reaching executive powers to EU agencies as an internal market harmonisation measure when they find it important for sustaining economic integration.[105] Demonstrating that the Treaty can be a flexible constitutional charter when a political compromise clearly in the interest of Europeans is mustered, the EU legislators have even claimed, unchallenged, that the SRM for the banking sector can be harmonised as an internal market matter.[106] This is a bold choice from the strictly legal perspective, considering that the internal market covers all EU countries, while it has been clear from day one that non-Eurozone countries would not be interested in joining the SRM.

These legal nuances are relevant for my point in this chapter, because ailing public policies and institutions at the national level undermine

[103] See, for example, Directive 2011/24/EU of the European Parliament and of the Council of 9 March 2011 on the application of patients' rights in cross-border healthcare, OJ 2011 No. L 88, 4 April 2011, pp. 45–65, which shares Art. 114 TFEU (internal market harmonisation) and Art. 168 TFEU (complementary and coordinating powers regarding public healthcare) as its legal bases.

[104] Art. 2(5) TFEU precludes harmonisation (directives) in the areas governed by supporting, coordinating and supplementary powers. *A fortiori*, nor should unification (regulations) be adopted in these situations.

[105] This particular feature stems from the 'ESMA doctrine', coined by the CJEU in case C-270/12, *UK* v. *Parliament and Council*, ECLI:EU:C:2014:18. For a broader discussion, see Dariusz Adamski, 'The ESMA Doctrine. A Constitutional Revolution and the Economics of Delegation', *European Law Review* 39 (2014): 812–834; Carl Fredrik Bergström, 'Shaping the New System for Delegation of Powers to EU Agencies: United Kingdom v. European Parliament and Council (Short Selling)', *Common Market Law Review* 52 (2015): 219–242.

[106] Regulation 806/2014 establishing uniform rules and a uniform procedure for the resolution of credit institutions and certain investment firms in the framework of a Single Resolution Mechanism and a Single Resolution Fund and amending Regulation 1093/2010, OJ 2014 No. L 225/1, 30 July 2014, p. 1–90. The SRM and a SRF are parts of the banking union. While in principle the latter can be joined by non-Eurozone countries, in practice these countries are strongly incentivised to retain banking supervision and resolution at the national level because this is where the LoLR for the national banking system (the national central bank) is located. For this reason it was quite predictable, when Regulation 806/2014 was enacted, that the non-Eurozone countries would not join the Single Resolution Mechanism.

competitive advantages of individual states and disrupt their ability to function properly (among others) on the internal market. This makes the case for treating the reform process of core socioeconomic policies and institutions as an internal market matter as well. General principles of EU law – of subsidiarity and proportionality in particular – point in the same direction. To see this it is first of all necessary to recall the point made in the previous chapter: some European societies have been quite successful in reforming their core socioeconomic policies and institutions exclusively through domestic processes. Many others have been failing in this respect. This gives different vectors to the same Treaty principles in different countries. In some, the principles of subsidiarity and proportionality should prevent EU actions in the field of national socioeconomic policies and institutions as superfluous and unnecessary, while clearly justifying them in others.[107]

The point about the role of the internal market as well as the principles of proportionality and subsidiarity in realigning structural funds and national reforms to socioeconomic policies and institutions is further corroborated by the failure of the OMC as a milder form of coordinating national economic and social policies. In the previous chapter I mentioned that this 'new governance' tool was devised in the late 1990s to reconcile the need to achieve economic convergence with the national control of the core socioeconomic policies and institutions on which the goal has hinged. But it has proven to be a paper tiger, a largely futile bureaucratic exercise unable to stymie centrifugal effects of national systems both in the Eurozone and outside of it. This is particularly important from the perspective of its proportionality. As the CJEU interpreted it, this principle 'requires that acts of the EU institutions be *appropriate* for attaining the legitimate objectives pursued by the legislation at issue and do not exceed the limits of *what is necessary in order to achieve those objectives*; when there is a choice between several appropriate measures, recourse must be had to the least onerous, and the disadvantages caused must not be *disproportionate to the aims pursued*'.[108] If the OMC is conspicuously unable to achieve its objectives, then it is

[107] The latter situation could be described by what Zuleeg calls 'inverse subsidiarity': Fabian Zuleeg, 'Can the Eurozone's Economic Governance Combine Political Accountability, Legitimacy and Effectiveness?', *EPC Discussion Paper*, 1 September 2015, 5, available at www.epc.eu/pub_details.php?cat_id=17&pub_id=5870&year=2015.

[108] Case C-358/14, *Poland* v. *Parliament and Council*, ECLI:EU:C:2016:323, § 78 and the case law cited therein (my emphasis). For broader accounts on the mechanics of the principle in EU law, see esp. Wolf Sauter, 'Proportionality in EU Law: A Balancing

both inappropriate and disproportionate to the aims pursued. In other words, the principle of proportionality should disqualify the OMC constitutionally, because this governance process has proven too facile to achieve its goals.

For the very same reasons, conditionality provisions in EU laws governing structural funds arguably fall short of what the principle of proportionality requires. They ought to be replaced by a much more meaningful governance paradigm.

The so-called Common Provisions Regulation (Regulation 1303/2013), setting up common rules for all the ESI Funds, establishes three types of conditionalities. The first, thematic conditionality, is to make sure that recipient countries and regions have necessary regulatory frameworks, strategic plans and institutional capacities in place to achieve the thematic objectives of the ESI Funds (e.g., ICTs, SMEs, low-carbon economy, transport and network infrastructure etc., mentioned earlier). The second, general conditionality, makes EU structural funding dependent on meeting seven basic EU priorities and principles.[109] If the recipient country disregards any of the two conditionality types, the Commission is authorised to suspend interim payments until compliance is restored.[110]

And then there is the third type, macroeconomic conditionality, the one most relevant in the present context. It allows the Commission to 'request a Member State to review and propose amendments' to the way it uses regional funding 'where this is necessary to support the implementation of relevant Council Recommendations' within the multilateral economic and fiscal surveillance (the Polish one, mentioned earlier, is one of such recommendations), 'or to maximise the growth and competitiveness impact of the ESI Funds in Member States receiving financial assistance'.[111] The Commission is also authorised to 'propose to the Council that it suspend part or all of the payments for the programmes

Act?', *Cambridge Yearbook of European Legal Studies* 15 (2013): 439–466; Tor-Inge Harbo, 'The Function of the Proportionality Principle in EU Law', *European Law Journal* 16 (2010): 158–185.

[109] They refer to the compliance with EU standards of: anti-discrimination, gender equality, protection of rights of persons with disabilities, public procurement, state aid, environmental legislation relating to Environmental Impact Assessments and Strategic Environmental Assessments, as well as statistical systems (Part II of Annex XI Regulation 1303/2013).

[110] Art. 19(5) Regulation 1303/2013.

[111] Art. 23(1) Regulation 1303/2013.

or priorities concerned' if 'the Member State fails to take effective action' in response to any such a Commission request.[112]

European institutions have never had much of an appetite to use macroeconomic conditionality in practice,[113] putting it on a collision course with the principle of proportionality. Similarly to the OMC, also within the ESI conditionality, national governments have an upper hand over the procedure, which discourages the Commission from anything other than complacency and renders the conditionality defunct. It makes the process entirely inadequate in the strictly legal sense and hence contrary to proportionality as a general principle of EU law.

All in all, the current cosy relationship between European institutions and national governments on the juncture of socioeconomic reforms and European redistribution has not been preordained by the Treaties. Quite to the contrary, the most sanctified general principles of EU law – when taken seriously – strongly oppose it.

8.8 Disdained Lessons of Development Economics

Even more importantly, the current power equilibrium is untenable in a longer perspective, because it triggers a powerful vortex of socioeconomic divergences and a serious waste of resources. Governments of the net contributors to the EU budget, facing growing pressure from the permanent austerity paradigm discussed in the previous chapter, can hardly be expected to sit back and watch how the twisted power equilibrium depletes their scarce public resources.

To grasp the point clearly we should return to the principle of shared management and the sobering experiences of Greece. I mentioned earlier that shared management puts national and regional decision-makers in the driving seat of the processes for which they have been

[112] Art. 23(6) Regulation 1303/2013. In some more egregious cases, where noncompliance has been vindicated by the Council, the Commission is obliged to submit to the Council a request 'to suspend part or all of the commitments or payments for the programmes of a Member State' – Art. 23(9) Regulation 1303/2013.

[113] Under the rules previously in force, in 2012 the Council suspended Hungarian cohesion funds for its disregard of EU recommendations within the excessive deficit procedure. After three months the suspension was lifted: Council of the European Union, 'Hungary: Council Lifts Cohesion Fund Suspension', Press Release No. 11648/12, 22 June 2012, available at www.consilium.europa.eu/uedocs/cms_data/docs/pressdata/en/ecofin/131129.pdf.

traditionally unprepared organisationally and culturally. For decades it has been believed that, with the additional funding available through the cohesion policy, these decision-makers would redefine their traditional behaviour. At the same time, however, the bonus resources have allowed regional and national politicians to nurture their influences, often with cataclysmic consequences. A Greek commentator captured it when he wrote in 2014 that this country's active labour market policies, generously supported by EU structural funds for years, do not reach 'the most vulnerable and disadvantaged unemployed persons but ... those with established network contacts with political party leaders ... These labour market measures function indirectly as a method of offering financial support to only part of the unemployed population, allowing politicians to manage the social problem of high unemployment in the context of traditional political networks by selecting the beneficiaries, thus valorizing extended clientelistic practices.'[114]

This picture should not be very surprising from the perspective of a fundamental insight behind development economics. Accordingly, societies are underdeveloped not so much because they lack the resources necessary to become prosperous, but because they have not developed capacities to effectively use the resources they possess. The best, therefore, foreign aid can achieve is to spur the 'capacity development' process.[115] This, however, cannot be accomplished under the grass-sprinkling paradigm of the cohesion policy. As long as 'the EU sees itself as a redistributor of funds and in no way as "donor"',[116] the Union redistribution should be expected to primarily petrify and aggrandise

[114] Constantine Dimoulas, 'Exploring the Impact of Employment Policy Measures in the Context of Crisis: The Case of Greece', *International Social Security Review* 67 (2014): 53; Asteris Huliaras and Sotiris Petropoulos, in 'European Money in Greece: In Search of the Real Impact of EU Structural Funds', *Journal of Common Market Studies* 54 (2016): 1332–1349, extend the argument to all EU Structural Funds, arguing that 'as with foreign aid, EUSF in Greece have ended up supporting a bloated bureaucracy, strengthening patronage patterns and reinforcing clientelistic networks. Also, they have had a strongly negative impact on incentives. They have been treated by Greek government officials with a sense of entitlement, rather than used as external support for domestic efforts', p. 1345.

[115] For more details on the concept, see, for example: Deborah Eade, *Capacity-building: An Approach to People-centred Development* (Oxford: Oxfam, 1997); Anita Ernstorfer and Albrecht Stockmayer, *Capacity Development for Good Governance* (Baden-Baden, Eschborn: Nomos, 2009); Alan Fowler, Naa-Aku Acquaye-Baddoo and Jan Ubels, *Capacity Development in Practice* (London: Routledge, 2010).

[116] Kálmán Mizsei and Ádám Kullmann, 'Struggling with an Opportunity: The First 10 years with the EU for Central Europe and the Baltics. A Few Lessons', *CEPS Essay* No. 12, 2 May 2014, 3, available at aei.pitt.edu/58409/1/Essay_No_12_NMS_at_10.pdf.

extant national governance processes, with all their flaws and inefficiencies, rather than to achieve sustainable capacity development and courageous socioeconomic reforms.

When this ironic mechanism is heeded, it should not be very surprising that the grass-sprinkling cohesion policy has nurtured cynicism towards the EU in the beneficiary societies and frustration in the contributor societies. For this reason the governance paradigm underlying the cohesion policy and producing these insidious effects is self-defeating. It should either be rectified, or the policy itself will cave in.

8.9 From 'Technical Assistance' to Reform Laboratories

Earlier, I argued that, to bring about the capacity development effects, regional funding ought to concentrate on the most significant public goods, rather than on private goods disguised as public. Now, after explaining why such an alteration is legally and politically viable, another tenet of such a reorientation must be elucidated. The EU acting as a donor – truly capacitated to drive structural policies at the national level – is another way of arguing for (much) more centralisation of the cohesion policy. But when such an argument is laid down, three serious counterarguments pop up immediately. First, European institutions lack the necessary resources, second, they are traditionally distant from domestic policymaking, and third, they tend to follow obscure, heavily bureaucratic processes unfit for the open-mindedness and creativity necessary to pursue viable socioeconomic reforms. Experiences of the countries visited by the Troika during the sovereign debt crisis can grossly serve as confirmation of all these institutional shortcomings.

To explain the point we must return to Greece. The first bailout package, agreed in 2010, was based on the assumption that the Greek state had the capacities necessary to pursue the reforms agreed with international creditors. It soon turned out, however, that – despite the initial commitment and devotion of the Greek government – the process was daunting for Greek authorities. They faced resistance from various special interests, and lacked resources and expertise. The following year, therefore, the Commission launched a programme of technical assistance coordinated by its internal body, called 'Task Force for Greece'.

For a few reasons the scheme was miscarried. The Task Force was broadly perceived as a local branch of the repressing and arrogant Troika, representing the interests of the creditors only and therefore broadly distrusted on the ground in Greece. To add injury to insult, it was very hastily set up. The establishment process underestimated the very important role this body should have performed in reconstructing the ailing Greek public policies and institutions. With a handful of largely inexperienced officials, no reasonable financing and no consistent mission creed, the body was a shadow of what it ought to have been. Four years later, in 2015, the Court of Auditors made this very clear when it contended that 'the urgency of responding to the crisis in Greece meant that the TFGR was set up very rapidly, without a full analysis of other options and without a dedicated budget. It had no single comprehensive strategic document for the delivery of TA [technical assistance] or for deciding between competing priorities, despite the TFGR's mandate to identify and coordinate the TA.'[117] In addition, the Task Force had no skin in the game, because no specific EU funding supporting the reforms was following its advice. Nor could its heavily clandestine, bureaucratic processes build legitimacy for its actions.

All the flaws have proven very intractable. The Support Group for Cyprus, established in March 2013, followed a similarly sloppy establishment process, and was similarly underfunded, underrated and inexperienced. In summer 2015, the Commission decided to replace the two ad-hoc teams with a permanent body. Its internal department, called Structural Reform Support Service (the Service), was tasked with supporting Member States with introducing 'key reforms, particularly those set out in our country-specific recommendations'.[118] The Service was designed to concentrate especially on 'revenue management and public financial management, improving the business environment and helping businesses, helping to facilitate and promote exports, assistance on employment, social inclusion and public health, developing efficient, modern, service-oriented public administrations and public procurement practices, effective rule of law and combating corruption'.[119]

Like its predecessors, this Service was born with no dedicated funding envelope and with serious governance flaws. Nonetheless, it was soon thrown into demanding reforms at the national level. In the months following its establishment, the unit was managing about sixty projects

[117] European Court of Auditors, 'More Attention to Results Needed to Improve the Delivery of Technical Assistance to Greece', *Special Report* No. 19/2015, 7, available at www.eca.europa.eu/Lists/ECADocuments/SR15_19/SR_TFGR_EN.pdf.

[118] Press Release, European Commission, 'Speaking Points of Vice-President Dombrovskis on the Commission's New Structural Reform Support Service', 17 June 2015, available at europa.eu/rapid/press-release_STATEMENT-15-5218_en.htm.

[119] Ibid.

in Greece and Cyprus, as well as an additional ten projects in seven other Member States (Slovakia, Slovenia, Romania, Bulgaria and three other countries whose governments never disclosed their identity).[120] In consequence, its staff was growing – from forty-seven officials in July 2015 to 135 in February 2017[121] – when a political agreement between the Commission, the Parliament and the Council secured it a budget of €143 million until 2020.[122] Justifying this financial appropriation, the Commission announced that a further ten Member States were seeking its assistance.[123]

Even after taking a more stable institutional root, the scheme's governance is very imperfect. Its significance has been seriously underestimated and misunderstood even by higher echelons of the Commission itself. The Service is tasked, for instance, both with reforms in vital socioeconomic policies and with orchestrating the (improbable) unification of Cyprus, while its head additionally coordinates the implementation of the EU–Turkey statement on migration management.[124] Its staff is therefore clearly overburdened. The unit still follows obscure, bureaucratic procedures, instead of attracting external expertise within open and participatory processes.[125] National governments, too, clearly strive to keep its cooperation with the Service under the radar of public opinion, undermining its legitimacy and achievable results in terms of cooperation with local stakeholders.

All of these features undermine the legitimacy and potential effectiveness of the Structural Reform Support Service. Yet, none is inevitable. It only requires a modicum of institutional ingenuity to overcome them: a dose small enough to be perfectly achievable by European

[120] Ryan Heath, 'Politico Brussels Playbook', *Politico*, 13 February 2017, available at www.politico.eu/newsletter/playbook/politico-brussels-playbook-presented-by-epp-group-european-commission-presidency-race-mogherini-snarks-trump/.

[121] Ibid.

[122] European Commission, Press release: 'Political Agreement Reached on Structural Reform Support Programme – A New Tool to Help Member States Implement Reforms', 8 February 2017, available at europa.eu/rapid/press-release_IP-17-233_en.htm.

[123] Ryan Heath, 'Politico Brussels Playbook'.

[124] The statement, issued on 18 March 2016, outlines conditions of cooperation with Turkey on stymieing the influx of irregular migrants from third countries.

[125] This point is not restricted to the Service. It is a sign of a broader dysfunctionality. While since the early 2000s the Commission has performed public consultations of its various initiatives, the opinion that 'the Commission's consultations are a sham time and time again. They just do box-checking exercises' (Ryan Heath, 'Politico Brussels Playbook') is prevalent among those who have ever participated in them.

institutions and national governments. If this is attained, the Service could be transformed into a serious, impartial driver of analytical and policy design work by experts from the countries assisted and from other EU countries where reforms have been successfully implemented,[126] as well as of coalition-building behind national reforms where otherwise national players face insurmountable political stalemates. If backed by serious financial flows now practically left for Member States to redistribute along the grass-sprinkling paradigm and by more robust governance processes, the Service could maximise the potential impact of EU redistribution on economic and social cohesion. If its reform-devising processes were open, inclusive and incentive-compatible, the Service could do wonders in the capacity-building process, aligning European redistribution with the most basic truths of development economics.

These governance developments are also necessary to set the Treaty requirement of independence – binding both on the Commission and European administration more generally[127] – straight at the juncture of socioeconomic reforms and European redistribution. Independence has various meanings in the European context.[128] It can mean non-dependence on external expertise and wisdom. Or it can betoken non-dependence on the dark side of politics: myopia, pork barrel and logrolling. So far the Service has largely followed the first of the two understandings, while schemes like the Investments Plan and the Youth Guarantee make it quite clear that the second type of the Commission's independence has been very imperfect. By the same token, the prevailing type of the Commission's – and of the European administration's more broadly – independence does not make it well predisposed to emulate the successes of the Swedish or German independent commissions, more broadly discussed in the previous chapter, in designing groundbreaking socioeconomic reforms.

[126] For instance, Austria may have a parochial family policy that can hardly serve as a blueprint for other EU countries. But it has been in the avant-garde of cost-effective reforms in healthcare. Portugal, on the other hand, has managed to seriously improve the effectiveness of its tax authorities and Sweden or the Netherlands have traditionally had some of the most effective tax authorities in Europe. Finland, Estonia and Slovenia have some of the best European educational systems both when it comes to students' performance and educational equity (according to the 2015 PISA assessment).

[127] Art. 245 TFEU in respect to the Commission and Art. 298 TFEU regarding European administration.

[128] Dominique Ritleng, ed., *Independence and Legitimacy in the Institutional System of the European Union* (Oxford: Oxford University Press, 2016).

By definition, however, the choice as to how to understand independence essentially belongs to the independent agent itself. It is, therefore, ultimately up to the Commission and to the European administration to decide if their independence is to be constructive or destructive. So far, it has hardly been constructive, partly under (most often both informal and illegitimate) pressure from national governments. The resultant approach of the Commission – too often very chaotic and theatrically superfluous – cannot get the Union very far, however. Redefining its independence is, therefore, important for the very survival of the European project.

Of course, even if the centralisation in managing European funds is reinforced, even if the funds are concentrated on vital national public goods and even if necessary reforms to national socioeconomic policies and institutions are devised through governance processes following the best possible understanding of independence, in any scenario European resources could cover only small parts of national bills for healthcare, education, tax collection or the administration of justice in ailing EU countries. But this is fair enough. For beneficiary countries the billions redistributed each year through the regional policy are a sufficiently attractive titbit to sway their actions in a systemic fashion. Consider, in particular, that in the 2018 EU budget of €156 billion, the resources committed to the cohesion policy amount to about €54 billion.[129] Even a small share of the budget could do wonders to national socioeconomic reforms if the cohesion policy was redesigned accordingly.

8.10 The Most Counterproductive of All: Farm Subsidies

But this is not yet the whole story. The share of the EU budget available for rebuilding national socioeconomic gardens could, and arguably definitely should, be augmented further by resources now committed to the most distortive and counterproductive European redistributive policy: the CAP.

Soon after the CAP was established in 1962 the Community achieved food self-sufficiency. In other words, the supply of food surpassed demand for it. At this point, the original goal of the CAP – mainlining high producer prices – could only generate growing policy costs,

[129] European Commission, 'Multiannual Financial Framework Adjusted for 2018', available at ec.europa.eu/budget/mff/figures/index_en.cfm.

because the growing supply of agricultural products was putting a downward pressure on market prices and therefore an upward pressure on the value of farm subsidies. In a string of reforms, propelled by the growing financial burden, by the new reality of global trade and, later on, by the incoming accessions of rural Eastern European countries, the CAP underwent reforms intended to change the farmers' incentive structure.[130] Export measures and market support funding, the main drivers of the earlier over-intensified production and oversupply, are now long gone, while a big share of direct payments to farmers has been decoupled from the levels of production outputs. They provide income maintenance, rather than product price maintenance.[131] Hence they also reduce the ecological damage of excessively intensified agriculture.[132]

130 The MacSharry reform of 1992, the Agenda 2000 reform of 1999 and the Fischler Reform of 2003. For more on the reforms, see esp. Isabelle Garzon, *Reforming the Common Agricultural Policy: History of a Paradigm Change* (London: Palgrave Macmillan, 2006); Arlindo Cunha and Alan Swinbank, *An Inside View of the CAP Reform Process: Explaining the MacSharry, Agenda 2000, and Fischler Reforms* (Oxford: Oxford University Press, 2011); Kennet Lynggaard and Peter Nedergaard, 'The Logic of Policy Development: Lessons Learned from Reform and Routine within the CAP 1980–2003', in: *The Common Agricultural Policy: Policy Dynamics in a Changing Context*, eds. Grace Skogstad and Amy Verdun (London: Routledge 2013): 25–43. For comprehensive discussions of more recent developments, see Johan F. M. Swinnen, ed., *The Political Economy of the 2014–2020 Common Agricultural Policy. An Imperfect Storm* (Brussels: CEPS and London: Rowman and Littlefield International, 2015); Alessandro Sorrentino and Roberto Henke, eds., *The Common Agricultural Policy after the Fischler Reform: National Implementations, Impact Assessment and the Agenda for Future Reforms* (London: Routledge, 2016).

131 Member States can still voluntarily couple a proportion (8 per cent as a general principle in the 2014–2020 Multiannual Financial Framework) of direct payments to certain products: Arts. 52–55 Regulation 1307/2013 of the European Parliament and of the Council of 17 December 2013 establishing rules for direct payments to farmers under support schemes within the framework of the CAP and repealing Council Regulation 637/2008 and Council Regulation 73/2009, OJ 2013 No. L 347/608, 20 December 2013, pp. 608–670.

132 Furthermore, since 2015 direct payments are subject to 'greening' requirements. According to Arts. 43–47 Regulation 1307/2013 Member States are to set aside 30 per cent of their direct payment budgets for agricultural practices that benefit the environment and the climate (diversifying crops, maintaining permanent grassland, or dedicating 5 per cent of arable land to 'ecologically beneficial elements' ['ecological focus areas']). For many observers the final wording of the provisions has been diluted to the level of a 'greenwash': see, for example, Emil Erjavec, Marko Lovec and Karmen Erjavec, 'From "Greening" to "Greenwash": The Drivers and Discourses of CAP 2020 "reform"', in: *The Political Economy of the 2014–2020 Common Agricultural Policy. An Imperfect Storm*, ed. Johan F. M. Swinnen (Brussels: CEPS and London: Rowman and Littlefield International, 2015): 215–244, esp. 238–239.

On the other hand, however, none of the reforms has managed to eliminate the original sin of the CAP: its giving a financial boost to the least productive economic sector,[133] bringing about oversupply of its products and nontrivial opportunity costs of the redistribution, which could otherwise be used much more productively.

This continuous inefficiency-amplifying mechanism has been constantly defended by the farm (and food processing) lobby, as well as by European institutions, on the grounds that agriculture is a sector like no other. One reason for this is economic: food prices are volatile and hardly predictable, while the supply is inelastic (at least in the short run) and exposed to unpredictable natural and environmental factors. In consequence, 'with … uncertainty over the two key variables in determining a farmers' revenue – quantity produced and price – farmers face enormous uncertainty over their income'.[134] The other reason is cultural and political. It appeals to the picture of a farmer as a custodian of the rural environment and of traditional social and cultural values superior to the economic calculus of the efficiency maximisation. As the Commission put it, 'in all EU Member States, farmers keep the countryside alive and maintain the rural way of life. If there were no farms or farmers, our hamlets, villages and market towns would be profoundly affected – for the worse.'[135]

Together, the reasons imply that because agriculture is unfit for free-market logic, farmers should be compensated by the sectors that can take fuller advantage of economic integration within the internal market. Using these arguments the farm lobby has been able to exploit the generally prevailing sympathy towards agriculture and farmers among Europeans. Because this lobby is very well-organised and clamorous, European policymakers have never mustered courage to confront it on any of the beliefs.

[133] In 2016, real labour productivity of the agricultural sector was slightly more than half of real labour productivity in entertaining, recreation and other services (the major low-wage sector), and more than five times lower than in the IT & Communications and Financial & Insurance sectors: Eurostat, National Accounts and GDP, Figure 6, available at ec.europa.eu/eurostat/statistics-explained/index.php/National_accounts_and_GDP.

[134] Robert Ackrill, *Common Agricultural Policy* (Sheffield: Sheffield Academic Press, 2000): 21.

[135] European Commission, 'The European Union Explained. The EU's Common Agricultural Policy (CAP): For Our Food, for Our Countryside, for Our Environment', Luxembourg 2017, 4, available at www.learneurope.eu/files/2513/7525/9029/Resumen_de_la_PAC_en.pdf.

As the years have gone by, however, all of the economic, social and political underpinnings of the CAP have been evaporating.

First, low-wage sectors have been burgeoning across European economies and structural unemployment has remained at stubbornly high levels in many EU countries. It has been all the less convincing, therefore, that more than a third of the EU budget should go to a sector generating 1.5 per cent of EU GDP (in 2016).[136] By subsidising it, the EU has helped retain higher employment there than otherwise would be the case, instead of funding socioeconomic policies boosting the creation of jobs in high-productivity and high-wage sectors. The growing number of workers in the low-wage sectors outside of agriculture can be expected to find redistribution to the shrinking farm sector increasingly illegitimate.

Second, the original idea of buying farmers into the European project with farm subsidies has also largely backfired. Polish farmers, for instance, are the core electorate of the Eurosceptic (currently governing) party. British farmers astonished observers by supporting the Leave campaign in the Brexit referendum.[137] French ones have massively flocked to the Front National, disappointed with France's funnelling of fiscal resources to the EU budget[138] only to see them largely transferred to the low-cost rural Eastern European countries with which French farmers find it extremely difficult to compete.[139] Because the CAP has found it increasingly hard to fulfil its main goal (income maintenance), new policy paradigms will more easily break through the political agenda.

Third, fading memories of food shortages and the recurring overproduction crises[140] should make it easier to understand the historic

136 Eurostat, Gross Value Added and Income by A*10 Industry Breakdowns.

137 See a blog post by Wyn Grant, 'How and Why Farmers Voted on Brexit', 26 December 2016, available at commonagpolicy.blogspot.com/2016/12/how-and-why-did-farmers-vote-on-brexit.html.

138 In 2016, the (negative) operating balance of France in the EU budget (its share in total EU operating expenditure minus its 'national contributions') was −€8.17 billion. This is comparable to the combined (positive) operating EU budgetary balances of Poland and Lithuania (€7.13 billion and €1.15 billion, respectively) the same year: European Commission, EU Expenditure and Revenue 2014–2020, available at ec.europa.eu/budget/figures/interactive/index_en.cfm.

139 David Chazan, 'French Farmers Hope Marine Le Pen Will Free Them from EU "Straitjacket"', *The Telegraph*, 25 February 2017; Johnny Cotton, 'France's Disillusioned Farmers Turn to Le Pen', *Reuters*, 28 February 2017, available at www.reuters.com/article/us-france-election-farmers-idUSKBN16627O.

140 The most recent one took place in the dairy sector in 2016. It was caused by a combination of farmers taking advantage of lifting milk quotas the previous

lesson of Eastern and Southern Europe, where insufficient means and incentives for the relocation of the labour force from agriculture to more productive sectors have seriously contributed to centuries-long stagnation and backwardness.[141]

Fourth, and most importantly, the example of New Zealand makes it clear that removing farm subsidies altogether is a viable method of boosting the productivity of agriculture. Prior to 1984, when the subsidies were lifted in New Zealand,[142] agriculture there was

> heavily protected via subsidies and price and income support. Protection led to market distortions, over-production and degradation of marginal lands [land not suited for pastoral agriculture] ... Production no longer matched demand as subsidy-based production soared; the government paid for the slaughter of sheep that could not be sold and in 1983, 6,000 tons of surplus sheep meat was turned into fertilizer. By 1984, agricultural output was worth less than the costs of producing and processing it.[143]

The policy reversal introduced then (expectedly, against farmers' protests) ushered in agricultural diversification, innovation and productivity, which boosted the international competitiveness of New Zealand's agriculture.[144] The usage of fertilisers and pesticides simultaneously went down, to limit production costs, and marginal lands were largely reforested, because without subsidies cultivating them was no longer profitable. Hence the policy shift proved very environmentally

year, of the Russian food embargo and of falling animal feed costs boosting milk production: Emmet Livingstone, 'Europe Offers €500 Million to Help Dairy Farmers', *Politico*, 15 July 2016, available at www.politico.eu/article/europe-awaits-last-ditch-effort-to-save-its-milk-farms-commission-overproduction/.

141 Andrew C. Janos, 'The Politics of Backwardness in Continental Europe, 1780–1945', *World Politics* 41 (1989): 325–358; See Andrew C. Janos, *East Central Europe in the Modern World: The Politics of the Borderlands from Pre- to Postcommunism* (Stanford, CA: Stanford University Press, 2000).

142 For details, see Ron Sandrey and Russell Reynolds, eds, *Farming without Subsidies: New Zealand's Recent Experience* (Wellington: GP Books, 1990), or Ralph Lattimore, 'Farm Subsidy Reform Dividends', Paper prepared for the North American Agrifood Market Integration Consortium Meetings, 31 May–2 June 2006, Calgary, Alberta, available from www.staff.ncl.ac.uk.

143 'Removal of Agricultural and Fisheries Subsidies', available at www.cbd.int/financial/fiscalenviron/newzealand-subsidyfish.pdf.

144 After dismantling the system of agricultural subsidies in mid-1980s, the total factor productivity of the agricultural sector in New Zealand rose from 1.5 to 2.5 per cent: New Zealand Ministry of Agriculture and Forestry, 'Agriculture in New Zealand: Past, Present and Future', New Zealand Ministry of Agriculture and Forestry 2006.

friendly.[145] After three decades of economising on the distortive fiscal transfers damaging agricultural productivity and the environment alike, New Zealand could boast a large (5 per cent of GDP), exceptionally diversified and ultra-competitive agricultural production (about 90 per cent of it being exported globally).[146]

The experience of New Zealand suggests that doing away with all farm subsidies could lead to economically beneficial restructuring and innovation. It would end the embarrassing reality of giant food companies receiving millions in farm subsidies,[147] or the phenomenon of 'sofa farmers'.[148] First of all, however, it demonstrates tremendous opportunity costs of the current European budget.

To mitigate criticism, CAP defenders might highlight that, while in 1984 agriculture expenditures accounted for 66 per cent of the Community budget, this share had declined to 41 per cent by 2014 and will decrease further to 36 per cent by 2020. This still, however, betokens very high – and, gauging by the experience of New Zealand, highly distortive – redistribution between countries, regions and sectors. In the whole period from 2014 to 2020, resources committed to agricultural market-related expenditure and direct payments – the two schemes intended to maintain farmers' incomes – will amount to €309 billion, a figure roughly equivalent to all EU payment appropriations in 2018 and 2019.[149] In other words, two EU budgets out of seven in the period from 2014 to 2020 will be deployed to artificially boost incomes in the least productive economic sector, undermining its productivity further and depleting the increasingly scarce fiscal resources which could otherwise be used for delivering crucial public goods – core socio-economic polices and institutions – on which national prosperity and European integration critically hinges.

145 Vangelis Vitalis, 'Agricultural Subsidy Reform and Its Implications for Sustainable Development: The New Zealand Experience', *Environmental Sciences* 4 (2007): 21–40.

146 Mark Ross and Chris Edwards, 'In New Zealand, Farmers Don't Want Subsidies', Huffington Post, 16 September 2012, available at www.huffingtonpost.com/mark-ross/farm-subsidies-new-zealand_b_1680259.html.

147 Relevant information can be browsed at farmsubsidy.openspending.org/.

148 Decoupled payments essentially subsidise farmland ownership. Production efforts are purposefully sidelined within this type of payments.

149 The payment appropriations for the two years are €155 billion and €159 billion: European Commission, 'Multiannual Financial Framework Adjusted for 2018'.

8.11 Memento

Euroscepticism feeds on the paradoxes and ironies of European redistribution tackled in this chapter. Instead of trying to eradicate them and adjust policy processes and goals to the necessities of the evolving reality, European elites have been turning their eyes in the other direction, encouraging Europeans to do the same. This can only nurture among European societies a sense of detachment and remoteness from policymakers and their inability to deliver where their actions are badly needed.

The condensing reality of permanent austerity makes this setup unsustainable in the longer term. With annual UK net contributions to the EU budget gone after Brexit and with other net contributor countries, France and Italy in particular, struggling fiscally and economically, the current redistribution paradigms of the EU cannot survive very long. Unless reformed, they will pull the whole project under.

As I argued in this chapter, much more perfect redistributive policies are possible. The European Union can improve the lives of Europeans in all of the aspects crucial for their well-being now and in the future. Of course, it takes quite some political courage and imagination to get there, while courageous and far-seeing politicians have recently become a species close to extinction in European politics. But without this courage, the decades of efforts to integrate the continent may turn to ashes. If European leaders do not prevent it, history will not fail to judge them for what happens next.

Even, however, if the reforms envisaged in this and the previous chapters are accomplished – if the Eurozone is fixed and European redistribution rethought – European societies will still face serious side effects of the other two policies at the very heart of the economic integration: the internal market and the commercial policy. In these two, like in the policies discussed so far, European policymakers have been entrapped by time-inconsistent incentives and stalemates produced by unevenly distributed costs and benefits. There, too, seriously disintegrating effects have been brewing for years now. They have been building up gradually and, unless corrected, will erupt vehemently at some point. Also in these two areas reforms are both possible and badly needed to sustain the European project and European unity. And there, too, a bit of thinking outside the box is a prerequisite.

The nature of the internal market and the commercial policy is ultimately similar, as both deal with international trade; the former between EU countries, the latter with third countries. Both, also, have been based on the conviction that international trade is a good thing. As I will explain in the rest of this book, the paradigm is neither entirely right nor fundamentally wrong. But, because the similarities end here, and the two policies differ quite significantly in their details, in the next two chapters I will discuss them separately.

The internal market follows first.

9 The Internal Market: Disunited in Diversity

9.1 Two Sides

In Art. I-8 – on 'the symbols of the Union' – the European Constitution of 2004 proclaimed that 'the motto of the Union shall be: "United in diversity"'. The referenda that blew this Constitution away the next year demonstrated, however, that the societies of the founding countries, the French in particular, perceived the idea of economic integration with the post-communist countries differently. Even in these economically prosperous times they did not feel 'united in diversity' with a Polish plumber.

Soon after, the essence of the 2004 draft Constitution was reintroduced with much less fanfare as the Lisbon Treaty. The 'United in diversity' motto was enshrined by sixteen EU countries in a declaration annexed to this Treaty[1] and enthusiastically embraced by the European institutions. But, nonetheless, the idea of sharing one market with a Lithuanian or a Romanian construction or social assistance worker has become even more distasteful for many of the more affluent European societies. Many of them have additionally supported bans on new disruptive online services, like Uber or Airbnb, and have generally contested the idea of market liberalisation. Dovetailing with changing attitudes to international trade (more on this in the next chapter), a 'permissive

[1] Declaration No. 52, which says 'Belgium, Bulgaria, Germany, Greece, Spain, Italy, Cyprus, Lithuania, Luxemburg, Hungary, Malta, Austria, Portugal, Romania, Slovenia and the Slovak Republic declare that the flag with a circle of twelve golden stars on a blue background, the anthem based on the "Ode to Joy" from the Ninth Symphony by Ludwig van Beethoven, the motto "United in diversity", the euro as the currency of the European Union and Europe Day on 9 May will for them continue as symbols to express the sense of community of the people in the European Union and their allegiance to it'.

consensus' backing up 'the area without internal frontiers in which the free movement of goods, persons, services and capital is ensured in accordance with the provisions of the Treaties' – as Art. 26(2) TFEU defines the internal market – has morphed into a 'constraining dissensus'.[2] The dissensus has erupted in periodic bouts of Euroscepticism, tides of protectionist populism, deepened cleavages among European societies and confusion among European institutions.

All of this has both reinforced the ailments of the Eurozone and built on the frustrations about the economic effects of the single currency. The puzzle of the internal market disuniting European societies in their diversity, however, reaches deeper than the Eurozone divergences themselves. It goes straight to the heart of European economic integration after World War II: to the paradigm that economic prosperity and free trade are two sides of the same coin.

According to this traditional paradigm – ten, twenty or thirty years ago universally supported by national governments and European institutions alike – the internal market has very positive, even if largely unrealised, effects for all of the societies involved. This orthodox view sees free trade in Europe as the best possible engine of economic prosperity and integration, and blames sustained short-sighted protectionism for economic stagnation wherever it occurs.

Yet, recently this narrative has been challenged by a different – heterodox – one. It conceives of the internal market as a source of disruption and a force dismantling the socioeconomic foundations on which the economically more developed societies have traditionally built their stability. The internal market, according to these optics, induces a pernicious race to the bottom. This view holds that the internal market among societies as diverse as those comprising the EU now inevitably leads to social dumping, to the relocation of production to low-cost countries and to unemployment in the remaining part, undermining the social and political contracts on which postwar prosperity had been founded.

The two narratives could not be more discordant. The traditional view builds on the very intuitive assumption that the internal market leads to more optimal allocation of economic resources, because it allows them to flow from the areas where they are undervalued, due

[2] Liesbet Hooghe and Gary Marks, 'A Postfunctionalist Theory of European Integration: From Permissive Consensus to Constraining Dissensus', *British Journal of Political Science* 39 (2009): 1–23.

to their oversupply, to the regions where they are priced higher. The first of the areas is spared the opportunity costs of underutilising its resources, while the latter benefits from its improved capacity. Welfare thus grows in both areas.

According to this argument, streamlined flows of the two crucial economic factors – capital and labour – particularly enhance the process. The labour force mobility is 'expected to be beneficial to the European economy as firms have access to a larger pool of workers to recruit from, attracting more qualified workers at lower cost and reducing skill mismatches. A similar predicament applies to the free circulation of capital, which should guarantee that funds reach the most productive investment opportunities and companies, eventually boosting growth.'[3] In addition, the two processes are expected to be mutually stabilising, because the free flow of capital mitigates emigration from the regions where labour is cheap. Capital owners are expected to locate foreign direct investments in these regions if they can enjoy the free movement of capital and entrepreneurship.

Welfare should also improve indirectly, according to the traditional view, due to the stronger competition produced by increased cross-border flows of economic factors (capital, enterprise, labour) and products (goods, services). This mechanism, the argument goes, 'reduces distortions of the price mechanism and enables a more efficient allocation of resources and higher productivity … Higher competitive pressure also increases the incentives for the management to organise work more efficiently and to reduce slack, as well as potential gains from exploiting increasing returns to scale as market size increases (productive efficiency). Finally, competition might also raise dynamic efficiency by increasing incentives for R&D activities and innovations and thereby boosting technological progress and growth of total factor productivity.'[4]

In other words, under the pressure of the enhanced competition produced by broadening product markets, companies are encouraged to innovate[5] and to grow bigger in order to exploit economies of

[3] Mario Mariniello, André Sapir and Alessio Terzi, 'The Long Road Towards the European Single Market', *Bruegel Working Paper* No. 2015/01, 16 March 2015, 2–3, available at bruegel.org/2015/03/the-long-road-towards-the-european-single-market/.

[4] Herald Badinger et al., 'Macroeconomic Effects of the Services Directive', in: *Services Liberalisation in the Internal Market*, eds. Fritz Breuss, Gerhard Fink and Stefan Griller (Vienna; New York: Springer 2008): 128.

[5] Innovation reduces production costs and/or creates new (segments of) markets, on which their creators can exploit the innovation rent (technological leadership): Michele Boldrin and David K. Levine, 'Perfectly Competitive Innovation',

scale.[6] In both cases their goal is the same: to lower production costs. In consequence, resources should move from the entrepreneurs unable to 'reinvent themselves' along these lines, to their more efficient competitors, following the Schumpeterian paradigm of creative destruction.[7]

The heterodox perspective does not dispute any of these findings. It undermines, however, an important implicit assumption of the traditional view: that the growth of the economic pie due to the less encumbered trade and investments should always be appreciated by the societies involved. This stance posits that the 'creative destruction' propelled by free trade concentrates its benefits in the hands of a few, undermining the economic and social stability of the many. Similarly to the UEFA Champions League, enhanced competition benefits the best players tremendously. It also motivates juniors to achieve what seems impossible at first sight. But by design only a few of them can make it to the top. And the disparities between the champions and average players widen (wage inequalities grow) when the pool of competitors broadens. A recent global football employment report brings this point home, when it concludes that while players from the Big Five European leagues – Premier League, Bundesliga, La Liga, Serie A, Ligue 1 – enjoy exceptionally good working conditions, the majority of footballers 'are under constant pressure to extend their careers in professional football and face precarious employment conditions, including a large degree of personal and contractual abuse'.[8]

Translating this sports comparison to the social reality: the fact that the few most skilled and fortuitous win much more than the rest of society[9] entails economic and social conflicts that can be durably

Journal of Monetary Economics 55 (2008): 435–453; Philippe Aghion, Peter Howitt and Susanne Prantl, 'Revisiting the Relationship between Competition, Patenting, and Innovation', in: *Advances in Economics and Econometrics (Tenth World Congress, Volume 1, Economic Theory)*, eds. Daron Acemoglu, Manuel Arellano and Eddie Dekel (Cambridge: Cambridge University Press, 2013): 451–455.

6 Bigger firms can reduce production costs by spreading fixed costs over larger volumes of production.

7 Richard E. Baldwin and Charles Wyplosz, *The Economics of European Integration* (London: McGraw-Hill Higher Education, 2015).

8 FIFPro, 'The 2016 Global Employment Report. Top Findings', November 2016, 2, available at fifpro.org/attachments/article/6706/2016%20FIFPro%20Global%20Survey%20-%20TopFindings_1128.pdf.

9 Ariel Burstein and Jonathan Vogel, 'International Trade, Technology, and the Skill Premium', February 2016, available at www.columbia.edu/~jev9/BV-TTSP.pdf; Hartmut Egger and Udo Kreickemeier, 'Firm Heterogeneity and the Labor Market Effects of Trade Liberalization', *International Economic Review* 50 (2009): 187–216.

pacified only by appropriately fast and adequate adaptations in socioeconomic policies. Such adaptations are impossible without very resilient governance and political processes, which – as argued in the previous two chapters – are a scarce commodity in many European countries. When national and international societies become increasingly polarised, socioeconomic policies are even more contestable and feeble, in a circular process leading to even more polarisation and political instability.

9.2 The Golden Era of the Permissive Consensus

Until the Eastern European accessions to the EU, the relationship informing the heterodox view had been veiled by the confluence of income levels in the incumbent countries. Of course, Ireland, Spain, Portugal and Greece stood out, but each was catching up fast without producing any clear damage to the rest of the club. Throughout the 1990s and most of the next decade, arguing it would be different with Eastern Europe seemed entirely counterintuitive. If European integration, driven by the concept of the internal market, only gained in popularity after the previous accessions of the peripheral countries, then why would it be any different if it were to reach out to Bug River or to the Carpathians?

It was also universally believed that, due to the agglomeration effects highlighted in the previous chapter, it is ultimately the poorer regions of the Community that risked more by joining the common market, because capital allocated there may not be able to offset the brain-drain they would experience as a consequence of the facilitated emigration.

In addition, between the late 1970s and the Great Recession, i.e., during the three decades of 'permissive consensus', there was no serious ideological alternative to freeing trade and freeing markets. Neo-liberal thinking permeated academia, international economic organisations and all policymaking circles. Globalisation seemed fruitful and unstoppable. The main institutional agents behind the internal market – the Commission and the Court of Justice – preached to the universally espoused ideologies and they were applauded as knowledgeable drivers of what seemed to be the only way to European prosperity and unity.[10]

[10] See also Wayne Sandholtz and John Zysman, '1992: Recasting the European Bargain', *World Politics* 42 (1989): 95–128. Alternative explanations why the single market programme was so successful in the 1980s, from intergovernmental institutionalism (Andrew Moravcsik, 'Negotiating the Single European Act: National Interests and

Today, when the internal market has largely become bogged down in conflicting expectations, ideologies and interests, it may seem startling that it took the first Delors Commission, which assumed office in January 1985, less than six months to publish the 'Completing the Internal Market' White Paper[11] enlisting about 300 legislative measures to be adopted by the end of 1992. Only one year into this Commission's term, the Single European Act was adopted. Expectations, ideologies and interests of all the stakeholders involved congealed fast on the neo-liberal foundation. Incontestable in its substance, the political process defining the internal market became extremely effective as a result, rendering the Commission unprecedently successful politically.[12]

The contribution of the Court of Justice to the evolution of the internal market during the period of the permissive consensus was equally significant. It enthusiastically apprehended the neo-liberal ideology simply because it is inherently integrationist. Take as an example the famous *Dassonville* formula for the free movement of goods ('all trading rules enacted by Member States which are capable of hindering, directly or indirectly, actually or potentially, intra-community trade are to be considered as measures having an effect equivalent to quantitative restrictions').[13] Certainly, it connotes the classical Hayekan liberal justification of an interstate federation.[14] But its neo-liberal flavour is merely a by-product of the formula's main goal of uniting desegregated national markets.

This integrationist strategy did not progress unreflectively. As students of European law know well, the market-liberating thrust of *Dassonville* was soon refined in the *Cassis de Dijon* decision of 1978,

Conventional Statecraft in the European Community', *International Organization* 45 [1991]: 19–56) to the political role of non-state actors (Maria Green Cowles, 'Setting the Agenda for a New Europe: The ERT and EC 1992', *Journal of Common Market Studies* 33 [1995]: 501–526) do not preclude this conclusion. Rather, they make it clear that the dominant ideology was congruent with the interests of the parties involved, which additionally facilitated decision-making.

11 COM(85)310, 14 June 1985.

12 For a more nuanced picture on the role of the Commission, see, for example, Liesbet Hooghe, *The European Commission and the Integration of Europe: Images of Governance* (Cambridge: Cambridge University Press, 2001); Mark A. Pollack, *The Engines of European Integration: Delegation, Agency, and Agenda Setting in the EU* (Oxford: Oxford University Press, 2003).

13 Case 8–74, *Procureur du Roi* v. *Dassonville*, ECLI:EU:C:1974:82, § 5.

14 Accordingly, political integration makes it more difficult for states to influence – or, actually, distort – welfare-enhancing operations of market forces: Friedrich August von Hayek, 'The Economic Conditions of Interstate Federalism', in: *Individualism and Economic Order* (Chicago: University of Chicago Press, 1948): 255–272.

in which the Court transformed (when it comes to the movement of goods, at least) the crude original Treaty setup of exceptions to the free movement principle into a much more nuanced principle of mutual recognition. Accordingly, an importing country is obliged to respect the requirements set for the given product by the exporting country. It can impose additional requirements on the imports only insofar as they are justified by a proportionally applied overriding public interest.[15]

Interestingly, in the 1980s, when the Commission was enjoying its greatest integrationist successes, the Court was still cautious in its approach to what the internal market should entail. It went the whole way in the 1990s, when the Commission's preferences for European integration encountered first push-backs from national capitals.

This is when the Court extended the internal market freedoms to the situations with very weak, or actually non-existing, relationships to intra-Community trade. A few days before the Maastricht Treaty entered into force, the Advocate General Tesauro still answered the question 'Is Article 30 of the Treaty[16] a provision intended to liberalize intra-Community trade or is it intended more generally to encourage the unhindered pursuit of commerce in individual Member States?' in the negative.[17] But in 1997 the Court changed its mind and decided to apply the four market freedoms to 'purely internal situations', if hypothetically intra-Community trade could be affected by a national provision contested by an individual seeking protection under European law.[18]

[15] For a more nuanced discussion of the principle, see esp. Kenneth Armstrong, 'Mutual Recognition', in: *The Law of the Single European Market: Unpacking the Premises*, eds. Catherine Barnard and Joanne Scott (Oxford; Portland, OR: Hart Publishing, 2002): 225–267; Christine Janssens, *The Principle of Mutual Recognition in EU Law* (Oxford: Oxford University Press, 2013); Susanne Schmidt, *Mutual Recognition as a New Mode of Governance* (London: Routledge, 2013); Fiorella Kostoris Padoa Schioppa, *The Principles of Mutual Recognition in the European Integration Process* (New York: Palgrave Macmillan, 2005).

[16] Now Art. 34 TFEU, prohibiting quantitative restrictions on imports and all measures with equivalent effect.

[17] Opinion of Mr Advocate General Tesauro delivered on 27 October 1993, Case C-292/92, Ruth Hünermund and others, § 1.

[18] Case C-321/94, *Pistre and others*, ECLI:EU:C:1997:229. The Court noted in this case that internal market freedoms (free movement of goods in this particular case) 'cannot be considered inapplicable simply because all the facts of the specific case before the national court are confined to a single Member State. In such a situation, the application of the national measure may also have effects on the free movement of

This turn mitigated the so-called reverse discrimination problem[19] and reduced the scope of national measures exempt from the scrutiny of the Luxembourg Court. It was also strongly integrationist and market-liberalising, after, in decisions issued in the early 1990s, the logic of the *Cassis de Dijon* case (again: originally designed for the free movement of goods) was extended to the free movement of services and workers in particular[20] and to all 'fundamental freedoms guaranteed by the Treaty' more generally.[21]

Years later, this activist stance provoked worries that the Court conceived the internal market not as 'a programmatic goal to be realized through political legislation but as a set of directly enforceable individual rights'.[22] Yet, in the 1990s no one in the mainstream thought of it that way. It was partly due to the fact that the EU legislators were also very active and creative on how to advance the internal market. And partly it was inherent in the Community method, which assumes that 'political legislators' may need prodding by the depoliticised European institutions to overcome their short-sighted bickering and logrolling. The legal principles of direct effects and primacy of EU law, which entitled individuals to use internal market

goods between Member States, in particular when the measure in question facilitates the marketing of goods of domestic origin to the detriment of imported goods. In such circumstances, the application of the measure, even if restricted to domestic producers, in itself creates and maintains a difference of treatment between those two categories of goods, hindering, at least potentially, intra-Community trade' (§ 44–45). Two months later, the Court conflated this revolutionary idea with the argument for uniform application of EU law ('where, in regulating purely internal situations, domestic legislation adopts the same solutions as those adopted in Community law … it is clearly in the Community interest that, in order to forestall future differences of interpretation, provisions or concepts taken from Community law should be interpreted uniformly, irrespective of the circumstances in which they are to apply'): Case C-28/95 *Leur-Bloem* ECLI:EU:C:1997:369, § 32). See also Harris Tagaras, 'Règles Communautaires de Libre Circulation, Discriminations à Rebours et Situations Dites Purement Internes', *Mélanges en hommage à Michel Waelbroeck*, Volume II, Bruylant, 1999.

19 Discrimination of a country's nationals against foreigners from other EU countries. See esp. Alina Tryfonidou, 'Purely Internal Situations and Reverse Discrimination in a Citizens' Europe: Time to "Reverse" Reverse Discrimination?', in: *Issues in Social Policy: A New Agenda. Jean Monnet Seminar Series*, ed. Peter G. Xuereb (Valletta: Progress Press, 2009): 11–29.

20 Janssens, *The Principle of Mutual Recognition*, 14–17.

21 Case C-55/94 *Gebhard*, ECLI:EU:C:1995:411, § 37.

22 Fritz Scharpf, 'Legitimacy in the Multilevel European Polity', *European Political Science Review* 1 (2009): 176.

freedoms as a weapon against domestic economic restrictions, now conflated with the market-liberalising stance of the Court of Justice. They both legitimised the policies of the 'depoliticised' supranational institutions and seriously broadened their influence. Europeans had individual stakes in the market liberalisation, and they could press for it in the courts. According to the view universally espoused back then, the Court of Justice would help liberate them from market-interfering grasps of national governments for the sake of higher economic growth and closer European integration. As Agustín Menéndez put it aptly, 'according to that understanding, European integration should be a matter of disempowering states and empowering economic actors through the assignment of hierarchical and normative priority to economic freedoms'.[23] Private autonomy, economic citizenship, non-discrimination and equality[24] would go hand-in-hand with market efficiency, enhanced competition and liberalisation. They would all be conceived of as supporting and reinforcing the European project.

9.3 The First Disruption: The Bolkestein Directive

And then, in a chain reaction, it all broke down soon after the Eastern European countries joined the EU. The hostility to the 'Polish plumber' in many Western societies marked the eve of the heterodox narrative, which pronouncedly gained traction in the aftermath of the Great Recession and the Eurozone crisis.

In January 2004, only a few months before the first 'Eastern' accession, the Commission published its draft Services Directive (the Bolkestein Directive).[25] In its four most controversial articles (Arts. 16–19) the draft provided as a general rule what could otherwise seem a logical next step in the evolution of the internal market. The Commission wanted to further refine the mutual recognition principle, which, as I mentioned earlier, governed the free movement of services since the landmark Court decisions in the 1990s, by specifying the circumstances in which

[23] Agustín Menéndez, 'The Existential Crisis of the European Union', *German Law Journal* 14 (2013): 472–473.

[24] See also Eleanor Spaventa, 'From Gebhard to Carpenter: Towards a (Non-) Economic European Constitution', *Common Market Law Review* 41 (2004): 743–773.

[25] COM(2004)2. For a discussion on the relationship between the directive and the French and Dutch referenda, see Emiliano Grossman and Cornelia Woll, 'The French Debate on the Bolkestein Directive', *Comparative European Politics* 9 (2011): 344–366.

the host country can exercise its powers to impose any additional mandatory requirements on service providers from other EU countries.

The intention was clearly to facilitate inter-country trade in services by making it more difficult for the host country to protect its service providers. Typically for the traditional approach to the internal market, it was assumed that more trade would lead to higher economic growth and to more jobs. Services, according to this argument, 'amount to 70% of the GDP of most Member States, but only to 20% of the cross-national exchange of goods and services … The potential of a liberalised market of the provision of services is thereby estimated to mount up to several hundred thousands of jobs.'[26]

The more heterodox perspective, which ultimately prevailed in the legislative process, held that further facilitations of the inter-state trade in services would propel a powerful 'regulatory competition'[27] process. The traditional view never denied this effect, assuming, instead, that it was a necessary precondition for the 'creative destruction': the main modernising force behind the internal market. It turned out, however, that many Western societies sensed that with the admission of several low-cost countries to the EU pains and gains of this competition would be very unequally distributed. They feared that the *creation* would tend to flow to the East, and the *destruction* to the West.

The final piece of legislation, adopted in late 2006[28] – when the European Constitution was already shattered as collateral damage of Western worries – was devoid of the country-of-origin principle. Instead, it envisaged a pattern of mutual recognition closely following the standard developed independently by the Court of Justice.[29]

[26] Armin Hatje, 'Services Directive – A Legal Analysis', in: *Services Liberalisation in the Internal Market*, eds. Fritz Breuss, Gerhard Fink and Stefan Griller (Vienna, New York: Springer 2008): 4.

[27] Bruno De Witte, 'Setting the Scene: How Did Services Get to Bolkestein and Why?', *EUI Working Paper* No. 2007/20.

[28] Adopted as directive 2006/123/EC of the European Parliament and of the Council of 12 December 2006 on services in the internal market, OJ 2006 No. L 376, 27 December 2006, pp. 36–68. For a comprehensive legal discussion, see Catherine Barnard, 'Unravelling the Services Directive', *Common Market Law Review* 45 (2008): 323–394.

[29] As Bruno De Witte noted in 'Setting the Scene', there is one exception to it. Namely, Art. 16(3) Directive 2006/123/EC establishes a closed list of overriding public interests justifying restrictions to the free movement (public policy, public security, public health or the protection of the environment), while the list of such public interests admitted by the Court of Justice when interpreting the Treaty is open-ended. This

Even in this watered-down version the Services Directive generated, according to the Commission's calculations published in 2012, 'an additional 0.81% of EU GDP, with the majority of effects materializing during the 5–10 years following implementation'.[30] The Commission's staff even argued that this estimation did not account for additional long-term effects of the increased cross-border trade in services and of cross-border foreign direct investments in the service sectors,[31] assessed at 7 and 4 per cent of EU GDP, respectively.[32]

On the one hand, these computations suggest merits of harmonisation (even when it amounts to codifying case-law only).[33] On the other, the Commission's estimates should be viewed with caution, because the Directive use suasion rather than any new obligations seriously altering the mechanics of the internal market as the means for achieving its goals. In consequence, those who analysed its implementation in the first few years after the directive was adopted came to the

does not make any practical difference, however, because the Court has been explicit that the conformity with secondary law does not exempt a national measure from the scrutiny under Treaty rules on the internal market. See Case C-211/08, *Commission v. Spain*, ECLI:EU:C:2010:340, § 45.

30 European Commission, 'Detailed Information on the Implementation of Directive 2006/123/EC on Services in the Internal Market Accompanying the Document Communication from the Commission to the European Parliament, the Council, the European Economic and Social Committee and the Committee of the Regions on the Implementation of the Services Directive. A Partnership for New Growth in Services 2012–2015', Brussels, 8 June 2012, SWD(2012)148, 7.

31 The effects on the foreign direct investments stem from the directive's provisions much less contestable than the country-of-origin principle. Namely, the directive nudged the Member States into simplifying administrative formalities related to the provision of services within its remit (Art. 5), into establishing points of single contact helping prospective service providers get through the related administrative formalities (Arts. 6 and 7) and into delivering e-government solutions facilitating interactions with national administrations (Art. 8). It also guided the Member States on how to handle administrative slack related to authorisation schemes preconditioning permanent service activity (Arts. 9–15).

32 Josefa Monteagudo, Aleksander Rutkowski and Dimitri Lorenzani, 'The Economic Impact of the Services Directive: A First Assessment Following Implementation', *European Economy, Economic Papers* No. 456, June 2012, Brussels, available at ec.europa.eu/economy_finance/publications/economic_paper/2012/pdf/ecp_456_en.pdf.

33 Interestingly, however, while in 2008 trade in services covered by the Services Directive amounted to 63 per cent of all intra-EU trade in services, the services within the remit of this Directive comprised only 28 per cent of intra-EU foreign direct investments in services: Federica Mustilli and Jacques Pelkmans, 'Securing EU Growth from Services', *CEPS Special Report* No. 67, October 2012, available at www.ceps.eu/system/files/Securing%20EU%20Growth%20from%20Services.pdf.

conclusion that this EU act was used as a liberalisation tool only where the governments otherwise pursued liberalisation agendas (esp. Poland and Ireland).[34] In addition, any remaining positive effects of the administrative streamlining on economic growth, if any, were soon dwarfed by the effects of the Great Recession and the Eurozone crisis.

Paradoxically, therefore, in economic terms the directive largely 'started as a tiger but ended as a bedside carpet'.[35] But politically it gave birth to a wild beast, catalysing the moment for the constraining dissensus to mature.

9.4 The Second Disruption: Patient Mobility

The fledgling constraining dissensus was reinforced by some of the Court's decisions, in which the internal market freedoms forayed into politically sensitive, and previously considered as firmly remaining within national prerogatives, policies governing patient mobility.[36]

The strand of cases on trans-border patient rights started in the 'good old 1990s' and gradually reached its apex in 2006, provoking a seemingly conformable legislative reaction, undergirded, however, by a deeper backlash and administrative resistance at the national level.[37]

It is less relevant for my argument here how the case law evolved.[38] More important is that in its 2006 decision the Court vindicated a claim

[34] Ulrich Stelkens, Wolfgang Weiß and Michael Mirschberger, *The Implementation of the EU Services Directive: Transposition, Problems and Strategies* (The Hague: TMC Asser Press by Springer, 2012). Other researchers studying thirteen EU countries and three service sectors (business services, construction and tourism) concluded that there was a great variation in national regulatory approaches and in the number of regulated professions (from sixteen in Finland to fifty-five in Germany): Centre for Strategy and Evaluation Services, 'Study to Provide an Inventory of Reserves of Activities Linked to Professional Qualifications Requirements in 13 Member States and Assessing Their Economic Impact', for DG Internal Market, European Commission, January 2012.

[35] Armin Hatje, 'Services Directive – A Legal Analysis', in: *Services Liberalisation in the Internal Market*, eds. Fritz Breuss, Gerhard Fink and Stefan Griller (Vienna; New York: Springer 2008): 2.

[36] For a broader account of the phenomenon see Hans-W Micklitz and Bruno De Witte, eds., *The European Court of Justice and the Autonomy of the Member States* (Cambridge; Antwerp; Portland, OR: Intersentia, 2012).

[37] For an authoritative discussion of the legal systemic context, see esp. Tamara K. Hervey and Jean V. McHale, *European Union Health Law. Themes and Implications* (Cambridge: Cambridge University Press, 2015).

[38] For broader discussions, see, for example, Dorte Sindbjerg Martinsen and Karsten Vrangbæk, 'The Europeanization of Health Care Governance: Implementing the Market Imperatives of Europe', *Public Administration* 86 (2008): 169–184; Julio Baquero Cruz, 'The Case Law of the European Court of Justice on the Mobility of Patients: An

of a UK patient, under the free movement of services, for reimbursement by the UK National Health Service (NHS) for her surgery undertaken in France, after she was put on a long waiting list for the same operation in the UK.[39] This decision was unexpected, to say the least, because UK healthcare is organised as a benefits-in-kind system. Patients may only receive the services it offers; they cannot be reimbursed for any treatment outside of it. Hence, the non-economic nature of the services provided by the NHS was very clear. And if there is no market, it is unclear at best why the internal market freedoms should still apply to it. In addition, the secondary law of the EU clearly provided that national authorities were competent to authorise patient mobility.[40] The Court's decision seemed to deprive them of this authority.

Congruently with the intrinsically market-liberalising nature of its case law, the Court disregarded such counterarguments, preordaining that because someone (e.g., a taxpayer) pays for healthcare services, and because the trans-border nature of the situation at hand was very obvious, the case should be scrutinised from the perspective of fundamental internal market freedoms.[41] After scrutiny it came to the conclusion that a prior authorisation to receive healthcare services abroad cannot be refused if the same or equally effective treatment cannot be given in good time in the Member State of residence of the person concerned.[42]

In this case, as well as in its subsequent decisions upholding this line, the Court emphasised that preventing the risk of serious harm to the financial balance of the social security system may in principle justify free-movement restrictions.[43] So can 'the objective of maintaining a balanced medical and hospital service open to all'.[44] But, typically for

Assessment', in: *Source Services and the EU Citizen*, ed. Frank S. Benyon (Oxford; Portland: Hart Publishing, 2013): 87–111.

[39] Case C-372/04, *Watts*, ECLI:EU:C:2006:325.

[40] Art. 22(1)(c) Regulation 1408/71 of the Council of 14 June 1971 on the application of social security schemes to employed persons and their families moving within the Community, O.J. 1971 L 149, 5 July 1971, pp. 2–50, provides that 'a worker who satisfies the conditions of the legislation of the competent State for entitlement to benefits' shall be entitled to 'receive appropriate treatment abroad' if (among others) '*authorised by the competent institution to go to the territory of another Member State*' (my emphasis).

[41] Case C-372/04, *Watts*, ECLI:EU:C:2006:325, § 86–90.

[42] In fact, this condition was inferred from *Watts* by subsequent case law. See Case C-268/13, *Petru*, ECLI:EU:C:2014:2271, § 31.

[43] Case C-341/08, *Petersen*, ECLI:EU:C:2010:4, § 45.

[44] Case C-490/09, *European Commission* v. *Grand Duchy of Luxemburg*, ECLI:EU:C:2011:34, § 43.

the traditional approach to the internal market, it has interpreted these interests restrictively through its demanding proportionality standard.

The patient mobility case law was confusing for national policymakers, because it instantiated a judicial micromanagement into national systems, inducing tensions in particular wherever the systems were construed as non-economic and solidaristic. It also posed the question of whether there are any inherently non-economic services shielded from the market-liberalising influence of the Court of Justice.[45]

The patient mobility decisions could not provoke accusations of any social dumping or a race to the bottom, however, because they were aimed to augment the pressure on some of the healthcare systems (those performing worse) and to generate more demand for healthcare services in others (those performing better). By the very same token they promised more revenues to well-organised systems and less demand for services in the systems offering lower quality. The message this entailed for the Member States was easy to comprehend and compelling: national healthcare systems should be efficient enough to meet the needs of patients. Otherwise, they may face the burden of reimbursing treatments abroad. The easiest third way, of failing to provide access to treatment at home and refusing it abroad, would not be tolerated.[46] The

[45] In a decision laid down in 2012, when the permissive consensus was already broken, the Court dismissed a Commission infringement case against Germany, in which the non-portability of German sickness benefits relating to the risk of reliance on care was questioned. In this case the Commission followed the argument, stemming from the case law on medical benefits, that payment modalities for the service are irrelevant in the assessment of the national measure under the internal market freedoms. The Court disagreed, positing, among others, that 'unlike sickness benefits in respect of medical treatment, benefits relating to the risk of reliance on care – being generally long-term benefits – are not, in principle, intended to be paid on a short-term basis' (Case C-562/10, *European Commission* v. *Federal Republic of Germany*, ECLI:EU:C:2012:442, § 51). This turnaround must have been baffling for the Commission, as in *Watts* the Court was explicit that 'Article 49 EC applies where a patient ... receives medical services ... for consideration in a Member State other than her State of residence, regardless of the way in which the national system with which that person is registered and from which reimbursement of the cost of those services is subsequently sought operates' (§ 90). Soon after, the Court held back attempts of private healthcare providers to force market deregulation in other areas as well. For a broader discussion of this case law, see Rebecca Zahn, 'The Regulation of Healthcare in the European Union: Member States' Discretion or a Widening of EU Law? Femarbel and Ottica New Line', *Common Market Law Review* 51 (2014): 1521–1538.

[46] See also Cases C-512/08 *European Commission* v. *French Republic*, ECLI:EU:C:2010:579 and C-173/09, *Elchinov*, ECLI:EU:C:2010:581, C-255/09, *European Commission* v. *Portuguese Republic*, ECLI:EU:C:2011:695. The most striking of all the cases is C-268/13 *Petru*, ECLI:EU:C:2014:2271, in which a Romanian patient sought access to German hospital

decisions could therefore be perplexing in the political terms of the distribution of powers between the EU and the national governments. But they could not seriously undermine the market-liberalising philosophy prevailing in the Court's approach to the internal market.

9.5 The Third Disruption: The Right to Strike

The situation changed, however, when in 2007 the Court applied the same philosophy to the conflict, which had already surfaced in the Services Directive debacle, between the interests of workers in the low-cost and the high-cost EU countries. This conflict was laid bare in particular in two decisions – *Laval* and *Viking*[47] – in which the fundamental market freedoms ultimately prevailed over the fundamental right to strike of workers in more affluent EU countries.

In the first of the two cases, collective actions of Swedish trade unions targeted entrepreneurs hiring Latvian posted workers (and remunerating them according to Latvian standards) to perform a construction contract in Sweden. In the other it aimed to dissuade a Finnish shipowner from reflagging a ferry from Finland to Estonia to reduce costs. In both the Court paid lip service to the right to collective action, finding, however, that it would disproportionally curtail internal market freedoms.

To many observers the Court went too far, so unambiguously prioritising internal market freedoms over the right to industrial action.[48] When the Great Recession and the sovereign debt crisis in the Eurozone additionally kindled anti-liberalisation moods, many EU law scholars – the vast majority of whom had previously supported the

treatment because the hospital in Romania 'did not have basic medical supplies such as painkillers, antiseptic/disinfectant, absorbent cotton wool or sterile dressings. Furthermore, the hospital had a high volume of patients, with, on average, three times as many patients as beds' (opinion of Advocate General Villalón delivered on 19 June 2014, par. 6). The CJEU agreed. See also Vassilis Hatzopoulos, 'Some Thoughts on the Fate of Poorer Member States' Healthcare Systems after the Ruling in Elena Petru', *European Law Review* 41 (2016): 424–430 and Barend van Leeuwen, 'The Doctor, the Patient, and EU Law: The Impact of Free Movement Law on Quality Standards in the Healthcare Sector', *European Law Review* 41 (2016): 638–654.

[47] Case C-438/05, *Viking*, ECLI:EU:C:2007:772; Case C-341/05, *Laval*, ECLI:EU:C:2007:809. The number of critical comments published in law journals only is already too big to quote here. For an extensive list of annotations (and one of very few defences of this case law), see Damjan Kukovec, 'Law and the Periphery', *European Law Journal* 21 (2015): 406–428.

[48] See note 47.

permissive consensus – now used the two cases as crown arguments that the traditional paradigm had gone astray. They argued that the case-law favours 'the asymmetrical bias that exists in the Union – simply put, capital extracts a bias by virtue of its greater mobility'.[49] By the same token the internal market, for decades conceived as a vehicle for economic welfare, prosperity and integration, now became a wedge between society and the market, driven by capital owners only to serve their anti-communal interests.

The Court of Justice, formerly praised for its individualistic and rights-based approach to the fundamental freedoms, was now deplored as an agent of social and political depravation. Ashiagbor, for instance, argued that 'the judicial efforts we can observe to re-embed the market have done so within a version of the social based on a narrow conception of social citizenship that is potentially destructive of the national version'.[50] Crespy and Menz asserted acerbically that the CJEU performs its market-building role 'in fairly aggressive and intrusive ways, meddling with the national regulation of labour markets and wage levels that are unprecedented and far-reaching in range'.[51] Other commentators went even further, claiming that 'the love of the CJEU for the individual European – the desire that all should be given opportunity – coincides happily with the frontier-busting universalism of neo-liberal precepts, and is transformed into a legal semantic of economic technology, which isolates and atomises the individual as a homo economicus … The European citizen is reborn as a unit of economic production and is divorced from the social collectives in which values of ethics and solidarity might be politically established.'[52]

Those who criticised the *Laval* and *Viking* decisions routinely claimed that the Court's understanding of the internal market developed throughout the decades of the permissive consensus violates a conceptual precept predating the neo-liberal thinking. According to it,

[49] Floris de Witte, 'EU Law, Politics, and the Social Question', *German Law Journal* 14 (2013): 607.

[50] Diamond Ashiagbor, 'Unravelling the Embedded Liberal Bargain: Labour and Social Welfare Law in the Context of EU Market Integration', *European Law Journal* 19 (2013): 319.

[51] Georg Menz and Amandine Crespy, 'Introduction: The Pursuit of Social Europe in the Face of Crisis', in: *Social Policy and the Eurocrisis: Quo Vadis Social Europe*, eds. Georg Menz and Amandine Crespy (Basingstoke: Palgrave Macmillan, 2015): 12.

[52] Michelle Everson and Christian Joerges, 'Reconfiguring the Politics–Law Relationship in the Integration Project through Conflicts–Law Constitutionalism', *European Law Journal* 18 (2012): 662.

disruptive consequences of market competition should not undermine the political and social reality in which markets are embedded. Because the proper operation of national markets depends on how they interact with the social and political contexts, the argument goes, by interfering with the latter the EU has destabilised the national markets upon which all the main goals of the integration depend. In particular the free movement rights, when approached as sweeping principles, push 'social market economies' towards 'liberal market economies' regardless of the will of national or European political institutions.[53] Accordingly, the Court undermined the basic requirements of subsidiarity[54] and of proportionality,[55] as well as rudimentary precepts of social cohesion and democratic self-determination[56] when ignoring this relationship.

Judges deciding both *Laval* and *Viking* must have been surprised by the merciless attacks their decisions attracted. After all, the two cases essentially boiled down to the question of whether EU law should tolerate industrial actions of trade unions, undertaken in accordance with national law but effectively driving companies trying to exercise internal market rights out of business. Answering the question in the affirmative would upend what the Court so assiduously defended for all the decades of the permissive consensus: that restrictions to the internal market should be interpreted restrictively and that economic protectionism should never justify them. The finding that a

[53] Fritz Scharpf, 'The Asymmetry of European Integration, or Why the EU Cannot Be a "Social Market Economy"', *Socio-Economic Review* 8 (2010): 211–250.

[54] In the context of labour market policies Elise Muir argued, for instance, that 'different Member States may have different perceptions of the needs, and the relevant national authorities are in a better position than the CJEU to assess these requirements': Elise Muir, *EU Regulation of Access to Labour Markets. A Case Study of EU Constraints on Member State Competences* (Alphen aan den Rijn: Kluwer Law International, 2012), 202.

[55] de Witte, 'EU Law, Politics', 607–608.

[56] Martin Höpner and Armin Schäfer, 'A New Phase of European Integration: Organized Capitalisms in Post-Ricardian Europe', *West European Politics* 33 (2010): 344–368; Diamond Ashiagbor, 'Collective Labor Rights and the European Social Model', *Law & Ethics of Human Rights* 3 (2009): 222–266; Floris de Witte, 'The Architecture of a 'Social Market Economy', *LSE Legal Studies Working Paper* No. 13/2015, June 2015; Ben Crum, 'Saving the Euro at the Cost of Democracy?', *Journal of Common Market Studies* 51 (2013): 614–630; Wolfgang Streeck, *Buying Time: The Delayed Crisis of Democratic Capitalism* (London: Verso Books, 2014); Chantal Euzéby, 'Social Protection to Achieve Sustainable Inclusion: A European Imperative in the Current Economic Crisis', *International Social Security Review* 65 (2012): 69–88; Fritz Scharpf, 'Perpetual Momentum: Directed and Unconstrained?', *Journal of European Public Policy* 19 (2012): 127–139.

collective action of trade unions hindering internal market freedoms is compliant with EU law whenever it complies with national law would also encourage national governments to block competition from Eastern European service providers merely by enabling trade unions to boycott Eastern European companies.[57] It would also put governments of the high-wage countries in a schizophrenic situation. They would be required to respect both the internal market freedoms of low-wage workers and the right of high-wage trade unions to prevent it.

Detractors of the Court of Justice were less interested in these legal nuances. Instead, they were asking a bigger question: should the EU tolerate the situation in which company management gets an upper hand over local workers simply by hinting it would replace them with much cheaper Eastern posted workers or it would relocate production to Eastern Europe? As I mentioned earlier, the permissive consensus implied an affirmative response to this question, just like it shrugged off the consequences of the most debilitating face of the internal market for the new countries: the very significant brain-drain stemming from wage differentials.[58] The constraining dissensus has been questioning this answer, however, highlighting deleterious social consequences of such an indifferent system.

9.6 The Upper Hand of National Politics

Even if the underlying concerns are perfectly legitimate, the next question is if they target the right villain when directed at the supranational institutions. No doubt the Eastern accessions profoundly changed the EU both politically and economically. But the internal market rules essentially remained the same after 2004. It is therefore natural that the Court of Justice (and the Commission) also stayed the course in interpreting what EU law allowed for, and what it prohibited,

[57] It would therefore undermine the very foundation of EU law on horizontal effects of the internal market freedoms. According to it, the freedoms restrain both 'the action of public authorities' and 'rules of any other nature aimed at regulating in a collective manner gainful employment and the provision of services'. Case 36/74 *Walrave and Koch* (Case 36/74) ECLI:EU:C:1974:140, § 17.

[58] For recent evidence on the scale of high-skill migration from the EU 12, see Aaron Clauset, 'The Negative Impact of EU Enlargement', *Science* 356 (2017), 14 April 2017, 149–150.

in this respect.[59] It is also expectable that in a different context the same interpretation would have different practical implications.

Cases like *Laval* or *Viking* vividly demonstrated the resultant tension and fed into the mounting constraining dissensus. The fact that the process was triggered by the Court of Justice naturally drew attention to its role, regardless of whether its decisions were really that significant in practice. An influential paper of Fritz Scharpf expressed the growing groundswell of suspicion towards the role of the Court on the internal market when it depicted Member State governments as largely helpless victims of European joint-decision traps, which hinder them from effectuating positive integration more generally, and from harmonising social policies in particular.[60] On the other hand, the rights-based toolbox of the Court of Justice does not allow it to substitute the legislators in establishing social entitlements. It can only liberalise and deregulate, the argument goes. And when it does so, national governments have no choice but to follow suit.

This depiction misses some important points, however. In the period of the permissive consensus the Court of Justice and the Commission could indeed hope that national governments would also play the same deregulating game. But in all of the thorny legal areas discussed so far in this chapter – the Services Directive, cross-border patient rights and the trade-off between the internal market and the right to industrial action – national governments firmly held an upper hand of the final legal and policy landscape. Neither the Commission nor the Court succeeded in challenging them.

As I mentioned earlier, the final Bolkestein Directive only codified the earlier EU law on the provision of services and employed soft suasion in advancing the freedom of establishment. It also dropped all of the more detailed contestable rules, like the obligation to incur

[59] Stephanie Reynolds argued that the legal salience of the internal market freedoms has been imposed by the logic of the Treaty: Stephanie Reynolds, 'Explaining the Constitutional Drivers behind a Perceived Judicial Preference for Free Movement over Fundamental Rights', *Common Market Law Review* 53 (2016): 643–677. As she concluded: 'The Rome Treaty presented free movement as a principal tool for the attainment of its primary goal of economic integration. Crucially, it made no provision for the protection of fundamental rights. The centrality of the market freedoms to core EEC objectives, as well as the textual structure of the free movement provisions, naturally invited a judicial approach to resolving tensions between free movement and opposing law and policy that prioritized the former' (p. 675).

[60] Scharpf, 'The Asymmetry of European Integration',

costs of treatments abroad by national social security systems.[61] This directive, therefore, was an outright victory for national governments and a crippling failure for the Commission.

Similarly, when a few years later the Commission endeavoured to imbue the draft directive on the application of patients' rights in cross-border healthcare[62] with a market-liberalising thrust, national governments held it back again, making sure the final text would not influence the organisation of national healthcare systems outside the narrow category of cross-border healthcare.[63] They also shunned administrative adjustments facilitating cross-border healthcare,[64] effectively depriving supranational institutions of their appetite to liberalise (or force national governments to create) healthcare markets.

Nor has the Commission's draft Monti II Regulation[65] – which strived to respond legislatively to the *Laval* and *Viking* decisions by transposing the Court's reading of the primary law to a piece of secondary legislation – flown anywhere. National parliaments successfully triggered the 'yellow card'[66] procedure and had the Commission withdraw the

[61] Art. 23 of the 2004 draft.

[62] Directive 2011/24/EU of the European Parliament and of the Council of 9 March 2011 on the application of patients' rights in cross-border healthcare, OJ 2011 No. L 88/45, 4 April 2011, p. 45–65.

[63] Art. 1(4) Directive 2011/24/EU provides that '[t]his Directive shall not affect laws and regulations in Member States relating to the organisation and financing of healthcare in situations not related to cross-border healthcare. In particular, nothing in this Directive obliges a Member State to reimburse costs of healthcare provided by healthcare providers established on its own territory if those providers are not part of the social security system or public health system of that Member State.'

[64] See also Scott Greer and Holly Jarman, 'Managing Risks in EU Health Services Policy: Spot Markets, Legal Certainty and Bureaucratic Resistance', *Journal of European Social Policy* 22 (2012): 259–272.

[65] Proposal for a Council Regulation on the exercise of the right to take collective action within the context of the freedom of establishment and the freedom to provide services, COM(2012)130.

[66] Under the so-called Early Warning System established by Protocol No. 2 on the Application of the Principles of Subsidiarity and Proportionality annexed to the Lisbon Treaty, 'any national Parliament or any chamber of a national Parliament may … send to the Presidents of the European Parliament, the Council and the Commission a reasoned opinion stating why it considers that the draft in question does not comply with the principle of subsidiarity' (Art. 6). If reasoned opinions on a draft legislative act's non-compliance with the principle of subsidiarity are submitted by at least one-third of all the votes allocated to the national Parliaments, 'the draft must be reviewed' (Art. 7(2)).

draft in September 2012.[67] This fact could seem on the face of it to corroborate the finding that internal market harmonisation has not been able to mitigate the effects of the Court's case law. But, instead, it marginalised the decisions of the Luxembourg Court. Without clear secondary law provisions to be internalised by national authorities, the Court's predicates have remained too vague to substantially alter national arrangements. As a result, the judicial decisions, initially conceived by many academics as particularly disruptive for national legal, social and political setups, have not been able to influence them in any systemic manner.[68]

9.7 Hoisted by Their Own (Posting of Workers) Petard

More recent initiatives to reform the Posting of Workers Directive have painted the same picture of national politics dominating the debate. Here, however, more than in any other area, the chasm between high-wage and low-wage countries has fuelled debilitating political processes, and the Commission more conspicuously than ever has broken up with the traditional approach to the internal market.

The Posting of Workers Directive[69] is devised for situations in which foreign service providers recruit workers in their countries of origin and post them to another Member State to carry out a service. It harmonises minimum conditions on which host Member States can impose terms and conditions of employment on posted workers.[70] Most

[67] The decision to withdraw the draft was published in OJ 2013 No. C 109/7. See also Marco Goldoni, 'The Early Warning System and the Monti II Regulation: The Case for a Political Interpretation', *European Constitutional Law Review*, 10 (2014): 90–108.

[68] The 2007 Court decisions have entailed legislative amendments only in Denmark and Sweden. In both cases they were couched very cautiously: see Jonas Malmberg, 'The Impact of the CJEU Judgements on Viking, Laval, Rueffert and Luxemburg on the Practice of Collective Bargaining and the Effectiveness of Social Action', European Parliament Study, May 2010, available at www.europarl.europa.eu/document/activities/cont/201107/20110718ATT24274/20110718ATT24274EN.pdf. See also Mark Freedland and Jeremias Prassl, eds., *Viking, Laval and Beyond* (Oxford: Hart Publishing, 2015); Michael Blauberger, 'With Luxembourg in Mind ... The Remaking of National Policies in the Face of CJEU Jurisprudence', *Journal of European Public Policy* 19 (2012): 109–126.

[69] Directive 96/71/EC of the European Parliament and of the Council of 16 December 1996 concerning the posting of workers in the framework of the provision of services, OJ 1997 No. L 18, 21 January 1997, pp. 1–6.

[70] Namely, maximum work periods and minimum rest periods; minimum paid annual holidays; the minimum rates of pay, including overtime rates; this point does not apply to supplementary occupational retirement pension schemes; the conditions of hiring-out of workers, in particular the supply of workers by temporary employment

importantly, its version in force when this book goes to press provides that host Member States can establish minimum rates of pay applicable to posted workers, but only by national legislation (or 'administrative provision'), or by universally applicable collective agreements.[71] By the same token, it precludes industry-level or company-level collective agreements from entailing similar effects.

In 1996, when the directive was adopted, it could be considered mainly as a method of disempowering trade unions, neatly dovetailing with the economic ideologies of the permissive consensus. It was weakening the position of the unions in any collective bargaining, because their outcome could not influence posted workers. Trade union leaders must have considered that by raising their expectations in the bargaining process, they reinforce the motivation of employers to replace local workers with cheaper posted foreigners. It was quite predictable that this process would reach a whole new level after the 2004 enlargement. But this was not something EU 15 leaders would necessarily dislike, because it allowed them to tighten their hold of trade unions. The directive was not amended, therefore, in the run-up to the enlargement.

This neo-liberal logic was clear to see for everyone involved, including European institutions. So while the preamble to the directive gives the Court some latitude to soften its constraints on the host countries,[72] this institution should not be condemned for not trying to openly reinterpret the directive's main – and unequivocal – provisions. What it could be expected to do when the topic became heavily political was to extend the leeway available to Member States when establishing minimum pay conditions for posted workers by means of non-discriminatory legislation.[73] Arguably, this stance has given national governments a chance

undertakings; health, safety and hygiene at work; protective measures with regard to the terms and conditions of employment of pregnant women or women who have recently given birth, of children and of young people; equality of treatment between men and women and other provisions on non-discrimination: Art. 3(1) Directive.

[71] Art. 3(1). In Art. 3(8) the Directive provides for an extended definition of what the phrase 'collective agreements or arbitration awards which have been declared universally applicable' means.

[72] 'The mandatory rules for minimum protection in force in the host country must not prevent the application of terms and conditions of employment which are more favourable to workers' (Sec. 17).

[73] Case C-115/14, *RegioPost*, ECLI:EU:C:2015:760. For a broader discussion, see Francesco Costamagna, 'Minimum Wage between Public Procurement and Posted Workers: Anything New after the RegioPost Case?', *European Law Review* 42 (2017): 101–111.

to address the main social dumping concerns without upending the main idea behind the Posting of Workers Directive. In times more conducive to the integration process, this judicial approach would probably suffice to depoliticise the directive, particularly as the posting of workers in the EU is not an economically significant phenomenon.

According to the Commission's calculations, posted workers represented only 0.9 per cent of total employment in 2015 (2.05 million workers).[74] Poland outnumbered other countries as a sending country, almost doubling the number of posted workers between 2010 and 2015 (to more than 450,000). But steep increases, from much lower initial levels, were also recorded by countries as diverse as Austria, Italy, Slovakia, Spain and, particularly, Slovenia. However, the country by far outstripping others in the growth of received posted workers between 2010 and 2015 was Germany (from about 250,000 workers hosted in 2010 to more than 400,000 five years later). While the numbers grew by 50,000 or more in Austria and Belgium as well, they rose by several thousand only in France, Sweden and the UK between 2010 and 2015, and actually fell during the same period in the Netherlands, Italy, Finland and Luxembourg.

From the political perspective all of these facts have proven much less significant than the finding that 'the number of posted workers has increased by 41.3% between 2010 and 2015'.[75] In the previous years of the permissive consensus, this fact could have been perceived as a sign of a better-functioning internal market propelling intra-EU trade in services more effectively. But, with the constraining dissensus mounting in many EU 15 countries, it has been seen the opposite way.

In a polarised Union, in which more than a third of its members are low-cost Eastern European countries, it could have been predicted that rewriting the rules of the game after the club was enlarged would not be easy. But the Commission, which made a remarkable about-face by openly joining the camp of constraining dissenters, nonetheless proposed an amendment of the Posting of Workers Directive in March 2016.[76] Its proposal was a modest version of a guideline by President

[74] All subsequent data in this paragraph is based on 'Posted Workers in the EU', available at ec.europa.eu/social/BlobServlet?docId=15181&langId=en.

[75] 'Posted Workers in the EU'.

[76] Proposal for a Directive of the European Parliament and of the Council amending Directive 96/71/EC of the European Parliament and of the Council of 16 December 1996 concerning the posting of workers in the framework of the provision of services, COM(2016)128.

Juncker: 'In our union, the same work at the same place should be remunerated in the same manner.'[77] Tabling it, the Commission emphasised that 'wage differences have increased, thereby creating unwanted incentives to use posting as a means to exploit these differences ... In addition, since posting companies must comply only with the minimum rates of pay of the host Member State, this frequently leads to stark wage differences between posted and local workers, especially in Member States with relatively high wage levels. Posted workers are reported to earn up to 50% less than local workers in some sectors and Member States.'[78]

The Guardian of the Treaties also commissioned a report that soon concluded that 'despite the relative low share of cross-border services in total EU-turnover of construction, amounting to just 0.8%, the import of services through the posting of workers could have undermined jobs for local employees ("job displacement effects"), labour tax revenues and the competitiveness of local employers'.[79]

The 2016 draft amendment proposed four main alterations to the Posting of Workers Directive. The first would extend host countries' rules on remuneration – defined either by law or by universally applicable collective agreements (and not only minimum rates of pay) – to all foreign posted workers. The effects of this alteration would be magnified by erasing the possibility for host countries to exempt foreign posted workers in certain sectors from universally applicable collective agreements.[80] Second, the Member States could decide that whenever the main contractor bound by collective agreements in the host country outsources the performance of the contract to providers from other countries, the latter would also be subject to all the collective

[77] 'Europe in Motion. President-elect Juncker's Main Messages from His Speech before the European Parliament. Statement in the European Parliament Plenary Session ahead of the Vote on the College Plenary Session, Strasbourg, 22 October 2014', available at ec.europa.eu/priorities/sites/beta-political/files/juncker-political-guidelines-speech_en_0.pdf.

[78] European Commission, 'Revision of the Posting of Workers Directive – Frequently Asked Questions', 8 March 2016, available at europa.eu/rapid/press-release_MEMO-16-467_en.htm.

[79] Frederic De Wispelaere and Jozef Pacolet, 'An Ad Hoc Statistical Analysis on Short Term Mobility – Economic Value of Posting of Workers', Research commissioned by DG EMPL within the framework of Contract VT/2015/096, available at lirias.kuleuven.be/bitstream/123456789/539523/1/The%20economic%20value%20of%20posting.pdf, 24–25.

[80] Proposal for new wording of Art. 3(1) Directive.

agreements the main contractor is bound by.[81] Third, the draft proposed that workers posted for periods longer than two years would be covered by all labour law protections in the host country.[82] Finally, fourth, the principle of equal treatment with local temporary agency workers would be extended to posted temporary agency workers.[83]

All four mechanisms of approximating the 'equal pay for equal work in the same place' principle in respect to posted workers would push the internal market back on its earlier evolutionary path. Workers in the high-wage countries should appreciate it, because the downward pressure on their wages in the sectors exposed to posted workers would be somewhat alleviated. By the same token, however, the ability of Eastern workers to exploit their cost advantage would diminish.

Unsurprisingly, therefore, seven labour ministers from high-wage countries openly supported the Commission's plans.[84] Equally predictably, two months later nine labour ministers from Eastern Europe sent a 'counter-letter'. As they argued, 'there is a danger that a revision will be used to undermine some of the fundamental principles of the EU, including the freedom to provide services. In this respect, we consider any references to equal pay for equal work in the same place as being misguided and incompatible with a genuine single market.'[85] In an unprecedented situation, therefore, a significant proportion of EU countries tightly stuck to the traditional paradigm of the internal market, against the Commission, which joined the dissenting camp. When the Commission published its draft, usually indifferent national parliaments stepped in. The parliaments of France, Italy, Portugal, Spain and the United Kingdom expressed their support for the draft when consulted by the Commission. Conversely, these from the recently admitted Eastern European countries (Bulgaria, Croatia, the

[81] Proposal of a new Art. 3(1a) Directive. Interestingly, this alteration would fall foul of the current interpretation of the Treaty provisions, interpreted in Case C-346/06 *Rüffert*, ECLI:EU:C:2008:189, § 36 et seq. as precluding precisely such national arrangements.

[82] Proposal of a new Art. 2a Directive.

[83] Proposal of a new Art. 3(1a) Directive.

[84] Letter of 18 June 2015, signed by ministers from Austria, Belgium, France, Germany, Luxembourg, the Netherlands and Sweden, available at www.gmb.org.uk/assets/media/gmbbrussels/EU%20Government%20ministers%20letter%20to%20Commissioner%20Thyssen%2018%20june%202015.pdf.

[85] Letter of 31 August 2015, signed by ministers of Bulgaria, Czechia, Estonia, Hungary, Lithuania, Latvia, Poland, Slovakia and Romania, available at arbetsratt.juridicum.su.se/euarb/15-03/nio_medlemsstater_utstationeriongsdirektivet_augusti_2015.pdf.

Czechia, Estonia, Hungary, Latvia, Lithuania, Poland, Romania and Slovakia) and from Denmark showed the Commission a yellow card within the so-called Early Warning System.[86] The latter group raised the otherwise bizarre argument (or, in fact, excuse) that the proposal violated the principle of subsidiarity.[87] No matter how inaccurate it was in substance, it heralded a conflict between high-wage and low-wage countries, as it is virtually impossible to legislate an amendment to the Posting of Workers Directive that would satisfy both sides. The one which will eventually have to yield in the legislative process is all but certain to become upset about the role of the internal market in European integration.

9.8 Equal Pay for Equal Work in the Same Place?

To the growing group of internal market critics this story vindicates the narrative of obnoxious Eastern Europeans dumping workers onto socially high-wage societies and exploiting the internal market freedoms to their advantage at the cost of other societies' social peace and economic prosperity. To those who share this view it is obvious that the principle of 'equal pay for equal work in the same place' highlighted by Commission President Juncker and the labour ministers from the high-wage countries should govern the Posting of Workers Directive. Otherwise similarly productive but more expensive local workers in the sectors where posted workers have made greatest forays (construction, manufacturing, health and social work services, or business services) will face growing pressure to accept lower wages to remain on *their* market. Or they will face unemployment.

[86] European Commission, Press release 'Posting of Workers: Commission Discusses Concerns of National Parliaments', 20 July 2016, available at europa.eu/rapid/press-release_IP-16-2546_en.htm.

[87] According to Art. 6 of Protocol (No 2) on the application of the principles of subsidiarity and proportionality the Commission can be addressed with reasoned opinions of legislative chambers only when 'it considers that the draft in question does not comply with the principle of subsidiarity'. Disentitled from using any other argument, the parliamentary chambers objecting the revision proposal clutched to the subsidiarity argument, even if in fact they could not correctly argue that a provision of services of an intrinsically interstate nature should be properly governed on the national level (which a proper argument invoking the principle of subsidiarity should entail). For a prescient and pointed broader critique of the Early Warning System from this perspective, see Davor Jančić, 'The Game of Cards: National Parliaments in the EU and the Future of the Early Warning Mechanism and the Political Dialogue', *Common Market Law Review* 52 (2015): 939–975.

Throughout the period of the permissive consensus the idea of 'equal pay for equal work in the same place' could have been deemed as unfairly discriminating the otherwise economically disadvantaged societies.[88] Back then it would have been immediately suppressed by the market efficiency argument: a downward pressure of posted workers on labour costs in high-wage countries makes products manufactured there cheaper and economies more competitive internationally. Even in the substantially watered down version proposed by the Commission, the idea would also have been rebuffed for the various practical problems it entails. Consider, for instance, a situation in which a winner of a public tender outsources a part of its contract to an Eastern European subcontractor who performs all of its tasks in an Eastern European country and then simply sends the outcome to the contractor.[89] Or how about a situation in which a truck driver only crosses the territory of one country while he is employed in a different one?[90]

[88] As Mustilli and Pelkmans argued: 'The economic effect of this is that the incipient demand for a given quality of any temporary service offered by providers from low-wage economies is drastically curtailed. This is anti-competitive. It is socially problematic, too. Whereas it does protect local workers in Sweden, Finland, Austria, Germany or Greece, it pre-empts Eastern European EU workers from exploiting their lower wages as a competitive advantage in the internal market! In fact, one can regard this constraint as a serious impediment of the free movement of temporary services, because, with equal (minimum) wages, the advantages of local firms in performing temporary contracts may squeeze the Eastern providers out of the market for the large majority of cases': Federica Mustilli and Jacques Pelkmans, 'Access Barriers to Services Markets. Mapping, Tracing, Understanding and Measuring', *CEPS Special Report* No. 77, 7 June 2013, 51, available at www.ceps.eu/publications/access-barriers-services-markets-mapping-tracing-understanding-and-measuring.

[89] This was exactly the factual background in Case C-549/13, *Bundesdruckerei GmbH* v. *Stadt Dortmund*, ECLI:EU:C:2014:2235. The Court held that the minimum wage legislation of the service recipient does not apply in such a situation.

[90] Germany, France and Austria introduced laws requiring that national minimum wage laws apply in this situation. The Commission countered with infringement proceedings: 'Commission Takes Legal Action against the Systematic Application of the French and German Minimum Wage Legislation to the Transport Sector', 16 June 2016, available at europa.eu/rapid/press-release_IP-16-2101_en.htm and Julia Fioretti, 'EU Challenges Austrian Minimum Wage Law for Truck Drivers', *Reuters*, 27 April 2017, available at uk.reuters.com/article/uk-austria-eu-minimumwage-idUKKBN17T1V4?il=0. On the other hand, the Commission proposed legislation requiring that minimum paid annual holidays and minimum rates of pay of the host country apply to international carriage operations if the period of posting to the host country is longer than three days during one calendar month (Art. 2(2) Proposal for a directive amending Directive 2006/22/EC as regards enforcement requirements and laying down specific rules with respect to Directive 96/71/EC and Directive 2014/67/EU for posting drivers in the road transport sector, COM(2017)278). Interestingly, a draft circulated

None of this, however, undermines the political sense of the 'equal pay for equal work in the same place' rallying cry and demonstrates its main underlying paradox. The posting of workers is the most visible channel of trade with low-cost EU countries, and therefore the most alarming one for local workers. The same workers do not see similarly vividly the other two avenues through which low-cost societies can exploit their economic advantage in international trade: through exports and by enticing foreign direct investments.[91] The latter processes attract far less political attention, even though they are systemically much more significant. This may explain why the Commission has not given up its traditional thinking about the role of the internal market in these areas, siding with its critics when it comes to the posting of workers. But doing so it has acted inconsistently, leaving Europeans legitimately puzzled. Is social dumping responsible for persistently high levels of unemployment in some EU countries? How significant is the posting of workers in practice and what are really its economic effects for the high-wage countries? Is trade with low-cost countries a good or a bad thing? Are direct investments? What should policy answers to all the questions be?

It is paradigmatic for the current debate on the internal market that answers to these questions are different for different countries, different sectors and different groups in each society. This strongly incentivises supranational institutions to take possibly cautious positions informed by current political calculations rather than any particular vision of the internal market.

9.9 The Digital Single Market Throttling Back

In the face of clearly conflicting distributional interests of different European societies, it should not be particularly surprising that the political drive behind the internal market has stalled in recent years.[92] It

only one day earlier recommended that the period of posting in international carriage operations excluding pay considerations from the scope of the Posting of Workers Directive was set at seven days: Catherine Stupp, 'Controversial EU Labour Rules Tackle Truck Drivers' Pay and Working Conditions', *Euractiv*, 31 May 2017, available at www.euractiv.com/section/road-safety/news/controversial-eu-labour-rules-tackle-truck-drivers-pay-and-working-conditions/. While both three- and seven-day periods are politically driven, they entail profoundly different distributional effects.

[91] Elena Vaccarino and Zsolt Darvas, '"Social Dumping" and Posted Workers: A New Clash within the EU', *Bruegel Blog Post*, 7 March 2016, available at bruegel.org/2016/03/social-dumping-and-posted-workers-a-new-clash-within-the-eu/.

[92] Quite tellingly, after more than two years in office, the Juncker Commission came up with four ideas how to 'unleash the full potential of the Single Market and make

has been clear to see even in the area of the internal market considered as key by the Juncker Commission: the digital single market.

For years now economic research has confirmed that improvements in productivity in service sectors are largely driven by information and communication technologies (ICTs).[93] How susceptible service sectors are to the transformative role of ICTs largely depends on the restrictiveness of labour market and services regulation, as well as on how firms are organised.[94] On all the accounts European companies are generally in a disadvantaged position compared to their main trading partners (the USA in particular), which may explain the stubbornly lower productivity growth in the EU's service markets since the mid-1990s.[95] On some very important markets (especially that of business services) the situation is even worse: the productivity of EU firms has not on average improved at all since 1980.[96]

Outdated, obtrusive regulations and the consequent hampered competition have become more pernicious in the technologically more advanced environment.[97] From this viewpoint the neo-liberal permissive

it the launchpad for European companies to thrive in the global economy': Press release 'A Services Economy That Works for Europeans', 10 January 2017, available at europa.eu/rapid/press-release_IP-17-23_en.htm. All four (a new European Services e-card, a proportionality assessment of national rules on professional services, guidance for national reforms in regulation of professions and improved notification of draft national laws on services) follow soft coordination patterns, resembling the OMC.

93 For example, Christian Kowalkowski, 'Service Productivity Gains through Information and Communication Technology Applications: A Service Marketing Approach', *International Journal of Knowledge Management Studies* 2 (2008): 96–114.

94 Salvador Barrios and Jean-Claude Burgelman, 'Europe Needs More Lisbon to Make ICT Investment Effective', *InterEconomics*, May–June 2008, 124–134; John Van Reenen et al., 'The Economic Impact of ICT', study for the European Commission, DG INFSO, SMART N. 2007/0020, LSE Enterprise, 2010.

95 See, for example, Vincent Aussilloux et al., 'Making the Best of the European Single Market', *Bruegel Policy Contribution* No. 3/2017, available at bruegel.org/wp-content/uploads/2017/02/PC-03-2017-single-market-010217-.pdf. As other Bruegel experts highlighted, the Eurozone in particular 'is suffering from excessively low growth in productivity. In 2002–2015, value added per employee grew by just 0.5% per year on average. The reason for that is not the industrial sector, where the figure is almost 2%, but the services sector, where productivity growth is very low and in some cases even negative. The services sector lacks innovative drive and investment': Marcel Fratzscher et al., 'Mere Criticism of the ECB Is No Solution', *Bruegel Blog Post*, 10 April 2016, available at bruegel.org/2016/04/mere-criticism-of-the-ecb-is-no-solution/.

96 Henk L. M. Kox, 'Unleashing Competition in EU Business Services', *CEPS Policy Brief* No. 284, 24 September 2012, available at aei.pitt.edu/36814/1/ceps_4.pdf.

97 Guglielmo Barone and Federico Cingano, 'Service Regulation and Growth: Evidence from OECD Countries', *Economic Journal* 121 (2011): 931–957. The Commission's position can be illustrated by this 2015 excerpt: 'More flexible regulation of services

consensus ushering in the 1980s the internal market programme could seem to have come right on time. What is more important, however, is that its market liberalisation thrust did not cut the same way across sectors. It did so smoothly in the financial sector, where incumbents were keenly interested in a broader market freedom and in technologically more advanced services. Yet it hit a wall in other sectors, where the incumbents were primarily interested in staving off potential competitors. Unexpectedly, the latter group gained new ammunition when the Great Financial Crisis demonstrated that in the financial sector the previous deregulation went astray. Many European societies, experiencing the aftershocks of the crisis, drew from it the simple conclusion that the orthodox narrative on deregulation and liberalisation for the sake of abstract efficiency gains was spurious across the board. Even if there were any efficiency gains, they argued, these gains have been distributed unequally between 'the toiling man' and the 'remorseless capitalist' wherever market liberalisation was successful. Instead of repeating the same mistake in the sectors previously spared by it, the argument follows, public authorities should control and restrain capital owners from pursuing their own interests under the guise of enhanced market efficiency. Rather than surrendering to the whims of international capitalists, the government should secure the traditional way of living and the traditional sources of economic prosperity.

This basic belief, from which the heterodox narrative largely springs, is equally hostile to foreign low-cost workers as it is inimical to highly productive and innovative companies. Upsetting the very bedrock of the internal market, it undermines the rationale behind European economic integration after World War II. It makes many European societies more defensive, and their national economic policies more parochial and obsolete. Yet, it is a natural side effect of an enhanced competition process, which offers higher winnings to champions and which multiplies the number of (even if only relative) losers.

As I was explaining in Chapter 7, using the Swedish example, striking its roots requires a resilient institutional tissue and smart

markets would lead to higher productivity and could ease the market entry of new players, reduce the price for services and ensure wider choices for consumers. In addition, the productivity of business services is critical for the competitiveness of certain economic sectors, for example manufacturing. Barriers to entry in these markets are high in some Member States': European Commission, 'Annual Growth Survey 2016. Strengthening the Recovery and Fostering Convergence', COM(2015) 690, 26 November 2015, p. 12.

socioeconomic policies calibrated to achieving benefits in the longer term. Such an environment does not prevail in the EU, though, while the various crises plaguing European countries in recent years have made it even more rare and endemic. Against this background initiatives of the Commission aimed at toppling national borders to innovative and competitive firms can easily backfire politically. The Monti Report, intended to set out internal market priorities for the second Barroso Commission, sounded ominous when it quoted Paul-Henri Spaak: 'All those who, in trying to meet the economic challenges set out by the treaty of Rome, neglected the political dimension have failed. As long as [those] challenges will be addressed exclusively in an economic perspective, disregarding their political angle, we will run – I am afraid – into repeated failures.'[98]

The moment the report was published – May 2010 – coincided unluckily with the explosion of the sovereign debt crisis and the devastation of national social contracts and trust in Europe it entailed. Yet, written before it all happened, the report paid a lot of attention to the economic benefits of the digital single market, highlighting that establishing it 'corresponds to a gain of almost €500 bn and means that the digital single market alone could have an impact similar to the 1992 internal market programme'.[99] In congruity with this 'economic angle' and contravening the 'political angle' – to paraphrase Spaak – it proposed very ambitious new initiatives to achieve the digital single market.[100]

The Commission showed more political sobriety when it published its digital Single Market Act II two years later, at the apex of the sovereign

[98] Paul-Henri Spaak, 'Discours à la Chambre des Représentants', 14 June 1961, quoted in Mario Monti, 'A New Strategy for the Single Market at the Service of Europe's Economy and Society. Report to the President of the European Commission José Manuel Barroso' 9 May 2010, 2, available at ec.europa.eu/internal_market/strategy/docs/monti_report_final_10_05_2010_en.pdf.

[99] Mario Monti, 'A New Strategy for the Single Market', 44.

[100] In particular, the Report proposed to create 'a seamless regulatory space for electronic communications, including proposals to reinforce EU level regulatory oversight, to introduce pan-European licensing and EU level frequency allocation and administration', 'harmonised rules for delivery, warranty and dispute resolution' in e-commerce, simplified 'business environment for cross-border retail transactions, including VAT rules, the cross border management of recycling rules and of copyright levies on blank media and equipment', 'an EU copyright law' and 'a legal framework for EU-wide online broadcasting'.

debt crisis.[101] It went down a few pegs with the ambitiousness of the proposed reforms, making them seemingly more feasible.

The years to follow witnessed new EU legislation in all of the areas prioritised in the Single Market Act II. A 2012 regulation lowered international roaming charges.[102] Two other directives – on measures to reduce the cost of deploying high-speed electronic communications networks[103] and on multi-territorial licensing of rights and collective rights management in musical works for online uses[104] – were enacted two years later. In late 2015, a regulation laying the foundations for the 'roam-like-at-home' principle and pursuing net neutrality was adopted,[105] while the next year the EU's data protection regime was overhauled.[106]

Characteristically, some of the legal acts were making the 'digital' economic activity easier, while others (new data protection and roaming rules in particular) made it more difficult. First of all,

[101] Communication COM(2012)573, 3 October 2012. It offered three key actions to build the European digital economy: supporting online services by making payment services in the EU more efficient, reducing the cost and increasing efficiency in the deployment of high-speed communication infrastructure, and making electronic invoicing the standard for public procurement.

[102] Regulation 531/2012 of the European Parliament and of the Council of 13 June 2012 on roaming on public mobile communications networks within the Union, OJ 2012 No. L 172, 30 June 2012, pp. 10–35.

[103] Directive 2014/61/EU of the European Parliament and of the Council of 15 May 2014 on measures to reduce the cost of deploying high-speed electronic communications networks, OJ 2014 No. L 155, 23 May 2014, pp. 1–14.

[104] Directive 2014/26/EU of the European Parliament and of the Council of 26 February 2014 on collective management of copyright and related rights and multi-territorial licensing of rights in musical works for online use in the internal market, OJ 2014 No. L 84, 20 March 2014, pp. 72–98.

[105] Regulation 2015/2120 of the European Parliament and of the Council of 25 November 2015 laying down measures concerning open Internet access and amending Directive 2002/22/EC on universal service and users' rights relating to electronic communications networks and services and Regulation 531/2012 on roaming on public mobile communications networks within the Union, OJ 2015 No. L 310, 26 November 2015, pp. 1–18.

[106] Regulation 2016/679 of the European Parliament and of the Council of 27 April 2016 on the protection of natural persons with regard to the processing of personal data and on the free movement of such data, and repealing Directive 95/46/EC, OJ 2016 No. L 119, 4 May 2016, pp. 1–88; Directive 2016/680 of the European Parliament and of the Council of 27 April 2016 on the protection of natural persons with regard to the processing of personal data by competent authorities for the purposes of the prevention, investigation, detection or prosecution of criminal offences or the execution of criminal penalties, and on the free movement of such data, and repealing Council Framework Decision 2008/977/JHA, OJ 2016 No. L 119, 4 May 2016, pp. 89–131.

however, none of them tackled the really big hurdles to the digital single market: like education, R&D policies, business environment, tax systems etc. Overcoming them would require going even further than the very ambitious recommendations of the Monti Report, for which – again – the political appetite vanished in many European societies in parallel to the solidification of the constraining dissensus. These societies that tended to put the blame for the economic travails on the previous European permissive consensus about the internal market, turning a blind eye to the short-sighted national economic, social and political processes, drifted further away from those still preaching economic flexibility and openness. In effect, national policies in the areas really important for technologically advanced entrepreneurship have become even more polarised and path-dependent. Whether successful or not, the tendency to follow national tracks along which the policies had developed in the past became deeper and more intractable as a result, dispelling hopes for a common digital motorway.

9.10 The Uber Debacle

National reactions to the so-called collaborative (on-demand) economy[107] – a group of disruptive new online platforms – is particularly telling in this respect. The collaborative economy has revolutionised the personal transport market, for instance. Uber and its smaller competitors (like Taxify or the French Heetch) immediately became very serious competitors to the traditional taxi syndicates. These new market players have brought about many of the benefits the internal market was promising: improved allocative efficiency, technological progress and improved consumer welfare. They have broadened the market both when it comes to the recipients and the providers, offering more convenient – and cheaper – alternatives to taxi services and rendering part-time driving fully feasible. The non-cash payments that the platforms enable make their customers safer, while due to geolocation routing is easy, even for drivers unfamiliar with the neighbourhood. All in all, these technological advancements

[107] For good introductions see Ilaria Maselli, Karolien Lenaerts and Miroslav Beblavý, 'Five Things We Need to Know about the On-demand Economy', *CEPS Essay* No. 21, 8 January 2016, available at papers.ssrn.com/sol3/papers.cfm?abstract_id=2715450 or Georgios Petropoulos, 'An Economic Review of the Collaborative Economy', *Bruegel Policy Contribution* No. 5/2017, 27 February 2017, available at bruegel.org/2017/02/an-economic-review-of-the-collaborative-economy/.

undermine the very ratio of state licensing and syndication on the taxi market. Of course, they also make the evasion of tax and car safety requirements easier. But these problems can be remedied with no extraordinary administrative constraints traditionally applied to the taxi market.

While, however, Uber and the likes epitomise the market liberalisation the traditional view of the internal market has striven to achieve (except for the non-European character of the leading platform), it also represents everything the heterodox view detests. It has strained national legal paradigms behind employee and consumer protection, upsetting at the same time the cohabitation of national authorities with local vested interests these authorities regulate and often protect from external competition. What is particularly significant from the perspective of the EU, is that it has also raised the question of whether EU law should defend Uber and its kin according to the traditional understanding of fundamental market freedoms, at the expense of risking even more anti-EU backlash from the growingly protectionist EU societies. Or should European institutions here too flirt with the heterodox sentiment, disavowing the original aspirations and goals of the internal market?

The growing polarisation of national attitudes, ideologies and policies has not made it any easier to answer these questions. In some – less etatist and/or more technology-friendly EU countries – public authorities have trodden the difficult path of protecting economic advantages entailed by such disruptive applications, while making sure they do not slip through basic antifraud, public safety and consumer protection requirements.[108] Estonia has spearheaded this group. In spring 2016, when this country adjusted its laws to make them accommodative to new applications of the collaborative economy, its prime minister said: 'Europe must embrace the digital revolution and Estonia has a definite wish to be on the forefront of it. So wouldn't it be reasonable – at a time when a large part of the world is finding protectionist reasons to prohibit the sharing economy – if we, Estonia, would be the first country to welcome Uber, Taxify and Airbnb?'[109] Shortly before the parliamentary vote on

[108] See also Vassilis Hatzopoulos and Sofia Roma, 'Caring for Sharing? The Collaborative Economy under EU Law', *Common Market Law Review* 54 (2017): 81–128.

[109] Kalle Palling, 'Why Estonia Introduced a Bill on Ridesharing', *The Baltic Times*, 5 March 2016, available at www.baltictimes.com/kalle_palling__why_estonia_introduced_a_bill_on_ridesharing/.

the legislation authorising collaborative economy platforms in Estonia, Andrus Ansip, former prime minister of Estonia and later the vice president of the European Commission responsible for the digital single market, struck the same chord: 'The Estonian Parliament doesn't have to vote for or against the collaborative economy – people have already embraced it. The parliament's task is now to adjust to what people want and remove barriers so that the collaborative economy can grow and expand in Estonia. And the same goes for Europe.'[110]

But Estonia has a highly open, liberal economy, a resilient social contract and an aspiration for being in the avant-garde of the high-tech revolution.[111] Throughout the previous decade, when the Lisbon Strategy's goal of becoming the world's most competitive and dynamic knowledge-based economy was universally preached, if not practised, in the EU, these features could have been acclaimed in many European capitals. But as Europeans were struggling with various crises, instead of reaping the benefits of the Lisbon Strategy,[112] Estonia has been engulfed in its approach, while some other national authorities have tried to hit back at the collaborative economy.

In most of EU countries the basic Uber application (called Uber POP) matching available drivers with potential clients was outlawed by court decisions soon after the company entered these markets.[113] The basic intuition behind all the injunctions was the same: Uber offers services functionally equivalent to the traditional taxis and, hence, even if it uses a different technological and organisational model, it should apply all of the local rules prescribed for the taxi market.

Of course, neither national courts nor public administration can be blamed for following the rule of law, rather than trying to adjust the laws to new circumstances. Quite to the contrary, the separation of powers implies that, as in Estonia, it is the legislator who should take

[110] 'Estonia Leads the Way on Regulated Ridesharing', *Medium*, 1 March 2016, available at medium.com/uber-under-the-hood/estonia-leads-the-way-on-regulated-ridesharing-28686a2fcf50#.ui4cs5kzb.

[111] Jorge Valero, 'How to Become a Successful "Tech-nation" from Scratch', *Euractiv*, 26 February 2016, available at www.euractiv.com/section/digital/news/how-to-become-a-successful-tech-nation-from-scratch/.

[112] Between 2009 and 2016, real wages fell every year in Greece, Croatia, Hungary, Portugal, Cyprus, the UK and Italy. They grew faster in this period than between 2001 and 2008 only in Germany, Poland and Bulgaria: European Trade Union Institute, 'Benchmarking Working Europe 2017', available at www.etui.org/Publications2/Books/Benchmarking-Working-Europe-2017.

[113] 'Uber Protests and Legal Actions', *Wikipedia*, available at en.wikipedia.org/wiki/Uber_protests_and_legal_actions.

a proactive stance, instead, in such a situation. In the majority of EU countries the legislator has not budged, however, which has implied a protection of the status quo. And even when a law has been passed, it has tended to go precisely in the opposite direction to the Estonian blueprint, which the French example testifies. There in particular taxi drivers and the government have held each other in check, because traditionally the government has been artificially capping the number of taxi licenses, raising their costs to exorbitant levels in the first step and securing rents (extraordinary profits produced by the artificial scarcity) to those who obtained them in the second.[114]

In October 2014, the French Parliament passed a bill (the *Thévenoud* Law)[115] aimed to secure the monopoly of the taxi syndicates by setting up four requirements intended to eliminate Uber from the French market. The first was that only taxis could charge per-kilometre fees. The second prohibited taxi competitors (chauffeured vehicles) from using geolocation applications showing available vehicles in the vicinity in real time. The third required that, after each ride, chauffeured vehicles return to their home base or stop where they are authorised to park. Fourth, the *Thévenoud* Law outlawed mobile applications that intermediated between non-professional drivers and potential customers.

A few months later, the *Conseil Constitutionnel* decided that only the first of the requirements violated the freedom of enterprise, while the other three were justified by the interest in preserving public order (with regard to the use of public roadways and parking places).[116] Soon after, taxi drivers, outraged by the loose enforcement of the new law, took to the streets. To them 'the law has never been enforced, and we think it's unenforceable … So we are demanding the elimination of

[114] As Uber highlights, between 1937 and now the number of licenses issued in Paris grew by only 14 per cent (from 14,000 to 15,900): Sophie Schmidt, 'From Scarcity to Abundance: Growing the Overall Transportation Pie', *Medium*, 12 January 2016, available at medium.com/uber-under-the-hood/from-scarcity-to-abundance-growing-the-overall-pie-by-sophie-schmidt-a2e5a24bbc71. In Paris the licenses sell for as much as €240,000; they are estimated to be worth €8 billion nationally: Nicholas Vinocur, 'French PM Calls for Truce in Taxi-Uber War', *Politico*, 26 January 2016, available at www.politico.eu/article/france-braces-for-new-taxi-uber-war-road-uberpop/.

[115] Law No. 2014-1104 of 1 October 2014 on Taxis and Chauffeured Transport Vehicles, orig. Loi No. 2014-1104 du 1er octobre 2014 relative aux taxis et aux voitures de transport avec chauffeur, available at www.legifrance.gouv.fr/affichTexte.do?cidTexte=JORFTEXT000029527162&dateTexte=&categorieLien=id.

[116] Decisions of the Conseil Constitutionnel of 22 May 2015 and of 29 September 2015.

VTCs ['voitures de tourisme avec chauffeur'], pure and simple, or compensation.'[117] While the then-Economy Minister Macron highlighted the benefits of this new model for employment, the rest of the government firmly sided with taxi drivers.[118]

The resultant picture has had nothing to do with legal predictability. Injunctions and laws banning Uber have often been defunct, while taxi authorisation schemes in many EU countries have remained as archaic and extortionary as they had been before. Uber has remained confronted with twenty-eight different regulatory approaches, only a few of which aimed to civilise its actions while harnessing the market potential.

Against very diverse national positions and preferences, the Commission hid behind non-binding recommendations, instead of trying to impose its view on how to integrate legislative and regulatory underpinnings of the collaborative economy. On the one hand, this institution issued a Communication entitled 'A European agenda for the collaborative economy'.[119] New market players could hardly agree more with its conclusion that 'the success of collaborative platforms are at times challenging for existing market operators and practices, but by enabling individual citizens to offer services, they also promote new employment opportunities, flexible working arrangements and new sources of income' (p. 2). They also certainly appreciate the Communication's dedication to the reading of the internal market as prohibiting national restrictions on the provision of services and entrepreneurship, unless such restrictions are narrowly tailored to an overriding public interest interpreted according to the demanding principles of proportionality and necessity.

On the other hand, however, the Commission balked at instigating infringement proceedings against the states quite obviously ignoring its reading of the fundamental internal market freedoms and disrespectfully defending the economic interests of the incumbent local lobbies instead.[120] Politico's Nicholas Hirst was on point when he argued that

[117] Amar Toor, 'French Taxi Drivers Clash with Police in Anti-Uber Strike', *The Verge*, 26 January 2016, available at www.theverge.com/2016/1/26/10832204/french-taxi-uber-strike-paris-vtc.

[118] Nicholas Vinocur, 'How France's Emmanuel Macron Lost the Uber War', *Politico*, 10 February 2016, available at www.politico.eu/article/how-frances-emmanuel-macron-lost-the-uber-war.

[119] COM(2016)356, 2 June 2016.

[120] The Commission was reported to have shied away from suing France in order not to boost Eurosceptics in the 2017 elections: Joanna Plucinska, Joshua Posaner and Ryan Heath, 'Uber Case on Hold over Le Pen Fears', *Politico*, 23 November 2016, available at www.politico.eu/pro/uber-complaint-falls-into-jean-claude-junckers-black-hole/.

the inactivity of European and national lawmakers in the Uber case 'has exposed bitter divisions among Europe's national capitals and laid bare the hypocrisy of the Commission, which supports Uber's case before the court but has shied away from enforcing politically sensitive complaints against Paris, Madrid and Berlin'.[121]

The Commission's fudging has put the Court of Justice, to which national courts referred their preliminary questions on the compatibility of Uber bans with EU law, in an awkward position. In one of the cases – *Elite Taxi*[122] – a Spanish court asked whether Uber should be classified as a provider of information society services in the sense of the so-called E-Commerce Directive,[123] and, if so, what consequences such a classification entails for national authorisation schemes. In another – *Uber Belgium*[124] – the referring Court was essentially asking whether internal market freedoms (and EU fundamental rights) can exempt drivers using an Uber application from national authorisation requirements imposed on taxi operators.

In both cases, therefore, national courts invited the Court of Justice to explain what internal market freedoms entail for often obsolete national taxi licensing requirements. Responding to it the Court could indeed exert market-liberalising – or market-improving – pressure.[125]

The legal path to get there could seem quite straightforward. Uber offers its drivers and users not only a technological platform, but the whole business model, and charges them for it. The model defines all important aspects of the service users receive and drivers provide. Nonetheless, because drivers are economically independent agents, they

121 Nicholas Hirst, 'Europe's Top Court Could Help Uber Where Commission Has Failed', *Politico*, 28 November 2016, available at www.politico.eu/article/uber-spain-sharing-economy-collaborative-economy/.

122 Case C-434/15 *Elite Taxi*, ECLI:EU:C:2017:364.

123 Directive 2000/31/EC of the European Parliament and of the Council of 8 June 2000 on certain legal aspects of information society services, in particular electronic commerce, in the Internal Market, OJ 2000 No. L 178, 17 July 2000, pp. 1–16. According to Art. 2(a) Directive 2000/31, read in conj. with Art. 1(2) Directive 98/34 as amended by Directive 98/48/EC of the European Parliament and of the Council of 20 July 1998 amending Directive 98/34/EC laying down a procedure for the provision of information in the field of technical standards and regulations, OJ 1998 No. L 217, 5 August 1998, pp. 18–26, an information society service is 'a service normally provided for remuneration, at a distance, by electronic means and at the individual request of a recipient of services'.

124 Case C-526/15 *Uber Belgium*, ECLI:EU:C:2016:830.

125 Even if, as the history of its market-liberalising endeavours a decade ago makes quite clear, the national governments (especially against a passive Commission) can find it easy to deflate any such a pressure.

can, and arguably should, be deemed to offer services separate from the platform that Uber delivers. If the tangible transportation service is thus separated from what Uber provides, the latter ought to be classified as an intangible one meeting the criteria of an information society service. This means that Uber itself would not be subject to taxi authorisation requirements, but the drivers using its application certainly would.

Due to a Treaty peculiarity, the freedom to provide services would not apply to the drivers.[126] But from the perspective of the Uber business model the freedom to provide services is largely irrelevant. Both Uber and 'its' drivers have actually questioned authorisation requirements for entering the taxi market. This aspect, in turn, triggers the freedom of establishment, instead of the freedom to provide services. In this situation, no Treaty provision allows the Court to forego its standard, fully-fledged analysis of whether national authorisation restrictions can be reconciled with the internal market.[127]

Equally important from the legal standpoint, the conclusion that Uber does not provide transport services should not lead to a profound enforcement dilemma, because the company hosts all of the information on the transactions underpinning the transport services enabled by its platform. This information centralisation makes it in many aspects similar to the once notorious Napster peer-to-peer file-sharing model. What should really matter from this perspective are conditions for liability exemptions established for hosting providers by the E-Commerce Directive.[128] If the conditions are not met, Uber could be held liable for law violations perpetrated by its users.

[126] According to Art. 58(1) TFEU, 'freedom to provide services in the field of transport shall be governed by the provisions of the Title relating to transport.' The latter Title is not built on the logic comparable to the internal market freedoms, pursuing non-discrimination, instead, and authorising the EU to establish a common transport policy.

[127] Similarly, in Case C-338/09, *Yellow Cab Verkehrsbetrieb*, ECLI:EU:C:2010:814, the Court opined that "urban or suburban services" (in this particular case public transport bus services within the territory of Vienna) 'do not constitute the national segment of a regular international service' (§ 32) and hence 'the national legislation at issue in the main proceedings falls to be assessed in the light of the provisions of the TFEU on freedom of establishment, which are applicable directly to transport, and not on the basis of the Title of that Treaty on transport' (§ 33).

[128] According to Art. 14(1) Directive 2000/31/EC 'where an information society service is provided that consists of the storage of information provided by a recipient of the service, Member States shall ensure that the service provider is not liable for the information stored at the request of a recipient of the service, on condition that: (a) the provider does not have actual knowledge of illegal activity or information and, as regards claims for damages, is not aware of facts or circumstances from which the illegal

Even if it were assumed that Uber's role is sufficiently passive to treat it as a hosting provider (the possibility of liability exemptions disappears, if it is not), no exemption could apply when a company 'is aware of facts or circumstances from which the illegal activity or information is apparent'.[129] In a context of ultimately similar services provided by an operator of an online marketplace (eBay), the Court unsurprisingly interpreted this premise as imposing on the intermediaries a standard of 'a diligent economic operator'.[130] Uber can hardly be classified as a passive service provider, and, in any case, it is fully aware that the drivers using its Uber Pop application do not possess taxi licenses. So it would be liable when its platform is used for an illegal activity. If, however, Uber is liable for violations of taxi authorisation requirements by 'its' drivers, then the really significant question of whether the requirements are permissible according to EU law resurfaces again. This gives the Court of Justice an opportunity to establish minimum requirements for road safety, consumer protection or tax compliance as legitimate restrictions to the freedom of establishment not only on the market of 'Uber drivers', but on the taxi market more generally.

Doing so the Court would expose itself to the criticisms of detractors contending that its liberalising pressure disrespects the autonomy of European local communities in determining taxi authorisation terms, ostensibly violating socially embedded local policies and regulatory diversity. But by the very same token the Court would do its bit – as inherent in the very concept of the internal market – in helping modernise national economies where their growth prospects are encumbered by obsolete regulations.

This is not, however, how the Uber cases have been unfolding. In *Uber Belgium* the Court did not even pick up the gauntlet, curiously claiming that the referring court failed to sufficiently describe 'the activity at issue, particularly with regard to the nature and modalities of the service concerned'.[131] It is a very bizarre justification, considering that the main

activity or information is apparent; or (b) the provider, upon obtaining such knowledge or awareness, acts expeditiously to remove or to disable access to the information.'

129 Art. 14(1)(a) Directive 2000/31/EC. The Court of Justice explained that a hosting provider subject to the safe harbour provisions of the E-Commerce Directive must be 'neutral, in the sense that its conduct is merely technical, automatic and passive, pointing to a lack of knowledge or control of the data which it stores': Joined Cases C-236/08 to C-238/08, *Google*, ECLI:EU:C:2008:389, § 114. See also Case C-324/09, *L'Oréal*, ECLI:EU:C:2011:474, § 107–117.

130 Case C-324/09, *L'Oréal*, ECLI:EU:C:2011:474, § 120.

131 Case C-526/15, *Uber Belgium*, ECLI:EU:C:2016:830, § 29.

features of Uber services are well known, globally uniform and available under the same names all around. A few months later Advocate General Szpunar recommended in his opinion to *Elite Taxi* that Uber be considered a transport company.[132] And, because the referring court had asked about taxi authorisation implications only in the event that Uber is classified as a provider of information society services, the advocate general ended his opinion without delving into this crucial aspect. Despite the referring court was clearly seeking to establish whether Uber could by liable for violations of authorisation requirements on taxi markets, the opinion does not even mention the crucial aspect of what the Treaty freedom of establishment entails for the market of taxis and 'Uber drivers' in the first place, and for Uber's liability in the second.

Ultimately, therefore, in line with the heterodox view of the internal market, and in stark contrast to its reading pursued throughout the period of the permissive consensus by the Commission and the Court, in the Uber cases the internal market law enforcers have deployed delaying tactics. They have shunned steering behaviour of national authorities, which are very often unable and unwilling to undermine the interests of vested local interests. By this omission, the European institutions have sided with local lobbies in their struggle against new organisational models driven by the technological revolution.

The systemic consequences of such status quo protection are significant for the whole collaborative economy. If the Commission and the Court maintain their circumspect stance, Airbnb – a disruptive lodging rental system despised by hotel lobbies for its competitive pressure and by some local residents for how effective it is in raising the number of tourists in their neighbourhoods[133] – should not hope for much support from the internal market freedoms. The same applies to Amazon,

[132] Opinion of Advocate General Szpunar, delivered on 11 May 2017, Case C-434/15, *Elite Taxi*, ECLI:EU:C:2017:364.

[133] In Brussels, for instance, renting an accommodation is allowed only after meeting high standards of insurance, urban planning, hygiene and fire safety standards, obtaining a police certificate of good conduct and a written consent of the owner (or co-owners) and registering the accommodation with the Brussels government: 'Nieuwe Regels Voor Airbnb in Brussel Goedgekeurd', *De Standaard*, 29 March 2016, available at www.standaard.be/cnt/dmf20160329_02207907. In Berlin, landlords can rent less than 50 per cent of the property's floor space and apply for official permits, granted discretionarily, to rent out entire apartments: Marta Cooper, 'Berlin Is Cracking Down on Short-term Apartment Rentals – and Airbnb Is Taking a Hit', *Quartz*, 1 May 2016, available at qz.com/673932/berlin-is-cracking-down-on-short-term-apartment-rentals-and-airbnb-is-taking-a-hit/.

which, for instance, hit a wall in Paris (for fears of decimating local retailers) when it strived to introduce there its fast delivery service of a broad range of products, including foodstuffs.[134]

9.11 Aground

Here, the different stories recounted throughout this chapter meet. During the permissive consensus era the internal market was deemed to support creative destructors: transnational healthcare providers, companies posting workers transnationally and technological pioneers. Jacques Delors, who famously used to say that 'nobody can fall in love with the single market' apparently sensed how heroic the task of pursuing creative destruction in the traditionally protectionist Europe was. As long as the traditional view of the internal market prevailed, however, it could have been hoped that overcoming the resistance of vested interests, as well as the traditional prejudices and concerns underpinning them, is just a question of time. But now, when unrestrained markets have been politically associated primarily with the Great Recession and with rising income inequalities,[135] this hope has been superseded by the constraining dissensus.

It is indicative in this context that the Juncker Commission's digital single market agenda[136] was backed by half the EU countries in a letter published in summer 2016. The letter called for 'a market-based approach where businesses do not face unjustified burdens, can operate freely across borders like they do in their home countries, and all legislation is digital by default'.[137] It was signed by ministers from

[134] See Communiqué de presse – Dimanche 19 juin 2016, Réaction de la Ville de Paris au nouveau service de livraison proposé par Amazon, available at presse.paris.fr/wp-content/uploads/2016/06/R%C3%A9action-de-la-Ville-de-Paris-au-nouveau-service-de-livraison-propos%C3%A9-par-Amazon.pdf.

[135] While the relationship between deregulation of financial markets in the previous decades and the Great Financial Crisis is uncontestable, it has been argued that income inequalities have actually subsided in Europe in the last two decades: Zsolt Darvas and Guntram Wolff, 'An Anatomy of Inclusive Growth in Europe', *Bruegel Blueprint* No. 26, 2016, available at bruegel.org/wp-content/uploads/2016/10/BP-26-26_10_16-final-web.pdf.

[136] Communication from the Commission: 'A Digital Single Market Strategy for Europe', COM(2015)192, 6 May 2015.

[137] Joint letter from Belgium, Bulgaria, Czechia, Denmark, Estonia, Finland, Ireland, Latvia, Lithuania, Luxembourg, Poland, Slovenia, Sweden and United Kingdom in preparation of the Transport, Telecommunications and Energy and Competitiveness Council meetings 26 May 2016, available at www.politico.eu/wp-content/uploads/2016/05/DSMletter23MemberStates.pdf.

the majority of Eastern European, Scandinavian and Benelux countries, as well as from the UK and Ireland. But others were remarkably missing from the list of signees.

This chasm not only undermines possible practical effects of the digital single market agenda, but it also demonstrates the politically very vulnerable position in which the Commission and the Court of Justice – the two major drivers of the internal market in the past – have found themselves.

Their previous, purely economic approach unequivocally supportive of fundamental internal market freedoms has subsided to a much more cautious and political calculus. Confronted with increases in skepticism towards the traditional view of the internal market, the Commission has been trying to show its more 'social' face, epitomised most accurately by the attempts to amend the Posting of Workers Directive. On the other hand, it has been more downbeat when facing a surge of economic protectionism in the East of the EU[138] and tellingly toothless in key areas on the digital frontier,[139] apparently sensing political backlash from national governments if it tried to pursue a more ambitious agenda. This has largely left the Luxembourg court to row the boat of the internal

[138] See, for example, Simon Marks, 'Eastern Europe Turns Back on Single Market', *Politico*, 11 May 2017, available at www.politico.eu/article/eastern-europe-versus-the-single-market/.

[139] The Commission has managed to secure political support for a few of its Digital Market initiatives: Regulation 2017/1128 of the European Parliament and of the Council of 14 June 2017 on cross-border portability of online content services in the internal market, OJ 2017 L 168, 30 June 2017, pp. 1–11; Decision 2017/899 of the European Parliament and of the Council of 17 May 2017 on the use of the 470–790 MHz frequency band in the Union, OJ 2017 L 138, 25 May 2017, pp. 131–137; Regulation 2017/920 of the European Parliament and of the Council of 17 May 2017 amending Regulation 531/2012 as regards rules for wholesale roaming markets, OJ 2017 L 147, 9 June 2017, pp. 1–8. On the other hand, its proposals on Internet connectivity and copyright (see press release: European Commision, 'State of the Union 2016: Commission Paves the Way for More and Better Internet Connectivity for All Citizens and Businesses', available at europa.eu/rapid/press-release_IP-16-3008_en.htm and State of the Union 2016: Commission Proposes Modern EU Copyright Rules for European Culture to Flourish and Circulate, available at europa.eu/rapid/press-release_IP-16-3010_en.htm, both of 14 September 2016) have been heavily criticised for their ambitionless: e.g., 'Incumbents Rule. The European Union's Online Reforms Help the Old More Than the New', *The Economist*, 17 September 2016, available at www.economist.com/news/business/21707189-european-unions-online-reforms-help-old-more-new-incumbents-rule or Chris Spillane, 'Copyright Conundrum: Tweeting This May Cost You', *Politico*, 26 October 2016, available at www.politico.eu/pro/copyright-conundrum-tweeting-this-may-cost-you/.

market on its own. But, satisfying those who do not like to see national choices swayed significantly by European institutions, the Court, too, has become cautious in its approach.[140]

The charges that the traditional thinking about the internal market disrespects sovereignty, democracy and the 'socially embedded' nature of the market have clearly left a mark here.[141] Yet what seems to matter even more in this respect are serious, systemically biased distributive effects produced by the internal market, with many EU-13 countries experiencing very low unemployment levels and some EU-15 countries struggling with persistent unemployment. The period of the permissive consensus did not anticipate such a dynamic. Importantly, however, this point does not question market competition. Rather, it first of all indicates that when some EU countries suffer from unsuitable monetary policy conditions, when many have been pursuing socioeconomic and institutional approaches making them unfit for the creative destruction propelled by the internal market and when very significant cost differences remain persistent, the internal market puts some economies in a systemically advantageous, and others is a systemically

[140] Even more evidently, the process has been visible on the junction of the free movement of persons, European citizenship and welfare payments. As Charlotte O'Brien summarised the trend, 'welfare nationalism is washing away the traces of EU citizenship, with decreasing resistance from the Court of Justice. In reassuring Member States that it is not traipsing over national sovereignty or green-lighting benefit tourism, the Court adopts a surprisingly deferential approach in a series of judgments that appear to roll back decades of citizenship construction': Charlotte O'Brien, 'Civis Capitalist Sum: Class as the New Guiding Principle of EU Free Movement Rights', *Common Market Law Review* 53 (2016): 937. For other particularly insightful recent analyses, see: Niamh Nic Shuibhne, 'What I Tell You Three Times Is True. Lawful Residence and Equal Treatment after Dano', *Maastricht Journal of European and Comparative Law* 23 (2016): 908–936 and Charlotte O'Brien, annotation to Case C-308/14, *Commission* v. *United Kingdom*, Judgment of the Court (First Chamber) of 14 June 2016, EU:C:2016:436, *Common Market Law Review* 54 (2017): 209–244, as well as the case law and literature cited therein. The Commission has adopted a similar stance in this respect. In late 2016 it proposed a regulation which would give Member States more leeway to restrict social benefits for EU migrants: proposal for a regulation amending Regulation 883/2004 on the coordination of social security systems and regulation 987/2009 laying down the procedure for implementing Regulation 883/200, COM(2016)815.

[141] Mounting especially during the sovereign debt crisis, the criticism has not subsided afterwards. In a 2017 paper, Sacha Garben concluded, for instance, that 'in the internal market … the balance between "the market" and "the social" has been decisively struck in favour of the former, to such an extent that it affects the overall balance of these values in the EU polity. Furthermore, we have established that this

disadvantageous, position. This in turn inevitably brings about more divisions and resentments, ultimately weakening the Union.

Furthermore, if the integration of EU markets is to bring about economic modernisation it was originally tasked with, it must be properly dovetailed with a profoundly rethought approach to the role of the EU in the socioeconomic realm. Without it the internal market has been degenerating towards the relocation of production from the high-wage countries to the low-wage countries, and to the reverse relocation of the most talented – potentially most productive – youth from the low-wage countries to the high-wage countries. In a longer term any such setup is a recipe for endless political recriminations and frictions. While any creative destruction, also the one the internal market was designed to enable, entails a backlash from the less productive workers who become its potential main victims, this cost is easier to accept when public authorities provide them with tools and incentives to enhance their productivity and when educational systems are calibrated to funnel younger cohorts towards the most productive sectors. As I argued in Chapter 7, invoking the examples of Sweden and Germany, some countries fare in this respect better than others. Yet, as the next chapter explained, this is not what the EU has ever consistently pursued or supported with its redistribution. And without such a shield, the internal market can be easily discredited as nothing more than a vehicle for unfair competition.

outcome is not the result of democratically legitimate procedures. It would thus seem that process and substantive outcome are interrelated': Sacha Garben, 'The Constitutional (Im)balance between "the Market" and "the Social" in the European Union', *European Constitutional Law Review* 13 (2017): 51.

10 The EU and the Hidden Costs of Maximum Globalisation

10.1 The Beauty of Comparative Advantage

Conflicts within the internal market between high-wage societies and low-wage societies depicted in the previous chapter are all amplified by accelerating globalisation. This, in turn, brings us to the question of why the paradigm of maximum globalization became so entrenched in policymaking circles; why it has been so broadly endorsed as a benediction.

The idea that unencumbered international trade is a blessing for every society participating in it springs from the brilliant yet general and counterintuitive economic idea of comparative advantage.[1] In the early nineteenth century, one of the great English economists of the day, David Ricardo, demonstrated in a simple numerical form that this advantage should render international trade a win-win situation for all parties involved.[2] He demonstrated that even when one country (A) is disadvantaged in its production costs of each and every good compared to another country (B), trade between the two can leave both better off

[1] See, for example, Robert Stern, ed., 'Comparative Advantage, Growth, and the Gains from Trade and Globalization: A Festschrift in Honor of Alan V Deardorff', *World Scientific Studies in International Economics* 16 (2011) or Steven Suranovic, 'The Ricardian Theory of Comparative Advantage. International Trade: Theory and Policy', *The International Economics Study Centre*, 2007, available at catalog.flatworldknowledge.com/bookhub/reader/28.

[2] For a formal explanation, see, for example, Richard Pomfret, *International Trade: Theory, Evidence and Policy* (New Jersey, London, Singapore, Beijing, Shanghai, Hong Kong, Taipei, Chennai, Tokyo: World Scientific Publishing 2016), ch. 2. The concept itself dates back to Robert Torrens, *Essay on the External Corn Trade* (London: Hatchard, 1815). David Ricardo, *On the Principles of Political Economy and Taxation* (London: John Murray, 1817), provides an example translating the intuition into a formal model. The idea of comparative advantage grew in salience especially after John Stuart Mill, *Principles of Political Economy* (London: Longmans, Green and Co., 1848).

nonetheless if A specialises in the production of the goods in which its disadvantage is smallest. In other words, even if country A has no absolute advantage on any of the markets compared to country B, it should have a comparative advantage over the latter on the markets on which its absolute disadvantage is smallest. This is because country B, despite being more productive on every market, will earn the highest profits if it concentrates on the markets where its absolute advantage is biggest, giving up the markets where its absolute advantage is smallest compared to A (i.e., where A has comparative advantage).[3] Economically speaking, therefore, the global output is maximised when countries specialise on the basis of their opportunity costs of production. The political conclusion stemming from this logic is simple: each country is better off if it peacefully coexists with others, delivering the goods in which it has comparative advantages.

Like many economic theories, this one too is general and restricted by various conditions and reservations detaching it from the real picture.[4] But nonetheless, many researchers have found that international trade has been benefitting developed and developing economies alike. First, it has been pointed out that enhanced competition leads to productivity gains, which in turn should be reflected in pay raises. For instance, in-house research of the Obama administration concluded in 2015 that 'the strong increase in exports over the 1990s and 2000s translates into an additional $1,300 in annual earnings for workers in today's dollars'.[5] Second, international trade boosts the purchasing power of the poorest social strata, because poorer consumers mainly buy products of the sectors which are traded more.[6] This is precisely where the price-suppressing forces of international trade are concentrated. Economists of the trade-friendly Obama administration computed the magnitude of the poor-skewed advantage: accordingly, the purchasing power of the

[3] Within the same unit of time country B can produce more units of the goods in which it has a comparative advantage than of the goods in which A has a comparative advantage.

[4] It assumes in particular labour as the only factor of production, homogeneous goods across firms and countries, homogeneous labour within a country but heterogeneous across countries, costless reallocation of labour between industries in each country but no reallocation of it between countries, full employment and perfectly competitive markets for both labour and goods.

[5] The Council of Economic Advisors, 'The Economic Benefits of U.S. Trade', May 2015, 19, available at obamawhitehouse.archives.gov/sites/default/files/docs/cea_trade_report_final_non-embargoed_v2.pdf.

[6] See also Pablo Fajgelbaum and Amit Khandelwal, 'Measuring the Unequal Gains from Trade', *The Quarterly Journal of Economics* 131 (2016): 1113–1180.

richest 10 per cent of Americans grew by only 3 per cent due to international trade since early 1990s, while the middle class gained 29 per cent and the purchasing power of the poorest 10 per cent of Americans soared by 62 per cent.[7] Third, the main source of concern caused by international trade among developed societies – the rapidly growing levels of imports from developing countries – often comprise value actually added in developed economies at various earlier stages of the global production chain.[8] Therefore, the argument that growing imports from developing countries undercut manufacturing in developed countries is inaccurate. Fourth, international trade can be expected to stimulate wage raises in developing countries, improving the purchasing power of their societies and demand for the goods (usually of higher added value) in which the developed societies have a comparative advantage, inducing more exports from the latter to the former. Fifth, there is a correlation between increased openness and better health, especially in developing countries.[9] And sixth, international trade can be beneficial for the environment as well: some researchers concluded that every percentage point of growth in international trade reduces the concentration of pollution by a comparable fraction.[10]

New trade deals negotiated bilaterally and regionally since the Great Recession were promising particularly hefty benefits. The Obama administration estimated that the Trans-Pacific Partnership (TPP) between twelve Pacific Rim countries (aborted by President Trump) would increase annual real incomes in the US by $131 billion (0.5 per cent of GDP) by 2030, its annual exports by $357 billion (9.1 per cent of total exports) and global annual incomes by $492 billion in the same period.[11] Another piece of research concluded that the Transatlantic

[7] The Council of Economic Advisors, 'The Economic Benefits', p. 13.

[8] Robert Koopman et al., 'Give Credit Where Credit Is Due: Tracing Value Added in Global Production Chains', *NBER Working Paper* No. 16426, September 2010, available at www.nber.org/papers/w16426, International Monetary Fund, 'Changing Patterns of Global Trade', 2011, available at www.imf.org/external/np/pp/eng/2011/061511.pdf.

[9] Ann L. Owen and Stephen Wu, 'Is Trade Good for Your Health?', *Review of International Economics* 15 (2007): 660–682.

[10] 'A trade liberalization that raises the scale of economic activity by 1% raises pollution concentration by 0.25 to 0.5% via the scale effect, but the accompanying increase in incomes per capita drives concentrations down by 1.25–1.5% via a technical effect': Brian R. Copeland and M. Scott Taylor, *Trade and the Environment: Theory and Evidence* (Princeton, NJ: Princeton University Press, 2013): 3.

[11] Peter Petri and Michael Plummer, 'The Economic Effects of the Trans-Pacific Partnership: New Estimates', *Peterson Institute for International Economics Working Paper* No. 16–2, January 2016, available at piie.com/system/files/documents/wp16-2_0.pdf.

Trade and Investment Partnership (TTIP) between the EU and the USA (again, aborted by President Trump) should improve EU income levels in all EU countries (except for Malta) by an additional 0.5 per cent on average.[12] It also estimated that this agreement would lead to export increases to the USA for all EU countries. EU wages would go up both for high- and low-skilled workers, by about 0.5 per cent, and yet the costs for EU and US producers would go down. Other research roughly confirmed these calculations, adding that, had TTIP been signed, EU exports to the USA would have grown by 27 per cent and imports from the USA would have increased by 35.7 per cent (though the EU trade surplus with the USA would nonetheless grow in absolute terms).[13] The EU and the USA would have gained additional economic output of €119 billion and €95 billion, respectively.[14]

10.2 The Downsides of Hyperglobalisation

As all of the exuberant analyses were being published, however, the gap between pundits pursuing a trade liberalisation agenda and the sentiment swelling among the post-industrial societies widened. And, what is particularly important for my point in this chapter, the anti-globalisation attitude has been more justified than the whizzes would like to admit.

This attitude, too, stems from the logic of comparative advantage preordaining that, in order to produce more in the sectors in which an economy has such an advantage, it has to give in some other sectors, even if also there it was originally more productive, in absolute terms, compared to its competitors. In other words, some 'good jobs' will inevitably migrate offshore, where they will be comparably less 'good' in terms of salaries, labour standards and protections. What is ultimately more important is that, while advanced economies usually have a comparative advantage in the more capital-intensive and less labour-intensive sectors, the boundary between the two is never clear enough.

12 World Trade Institute, 'TTIP and the EU Member States', University of Bern, January 2016.

13 Ecorys, 'Trade SIA on the Transatlantic Trade and Investment Partnership (TTIP) between the EU and the USA', 2016, available at www.trade-sia.com/ttip/wp-content/uploads/sites/6/2014/02/TSIA-TTIP-draft-Interim-Technical-Report.pdf.

14 Joseph Francois et al., 'Reducing Transatlantic Barriers to Trade and Investment – An Economic Assessment', *Final Project Report*, CEPR, London, March 2013, available at trade.ec.europa.eu/doclib/docs/2013/march/tradoc_150737.pdf.

Nor does the comparative advantage explain what governments of post-industrial countries should do when powerful international players (like China) enter the (high value added) markets in which they previously had comparative disadvantage. Furthermore, the Ricardian model posits perfect competition, while the reality is dominated by industrial policies skewing exchange rates, competition rules, fiscal policies and financial intermediation for the benefit of domestic companies. And finally, this model does not tackle the ultimately most fundamental problem: higher labour and environment protection standards inevitably lead to higher production costs. Stark discrepancies between trading societies in these respects will trigger the relocation of the industries in which natural resources and labour matter most to the countries where the standards are lowest. Contrary to the findings that more trade is good for health and the environment, the logic of comparative advantage should therefore spur powerful externalities and a race to the bottom, to the detriment of the values determining well-being beyond mere economic output and consumption.

Some renowned economists have warned against these downsides of maximum globalisation for a long time now. In a 1992 paper, Harvard's Dani Rodrik claimed that every $1 of net efficiency gains produced by international trade would cause an additional $5 of income redistribution.[15] In other words, before the WTO came into existence and when China was an industrial lightweight, it could have been expected that international trade would seriously reshuffle wealth within individual societies. According to Rodrik's calculations, the winners were likely to gain $5 in addition to every $1 of net efficiency gains due to international trade. As a flipside, however, someone else within the same society was about to lose $5, gaining nothing in return. This ratio of redistribution to efficiency would only grow as tariffs go down, Rodrik predicted.[16] Hence globalisation, largely fuelled by international trade, may aggregate consumption and outputs, but it also undermines domestic social stability by pitching 'losers'

[15] Dani Rodrik, 'The Rush to Free Trade in the Developing World: Why So Late? Why Now? Will it Last?', *NBER Working Paper* No. 3947, January 1992, available at www.nber.org/papers/w3947.pdf.

[16] In a 2011 book, Rodrik argued that 'in an economy like the United States, where average tariffs are below 5%, a move to complete free trade would reshuffle more than $50 of income among different groups for each dollar of efficiency or "net" gain created!': Dani Rodrik, *The Globalization Paradox: Democracy and the Future of the World Economy* (New York: Norton, 2012): 57.

against 'winners'.[17] The redistributive effects would happen not only within societies, but – even more remarkably – between them. Paul Samuelson, a Nobel Prize laureate, demonstrated soon after China was admitted to the WTO in 2001 that, within the Ricardian model, 'sometimes free trade globalization can convert a technical change abroad into a benefit for both regions; but sometimes a productivity gain in one country can benefit that country alone, while permanently hurting the other country by reducing the gains from trade that are possible between the two countries'.[18]

In line with this finding, one important paper, published in early 2016, when both the EU and the Obama administration were pursuing in earnest their trade liberalisation agendas, argued that job losses in the USA from increasing Chinese import competition between 1999 and 2011 were in the non-negligible range of 2.0–2.4 million.[19] Joseph Stiglitz argued soon after that 'in the US, the bottom 90% has endured income stagnation for a third of a century. Median income for full-time male workers is actually *lower* in real (inflation-adjusted) terms than it was 42 years ago. At the bottom, real wages are comparable to their level 60 years ago.'[20] When you add to the picture that in 2012 about three million American children spent at least a quarter of the year on virtually no money,[21] the mainstream picture of international trade as a pure blessing for advanced economies becomes much more obscure.[22] Of course, very slow or non-existing wage gains in the middle and lower ranges of the earnings distribution are not an indigenous American problem. It has affected the vast majority of OECD countries

[17] See also Dani Rodrik, *Has Globalization Gone Too Far?* (Washington, DC: Peterson Institute for International Economics, 1997).

[18] Paul A. Samuelson, 'Where Ricardo and Mill Rebut and Confirm Arguments of Mainstream Economists Supporting Globalization', *Journal of Economic Perspectives* 18 (2004): 142.

[19] Daron Acemoglu et al., 'Import Competition and the Great US Employment Sag of the 2000s', *Journal of Labor Economics* 34 (Part 2, January 2016): 141–198.

[20] Joseph Stiglitz, 'Globalization and Its New Discontents', *Project Syndicate*, 5 August 2016, available at www.project-syndicate.org/commentary/globalization-new-discontents-by-joseph-e–stiglitz-2016-08. According to the Economic Policy Institute, between 1973 and 2015, US productivity increased by 73 per cent, while compensation (adjusted for inflation) increased by 11 per cent: EPI, 'The Productivity–Pay Gap', available at www.epi.org/productivity-pay-gap/.

[21] Kathryn J. Edin and H. Luke Shaefer, *$2.00 a Day: Living on Almost Nothing in America* (New York: Houghton Mifflin Harcourt, 2015).

[22] Branko Milanovic, *Global Inequality. A New Approach for the Age of Globalization* (Cambridge, MA; London: The Belknap Press of Harvard University Press, 2016).

during the last decade.[23] And while all the downsides have also been fuelled by other factors, from technological change to swings in welfare policies, international trade, too, has seriously contributed to the sentiment spreading among the working classes of the advanced economies: that globalisation has put them on the losing side.

10.3 China Cut Loose

Chinese economic advancements have been particularly disturbing from this perspective. This country's very effective export-oriented industrial policy has been casting a long shadow on the logic of comparative advantage ever since the country was admitted to the WTO. With only rudimentary social protections, with intensive investments in education and science,[24] with currency manipulations to stimulate exports, like the one following the Shanghai stock exchange crash in August 2015, with the state-owned financial system mobilised to support exports,[25] with aggressive industrial policy,[26] as well as with subsidised energy, China has been offering unbeatable prices for a growing range of products.[27]

23 OECD, OECD Employment Outlook 2016.

24 'The increase in Chinese and Korean business R&D expenditure has been remarkable, particularly China's. China is now the world's second biggest R&D spender, after the US, and is similar in R&D size to Germany, France and Italy combined': Francesca Barbiero et al., *Manufacturing Europe's Future*, ed. Reinhilde Veugelers (Bruegel Blueprint, 1 October 2013), 18, available at bruegel.org/wp-content/uploads/imported/publications/Blueprint_XXI_web_181113a.pdf.

25 The World Bank indicated in its 2015 China Economic Update, June 2015, 28–29, that 'instead of promoting the foundations for sound financial development, the state has interfered extensively and directly in allocating resources through administrative and price controls, guarantees, credit guidelines, pervasive ownership of financial institutions, and regulatory policies. These interventions have no parallel in modern market economies.' Interestingly, the whole chapter of the report on the financial sector was subsequently redacted: see also Gabriel Wildau, 'World Bank Redacts Report Critical of China Financial System', *Financial Times*, 3 July 2015, available at www.ft.com/content/23dcc148-2152-11e5-aa5a-398b2169cf79?mhq5j=e2. In a disclaimer at the beginning of the document's final version the institution wrote that this part 'had not gone through the World Bank's usual internal review and clearance procedures' (p. 1).

26 For an overview of literature documenting it see Robert Kalcik, 'Is China's Innovation Strategy a Threat?', *Bruegel Blog Post*, 3 April 2017, available at bruegel.org/2017/04/19927/.

27 The issue of state-subsidised investments in Europe has also stirred debate in the EU. For an overview see: Gisela Grieger, 'Foreign Direct Investment Screening. A Debate in Light of China-EU FDI Flows', *European Parliamentary Research Service*, May

The economic profile championed by China has been advancing consumer welfare by giving the world's consumers access to products otherwise unavailable to many of them. But it has also raised the issue of fair competition and job leakages, intermittently erupting in serious trade disputes over suspiciously cheap export prices, from solar panels to steel.

For the first fifteen years of China in the WTO (i.e., between December 2001 and December 2016), European authorities had their trade defence tasks facilitated by the China Accession Protocol. Its Art. 15 (a)(ii), in force until December 2016,[28] provided that 'the importing WTO Member may use a methodology that is not based on a strict comparison with domestic prices or costs in China if the producers under investigation cannot clearly show that market economy conditions prevail in the industry producing the like product'. In other words, unless China had been recognised as a market economy by the EU during its first fifteen years in the WTO, which did not happen, European institutions could forego the 'normal value' methodology (which strictly requires that export prices be only gauged by direct costs and prices in the country of origin), when determining whether a Chinese product is dumped on the EU market.[29] Instead, they could use alternative methods of establishing the reference price when judging whether dumping takes place. And the EU authorities did so, comparing export prices of all non-market economies (including China) with prices in analogous market economies.[30] This method allowed trade defence

2017, available at www.europarl.europa.eu/RegData/etudes/BRIE/2017/603941/EPRS_BRI(2017)603941_EN.pdf.

[28] According to Art. 15(d) Protocol: 'in any event, the provisions of subparagraph (a)(ii) shall expire 15 years after the date of accession'.

[29] According to Art. VI of the 1994 GATT agreement a price of the product exported from one country to another is below its normal value if it:

- (a) is less than the comparable price, in the ordinary course of trade, for the like product when destined for consumption in the exporting country, or,
- (b) in the absence of such domestic price, is less than either
  - (i) the highest comparable price for the like product for export to any third country in the ordinary course of trade, or
  - (ii) the cost of production of the product in the country of origin plus a reasonable addition for selling cost and profit.

[30] Art. 2(7)(a) Council Regulation 1225/2009 of 30 November 2009 on protection against dumped imports from countries not members of the European Community, OJ 2009 No. L 343, 22 December 2009, pp. 51–73 provided that, as a general rule, 'In the case of imports from non-market economy countries, normal value shall be determined on the basis of the price or constructed value in a market economy third country, or the price from such a third country to other countries, including the Community,

measures to be triggered against Chinese products whenever EU institutions concluded that Chinese export prices were below international reference standards.[31]

Until 2016, the majority of EU countries were rather agnostic about the prospect of switching export price gauging to the normal value methodology,[32] intrinsically more friendly to Chinese exports. But as the popular perception of international trade worsened and as Chinese overcapacities in the steel and aluminium sectors mounted,[33] the political atmosphere changed. Of course, European producers of capital goods, all sorts of machineries in particular, could be rubbing their hands at the prospect of switching to the 'normal value' methodology, because Chinese overproduction was sending prices of raw materials to historic lows. Yet the outlook of switching to the 'normal value' methodology, more friendly to Chinese imports than the earlier one, was sending jitters across European steel and aluminium producers, who became anxious that European production would be obliterated were the trade defence measures weakened. Trade pundits confirmed these qualms. One analysis concluded that up to 211,000 jobs would be lost directly if the EU switched to the standard anti-dumping methodology

or where those are not possible, on any other reasonable basis, including the price actually paid or payable in the Community for the like product, duly adjusted if necessary to include a reasonable profit margin'.

31 The EU was quite cautious when using the powers it had, however. Authors of a study commissioned by the European Parliament calculated that the EU's anti-dumping measures affected less than 2 per cent of bilateral imports at the end of 2014; on average, the duties were 44 per cent, compared to 142 per cent for the USA and 80 per cent for India: Erdal Yalcin, Gabriel Felbermayr and Alexander Sandkamp, 'New Trade Rules for China? Opportunities and Threats for the EU', study commissioned by the European Parliament's Committee on International Trade, 2016, 5, available at www.europarl.europa.eu/RegData/etudes/STUD/2016/535021/EXPO_STU(2016)535021_EN.pdf.

32 François Godement, 'China's Market Economy Status and the European Interest', *European Council on Foreign Relations Policy Brief* No. 180, June 2016, available at www.ecfr.eu/page/-/ECFR_180_-_CHINA_MARKET_ECONOMY_STATUS_AND_THE_EUROPEAN_INTEREST_(002).pdf.

33 As the Commission emphasised in autumn 2016, 'the steel overcapacity in China alone has been estimated at around 350 million tonnes, almost the double of the Union's annual production. Steel imports from China to the EU have surged in the last three years. Market prices for some steel products fell by up to 40% due to the surge of volumes … Overcapacities are also developing very fast in other sectors, for instance aluminium. China has almost 10 million tons of excess aluminium capacity, doubled from five years ago': European Commission, 'Communication: Towards a Robust Trade Policy for the EU in the Interest of Jobs and Growth', COM(2016)690, 18 October 2016.

in respect to China.[34] According to another, which also took into account more far-reaching effects, between 1.7 million and 3.5 million European jobs would be at risk, while Europe would lose 1 to 2 per cent of GDP of output.[35]

These figures agitated European policymakers. As a consequence, the Basic Anti-Dumping Regulation, enacted in 2016, provided that the 'normal value' methodology would apply only to the Chinese producers who are capable of demonstrating that 'market-economy conditions prevail for this producer or producers in respect of the manufacture and sale of the like product concerned'.[36] Second, the Basic Regulation was amended in December 2017.[37] The amendment, which in practice entails similar effects to the previous rules, is intended, first, to capture significant market distortions caused by state interventions disguising the true extent of dumping practices, in order to determine whether a 'particular market situation' required by Art. 2.2 of the Anti-Dumping Agreement to justify an exemption to the basic methodology,[38] exists.[39] Second, where such distortions occur, prices and costs in the exporting country would be disregarded. Instead, in order to determine whether

[34] European Commission, 'Change in the Methodology for Anti-dumping Investigations Concerning China', 5 February 2016, available at trade.ec.europa.eu/doclib/docs/2016/february/tradoc_154241.pdf.

[35] Robert Scott and Xiao Jiang, 'Unilateral Grant of Market Economy Status to China Would Put Millions of EU Jobs at Risk', *Economic Policy Institute Briefing Paper* No. 407, 18 September 2015, available at www.epi.org/publication/eu-jobs-at-risk/.

[36] Art. 2(7)(b) Regulation 2016/1036.

[37] Regulation 2017/2321 of the European Parliament and of the Council of 12 December 2017 amending Regulation (EU) 2016/1036 on protection against dumped imports from countries not members of the European Union and Regulation (EU) 2016/1037 on protection against subsidised imports from countries not members of the European Union, OJ 2017 No. L 338, 19 December 2017, pp. 1–7.

[38] Art. 2.2 WTO Anti-Dumping Agreement establishes an exception to the 'normal value' methodology. It provides that 'when, because of the particular market situation' sales of the like product in the ordinary course of trade in the domestic market of the exporting country 'do not permit a proper comparison, the margin of dumping shall be determined by comparison with a comparable price of the like product when exported to an appropriate third country, provided that this price is representative'.

[39] To assess whether the distortions occur, European institutions would consider several criteria, such as the widespread presence of enterprises controlled by public authorities, distorted wage costs, discrimination in favour of domestic companies, the lack, discriminatory application or inadequate enforcement of bankruptcy, corporate or property laws and prevalence of financial sector institutions implementing public policy objectives: new Art. 2(6a)(b) Regulation 2016/1036.

dumping is taking place, the Commission would use other available benchmarks, including costs and prices in other economies.[40]

Neither the rules of the 2016 Basic Regulation nor the amendment could satisfy China, which took the case against the EU to the WTO's Dispute Resolution Body immediately after its Accession Agreement's transitional period expired.[41] It also mounted political pressure on Germany in particular, to temper the European stance.[42]

The WTO will rather inevitably uphold the Chinese case. Until October 2016, EU policymakers could hope that either the 2016 Basic Regulation or a more refined version of it would meet WTO standards. Yet, a month before the Commission tabled its draft amendment to the Basic Regulation in November 2016, the WTO's Dispute Settlement Body's second instance found a similar anti-dumping measure imposed by the Council on imports of biodiesel from Argentina[43] incongruent with Art. 2.2 Anti-Dumping Agreement.[44] In that case the Council argued that export prices for soybeans used as inputs for biodiesel in Argentina were distorted by much higher export taxes levied there, compared to the taxes on the finished product (biodiesel). In consequence, the Council ignored the costs reported in the Argentine exporters' records for soybeans. In

[40] According to the amendment to Regulation 2016/1036 (new Art. 2(6a)(a)) 'the normal value shall be constructed exclusively on the basis of costs of production and sale reflecting undistorted prices or benchmarks'. For this purpose, the sources that may be used include in particular 'undistorted international prices, costs, or benchmarks', 'corresponding costs of production and sale in an appropriate representative country with a similar level of economic development as the exporting country, provided the relevant cost data are readily available', or 'domestic costs, but only to the extent that they are positively established not to be distorted, on the basis of accurate and appropriate evidence'. This tenet is apparently to instantiate the 'comparison with a comparable price' requirement of Art. 2.2 of the Anti-Dumping Agreement.

[41] Case DS516: European Union – Measures Related to Price Comparison Methodologies, file available at www.wto.org/english/tratop_e/dispu_e/cases_e/ds516_e.htm.

[42] In spring 2017, Chinese authorities warned that they were contemplating an introduction of a car quota: Hans von der Burchard and Jakob Hanke, 'China Turns Trade Screws on German Cars', *Politico*, 30 May 2017, available at www.politico.eu/article/china-turns-screws-on-german-cars-to-swing-eu-trade-policy/.

[43] Implementing Regulation 1194/2013 imposing a definitive anti-dumping duty and collecting definitively the provisional duty imposed on imports of biodiesel originating in Argentina and Indonesia, OJ 2013 No. L 315, 26 November 2013, pp. 2–26.

[44] Case DS 473: European Union – Anti-Dumping Measures on Biodiesel from Argentina, file available at www.wto.org/english/tratop_e/dispu_e/cases_e/ds473_e.htm. Indonesia also sued the EU before the WTO's DSB (case DS 480: European Union – Anti-Dumping Measures on Biodiesel from Indonesia, file available at www.wto.org/english/tratop_e/dispu_e/cases_e/ds480_e.htm).

lieu of that it construed the reference value of the Argentine products by replacing recorded costs of the producers with international reference prices published by its government. The Council opined that these prices more properly reflected the level of comparable prices on markets with no distortions induced by government actions. The WTO panel disagreed, however, asserting, among other things, that in any scenario under Art. 2.2 Anti-Dumping Agreement the authority undertaking an investigation should strive to establish costs of production in the country of origin. According to the panel, this applies also when there are market distortions.[45] The stance of EU law towards China is very similar to the disputed 2013 Argentine measures, putting it in a similarly vulnerable legal position.

The case for any such a defence measure is further weakened by the wording of China's Accession Protocol. It is straightforward that, since December 2016 '[i]n determining price comparability ... the importing WTO Member shall use ... Chinese prices or costs for the industry under investigation' – i.e., the 'normal value' methodology – as the only gauge available to China's trading partners. In other words, China's Accession Protocol apparently seeks to make sure that after the transition period only the basic methodology, most favourable to Chinese products, applies. Considering this additional aspect, a WTO panel can be even less expected to accept any attempts to apply to China any methodology similar to what the EU strived to use in respect to Argentine biodiesel.

After the Argentine biodiesel case was decided in autumn 2016, the EU has faced a dilemma. It can nonetheless try to rectify the excessively

[45] As the Appellate Body noted in its report in Case European Union – Anti-Dumping Measures on Biodiesel from Argentina, WTO case WT/DS473/AB/R of 6 October 2016, Sec. 6.81, 'when relying on any out-of-country information to determine the "cost of production in the country of origin" under Article 2.2 of the Anti-Dumping Agreement, an investigating authority has to ensure that such information is used to arrive at the "cost of production in the country of origin" ... Other than pointing to the deduction of fobbing costs, the European Union has not asserted, either before the Panel or before us, that the EU authorities adapted, or even considered adapting, the information used in their calculation in order to ensure that it represented the cost of production in Argentina. On the contrary, the EU authorities specifically selected the surrogate price for soybeans to remove the perceived distortion in the cost of soybeans in Argentina. As the Panel stated, the EU authorities selected and used this particular information precisely because it did not represent the cost of soybeans in Argentina. Thus, we agree with the Panel that the surrogate price for soybeans used by the EU authorities did not represent the cost of soybeans in Argentina for producers or exporters of biodiesel.'

optimistic assumption of China's Accession Protocol that this country would certainly be a market economy by the end of 2016, sticking to its different anti-dumping methodology. In that scenario, however, it faces hefty Chinese retaliatory measures authorised by the WTO's Dispute Settlement Body. Or it can buckle under. The latter decision will mean, however, that the economies in more open competition with Chinese products will face further job haemorrhaging.

More generally, the dilemma of China's WTO Accession Protocol has pointed to the question of negative externalities: the costs of producing a certain good not reflected in its price and hence borne by society at large. I mentioned earlier that because Chinese workers receive only rudimentary social protections and because they compete with European workers enjoying comparably very high social protections, the Chinese competition should put a significant downward pressure on the protections in Europe, particularly in the exposed sectors, entailing job destructions where the standards are not sufficiently aligned downwards.

In fact, international trade wizards have never denied this effect. What they have highlighted, instead, is that this mechanism should apply to some sectors only, while other sectors, both non-tradeable and more technologically advanced, would retain the advantages of social protections and the economic boost from broadened markets.

As I highlighted in Chapter 7, discussing the evolution of the Swedish socioeconomic model, such a strategy could indeed work, as far as the government is capable of continuously shepherding workers towards the sectors in which the comparative advantage can be maintained. This type of institutional effectiveness and agility is beyond the reach of many (in fact, most) EU governments, however. And otherwise the idea becomes politically disruptive, because European societies are naturally confused by better job opportunities for the most productive workers and by the suppression of consumer prices whenever they are accompanied by the externalities of more precarious jobs and higher unemployment in other sectors.

10.4 The Curiosities of the European Climate Policy

Yet another type of externality is even more problematic in the longer term. It is the environmental damage and climate change inadvertently reinforced by the current paradigms of international trade, which is hurting both the developed and developing societies much more than the increasing long-term unemployment and social unrest from which some of them suffer.

For more than a decade now, the EU's climate policy has relied on three main principles: the first is to cut greenhouse gas (GHG) emissions compared to 1990 levels, the second focuses on raising the share of EU energy from renewable resources, and the third is to improve energy efficiency. The European Council agreed in March 2007 that the EU would improve its performance on all three accounts by 20 per cent by 2020. Initially, it seemed that the EU emissions trading system (ETS) would be the main engine of the policy in the first of its three aspects. The ETS, established in 2005 to cover around 45 per cent of the EU's GHG emissions, was intended to reduce them 'in a cost-effective and economically efficient manner'[46] by introducing a pricing system for CO_2.[47] In addition, to curb the effects of the remaining 55 per cent emissions on climate change, the Effort Sharing Decision, enacted in 2009,[48] set national reduction targets of GHG emissions for 2020. In the same year, the EU legislator passed a directive instrumental to achieving the goal on renewables,[49] while yet another one, signed into law in 2012,[50] defined the toolbox for achieving the energy efficiency goal.

[46] Art. 1 Directive 2003/87/EC of the European Parliament and of the Council of 13 October 2003 establishing a scheme for GHG emission allowance trading within the Community and amending Council Directive 96/61/EC, OJ 2003 No. L 275, 25 October 2003, pp. 32–46.

[47] The ETS is a cap-and-trade system, in which the amount of GHGs that the sectors covered can emit is regulated. Companies trade permits to emit GHGs, which they originally buy in auctions. This market mechanism naturally raises the price for permits if the demand to emit GHGs grows, but it also causes price falls if the demand drops, as it has been the case in the EU since the inception of the economic crisis in 2008.

[48] Decision No 406/2009/EC of the European Parliament and of the Council of 23 April 2009 on the effort of Member States to reduce their GHG emissions to meet the Community's GHG emission reduction commitments up to 2020, OJ 2009 No. L 140, 5 June 2009, pp. 136–148.

[49] Directive 2009/28/EC of the European Parliament and of the Council of 23 April 2009 on the promotion of the use of energy from renewable sources and amending and subsequently repealing Directives 2001/77/EC and 2003/30/EC, OJ 2009 No. L 140, 5 June 2009, pp. 16–62.

[50] Directive 2012/27/EU of the European Parliament and of the Council of 25 October 2012 on energy efficiency, amending Directives 2009/125/EC and 2010/30/EU and repealing Directives 2004/8/EC and 2006/32/EC, OJ 2012 No. L 315, 14 November 2012, pp. 1–56.

By the time all the puzzles were put in place, however, it became evident that the emissions trading system was dysfunctional.[51] Largely in order to avoid carbon leakage – the relocation of energy-intensive sectors to locations outside the EU – the number of permits to pollute handed out to each of the factories and power stations covered by the scheme was set too high from the very beginning to achieve their scarcity, carbon price rises and emission reductions. Between 2005 and 2008, carbon prices hovered between €15 and €25+ per tonne of CO_2. By mid-2008 they went up to almost €30 per tonne of CO_2. Then, however, they collapsed, reaching less than €5 per tonne of CO_2 five years later. Despite the Commission's attempts to restore the price by postponing the auctioning of some permits until 2019–2020 and by reducing auction volumes,[52] carbon prices hit the floor of €5 per tonne of CO_2 again in 2016. This price level, prevailing for the next several months, is 80 per cent below what the OECD called 'a conservative minimum estimate of the damage that results from emitting one tonne of carbon'.[53]

Yet, what sent carbon prices so low – the economic crisis, technological advances and the growth of wind and solar electricity production[54] – was

[51] It has also turned out that transport emissions (a quarter of all emissions) have been growing unencumbered. Directive 2009/28/EC was based on the assumption that 'the Community and the Member States should strive to reduce total consumption of energy in transport and increase energy efficiency in transport. The principal means of reducing consumption of energy in transport include transport planning, support for public transport, increasing the share of electric cars in production and producing cars which are more energy efficient and smaller both in size and in engine capacity' (preamble, § 28). Contrary to these expectations, transport emissions have grown so pronouncedly that they caused a rise of total emissions in 2015: European Environment Agency, 'EU Greenhouse Gas Emissions from Transport Increase for the Second Year in a Row', 1 June 2017, available at www.eea.europa.eu/highlights/eu-greenhouse-gas-emissions-from-transport-increased.

[52] Commission Regulation 176/2014 of 25 February 2014 amending Regulation 1031/2010 in particular to determine the volumes of GHG emission allowances to be auctioned in 2013–2020, OJ 2014 No. L 56, 26 February 2014, pp. 11–13. The Commission also proposed further tightening of the system: Proposal for a directive amending Directive 2003/87/EC to enhance cost-effective emission reductions and low-carbon investments (COM(2015)337). In early 2017, the Council backed it up, delaying the process of cancelling surplus permits until 2024, however. For an overview see Robert-Jan Bartunek and Alissa de Carbonnel, 'EU Nations Thrash Out Deal on Carbon Market Reform', *Reuters*, 3 March 2017, available at http://uk.reuters.com/article/uk-eu-carbon-idUKKBN16718Q?il=0.

[53] OECD, *Effective Carbon Rates: Pricing CO2 through Taxes and Emissions Trading Systems* (Paris: OECD Publishing, 2016).

[54] Specific causations behind the price drop are not very clear, however. See, for example, Nicolas Koch et al., 'Causes of the EU ETS Price Drop: Recession, CDM, Renewable Policies or a Bit of Everything? – New Evidence', *Energy Policy* 73 (2014): 676–685.

nonetheless rendering the EU's target on emission reductions easy to reach. In consequence GHG emissions in EU 28 decreased by 23.7 per cent between 1990 and 2015.[55]

Aware of this overperformance, EU leaders decided to established more ambitious targets for 2030, setting the GHG emissions reduction target for 2030 at 40 per cent less than in 1990 and raising the targets for the share of renewable energy and the improvement in energy efficiency by an additional seven percentage points (i.e., to 27 per cent).[56] In doing so, the EU placed itself in the avant-garde of the international community, which played out in December 2015, when a United Nations conference on climate change brought about the so-called Paris accord outlining a global agreement to keep global temperature rise to 2°C and to strive to limit warming to 1.5°C. When, nine months later, the Environment Council approved the ratification of the Paris Agreement by the European Union, the EU Commissioner for Climate Action and Energy, Miguel Arias Cañete, was beaming with pride. As he avowed, 'they said Europe is too complicated to agree quickly. They said we had too many hoops to jump through. They said we were all talk. Today's decision shows what Europe is all about: unity and solidarity as Member States take a European approach, just as we did in Paris. We are reaching a critical period for decisive climate action. And when the going gets tough, Europe gets going.'[57]

The question, however, is how far the EU's climate action will go in the reality of maximum globalisation even when 'Europe gets going'. Its climate policy has always relied on the assumption that the protection of the environment can go hand-in-hand with unencumbered international trade. It has presumed that Europe can influence global climate action by spearheading emission reductions and by 'providing leadership with the "soft power" of ideas from the high moral ground

[55] European Environmental Agency, 'EEA Report, 2017. Annual European Union Greenhouse Gas Inventory 1990–2015 and Inventory Report 2017', May 2017, vii, available at www.eea.europa.eu/publications/european-union-greenhouse-gas-inventory-2017 and European Environment Agency, 'EU Greenhouse Gas Emissions from Transport Increase for the Second Year in a Row', 1 June 2017, available at www.eea.europa.eu/highlights/eu-greenhouse-gas-emissions-from-transport-increased.

[56] European Council (23 and 24 October 2014), conclusions available at www.consilium.europa.eu/uedocs/cms_data/docs/pressdata/en/ec/145397.pdf.

[57] European Commission, 'Ministers Approve EU Ratification of Paris Agreement', 30 September 2016, available at ec.europa.eu/clima/news/articles/news_2016093001_en.htm.

of global environmental protection'.[58] It conjectured that other countries would follow its efforts if only they were encouraged diplomatically or enticed financially to do so.

In practice, however, these assumptions have posed an unanswerable question, making the EU's climate policy extremely vulnerable: how credible can the EU's suasion as a leadership tool be, considering that the organisation has been declining industrially compared to other world's regions, with its share in global emissions decreasing precipitously as a result?

In 2014, for instance (the most recent year for which comprehensive data is available), global GHG emissions (excluding the so-called Land-Use Change and Forestry[59]) were about 50 per cent higher than in 1990.[60] China has mainly contributed to this trend, with its emissions increasing almost fourfold in the same period.[61] But also developed economies facing the relocation of industrial production to developing countries, like the USA, Australia or Canada, were doing more damage to the environment in 2014 than in 1990. Europe has therefore been exceptional in its emissions reduction feat. Also incomparable was the European mix of factors leading up to its globally unusual stance: heavy redistribution from consumers and taxpayers to the producers of green energy in some countries,[62] deindustrialisation, technological

[58] Andrei Marcu, 'Paris 2015: What's in It for the EU?', *CEPS Commentary*, 8 May 2015, available at www.ceps.eu/publications/paris-2015-what's-it-eu.

[59] I.e., excluding 'a greenhouse gas inventory sector that covers emissions and removals of greenhouse gases resulting from direct human-induced land use, land-use change and forestry activities': United Nations Framework Convention on Climate Change, Glossary of climate change acronyms and terms, available at unfccc.int/essential_background/glossary/items/3666.php#L.

[60] 45,741 MtCO2e in 2014 and 29,964 in 1990: World Resources Institute, CAIT Climate Data Explorer, Historical Emissions, available at cait.wri.org.

[61] From 3,154 $MtCO_2e$ in 1990 to 11,912 $MtCO_2e$ in 2014: ibid.

[62] This redistribution was endorsed by the Court of Justice early on, when it authorised the Member States to require private power firms to purchase renewable energy 'at minimum prices higher than the real economic value of that type of electricity, and, second, distribute the financial burden resulting from that obligation' to their consumers, arguing that renewable energy is instrumental to reducing 'emissions of greenhouse gases which are amongst the main causes of climate change which the European Community and its Member States have pledged to combat': Case C-379/98, *PreussenElektra*, ECLI:EU:C:2001:160, § 56, 73. EU law also authorises state aids to renewables, if they meet certain basic conditions: Sec. 7 of Commission Regulation 651/2014 of 17 June 2014 declaring certain categories of aid compatible with the internal market in application of Articles 107 and 108 of the Treaty, OJ 2014 No. L 187, 26 June 2014, pp. 1–78; Guidelines on State aid for environmental protection and energy 2014–2020, OJ 2014 No. C 200, 28 June 2014, pp. 1–55; Guidelines on certain State aid measures in the context of the greenhouse gas emission allowance trading scheme post-2012, OJ 2012 No. C 158, 5 June 2012, pp. 4–22.

improvements, especially in the once-heavily polluting Eastern Europe, and the protracted economic crisis. In consequence of all these factors, while in 1990 the current EU was responsible for 17.5 per cent of global GHG emissions,[63] in 2014 this share slid down to 8.9 per cent.[64]

It can be argued that this fact makes it easier for the EU to be a role model and to spearhead global efforts to stymie climate change. The role European countries played in winning the international community to the Paris accord – the first ever universally binding climate change agreement – can be seen as a confirmation of this stance. But the Paris accord has not been a remedy to the climate change problem, even had the USA not pulled out of it. Soon after it was signed, scientists realised that individual country pledges to emission reductions this accord ushers in would likely cause temperatures to be higher than 2.6 to 3.1°C by the year 2100 compared to pre-industrial levels.[65] The picture will not change much, even if the EU doubles its efforts to reduce its emissions. The main implication for the trade policy is that, as Paul De Grauwe noted, when those pushing for maximum trade liberalisation 'argue that trade agreements will lead to higher GDPs, they are right, but they forget to say that this will be accompanied by rising environmental costs. If we subtract the latter from the former, it is not certain that this leaves something positive.'[66]

10.5 Carbon Adjustments

All in all, therefore, the moral suasion and economic sacrifices[67] of such an insignificant emitter as the EU cannot alone make its climate policy successful, while reinforced international trade further corrodes its efforts on this front. This does not mean that European environmental ambitions are erroneous. Instead, it implies that the EU should

[63] 5,244 $MtCO_2e$ EU28, against 29,964 $MtCO_2e$ World: World Resources Institute, CAIT Climate Data Explorer.

[64] 4,054 MtCO2e EU28, against 45,741 MtCO2e World: Ibid.

[65] Joeri Rogelj et al., 'Paris Agreement Climate Proposals Need a Boost to Keep Warming Well below 2°C', *Nature* (2016): 631–639.

[66] Paul De Grauwe, 'How Far Should We Push Globalisation?', *CEPS Commentary*, 4 November 2016, 2, available at www.ceps.eu/publications/how-far-should-we-push-globalisation.

[67] The Commission itself admits that in order to cut EU emissions by 80 per cent by 2050 (compared to 1990) 'the EU would need to invest an additional €270 bn (or on average 1.5% of its GDP annually) over the next 4 decades': available at the European Commission's website '2050 Low-carbon Economy', available at ec.europa.eu/clima/policies/strategies/2050_en.

do much more to reconcile its climate policy goals with international trade. Or, to put the same somewhat differently, European climate goals are unachievable, unless the EU supplements its commercial policy's current toolbox with new, incentive-compatible instruments capable of mitigating the self-inflicted costs of domestic emission reductions.

This instrument – a charge on imports aimed to equalise the price for carbon, regardless of the product's origin – has so far largely languished at the margins of policy debates.[68] The idea of a carbon tariff, once championed by French President Sarkozy, and then revived by Arnaud Montebourg – a French Minister of Industrial Revival under President Hollande[69] – has been consistently rejected by European decision-makers. Back in 2009, the *Financial Times* reported Environment Commissionaire Stavros Dimas saying: '"I don't think it should be used as a means of pressure" … arguing that instead poor countries "should be offered finance to help them to tackle climate change"'.[70] The Commission has not changed its mind since. The Climate Commissioner in the Juncker Commission, Arias Cañete, when asked in late 2016 about the possibility of imposing such a tax on American exports if the Trump administration pulls out of the Paris accord (which indeed happened the next year), retorted: 'We have always said we didn't like carbon taxes – both before the US election and after.'[71] A few years earlier, another EU commissionaire – Karl De Gucht – explained why: 'The big risk is that there will be slippage into a trade war with people outbidding each other on such measures.'[72]

[68] See esp. Madison Condon and Ada Ignaciuk, 'Border Carbon Adjustment and International Trade: A Literature Review', *OECD Trade and Environment Working Papers* No. 2013/06 (Paris: OECD Publishing, 2013), available at papers.ssrn.com/sol3/papers.cfm?abstract_id=2693236.

[69] Frédéric Simon, 'French to Revive Sarkozy's EU Carbon Tariff Idea', *Euractiv*, 18 May 2012, available at www.euractiv.com/section/climate-environment/news/french-to-revive-sarkozy-s-eu-carbon-tariff-idea/.

[70] Joshua Chaffin and Fiona Harvey, 'EU Attacks Carbon Border Tax Initiative', *Financial Times*, 14 October 2009, available at www.ft.com/content/7cba7a90-b8e3-11de-98ee-00144feab49a.

[71] "Berlin, Brussels Dismiss Call for CO2 Tax on Trump's US', *Euractiv.com with Reuters*, 15 November 2016, available at www.euractiv.com/section/climate-environment/news/berlin-brussels-dismiss-call-for-co2-tax-on-us-under-trump/.

[72] 'EU Trade Chief-designate Rejects Carbon Border Tariffs', *Euractiv*, 13 January 2010, available at www.euractiv.com/section/trade-society/news/eu-trade-chief-designate-rejects-carbon-border-tariffs/. For a more nuanced argumentation ultimately leading to the same conclusion, see Henrik Horn and André Sapir, 'Can Border Carbon Taxes Fit into the Global Trade Regime?', *Bruegel Policy Brief* No. 2013/06, 9 December 2013, available at bruegel.org/wp-content/uploads/imported/publications/pb_2013_06__01.pdf.

Is it really what would follow, though? As I will explain more thoroughly later in this chapter, had carbon border taxes been imposed only for environmental protection purposes, they would perfectly square with WTO law.[73] Because the EU emission reduction system is more demanding than anywhere else in the world, other WTO members would not be able to respond similarly to the European tax, as long at least as it targets third-country sectors comparably to how EU tools to cut GHG emissions influence European sectors. On the one hand, it would eliminate the major argument of those who claim that meaningful emission reduction measures within the EU would only lead to carbon leakage and that they undermine European competitive advantages, leading to further relocation of production in energy-intensive sectors elsewhere. This would help rejuvenate the EU emissions trading system and facilitate the achievement of emission reductions targets,[74] because European industries and societies would find it easier to accept sacrifices necessary to achieve the low-carbon economy had the EU been able to demonstrate it puts its global competitors under a similar pressure.[75] On the other hand, the border carbon tax could provide the Union with additional resources to fund research and investments in clean energy.[76] Joseph Stiglitz accurately called the effects of imposing such a tax 'a welfare trifecta': 'Higher growth as firms retrofit to reflect the increased costs of carbon dioxide

[73] See also Carolyn Fischer, 'Options for Avoiding Carbon Leakage', in: *Towards an Effective and Sustainable Climate Regime*, eds. Scott Barrett, Carlo Carraro and Jaime de Melo, 2015: 297–311, available at http://voxeu.org/sites/default/files/image/FromMay2014/Climate%20change%20book%20for%20web.pdf.

[74] As I mentioned earlier, in October 2014 EU leaders agreed on a binding economy-wide domestic emission reductions target of at least 40 per cent by 2030. As they added, the sectors not covered by the EU ETS would reduce emissions by 30 per cent by 2030 compared to 2005. The majority of EU countries have been remarkably unambitious during the legislative process on the rules fleshing out the 2021–2030 GHG reduction targets. See Transport & Environment, 'The EU Climate Leader Board', 28 March 2017, available at www.transportenvironment.org/publications/eu-climate-leader-board.

[75] Especially that an alternative method of pursuing the same goal – environment-related provisions of the regional trade agreements – has proven patently toothless: José-Antonio Monteiro, 'Typology of Environment-Related Provisions in Regional Trade Agreements', *WTO Working Paper* No. ERSD-2016-13, July 2016, available at www.wto.org/english/res_e/reser_e/ersd201613_e.pdf.

[76] For an overview of the relationship between the climate policy and R&D, see esp. Georg Zachmann, 'Making Low-Carbon Technology Support Smarter', *Bruegel Policy Brief* No. 2015/02, 18 August 2015, available bruegel.org/2015/08/making-low-carbon-technology-support-smarter/.

emissions; a cleaner environment; and revenue that could be used to finance infrastructure and direct efforts to narrow [the] economic divide.'[77]

Of course, the border carbon tax cannot solve global climate change problems as long as it is not universally accepted, which is improbable. But, nonetheless, Daniel Gros was absolutely right when he asserted that 'the world would benefit from the imposition of a (small) carbon import tariff by the EU (the only significant country with a cap-and-trade system in operation)'.[78] This tariff would alleviate the current situation, in which producers of negative externalities are incentivised to enhance their activities, as they do not incur their costs.

10.6 What Does Palm Oil Teach Us?

Earlier on in this chapter, I invoked research arguing that international trade is good for the environment, mainly because it induces technological progress in the developing countries and supports wealth creation there, which in turn is necessary to become environmentally aware and to have the resources necessary to translate this awareness into action. So are there any negative externalities the carbon tax would cancel out or not?

There are, and they have been very significant. Take palm oil, for instance. It is used in foods, cosmetics, cleaning products and, especially, in biodiesel production.[79] In 2016, Indonesia, the world's leading producer, harvested 35,000 million tons of this oil – almost ten times more than it did in 1993.[80] To make room for its plantations, rainforests have been cleared on an unprecedented scale there. From the climate change perspective this is doubly vexing: first because burning down the forests

[77] Joseph Stiglitz, 'What America's Economy Needs from Trump', *Project Syndicate*, 13 November 2016, available at www.project-syndicate.org/commentary/trump-agenda-america-economy-by-joseph-e–stiglitz-2016-11.

[78] Daniel Gros, 'A Border Tax to Protect the Global Environment?', *VOX CEPR's Policy Portal*, 9 December 2009, available at voxeu.org/article/why-eu-needs-border-tax-carbon#fn.

[79] As Transport & Environment calculated, 'The use of palm oil for biodiesel has been increasing in the EU; 3.35 million tonnes of it was used in 2015. Currently 46% of palm oil imported to the EU is used for biodiesel, requiring around 1 million hectares of tropical land': Transport & Environment, 'Europe Keeps Burning More Palm Oil in Its Diesel Cars and Trucks', November 2016, available at www.transportenvironment.org/sites/te/files/2016_11_Briefing_Palm_oil_use_continues_to_grow.pdf.

[80] Indexmundi, 'Indonesia Palm Oil Production by Year', available at www.indexmundi.com/agriculture/?country=id&commodity=palm-oil&graph=production.

standing on tropical peat soils releases enormous amounts of GHGs. Second, with rainforests logged down, the planet loses its natural lungs.

In the previous decade the palm oil industry formed what it called the Roundtable on Sustainable Palm Oil, allegedly to tackle the problem through self-regulation (setting standards and certification of environmentally friendly palm oil). Soon after, the Indonesian government signed a moratorium on the clearing of primary forests and peat lands, to be effective from 2011 till 2015.

In reality, however, Indonesia has been going in the opposite direction. A recent study found that between 2000 and 2012 this country lost almost twice as much primary forest as did Brazil.[81] According to the same research, the surface area of rainforest lost in 2014 alone was almost as large as the territory of Cyprus, and in the period 2000–2012 the loss of primary forests in Indonesia was equivalent to an area twice the size of Belgium.

This process is immediately measurable in GHG emissions. In 2014, for instance, the Indonesian so-called 'Total GHG Emissions Excluding Land-Use Change and Forestry', which does not account for the emissions caused by deforestation, was close to the UK and Spanish emissions combined.[82] But if you include the Land-Use Change and Forestry factor, in 2014 total Indonesian CO_2 emissions were more than three times as high in Indonesia as without it, and were equal to two-thirds of all EU 28 emissions of the same type in the same year.[83] And then the Indonesian problem only exacerbated. During the peak of the fire season in autumn 2015, in what was called the 'Asian haze crisis', in just four weeks the country emitted more GHG gases than did Germany during the whole year.[84]

This did not discourage the Indonesian government from pledging, right in the middle of the 2015 haze crisis, that it would cut its emissions by 29 per cent by 2030 compared to a no-intervention scenario, and that it would reduce them by a further 12 per cent if it receives $6 billion of financial and technological support from industrialised

[81] Belinda Arunarwati Margono et al., 'Primary Forest Cover Loss in Indonesia over 2000–2012', *Nature Climate Change* 4 (2014): 730–735.

[82] 789 $MtCO_2e$: World Resources Institute, CAIT Climate Data Explorer.

[83] 2,472 $MtCO_2e$ and 3,625 $MtCO_2e$, respectively.

[84] Nancy Harris et al., 'Indonesia's Fire Outbreaks Producing More Daily Emissions Than Entire US Economy', *World Resources Institute*, 16 October 2015, available at www.wri.org/blog/2015/10/indonesia%E2%80%99s-fire-outbreaks-producing-more-daily-emissions-entire-us-economy.

nations by that date. You are excused if you wonder how a government unable to prevent a major environmental disaster despite its voluntarily adopted moratorium on activities leading to this very disaster could meet such a – much more demanding – commitment. But even if it miraculously does so, the emission reduction it proposed in 2015, according to researchers brought together in the reputable Climate Action Tracker, is 'at the least ambitious end of what would be a fair contribution, and is not consistent with limiting warming to below 2°C, let alone with the the Paris Agreement's stronger 1.5°C limit, unless other countries make much deeper reductions and comparably greater effort'.[85]

This leads us to a major paradox. On the one hand, due to intensifying globalisation the whole world discovered palm oil: a cheap, greatly desired and extremely profitable product, which is in addition healthier for consumers than its substitutes. Its production boosts Indonesian exports and employment (the palm oil industry estimates it gives jobs to more than 4.5 million people in Indonesia and Malaysia alone).[86]

On the other hand, palm oil is emblematic of the worst negative externalities produced by unencumbered international trade. This good can be bought so cheaply because plantation workers receive miserable wages of less than $1.50 to $5 a day[87] and because the Indonesian environment is devastated to make room for plantations, with global climate repercussions that the palm oil prices do not capture. Nor do they take into account the death toll of forest blazes. According to some estimates, the toll is as high as 100,000 people in Indonesia, Malaysia and Singapore as a consequence of the 2015 Asian haze crisis.[88] Even the seeming benefit of putting a downward pressure on prices for all

[85] Climate Action Tracker, Indonesia, available at climateactiontracker.org/countries/indonesia.html.

[86] Roundtable on Sustainable Palm Oil, Impact Report 2016, 23, available at www.rspo.org/key-documents/impact-reports.

[87] Rainforest Action Network, 'The Human Cost of Conflict Palm Oil', 2016, 25, available at d3n8a8pro7vhmx.cloudfront.net/rainforestactionnetwork/pages/15889/attachments/original/1467043668/The_Human_Cost_of_Conflict_Palm_Oil_RAN.pdf?1467043668 (for the lower figure) and Roundtable on Sustainable Palm Oil Certification, Assessment Report (for the upper figure).

[88] Shannon Koplitz et al., 'Public Health Impacts of the Severe Haze in Equatorial Asia in September–October 2015: Demonstration of a New Framework for Informing Fire Management Strategies to Reduce Downwind Smoke Exposure', *Environmental Research Letters* 11 (2016), available at iopscience.iop.org/article/10.1088/1748-9326/11/9/094023.

edible oils (the effect partly offset by the European biofuel policy aimed to give a fillip to demand for all biofuels, including palm oil)[89] is problematic from this perspective, because this downward pressure induces anxieties among European farmers and strengthens their dependence on farm subsidies. This additional negative externality is not captured in the price of palm oil, either.

10.7 Pigovian Taxes Not So Unreal

Detractors of the border carbon tax, or indeed of any Pigovian tax, i.e., a tax levied in order to correct negative externalities,[90] may retort at this point that imposing it on any imported good carrying externalities would most probably ratchet up prices not only for this good, but also for its substitutes produced domestically, because the demand for these substitutes would grow. This would happen even if the production of these substitutes does not entail externalities. Furthermore, foreign producers could recoup the slump in demand for the products covered by the tax in one jurisdiction on other markets pursuing different

[89] In order to promote the use of renewable energy in transport, Directive 2003/30/EC of the European Parliament and of the Council of 8 May 2003 on the promotion of the use of biofuels or other renewable fuels for transport, OJ 2003 No. L 123, 17 May 2003, pp. 42–46, established a binding target of 5.75 per cent for energy from renewable sources in transport by 2010. Subsequently, Directive 2009/28/EC of the European Parliament and of the Council of 23 April 2009 on the promotion of the use of energy from renewable sources and amending and subsequently repealing Directives 2001/77/EC and 2003/30/EC, OJ 2009 No. L 140/16, 5 June 2009, p. 16–62, increased this ratio to 10 per cent for 2020. In 2015, another EU act – Directive 2015/1513 of the European Parliament and of the Council of 9 September 2015 amending Directive 98/70/EC relating to the quality of petrol and diesel fuels and amending Directive 2009/28/EC on the promotion of the use of energy from renewable sources, OJ 2015 No. L 239, 15 September 2015, pp. 1–29 – introduced a cap of 7 per cent towards the 10 per cent target of conventional biofuels, i.e., crop-based biofuels, and required that the (at least) 3 per cent that remained should come from other renewables such as advanced biofuels or renewable electricity. Nonetheless, subsequent research revealed that, even when reformed, the EU biofuel policy would actually increase emissions by 2020, mainly due to peatland drainage in Indonesia and Malaysia: see Hugo Valin et al., 'The Land Use Change Impact of Biofuels Consumed in the EU', study for the European Commission, 27 August 2015, available at ec.europa.eu/energy/sites/ener/files/documents/Final%20Report_GLOBIOM_publication.pdf; Transport & Environment, 'Globiom: The Basis for Biofuel Policy Post-2020', April 2016, available at www.transportenvironment.org/sites/te/files/publications/2016_04_TE_Globiom_paper_FINAL_0.pdf.

[90] For a much more comprehensive take on Pigovian taxes in the very contemporary context, see esp. Luc Nijs, *Neoliberalism 2.0: Regulating and Financing Globalizing Markets: A Pigovian Approach for 21st Century Markets* (New York: Palgrave Macmillan, 2016).

trade policies (for instance the USA, China, India). In effect, externalities would not be halted, while consumers would take the economic brunt of the border tax where it is imposed. Their purchasing power, and hence consumption, would be reduced, and so would economic growth.

Yet, again, the point I am making here is not that the EU can on its own solve any of the global externality problems by imposing Pigovian taxes on imports. Instead, such taxes would make the EU's policies more consistent and more effective compared to its current paradigm of constraining externalities (like carbon emissions) at home and willingly contributing to producing them abroad. While price hikes would indeed weaken the purchasing power of Europeans (worse even, it can be predicted that the poorer social strata would foot a comparably bigger bill[91]), the growth in demand for European substitutes, produced without comparable externalities, can be expected to translate into more jobs in the respective sectors. This counteracts the process in which 'good jobs' are exchanged for 'cheap goods' from abroad, where the goods can be produced cheaply because they cause damage their prices do not reflect. The issue falls into the commercial policy, which in turn is an exclusive competence of the EU.[92] Hence, the organisation is empowered to use Pigovian taxes. What is equally significant, in practice, it can do so much more effectively than any single European country could, considering that it still accounts for a fifth of all world trade.[93]

[91] E.g., Silvia Merler, 'Tariffs and the American Poor', *Bruegel Blog Post*, 23 January 2017, available at bruegel.org/2017/01/tariffs-and-the-american-poors/.

[92] The common commercial policy, governed at the Treaty level by Arts. 206 and 207 TFEU, is one of the few areas in which the EU has the so-called exclusive competences (Art. 3(1)(e) TFEU). According to consistent case law of the CJEU an EU act falls within the common commercial policy 'if it relates specifically to such trade in that it is essentially intended to promote, facilitate or govern such trade and has direct and immediate effects on it' (e.g., Opinion 2/15 of the Court of 16 May 2017, § 36, ECLI:EU:C:2017:376). This is clearly the case of Pigovian taxes in the context of international trade. Therefore 'only the Union may legislate and adopt legally binding acts' in the area, 'the Member States being able to do so themselves only if so empowered by the Union or for the implementation of acts of the Union' (Damian Chalmers, Gareth Davies and Giorgio Monti, *European Union Law: Text and Materials* [Cambridge: Cambridge University Press, 2014: 210]) because 'a given competence is exclusive when it has been completely transferred by the Member State to the Community and there is no residual concurrent competence retained by the Member States' (Elena Fierro, *European Union's Approach to Human Rights Conditionality in Practice* [The Hague: Martinus Nijhoff Publishers, 2003: 35]).

[93] Immediately after the French Parliament proposed a palm oil tax provision in its Biodiversity Bill of 2016, Indonesian authorities delayed an approval

Of course, the point is not restricted solely to palm oil or to Indonesia. The same applies to a large proportion of agricultural products harvested in developing countries and causing environmental damage not reflected in their prices. More importantly, environmental damage and climate change charades are not the only externalities a Pigovian border tax could mitigate. The same applies to the externalities produced by offshoring manufacturing and services to locations lacking basic social and labour protections.

10.8 GSPs and the Forgotten Rana Plaza Disaster

Since the early 1970s, developed countries have been fostering trade with developing countries through generalised tariff preferences schemes.[94] The European Generalised Scheme of Preferences (GSP), now based on a 2012 regulation,[95] provides for three slightly different types of tariff preferences. Within the first of them – the general arrangement – all developing countries, except for those where income levels are high or upper-middle, are granted autonomous trade preferences.[96] Since 2001, about fifty least developed of them have enjoyed further concessions under another scheme of trade preferences, called 'Everything but Arms' (EBA). The latter extends the unrestricted duty-free access to all goods produced in these countries, except for arms and munitions.[97] The third scheme, called 'special incentive arrangement for sustainable development and good governance'

of a food safety agreement between the two countries. Soon after 'French politicians have dropped the proposed palm oil tax, leading some politicians to say the country is being blackmailed by producer countries': Niamh Michail, 'French MPs Drop Palm Oil Tax – But Accuse Producer Countries of Blackmail', *Foodnavigator*, 27 June 2016, available at: www.foodnavigator.com/Policy/French-MPs-drop-palm-oil-tax-but-accuse-producer-countries-of-blackmail.

[94] A system of tariff preferences for developing countries was originally enshrined by the first United Nations Conference on Trade and Development (UNCTAD) as a part of the so-called New International Economic Order. See also Jeffrey A. Hart, *The New International Economic Order. Conflict and Cooperation in North-South Economic Relations, 1974–77* (London: Palgrave Macmillan, 1983).

[95] Regulation 978/2012 of the European Parliament and of the Council of 25 October 2012 applying a scheme of generalised tariff preferences and repealing Council Regulation 732/2008, OJ 2012 No. L 303, 31 October 2012, pp. 1–82.

[96] The preferences comprise a suspension of all customs duties on non-sensitive products originating in developing countries, while for sensitive products the Common Customs Tariff for ad valorem duties is reduced by 3.5 per cent as a general rule. For further conditions see Arts. 7 and 8 Regulation 978/2012.

[97] Art. 18 Regulation 978/2012.

(GSP+) provides special trade incentives for these GSP countries which 'are vulnerable due to a lack of diversification and insufficient integration into the international trading system'.[98] In exchange for additionally facilitated market access,[99] the GSP+ arrangement is offered as a 'positive conditionality'[100]: it is to be available only to the beneficiaries that 'effectively implement' twenty-seven core international conventions on human and labour rights, good governance and environmental protection.

More than half of all GSP Preferential Imports to the EU come from India after China group in 2015, and more than 90 per cent of the remaining part originates in Vietnam and Indonesia.[101] In the GSP+ group about 70 per cent of EU imports come from Pakistan and in the EBA group from Bangladesh.[102]

In the heyday of maximum globalisation, back in 2004, the Commission asserted that 'trade has proved to be one of the most effective tools to foster development. Increased trade with developing countries will enhance their export earnings, promote their industrialisation, encourage the diversification of their economies and accelerate their economic growth.'[103] Indeed, it is hard to dispute such a depiction. Nonetheless, it overlooks the dark side of the process: environmental devastation and social deprivation accompanying the same entanglement of forces.

These effects are in particular at odds with the international conventions to be implemented in the developing countries as a precondition of the GSP+ status. It is because, again, this tariff preference should be available only to the world's good citizens among developing countries. And, yet, the reality is quite different. The Commission finds

98 Art. 9(1)(a) Regulation 978/2012.

99 As a general principle, Common Customs Tariff *ad valorem* duties on the products originating in a GSP+ beneficiary country (and listed in an annex to Regulation 978/2012) are suspended: Arts. 11 and 12 Regulation 978/2012.

100 Lorand Bartels, 'The WTO Enabling Clause and Positive Conditionality in the European Community's GSP Program', *Journal of International Economic Law* 6 (2003): 507–532.

101 Report from the Commission on the Generalised Scheme of Preferences covering the period 2014–15, COM(2016)29, 28 January 2016, 7 (2014 data).

102 Report from the Commission on the Generalised Scheme of Preferences covering the period 2014–15, COM(2016)29, 28 January 2016, 10 and 8, respectively (2014 data).

103 European Commission, 'The European Union's Generalised System of Preferences GSP', 2004, 2, available at trade.ec.europa.eu/doclib/docs/2004/march/tradoc_116448.pdf.

courage to admit it,[104] but it hardly ever dares to do what EU law requires in such a situation: to temporarily withdraw trade preferences.[105]

The story of Bangladesh – the world's main beneficiary of the EBA tariff preferences – paints an even more ambiguous picture.

On the one hand, the EBA scheme has been hailed as 'the showcase of the development-friendly nature of EU trade policy'.[106] The Bangladeshi apparel industry in particular has thrived on it since the 1980s. While in 1984 the value of the country's ready-made garment exports was a paltry $32 million (less than 4 per cent of all of the country's exports), in 2016 the same sector exported apparels worth $28.09 billion (82 per cent of Bangladeshi exports).[107] The EU accounted for almost two-thirds of them.[108] This sector employs about four million people in Bangladesh,[109] robustly augmenting the country's GDP year after year. Thanks to

[104] Consider the Commission's following cagey yet unambiguous assessment of Pakistan: 'A cross-cutting issue, not restricted to human rights, is the poor implementation and enforcement of legal safeguards … Problems related to implementation are multifaceted and include prejudice and entrenched stereotypes, for example on the role of women, running contrary to basic human rights, the weakness of state institutions (notably the police and the judiciary), and the legal uncertainties and capacity gaps … Altogether, this means that the work done to adopt new legislation may not always translate into tangible improvement on the ground': European Commission, 'The EU Special Incentive Arrangement for Sustainable Development and Good Governance ('GSP+') Covering the Period 2014–2015', *Joint Staff Working Document* 8 (2016), 28 January 2016, 189, available at eeas.europa.eu/sites/eeas/files/european_commission._2016._report_on_the_generalised_scheme_of_preferences_during_the_period_2014-2015.pdf.

[105] Art. 15(1) Regulation 978/2012 provides that the GSP+ arrangement 'shall be withdrawn temporarily, in respect of all or of certain products originating in a GSP+ beneficiary country, where in practice that country does not respect its binding undertakings'. This wording is clearly to limit the Commission's discretion in this respect to the absolute minimum. Nonetheless, the GSP+ status has been so far withdrawn only in the case of Belarus, Myanmar and Sri Lanka (in the latter two cases to be subsequently reinstated). For a more (and arguably overly) sanguine account see James Yap, 'Beyond "Don't Be Evil": The European Union GSP+ Trade Preference Scheme and the Incentivisation of the Sri Lankan Garment Industry to Foster Human Rights', *European Law Journal* 19 (2013): 283–301.

[106] Gerrit Faber and Jan Orbie, 'Everything but Arms: Much More Than Appears at First Sight', *Journal of Common Market Studies* 47 (2009): 768.

[107] Bangladesh Garment Manufacturers and Exporters Association, Table 'Comparative Statement on Export of RMG and Total Export of Bangladesh', available at bgmea.com.bd/home/pages/TradeInformation.

[108] 62.6 per cent of World Exports: Bangladesh Garment Manufacturers and Exporters Association, Table, 'Bangladesh's RMG Export to World 2014 to 2016', available at bgmea.com.bd/home/pages/TradeInformation.

[109] Bangladesh Garment Manufacturers and Exporters Association, Table 'Membership and Employment', available at bgmea.com.bd/home/pages/TradeInformation.

thousands of textile factories producing for the Western brands, 'few Bangladeshi starve to death any more. This wasn't the case a generation ago when 80 percent of the country subsisted on agriculture, survival being by no means guaranteed.'[110] Some intellectuals, following Thomas Nagel,[111] may therefore claim that developed countries commit a moral wrong when they defend their economies against imports from places like Bangladesh. And, more practically, as a result of the unencumbered growth in garment trade with Bangladesh, European fashion companies can impressively multiply their turnover and profits, at the same time letting consumers shop for unprecedentedly low prices.

Yet when in 2013 more than 1,100 people died in the rubble of a collapsed building hosting some of the garment factories producing for world-renowned brands (the catastrophe known as the Rana Plaza collapse), the world learnt the dark side of this process: shoddy sweatshops in which fashionable Western clothes are produced, workers harassed and exploited in extremely unsafe working conditions, wages barely enough to scrape by on. Hardly ever do seamstresses earn more than the Bangladeshi minimum wage of less than €60 a month, while the national poverty line is about €70 a month.[112] Child labour remains routine, against international conventions and indeed against Bangladeshi laws.[113] And the 2013 calamity has changed the picture for anything but the worse, leading to repeated protests.[114] According to one Bangladeshi former child factory worker and a labour rights activist, 'since the disaster, employees have to work harder ... They have higher production targets. If they cannot fulfil them they have to work extra hours but with no overtime. It is very tough; they cannot go for toilet breaks or to drink water. They become sick.'[115]

[110] Zafar Sobhan, 'Progress and Globalization in Bangladesh: The Tazreen Fashions Garment Factory Fire', *VICE*, 2 December 2012, available at www.vice.com/read/progress-and-globalization-in-bangladesh-the-tazreen-fashions-garment-factory-fire.

[111] Thomas Nagel, 'The Problem of Global Justice', *Philosophy and Public Affairs* 33 (2005): 113–147.

[112] BDT 5,300 and 6,336, respectively, according to publically available data available at wageindicator-wages-in-context.silk.co/page/Bangladesh.

[113] Niaz Asadullah and Zaki Wahhaj, 'Minimum Wage Attracts Girls to Factories', *Development and Cooperation*, 3 January 2016, available at www.dandc.eu/en/article/higher-wages-bangladeshs-garments-sector-mean-better-income-push-girls-work-child.

[114] Like the one in December 2016: Michael Safi, 'Bangladesh Garment Factories Sack Hundreds after Pay Protests', *Guardian*, 27 December 2016, available at www.theguardian.com/world/2016/dec/27/bangladesh-garment-factories-sack-hundreds-after-pay-protests.

[115] Simon Parry, 'The True Cost of Your Cheap Clothes: Slave Wages for Bangladesh Factory Workers', *Post Magazine*, 31 March 2017, available at www.scmp.com/magazines/post-magazine/article/1970431/true-cost-your-cheap-clothes-slave-wages-bangladesh-factory.

The Bangladeshi garment industry is not exceptional. Another high-profile example is the Cambodian sugar industry, which has also greatly benefitted from this country's EBA status. And there, too, the process has been accompanied by massive human rights abuses and environmental damage.[116]

10.9 The Middle Ground

All in all, therefore, there are many short-term benefits of trade arrangements with Indonesia, Bangladesh or Cambodia. But in the longer perspective they also entail serious costs. Hence, they raise the familiar question of time inconsistencies. Any good produced by semi-slaves entails dumping effects on the importing country, because the societies respecting working safety conditions and minimum social rights as well as a living wage cannot compete with the producers taking advantage of disobeying them. Those who follow the rules lose the market to those who do not.

Having no tariffs on products exported by a developing country resembles a situation in which massive immigration of this country's workers to Western countries takes place and in which they are employed there in conditions violating any civilised international standards. A paradigm based on such a pattern harms (the part of) the competing industries in the importing countries that employ local workers, constraining job opportunities among its poorest (and least educated) citizens as well as putting downward pressure on their wages. In more technical terms, the increasing elasticity of demand for labour among multinational companies enhances wage and unemployment volatility in developed countries.[117] Job insecurity escalates in such a situation, with its political implications gradually growing when the losers demand more fiscal redistribution.[118] It should not be

[116] Jack Davies, 'Europe's "Blood Sugar"', *Politico*, 4 April 2017, available at www.politico.eu/article/europe-blood-sugar-cambodia-human-rights-trade/. As one of the local activists quoted there remarked bitterly, 'when the sugar companies, one by one, seized the land and property of thousands of people by force, torching homes and slashing forests, the EU sat back silently and continued to subsidize these criminal enterprises by granting them preferential access to the European market'.

[117] Kenneth Sheve and Matthew Slaughter, 'Economic Insecurity and the Globalization of Production', *American Journal of Political Science* 48 (2004): 662–674.

[118] Dani Rodrik, 'Why Do More Open Economies Have Bigger Governments?', *Journal of Political Economy* 106 (1998): 997–1032.

surprising from this perspective that the nations losing their shares in international trade in a particularly precipitous pace also see their public debt levels growing. Public expenditure cuts, which at some point start dominating the political agenda as a response to the consequent fiscal strain, are then naturally concentrated on discretionary spending – read: investments – because this is where spending cuts are easiest to implement.[119] This, however, translates into more insecurity in the longer term, because tangible and intangible foundations of the nation's prosperity are further eroded.

Of course, one can nonetheless argue that, as a flipside of this process, the world's real poor in developing countries gain a modicum of stability. They may work in ghastly conditions, but at least they do not starve to death anymore. This is true, but in no way does it undermine my point here. Accepting the race to the bottom in social and environmental standards, the developed societies obtain access to very cheap products. Yet, along the self-inflicted damage to their social contracts and political as well as economic stability, they also forego their leverage over environmental and social standards in the developing countries. More specifically, tariffs reversely proportional to social and working conditions standards in developing countries (the worse the conditions, the higher the tariffs) would not only make globalisation more congestible for economically advanced societies. They would also incentivise the governments of the developing countries to eradicate semi-slavery as well as other forms of exploitation and devastation now accompanying the maximum globalisation paradigm.

In stark contrast to this pattern, aimed to tackle the long-term costs of globalisation, the policy paradigm behind international trade during the last three decades has firmly prioritised short-term benefits for customers and multinational companies. Long-term costs of such policies have either been ignored at the stage of the legislative process, or – as the plight of the positive conditionality behind the GSP+ scheme demonstrates – they have fizzled out later on, at the stage of enforcement.

Even the countries, like Germany, portraying themselves as good global citizens and economic winners of globalisation have faced

[119] Zsolt Darvas and Olga Tschekassin, 'Poor and under Pressure: The Social Impact of Europe's Fiscal Consolidation', *Bruegel Policy Contribution* No. 2015/04, March 2015, available at bruegel.org/wp-content/uploads/imported/publications/Poor_and_under_pressure.pdf.

long-term costs of the flawed policy patterns focussed exclusively on short-term benefits from international trade. They too have experienced growing inequality, wage moderations among unskilled workers (more on this in Chapter 7) and the effects of global climate change. Others, with less flexible and less resilient domestic governance, like Italy or France, have experienced the long-term costs undermining the short-term benefits much more clearly.

This conclusion is an anathema to free-trade zealots, because it implies that (moderate) tariffs may actually have positive effects on the economies involved. Restrictions to free trade, they argue, are never good. Take the example of the infamous Smoot–Hawley Act. This US law, enacted in 1930, was aimed to boost demand for US products by raising tariffs on dutiable goods to an average of 45 per cent. Many economists already opposed it when it was undergoing the legislative process. Decades later, Ben Bernanke professed that 'economists still agree that Smoot-Hawley and the ensuing tariff wars were highly counterproductive and contributed to the depth and length of the global Depression'.[120] Another commentator even went as far as to assert that President Hoover committed 'the most disastrous single mistake any U.S. president has made in international relations' when signing the Smoot–Hawley Act into law.[121] Others have claimed that these statements are seriously exaggerated.[122] But, nonetheless, it is impossible to find an economist intimating that this piece of legislation had any positive effects on the US economy. None could contend that the Roosevelt administration made a mistake repealing the Smoot–Hawley Act a few years later.

There is no doubt that in this particular moment and in this particular place a surge of protectionism did not help the economy. On the other hand, however, throughout history tariffs have often been

[120] Ben Bernanke, speech 'Monetary Policy and the Global Economy', at the London School of Economics, 25 March 2013, available at www.federalreserve.gov/newsevents/speech/bernanke20130325a.htm.

[121] Richard N. Cooper, 'Trade Policy as Foreign Policy', in: *U.S. Trade Policies in a Changing World Economy*, ed. Robert M. Stern (Cambridge, MA: MIT Press, 1987): 291.

[122] In fact, most economists opine that the distortive impact of Smoot–Hawley at the aggregate level was relatively modest, even if it contributed to instability on the stock market. For a review of literature see Alfred E. Eckes Jr., *Opening America's Market: U.S. Foreign Trade Policy Since 1776* (Chapel Hill: University of North Carolina Press, 1995): chapter 4. More recently, and similarly, Eric W. Bond et al., 'Misallocation and Productivity Effects of the Smoot-Hawley Tariff', *NBER Working Paper* No. 18034, May 2012, available at www.nber.org/papers/w18034.pdf.

deployed successfully as a method of gaining a long-term economic advantage by the nations aspiring to build a strong technological base to be later deployed as a source of comparative advantages on international markets.[123] England in the seventeenth and eighteenth centuries, the USA and Germany in the second half of the nineteenth century, Japan in the first half of the twentieth century, South Korea a few decades later: all these subsequent free trade proselytes were first heavily protectionist.

All in all, therefore, context matters. In the context of the current, global world any diehard protectionism would be disastrous, no doubt about it. In the European context any such a policy reorientation could hardly be expected to allow its globalisation laggards to build a meaningful technological springboard, while history teaches us that this is the only rational reason for choosing protectionism. At the same time this paradigm shift would deprive the current European trade champions, like Germany, the Netherlands, Denmark, or Sweden, of the main economic foundation for their relative economic, political and social stability.

Yet, imagine a middle ground of a border Pigovian tax to be used as an anti-dumping measure aimed only to ameliorate long-term costs caused by exceedingly low working, environmental and social protections in the developing world. Traditionally, these long-term costs have been entirely ignored in determining whether a 'particular market situation' justifying an exemption from basic anti-dumping rules according to Art. 2.2 of the WTO Anti-Dumping Agreement should apply. And yet, starkly diverging working and social standards around the world render international trade increasingly unstable and vulnerable politically.

But how to factor the costs in? To start with, as a principle only trading partners from the countries with their 'national social protection floors' in place could be allowed to trade with Europe duty-free. The notion of 'national social protection floor' is now well-recognised. Its details have been chiselled by international organisations, which by now have agreed that such a floor is maintained when the state offers the following five social security guarantees to all of its residents: access to essential healthcare, including maternity care; basic income security for children; access to nutrition, education, care and any other necessary

[123] Ha-Joon Chang, *Bad Samaritans: The Myth of Free Trade and the Secret History of Capitalism* (New York: Bloomsbury Publishing, 2010); Dani Rodrik, The Globalization Paradox.

goods and services; basic income security for persons in active age who are unable to earn sufficient income, in particular in cases of sickness, unemployment, maternity and disability; and basic income security for older persons.[124]

Such a 'positive conditionality' for exempting a country from Pigovian taxes should also arguably apply to the poorest countries (covered by the ABA arrangement). Because none of them can afford any comprehensive social protection floor, however, the EU could guarantee that whatever tariffs are levied on products of the countries would be returned to them to fund their crucial socioeconomic policies and institutions, on which the achievement of the national social protection floors depends in turn.

Certainly, overseeing working and living conditions throughout the world within any such arrangement, and working with local governments on developing them, would be challenging. For the very same reason it would be difficult to make sure that the tariffs only compensate for the actual externalities. But these technical constraints could be reduced to the minimum in an open and transparent manner.

10.10 How About the WTO?

A defender of the current paradigm may retort at this point that, for better or worse, the current system is the one envisaged by the WTO regime. An alternative cannot be put in place without seriously upsetting the legal framework behind the international trade and without triggering tariff wars. This argument, however, is partly misleading. And in its correct element it simply points to a problem already produced by the spat over the anti-dumping methodology to be used in respect to China.

To start with, the carbon border tax, as I mentioned earlier, neatly squares with the GATT's so-called general exception clause when it is calibrated to account for the effects of the cap-and-trade system used in the EU. This GATT's clause provides that

> subject to the requirement that such measures are not applied in a manner which would constitute a means of arbitrary or unjustifiable discrimination

[124] International Labour Organization, Recommendation No. 202 concerning National Floors of Social Protection, adopted 14 June 2012.

between countries where the same conditions prevail, or a disguised restriction on international trade, nothing in this Agreement shall be construed to prevent the adoption or enforcement by any contracting party of measures ... necessary to protect human, animal or plant life or health and relating to the conservation of exhaustible natural resources if such measures are made effective in conjunction with restrictions on domestic production or consumption.[125]

The heavily conditional character of this exception seriously limits its applicability. Yet, when striking down a US measure failing to address its requirements, a WTO panel also underscored that 'we have not decided that the protection and preservation of the environment is of no significance to the Members of the WTO. Clearly, it is ... And we have not decided that sovereign states should not act together bilaterally, plurilaterally or multilaterally, either within the WTO or in other international fora, to protect endangered species or to otherwise protect the environment. Clearly, they should and do.'[126]

All in all, therefore, the carbon border tax, carefully synchronised with the European emission reduction efforts, should pass the test of the WTO rules.

Conversely, the WTO is unfamiliar with the idea that the costs of lacking social or working standards should be taken into account when determining dumping effects. There is no general exception clause allowing for it. Even if you treat Pigovian taxes not as a general tariff system, but as an anti-dumping scheme, they ostensibly hit the wall of the 'normal value methodology' mentioned earlier in the Chinese context. Within this methodology, used as a default mechanism of determining whether dumping takes place, 'costs shall normally be calculated on the basis of records kept by the exporter or producer under investigation, provided that such records are in accordance with the generally accepted accounting principles of the exporting country and reasonably reflect the costs associated with the production and sale of the product' (Art. 2.2.1.1

[125] Art. XX, esp. letters b and g. For more nuanced analyses see esp. Joost Pauwelyn, 'Carbon Leakage Measures and Border Tax Adjustments under WTO Law', March 21, 2012, available at https://papers.ssrn.com/sol3/papers.cfm?abstract_id=2026879. See also Ross Astoria, "Design of an International Trade Law Compliant Carbon Border Tax Adjustment," *Arizona Journal of Environmental Law & Policy* 6 (2015): 491–54 and Condon and Ignaciuk, "Border Carbon Adjustment," 17–22.

[126] Case United States – Import Prohibition of Certain Shrimp and Shrimp Products, WTO case WT/DS58/AB/R of 12 October 1998, § 185.

of the Anti-Dumping Agreement). By their very definition, externalities are not captured by any record of any exporter or producer, while working or social sub-standards allow for limiting the costs reported in full accordance with the generally accepted accounting principles.

However, the last part of the provision just quoted contains an escape clause for the situations in which the costs reported by producers or exporters do not 'reasonably reflect the costs associated with the production and sale of the product'. Externalities are precisely such costs, which production entails but the price fails to capture. This point is crucial from the legal perspective, because the EU lost the Argentine biodiesel case not because some additional costs associated with the production yet not captured by the export price were taken into account by the European methodology (which a Pigovian tax would aim to achieve). The EU lost this case because it disregarded the costs actually borne (or externalised) by producers altogether. It is precisely the same conceptual shortcut that renders the Basic Regulation and its 2017 amendment so vulnerable in the Chinese case. This shortcut prevents the EU from achieving what Rodrik called 'smart globalization, not maximum globalization'.[127]

Rectifying this situation is so crucial because maximum globalisation is irrational and counterproductive. Ricardo's idea of comparative advantage simply does not apply to market circumstances distorted to the point where all the conditions of this idea are absent. What sense does it make to stick to high standards at home and turn a blind eye to very different policy patterns abroad? How can one expect that developed societies can maintain their economic, social and political models when at the same time they are exposed to competition with policy models based on the exploitation of workers and resources unseen in the advanced world since at least World War I? Arguably the rules of international trade should not foster unsound answers to these questions. They ought to allow for cost advantages to play out, while mitigating concomitant negative externalities. This is what rational, smart globalisation requires.

[127] Rodrik, *The Globalization Paradox*, p. xix.

10.11 Vestager-Like Leadership

What is rational, however, from the long-term economic and political perspectives as well as doable legally may not be achievable for short-term political reasons, a detractor can retort. Throughout the last decades there has been a lot of cheap talk about sustainable development, social and economic progress and fair competition in the context of international trade. But in reality international trade has always been about power and influence, while the most influential and powerful groups, with their interests most concentrated, naturally walk away from the table with the best treasure. This is what the logic of collective action clearly predicts.[128] Because they are too weak and too divided, the argument goes, European governments and European institutions suffer from collective action problems making them unable to countenance these special interests.

This point chimes with another shrewd remark by Dani Rodrik, who elucidated that 'trade policies driven by domestic political lobbying and special interests are beggar-thyself policies. They may have beggar-thy-neighbor consequences, but that is not their motive. They reflect power asymmetries and political failures within societies ... Addressing beggar-thyself policies requires improving domestic governance, not establishing international rules.'[129] Flaws in domestic governance setups have allowed multinationals to dominate the policy design, tailoring it to their needs, as well as to the expectations of their customers, who seek ever lower prices. This collusion between producers, consumers and policymakers has made the current paradigm of maximum globalisation seemingly unreformable.

Yet, consumers are also employees and citizens. The allergic reaction of Europeans to investor protection clauses in both the comprehensive trade deal with Canada, ultimately signed after a very tortuous process, and in the hindered attempt to design a similar one with the USA[130] makes it quite clear that the trade paradigm that tips the

[128] Mancur Olson, *The Logic of Collective Action* (Cambridge, MA: Harvard University Press, 1965).

[129] Dani Rodrik, 'Don't Cry over Dead Trade Agreements', *Project Syndicate*, 8 December 2016, available at www.project-syndicate.org/commentary/no-mourning-dead-trade-agreements-by-dani-rodrik-2016-12.

[130] This refers especially to Investor-State Dispute settlement (ISDS) arrangements, enabling individual foreign companies to sue countries before an arbitration tribunal for alleged discriminatory practices. These arrangements were crucial for catalysing popular backlash, manifested in more than three million signatures under

balance between public authorities and investors in international trade towards the latter is explosive politically. Even the societies, like the German one, which largely maintain their competitive advantages on international markets, are not patient about it any longer.[131] A different paradigm would entail less international trade, no doubt about it, and it would require strong institutions to resist lobbying by special interests as well as to coordinate a network of NGOs overseeing social and working conditions in developing countries. But if implemented properly, it would motivate governments of these countries to introduce basic social, economic and environmental policies on which the sustainability of their prosperity is contingent. It would lead to more 'harmonious development of world trade', as Art. 206 TFEU requires.

Furthermore, the fact that the commercial policy is an exclusive EU competence makes it reformable if only the EU's institutions muster enough leadership and policy imagination to choose a new course. This point is undergirded by a recent policy shift in another area in which the EU has been given exclusive competences: state aid control. For decades the Commission had not tried to use its powers in this area against special corporate tax arrangements offered by some EU governments to foreign investors, despite Art. 107 TFEU clearly providing that 'any aid granted by a Member State or through state resources in any form whatsoever which distorts or threatens to distort competition by favouring certain undertakings or the production of certain goods shall … be incompatible with the internal market'.[132] And then all of a sudden

petitions against Comprehensive Economic and Trade Agreement (with Canada) and Transatlantic Trade and Investment Partnership (with the USA) and more than 2,000 municipalities declaring themselves TTIP- and CETA-free. See stop-ttip.org/blog/eci-is-closed-signature-gathering-continues/?noredirect=en_GB (petitions) and foeeurope.org/2000-CETA-and-TTIP-free-zones-in-Europe (CETA- and TTIP-free zones).

131 A YouGov survey conducted in February 2016 revealed that only 56 per cent of Germans considered international trade as a good thing and 27 per cent had a negative opinion. This is in stark contrast to the opinions prevailing only two years earlier, when 88 per cent had a positive opinion of international trade, and only 9 per cent were against it: Christian Bluth, 'Attitudes to Global Trade and TTIP in Germany and the United States', *Global Economic Dynamics Study*, Bertelsmann Stiftung 2016, available at www.bertelsmann-stiftung.de/en/publications/publication/did/attitudes-to-global-trade-and-ttip-in-germany-and-the-united-states/.

132 This, in turn, has stemmed from tax competition provoked by cumbersome harmonisation decision-making in the area of direct taxes. For a concise introduction, see André Meyer, 'A Common Tax Policy for Europe', in: *EU Law after the Financial Crisis*, eds. Jessica Schmidt, Carlos Esplugues and Rafael Arenas (Cambridge: Intersentia, 2016): 97–106.

Commissioner Vestager changed course in summer 2016 without raising a brow of any of her Commission colleagues. In an unprecedentedly far-reaching decision the Commission first concluded[133] that for many years Apple had been receiving illegal state aid from the Irish government, due to special tax arrangements tailored by the Irish authorities to the needs of this tech giant and allowing it to pay income tax at an effective tax rate of 0.005 per cent. Second, it requested the Irish government to reclaim about €13 billion from Apple.

Granted, in the field of competition policy the Commission enjoys the position of a 'tsar', largely insulating it from formal pressures by either national or European politicians. Hence, it enjoys a very strong sway over the policy course. The common commercial policy, conversely, may be an exclusive competence of the EU, but here the Commission is essentially only an agent of its trade policy principals – the Council and the Parliament – when it comes to major policy decisions.[134] In consequence, even if the policy reorientation discussed in this chapter does not raise the thorny question of whether national authorities should also have a direct say on it,[135] the ability of the Commission to flex its muscles in the commercial policy is much weaker. With its institutional clout so much facilitated in competition policy, the Commission can pursue its own agenda and impose hefty fines for breaching Treaty rules. Within commercial policy, on the other hand, it is overwhelmed by the pressure of various special interests, most of which lobby for unfettered international trade.

Remember, however, that the junction of the tax and competition policies has not been traditionally recognised to be a locus of

[133] Commission Decision of 30 August 2016 on state aid SA.38373 (2014/C) (ex 2014/NN) (ex 2014/CP) implemented by Ireland to Apple, C(2016) 5605.

[134] According to Art. 207(2) TFEU 'the European Parliament and the Council, acting by means of regulations in accordance with the ordinary legislative procedure, shall adopt the measures defining the framework for implementing the common commercial policy'. See also Marc Bungenberg, 'Going Global? The EU Common Commercial Policy after Lisbon', *European Yearbook of International Economic Law* 1 (2010): 123–151; Angelos Dimopoulos, 'The Common Commercial Policy after Lisbon: Establishing Parallelism between Internal and External Economic Relations?', *Croatian Yearbook of European Law and Policy* 4 (2008): 101–129; Marc Bungenberg and Christoph Herrmann, eds., *Common Commercial Policy after Lisbon* (Heidelberg: Springer, 2013).

[135] Questions of sustainable development, encompassing both environmental and social aspects, firmly fall within the common commercial policy and, hence, within the exclusive competence of the European Union: Opinion 2/15 of the Court of 16 May 2017, ECLI:EU:C:2017:376, § 141–167.

tsar-like powers. Here the Commission is under similar pressure of the interests championing maximum globalisation and the state dis-empowerment paradigm to those recognisable in the commercial policy. And, yet, at some point it was realised that this paradigm produces too many long-term costs the governments of individual countries are unable to mitigate. It is this intellectual breakthrough, rather than a particular institutional pattern, which can explain why the Commission ventured the sudden U-turn in its assessment of special tax arrangements under the state aid law. Trade Commissioner Malmström has not managed a similar transition. Conversely, she has been desperately clinging to the vulnerable paradigm of maximum globalisation, despite the Wallonia debacle[136] and then an upshot of the 2016 US presidential elections.

The question now is not whether 'maximum globalisation' is the only, or the best, policy paradigm. It is not. The question is how not undermine the brilliant Ricardo's idea of comparative advantage, by pursuing policies in too many respects producing serious side effects. The question, in other words, is how to achieve smart globalisation. As I tried to explain in this chapter, smart globalisation is not a chimera; it is right around the corner. All it needs to get there is a bit of political courage, leadership and thinking outside the box. As the recent flip-flop in the state aid policy demonstrates, Europe can still get there.

[136] On 14 October 2016, the regional parliament of Belgian Wallonia voted to block the Comprehensive Economic and Trade Agreement – a new-generation trade deal between the EU and Canada. It was holding both sides to the deal its hostage for almost two weeks, until leaders of the five Belgian regional parliaments reached an agreement with the federal government, rescinding the Wallonia veto.

Summary: Rerouting the European Project

The series of defeats dealt to anti-European political forces in national elections during the first half of 2017 and the EU's unexpectedly good economic performance had some thinking that the 'Lost Continent rediscovers its mojo'.[1] According to this belief, European integration has proven more resilient and stable than even Euro-enthusiasts could have imagined a few years ago. Policymakers may have not done much to fix its deep problems in recent years, the argument goes, but apparently they have done enough to keep it attractive for European voters.

This thinking is all music to the ears of incumbent politicians, encouraging them to go ahead with their favourite strategy of mutual congratulations underpinning the business-as-usual model. But because it entails quick fixes staving off immediate policy disasters in lieu of actual reforms, the moments when European integration seems to be on track again can easily become as deceptive as desert mirages. They propel the circle of crisis, response, improvement and complacency, with growing risks pushed down the road.

Elation is therefore hardly a viable way forward. While the societies of continental Europe clearly do not want to see the EU unravelled, European economic integration is profoundly endangered as long as policymakers reshuffle risks produced by malfunctioning economic policies, instead of addressing the roots of their ailments. Ephemeral mojo moments engendered by predominantly pro-European attitudes are no alternative to it. Another commentator grasped this clearly, when he argued that the results of the June 2017 snap election in the UK and the French elections should rather be perceived as the most recent

[1] The title of an article by Matthew Karnitschnig, published in *Politico*, 12 June 2017, available at www.politico.eu/article/lost-continent-rediscovers-its-mojo/.

episodes in 'the revolt of the citizens'.[2] From this perspective political developments throughout Europe in recent years have demonstrated that voters desperately seek political forces promising a sense of stability and prosperity in the reality of mounting economic and social risks. The European project is as endangered as incumbent politicians if it fails to deliver on this account. The author of the commentary put it neatly when he argued that 'as the economic crisis fuelled social unrest, voters turned to those who offered answers, albeit simple ones, to their concerns. Faced with increased populism across Europe, EU leaders pledged to start listening to their citizens more closely. But Europe needs more than responsive politicians and half a dozen reflection papers to relaunch its project. It needs a new approach to rebuild Europe.'[3]

This book entirely corroborates this statement and develops it a few steps further. First, it documents how the original hopes and beliefs about the trajectories of the major European economic policies have either backfired or produced deleterious and unexpected side effects. Second, it demonstrates that any alterations to these major policies adopted recently have been exceedingly superficial.

In particular, the EMU is essentially as prone to systemic crises now as it ever was. The alchemy of the monetary policy has been able to ward off its demise, but it has not brought the Eurozone any closer to the optimum currency area than it was ten or fifteen years ago. It is also naïve to believe that this flaw can be remedied in the foreseeable future. The dangerous fallouts of the single currency are seriously amplified in the countries with ineffective and parochial national socioeconomic policies and institutions. European redistribution does not help remedy this crucial blind spot of integration, while the internal market and the dominating approach to international trade make it more difficult for vulnerable economies to avoid skids.

The underlying processes are unobvious and contestable even for specialists. And they are entirely impenetrable for average citizens, arguably due to what Anthony Downs once called 'rational ignorance'.[4]

[2] Jorge Valero, 'The Revolt of the Citizens', *Euractiv*, 9 June 2017, available at www.euractiv.com/section/all/news/the-brief-the-revolt-of-the-citizens/.

[3] Ibid.

[4] Downs argued that because information absorption entails costs of assimilation, rational actors adjust the amount of information comprehended to the expected significance of the decisions taken thereupon. He also realised that in politics there is hardly any relationship between a single vote – the role of a single voter – and the electoral outcome, because universal elections are never decided by a single vote.

This obscureness and contestability of alternatives to major European policies have made it easier for European leaders to sustain their preferred muddle-through strategy on all the crucial accounts of European integration. The strategy of quick fixes, driven by the political irresistibility of time-inconsistent responses to surfacing flaws, has prevailed as a result.

This approach has been clear to see within all major European policies. As its upshot, the ECB has been manoeuvred into monetary financing disguised as quantitative easing when European leaders failed to tackle the Eurozone's debacle of growing debts head-on. Arguably for the same reason, Brexit – the golden opportunity to rectify inefficiencies of European redistributive policies – can hardly be predicted to usher in a fundamental redefinition of how the EU budget is spent. Similarly, the way the Commission and the Court have tried to accommodate the growing disillusionment with the internal market sums up to anything but a set of quick, sometimes inconsistent, fixes. Finally, in the domain of the common commercial policy the Commission has offered immediate remedies to the most controversial facets of it – like secrecy of its free trade agreement negotiations, or the politically disruptive question of the investor-state dispute settlement, or dumping concerns related to Chinese exports – without scratching the deeper worries produced by the paradigm of maximum globalisation.

This tinkering has made the European project exceedingly vulnerable. Even if rationally ignorant about the complexities of economic policies, Europeans have not failed to notice that the underlying paradigms, as touted by mainstream political forces for decades, have often backfired, and that deeper policy flaws have not been uprooted. A recent poll is particularly telling in this respect. It revealed that only 34 per cent of the public in the EU countries feel they have benefited from the EU (compared with 71 per cent of the elite) and 54 per cent of the public think their country was a better place to live twenty years ago.[5]

So voters have a very limited incentive to solicit information necessary for rational, informed political choices on complex policy issues: Anthony Downs, *An Economic Theory of Democracy* (New York: Harper, 1957).

[5] Thomas Raines, Matthew Goodwin and David Cutts, 'The Future of Europe. Comparing Public and Elite Attitudes', Chatham House, June 2017, available at www.chathamhouse.org/sites/files/chathamhouse/publications/research/2017-06-20-future-europe-attitudes-raines-goodwin-cutts-final.pdf.

In some societies this vulnerability has been exploited by Eurosceptics. Most of the time, however, Europeans have not found it excessively difficult to realise that prescriptions offered by anti-European forces are even more pernicious; that isolation can only lead to sidelining and decline. The 'revolt of the citizens' should therefore be understood as an attempt to break out of the deadlock between old policy paradigms pursued by unreformable mainstream politicians, on the one hand, and by the self-defeating Euroscepticism, on the other.

As I argued in this book, the way out of the clutch between the two compromised approaches is fully feasible. The European project can be recalibrated to give Europeans hope and to improve their lives without producing the current serious long-term costs undermining short-term benefits. Getting there is less risky and less costly than diehards of the muddling-through approach assert.

On balance, the most difficult step, as is often so, is to understand the lessons of the past. We know by now in particular that framing the single currency as a political project was a very serious mistake committed three decades ago. We know that the idea of a stable currency is devastating for the economies unsuited to its discipline and that this unsuitability does not disappear as time goes by, producing bouts of high unemployment and debt overhang as a side effect. We know that the picture of regional policy or the CAP bringing Europeans closer together is not accurate any longer. That the internal market and international trade do not necessarily lead to win-win outcomes and that public policies should strive to prevent the concomitant negative externalities even at the expense of reduced economic exchange. And we know that what really matters for the success of European integration is not yet another grandiose, half-baked political project. Instead, it is a specific and constructive set of actions improving crucial institutions and public policies on which the prosperity and stability of European societies largely depend.

These hardly contestable findings logically impose the way forward.

The priority should be to disarm the Eurozone's ticking time bomb of a monetary system too conducive to asymmetric shocks manageable only through very inefficient and costly debt management operations. In some cases, dismantling this bomb requires redenominations, which have been unjustly vilified as ostensibly leading to uncontrollable economic contagion and as irreconcilable with the Treaties. Especially in the case of redenominations the EU has a paramount role to play in redefining and reinforcing (also financially) the national socioeconomic policies and institutions crucial to overcoming monetary transitions. In essence, therefore, while the EMU experiment requires a dose of dissolution if it is not to perpetuate the debt accumulation and its politically damaging effects across the Eurozone, it also necessitates much more punchy and agile European redistributive policies in lieu of the current 'grass-sprinkling' cohesion policy and the CAP. A dose of disintegration where integration has become deleterious (monetary policy) should be compensated by reinforced integration where it is salient for the prosperity of European societies (redistributive policies).

Concentrating European resources in the areas with a particular potential to boost productivity is also crucial for the internal market. The latter has not been traditionally associated with education, research, business environment or retraining – the key enablers of productivity improvements. But without effective policies directing and fostering national efforts on all these accounts, coordinated at the EU level, a 'naked' internal market preoccupied only with the relocation of factors of production and their outcomes does not promise seamless economic development. Instead, it is conducive to social and political upheavals when market competition produces systemically biased outcomes. The internal market, therefore, is likely to become increasingly contestable and unconvincing for European societies, unless it is redefined as a much more sophisticated tool of productivity enhancement than what has been the case so far.

The same applies to the common commercial policy. The idea of smart globalisation advocated in this book is very far from praising economic protectionism. Instead, it highlights the debilitating effects of negative externalities ignored by the current paradigm of maximum globalisation. It calls for improvements mitigating them. It is significant from the perspective of European integration that such a realignment does not entail a weaker, more defensive policy. Quite to the contrary: it requires a broader and more ambitious one. Pursuing it would inevitably impose an additional layer of complexities on the already very complex trade negotiations. But otherwise their outcomes, especially in relations with developing countries, will become increasingly disruptive politically and socially in Europe.

The adjustments sketched above may entail retreats from the current integration paths wherever these paths have been visibly leading the European project towards economic, social and political marshland.

But they also necessitate serious advancements of integration in the areas on which shared long-term prosperity crucially depends, and on which many European societies have been conspicuously blundering. All in all, the alterations are therefore two steps back from the paths towards the cul-de-sac of integration and three steps towards directions promising a more viable integrationist project. What is also important is that this rerouting is achievable without upsetting the current Treaty framework.

It may be contestable, however, that the most important part of such a rerouting is to re-conceptualise European economic integration. In other words, you may wonder if the European project can only really be rejuvenated when inherited dogmas and unproductive intellectual conventions are overcome.

From the political perspective, yet another aspect looms as an obstacle much more difficult to surmount. Redefining European economic integration entails serious redistribution from those who have benefitted from the current arrangements towards those who have been less privileged. Even if policymakers agree that the current policies are unsustainable in a longer perspective, those who stand to lose from reforming them can only be expected to fight tooth and nail to defend the status quo. If they have been able to pursue their interests so far, it would be naïve to believe that their leverage can now vanish under some superior idea of a more perfect future Union.

This is, however, where the 'revolt of the citizens' returns to the picture. The changing landscape of European politics should arguably be read first and foremost as a harbinger of political coalitions of the past being unravelled by those who have felt disenfranchised and disadvantaged by the current setup; by those who have incurred the costs of the policies benefitting someone else. Various debt management operations have managed to recycle a big share of the costs into (mounting) risks accumulated by governments, central banks, or banking systems. Because in consequence the costs are less visible, the traditional coalitions remain stronger as a result and the 'revolt of the citizens' is naturally delayed. But unless the remedies address the source problems of ineffective social contracts, obsolete economic models and political inaptitude, the risks will resurface again in the future, leading to high unemployment, mounting debts, emigration of talents, deterioration of public institutions and a widespread sense of political and economic disempowerment.

One of this book's main arguments is that the current European policies are not properly calibrated to eliminate the underlying risks. Politicians – national and European – have been busy removing them from the radar of public opinion, often by shifting the costs of policy failures into the future. But they have not reduced them. More ominously, the time-inconsistent nature of the quick fixes has implied that current benefits of temporary solutions will sooner or later rear their heads. There will be a price – of a more disruptive 'revolt of the citizens' – to pay for the current 'mojo moments', unless the moments are used to draw lessons from the concerns of Europeans. The most crucial, and legitimate, concern is that public policies have concentrated their benefits in some well-connected groups at the expense of the rest of society. Sometimes the well-connected group is big corporations and sometimes small entrepreneurs. It can be the older generation, labour market insiders, farmers, or many other groups. And it is always policymakers themselves.

The left–right division does not delineate the line of the conflict here. Nor can it be drawn between 'the market' and 'society'. The conflict is essentially between those who have been benefitting from dysfunctional policy paradigms in the short term and those who stand to lose from them in the longer perspective. The current status quo is arguably maintainable only as long as the policy dysfunctionalities, or the relationship between them and their distributional effects, can somehow be swept under the rug. But because these distributional effects gradually grow, it will become increasingly difficult to keep them invisible. At some point they will trigger a backlash breaking up the current status quo. And when it happens, Europe's future will depend on whether the first step to achieve a more perfect Union is made: whether European leaders overcome the intellectual traps, habits and simplified worldviews responsible for the current stalemate of European integration. If they are able to do so, the integration can reach a whole new level, for the good of European societies. If not, anti-European rhetoric is likely to prevail, devastating the European edifice and ushering in economic, social and political mayhem.

This latter scenario is certainly not what Europeans want, nor what they deserve.

Bibliography

Acemoglu, Daron et al. 'Import Competition and the Great US Employment Sag of the 2000s', *Journal of Labor Economics* 34 (Part 2, January 2016): 141–198.

Acemoglu, Daron, García-Jimeno, Camilo and Robinson, James A. 'The Role of State Capacity in Economic Development', *The Political Economist* XI (1) (2015): 7–9.

Acharya, Viral V. and Steffen, Sascha. 'The "Greatest" Carry Trade Ever? Understanding Eurozone Bank Risks', *Journal of Financial Economics* 115 (2015): 215–236.

Ackrill, Robert. *Common Agricultural Policy* (Sheffield: Sheffield Academic Press, 2000).

Adamski, Dariusz. 'The ESMA Doctrine. A Constitutional Revolution and the Economics of Delegation', *European Law Review* 39 (2014): 812–834.

'Economic Policy Coordination as a Game Involving Economic Stability and National Sovereignty', *European Law Journal* 22 (2016): 180–203.

Adascalitei, Dragos. 'Welfare State Development in Central and Eastern Europe: A State of the Art Literature Review', *Studies of Transition States and Societies* 4 (2012): 59–70, available at www.ssoar.info/ssoar/bitstream/handle/document/36268/ssoar-stss-2012-2-adascalitei-Welfare_State_Development_in_Central.pdf?sequence=1.

Aghion, Philippe, Howitt, Peter and Prantl, Susanne. 'Revisiting the Relationship between Competition, Patenting, and Innovation', in: *Advances in Economics and Econometrics (Tenth World Congress, Volume 1, Economic Theory)*, eds. Daron Acemoglu, Manuel Arellano and Eddie Dekel (Cambridge: Cambridge University Press 2013): 451–455.

Aizenman, Joshua and Pasricha, Gurnain K. 'Net Fiscal Stimulus During the Great Recession', *NBER Working Papers* No. 16779, February 2011, available at www.nber.org/papers/w16779.

Alcidi, Cinzia and Gros, Daniel. 'Adjustment Difficulties and Debt Overhangs in the Eurozone Periphery', *CEPS Working Document*

No. 347, 4 May 2011, available at www.ceps.eu/publications/adjustment-difficulties-and-debt-overhangs-eurozone-periphery.

Alcidi, Cinzia, Busse, Matthias and Gros, Daniel. 'Is There a Need for Additional Monetary Stimulus? Insights from the Original Taylor Rule', *CEPS Policy Brief* No. 342, April 2016, available at www.ceps.eu/system/files/PB342TaylorRule.pdf.

Alcidi, Cinzia, Giovannini, Alessandro and Piedrafita, Sonia. 'Enhancing the Legitimacy of EMU Governance', *CEPS Special Report* No. 98, 18 December 2014, available at www.ceps.eu/publications/enhancing-legitimacy-emu-governance.

Alesina Alberto F. and Ardagna, Silvia. 'Large Changes in Fiscal Policy: Taxes versus Spending', *NBER Working Paper* No. 15438, October 2009.

Alesina, Alberto F., Favero, Carlo and Giavazzi, Francesco. 'The Output Effect of Fiscal Consolidations', *NBER Working Paper* No. 18336, August 2012.

Allard, Céline et al. 'Toward a Fiscal Union for the Euro Area', *IMF Staff Discussion Note*, September 2013, available at www.imf.org/external/pubs/ft/sdn/2013/sdn1309.pdf.

Andersen, Torben M. et al. 'Tuning Secondary Education', *The EEAG Report on the European Economy* (Munich: CESifo 2016): 70–84.

Andor, László. 'Basic European Unemployment Insurance – The Best Way Forward in Strengthening the EMU's Resilience and Europe's Recovery', *Intereconomics* 49 (2014): 184–189.

András, Pethő and Blanka, Zöldi. 'How EU-funded Projects Secretly Contributed to the Orbán Family's Enrichment', *DIREKT36*, 9 May 2017, available at www.direkt36.hu/en/2017/05/09/rejtett-allami-munkakbol-is-jott-penz-az-orban-csalad-gyorsan-szerzett-milliardjaihoz/.

ANSA. 'Juncker says Italy "can't complain"', 11 December 2014, available at www.ansa.it/english/news/2014/12/11/juncker-says-italy-cant-complain_2cb65dde-cf3b-4d40-9646-fa97b89293a0.html.

Armingeon, Klaus and Baccaro, Lucio. 'Political Economy of the Sovereign Debt Crisis: The Limits of Internal Devaluation', *Industrial Law Journal* 41 (2012): 254–275.

Armstrong, Kenneth. 'Mutual Recognition', in: *The Law of the Single European Market: Unpacking the Premises*, eds. Catherine Barnard and Joanne Scott (Oxford; Portland, OR: Hart Publishing, 2002): 225–267.

Artavanis, Nikolaos, Morse, Adair and Tsoutsoura, Margarita. 'Measuring Income Tax Evasion Using Bank Credit: Evidence from Greece', 25 September 2015, available at faculty.haas.berkeley.edu/morse/research/papers/ArtavanisMorseTsoutsouraTaxEvasionGreece.pdf.

Arunarwati Margono, Belinda et al. 'Primary Forest Cover Loss in Indonesia over 2000–2012', *Nature Climate Change* 4 (2014): 730–735.

Asadullah, Niaz and Wahhaj, Zaki. 'MinimumWage Attracts Girls to Factories', *Development and Cooperation*, 3 January 2016, available at www.dandc.eu/en/article/higher-wages-bangladeshs-garments-sector-mean-better-income-push-girls-work-child.

Ascoli, Ugo and Pavolini, Emmanuele. *The Italian Welfare State in a European Perspective: A Comparative Analysis* (Bristol: Policy Press, 2016).

Asdrubali, Pierfederico, Sorensen, Bent E. and Yosha, Oved. 'Channels of Interstate Risk Sharing: United States 1963–1990', *Quarterly Journal of Economics* 111 (1996): 1081–1110.

Ashiagbor, Diamond. 'Collective Labor Rights and the European Social Model', *Law & Ethics of Human Rights* 3 (2009): 222–266.

'Unravelling the Embedded Liberal Bargain: Labour and Social Welfare Law in the Context of EU Market Integration', *European Law Journal* 19 (2013): 303–324.

Åslund, Anders. *The Last Shall Be the First: The East European Financial Crisis* (Washington, DC: Peterson Institute for International Economics, 2010).

Astoria, Ross. 'Design of an International Trade Law Compliant Carbon Border Tax Adjustment', *Arizona Journal of Environmental Law & Policy* 6 (2015): 491–454.

Athanasoulis, Stefano and van Wincoop, Eric. 'Risk Sharing within the United States: What Do Financial Markets and Fiscal Federalism Accomplish?', *The Review of Economics and Statistics* 83 (2001): 688–698.

Athanassiou, Phoebus. 'Withdrawal and Expulsion from the EU and EMU. Some Reflections', *ECB's Legal Working Paper Series* No. 10, December 2009, available at www.ecb.europa.eu/pub/pdf/scplps/ecblwp10.pdf.

Aussilloux, Vincent et al. 'Making the Best of the European Single Market', *Bruegel Policy Contribution* No. 3/2017, available at bruegel.org/wp-content/uploads/2017/02/PC-03-2017-single-market-010217-.pdf.

Azoulai, Loic et al. 'Another Legal Monster? An EUI Debate on the Fiscal Compact Treaty', ed. Anna Kocharov, *EUI Working Papers LAW* 09 (2012): available at cadmus.eui.eu/handle/1814/21496.

Baccaro, Lucio and Howell, Chris. 'A Common Neoliberal Trajectory: The Transformation of Industrial Relations in Advanced Capitalism', *Politics & Society* 39 (2011): 521–563.

Bachtler, John and Mendez, Carlos. 'Who Governs EU Cohesion Policy? Deconstructing the Reforms of the Structural Funds', *Journal of Common Market Studies* 45 (2007): 535–564.

Bachtler, John, Mendez, Carlos and Wishlade, Fiona. *EU Cohesion Policy and European Integration: The Dynamics of EU Budget and Regional Policy Reform* (Farnham: Ashgate Publishing, 2014).

Bachtler, John and Michie, Rona. 'Strengthening Economic and Social Cohesion? The Revision of the Structural Funds', *Regional Studies* 28 (1994): 789–796.

Bäckman, Olof and Bergmark, Åke. 'Escaping Welfare? Social Assistance Dynamics in Sweden', *Journal of European Social Policy* 21 (2011): 486–500.

Badinger, Herald et al. 'Macroeconomic Effects of the Services Directive', in: *Services Liberalisation in the Internal Market*, eds. Fritz Breuss, Gerhard Fink and Stefan Griller (Vienna, New York: Springer 2008): 125–165.

Balcerowicz, Leszek. 'On the Prevention of Crises in the Eurozone', in: Governance for the Eurozone: Integration or *Disintegration?*, eds. Allen Franklin, Elena Carletti and Saverio Simonelli, 2012, available at www.eui.eu/DepartmentsAndCentres/Economics/SeminarsEvents/Conferences/GovernanceoftheEurozoneIntegrationorDisintegration.aspx: 75–88

Baldwin, Richard E. and Wyplosz, Charles. *The Economics of European Integration* (London: McGraw-Hill Higher Education, 2015).

Bank for International Settlements. '83rd Annual Report', 23 June 2013, available at www.bis.org/publ/arpdf/ar2013e.pdf.

Bank of International Settlements. '85th Annual Report', 28 June 2015, available at www.bis.org/publ/arpdf/ar2015_ec.pdf.

Bank of Ireland Economic Research Unit. 'The Outlook. A Quarterly Analysis of Trends in the Irish Economy', October 2010, available at www.bankofireland.com/fs/doc/wysiwyg/outlook_oct10.pdf.

Baquero Cruz, Julio. 'The Case Law of the European Court of Justice on the Mobility of Patients: An Assessment', in: *Source Services and the EU Citizen*, ed. Frank S. Benyon (Oxford; Portland: Hart Publishing, 2013): 87–111.

Barbiero, Francesca et al. *Manufacturing Europe's Future*, ed. Reinhilde Veugelers (Bruegel Blueprint, 1 October 2013), available at bruegel.org/wp-content/uploads/imported/publications/Blueprint_XXI_web_181113a.pdf.

Barkbu, Bergljot, Eichengreen, Barry and Mody, Ashoka. 'Financial Crises and the Multilateral Response: What the Historical Record Shows', *Journal of International Economics* 88 (2012): 422–435.

'The Euro's Twin Challenges. Experience and Lessons', in: *The Political and Economic Dynamics of the Eurozone Crisis*, eds. James A. Caporaso and Martin Rhodes (Oxford: Oxford University Press, 2016): 48–78.

Barnard, Catherine. 'Unravelling the Services Directive', *Common Market Law Review* 45 (2008): 323–394.

EU Employment Law (Oxford: Oxford University Press, 2012).

Barone, Guglielmo and Cingano, Federico. 'Service Regulation and Growth: Evidence from OECD Countries', *Economic Journal* 121 (2011): 931–957.

Barrios, Salvador and Burgelman, Jean-Claude. 'Europe Needs More Lisbon to Make ICT Investment Effective', *InterEconomics*, May–June 2008, 124–134.

Barro, Robert and Tenreyro, Silvana. 'Economic Effects of Currency Unions', *Economic Inquiry* 45 (2007): 1–23.

Barslund, Mikkel and von Werder, Marten. 'Measuring Ageing and the Need for Longer Working Lives in the EU', *CEPS Working Document* No. 417, February 2016, available at www.ceps.eu/system/files/WD417%20MB%20%26%20MVW%20Measuring%20ageing%20and%20need%20for%20longer%20working%20lives%20%281%29.pdf.

Bartels, Lorand. 'The WTO Enabling Clause and Positive Conditionality in the European Community's GSP Program', *Journal of International Economic Law* 6 (2003): 507–532.

Bartunek, Robert-Jan and de Carbonnel, Alissa. 'EU Nations Thrash Out Deal on Carbon Market Reform', *Reuters*, 3 March 2017, available at uk.reuters.com/article/uk-eu-carbon-idUKKBN16718Q?il=0.

Bauer, Michael W. and Becker, Stefan. 'The Unexpected Winner of the Crisis: The European Commission's Strengthened Role in Economic Governance', *Journal of European Integration* 36 (2014): 213–229.

Baun, Michael and Marek, Dan. *Cohesion Policy in the European Union* (New York: Palgrave Macmillan, 2014).

Beblavý, Miroslav et al. 'Common Unemployment Insurance Scheme for the Euro Area', Annex I to 'Common Unemployment Insurance Scheme for the Euro Area. Cost of Non-Europe Report', European Parliamentary Research Service, September 2014, available at www.europarl.europa.eu/RegData/etudes/STUD/2014/510984/EPRS_STU(2014)510984_REV1_EN.pdf.

Beblavý, Miroslav, Gros, Daniel and Maselli, Ilaria 'Reinsurance of National Unemployment Benefit Schemes', *CEPS Working Document* No. 401, January 2015, available at www.ceps.eu/system/files/wd401.pdf.

Beblavý, Miroslav, Lenaerts, Karolien and Maselli, Ilaria. 'Design of a European Unemployment Benefit Scheme', *CEPS Research Report* No 2017/04, February 2017, available at www.ceps.eu/system/files/Design%20of%20EUBS%20RRpt%20No%202017-04.pdf.

Beblavý, Miroslav and Martellucci, Elisa. 'Extending Working Lives. A Comparative Analysis of How Governments Influence Lifelong Learning', *CEPS Special Report* No. 111, July 2015, available at www.ceps.eu/system/files/No%20111%20Beblavy%20%26%20Martelucci%20Mopac%20FINAL.pdf.

Begg, Iain. 'Cohesion in the European Community: A Key Imperative for the 1990s?', *Regional Science and Urban Economics* 23 (1993): 427–448.

Bekaert, Geert, Harvey, Campbell R. and Lundblad, Christian. 'Growth Volatility and Financial Liberalization', *Journal of International Money and Finance* 25 (2006): 370–403.

Belke, Ansgar. '3-year LTROs – A First Assessment of a Non-Standard Policy Measure', Briefing paper prepared for the April 2012 Monetary Dialogue at the European Parliament, available at www.europarl.europa.eu/document/activities/cont/201204/20120423ATT43715/20120423ATT43715EN.pdf.

'Gold-backed Sovereign Bonds: An Effective Alternative to OMTs', in: *Financial Crises, Sovereign Risk and the Role of Institutions*, eds. Dominik Maltritz and Michael Berlemann (Cham: Springer, 2014): 7–24.

Belke, Ansgar, Domnick, Clemens and Gros, Daniel. 'Business Cycle Synchronization in the EMU: Core vs. Periphery', *CEPS Working Document*, No. 427, 14 November 2016, available at www.ceps.eu/publications/business-cycle-synchronization-emu-core-vs-periphery.

Belke, Ansgar and Osowski, Thomas. 'Measuring Fiscal Spillovers in EMU and Beyond: A Global VAR Approach', *CEPS Working Document* No. 428, December 2016, available at www.ceps.eu/system/files/WD428%20Fiscal%20spillover.pdf.

Belke, Ansgar and Polleit, Thorsten. 'How Much Fiscal Backing Must the ECB Have? The Euro Area Is Not (Yet) the Philippines', *International Economics* 124 (2010): 5–30.

Benner, Mats and Bundgaard Vad, Torben. 'Sweden and Denmark Defending the Welfare State', in *Welfare and Work in the Open Economy Volume II: Diverse Responses to Common Challenges in Twelve Countries*, eds. Fritz Scharpf and Vivien A. Schmidt (Oxford: Oxford University Press, 2000): 399–466.

Bergström, Carl Fredrik. 'Shaping the New System for Delegation of Powers to EU Agencies: United Kingdom v. European Parliament and Council (Short Selling)', *Common Market Law Review* 52 (2015): 219–242.

Bernanke, Ben. 'Monetary Policy and the Global Economy', 2013, available at www.federalreserve.gov/newsevents/speech/bernanke20130325a.htm.

Bernhard, Helen, Fischbacher, Urs and Fehr, Ernst. 'Parochial Altruism in Humans', *Nature* 442 (2006): 912–915.

Bertola Giuseppe et al. 'Price, Wage and Employment Response to Shocks: Evidence from the WDN Survey', *ECB Working Paper Series* No. 1164, March 2010, available at www.ecb.europa.eu/pub/pdf/scpwps/ecbwp1164.pdf.

Bieler, Andreas. 'European Integration and the Transnational Restructuring of Social Relations: The Emergence of Labour as a Regional Actor', *Journal of Common Market Studies* 43 (2005): 461–484.

Biggs, Michael and Mayer, Thomas. 'Latvia and Greece: Less Is More', *CEPS High-Level Brief*, 12 February 2014, available at www.ceps.eu/publications/latvia-and-greece-less-more.

Bijlsma, Michiel and Lukkezen, Jasper. 'TARGET 2 of the ECB vs. Interdistrict Settlement Account of the Federal Reserve', *Bruegel Blog Post*, 6 March 2012, available at bruegel.org/2012/03/target-2-of-the-ecb-vs-interdistrict-settlement-account-of-the-federal-reserve/.

Bini Smaghi, Lorenzo. *Austerity: European Democracies Against the Wall* (Brussels: CEPS Paperback, July 2013): available at aei.pitt.edu/47681/1/LBS_Austerity.pdf.

Blanchard, Olivier. 'Country Adjustment within Euroland: Lessons after Two Years', *Monitoring the European Central Bank*, annual CEPR report, March 2001.

Blanchard, Olivier, Mauro, Paolo and Acalin, Julien. 'The Case for Growth-indexed Bonds in Advanced Economies Today', *Peterson Institute for International Economics Policy Brief* No. 16-2, February 2016, available at piie.com/publications/policy-briefs/case-growth-indexed-bonds-advanced-economies-today.

Blanchard, Olivier and Wolfers, Justin. 'The Role of Shocks and Institutions in the Rise of European Unemployment: The Aggregate Evidence', *NBER Working Paper* No. 7282, August 1999, available at www.nber.org/papers/w7282.pdf.

Blauberger, Michael. 'With Luxembourg in Mind ... the Remaking of National Policies in the Face of ECJ Jurisprudence', *Journal of European Public Policy* 19 (2012): 109–126.

Bleses, Peter and Seeleib-Kaiser, Martin. *The Dual Transformation of the German Welfare State* (Basingstoke: Palgrave Macmillan, 2004).

Bluth, Christian. 'Attitudes to Global Trade and TTIP in Germany and the United States', *Global Economic Dynamics Study*, Bertelsmann Stiftung 2016, available at www.bertelsmann-stiftung.de/en/publications/publication/did/attitudes-to-global-trade-and-ttip-in-germany-and-the-united-states/.

Bofinger, Peter et al. 'A Redemption Pact for Europe: Time to Act Now', *VOX CEPR's Policy Portal*, 25 July 2012, available at voxeu.org/article/redemption-pact-europe-time-act-now.

Boggero, Giovanni and Annicchino, Pasquale. '"Who Will Ever Kick Us Out?": Italy, the Balanced Budget Rule and the Implementation of the Fiscal Compact', *European Public Law* 20 (2014): 247–261.

Boldrin, Michele and Levine, David K. 'Perfectly Competitive Innovation', *Journal of Monetary Economics* 55 (2008): 435–453.

Bonatti, Luigi and Fracasso, Andrea. 'The German Model and the European Crisis', *Journal of Common Market Studies* 51 (2013): 1023–1039.

Bond, Eric W. et al. 'Misallocation and Productivity Effects of the Smoot-Hawley Tariff', *NBER Working Paper* No. 18034, May 2012, available at www.nber.org/papers/w18034.pdf.

Bonoli, Giuliano. 'Classifying Welfare States: A Two-Dimension Approach', *Journal of Social Policy* 26 (1997): 351–372.

Bonoli, Giuliano and Natali, David. 'The Politics of the "New" Welfare States: Analysing Reforms in Western Europe', in: *The Politics of the New Welfare State*, eds. Giuliano Bonoli and David Natali (Oxford: Oxford University Press, 2012): 3–17.

Bootle, Roger. 'Leaving the Euro: A Practical Guide', *Capital Economics*, 4 June 2012, available at www.capitaleconomics.com/wp-content/uploads/2016/11/wolfson-prize-submission.pdf.

Bordo, Michael D. and Eichengreen, Barry, eds. *A Retrospective on the Bretton Woods System: Lessons for International Monetary Reform* (Chicago: University of Chicago Press, 1993).

Bordo, Michael D., Markiewicz, Agnieszka and Jonung, Lars. 'A Fiscal Union for the Euro: Some Lessons from History', *NBER Working Paper* 17380, September 2011, available at www.nber.org/papers/w17380.

Borger, Vestert. 'How the Debt Crisis Exposes the Development of Solidarity in the Euro Area', *European Constitutional Law Review* 9 (2013): 23–24.

Bosch, Gerhard and Weinkopf, Claudia. *Low-Wage Work in Germany* (New York: Russell Sage Foundation, 2008).

Bouget, Denis et al., 'Social Investment in Europe. A Study of National Policies', April 2015, available at ec.europa.eu/social/BlobServlet?docId=15131&langId=en.

Brandolini, Andrea, Carta, Francesca and D'Amuri, Francesco. 'A Feasible Unemployment-Based Shock Absorber for the Euro Area', Banca D'Italia, Questioni di Economia e Finanza (Occasional papers) No. 254, November 2014, available at www.bancaditalia.it/pubblicazioni/qef/2014-0254/QEF_254.pdf.

Brender, Anton, Pisani, Florence and Gagna, Emile. *The Sovereign Debt Crisis. Placing a Curb on Growth* (CEPS, 2012): available at www.ceps.eu/publications/sovereign-debt-crisis-placing-curb-growth.

Money, Finance and the Real Economy: What Went Wrong? (CEPS Paperback, 17 March 2015): available at www.ceps.eu/publications/money-finance-and-real-economy-what-went-wrong.

Brenner, Neil, Peck, Jamie and Theodore, Nik. 'Variegated Neoliberalization: Geographies, Modalities, Pathways', *Global Networks. A Journal of Transnational Affairs* 10 (2010): 182–222.

Breunig, Christian and Busemeyer, Marius R. 'Fiscal Austerity and the Trade-off between Public Investment and Social Spending', *Journal of European Public Policy* 19 (2012): 921–938.

Brown, Ellen. 'Thinking Outside the Box: How a Bankrupt Germany Solved Its Infrastructure Problems', *The Web of Debt*, 9 August 2007, available at www.webofdebt.com/articles/bankrupt-germany.php.

Brülhart, Marius and Torstensson, Johan. 'Regional Integration, Scale Economies and Industry Location in the European Union', *CEPR Discussion Paper 1435* (London: Centre for Economic Policy Research, 1996).

Brunnermeier, Markus K., James, Harold and Landau, Jean-Pierre. *The Euro and the Battle of Ideas* (Princeton, NJ: Princeton University Press, 2016).

Buchanan, James M. and Wagner, Richard E. *Democracy in Deficit. The Political Legacy of Lord Keynes* (New York: Academic Press, 1977).

Buchanan, James M. et al. 'The Political Biases of Keynesian Economics', in: *Fiscal Responsibility in Constitutional Democracy*, eds. James M. Buchanan and Richard E. Wagner (Leiden: Martinus Nijhoff, 1978): 79–100.

Buchheit, Lee C., Gulati, G. Mitu, and Tirado, Ignacio. 'The Problem of Holdout Creditors in Eurozone Sovereign Debt Restructurings', Draft, 22 January 2013, available at pdfs.semanticscholar.org/bbb9/94b33376f0352cbe9dd6f1e1c27155b24a59.pdf.

Buiter, Willem H. 'Helicopter Money: Irredeemable Fiat Money and the Liquidity Trap', *NBER Working Paper* No. 10163, December 2003, available at www.nber.org/papers/w10163.pdf.

Buiter, Willem H. and Rahbari, Ebrahim. 'The European Central Bank as Lender of Last Resort for Sovereigns in the Eurozone', *Journal of Common Market Studies* 50 (2012) Annual Review: 6–35.

Bunea, Daniela et al. 'Profit Distribution and Loss Coverage Rules for Central Banks', *ECB's Occasional Paper* No. 169, April 2016, available at www.ecb.europa.eu/pub/pdf/scpops/ecbop169.en.pdf?f7073b79c2f6f62c79918dc24088dd00.

Bungenberg, Marc. 'Going Global? The EU Common Commercial Policy after Lisbon', *European Yearbook of International Economic Law* 1 (2010): 123–151.

Bungenberg, Marc and Herrmann, Christoph, eds. *Common Commercial Policy after Lisbon* (Heidelberg: Springer, 2013).

Burstein, Ariel and Vogel, Jonathan. 'International Trade, Technology, and the Skill Premium', February 2016, available at www.columbia.edu/~jev9/BV-TTSP.pdf.

Busemeyer, Marius R. and Schlicht-Schmälzle, Raphaela. 'Partisan Power, Economic Coordination and Variations in Vocational Training Systems in Europe', *European Journal of Industrial Relations* 20 (2014): 55–71.

Buti, Marco and Carnot, Nicolas. 'The EMU Debt Crisis: Early Lessons and Reforms', *Journal of Common Market Studies* 50 (2012): 899–911.

Canotilho, Mariana, Violante, Teresa and Lanceiro, Rui. 'Austerity Measures under Judicial Scrutiny: The Portuguese Constitutional Case-law: Portuguese Constitutional Court Decision 399/2010 (Surtax on Personal Income Tax 2010) Decision 396/2011 (State Budget 2011) Decision 353/2012 (State Budget 2012) Decision 187/2013 (State Budget 2013) Decision 474/2013 (Public Workers Requalification) Decision 602/2013 (Labour Code) Decision 794/2013 (40-Hour Work Week) Decision 862/2013 (Pensions Convergence) Decision 413/2014 (State Budget 2014) Decision 572/2014 (Special Solidarity Contribution 2014) Decision 574/2014 (Pay cuts 2014–2018) Decision 575/2014 (Special Sustainability Contribution)', *European Constitutional Law Review* 11 (2015): 155–183.

Cappelen, Aadne et al. 'The Impact of EU Regional Support on Growth and Convergence in the European Union', *Journal of Common Market Studies* 41 (2003): 621–644.

Carletti, Elena and Simonelli, Saverio, in: *Governance for the Eurozone: Integration or Disintegration?*, eds. Allen Franklin, Elena Carletti and Saverio Simonelli, 2012: 75–88, available at www.eui.eu/DepartmentsAndCentres/Economics/SeminarsEvents/Conferences/GovernancefortheEurozoneIntegrationorDisintegration.aspx.

Castles, Francis G. and Obinger, Herbert. 'Worlds, Families, Regimes: Country Clusters in European and OECD Area Public Policy', *West European Politics* 31 (2008): 321–344.

Centre for Strategy and Evaluation Services. 'Study to Provide an Inventory of Reserves of Activities Linked to Professional Qualifications Requirements in 13 Member States and Assessing Their Economic Impact', for DG Internal Market, European Commission, January 2012.

Center on Budget and Policy Priorities. 'Policy Basics: Where Do Our Federal Tax Dollars Go?', 4 March 2016.

CESifo. 'EEAG Report on the European Economy 2011', available at www.cesifo-group.de.

Chaffin, Joshua and Harvey, Fiona. 'EU Attacks Carbon Border Tax Initiative', *Financial Times*, 14 October 2009, available at www.ft.com/content/7cba7a90-b8e3-11de-98ee-00144feab49a.

Chalmers, Damian, Davies, Gareth and Monti, Giorgio. *European Union Law: Text and Materials* (Cambridge: Cambridge University Press, 2014).

Chang, Ha-Joon. *Bad Samaritans: The Myth of Free Trade and the Secret History of Capitalism* (New York: Bloomsbury Publishing, 2010).

Chazan, David. 'French Farmers Hope Marine Le Pen Will Free Them from EU "Straitjacket"', *The Telegraph*, 25 February 2017.

Cisotta, Roberto and Gallo, Daniel. 'The Portuguese Constitutional Court Case Law on Austerity Measures: A Reappraisal', in: *Social Rights in Times of Crisis in the Eurozone: The Role of Fundamental Rights' Challenges*, eds. Claire Kilpatrick and Bruno De Witte, *EUI Working Papers LAW* 5 (2014): 85–94, available at cadmus.eui.eu/handle/1814/31247.

Claessens, Stijn, Mody, Ashoka and Vallée, Shahin. 'Paths to Eurobonds', *IMF Working Paper* No. WP/12/172, 1 July 2012, available at www.imf.org/en/Publications/WP/Issues/2016/12/31/Paths-to-Eurobonds-26034.

Claeys, Grégory. 'The (not so) Unconventional Monetary Policy of the European Central Bank since 2008', Bruegel External Publication for the European Parliament's Montary Dialogue with the President of the European Central Bank Mario Draghi, June 2014, available at bruegel.org/2014/07/the-not-so-unconventional-monetary-policy-of-the-european-central-bank-since-2008/.

Claeys, Grégory. 'Low Long-term Rates: Bond Bubble or Symptom of Secular Stagnation?', *Bruegel Policy Contribution* No. 15/2016, 26 September 2016, available at bruegel.org/2016/09/low-long-term-rates-bond-bubble-or-symptom-of-secular-stagnation/.

Claeys, Grégory, Darvas, Zsolt and Leandro, Alvaro. 'A Proposal to Revive the European Fiscal Framework', *Bruegel Policy Contribution* No. 2016/07, 29 March 2016, available at bruegel.org/wp-content/uploads/2016/03/pc_2016_07.pdf.

Claeys, Grégory, Darvas, Zsolt and Wolff, Guntram 'Benefits and Drawbacks of European Unemployment Insurance', *Bruegel Policy Brief* No. 2014/06, 12 September 2014, available at bruegel.org/2014/09/benefits-and-drawbacks-of-european-unemployment-insurance/.

Claeys, Grégory, Leandro, Álvaro and Mandra, Allison. 'European Central Bank Quantitative Easing: The Detailed Manual', *Bruegel Policy Contribution* No. 2015/02, 11 March 2015, available at bruegel.org/2015/03/european-central-bank-quantitative-easing-the-detailed-manual/.

Clasen, Jochen. *Reforming Welfare States – Germany and the UK Compared* (Oxford: Oxford University Press, 2005).

Clauset, Aaron. 'The Negative Impact of EU Enlargement', *Science* 356 (2017): 14 April 2017, 149–150.

Climate Action Tracker. Indonesia, available at climateactiontracker.org/countries/indonesia.html

Cœuré, Benoît. 'Outright Monetary Transactions, One Year On', 2 September 2013, available at www.ecb.europa.eu/press/key/date/2013/html/sp130902.en.html.

Cœuré, Benoît. 'People Are Not Only Savers', Frankfurter Allgemeine Sonntagszeitung, 1 May 2016, available at www.ecb.europa.eu/press/key/date/2016/html/sp160501.en.html.

'Comments on the latest Greek proposals', 10 July 2015, available at www.sven-giegold.de/wp-content/uploads/2015/07/grexit_bundesregierung_non_paper_10_juli_2015.pdf.

Commission of the European Communities. 'Report of the Study Group on the Role of Public Finance in European Integration', 1 (1977): April 1977, available at ec.europa.eu/archives/emu_history/documentation/chapter8/19770401en73macdougallrepvol1.pdf.

'Completing the Internal Market', White Paper, COM(85)310, 14 June 1985.

'Community Structural Funds 1994–1999. Revised Regulations and Comments', August 1993, available at aei.pitt.edu/1750/1/structure_funds_93_commentary.pdf.

'European Social Policy – A Way Forward for the Union – A White Paper', COM(94)333.

Committee for the Study of Economic and Monetary Union. 'Report on Economic and Monetary Union in the European Community', April 1989, available at aei.pitt.edu/1007/1/monetary_delors.pdf.

Condon, Madison and Ignaciuk, Ada. 'Border Carbon Adjustment and International Trade: A Literature Review', *OECD Trade and Environment Working Papers* No. 2013/06 (Paris: OECD Publishing, 2013): available at papers.ssrn.com/sol3/papers.cfm?abstract_id=2693236.

Connolly, Michael and Cheng Li, 'Government Spending and Economic Growth in the OECD Countries', *Journal of Economic Policy Reform* 19 (2016): 386–395.

Constâncio, Vítor. 'Resolving Europe's NPL Burden: Challenges and Benefits', 3 February 2017, available at bruegel.org/2017/02/resolving-europes-npl-burden-challenges-and-benefits/.

Cooper, Marta. 'Berlin Is Cracking Down on Short-Term Apartment Rentals – and Airbnb Is Taking a Hit', *Quartz*, 1 May 2016, available at qz.com/673932/berlin-is-cracking-down-on-short-term-apartment-rentals-and-airbnb-is-taking-a-hit/.

Cooper, Richard N. 'Trade Policy as Foreign Policy', in: *U.S. Trade Policies in a Changing World Economy*, ed. Robert M. Stern (Cambridge, MA: MIT Press, 1987): 290–321.

Copeland, Brian R. and Taylor, M. Scott. *Trade and the Environment: Theory and Evidence* (Princeton, NJ: Princeton University Press, 2013).

Costamagna, Francesco. 'The Internal Market and the Welfare State: Anything New After Lisbon?', in: *The Treaty of Lisbon and the Future of European Law and Policy*, eds. Martin Trybus and Luca Rubini (Cheltenham; Northampton, MA: Edward Elgar Publishing, 2012): 381–397.

'Minimum Wage between Public Procurement and Posted Workers: Anything New after the RegioPost Case?', *European Law Review* 42 (2017): 101–111.

Cotton, Johnny. 'France's Disillusioned Farmers Turn to Le Pen', *Reuters*, 28 February 2017, available at www.reuters.com/article/us-france-election-farmers-idUSKBN16627O.

Coucheir, Michael, Strban, Grega and Hauben, Harald. 'The Legal and Operational Feasibility of a European Unemployment Benefits Scheme at the National Level', *CEPS Special Report* No. 145, 26 September 2016, available at www.ceps.eu/publications/legal-and-operational-feasibility-european-unemployment-benefits-scheme-national-level.

Council of Economic Advisors. 'The Economic Benefits of U.S. Trade', May 2015, available at obamawhitehouse.archives.gov/sites/default/files/docs/cea_trade_report_final_non-embargoed_v2.pdf.

Council of the European Union. 'Hungary: Council Lifts Cohesion Fund Suspension', Press release No. 11648/12, 22 June 2012, available at www.consilium.europa.eu/uedocs/cms_data/docs/pressdata/en/ecofin/131129.pdf.

'Opinion of the Legal Service', Ref 7739/15, 7 April 2015.

Countouris, Nicola and Freedland, Mark. 'Epilogue: Resocialising Europe – Looking Back and Thinking Forward', in: *Resocialising Europe in a Time of Crisis*, eds. Nicola Countouris and Mark Freedland (Cambridge: Cambridge University Press, 2013): 493–503.

'Preface', in: *Resocialising Europe in a Time of Crisis*, eds. Nicola Countouris and Mark Freedland (Cambridge: Cambridge University Press, 2013): ix–xi.

Court of Auditors. 'Youth Unemployment – Have EU Policies Made a Difference? An Assessment of the Youth Guarantee and the Youth Employment Initiative', *Special Report* No. 5/2017, available at www.eca.europa.eu/Lists/ECADocuments/SR17_5/SR_YOUTH_GUARANTEE_EN.pdf.

Craig, Paul. 'Guest Editorial. Pringle: Legal Reasoning, Text, Purpose and Teleology', *Maastricht Journal of European Law* 20 (2013): 3–11.

Cruces Juan J. and Trebesch, Christoph. 'Sovereign Defaults: The Price of Haircuts', *American Economic Journal: Macroeconomics* 5 (2013): July 2013, 85–117, available at www.aeaweb.org/articles?id=10.1257/mac.5.3.85.

Crum, Ben. 'Saving the Euro at the Cost of Democracy?', *Journal of Common Market Studies* 51 (2013): 614–630.

Cunha, Arlindo and Swinbank, Alan. *An Inside View of the CAP Reform Process: Explaining the MacSharry, Agenda 2000, and Fischler Reforms* (Oxford: Oxford University Press, 2011).

Da Costa Cabral, Nazaré. 'Which Budgetary Union for the E(M)U?', *Journal of Common Market Studies*, 54 (2016): 1280–1295.

Dahan, Samuel. 'The EU/IMF Financial Stabilisation Process in Latvia and Its Implications for Labour Law and Social Policy', *Industrial Law Journal* 41 (2012): 305–327.

Daley, Janet. 'This Was the Week That European Democracy Died', *The Telegraph*, 29 October 2011, available at www.telegraph.co.uk/finance/financialcrisis/8857533/This-was-the-week-that-European-democracy-died.html.

Daly, Mary. 'Welfare States under Pressure: Cash Benefits in European Welfare States over the Last Ten Years', *Journal of European Social Policy* 7 (1997): 129–146.

Damjanovic, Dragana and De Witte, Bruno. 'Welfare Integration through EU Law: The Overall Picture in the Light of the Lisbon Treaty', *EUI Working Papers LAW* No. 2008/34.

Danescu, Elena. 'Economists v. Monetarists – Agreements and Clashes in the Drafting of the Werner Report', *Centre virtuel de la connaissance sur l'Europe*

2012, available at www.cvce.eu/content/publication/2012/4/3/875a85f1-e099-4013-acbf-68b2c50a6879/publishable_en.pdf.

Danforth, Benjamin. 'Worlds of Welfare in Time: A Historical Reassessment of the Three-World Typology', *Journal of European Social Policy* 24 (2014): 164–182.

Darvas, Zsolt. 'A Tale of Three Countries: Recovery after Banking Crises', Bruegel Policy Contribution No. 2011/19, 29 December 2011, available at bruegel.org/2011/12/a-tale-of-three-countries-recovery-after-banking-crises/.

'The Greek Debt Trap: An Escape Plan', Bruegel Policy Contribution No. 2012/19, 9 November 2012, available at bruegel.org/2012/11/the-greek-debt-trap-an-escape-plan/.

'Regional and Global Financial Safety Nets: The Recent European Experience and Its Implications for Regional Cooperation in Asia', Bruegel Working Paper No. 6/2017, 20 April 2017, available at bruegel.org/2017/04/regional-and-global-financial-safety-nets-the-recent-european-experience-and-its-implications-for-regional-cooperation-in-asia/.

Darvas, Zsolt and Hüttl, Pia. 'Is Greek Public Debt Unsustainable?', *Bruegel Blog Post*, 7 May 2016, available at bruegel.org/2016/05/is-greek-public-debt-unsustainable/.

Darvas, Zsolt and Leandro, Álvaro. 'The Limitations of Policy Coordination in the Euro Area under the European Semester', Bruegel Policy Contribution No. 2015/19, 12 November 2015.

Darvas, Zsolt and Tschekassin, Olga. 'Poor and under Pressure: The Social Impact of Europe's Fiscal Consolidation', Bruegel Policy Contribution No. 2015/04, March 2015, available at bruegel.org/wp-content/uploads/imported/publications/Poor_and_under_pressure.pdf.

Darvas, Zsolt and Wolff, Guntram. 'An Anatomy of Inclusive Growth in Europe', Bruegel Blueprint No. 26, 2016, available at bruegel.org/wp-content/uploads/2016/10/BP-26-26_10_16-final-web.pdf.

'Memos to the New EU Leadership. To the Commissioner for Economic and Monetary Affairs', Bruegel EU to do in 2015–2019, available at eu2do.bruegel.org/economic-and-monetary-affairs/.

Darvas, Zsolt, Sapir, André and Wolff, Guntram. 'The Long Haul: Managing Exit from Financial Assistance', Bruegel Policy contribution, 20 February 2014, available at bruegel.org/2014/02/the-long-haul-managing-exit-from-financial-assistance/.

Davies, Jack. 'Europe's "Blood Sugar"', *Politico*, 4 April 2017, available at www.politico.eu/article/europe-blood-sugar-cambodia-human-rights-trade/.

Dawson, Mark. *New Governance and the Transformation of European Law: Coordinating EU Social Law and Policy* (Cambridge: Cambridge University Press, 2011).

Dawson, Mark and De Witte, Floris. 'Constitutional Balance in the EU After the Euro-Crisis', *The Modern Law Review* 76 (2013): 817–844.

De Grauwe, Paul. 'The Governance of a Fragile Eurozone', *CEPS Working Document* No. 346, May 2011, available at www.ceps.eu/system/files/book/2011/05/WD%20346%20De%20Grauwe%20on%20Eurozone%20 Governance .pdf.

'How to Avoid a Double-dip Recession in the Eurozone', *CEPS Commentary*, 15 November 2012, available at www.ceps.eu/publications/how-avoid-double-dip-recession-eurozone.

Economics of the Monetary Union (Oxford: Oxford University Press, 2012).

'Design Failures in the Eurozone: Can They Be Fixed?', *LSE Europe in Question Paper Series* No. 57/2013, February 2013, available at www.lse.ac.uk/europeanInstitute/LEQS%20Discussion%20Paper%20Series/LEQSPaper 57.pdf.

De Grauwe, Paul et al. 'The Future of Europe's Economy: Disaster or Deliverance?', *Centre for European Reform Report*, 18 September 2013, available at www.cer.org.uk/publications/archive/report/2013/future-europes-economy-disaster-or-deliverance.

De Grauwe, Paul. 'How Far Should We Push Globalisation?', *CEPS Commentary*, 4 November 2016, available at www.ceps.eu/publications/how-far-should-we-push-globalisation.

De Grauwe, Paul and Ji, Yuemei. 'Self-Fulfilling Crises in the Eurozone: An Empirical Test', *CEPS Working Document* No. 367, June 2012, available at www.ceps.eu/system/files/WD%20No%20367%20Empirical%20Test%20 Fragility%20Eurozone.pdf.

'The Legacy of Austerity in the Eurozone', *CEPS Commentary*, 4 October 2013, available at www.ceps.eu/publications/legacy-austerity-eurozone.

'Disappearing Government Bond Spreads in the Eurozone – Back to Normal?', *CEPS Working Document* No. 396, 14 May 2014.

'Why the ECB Should Not Insist on Repayment of Its Greek Bonds', *VOX CEPR's Policy Portal*, 16 July 2015, available at voxeu.org/article/why-ecb-should-not-insist-repayment-its-greek-bonds.

'Flexibility Versus Stability. A Difficult Trade-off in the Eurozone', *CEPS Working Document* No. 422, 29 April 2016, available at www.ceps.eu/publications/flexibility-versus-stability-difficult-trade-eurozone.

De Groen, Willem Pieter. 'Carving Out Legacy Assets: A Successful Tool for Bank Restructuring?', *In-Depth Analysis for the European Parliament*, March 2017, available at www.europarl.europa.eu/RegData/etudes/IDAN/2017/587398/IPOL_IDA(2017)587398_EN.pdf.

De la Porte, Caroline. 'The European Level Development and National Level Influence of the Open Method of Coordination: The Cases of Employment and Social Inclusion' (PhD diss., European University Institute, 2008), available at cadmus.eui.eu//handle/1814/10463.

De Lhoneux, Etienne and Vassilopoulos, Christos. *The European Stability Mechanism before the Court of Justice of the European Union. Comments on the Pringle Case* (Cham: Springer, 2014).

Delors, Jacques. 'Regional Implications of Economic and Monetary Integration', in *Report on Economic and Monetary Union in the European Community. Collection of Papers Submitted to the Committee for the Study of Economic and Monetary Union*, ed. Committee for the Study of Economic and Monetary Union, 1989, 81–89, available at aei.pitt.edu/1008/1/monetary_delors_collected_papers.pdf.

De Wispelaere, Frederic and Pacolet, Jozef. 'An Ad Hoc Statistical Analysis on Short Term Mobility – Economic Value of Posting of Workers', Research commissioned by DG EMPL within the framework of Contract VT/2015/096, available at ec.europa.eu/social/BlobServlet?docId=15425&langId=en.

De Witte, Bruno. 'Setting the Scene: How Did Services Get to Bolkestein and Why?', *EUI Working Paper* No. 2007/20.

De Witte, Floris. 'EU Law, Politics, and the Social Question', *German Law Journal* 14 (2013): 581–612.

'The Architecture of a "Social Market Economy"', *LSE Legal Studies Working Paper* No. 13/2015, June 2015.

Debrun, Xavier and Kapoor, Radhicka. 'Fiscal Policy and Macroeconomic Stability: Automatic Stabilizers Work, Always and Everywhere', *IMF* working paper No. 10/111, 1 May 2010, available at www.imf.org/en/Publications/WP/Issues/2016/12/31/Fiscal-Policy-and-Macroeconomic-Stability-Automatic-Stabilizers-Work-Always-and-Everywhere-23818.

Dellmuth, Lisa Maria, Schraff, Dominik and Stoffel, Michael F. 'Distributive Politics, Electoral Institutions and European Structural and Investment Funding: Evidence from Italy and France', *Journal of Common Market Studies* 55 (2017): 275–293.

DeLong, J. Bradford and H. Summers, Lawrence. 'Fiscal Policy in a Depressed Economy', *Brookings Paper on Economic Activity*, Spring 2012, available at www.brookings.edu/bpea-articles/fiscal-policy-in-a-depressed-economy/.

Delpla, Jacques and von Weizsäcker, Jakob. 'The Blue Bond Proposal', *Bruegel Policy Brief*, No. 2010/03, May 5, 2010, available at www.bruegel.org/publications/publication-detail/publication/403-the-blue-bond-proposal.

Demertzis, Maria and Lehmann, Alex. 'Tackling Europe's Crisis Legacy: A Comprehensive Strategy for Bad Loans and Debt Restructuring', *Bruegel Policy Contribution* No. 11/2017, 21 April 2017, available at bruegel.org/2017/04/tackling-europes-crisis-legacy-a-comprehensive-strategy-for-bad-loans-and-debt-restructuring/.

Demertzis, Maria and Wolff, Guntram 'What Impact Does the ECB's Quantitative Easing Policy Have on Bank Profitability?', *Bruegel Policy Contribution* No. 20/2016, 30 November 2016, available at bruegel.org/2016/11/what-impact-does-the-ecbs-quantitative-easing-policy-have-on-bank-profitability/.

Demyanyk, Yuliya, Ostergaard, Charlotte and Sørensen, Bent E. 'Risk Sharing and Portfolio Allocation in EMU', *Economic Papers* 334 (2008): European Commission.

Dennis, Brady. 'Iceland Makes Fledgling Recovery from Its Economic Meltdown', *The Washington Post*, 16 January 2012, available at www.washingtonpost.com/business/economy/iceland-makes-fledgling-recovery-from-its-economic-meltdown/2012/01/12/gIQAW1q83P_story.html?utm_term=.3783fbaf817f.

Dias Sanchez, Jose L. and Varoudakis, Aristomene. 'Tracking the Causes of Eurozone External Imbalances: New Evidence', *VOX CEPR's Policy Portal*, 6 February 2014, available at www.voxeu.org/article/causes-eurozone-external-imbalances.

Dimopoulos, Angelos. 'The Common Commercial Policy after Lisbon: Establishing Parallelism between Internal and External Economic Relations?', *Croatian Yearbook of European Law and Policy* 4 (2008): 101–129.

'The Use of International Law as a Tool for Enhancing Governance in the Eurozone and Its Impact on EU Institutional Integrity', in: *The Constitutionalization of European Budgetary Constraints*, eds. Maurice Adams, Federico Fabbrini and Pierre Larouche (Oxford: Hart Publishing, 2014).

Dimoulas, Constantine. 'Exploring the Impact of Employment Policy Measures in the Context of Crisis: The Case of Greece', *International Social Security Review* 67 (2014): 49–55.

Dolls, Mathias et al. 'An Unemployment Insurance Scheme for the Euro Area? A Comparison of Different Alternatives Using Micro Data', *Centre for European Economic Research-ZEW Discussion Paper* No. 14–084, 28 October 2014, available at ftp.zew.de/pub/zew-docs/dp/dp14095.pdf.

Dolls, Mathias and Fuest, Clemens and Peichl, Andreas. 'Automatic Stabilizers and Economic Crisis: US vs Europe', *Journal of Public Economics* 96 (2012): 279–294.

Donaldson, Cam. *Credit Crunch Health Care: How Economics Can Save Our Publicly Funded Health Services* (Bristol: Policy Press, 2011).

Downs, Anthony. *An Economic Theory of Democracy* (New York: Harper, 1957).

Dräbing, Verena. 'The Role of the State: Reform Pressures and Welfare Reform Towards Social Investment', in: *Let's Get to Work! The Future of Labour in Europe, Vol. 1*, eds. Miroslav Beblavý, Ilaria Maselli and Marcela Veselková, CEPS 2014, 159–184, available at www.ceps.eu/system/files/NEUJOBS%20Future%20of%20Labour%20Vol%20I_FINAL_1_0.pdf.

Draghi, Mario. Speech by the President of the European Central Bank at the Global Investment Conference in London, 26 July 2012, available at www.ecb.europa.eu/press/key/date/2012/html/sp120726.en.html.

'The Future of the Euro: Stability through Change', published in *Die Zeit*, 29 August 2012, available at www.ecb.europa.eu/press/key/date/2012/html/sp120829.en.html.

'Introductory Statement to the Press Conference (with Q&A)', 6 September 2012, available at www.ecb.europa.eu/press/pressconf/2012/html/is120906.en.html.

'Europe's Pursuit of "a More Perfect Union"', 9 October 2013, available at www.ecb.europa.eu/press/key/date/2013/html/sp131009_1.en.html.

'Financial Integration and Banking Union', in: *Progress through Crisis? Proceedings of the Conference for the 20th Anniversary of the Establishment of the European Monetary Institute*, eds. Ivo Maes and Frank Moss (Frankfurt am Main: ECB, 2014): 151–159.

'Introductory Statement to the Press Conference (with Q&A): Frankfurt am Main', 22 January 2015, available at www.ecb.europa.eu/press/pressconf/2015/html/is150122.en.html.

'Introductory Statement to the Press Conference (with Q&A)', 21 April 2016, available at www.ecb.europa.eu/press/pressconf/2016/html/is160421.en.html.

Drehmann, Mathias, Borio, Claudio and Tsatsaronis, Kostas. 'Characterising the Financial Cycle: Don't Lose Sight of the Medium-term!' *BIS Working Paper* No. 380, June 2012.

Duffy, Jack. 'Schaeuble: Plan for Greece "Timeout" Was Widely Backed', 20 October 2015, available at www.marketnews.com/content/schaeuble-plan-greece-timeout-was-widely-backed-press.

Dullien, Sebastian. 'The Macroeconomic Stabilisation Impact of a European Basic Unemployment Insurance Scheme', *Intereconomics* 49 (2014): 189–193.

Dupont, Jonathan and Kwarteng, Kwasi. 'Binding the Hands of Government – a Credible Fiscal Rule for the UK', *The Institute of Economic Affairs Current Controversies Paper* No. 36, May 2012, available at iea.org.uk/wp-content/uploads/2016/07/Binding%20the%20hands%20of%20government-1.pdf.

Dyson, Kenneth H. F. 'Germany and the Euro: Redefining EMU, Handling Paradox and Managing Uncertainty and Contingency', in: *European States and the Euro: Europeanization, Variation, and Convergence*, ed. Kenneth Dyson (New York: Oxford University Press, 2002): 173–211.

Dyson, Kenneth H. F. and Featherstone, Kevin. *The Road to Maastricht: Negotiating Economic and Monetary Union* (Oxford: Oxford University Press, 1999).

Eade, Deborah. *Capacity-building: An Approach to People-centred Development* (Oxford: Oxfam, 1997).

Earles, Kimberly. 'Swedish Family Policy – Continuity and Change in the Nordic Welfare State Model', *Social Policy & Administration* 45 (2011): 180–193.

Eckes Jr., Alfred E. *Opening America's Market: U.S. Foreign Trade Policy Since 1776* (Chapel Hill: University of North Carolina Press, 1995).

Economist. 'Incumbents Rule. The European Union's Online Reforms Help the Old More Than the New', 17 September 2016, available at www.economist.com/news/business/21707189-european-unions-online-reforms-help-old-more-new-incumbents-rule.

Ecorys. 'Trade SIA on the Transatlantic Trade and Investment Partnership (TTIP) between the EU and the USA', 2016, available at www.trade-sia.com/ttip/wp-content/uploads/sites/6/2014/02/TSIA-TTIP-draft-Interim-Technical-Report.pdf.

Edin, Kathryn J. and Shaefer, H. Luke. *$2.00 a Day: Living on Almost Nothing in America* (New York: Houghton Mifflin Harcourt, 2015).

Besselink, Leonard and Reestman, Jan-Herman (Editorial). 'The Fiscal Compact and the European Constitutions: "Europe Speaking German"', *European Constitutional Law Review* 8 (2012): 6.

Economic Policy Institute. 'The Productivity–Pay Gap', available at www.epi.org/productivity-pay-gap/.

Edlund, Jonas and Johansson Sevä, Ingemar. 'Is Sweden Being Torn Apart? Privatization and Old and New Patterns of Welfare State Support', *Social Policy & Administration* 47 (2013): 542–564.

Egger, Hartmut and Kreickemeier, Udo. 'Firm Heterogeneity and the Labor Market Effects of Trade Liberalization', *International Economic Review* 50 (2009): 187–216.

Eichengreen, Barry. 'Is Europe an Optimum Currency Area?', *NBER Working Paper* No. 3579, January 1991.

'After the Stability Pact', University of California, Berkeley, 19 November 2003, available from eml.berkeley.edu/~eichengr/reviews/die-zeitnov20-03.pdf.

'Europe, the Euro and the ECB: Monetary Success, Fiscal Failure', *Journal of Policy Modeling*, 27 (2005): 427–439.

'Imbalances in the Euro Area', University of California, Berkeley, unpublished paper, November 2010, available at eml.berkeley.edu/~eichengr/Imbalances_Euro_Area_5-23-11.pdf.

Exorbitant Privilege: The Rise and Fall of the Dollar and the Future of the International Monetary System (Oxford: Oxford University Press, 2011).

'European Monetary Integration with Benefit of Hindsight', *Journal of Common Market Studies* 50 (2012): 123–136.

Eichengreen, Barry and Wyplosz, Charles 'The Stability Pact: More Than a Minor Nuisance?', *Economic Policy* 13 (1998): 65–114.

Eichhorst, Werner and Marx, Paul. 'Reforming German Labour Market Institutions: A Dual Path to Flexibility', *Journal of European Social Policy* 21 (2011): 73–87.

El-Erian, Mohamed A. *The Only Game in Town: Central Banks, Instability, and Avoiding the Next Collapse* (New York: Random House, 2016).

Elango, Sneha et al. 'Early Childhood Education', 4 November 2015, available at heckmanequation.org/assets/2017/01/FINALMoffitt-ECE-Paper2015.pdf.

Elliott, Larry. 'No EU Bailout for Greece as PM Promises to "Put Our House in Order"', *Guardian*, 28 January 2010, available at www.guardian.co.uk/business/2010/jan/28/greece-papandreou-eurozone.

Emerson, Michael et al. *One Market, One Money. An Evaluation of the Potential Benefits and Costs of Forming an Economic and Monetary Union* (New York: Oxford University Press, 1992).

Enderlein, Henrik, Guttenberg, Lucas and Spiess, Jann. 'Blueprint for a Cyclical Shock Insurance in the Euro Area', *Notre Europe-Jacques Delors Institute Studies and Reports*, September 2013, available at www.institutdelors.eu/media/blueprintforacyclicalshockinsurancene-jdisept2013.pdf?pdf=ok.

Engler, Philipp and Voigts, Simon. 'A Transfer Mechanism for a Monetary Union', *SFB 649 Discussion Paper* No. 2013-013, 5 March 2013, available at sfb649.wiwi.hu-berlin.de/papers/pdf/SFB649DP2013-013.pdf.

English, William. 'Understanding the Costs of Sovereign Default: American State Debts in the 1840s', *American Economic Review* 86 (1996): 259–275.

Englund, Peter. 'The Swedish Banking Crisis: Roots and Consequences', *Oxford Review of Economic Policy* 15 (1999): 80–97.

Epaulard, Anne. 'Contingent vs. Non-Contingent Unemployment Benefit Scheme for the EMU', paper for conference 'Economic Shock Absorbers for the Eurozone' in Brussels, 20 June 2014, available at ec.europa.eu/social/BlobServlet?docId=11889&langId=en.

Erixon, Lennart. 'The Rehn-Meidner Model in Sweden: Its Rise, Challenges and Survival', *Journal of Economic Issues* 44 (2010): 677–715.

Erjavec, Emil, Lovec, Marko and Erjavec, Karmen. 'From "Greening" to "Greenwash": The Drivers and Discourses of CAP 2020 "Reform"', in: *The Political Economy of the 2014–2020 Common Agricultural Policy. An Imperfect Storm*, ed. Johan F. M. Swinnen (Brussels: CEPS and London: Rowman and Littlefield International, 2015): 215–244.

Ernstorfer, Anita and Stockmayer, Albrecht. *Capacity Development for Good Governance* (Baden-Baden: Eschborn: Nomos, 2009).

Esping-Andersen, Gøsta. 'Prologues: What Does It Mean to Break with Bismarck?', in: *A Long Goodbye to Bismarck?*, ed. Bruno Palier (Amsterdam: Amsterdam University Press 2010): 11–18.

Esping-Andersen, Gøsta. *The Three Worlds of Welfare Capitalism* (Cambridge: Polity Press, 1990).

Esser, Ingrid et al. 'Unemployment Benefits in EU Member States', paper prepared for the European Commission, Directorate-General for Employment, Social Affairs and Inclusion, 2013.

Euractiv. 'EU Trade Chief-designate Rejects Carbon Border Tariffs', *Euractiv*, 13 January 2010, available at www.euractiv.com/section/trade-society/news/eu-trade-chief-designate-rejects-carbon-border-tariffs/.

Euractiv and Reuters. 'Berlin, Brussels Dismiss Call for CO2 Tax on Trump's US', 15 November 2016, available at www.euractiv.com/section/climate-environment/news/berlin-brussels-dismiss-call-for-co2-tax-on-us-under-trump/.

Eurogroup. 'Statement on Greece', 9 May 2016, available at www.consilium.europa.eu/en/press/press-releases/2016/05/09-eg-statement-greece/.

'Statement on Greece', 25 May 2016, available at www.esm.europa.eu/press-releases/eurogroup-statement-greece-25-may-2016.

European Central Bank. 'ECB Decides on Measures to Address Severe Tensions in Financial Markets', 10 May 2010, available at www.ecb.europa.eu/press/pr/date/2010/html/pr100510.en.html.

'Consolidated Financial Statement of the Eurosystem as at 28 October 2011', 1 November 2011, available at www.ecb.europa.eu/press/pr/wfs/2011/html/fs111101.en.html.

'ECB Announces Measures to Support Bank Lending and Money Market Activity', 8 December 2011, available at www.ecb.europa.eu/press/pr/date/2011/html/pr111208_1.en.html.

European Central Bank. Monthly Bulletin May 2013, 112, available at www.ecb.europa.eu/pub/pdf/mobu/mb201305en.pdf.

European Central Bank. 'Technical Features of Outright Monetary Transactions', 6 September 2012, available at www.ecb.europa.eu/press/pr/date/2012/html/pr120906_1.en.html.

'Aggregate Report on the Comprehensive Assessment', October 2014, available at www.ecb.europa.eu/pub/pdf/other/aggregatereportonthecomprehensiveassessment201410.en.pdf.

'ECB Announces Expanded Asset Purchase Programme', 22 January 2015, available at www.ecb.europa.eu/press/pr/date/2015/html/pr150122_1.en.html.

'Account of the Monetary Policy Meeting of the Governing Council of the European Central Bank Held in Frankfurt am Main on Wednesday and Thursday, 21–22 January 2015', available at www.ecb.europa.eu/press/accounts/2015/html/mg150219.en.html.

'Financial Integration in Europe', April 2015, available at www.ecb.europa.eu/pub/pdf/other/financialintegrationineurope201504.en.pdf?ec20b5e9b09b9003ce3e08ab27a6acb8.

European Central Bank. Economic Bulletin, Issue 7/2015, November 2015, 56.

European Central Bank. 'ECB Adds Corporate Sector Purchase Programme (CSPP) to the Asset Purchase Programme (APP) and Announces Changes to APP', 10 March 2016, available at www.ecb.europa.eu/press/pr/date/2016/html/pr160310_2.en.html.

'ECB Announces New Series of Targeted Longer-term Refinancing Operations (TLTRO II)', 10 March 2016, available at www.ecb.europa.eu/press/pr/date/2016/html/pr160310_1.en.html.

'Financial Stability Review', May 2016, available at www.ecb.europa.eu/pub/pdf/other/financialstabilityreview201605.en.pdf?e1a2bef79ed901d8ceaee004f2fcecdd.

'ECB Reinstates Waiver Affecting the Eligibility of Greek Bonds Used as Collateral in Eurosystem Monetary Policy Operations', 22 June 2016, available at www.ecb.europa.eu/press/pr/date/2016/html/pr160622_1.en.html).

'ECB Reinstates Waiver Affecting the Eligibility of Greek Bonds Used as Collateral in Eurosystem Monetary Policy Operations', 22 June 2016, available at www.ecb.europa.eu/press/pr/date/2016/html/pr160622_1.en.html.

'Report on Financial Structures', October 2017, available at www.ecb.europa.eu/pub/pdf/other/reportonfinancialstructures201710.en.pdf.

'ECB Adjusts Parameters of Its Asset Purchase Programme (APP)', 8 December 2016, available at www.ecb.europa.eu/press/pr/date/2016/html/pr161208_1.en.html.

'Monetary Policy Decisions', 9 March 2017, available at www.ecb.europa.eu/press/pr/date/2017/html/pr170309.en.html.

'Monetary Policy Decisions', 26 October 2017, available at www.ecb.europa.eu/press/pr/date/2017/html/ecb.mp171026.en.html.

'The Definition of Price Stability', n. d., available at www.ecb.europa.eu/mopo/strategy/pricestab/html/index.en.html.

European Commission. 'Investment Plan for Europe. Country Factsheet: Italy', available at www.eib.org/projects/pipelines/pipeline/20150563.

'One Market, One Money. An Evaluation of the Potential Benefits and Costs of Forming an Economic and Monetary Union', European Economy No. 44, October 1990, available at ec.europa.eu/economy_finance/publications/pages/publication7454_en.pdf.

'EMU after Five Years', *European Economy*, Special Report No 1/2004, available at docentes.fe.unl.pt/~jamador/Textos/eesp104en.pdf.

'The European Union's Generalised System of Preferences GSP', 2004, available at trade.ec.europa.eu/doclib/docs/2004/march/tradoc_116448.pdf.

'Economic Assessment of the Stability Programme of Spain', 20 March 2007, ECFIN/50968/07-EN.

'The Economic Adjustment Programme for Greece', *European Economy Occasional Paper* No. 61, May 2010, available at ec.europa.eu/economy_finance/publications/occasional_paper/2010/pdf/ocp61_en.pdf.

'Communication: Reinforcing Economic Policy Coordination', COM(2010)250, 12 May 2010.

European Commission, 'European Economic Forecast - Spring 2011', *European Economy* No. 1/2011, available at ec.europa.eu/economy_finance/publications/european_economy/2011/pdf/ee-2011-1_en.pdf.

European Commission. 'European Economic Forecast Autumn 2012', *European Economy* No. 7/2012, available at ec.europa.eu/economy_finance/publications/european_economy/2012/pdf/ee-2012-7_en.pdf.

'Detailed Information on the Implementation of Directive 2006/123/EC on Services in the Internal Market Accompanying the Document Communication from the Commission to the European Parliament, the Council, the European Economic and Social Committee and the Committee of the Regions on the Implementation of the Services Directive. A Partnership for New Growth in Services 2012–2015', Brussels, 8 June 2012, SWD(2012)148.

'Scoreboard for the Surveillance of Macroeconomic Imbalances', *European Economy*, Occasional Paper 92, February 2012, available at ec.europa.eu/economy_finance/publications/occasional_paper/2012/pdf/ocp92_en.pdf.

'Detailed Information on the Implementation of Directive 2006/123/EC on Services in the Internal Market Accompanying the Document Communication from the Commission to the European Parliament, the Council, the European Economic and Social Committee and the Committee of the Regions on the Implementation of the Services Directive. A Partnership for New Growth in Services 2012–2015', Brussels, 8 June 2012, SWD(2012)148.

European Commission: 'Communication: A Blueprint for a Deep and Genuine Economic and Monetary Union. Launching a European Debate', COM(2012)777, 28 November 2012.

European Commission. 'Report on Public Finances in EMU 2013', *European Economy* No. 4/2013, available at ec.europa.eu/economy_finance/publications/european_economy/2013/pdf/ee-2013–4.pdf.

'Paper on Automatic Stabilisers', 4 October 2013.

'Communication: 2014 Draft Budgetary Plans of the Euro Area: Overall Assessment of the Budgetary Situation and Prospects', COM(2013)900, 15 November 2013.

'Europe in Motion. President-elect Juncker's Main Messages from His Speech before the European Parliament. Statement in the European Parliament Plenary Session Ahead of the Vote on the College Plenary Session, Strasbourg, 22 October 2014', available at ec.europa.eu/priorities/sites/beta-political/files/juncker-political-guidelines-speech_en_0.pdf.

'Communication: An Investment Plan for Europe', COM(2014)903, 26 November 2014.

'Communication: 2015 Draft Budgetary Plans. Overall Assessment', COM(2014)907, 28 November 2014.

'2015 Ageing Report', *European Economy* No. 3/2015, available at ec.europa.eu/economy_finance/publications/european_economy/2015/pdf/ee3_en.pdf.

'Communication: A Digital Single Market Strategy for Europe', COM(2015)192, 6 May 2015.

'Speaking Points of Vice-President Dombrovskis on the Commission's New Structural Reform Support Service', 17 June 2015, available at europa.eu/rapid/press-release_STATEMENT-15-5218_en.htm.

'Communication: Action Plan on Building a Capital Markets Union', COM(2015)468, 30 September 2015.

'Communication: 2016 Draft Budgetary Plans. Overall Assessment', COM(2015)800, 16 November 2015.

'Annual Growth Survey 2016. Strengthening the Recovery and Fostering Convergence', COM(2015)690, 26 November 2015.

'State of the Union 2016: Commission Paves the Way for More and Better Internet Connectivity for All Citizens and Businesses', available at europa.eu/rapid/press-release_IP-16-3008_en.htm.

'Study and Reports on the VAT Gap in the EU-28 Member States: 2016 Final Report', TAXUD/2015/CC/131, 23 August 2016, available at ec.europa.eu/taxation_customs/sites/taxation/files/study_and_reports_on_the_vat_gap_2017.pdf.

'Report on the Generalised Scheme of Preferences Covering the Period 2014–2015', COM(2016)29, 28 January 2016.

'The EU Special Incentive Arrangement for Sustainable Development and Good Governance ("GSP+") Covering the Period 2014–2015', *Joint Staff Working Document* 8 (2016), 28 January 2016, available at eeas.europa.eu/sites/eeas/files/european_commission._2016._report_on_the_generalised_scheme_of_preferences_during_the_period_2014-2015.pdf.

'Change in the Methodology for Anti-dumping Investigations Concerning China', 5 February 2016, available at trade.ec.europa.eu/doclib/docs/2016/february/tradoc_154241.pdf.

'Revision of the Posting of Workers Directive – Frequently Asked Questions', 8 March 2016, available at europa.eu/rapid/press-release_MEMO-16-467_en.htm.

'Communication on an Action Plan on VAT. Towards a Single EU VAT Area: Time to Decide', COM(2016)148, 7 April 2016.

'European Financial Stability and Integration Review (EFSIR): A Focus on Capital Markets Union', SWD(2016)146, 25 April 2016, available at ec.europa.eu/info/system/files/efsir-2016-25042016_en.pdf.

'Communication: A European Agenda for the Collaborative Economy', COM(2016)356, 2 June 2016.

'Commission Takes Legal Action Against the Systematic Application of the French and German Minimum Wage Legislation to the Transport Sector', 16 June 2016, available at europa.eu/rapid/press-release_IP-16-2101_en.htm.

'9 Ways Cohesion Policy Works for Europe – Main Results 2007–2013', 10 July 2016, available at ec.europa.eu/regional_policy/sources/docgener/evaluation/pdf/expost2013/wp1_synthesis_factsheet_en.pdf.

'Posting of Workers: Commission Discusses Concerns of National Parliaments', 20 July 2016, available at europa.eu/rapid/press-release_IP-16-2546_en.htm.

'Ministers Approve EU Ratification of Paris Agreement', 30 September 2016, available at ec.europa.eu/clima/news/articles/news_2016093001_en.htm.

'Communication: The Youth Guarantee and Youth Employment Initiative Three Years On', COM(2016)646, 4 October 2016.

'Communication: Towards a Robust Trade Policy for the EU in the Interest of Jobs and Growth', COM(2016)690, 18 October 2016.

European Commission, 'Flash Eurobarometer 446 "The Euro Area"', December 2016, available at ec.europa.eu/COMMFrontOffice/publicopinion/index.cfm/ResultDoc/download/DocumentKy/76001.

European Commission. 'Multiannual Financial Framework Adjusted for 2018', available at ec.europa.eu/budget/mff/figures/index_en.cfm.

'The European Union Explained. The EU's Common Agricultural Policy (CAP): For Our Food, for Our Countryside, for Our Environment', Luxembourg 2017, available at www.learneurope.eu/files/2513/7525/9029/Resumen_de_la_PAC_en.pdf.

'A Services Economy That Works for Europeans', 10 January 2017, available at europa.eu/rapid/press-release_IP-17-23_en.htm.

'Political Agreement Reached on Structural Reform Support Programme – A New Tool to Help Member States Implement Reforms', 8 February 2017, available at europa.eu/rapid/press-release_IP-17-233_en.htm.

'Investment Plan for Europe: 55 000 Small Companies in Italy to Benefit from EUR 3.5 billion', 15 February 2017, available at ec.europa.eu/

commission/commissioners/2014–2019/katainen/announcements/investment-plan-europe-55-000-small-companies-italy-benefit-eur-0_en.

'Report from the Commission Presented under Article 8 of the Treaty on Stability, Coordination and Governance in the Economic and Monetary Union', C(2017)1201, 22 February 2017.

'Key Achievements of Regional Policy', available at ec.europa.eu/regional_policy/en/policy/what/key-achievements/.

European Constitutional Law Review. 'The Fiscal Compact and the European Constitutions: "Europe Speaking German"', Editorial, 8 (2012): 1–7.

European Council. (23 and 24 October 2014) conclusions available at www.consilium.europa.eu/uedocs/cms_data/docs/pressdata/en/ec/145397.pdf.

European Court of Auditors. 'More Attention to Results Needed to Improve the Delivery of Technical Assistance to Greece', *Special Report* No. 19/2015, available at www.eca.europa.eu/Lists/ECADocuments/SR15_19/SR_TFGR_EN.pdf.

European Economic Advisory Group. 'Intergenerational Fairness', in: *2016 The EEAG Report on the European Economy* (Munich: CESifo, 2016): 54–69.

European Environmental Agency. 'EEA Report, 2017. Annual European Union Greenhouse Gas Inventory 1990–2015 and Inventory Report 2017', May 2017, available at www.eea.europa.eu/publications/european-union-greenhouse-gas-inventory-2017.

European Environment Agency. 'EU Greenhouse Gas Emissions from Transport Increase for the Second Year in a Row', 1 June 2017, available at www.eea.europa.eu/highlights/eu-greenhouse-gas-emissions-from-transport-increased.

'EU Greenhouse Gas Emissions from Transport Increase for the Second Year in a Row', 1 June 2017, available at www.eea.europa.eu/highlights/eu-greenhouse-gas-emissions-from-transport-increased.

European Investment Bank. 'What Is the European Fund for Strategic Investments (EFSI)?', available at www.eib.europa.eu/efsi/what-is-efsi/index.htm.

European Social Fund. 'The ESF in the News: Support for Young People in France to Restart Education', 3 March 2017, available at ec.europa.eu/esf/main.jsp?catId=67&langId=en&newsId=2752.

'The ESF in the News: Breaking Down Social Barriers in Spain', 10 March 2017, available at ec.europa.eu/esf/main.jsp?catId=67&langId=en&newsId=2760.

European Trade Association for Business Angels, Seed Funds, and Other Early Stage Market Players. 'European Early Stage Market Statistics. 2015', May 2016, available at www.eban.org/wp-content/uploads/2016/06/Early-Stage-Market-Statistics-2015.pdf.

European Trade Union Confederation. 'The Athens Manifesto', 2011, available at www.etuc.org/athens-manifesto-0.

European Trade Union Institute. 'Benchmarking Working Europe 2017', available at www.etui.org/Publications2/Books/Benchmarking-Working-Europe-2017.

Euzéby, Chantal. 'Social Protection to Achieve Sustainable Inclusion: A European Imperative in the Current Economic Crisis', *International Social Security Review* 65 (2012): 69–88.

Evans, Peter B. 'In Search of the 21st Century Developmental State', *The Centre for Global Political Economy at the University of Sussex*, Working Paper No. 4, December 2008, available at www.sussex.ac.uk/webteam/gateway/file .php?name=cgpe-wp04-peter-evans.pdf&site=359.

Evans-Pritchard, Ambrose. 'France and Germany Smash Euro Pact', *The Telegraph*, 26 November 2003, available at www.telegraph.co.uk/finance/ 2870055/France-and-Germany-smash-Euro-pact.html.

'Debt Crisis: Germany Signals Shift on €2.3 Trillion Redemption Fund for Europe', *The Telegraph*, 13 June 2012, available at www.telegraph.co.uk/ finance/financialcrisis/9330398/Debt-crisis-Germany-signals-shift-on-2.3-trillion-redemption-fund-for-Europe.html.

Evers, Michael P. 'Federal Fiscal Transfer Rules in Monetary Unions', *European Economic Review* 56 (2012): 507–525.

Everson, Michelle and Joerges, Christian. 'Reconfiguring the Politics–Law Relationship in the Integration Project through Conflicts–Law Constitutionalism', *European Law Journal* 18 (2012): 644–666.

Eyraud, Luc and Weber, Anke. 'The Challenge of Debt Reduction during Fiscal Consolidation', *IMF Working Paper* No. 13/67, March 2013.

Eyraud, Luc, Gaspar, Vitor and Poghosyan, Tigran. 'Fiscal Politics in the Euro Area', *IMF Working Paper* No. 17/18, 30 January 2017, available at www.imf.org/en/Publications/WP/Issues/2017/01/30/ Fiscal-Politics-in-the-Euro-Area-44601.

Faber, Gerrit and Orbie, Jan. 'Everything but Arms: Much More Than Appears at First Sight', *Journal of Common Market Studies* 47 (2009): 767–787.

Fajgelbaum, Pablo and Khandelwal, Amit. 'Measuring the Unequal Gains from Trade', *The Quarterly Journal of Economics* 131 (2016): 1113–1180.

Falkner, Gerda. *EU Social Policy in the 1990s: Towards a Corporatist Policy Community* (London: Routledge, 1998).

Farhi, Emmanuel and Werning, Iván. 'Fiscal Unions', July 2014, available at scholar.harvard.edu/files/farhi/files/fiscal-unions_july_2014_0.pdf.

Fatih Aysan, Mehmet and Beaujot, Roderic. 'Welfare Regimes for Aging Populations: No Single Path for Reform', *Population and Development Review* 35 (2009): 701–720.

Featherstone, Kevin and Papadimitriou, Dimitris. *The Limits of Europeanization: Reform Capacity and Policy Conflict in Greece* (Basingstoke: Palgrave Macmillan, 2008).

Featherstone, Kevin. 'The Greek Sovereign Debt Crisis and EMU: A Failing State in a Skewed Regime', *Journal of Common Market Studies* 49 (2011): 193–217.

'External Conditionality and the Debt Crisis: The "Troika" and Public Administration Reform in Greece', *Journal of European Public Policy*, 22 (2015): 295–314.

Federal Deposit Insurance Corporation. 'Deposit Insurance Fund Management', available at www.fdic.gov/deposit/insurance/fund.html.

Feld, Lars P. and Osterloh, Steffen. 'Is a Fiscal Capacity Really Necessary to Complete EMU?', *Freiburger Diskussionspapiere zur Ordnungsökonomik*, No. 13/5, October 2013, available at www.econstor.eu/bitstream/10419/88113/1/77216021X.pdf.

Feldman, Robert. 'Cobwebs and CRICs', *Morgan Stanley Dean Witter's Japan Economics*, 4 April 2001, available at www.yumpu.com/en/document/view/4429905/cobwebs-and-crics-japan-economics.

Fergusson, Adam. *When Money Dies: The Nightmare of Deficit Spending, Devaluation, and Hyperinflation in Weimar Germany* (New York: PublicAffairs, 2010).

Fernández-Villaverde, Jésus, Garicano, Luis and Santos, Tano. 'Political Credit Cycles: The Case of the Euro Zone', *NBER Working Paper No. 18899*, 15 March 2013, available at economics.sas.upenn.edu/~jesusfv/Political_Credit_Cycles.pdf.

Ferrera, Maurizio. 'The "Southern Model" of Welfare in Social Europe', *Journal of European Social Policy* 6 (1996): 17–37.

Fierro, Elena. *European Union's Approach to Human Rights Conditionality in Practice* (The Hague: Martinus Nijhoff Publishers, 2003).

FIFPro. 'The 2016 Global Employment Report. Top Findings', November 2016, available at fifpro.org/attachments/article/6706/2016%20FIFPro%20Global%20Survey%20-%20TopFindings_1128.pdf.

Finfacts. 'Irish Bank Senior Debt and Subordinated Debt Outstanding February 2011', 2 March 2011, available at www.finfacts.ie/irishfinancenews/article_1021762.shtml.

Finland – Concluding Statement for the 2015 Article IV Consultation, 15 September 2015, available at www.imf.org/external/np/ms/2015/091515.htm.

Fioretti, Julia. 'EU Challenges Austrian Minimum Wage Law for Truck Drivers', *Reuters*, 27 April 2017, available at uk.reuters.com/article/uk-austria-eu-minimumwage-idUKKBN17T1V4?il=0.

Fischer, Carolyn. 'Options for Avoiding Carbon Leakage', in: *Towards an Effective and Sustainable Climate Regime*, eds. Scott Barrett, Carlo Carraro and Jaime de Melo, 2015, available at voxeu.org/sites/default/files/image/FromMay2014/Climate%20change%20book%20for%20web.pdf.

FitzGerald, John and Kearney, Ide. 'Irish Government Debt and Implied Debt Dynamics: 2011–2015', *The Economic and Social Research Institute Quarterly Economic Commentary*, 6 September 2011, available at www.esri.ie/publications/irish-government-debt-and-implied-debt-dynamics-2011–2015/.

Fleckenstein, Timo. 'Restructuring Welfare for the Unemployed: The Hartz Legislation in Germany', *Journal of European Social Policy* 18 (2008): 177–188.

Foglietta, Fosco and Toniolo, Franco. *New Models of Governance and Health System Integration* (Milano: FrancoAngeli 2013).

Fontagné, Lionel and Freudenberg, Michael. 'Endogenous Symmetry of Shocks in a Monetary Union', *Open Economies Review* 10 (1999): 263–287.

Fouskas, Vassilis and Dimoulas, Constantine. *Greece, Financialization and the EU: The Political Economy of Debt and Destruction* (International political economy series, Basingstoke: Palgrave Macmillan, 2013).

Fowler, Alan, Acquaye-Baddoo, Naa-Aku and Ubels, Jan. *Capacity Development in Practice* (London: Routledge, 2010).

Francois, Joseph et al. 'Reducing Transatlantic Barriers to Trade and Investment – An Economic Assessment', *Final Project Report*, CEPR, London, March 2013, available at trade.ec.europa.eu/doclib/docs/2013/march/tradoc_150737.pdf.

Frankel, Jeffrey A. and Rose, Andrew K. 'The Endogeneity of the Optimum Currency Area Criteria', *NBER Working Paper* No 5700, August 1996, available at www.nber.org/papers/w5700.pdf.

Frankel, Jeffrey A. and Schreger, Jesse. 'Over-Optimistic Official Forecasts in the Eurozone and Fiscal Rules', *NBER Working Paper* No. 18283, August 2012.

Fratzscher, Marcel et al. 'Mere Criticism of the ECB Is No Solution', *Bruegel Blog Post*, 10 April 2016, available at bruegel.org/2016/04/mere-criticism-of-the-ecb-is-no-solution/.

Freedland, Mark and Prassl, Jeremias, eds. *Viking, Laval and Beyond* (Oxford: Hart Publishing, 2015).

Frieden, Jeffry. 'Lessons for the Euro from Early American Monetary and Financial History', *Bruegel Essay and Lecture Series*, May 2016, available at bruegel.org/wp-content/uploads/2016/05/essay_frieden_may16.pdf.

Friedman, Milton. 'The Case for Flexible Exchange Rates', in: *Essays in Positive Economics* (Chicago, IL: University of Chicago Press, 1953): 157–203.

'The Euro: Monetary Unity to Political Disunity?', *Project Syndicate*, 28 August 1997, available at www.project-syndicate.org/commentary/the-euro--monetary-unity-to-political-disunity.

Fuest, Clemens. 'Stabile Fiskalpolitische Institutionen für die Europäische Währungsunion', *Wirtschaftsdienst* 10 (1993): 539–545.

Fujita, Masahisa, Krugman, Paul and Venables, Anthony J. *The Spatial Economy: Cities, Regions and International Trade* (Cambridge, MA: MIT Press, 1999).

Furceri, Davide and Zdzienicka, Aleksandra. 'The Euro Area Crisis: Need for a Supranational Fiscal Risk Sharing Mechanism?', *IMF Working Paper* No. WP/13/198, September 2013, available at www.imf.org/external/pubs/ft/wp/2013/wp13198.pdf.

Gabrisch, Hubert and Staehr, Karsten. 'The Euro Plus Pact: Competitiveness and External Capital Flows in the EU Countries', *ECB Working Paper Series* No. 1650, March 2014, available at www.ecb.europa.eu/pub/pdf/scpwps/ecbwp1650.pdf?b634be5ae6e3564a096c8dc2cf9e3203.

Gandrud, Christopher and Hallerberg, Mark. 'How Not to Create Zombie Banks: Lessons for Italy from Japan', *Bruegel Policy Contribution* No. 6/2017,

8 March 2017, available at bruegel.org/2017/03/how-not-to-create-zombie-banks-lessons-for-italy-from-japan/.

Garben, Sacha. 'The Constitutional (Im)balance between "the Market" and "the Social" in the European Union', *European Constitutional Law Review*, 13 (2017): 23–61.

Garzon, Isabelle. *Reforming the Common Agricultural Policy: History of a Paradigm Change* (London: Palgrave Macmillan, 2006).

Genschel, Philipp and Schwarz, Peter. 'Tax Competition and Fiscal Democracy', in: *Politics in the Age of Austerity*, eds. Wolfgang Streeck and Armin Schafer (Cambridge: Polity Press, 2013): 59–83.

Giannetti, Mariassunta and Ongena, Steven. 'Financial Integration and Firm Performance: Evidence from Foreign Bank Entry in Emerging Markets', *Review of Finance* 13 (2009): 181–223.

Giles, Chris. 'Ditch This Daft Concept and Expose Economists to Reality', *Financial Times*, 13 June 2012.

Gitis, Ben. 'Primer: Unemployment Compensation and Labor Market Recovery', *American Action Forum*, 9 January 2015, available at www.americanactionforum.org/research/primer-unemployment-compensation-and-labor-market-recovery/#_ftnref6.

Giugliano, Ferdinando. 'Greece's Debt Pile: Is It Really Unsustainable?', *Financial Times*, 25 January 2015.

Global Competitiveness Report. 2016–2017, available at www.weforum.org/reports/the-global-competitiveness-report-2016-2017-1.

Godement, François. 'China's Market Economy Status and the European Interest', *European Council on Foreign Relations Policy Brief* No. 180, June 2016, available at www.ecfr.eu/page/-/ECFR_180_-_CHINA_MARKET_ECONOMY_STATUS_AND_THE_EUROPEAN_INTEREST_(002).pd.

Godley, Wynne. 'Maastricht and All That', *London Review of Books* 14 (1992): 3–4, available at www.lrb.co.uk/v14/n19/wynne-godley/maastricht-and-all-that.

Goetschy, Janine. 'The European Employment Strategy: Genesis and Development', *European Journal of Industrial Relations* 5 (1999): 117–137.

Goldoni, Marco. 'The Early Warning System and the Monti II Regulation: The Case for a Political Interpretation', *European Constitutional Law Review*, 10 (2014): 90–108.

Gomes, Júlio. 'Social Rights in Crisis in the Eurozone. Work Rights in Portugal', in: *Social Rights in Times of Crisis in the Eurozone: The Role of Fundamental Rights' Challenges*, eds. Claire Kilpatrick and Bruno De Witte, *EUI Working Papers LAW* 5 (2014): 78–84, available at cadmus.eui.eu/handle/1814/31247.

Goodhart, Charles. 'The United Kingdom and the Eurozone: How to Co-exist', in: *Governance for the Eurozone: Integration or Disintegration?*, eds. Franklin Allen, Elena Carletti and Saverio Simonelli (Florence, PA: European University Institute and Wharton Financial Institutions Center, 2012): 161–171.

'GDP Bonds Are Answer to Greek Debt Problem', *Financial Times*, 5 August 2015.

Gräf, Bernhard et al. 'Focus Germany: Structural National Improvements Support Exceptional Position', *Research Brief Deutsche Bank*, 1 July 2013.

Grant, Wyn. 'How and Why Farmers Voted on Brexit', 26 December 2016, available at commonagpolicy.blogspot.com/2016/12/how-and-why-did-farmers-vote-on-brexit.html.

Graziano, Paolo R., Jacquot, Sophie and Palier, Bruno. 'Introduction: The Usages of Europe in National Employment-friendly Welfare State Reforms', in: *The EU and the Domestic Politics of Welfare State Reforms*, eds. Paolo R. Graziano, Sophie Jacquot and Bruno Palier (London: Palgrave Macmillan, 2011): 1–18.

Green Cowles, Maria. 'Setting the Agenda for a New Europe: The ERT and EC 1992', *Journal of Common Market Studies* 33 (1995): 501–526.

Greer, Scott and Jarman, Holly. 'Managing Risks in EU Health Services Policy: Spot Markets, Legal Certainty and Bureaucratic Resistance', *Journal of European Social Policy* 22 (2012): 259–272.

Grieger, Gisela. 'Foreign Direct Investment Screening. A Debate in Light of China-EU FDI Flows', *European Parliamentary Research Service*, May 2017, available at www.europarl.europa.eu/RegData/etudes/BRIE/2017/603941/EPRS_BRI(2017)603941_EN.pdf.

Groeneveld, Johannes M. *Inflation Patterns and Monetary Policy: Lessons for the European Central Bank* (Cheltenham; Northampton, MA: Edward Elgar, 1998).

Gros, Daniel. 'A Border Tax to Protect the Global Environment?', *VOX CEPR's Policy Portal*, 9 December 2009, available at voxeu.org/article/why-eu-needs-border-tax-carbon#fn.

'Banking Union Instead of Fiscal Union?', in: *Governance for the Eurozone: Integration or Disintegration?*, eds. Allen Franklin, Elena Carletti and Saverio Simonelli, 2012: 65–78, available at www.eui.eu/DepartmentsAndCentres/Economics/SeminarsEvents/Conferences/GovernancefortheEurozoneIntegrationorDisintegration.aspx.

'On the Stability of Public Debt in a Monetary Union', *Journal of Common Market Studies* 50 (2012) Annual Review: 36–48.

'Germany as Scapegoat', *CEPS Commentary*, 10 December 2013, available at www.ceps.eu/system/files/Germany%20as%20Scapegoat.pdf.

'The Greek Austerity Myth', *CEPS Commentary*, 10 February 2015, available at www.ceps.eu/system/files/COMDGGreekAusterityMyth.pdf.

'Countries under Adjustment Programmes: What Role for the ECB?', *CEPS Special Report* No. 124, 10 December 2015, available at www.ceps.eu/publications/countries-under-adjustment-programmes-what-role-ecb.

'The Silent Death of Eurozone Governance', *Project Syndicate*, 10 August 2016, available at www.project-syndicate.org/commentary/eu-fiscal-rules-not-enforced-spain-portugal-by-daniel-gros-2016-08?barrier=accessreg.

'Ultra-low or Negative Yields on Euro-Area Long-term Bonds: Causes and Implications for Monetary Policy', *CEPS Working Document* No. 426, September 2016, available at www.ceps.eu/publications/ultra-low-or-negative-yields-euro-area-long-term-bonds-causes-and-implications-monetary.

'One Market, One Money – A Mistaken Argument (Post Factum)?', *CEPS Policy Insight* No. 2017/05, 16 February 2017, available at www.ceps.eu/system/files/DG_OneMarketOneMoney_0.pdf

Gros, Daniel and Belke, Ansgar. *Banking Union as a Shock Absorber. Lessons for the Eurozone from the US* (Brussels: CEPS and London: Rowman & Littlefield International, 2015), available at aei.pitt.edu/70406/1/Banking_Union_as_Shock_Absorber.pdf.

Gros, Daniel and de Groen, Willem Pieter. 'A Radical Cure for Italy's Banking Problems: A Combination of Good Banks and Soft Bail-in', *CEPS Policy Brief* No. 351, December 2016, available at www.ceps.eu/publications/radical-cure-italy's-banking-problems-combination-good-banks-and-soft-bail.

Gros, Daniel et al. *Implementation of the Macroeconomic Adjustment Programmes in the Euro Area. State-of-Play* (CEPS E-BOOK, 2014): available at www.ceps.eu/system/files/Macroeconomic%20Adjustment%20Programmes%20in%20Euro%20Area%20e-book.pdf.

Gros, Daniel and Giovannini, Alessandro. 'The "Relative" Importance of EMU Macroeconomic Imbalances in the Macroeconomic Imbalance Procedure', CEPS, 25 March 2014, available at www.ceps.eu/publications/'relative'-importance-emu-macroeconomic-imbalances-macroeconomic-imbalance-procedure.

Gros, Daniel and Roth, Felix. 'The Europe 2020 Strategy. Can It Maintain the EU's Competitiveness in the World?', CEPS 2012, available at www.ceps.eu/system/files/Europe%202020.pdf.

Gros, Daniel, Valiante, Diego and De Groen, Willem Pieter. 'The ECB's Latest Gimmick. Cash for Loans', *CEPS Policy Brief* No. 341, March 2016, available at www.ceps.eu/system/files/ECBLoanSubsidies.pdf.

Grossman, Emiliano and Woll, Cornelia. 'The French Debate on the Bolkestein Directive', *Comparative European Politics* 9 (2011): 344–366.

Gruenberg, Martin J., 'Statement of Acting Chairman: Federal Deposit Insurance Corporation on Enhanced Oversight after the Financial Crisis: Wall Street Reform at One Year before the Committee on Banking, Housing and Urban Affairs', US Senate, 21 July 2011, available at www.fdic.gov/news/news/speeches/archives/2011/spjul2111.html.

Guarascio, Francesco. 'EU Gives Budget Leeway to France "Because it is France" – Juncker', *Reuters*, 31 May 2016, available at uk.reuters.com/article/uk-eu-deficit-france-idUKKCN0YM1N0.

'IMF to Join Greece Bailout, but No Funds Until Debt Relief Deal: Lagarde', *Reuters*, 15 June 2017, available at www.reuters.com/article/us-eurozone-greece-imf-idUSKBN1962PX.

Guardian. 'Three Days That Saved the Euro', 22 October 2015, available at www.theguardian.com/world/2015/oct/22/three-days-to-save-the-euro-greece.

Gunther, Richard, Diamandouros, P. Nikoros and Sotiropoulos, Dimitri A., eds. *Democracy and the State in the New Southern Europe* (New York: Oxford University Press, 2006).

Gurría, Angel. 'Launch of the 2017 Economic Survey of Sweden', 8 February 2017, available at www.oecd.org/about/secretary-general/launch-of-the-2017-economic-survey-of-sweden.htm.

Haas, Linda. 'Family Policy in Sweden', *Journal of Family and Economic Issues* 17 (1996): 47–92.

Hagedorn, Marcus et al. 'Unemployment Benefits and Unemployment in the Great Recession: The Role of Macro Effects', *Federal Reserve Bank of New York Staff Reports* No. 646, October 2013, revised February 2015, available at pdfs.semanticscholar.org/c726/0118ccd96e3ad6e7eb6f966584b3b18ee228.pdf.

Hall, Peter A. and Soskice, David. *Varieties of Capitalism: The Institutional Foundations of Comparative Advantage* (Oxford: Oxford University Press, 2001).

Hancké, Bob, Rhodes, Martin and Thatcher, Mark, eds. *Beyond Varieties of Capitalism. Conflict, Contradictions, and Complementarities in the European Economy* (Oxford: Oxford University Press, 2008).

Hand, Lise. 'The Week Ireland Gave Up its Sovereignty', *Irish Independent*, 1 December 2013, available at www.independent.ie/lifestyle/the-week-ireland-gave-up-its-sovereignty-29796376.html.

Harbo, Tor-Inge. 'The Function of the Proportionality Principle in EU Law', *European Law Journal* 16 (2010): 158–185.

Harris, Nancy et al. 'Indonesia's Fire Outbreaks Producing More Daily Emissions Than Entire US Economy', *World Resources Institute*, 16 October 2015, available at www.wri.org/blog/2015/10/indonesia%E2%80%99s-fire-outbreaks-producing-more-daily-emissions-entire-us-economy.

Hart, Jeffrey A. *The New International Economic Order. Conflict and Cooperation in North-South Economic Relations, 1974–77* (London: Palgrave Macmillan, 1983).

Hatje, Armin. 'Services Directive – a Legal Analysis', in: *Services Liberalisation in the Internal Market*, eds. Fritz Breuss, Gerhard Fink and Stefan Griller (Vienna, New York: Springer 2008): 1–20.

Hatzopoulos, Vassilis. 'Some Thoughts on the Fate of Poorer Member States' Healthcare Systems after the Ruling in Elena Petru', *European Law Review* 41 (2016): 424–430.

Hatzopoulos, Vassilis and Roma, Sofia. 'Caring for Sharing? The Collaborative Economy under EU Law', *Common Market Law Review* 54 (2017): 81–128.

Heath, Ryan. 'Politico Brussels Playbook', *Politico*, 15 September 2016, available at www.politico.eu/newsletter/playbook/politico-brussels-playbook-presented-by-epp-group-eu-reset-two-dueling-presidents-soteu-wrap/.

'Politico Brussels Playbook', *Politico*, 13 February 2017, available at www.politico.eu/newsletter/playbook/politico-brussels-playbook-presented-by-epp-group-european-commission-presidency-race-mogherini-snarks-trump/.

Helliwell, John, Layard, Richard and Sachs, Jeffrey, eds. *World Happiness Report 2017*, available at www.worldhappiness.report/wp-content/uploads/sites/2/2017/03/HR17.pdf.

Hellwig, Martin. 'Financial Stability, Monetary Policy, Banking Supervision, and Central Banking', *Preprints of the Max Planck Institute for Research on Collective Goods*, Bonn 2014/9, available at www.mpp-rdg.mpg.de/pdf_dat/2014_09online.pdf.

'Yes Virginia, There Is a European Banking Union! But It May Not Make Your Wishes Come True', *Preprints of the Max Planck Institute for Research on Collective Goods*, Bonn 2014/12, August 2014, available at www.coll.mpg.de/pdf_dat/2014_12online.pdf.

Hemerijck, Anton. *Changing Welfare States* (Oxford: Oxford University Press, 2013).

'Making Social Investment Happen for the Eurozone', *Intereconomics* 51 (2016): 341–347.

Hemerijck, Anton, ed. *The Uses of Social Investment* (Oxford: Oxford University Press, 2017).

Hemerijck, Anton and Marx, Ive. 'Continental Welfare at a Crossroads: The Choice between Activation and Minimum Income Protection in Belgium and the Netherlands', in: *A Long Goodbye to Bismarck?*, ed. Bruno Palier (Amsterdam: Amsterdam University Press, 2010): 129–155.

Hemerijck, Anton and Visser, Jelle. 'Policy Learning in European Welfare States', *Center for European Studies*, October 2003.

Hemerijck, Anton et al. 'Assessing Social Investment Synergies (ASIS)', October 2016, available at ec.europa.eu/social/BlobServlet?docId=16878&langId=en.

Hernández de Cos, Pablo, Lacuesta, Aitor and Moral-Benito, Enrique. 'An Exploration of Real-Time Revisions of Output Gap Estimates across European Countries', *Banco de Espana Occasional Paper* No. 1605, 28 July 2016.

Herszenhorn, David M. 'Alexander Stubb: Europe's Endangered Liberal Future', *Politico*, 26 December 2016, available at www.politico.eu/article/alexander-stubb-europes-endangered-liberal-future-populism-finnish-party/.

Hervey, Tamara K. and McHale, Jean V. *European Union Health Law. Themes and Implications* (Cambridge: Cambridge University Press, 2015).

Herzberg, Angelique. *Sustainability of External Imbalances: A Critical Appraisal* (Cham: Springer 2014).

Hild, Alexandra, Herz, Bernhard and Bauer, Christian. 'Structured Eurobonds: Limiting Liability and Distributing Profits', *Journal of Common Market Studies* 52 (2014): 250–267.

Hinarejos, Alicia. 'Fiscal Federalism in the European Union: Evolution and Future Choices for EMU', *Common Market Law Review* 50 (2013): 1621–1642.

Hinrichs, Karl. 'A Social Insurance State Withers Away. Welfare State Reforms in Germany – Or: Attempts to Turn Around in a Cul-de-Sac', in: *A Long Goodbye to Bismarck?*, ed. Bruno Palier (Amsterdam: Amsterdam University Press, 2010): 45–72.

Hirst, Nicholas, 'Europe's Top Court Could Help Uber Where Commission Has Failed', *Politico*, 28 November 2016, available at www.politico.eu/article/uber-spain-sharing-economy-collaborative-economy/.

Hofmann, Boris and Remsperger, Hermann. 'Inflation Differentials among the Euro Area Countries: Potential Causes and Consequences', *Journal of Asian Economics* 16 (2005): 403–419.

Hofmann, Christian. 'Greek Debt Relief', *Oxford Journal of Legal Studies* 37 (2017): 1–30.

Homar, Timotej and van Wijnbergen, Sweder. 'Bank Recapitalisation and Economic Recovery after Financial Crises', *VOX CEPR's Policy Portal*, 13 February 2016, available at voxeu.org/article/bank-recapitalisation-and-economic-recovery-after-financial-crises.

Hooghe, Liesbet, ed. *Cohesion Policy and European Integration: Building Multi-level Governance* (Oxford: Oxford University Press, 1996).

Hooghe, Liesbet. *The European Commission and the Integration of Europe: Images of Governance* (Cambridge: Cambridge University Press, 2001).

Hooghe, Liesbet and Marks, Gary. 'A Postfunctionalist Theory of European Integration: From Permissive Consensus to Constraining Dissensus', *British Journal of Political Science* 39 (2009): 1–23.

Multi-level Governance and European Integration (Lanham, MD: Rowman & Littlefield, 2001).

Höpner, Martin and Schäfer, Armin. 'A New Phase of European Integration: Organized Capitalisms in Post-Ricardian Europe', *West European Politics* 33 (2010): 344–368.

Horn, Henrik and Sapir, André. 'Can Border Carbon Taxes Fit into the Global Trade Regime?', *Bruegel Policy Brief* No. 2013/06, 9 December 2013, available at bruegel.org/wp-content/uploads/imported/publications/pb_2013_06__01.pdf.

Huliaras, Asteris and Petropoulos, Sotiris. 'European Money in Greece: In Search of the Real Impact of EU Structural Funds', *Journal of Common Market Studies* 54 (2016): 1332–1349.

Independent Evaluation Office of the IMF, 'The IMF and the Crises in Greece, Ireland, and Portugal: An Evaluation by the Independent Evaluation Office', 8 July 2016, available at www.ieo-imf.org/ieo/files/completedevaluations/EAC__REPORT%20v5.PDF.

Indexmundi, 'Indonesia Palm Oil Production by Year', n.d., available at www.indexmundi.com/agriculture/?country=id&commodity=palm-oil&graph=production

Inman, Phillip. 'Irish Economy Surges 26% as Revised Figures Take in Foreign Investment', *Guardian*, 12 July 2016, available at www.theguardian.com/business/2016/jul/12/irish-economic-growth-revised-figures-foreign-investment-aircraft.

Inman, Robert. 'Managing Country Debts in the European Monetary Union: Stronger Rules or Stronger Union?', in: *Political, Fiscal and Banking Union in the Eurozone?*, eds. Franklin Allen, Elena Carletti and Joanna Gray (Philadelphia: FIC Press 2013): 79–102.

International Monetary Fund. 'Access Policy in Capital Account Crises', (SM/02/246; 7/30/02), 29 July 2002, available at www.imf.org/external/np/tre/access/2003/pdf/072902.pdf.

'Spain: 2007 Article IV Consultation – Staff Report', IMF Country Report No. 07/175, May 2007.

'Euro Area Policies: 2008 Article IV Consultation', IMF Country Report No. 08/262, August 2008, available at www.imf.org/external/pubs/ft/scr/2008/cr08262.pdf.

'Greece: Staff Report on Request for Stand-By Arrangement', *IMF Country Report* No. 10/110, May 2010, 25, available at www.imf.org/external/pubs/ft/scr/2010/cr10110.pdf.

'Changing Patterns of Global Trade', 2011, available at www.imf.org/external/np/pp/eng/2011/061511.pdf.

'Spain–Staff Report for the 2011 Article IV Consultation', IMF Country Report No. 11/215, July 2011.

'Cyprus: Staff Report for the 2011 Article IV Consultation', *IMF Country Report* No. 11/331, 3 November 2011, available at www.imf.org/external/pubs/ft/scr/2011/cr11331.pdf.

'Greece: Ex Post Evaluation of Exceptional Access under the 2010 Stand-By Arrangement', *IMF Country Report* No. 13/156, June 2013, available at www.imf.org/external/pubs/ft/scr/2013/cr13156.pdf.

'World Economic Outlook. Coping with High Debt and Sluggish Growth', October 2012.

'Access Policy and Limits in the Credit Tranches and under the Extended Fund Facility and on Overall Access to the Fund's General Resources, and Exceptional Access Policy – Review and Modification', prepared by the Legal Department of the IMF, as updated as of 31 December 2013, available at www.imf.org/external/pubs/ft/sd/index.asp?decision=14064-(08/18).

'Greece: Grounds for Cautious Optimism', *IMF Survey*, 10 June 2014, available at www.imf.org/external/pubs/ft/survey/so/2014/car060914a.htm.

'Greece: Preliminary Draft Debt Sustainability Analysis', *IMF Country Report* No. 15/165, 26 June 2015, available at www.imf.org/external/pubs/ft/scr/2015/cr15165.pdf.

'2016 Article IV Consultation Country on Greece', Report No. 17/40, 7 February 2017, available at www.imf.org/en/Publications/CR/Issues/2017/02/07/Greece-2017-Article-IV-Consultation-Press-Release-Staff-Report-and-Statement-by-the-44630.

'Greece: Debt Sustainability Summary Note', available at www.documentcloud.org/documents/2840552-IMF-Greece.html.

International Monetary Fund Finance Department. 'Ireland: Ex Post Evaluation of Exceptional Access under the 2010 Extended Arrangement', International Monetary Fund, 29 January 2015, available at www.imf.org/external/pubs/cat/longres.aspx?sk=42656.0.

InvestEurope. '2016 European Private Equity Activity. Statistics on Fundraising, Investments & Divestments', available at www.investeurope.eu/media/651727/invest-europe-2016-european-private-equity-activity-final.pdf?utm_source=POLITICO.EU&utm_campaign=ea29f1e5c9-EMAIL_CAMPAIGN_2017_05_16&utm_medium=email&utm_term=0_10959edeb5-ea29f1e5c9-188989817.

Ioannou, Christos. 'Greek Public Service Employment Relations: A Gordian Knot in the Era of Sovereign Default', *European Journal of Industrial Relations* 19 (2013): 295–308.

Italianer, Alexander and Pisani-Ferry, Jean. 'Systèmes Budgétaires et Amortissement des Chocs Régionaux: Implications pour l'Union Économique et Monétaire', *Économie de Prospective Internationale*, n 51, CEPII, Paris, 3e trimestre 1992.

Italianer, Alexander and Vanheukelen, Marc. 'Proposals for Community Stabilization Mechanisms: Some Historical Applications', in: *The Economics of Community Public Finance*, European Economy No. 5, 1993: 493–510.

Izsak, Kincsö, Markianidou, Paresa and Radošević, Slavo. 'Convergence of National Innovation Policy Mixes in Europe – Has It Gone Too Far? An Analysis of Research and Innovation Policy Measures in the Period 2004–12', *Journal of Common Market Studies* 53 (2015): 786–802.

Jackson, Gregory and Deeg, Richard. 'The Long-term Trajectories of Institutional Change in European Capitalism', *Journal of European Public Policy* 19 (2012): 1109–1125.

Jacobsen, Henriette. 'Private Clinics Deny Patients Treatment as Greece's Health System Collapses', *Euractiv*, 31 October 2013, available at www.euractiv.com/section/health-consumers/news/private-clinics-deny-patients-treatment-as-greece-s-health-system-collapses/.

'Merkel Admits EU's Youth Unemployment Initiative Has Been a Failure', *Euractiv*, 30 June 2014, available at www.euractiv.com/section/social-europe-jobs/news/merkel-admits-eu-s-youth-unemployment-initiative-has-been-a-failure/.

James, Harold. *Making the European Monetary Union* (Cambridge, MA: Harvard University Press, 2012.

Jančić, Davor. 'The Game of Cards: National Parliaments in the EU and the Future of the Early Warning Mechanism and the Political Dialogue', *Common Market Law Review* 52 (2015): 939–975.

Janning, Josef. 'The Ultimate Test for Merkel's "Muddle Through" Model', *European Council on Foreign Relations*, 10 July 2015, available at www.ecfr.eu/article/commentary_the_ultimate_test_for_merkels_muddle_through_model3066.

Janos, Andrew C. 'The Politics of Backwardness in Continental Europe, 1780–1945', *World Politics* 41 (1989): 325–358.

East Central Europe in the Modern World: The Politics of the Borderlands From Pre- to Postcommunism (Stanford, CA: Stanford University Press, 2000).

Janssens, Christine. *The Principle of Mutual Recognition in EU Law* (Oxford: Oxford University Press, 2013).

Jessoula, Matteo and Alti, Tizziana. 'Italy: An Uncompleted Departure from Bismarck', in: *A Long Goodbye to Bismarck?*, ed. Bruno Palier (Amsterdam: Amsterdam University Press, 2010): 157–181.

Jimeno, Juan and Thomas, Carlos. 'Collective Bargaining, Firm Heterogeneity, and Unemployment', *European Economic Review* 59 (2013): 63–79.

Joerges, Christian. 'Europe's Economic Constitution in Crisis and the Emergence of a New Constitutional Constellation', *ZENTRA Working Papers In Transnational Studies* 6 (2012), available at papers.ssrn.com/sol3/papers.cfm?abstract_id=2179595##.

'Law and Politics in Europe's Crisis: On the History of the Impact of an Unfortunate Configuration', *EUI Working Papers LAW* 9 (2013).

Joerges, Christian and Dehousse, Renaud, eds. *Good Governance in Europe's Integrated Market* (Oxford: Oxford University Press, 2002).

Jowett, Matthew et al. 'Spending Targets for Health: No Magic Number', *WHO Health Financing Working Paper* No. 1, 2016, available at apps.who.int/iris/bitstream/10665/250048/1/WHO-HIS-HGF-HFWorkingPaper-16.1-eng.pdf.

Juncker, Jean-Claude. 'A New Start for Europe: My Agenda for Jobs, Growth, Fairness and Democratic Change. Political Guidelines for the Next European Commission. Opening Statement in the European Parliament Plenary Session', Strasbourg, 15 July 2014, available at ec.europa.eu/commission/publications/president-junckers-political-guidelines_en.

Juncker, Jean-Claude, speech 'Investing in Europe: Speech by President Juncker in the European Parliament Plenary Session on the €315 bn Investment Plan', delivered in the European Parliament on 26 November 2014, available at europa.eu/rapid/press-release_SPEECH-14-2160_en.htm.

Juncker, Jean-Claude, Tusk, Donald, Dijsselbloem, Jeroen, Draghi, Mario and Schulz, Martin. 'The Five Presidents' Report: Completing Europe's Economic and Monetary Union', 22 June 2015, available at ec.europa.eu/priorities/publications/five-presidents-report-completing-europes-economic-and-monetary-union_en.

Kalcik, Robert. 'Is China's Innovation Strategy a Threat?', *Bruegel Blog Post*, 3 April 2017, available at bruegel.org/2017/04/19927/.

Kaletsky, Anatole. 'Roman Europe?', *Project Syndicate*, 26 April 2016, available at www.project-syndicate.org/commentary/italy-not-germany-leads-europe-by-anatole-kaletsky-2016-04?barrier=accessreg.

Kallaste, Epp and Woolfson, Charles. 'The Paradox of Post-communist Trade Unionism: You Can't Want What You Can't Imagine', *The Economic and Labour Relations Review* 20 (2009): 93–109.

Kaltenthaler, Karl. *Germany and the Politics of Europe's Money* (Durham, NC: Duke University Press, 1998).

Kammer, Andreas, Niehues, Judith and Peichl, Andreas. 'Welfare Regimes and Welfare State Outcomes in Europe', *Journal of European Social Policy* 22 (2012): 455–471.

Karnitschnig, Matthew. 'Lost Continent Rediscovers Its Mojo', *Politico*, 12 June 2017, available www.politico.eu/article/lost-continent-rediscovers-its-mojo/.

Kasparek, Annika. 'Fiscal Policy in US States', *Deutsche Bank Research Current Issues*, December 2011.

Katsios, Stavros. 'The Shadow Economy and Corruption in Greece', *South-Eastern Europe Journal of Economics* 1 (2006): 61–80.

Kazepov, Yuri and Ranci, Costanzo. 'Is Every Country Fit for Social Investment? Italy as an Adverse Case', *Journal of European Social Policy* 27 (2017): 90–104.

KeepTalkingGreece. 'Lagarde: 3.5% Primary Surplus Might Be Achievable in Short-term with Heroic Efforts by Greek People', 14 April 2016, available at www.keeptalkinggreece.com/2016/04/14/lagarde-3-5-primary-surplus-might-be-achievable-in-short-term-with-heroic-efforts-by-greek-people/.

Kenen, Peter. 'The Theory of Optimum Currency Areas: An Eclectic View', in: *Monetary Problems of the International Economy*, eds. Robert Mundell and Alexander Swoboda (Chicago: University of Chicago Press, 1969): 41–60.

Kilpatrick, Claire. 'Constitutions, Social Rights and Sovereign Debt States in Europe: A Challenging New Area of Constitutional Inquiry', *EUI Working Papers LAW* 34 (2015).

Knuth, Matthias. 'Broken Hierarchies, Quasi-markets and Supported Networks – A Governance Experiment in the Second Tier of Germany's Public Employment Service', *Social Policy & Administration* 48 (2014): 240–261.

Koch, Nicolas et al. 'Causes of the EU ETS Price Drop: Recession, CDM, Renewable Policies or a Bit of Everything? – New Evidence', *Energy Policy* 73 (2014): 676–685.

Kohl, Heribert and Platzer, Hans, eds. *Industrial Relations in Central and Eastern Europe: Transformation and Integration: A Comparison of the Eight New EU Member States* (Brussels: European Trade Union Institute, 2004).

Kolb, Robert W. *Sovereign Debt: From Safety to Default* (Hoboken, NJ: John Wiley & Sons, 2011).

Kolmar, Martin. 'Beveridge Versus Bismarck Public-pension Systems in Integrated Markets', *Regional Science and Urban Economics* 37 (2007): 649–669.

Koo, Richard C. 'The World in Balance Sheet Recession: Causes, Cure, and Politics', *Real-World Economics Review* 58 (2011): 19–37.

Koopman, Robert et al. 'Give Credit Where Credit Is Due: Tracing Value Added in Global Production Chains', *NBER Working Paper* No. 16426, September 2010, available at www.nber.org/papers/w16426.

Koplitz, Shannon et al. 'Public Health Impacts of the Severe Haze in Equatorial Asia in September–October 2015: Demonstration of a New Framework for Informing Fire Management Strategies to Reduce Downwind Smoke Exposure', *Environmental Research Letters* 11 (2016), available at iopscience.iop.org/article/10.1088/1748-9326/11/9/094023/pdf.

Koranyi, Balazs. 'Europe's Inequality Highly Destabilising, ECB's Draghi Says', *Reuters*, 26 June 2017, available from uk.reuters.com.

Korioth, Stefan. 'Das Rechtsregime für die Unterstützung Notleidender Staaten des Euro-Raums – Analyse nach Maßgabe des Nationalen und des Unionsrechts', in: *Grundlagen, Aktuelle Entwicklungen und Perspektiven der Europäischen Währungsunion*, eds. Eckhard Pache and Kyrill-A. Schwarz (Baden-Baden: Nomos, 2012): 61–97.

Kornai, János, Maskin, Eric and Roland, Gérard. 'Understanding the Soft Budget Constraint', available at www.sss.ias.edu/files/papers/econpaper19.pdf.

Kostoris Padoa Schioppa, Fiorella. *The Principles of Mutual Recognition in the European Integration Process* (New York: Palgrave Macmillan, 2005).

Koukiadaki, Aristea and Kretsos, Lefteris. 'Opening Pandora's Box: The Sovereign Debt Crisis and Labour Market Regulation in Greece', *Industrial Law Journal* 41 (2012): 276–304.

Kowalkowski, Christian. 'Service Productivity Gains through Information and Communication Technology Applications: A Service Marketing Approach', *International Journal of Knowledge Management Studies* 2 (2008): 96–114.

Kox, Henk L. M. 'Unleashing Competition in EU Business Services', *CEPS Policy Brief* No. 284, 24 September 2012, available at aei.pitt.edu/36814/1/ceps_4.pdf.

Krugman, Paul. *Geography and Trade* (Cambridge, MA: MIT Press, 1991).

'Lessons of Massachusetts for EMU', in: *Adjustment and Growth in the European Monetary Union*, eds. Francesco Giavazzi and Francisco Torres (Cambridge: Cambridge University Press, 1993): 241–261.

'Japan's Trap', May 1998, available at web.mit.edu/krugman/www/japtrap.html.

Kukovec, Damjan. 'Law and the Periphery', *European Law Journal* 21 (2015): 406–428.

Kumm, Mattias. 'What Kind of a Constitutional Crisis Is Europe in and What Should Be Done About It?', *WZB Discussion Paper*, February 2013, available at bibliothek.wzb.eu/pdf/2013/iv13-801.pdf.

La Spina, Antonio and Sciortino, Giuseppe. 'Common Agenda, Southern Rules: European Integration and Environmental Change in the Mediterranean States', in: *European Integration and Environmental Policy*, eds. Duncan Liefferink, Philip Lowe and Arthur Moll (London: Belhaven Press, 1993): 217–236.

Lain, David, Vickerstaff, Sarah and Loretto, Wendy. 'Reforming State Pension Provision in "Liberal" Anglo- Saxon Countries: Re-Commodification, Cost-Containment or Recalibration?', *Social Policy and Society* 12 (2013): 77–90.

Lambert, Priscilla A. 'The Comparative Political Economy of Parental Leave and Child Care: Evidence from Twenty OECD Countries' *Social Politics* 15 (2008): 315–344.

Lamo, Ana, Pérez, Javier and Schuknecht, Ludger. 'Public and Private Sector Wages: Co-movement and Causality', *ECB Working Paper Series* No. 963, November 2008, available at www.ecb.europa.eu/pub/pdf/scpwps/ecbwp963.pdf.

Lamping, Wolfram and Rüb, Friedbert W. 'From the Conservative Welfare State to an "Uncertain Something Else": German Pension Politics in Comparative Perspective', *Policy & Politics* 32 (2004): 169–191.

Lane, Timothy. 'Market Discipline', *IMF Working Paper* No. 92/42, June 1992, available at papers.ssrn.com/sol3/papers.cfm?abstract_id=884774.

Lannoo, Karel. 'EU Federalism in Crisis', *CEPS Policy Brief* No. 259, October 2011, available at www.ceps.eu/publications/eu-federalism-crisis.

Lattimore, Ralph. 'Farm Subsidy Reform Dividends', *Paper Prepared for the North American Agrifood Market Integration Consortium Meetings*, 31 May–2 June 2006, Calgary, Alberta, available from www.staff.ncl.ac.uk.

Laulom Sylvaine et al. 'How Has the Crisis Affected Social Legislation in Europe?' *ETUI Policy Brief. European Economic, Employment and Social Policy* No. 2/2012, available at www.etui.org/Publications2/Policy-Briefs/European-Economic-Employment-and-Social-Policy/How-has-the-crisis-affected-social-legislation-in-Europe.

Legorano, Giovanni. 'Italy Sets Up Fund to Help Troubled Banks', *Wall Street Journal*, 23 December 2016, available at www.wsj.com/articles/italy-sets-up-fund-to-help-troubled-banks-1482458087.

Lehmann, Alexander. 'Credit Recovery in Spain: NPL Resolution Was Essential, But Success Depended on Broader Sector Reform', *Bruegel Blog Post*, 21 November 2016, available at bruegel.org/2016/11/credit-recovery-in-spain-npl-resolution-was-essential-but-success-depended-on-broader-sector-reform/ sets it against a broader context.

'Carving Out Legacy Assets: A Successful Tool for Bank Restructuring?' *Bruegel Policy Contribution* No. 9/2017, available at bruegel.org/wp-content/uploads/2017/03/PC-09-2017-NPL-29317.pdf.

Leibfried, Stephan and Pierson, Paul. *European Social Policy: Between Fragmentation and Integration* (Washington, DC: Brookings Institution Press, 1995).

Leino, Päivi and Saarenheimo, Tuomas. 'Sovereignty and Subordination: On the Limits of EU Economic Policy Co-ordination', *European Law Review* 42 (2017): 166–189.

Lellouch, Thomas and Sode, Arthur. 'An Unemployment Insurance Scheme for the Euro Area', *Trésor-Economics* No. 132, June 2014, available at www.tresor.economie.gouv.fr/File/403124.

Lenaerts, Koen. 'EMU and the European Union's Constitutional Framework', *European Law Review* 39 (2014): 753–769.

Lindbeck, Assar et al. 'Options for Economic and Political Reform in Sweden', *Economic Policy* 8 (1993): 219–263.

Lindbom, Anders. 'Dismantling the Social Democratic Welfare Model? Has the Swedish Welfare State Lost Its Defining Characteristics?', *Scandinavian Political Studies* 24 (2001): 171–193.

Linklaters. 'Eurozone Bulletin: Capital and Exchange Controls', April 2013, available at www.linklaters.com/pdfs/mkt/london/Eurozone-Bulletin-Capital-Exchange-Controls.pdf.

Lipsey, Richard and Chrystal, Alec. *Economics* (Oxford: Oxford University Press, 2015).

Livingstone, Emmet. 'Europe Offers €500 Million to Help Dairy Farmers', *Politico*, 15 July 2016, available at www.politico.eu/article/europe-awaits-last-ditch-effort-to-save-its-milk-farms-commission-overproduction/.

Lof, Matthijs and Malinen, Tuomas. 'Determinants of the Growth and Sovereign Debt Correlation', *VOX CEPR's Policy Portal*, 25 May 2014, available at voxeu.org/article/growth-and-sovereign-debt-correlation.

Lowe, Philip. 'The Reform of the Community's Structural Funds', *Common Market Law Review* 25 (1988): 503–521.

Lynggaard, Kennet and Nedergaard, Peter. 'The Logic of Policy Development: Lessons Learned from Reform and Routine within the CAP 1980–2003', in: *The Common Agricultural Policy: Policy Dynamics in a Changing Context*, eds. Grace Skogstad and Amy Verdun (London: Routledge 2013): 25–43.

Mabbett, Deborah. 'The Minimum Wage in Germany: What Brought the State In?', *Journal of European Public Policy* 23 (2016): 1240–1258.

Macartney, Huw. *Variegated Neoliberalism: EU Varieties of Capitalism and International Political Economy* (New York; London: Routledge, 2011).

Maes, Ivo and Moss, Frank. *Progress through Crisis? Proceedings of the Conference for the 20th Anniversary of the Establishment of the European Monetary Institute* (Frankfurt am Main: ECB, 2014).

Maino, Franca and Neri, Stefano. 'Explaining Welfare Reforms in Italy between Economy and Politics: External Constraints and Endogenous Dynamics', *Social Policy & Administration* 45 (2011): 445–464.

Malmberg, Jonas. 'The Impact of the ECJ Judgements on Viking, Laval, Rueffert and Luxemburg on the Practice of Collective Bargaining and the Effectiveness of Social Action', European Parliament Study, May 2010, available at www.europarl.europa.eu/document/activities/cont/201107/20110718ATT24274/20110718ATT24274EN.pdf.

Marchegiani, Giannangelo. 'The European Investment Bank after the Treaty of Lisbon', *European Law Review* 37 (2012): 70–78.

Marcu, Andrei. 'Paris 2015: What's in It for the EU?', *CEPS Commentary*, 8 May 2015, available at www.ceps.eu/publications/paris-2015-what's-it-eu.

Marin, Dalia, Schymik, Jan and Tscheke, Jan. 'Europe's Exports Superstar – It's the Organisation', *Bruegel Working Paper* No. 2015/05, 14 July 2015, available at bruegel.org/2015/07/europes-exports-superstar-its-the-organisation/.

Mariniello, Mario, Sapir, André and Terzi, Alessio. 'The Long Road towards the European Single Market', *Bruegel Working Paper* No. 2015/01, 16 March 2015, available at bruegel.org/2015/03/the-long-road-towards-the-european-single-market/.

Marks, Gary. 'Structural Policy and Multilevel Governance in the EC', in: *The State of the European Community, Vol. 2: The Maastricht Debates and Beyond*, eds. Alan W. Cafruny and Glenda G. Rosenthal (Boulder, CO: Lynne Rienner Publishers, Inc. and Harlow, Essex: Longman Group U.K. Ltd., 1993): 391–410.

'JCMS Annual Lecture 2011 Europe and Its Empires: From Rome to the European Union', *Journal of Common Market Studies* 50 (2012): 1–20.

Marks, Simon. 'Eastern Europe Turns Back on Single Market', *Politico*, 11 May 2017, available at www.politico.eu/article/eastern-europe-versus-the-single-market/.

Martin, Philippe. 'Are European Regional Policies Delivering?', CERAS-ENPC, Paris and CEPR, 1999, available at willmann.com/~gerald/euroecon-04/martin-paper.pdf.

Maselli, Ilaria, Lenaerts, Karolien and Beblavý, Miroslav. 'Five Things We Need to Know About the On-demand Economy', *CEPS Essay* No. 21, 8 January 2016, available at papers.ssrn.com/sol3/papers.cfm?abstract_id=2715450.

Maskin, Eric S. 'Theories of the Soft Budget-constraint', *Japan and the World Economy* 8 (1996): 125–133.

Mathias Dolls et al. Annex II to 'Common Unemployment Insurance Scheme for the Euro Area. Cost of Non-Europe Report', European Parliamentary Research Service, September 2014, II-49, available at www.europarl.europa.eu/RegData/etudes/STUD/2014/510984/EPRS_STU(2014)510984_REV1_EN.pdf.

Matsaganis, Manos. 'The Welfare State and the Crisis: The Case of Greece', *Journal of European Social Policy* 21 (2011): 501–512.

Matsubayashi, Yoichi. 'The Effort to Stabilise the Financial System in Japan: An Outline and the Characteristics of the Programme for Financial Revival', *Bruegel Working Paper* No. 2015/02, 18 March 2015, available at bruegel.org/2015/03/the-effort-to-stabilise-the-financial-system-in-japan-an-outline-and-the-characteristics-of-the-programme-for-financial-revival/.

McKinnon, Ronald. 'Optimum Currency Areas', *American Economic Review*, 53 (1963): 717–724.

McKinnon, Ronald. 'Optimum Currency Areas and Key Currencies: Mundell I versus Mundell II', *Journal of Common Market Studies* 42 (2004): 689–715.

Mclaughlin, Eithne. *Understanding Unemployment: New Perspectives on Active Labour Market Policies* (London, New York: Routledge, 2013).

McNamara, Kathleen R. 'The Forgotten Problem of Embeddedness. History Lessons for the Euro', in: *The Future of the Euro*, eds. Matthias Matthijs and Mark Blyth (Oxford: Oxford University Press, 2015): 21–43.

Medium. 'Estonia Leads the Way on Regulated Ridesharing', 1 March 2016, available at medium.com/uber-under-the-hood/estonia-leads-the-way-on-regulated-ridesharing-28686a2fcf50#.ui4cs5kzb.

Melitz, Jacques and Zumer, Frederic. 'Regional Redistribution and Stabilization by the Center in Canada, France, the UK and the US: A Reassessment and New Tests', *Journal of Public Economics* 86 (2002): 263–286.

Menéndez, Agustín. 'The Existential Crisis of the European Union', *German Law Journal* 14 (2013): 453–526.

Menz, Georg and Crespy, Amandine. 'Introduction: The Pursuit of Social Europe in the Face of Crisis', in: *Social Policy and the Eurocrisis: Quo Vadis Social Europe*, eds. Georg Menz and Amandine Crespy (Basingstoke: Palgrave Macmillan, 2015): 1–23.

Merler, Silvia. 'Banking Union: Progresses and Problems', *Banking Union and beyond Discussion Papers*, 28 January 2014, available at bruegel.org/2014/01/banking-union-and-beyond-discussion-papers-for-brussels-think-tank-dialogue/.

'Income Convergence during the Crisis: Did EU Funds Provide a Buffer?', *Bruegel Working Paper* No. 6/2016, 18 October 2016, available at bruegel.org/2016/10/income-convergence-did-eu-funds-provide-a-buffer/.

'Tariffs and the American Poor', *Bruegel Blog Post*, 23 January 2017, available at bruegel.org/2017/01/tariffs-and-the-american-poors/.

Merler, Silvia and Pisani-Ferry, Jean. 'Sudden Stops in the Euro Area', *Bruegel Policy Contribution* No. 2012/06, 29 March 2012, available at bruegel.org/2012/03/sudden-stops-in-the-euro-area-2/.

Merler, Silvia and Wolff, Guntram. 'Ending Uncertainty: Recapitalisation under European Central Bank Supervision', *Bruegel Policy Contribution* No. 2013/18, 17 December 2013, available at bruegel.org/2013/12/ending-uncertainty-recapitalisation-under-european-central-bank-supervision/.

Merler, Silvia, Pisani-Ferry, Jean and Wolff, Guntram. 'The Role of the ECB in Financial Assistance: Some Early Observations', June 2012, available at www.europarl.europa.eu/document/activities/cont/201207/20120702ATT48160/20120702ATT48160EN.pdf.

Merritt, Giles. 'Euro-dole: A German Initiative That Berlin Doesn't Welcome', *Friends of Europe*, 23 November 2016, available at www.friendsofeurope.org/future-europe/frankly-speaking-euro-dole-german-initiative-berlin-doesnt-welcome/.

Meyer, André. 'A Common Tax Policy for Europe', in: *EU Law after the Financial Crisis*, eds. Jessica Schmidt, Carlos Esplugues and Rafael Arenas (Cambridge: Intersentia, 2016): 97–106.

Michail, Niamh. 'French MPs Drop Palm Oil Tax – But Accuse Producer Countries of Blackmail', *Foodnavigator*, 27 June 2016, available at: www.foodnavigator.com/Policy/French-MPs-drop-palm-oil-tax-but-accuse-producer-countries-of-blackmail.

Michie, Rona and Fitzgerald, Rona. 'The Evolution of the Structural Funds', in: *The Coherence of EU Regional Policy: Contrasting Perspectives on the Structural Funds*, eds. John Bachtler and Ivan Turok (London: Routledge, 2013).

Micklitz, Hans-W. and De Witte, Bruno, eds. *The European Court of Justice and the Autonomy of the Member States* (Cambridge; Antwerp; Portland: Intersentia, 2012).

Micossi, Stefano, Bruzzone, Ginevra and Cassella, Miriam. 'Fine-tuning the Use of Bail-in to Promote a Stronger EU Financial System', *CEPS Special Report* No. 136, 21 April 2016, available at www.ceps.eu/publications/fine-tuning-use-bail-promote-stronger-eu-financial-system.

Milanovic, Branko. *Global Inequality. A New Approach for the Age of Globalization* (Cambridge, MA; London: The Belknap Press of Harvard University Press, 2016).

Mill, John Stuart. *Principles of Political Economy* (London: Longmans, Green and Co., 1848).

Miller, Marcus and Sutherland, Alan. 'The "Walters" Critique of the EMS: A Case of Inconsistent Expectations', *CEPR Discussion Paper* No. 480, November 1990, available at cepr.org/active/publications/discussion_papers/dp.php?dpno=480#.

Milward, Alan. *The European Rescue of the Nation-State* (London: Routledge, 1992).

Minas, Christos et al. 'Welfare Regime, Welfare Pillar and Southern Europe', *Journal of European Social Policy* 24 (2014): 135–149.

Minenna, Marcello, Boi, Giovanna Maria and Verzella, Paulo. *The Incomplete Currency: The Future of the Euro and Solutions for the Eurozone* (Chichester: John Wiley & Sons, 2016).

Mingardi, Alberto. 'What Europe Can Learn from Italy', *Politico*, 2 March 2017, available at www.politico.eu/article/what-europe-can-learn-from-italy-economics-budget-monetary-union/.

Mitchell, William. *Eurozone Dystopia* (Cheltenham: Edward Elgar Publishing, 2015).

Mizsei, Kálmán and Kullmann, Ádám. 'Struggling with an Opportunity: The First 10 Years with the EU for Central Europe and the Baltics. A Few Lessons', *CEPS Essay* No. 12, 2 May 2014, available at aei.pitt.edu/58409/1/Essay_No_12_NMS_at_10.pdf.

Mody, Ashoka. 'A Schuman Compact for the Euro Area', *Bruegel Essay and Lecture Series*, 20 November 2013, available at bruegel.org/2013/11/a-schuman-compact-for-the-euro-area/.

'Sovereign Debt and Its Restructuring Framework in the Eurozone', *Oxford Review of Economic Policy* 29 (2013): 715–744.

Mohlmann, Jan and Suyker, Wim. 'An Update of Blanchard's and Leigh's Estimates in "Growth Forecast Errors and Fiscal Multipliers"', *CEPR Policy Portal*, 1 December 2015, available at www.voxeu.org/article/blanchard-and-leigh-s-fiscal-multipliers-revisited.

Moloney, Niamh. 'Capital Markets Union: "Ever Closer Union" for the EU Financial System?', *European Law Review* 41 (2016): 307–337.

Monnet, Jean. *Mémoires* (Paris: Fayard 1976).

Monteagudo, Josefa, Rutkowski, Aleksander and Lorenzani, Dimitri. 'The Economic Impact of the Services Directive: A First Assessment Following Implementation', *European Economy, Economic Papers* No. 456, June 2012, Brussels, available at ec.europa.eu/economy_finance/publications/economic_paper/2012/pdf/ecp_456_en.pdf.

Monteiro, José-Antonio. 'Typology of Environment-Related Provisions in Regional Trade Agreements', *WTO Working Paper* No. ERSD-2016-13, July 2016, available at www.wto.org/english/res_e/reser_e/ersd201613_e.pdf.

Monti, Mario. 'A New Strategy for the Single Market at the Service of Europe's Economy and Society. Report to the President of the European Commission José Manuel Barroso', 9 May 2010, available at ec.europa.eu/internal_market/strategy/docs/monti_report_final_10_05_2010_en.pdf.

Moravcsik, Andrew. 'Negotiating the Single European Act: National Interests and Conventional Statecraft in the European Community', *International Organization* 45 (1991): 19–56.

Morel, Nathalie, Palier, Bruno and Palme, Joakim. *Towards a Social Investment Welfare State? Ideas, Policies and Challenges* (Bristol: Policy Press, 2012).

Mossialos, Elias and Petmesidou, Maria, eds. *Social Policy Developments in Greece* (London: Routledge, 2006).

Muir, Elise. *EU Regulation of Access to Labour Markets: A Case Study of EU Constraints on Member State Competences* (Alphen aan den Rijn: Kluwer Law International, 2012).

Müller, Jan-Werner. 'Beyond Militant Democracy?', *New Left Review* 73 (2012): 33–42.

Mundell, Robert. 'A Theory of Optimum Currency Areas', *American Economic Review* 51 (1961): 509–517.

'Uncommon Arguments for Common Currencies', in: *The Economics of Common Currencies*, eds. Harry Johnson and Alexander Swoboda (London: Allen & Unwin 1973): 114–132.

Munkhammar, Johnny. 'The Swedish Model. It's the Free-market Reforms, Stupid', *The Wall Street Journal Europe*, 26 January 2011, available at www.wsj.com/articles/SB10001424052748704698004576104023432243468.

Muñoz de Bustillo, Rafael. 'Questioning the Myth of Expansionary Austerity: European Macroeconomic Policy during the Crisis and Its Aftermath', in: *The Economic Crisis and Governance in the European Union: A Critical Assessment*, ed. Javier Bilbao-Ubillos (London: Routledge, 2014): 114–133.

Musgrave, Richard. *The Theory of Public Finance: A Study in Public Economy* (New York: McGraw Hill, 1959).

Mustilli, Federica and Pelkmans, Jacques. 'Access Barriers to Services Markets. Mapping, Tracing, Understanding and Measuring', *CEPS Special Report* No. 77, 7 June 2013, available at www.ceps.eu/publications/access-barriers-services-markets-mapping-tracing-understanding-and-measuring.

'Securing EU Growth from Services', *CEPS Special Report* No. 67, October 2012, available at www.ceps.eu/system/files/Securing%20EU%20 Growth%20from%20Services.pdf.

Nagel, Thomas. 'The Problem of Global Justice', *Philosophy and Public Affairs* 33 (2005): 113–147.

Nakano, Satoshi. 'Maastricht Social Protocol Revisited: Origins of the European Industrial Relations System', *Journal of Common Market Studies* 52 (2014): 1053–1069.

Naldini, Manuela and Jurado, Teresa. 'Family and Welfare State Reorientation in Spain and Inertia in Italy from a European Perspective', *Population Review* 52 (2013): 43–61.

Nelson, Stephen C. 'Playing Favorites: How Shared Beliefs Shape the IMF's Lending Decisions', *International Organization* 68 (2014): 297–328.

New Zealand Ministry of Agriculture and Forestry, 'Agriculture in New Zealand: Past, Present and Future', New Zealand Ministry of Agriculture and Forestry, 2006

Ngai, Victor. 'Appendix. Introduction to the Stability and Growth Pact', in: *Governance for the Eurozone: Integration or Disintegration?*, eds. Allen Franklin, Elena Carletti and Saverio Simonelli, 2012: 213–228, available at www.eui.eu/DepartmentsAndCentres/Economics/SeminarsEvents/Conferences/GovernancefortheEurozoneIntegrationorDisintegration.aspx.

Nic Shuibhne, Niamh. 'What I Tell You Three Times Is True. Lawful Residence and Equal Treatment after Dano', *Maastricht Journal of European and Comparative Law* 23 (2016): 908–936.

Nicolaïdis, Kalypso. 'European Demoicracy and Its Crisis', *Journal of Common Market Studies* 51 (2013): 351–369.

Nijs, Luc. *Neoliberalism 2.0: Regulating and Financing Globalizing Markets: A Pigovian Approach for 21st Century Markets* (New York: Palgrave Macmillan, 2016).

Nogueira de Brito, Miguel. 'Putting Social Rights in Brackets? The Portuguese Experience with Welfare Challenges in Times of Crisis', in: *Social Rights in Times of Crisis in the Eurozone: The Role of Fundamental Rights' Challenges*, eds. Claire Kilpatrick and Bruno De Witte, *EUI Working Papers LAW* 5 (2014): 67–77, available at cadmus.eui.eu/handle/1814/31247.

Nölke, Andreas and Vliegenthart, Arjan. 'Enlarging the Varieties of Capitalism: The Emergence of Dependent Market Economies in East Central Europe', *World Politics* 61 (2009): 670–702.

O'Brien, Charlotte. 'Civis Capitalist Sum: Class as the New Guiding Principle of EU Free Movement Rights', *Common Market Law Review* 53 (2016): 937–978.

'Annotation to Case C-308/14, *Commission* v. *United Kingdom*, Judgment of the Court (First Chamber) of 14 June 2016, EU:C:2016:436', *Common Market Law Review* 54 (2017): 209–244.

Oates, Wallace E. 'An Essay on Fiscal Federalism', *Journal of Economic Literature* 37 (1999): 1120–1149.

'On the Theory and Practice of Fiscal Decentralization', *IFIR Working Paper* No. 2006-05, May 2006.

Fiscal Federalism (New York: Harcourt Brace Jovanovich, 1972).

Obstfeld, Maurice, Shambaugh, Jay C. and Taylor, Alan M. 'The Trilemma in History: Tradeoffs among Exchange Rates, Monetary Policies, and Capital Mobility', *The Review of Economics and Statistics* 87 (2005): 423–438.

OECD. *Effective Carbon Rates: Pricing CO2 through Taxes and Emissions Trading Systems* (Paris: OECD Publishing, 2016).

OECD Employment Outlook 2016.

The 2016 OECD Economic Surveys: Germany 2016 (Paris: OECD Publishing, 2016).

Working Together: Skills and Labour Market Integration of Immigrants and Their Children in Sweden (Paris: OECD Publishing, 2016).

The 2017 OECD Economic Surveys: Japan 2017 (Paris: OECD Publishing, 2017).

The 2017 OECD Economic Surveys: Sweden 2017 (Paris: OECD Publishing, 2017).

Olson, Mancur. *The Logic of Collective Action: Public Goods and the Theory of Groups* (Cambridge, MA; London, England: Harvard University Press, 1965).

Orphanides, Athanasios. 'Taylor Rules', *Finance and Economics Discussion Series, Board of the Federal Reserve System*, January 2007, available at www.federalreserve.gov/pubs/feds/2007/200718/200718pap.pdf.

Osborn, Andrew. 'Prodi Disowns "Stupid" Stability Pact', *Guardian*, 18 October 2002, available at www.theguardian.com/business/2002/oct/18/theeuro.europeanunion.

Osterloh, Steffen, Heinemann, Friedrich and Mohl, Philipp. 'EU Budget Reform Options and the Common Pool Problem', *Centre for European Economic Research ZEW*, August 2008.

Owen, Ann L. and Wu, Stephen. 'Is Trade Good for Your Health?', *Review of International Economics* 15 (2007): 660–682.

Padoa-Schioppa, Tommaso. 'An Institutional Glossary of the Eurosystem', prepared for the conference on 'The Constitution of the Eurosystem: The Views of the EP and the ECB', 8 March 2000, available at www.ecb.europa.eu/press/key/date/2000/html/sp000308_1.en.html.

Padoan, Pier Carlo, Sila, Urban and van den Noord, Paul. 'Avoiding Debt Traps: Fiscal Consolidation, Financial Backstops and Structural Reforms', *OECD Journal: Economic Studies* 2012, available at www.oecd.org/eco/public-finance/AvoidingdebttrapsFiscalconsolidationfinancialbackstopsandfinancialreforms.pdf.

Paetzold, Jörg and van Vliet, Olaf. 'EU Co-Ordination and the Convergence of Domestic Unemployment Protection Scheme', *Journal of Common Market Studies* 52 (2014): 1070–1089.

Palast, Greg. 'Robert Mundell, Evil Genius of the Euro', *Guardian*, 26 June 2012, available at www.theguardian.com/commentisfree/2012/jun/26/robert-mundell-evil-genius-euro.

Palier, Bruno. 'Ordering Change: Understanding the "Bismarckian" Welfare Reform Trajectory', in: *A Long Goodbye to Bismarck?*, ed. Bruno Palier (Amsterdam: Amsterdam University Press, 2010): 19–44.

'The Dualizations of the French Welfare System', in: *A Long Goodbye to Bismarck?*, ed. B. Palier (Amsterdam: Amsterdam University Press, 2010): 73–100.

Palling, Kalle. 'Why Estonia Introduced a Bill on Ridesharing', *The Baltic Times*, 5 March 2016, available at www.baltictimes.com/kalle_palling__why_estonia_introduced_a_bill_on_ridesharing/.

Palmstorfer, Rainer. 'The Reverse Majority Voting under the "Six-Pack": A Bad Turn for the Union?', *European Law Journal* 20 (2014): 186–203.

Panizza, Ugo. 'Do We Need a Mechanism for Solving Sovereign Debt Crises? A Rule-based Discussion', *Graduate Institute of International and Development Studies Working Paper* No. 03/2013, February 2013, available at www.econstor.eu/bitstream/10419/77428/1/736082816.pdf.

Papaioannou, Elias. 'Needed: A European Institutional Union', in: *How to Fix Europe's Monetary Union. Views of Leading Economists*, eds. Richard Baldwin and Francesco Giavazzi (London: CEPR, 2016): 207–225.

Pappas, Takis S. 'Why Greece Failed', *Journal of Democracy* 24 (2013): 31–45.

Pâris, Pierre and Wyplosz, Charles. 'PADRE 2.0:Politically Acceptable Debt Restructuring in the Eurozone', May 2014, available at graduateinstitute.ch/files/live/sites/iheid/files/sites/international_economics/shared/international_economics/prof_websites/wyplosz/Papers/PADRE%202.pdf/.

Pâris, Pierre and Wyplosz, Charles. 'PADRE. Politically Acceptable Debt Restructuring in the Eurozone', *Geneva Reports on the World Economy Special Report* No. 3, CEPR, January 2014, available at www.cepr.org/sites/default/files/geneva_reports/GenevaP252.pdf.

Parry, Simon. 'The True Cost of Your Cheap Clothes: Slave Wages for Bangladesh Factory Workers', *Post Magazine*, 31 March 2017, available at www.scmp.com/magazines/post-magazine/article/1970431/true-cost-your-cheap-clothes-slave-wages-bangladesh-factory.

Pauwelyn, Joost. 'Carbon Leakage Measures and Border Tax Adjustments under WTO Law', 21 March 2012, available at papers.ssrn.com/sol3/papers.cfm?abstract_id=2026879.

Peel, Quentin. 'German MPs Clash on Future of Eurozone', *Financial Times*, 15 December 2010, available at www.ft.com/content/bb9bea42-085f-11e0-8527-00144feabdc0?mhq5j=e2.

Persson, Torsten and Tabellini, Guido. 'Federal Fiscal Constitutions: Risk Sharing and Moral Hazard', *Econometrica* 64 (1996): 623–646.

Petmesidou, Maria and Guillén, Ana. '"Southern Style" National Health Services? Recent Reforms and Trends in Spain and Greece', *Social Policy and Administration* 42 (2008): 106–124.

Petri, Peter and Plummer, Michael. 'The Economic Effects of the Trans-Pacific Partnership: New Estimates', *Peterson Institute for International Economics Working Paper* No. 16–2, January 2016, available at piie.com/system/files/documents/wp16-2_0.pdf.

Petropoulos, Georgios. 'An Economic Review of the Collaborative Economy', *Bruegel Policy Contribution* No. 5/2017, 27 February 2017, available at bruegel.org/2017/02/an-economic-review-of-the-collaborative-economy/.

Phillips, Leigh. 'EU Ushers in "Silent Revolution" in Control of National Economic Policies', *EUObserver*, 16 March 2011, available at euobserver.com/institutional/31993.

Piattoni, Simona. *The Theory of Multi-level Governance: Conceptual, Empirical, and Normative Challenges* (Oxford: Oxford University Press, 2010).

Pierson, Paul. 'Coping with Permanent Austerity: Welfare State Restructuring in Affluent Democracies', in: *The New Politics of the Welfare State*, ed. Paul Pierson (New York: Oxford University Press, 2001): 410–456.

'From Expansion to Austerity. The New Politics of Taxing and Spending', in: *Seeking the Center: Politics and Policymaking at the New Century*, eds. Martin A. Levin, Marc K. Landy and Martin Shapiro (Washington, DC: Georgetown University Press, 2001): 54–80.

'The Path to European Integration: A Historical Institutionalist Analysis', *Comparative Political Studies* 29 (1996): 123–163.

'Irresistible Forces, Immovable Objects: Post-Industrial Welfare States Confront Permanent Austerity', *Journal of European Social Policy* 5 (1998): 539–560.

Pill, Huw. 'The ECB Can't Substitute for Periphery Financial Reform', *The Economist Free Exchange*, 20 May 2013, available at www.economist.com/blogs/freeexchange/2013/05/european- central-bank-5.

Pisani-Ferry, Jean. 'Only One Bed for Two Dreams: A Critical Retrospective on the Debate over the Economic Governance of the Euro Area', *Journal of Common Market Studies* 44 (2006): 823–844.

The Euro Crisis and Its Aftermath (New York: Oxford University Press, 2014).

Pisani-Ferry, Jean and Wolff, Guntram. 'Propping up Europe?', *Bruegel Policy Contribution* No. 2012/07, 23 April 2012, available at bruegel.org/2012/04/propping-up-europe/.

Pisani-Ferry, Jean, Sapir, André and Wolff, Guntram. 'EU-IMF Assistance to Euro Area Countries: An Early Assessment', *Bruegel Blueprint Series* No. 19/2013, 16 June 2013, available at bruegel.org/2013/06/eu-imf-assistance-to-euro-area-countries-an-early-assessment/.

Pisani-Ferry, Jean, Vihriälä, Erkki and Wolff, Guntram. 'Options for a Euro-area Fiscal Capacity', *Bruegel Policy Contribution* No. 2013/01, 10 January 2013, available at bruegel.org/2013/01/options-for-a-euro-area-fiscal-capacity/.

Plucinska, Joanna, Posaner, Joshua and Heath, Ryan. 'Uber Case on Hold over Le Pen Fears', *Politico*, 23 November 2016, available at www.politico.eu/pro/uber-complaint-falls-into-jean-claude-junckers-black-hole/.

Poiares Maduro, Miguel. 'A New Governance for the European Union and the Euro: Democracy and Justice', RSCAS Policy Paper No. 2012/11, 30 August 2012.

Pollack, Mark A. *The Engines of European Integration: Delegation, Agency, and Agenda Setting in the EU* (Oxford: Oxford University Press, 2003).

Pomfret, Richard. *International Trade: Theory, Evidence and Policy* (New Jersey, London, Singapore, Beijing, Shanghai, Hong Kong, Taipei, Chennai, Tokyo: World Scientific Publishing, 2016).

Pop, Luana. 'The Decoupling of Social Policy Reforms in Romania', *Social Policy & Administration* 47 (2013): 161–181.

Popper, Helen. 'The Erosion of Greece's Future', *Politico*, 13 July 2015, available at www.politico.eu/article/greece-future-youth-unemployment-grexit-crisis-eurozone/.

Proctor, Charles. 'The Future of the Euro – What Happens if a Member State Leaves?', *European Business Law Review* 17 (2006): 909–937.

Prosser, Thomas. 'Economic Union without Social Union: The Strange Case of the European Social Dialogue', *Journal of European Social Policy* 26 (2016): 460–472.

Puntscher Riekmann, Sonja and Wydra, Doris. 'Representation in the European State of Emergency: Parliaments against Governments?', *Journal of European Integration* 35 (2013): 565–582.

Putnam, Robert. 'Diplomacy and Domestic Politics: The Logic of Two-level Games', *International Organization* 42 (1988): 427–460.

Quaglia, Lucia, Howarth, David and Liebe, Moritz. 'The Political Economy of European Capital Markets Union', *Journal of Common Market Studies*, 54 (2016): 185–203.

Raines, Thomas, Goodwin, Matthew and Cutts, David. 'The Future of Europe. Comparing Public and Elite Attitudes', Chatham House, June 2017, available at www.chathamhouse.org/sites/files/chathamhouse/publications/research/2017-06-20-future-europe-attitudes-raines-goodwin-cutts-final.pdf.

Rainforest Action Network. 'The Human Cost of Conflict Palm Oil', 2016, available at d3n8a8pro7vhmx.cloudfront.net/rainforestactionnetwork/pages/15889/attachments/original/1467043668/The_Human_Cost_of_Conflict_Palm_Oil_RAN.pdf?1467043668.

Raudla, Ringa and Kattel, Rainer. 'Why Did Estonia Choose Fiscal Retrenchment after the 2008 Crisis?', *Journal of Public Policy* 31 (2011): 163–186.

Raymond, Robert. 'From the Maastricht Treaty to the Euro: The Role of the EMI', in: *Progress through Crisis? Proceedings of the Conference for the 20th Anniversary of the Establishment of the European Monetary Institute*, eds. Ivo Maes and Frank Moss (Frankfurt am Main: ECB, 2014): 71–77.

Reinhart Carmen M. and Rogoff, Kenneth S. 'Growth in a Time of Debt', *American Economic Review* 100 (2010): 573–578.

Reinhart, Carmen M. and Rogoff, Kenneth S. *This Time Is Different – Eight Centuries of Financial Folly* (Princeton, NJ: Princeton University Press, 2010).

Repasi, René. 'Legal Options and Limits for the Establishment of a European Unemployment Benefit Scheme', January 2017, available at ec.europa.eu/social/BlobServlet?docId=16886&langId=en.

Reuters. 'Italy's Renzi to Tell Germany to Accept Greece Deal', 12 July 2015, available at www.reuters.com/article/us-eurozone-greece-renzi-idUSKCN0PM08320150712.

Reynolds, Stephanie. 'Explaining the Constitutional Drivers behind a Perceived Judicial Preference for Free Movement over Fundamental Rights', *Common Market Law Review* 53 (2016): 643–677.

Ricardo, David. *On the Principles of Political Economy and Taxation* (London: John Murray, 1817).

Rinaldi, David and Núñez Ferrer, Jorge. 'The European Fund for Strategic Investments as a New Type of Budgetary Instrument', *CEPS Research Report* No. 2017/07, 5 April 2017, available at www.ceps.eu/publications/european-fund-strategic-investments-new-type-budgetary-instrument.

Ritleng, Dominique, ed. *Independence and Legitimacy in the Institutional System of the European Union* (Oxford: Oxford University Press, 2016).

Roberts, Alasdair. '"An Ungovernable Anarchy": The United States' Response to Depression and Default, 1837–1848', *Intereconomics* 45 (2010): 196–202.

Rocholl, Jörg and Stahmer, Axel. 'Where Did the Greek Bailout Money Go?', *ESMT White Paper* No. WP–16–02, 2016.

Rodríguez-Pose, Andrés. 'Do Institutions Matter for Regional Development?', *Regional Studies* 47 (2013): 1034–1047.

Rodrik, Dani. 'The Rush to Free Trade in the Developing World: Why So Late? Why Now? Will It Last?', *NBER Working Paper* No. 3947, January 1992, available at www.nber.org/papers/w3947.pdf.

Has Globalization Gone Too Far? (Washington, DC: Peterson Institute for International Economics, 1997).

'Why Do More Open Economies Have Bigger Governments?', *Journal of Political Economy* 106 (1998): 997–1032.

'Don't Cry over Dead Trade Agreements', *Project Syndicate*, 8 December 2016, available at www.project-syndicate.org/commentary/no-mourning-dead-trade-agreements-by-dani-rodrik-2016-12.

The Globalization Paradox: Democracy and the Future of the World Economy (New York: Norton, 2012).

Rogelj, Joeri et al. 'Paris Agreement Climate Proposals Need a Boost to Keep Warming Well below 2°C', *Nature* (2016): 631–639.

Ross, Mark and Edwards, Chris. 'In New Zealand, Farmers Don't Want Subsidies', *Huffington Post*, 16 September 2012, available at www.huffingtonpost.com/mark-ross/farm-subsidies-new-zealand_b_1680259.html.

Roundtable on Sustainable Palm Oil Certification. Assessment Report, 2012, available at www.rspo.org/sites/default/files/PT_Adei_Plantation_RSPO_Assessment_Report__Final2_-8.pdf.

Roundtable on Sustainable Palm Oil. Impact Report 2016, available at www.rspo.org/key-documents/impact-reports.

Rueda, David. *Social Democracy Inside Out: Partisanship and Labour Market Policy in Industrialised Democracies* (Oxford: Oxford University Press, 2007).

Ruffert, Matthias. 'The European Debt Crisis and European Union Law', *Common Market Law Review* 48 (2011): 1777–1805.

Rute Cardoso, Ana and Portela, Miguel. 'Micro Foundations for Wage Flexibility: Wage Insurance at the Firm Level', *The Scandinavian Journal of Economics* 111 (2009): 29–50.

Sabel, Charles F. and Zeitlin, Jonathan, eds. *Experimentalist Governance in the European Union* (Oxford: Oxford University Press, 2012).

Sachs, Jeffrey. 'Institutions Matter, but Not for Everything', *Finance and Development* 40 (2003): 38–41, available at www.imf.org/external/pubs/ft/fandd/2003/06/.

Safi, Michael. 'Bangladesh Garment Factories Sack Hundreds after Pay Protests', *Guardian*, 27 December 2016, available at www.theguardian.com/world/2016/dec/27/bangladesh-garment-factories-sack-hundreds-after-pay-protests.

Safire, William. 'On Language: Third Rail', *The New York Times*, 18 February 2007, available at www.nytimes.com/2007/02/18/magazine/18wwlnsafire.t.html.

Salomon, Margot E. 'Of Austerity, Human Rights and International Institutions', *European Law Journal* 21 (2015): 521–545.

Samuelson, Paul A. 'Where Ricardo and Mill Rebut and Confirm Arguments of Mainstream Economists Supporting Globalization', *Journal of Economic Perspectives* 18 (2004): 135–146.

Sandholtz, Wayne and Zysman, John. '1992: Recasting the European Bargain', *World Politics* 42 (1989): 95–128.

Sandrey, Ron and Reynolds, Russell, eds. *Farming without Subsidies: New Zealand's Recent Experience* (Wellington: GP Books, 1990).

Sapir, André et al. 'An Agenda for a Growing Europe. Making the EU Economic System Deliver', July 2003, available at cejm.univ-rennes.eu/digitalAssets/24/24407_sapirreport.pdf.

Sapir, André and Wolff, Guntram. 'Euro-area Governance: What to Reform and How to Do It', *Bruegel Policy Brief* No. 2015/01, February 2015, available at bruegel.org/2015/02/euro-area-governance-what-to-reform-and-how-to-do-it/.

Sapir, André and Wolff, Guntram. 'The Neglected Side of Banking Union: Reshaping Europe's Financial System', Note presented at the informal ECOFIN 14 September 2013, Vilnius, available at bruegel.org/wp-content/uploads/imported/publications/20130913SapirWolff_final_.pdf.

Sauter, Wolf. 'Proportionality in EU Law: A Balancing Act?', *Cambridge Yearbook of European Legal Studies* 15 (2013): 439–466.

Scarth, William. *Macroeconomics: The Development of Modern Methods for Policy Analysis* (Cheltenham: Edward Elgar Publishing, 2014).

Scharpf, Fritz. 'Legitimacy in the Multilevel European Polity', *European Political Science Review* 1 (2009): 173–204.

Scharpf, Fritz 'The Asymmetry of European Integration, or Why the EU Cannot Be a "Social Market Economy"', *Socio-Economic Review* 8 (2010): 211–250.

Scharpf, Fritz. 'Monetary Union, Fiscal Crisis and the Preemption of Democracy', *MPIfG Discussion Paper* No. 11/11, July 2011, available at www.mpifg.de/pu/mpifg_dp/dp11-11.pdf.

'Perpetual Momentum: Directed and Unconstrained?', *Journal of European Public Policy* 19 (2012): 127–139.

Schmidt, Susanne. *Mutual Recognition as a New Mode of Governance* (London: Routledge, 2013).

Schmidt, Sophie. 'From Scarcity to Abundance: Growing the Overall Transportation Pie', *Medium*, 12 January 2016, available at medium.com/uber-under-the-hood/from-scarcity-to-abundance-growing-the-overall-pie-by-sophie-schmidt-a2e5a24bbc71.

Schnyder, Gerhard. 'Like a Phoenix from the Ashes? Reassessing the Transformation of the Swedish Political Economy Since the 1970s', *Journal of European Public Policy* 19 (2012): 1126–1145.

Schuknecht, Ludger et al. 'The Stability and Growth Pact: Crisis and Reform', *ECB Occasional Paper Series* No. 129, September 2011, available at pdfs.semanticscholar.org/3975/f02101490ea78caec8cffbaaf8b3017a7a59.pdf.

Scott, Hal S. 'When the Euro Falls Apart – A Sequel', *Harvard Public Law Working Paper* No. 12-16, 31 January 2012, available at papers.ssrn.com/sol3/papers.cfm?abstract_id=1998356.

Scott, Robert and Jiang, Xiao. 'Unilateral Grant of Market Economy Status to China Would Put Millions of EU Jobs at Risk', *Economic Policy Institute Briefing Paper* No. 407, 18 September 2015, available at www.epi.org/publication/eu-jobs-at-risk/.

Seikel, Daniel. 'Flexible Austerity and Supranational Autonomy. The Reformed Excessive Deficit Procedure and the Asymmetry between Liberalization and Social Regulation in the EU', *Journal of Common Market Studies*, 54 (2016): 1398–1416.

Sheve, Kenneth and Slaughter, Matthew. 'Economic Insecurity and the Globalization of Production', *American Journal of Political Science* 48 (2004): 662–674.

Shuster, Simon. 'Germany Finds Itself Cast as the Villain in Greek Drama', *The Time*, 15 July 2015, available at time.com/3959164/germany-greece-bailout-deal-athens-merkel/.

Sigmalive. 'We Are a Rule-based Monetary Union: Dijsselbloem', 13 July 2015, available at www.sigmalive.com/en/news/greece/132105/we-are-a-rulebased-monetary-union-dijsselbloem.

Simon, Frédéric. 'French to Revive Sarkozy's EU Carbon Tariff Idea', *Euractiv*, 18 May 2012, available at www.euractiv.com/section/climate-environment/news/french-to-revive-sarkozy-s-eu-carbon-tariff-idea/.

Sindbjerg Martinsen, Dorte and Vrangbæk, Karsten. 'The Europeanization of Health Care Governance: Implementing the Market Imperatives of Europe', *Public Administration* 86 (2008): 169–184.

Single Resolution Board. 'The SRB Will Not Take Resolution Action in Relation to Banca Popolare di Vicenza and Veneto Banca', 23 June 2017, available at srb.europa.eu/en/node/341.

Sinn, Hans-Werner. 'Responsibility of States and Central Banks in the Euro Crisis', Expert report commissioned by the German Constitutional Court, Second Senate, Session of 11 and 12 June 2013, available at www.cesifo-group.de/portal/page/portal/DocBase_Content/ZS/ZS-CESifo_Forum/zs-for-2014/zs-for-2014-1/forum1-14-1.pdf.

The Euro Trap: On Bursting Bubbles, Budgets, and Beliefs (New York: Oxford University Press, 2014).

Sirletti, Sonia and Weber, Alexander. 'Italy Commits $19 Billion for Veneto Banks in Biggest Rescue', 25 June 2017, available at www.bloomberg.com/news/articles/2017-06-25/italy-mobilizes-up-to-19-billion-to-keep-veneto-banks-afloat.

Smith-Meyer, Bjarke. 'Commission Decides Against Fining Portugal, Spain for Budget Breaches', *Politico*, 27 July 2016, available at www.politico.eu/pro/commission-decides-against-fining-portugal-spain-for-budget-breaches/.

Smits, René. 'The European Constitution and EMU: An Appraisal', *Common Market Law Review* 42 (2005): 425–468.

Snell, Jukka. 'The Trilemma of European Economic and Monetary Integration, and Its Consequences', *European Law Journal* 22 (2016): 157–179.

Snowdon, Brian and Vane, Howard R. *Modern Macroeconomics: Its Origins, Development and Current State* (Cheltenham; Northampton, MA: Edward Elgar Publishing, 2005).

Sobhan, Zafar. 'Progress and Globalization in Bangladesh: The Tazreen Fashions Garment Factory Fire', *VICE*, 2 December 2012, available at www.vice.com/read/progress-and-globalization-in-bangladesh-the-tazreen-fashions-garment-factory-fire.

Sommers, Jeffrey and Woolfson, Charles, eds. *The Contradictions of Austerity: The Socio-Economic Costs of the Neoliberal Baltic Model* (Abingdon: Routledge, 2014).

Sörensen, Bent E. et al. 'Home Bias and International Risk Sharing: Twin Puzzles Separated at Birth', *Journal of International Money and Finance* 26 (2007): 587–605.

Sorrentino, Alessandro and Henke, Roberto, eds. *The Common Agricultural Policy after the Fischler Reform: National Implementations, Impact Assessment and the Agenda for Future Reforms* (London: Routledge, 2016).

Sotiropoulos, Dimitri. 'Usages of "Europe" in Welfare Policies in Greece, 1981–2010', in: *The EU and the Domestic Politics of Welfare State Reforms*, eds. Paolo R. Graziano, Sophie Jacquot and Bruno Palier (London: Palgrave Macmillan, 2011): 121–147.

Spaventa, Eleanor. 'From Gebhard to Carpenter: Towards a (Non-)Economic European Constitution', *Common Market Law Review* 41 (2004): 743–773.

Speciale, Alessandro. 'Draghi Says Euro Is Irreversible as Le Pen Urges French Exit', *Bloomberg Markets*, 6 February 2017, available at www.bloomberg.com/news/articles/2017-02-06/draghi-says-euro-is-irreversible-as-le-pen-urges-french-exit.

Spiegel, Peter. 'Varoufakis Unplugged: The London Call Transcript', *Financial Times*, 27 July 2015, available at blogs.ft.com/brusselsblog/2015/07/27/varoufakis-unplugged-the-london-call-transcript/.

Spillane, Chris. 'Copyright Conundrum: Tweeting This May Cost You', *Politico*, 26 October 2016, available at www.politico.eu/pro/copyright-conundrum-tweeting-this-may-cost-you/.

Standaard. 'Nieuwe Regels voor Airbnb in Brussel Goedgekeurd', 29 March 2016, available at www.standaard.be/cnt/dmf20160329_02207907.

Steinbach, Armin. *Economic Policy Coordination in the Euro Area* (London and New York: Routledge, 2014).

'The "Haircut" of Public Creditors under EU Law', *European Constitutional Law Review* 12 (2016): 223–239.

'The Lender of Last Resort in the Eurozone', *Common Market Law Review* 53 (2016): 361–384.

Steinhauser, Gabriele. 'Schäuble's Timeout Plan for Greece Was "Courageous," Says Slovak Minister', *The Wall Street Journal*, 15 July 2015, available at blogs.wsj.com/brussels/2015/07/15/schaubles-timeout-plan-for-greece-was-courageous-says-slovak-minister/.

Steinmo, Sven. 'Governing as an Engineering Problem: The Political Economy of Swedish Success', in: *Politics in the Age of Austerity*, eds. Wolfgang Streeck and Armin Schafer (Cambridge: Polity Press, 2013): 84–107.

Stelkens, Ulrich, Weiß, Wolfgang and Mirschberger, Michael. *The Implementation of the EU Services Directive: Transposition, Problems and Strategies* (The Hague: TMC Asser Press by Springer, 2012).

Stella, Gian Antonio and Rizzo, Sergio. *Se Muore il Sud* (Milano: Feltrinelli, 2013).

Stern, Robert, ed. 'Comparative Advantage, Growth, and the Gains from Trade and Globalization: A Festschrift in Honor of Alan V. Deardorff', *World Scientific Studies in International Economics* 16 (2011).

Stiglitz, Joseph. 'Globalization and Its New Discontents', *Project Syndicate*, 5 August 2016, available at www.project-syndicate.org/commentary/globalization-new-discontents-by-joseph-e–stiglitz-2016-08.

The Euro: How a Common Currency Threatens the Future of Europe (New York: W. W. Norton, 2016).

'What America's Economy Needs from Trump', *Project Syndicate*, 13 November 2016, available at www.project-syndicate.org/commentary/trump-agenda-america-economy-by-joseph-e–stiglitz-2016-11.

Stokes, Bruce, Wike, Richard and Manevich, Dorothy. 'Post-Brexit, Europeans More Favorable toward EU', Pew Research, 15 June 2017, available at assets.pewresearch.org/wp-content/uploads/sites/2/2017/06/19101129/Pew-Research-Center_Post-Brexit-European-Views-of-EU_Full-Report_06.15.2017.pdf.

Streeck, Wolfgang. *Buying Time: The Delayed Crisis of Democratic Capitalism* (London: Verso Books, 2014).

Re-Forming Capitalism. Institutional Change in the German Political Economy (Oxford: Oxford University Press, 2010).

Streeck, Wolfgang and Elsässer, Lea. 'Monetary Disunion: The Domestic Politics of Euroland', *Journal of European Public Policy* 23 (2016): 1–24.

Streeck, Wolfgang and Mertens, Daniel. 'Fiscal Austerity and Public Investment: Is the Possible the Enemy of the Necessary?', *MPIfG Discussion Paper* No. 11/12.

'Public Finance and the Decline of State Capacity in Democratic Capitalism', in: *Politics in the Age of Austerity*, eds. Wolfgang Streeck and Armin Schafer (Cambridge: Polity Press, 2013): 26–58.

Strøby Jensen, Carsten. 'Neofunctionalism', in: *European Union Politics*, eds. Michelle Cini and Nieves Pérez-Solórzano Borragán (Oxford: Oxford University Press, 2016): 53–64.

Stupp, Catherine. 'Controversial EU Labour Rules Tackle Truck Drivers' Pay and Working Conditions', *Euractiv*, 31 May 2017, available at www.euractiv.com/section/road-safety/news/controversial-eu-labour-rules-tackle-truck-drivers-pay-and-working-conditions/.

Suranovic, Steven. 'The Ricardian Theory of Comparative Advantage. International Trade: Theory and Policy', *The International Economics Study Centre*, 2007, available at catalog.flatworldknowledge.com/bookhub/reader/28.

Swank, Duane. 'Social Democratic Welfare States in a Global Economy: Scandinavia in a Comparative Perspective', in: *Globalization, Europeanization, and the End of Scandinavian Social Democracy?*, ed. Robert Geyer (London: Macmillan, 1998): 85–138.

Swann, Dennis. *The Economics of Europe: From Common Market to European Union* (London: Penguin, 2000).

Swenson, Peter A. *Capitalists against Markets: The Making of Labor Markets and Welfare States in the United States and Sweden* (New York: Oxford University Press, 2002).

Swinnen, Johan F. M., ed. *The Political Economy of the 2014–2020 Common Agricultural Policy. An Imperfect Storm* (Brussels: CEPS and London: Rowman and Littlefield International, 2015).

Tagaras, Harris. 'Règles Communautaires de Libre Circulation, Discriminations à Rebours et Situations Dites Purement Internes', *Mélanges en hommage à Michel Waelbroeck*, Volume II, Bruylant, 1999.

Tamesberger, Dennis, Leitgöb, Heinz and Bacher, Johann. 'How to Combat NEET? Evidence from Austria', *Intereconomics* 49 (2014): 221–227.

Task Force to the European Council, 'Strengthening Economic Governance in the EU', October 2010, available at www.consilium.europa.eu/uedocs/cms_data/docs/pressdata/en/ec/117236.pdf.

Telegraph. 'Ireland "Pushed into Bailout"', 18 June 2015, available at www.telegraph.co.uk/finance/economics/11683995/Ireland-pushed-into-bailout.html.

Terzi, Alessio. 'An Italian Job: The Need for Collective Wage Bargaining Reform', *Bruegel Policy Contribution* No. 2016/11, 6 July 2016, available at bruegel.org/2016/07/an-italian-job-the-need-for-collective-wage-bargaining-reform/.

'Reform Momentum and Its Impact on Greek Growth', *Bruegel Policy Contribution* No. 12/2015, 29 July 2015, available at bruegel.org/2015/07/reform-momentum-and-its-impact-on-greek-growth/.

Thelen, Kathleen. *Varieties of Liberalization: The New Politics of Social Solidarity* (New York: Cambridge University Press, 2014).

Thieffry, Gilles. 'The Not So Unthinkable – The Break-up of the European Monetary Union', *International Financial Law Review*, 1 July 2005, 15–17.

Thiele, Alexander. '(No) Haircut for Hellas? A Short and Critical Reply to Armin Steinbach, "The 'Haircut' of Public Creditors under EU Law", EuConst (2016) p. 223', *European Constitutional Law Review* 12 (2016): 520–537.

Thietmar of Merseburg. *Ottonian Germany: The Chronicon of Thietmar of Merseburg*, trans. and annot. by David A. Warner (Manchester: Manchester University Press, 2001).

Thirion, Gilles. 'European Fiscal Union: Economic Rationale and Design Challenges', *CEPS Working Document* No. 2017/01, 20 January 2017, available at www.ceps.eu/publications/european-fiscal-union-economic-rationale-and-design-challenges.

Thomadakis, Apostolos. 'How Close Are We to a Capital Markets Union?', *ECMI Commentary* No. 44, 17 March 2017, available at www.ceps.eu/publications/how-close-are-we-capital-markets-union.

Tinios, Platon. 'International Accounting Standards as Catalysts for Pension Reform: Greek Pensions and the Public/Private Boundary', *Journal of European Social Policy* 21 (2011): 164–177.

Toor, Amar. 'French Taxi Drivers Clash with Police in Anti-Uber Strike', *The Verge*, 26 January 2016, available at www.theverge.com/2016/1/26/10832204/french-taxi-uber-strike-paris-vtc.

Torrens, Robert. *Essay on the External Corn Trade* (London: Hatchard, 1815).

Trabandt, Mathias and Uhlig, Harald. 'How Do Laffer Curves Differ across Countries?' *NBER Working Paper* No. 17862, February 2012, available at www.nber.org/papers/w17862.

Transport&Environment. 'Europe Keeps Burning More Palm Oil in Its Diesel Cars and Trucks', November 2016, available at www.transportenvironment.org/sites/te/files/2016_11_Briefing_Palm_oil_use_continues_to_grow.pdf.

Transport & Environment. 'Globiom: The Basis for Biofuel Policy Post-2020', April 2016, available at www.transportenvironment.org/sites/te/files/publications/2016_04_TE_Globiom_paper_FINAL_0.pdf.

Transport & Environment. 'The EU Climate Leader Board', 28 March 2017, available at www.transportenvironment.org/publications/eu-climate-leader-board.

Trantidis, Aris. 'Clientelism and Economic Policy: Hybrid Characteristics of Collective Action in Greece', *Journal of European Public Policy* 23 (2016): 1460–1480.

Tryfonidou, Alina. 'Purely Internal Situations and Reverse Discrimination in a Citizens' Europe: Time to "Reverse" Reverse Discrimination?', in: *Issues in Social Policy: A New Agenda. Jean Monnet Seminar Series*, ed. Peter G. Xuereb (Valletta: Progress Press, 2009): 11–29.

Tuori, Kaarlo. 'The European Financial Crisis – Constitutional Aspects and Implications', *EUI Working Papers LAW* 28 (2012): available at cadmus.eui.eu/handle/1814/24301.

Turner, Zeke. 'Money Matters: A Capital Markets Union Primer', *Politico*, 27 June 2015, available at www.politico.eu/article/moving-money-a-capital-markets-union-primer/.

Türk, Alexander H. *Judicial Review in EU Law* (Cheltenham; Northamption, MA: Edward Elgar Publishing, 2010).

Vaccarino, Elena and Darvas, Zsolt. '"Social Dumping" and Posted Workers: A New Clash within the EU', *Bruegel Blog Post*, 7 March 2016, available at bruegel.org/2016/03/social-dumping-and-posted-workers-a-new-clash-within-the-eu/.

Valero, Jorge. 'Member States Limit New Flexibility Clauses in EU Fiscal Pact', *EurActiv*, 9 December 2015, available at www.euractiv.com/section/euro-finance/news/member-states-limit-new-flexibility-clauses-in-eu-fiscal-pact/.

'How to Become a Successful "Tech-nation" from Scratch', *Euractiv*, 26 February 2016, available at www.euractiv.com/section/digital/news/how-to-become-a-successful-tech-nation-from-scratch/.

'EU Banking Resolution Rules Pass Credibility Test with Banco Popular', Euractiv, 7 June 2017, available at www.euractiv.com/section/banking-union/news/eu-banking-resolution-rules-pass-credibility-test-with-banco-popular/.

'The Revolt of the Citizens', *Euractiv*, 9 June 2017, available at www.euractiv.com/section/all/news/the-brief-the-revolt-of-the-citizens/.

Valiante, Diego. 'Banking Union in a Single Currency Area: Evidence on Financial Fragmentation', *Journal of Financial Economic Policy* 7 (2015): 251–274.

'Europe's Untapped Capital Market: Rethinking Integration after the Great Financial Crisis', CEPS Paperback (London: Rowman & Littlefield International, 2016), available also at www.ceps.eu/publications/europe%E2%80%99s-untapped-capital-market-rethinking-integration-after-great-financial-crisis.

'Harmonising Insolvency Laws in the Euro Area. Rationale, Stocktaking and Challenges', *CEPS Special Report* No. 153, 1 December 2016, available at www.ceps.eu/publications/harmonising-insolvency-laws-euro-area-rationale-stocktaking-and-challenges.

Valin, Hugo et al. 'The Land Use Change Impact of Biofuels Consumed in the EU', study for the European Commission, 27 August 2015, available at ec.europa.eu/energy/sites/ener/files/documents/Final%20Report_GLOBIOM_publication.pdf.

Vandenbroucke, Frank et al. 'Institutional Moral Hazard in the Multi-Tiered Regulation of Unemployment and Social Assistance Benefits', *CEPS Special*

Report No. 137, 27 April 2016, available at www.ceps.eu/publications/institutional-moral-hazard-multi-tiered-regulation-unemployment-and-social-assistance.

Van Gerven, Minna. 'The Broad Tracks of Path Dependent Benefit Reforms. A Longitudinal Study of Social Benefit Reforms in Three European Countries, 1980–2006', 2008, available at pure.uvt.nl/ws/files/1032352/van_Gerven_tutkimuksia_100.pdf.

Van Kersbergen, Kees and Vis, Barbara. *Comparative Welfare State Politics: Development, Opportunities, and Reform* (New York: Cambridge University Press, 2014).

Van Leeuwen, Barend. 'The Doctor, the Patient, and EU Law: The Impact of Free Movement Law on Quality Standards in the Healthcare Sector', *European Law Review* 41 (2016): 638–654.

Van Oorschot, Wim. 'The Dutch Welfare State: Recent Trends and Challenges in Historical Perspective', *European Journal of Social Security* 8 (2006): 57–76.

Van Poeck, André. 'One Money and Sixteen Needs: Has the ECB's Monetary Policy Become More Balanced towards the Needs of the Member States?', *De Economist* 158 (2010): 43–60.

Van Reenen, John. 'Fiscal Consolidation: Too Much of a Good Thing?', *CEPR's Policy Portal*, 27 April 2012, available at www.voxeu.org/article/fiscal-consolidation-too-much-good-thing.

Van Reenen, John et al. 'The Economic Impact of ICT', study for the European Commission, DG INFSO, SMART N. 2007/0020, LSE Enterprise, 2010.

Van Rie, Tim and Marx, Ive. 'The European Union at Work? The European Employment Strategy from Crisis to Crisis', *Journal of Common Market Studies* 50 (2012): 335–356.

Van Rompuy, Herman, Barroso, José Manuel, Juncker, Jean-Claude and Draghi, Mario. 'Towards a Genuine Economic and Monetary Union', 5 December 2012, available at www.consilium.europa.eu/uedocs/cms_Data/docs/pressdata/en/ec/134069.pdf.

Varoufakis, Yanis. *The Global Minotaur: America, Europe and the Future of the Global Economy* (London, New York: Zed Books, 2011).

'A New Approach to Eurozone Sovereign Debt', *Project Syndicate*, 17 August 2015, available at www.project-syndicate.org/commentary/eurozone-sovereign-debt-solution-by-yanis-varoufakis-2015-08?barrier=accessreg.

Venn, Danielle. 'Eligibility Criteria for Unemployment Benefits: Quantitative Indicators for OECD and EU Countries', *OECD Social, Employment and Migration Working Papers* 131, 9 January 2012, available at www.oecd-ilibrary.org/social-issues-migration-health/eligibility-criteria-for-unemployment-benefits_5k9h43kgkvr4-en.

Veugelers, Reinhilde. 'The European Union's Growing Innovation Divide', *Bruegel Policy Contribution* No. 2016/06, 7 April 2016, available at bruegel.org/2016/04/the-european-unions-growing-innovation-divide/.

Vinocur, Nicholas. 'French PM Calls for Truce in Taxi-Uber War', *Politico*, 26 January 2016, available at www.politico.eu/article/france-braces-for-new-taxi-uber-war-road-uberpop/.

'How France's Emmanuel Macron Lost the Uber War', *Politico*, 10 February 2016, available at www.politico.eu/article/how-frances-emmanuel-macron-lost-the-uber-war.

Vitalis, Vangelis. 'Agricultural Subsidy Reform and Its Implications for Sustainable Development: The New Zealand Experience', *Environmental Sciences* 4 (2007): 21–40.

Von der Burchard, Hans and Hanke, Jakob. 'China Turns Trade Screws on German Cars', *Politico*, 30 May 2017, available at www.politico.eu/article/china-turns-screws-on-german-cars-to-swing-eu-trade-policy/.

Von Hagen, Jürgen. 'Common Pools – Why a European Fiscal Union Will Make Things Worse', *Bonn Journal of Economics* 1 (2012): 65–73.

Von Hayek, Friedrich August. 'The Economic Conditions of Interstate Federalism', in: *Individualism and Economic Order*, ed. Friedrich August von Hayek (Chicago: University of Chicago Press, 1948).

Wagstyl, Stefan and Jones, Claire. 'Germany Blames Mario Draghi for Rise of Rightwing AfD Party', *Financial Times*, 10 April 2016.

Wallis, John Joseph, Sylla, Richard E. and Grinath, Arthur. 'Sovereign Debt and Repudiation: The Emerging-market Debt Crisis in the US States, 1839–1843', *NBER Working Paper* No. 10753, September 2004, available at www.nber.org/papers/w10753.

Walter, Stefanie. *Financial Crises and the Politics of Macroeconomic Adjustments* (New York: Cambridge University Press, 2013).

Walters, Alan. *Sterling in Danger: The Economic Consequences of Pegged Exchange Rates* (London: Fontana/Collins, 1990).

Wang, Shaoguang. 'The Rise of the Regions: Fiscal Reform and the Decline of Central State Capacity in China', in: *The Waning of the Communist State: Economic Origins of Political Decline in China and Hungary*, ed. Andrew Walder (Berkeley; Los Angeles; Oxford: University of California Press, 1995): 87–113.

Weishaupt, Timo. 'A Silent Revolution? New Management Ideas and the Reinvention of European Public Employment Services', *Socio-Economic Review* 8 (2010): 461–486.

'Germany after a Decade of Social Democrats in Government: The End of the Continental Model?', *German Politics* 19 (2010): 105–122.

Werner, Pierre et al. 'Report to the Council and the Commission on the Realisation of Economic and Monetary Union in the Community', 1970, available at ec.europa.eu/economy_finance/publications/publication6142_en.pdf.

Whelan, Karl. 'The ECB's Role in Financial Assistance Programmes', June 2012, available at www.europarl.europa.eu/document/activities/cont/201207/20120705ATT48408/20120705ATT48408EN.pdf.

Whittaker, John. 'Intra-eurosystem Debts', Lancaster University Management School, 30 March 2011, available at ssrn.com/abstract=1836470.

Whittaker, Julie M. and Isaacs, Katelin P. 'Extending Unemployment Compensation Benefits during Recessions', *Congressional Research Service* No. RL34340, 2 May 2013, available at www.fas.org/sgp/crs/misc/RL 34340.pdf.

Wibbels, Erik. 'Bailouts, Budget Constraints, and Leviathans: Comparative Federalism and Lessons from the Early United States', *Comparative Political Studies* 36 (2003): 475–508.

Wikipedia. 'Uber Protests and Legal Actions', available at en.wikipedia.org/ wiki/Uber_protests_and_legal_actions.

Wildau, Gabriel. 'World Bank Redacts Report Critical of China Financial System', *Financial Times*, 3 July 2015, available at www.ft.com/content/ 23dcc148-2152-11e5-aa5a-398b2169cf79?mhq5j=e2.

Wilkinson, Michael A. 'The Specter of Authoritarian Liberalism: Reflections on the Constitutional Crisis of the European Union', *German Law Journal* 14 (2013): 527–560.

Wolf, Martin. 'What Was Spain Supposed to Have Done?', *Martin Wolf's Exchange*, *Financial Times Blogs*, 25 June 2012.

Wood, Philip R. *Principles of International Insolvency* (London: Sweet & Maxwell, 2007).

World Bank. 'World Bank Lending Helps Latvia Improve Social Safety Nets', 26 May 2011, www.worldbank.org/en/news/press-release/2011/05/26/ world-bank-lending-helps-latvia-improve-social-safety-nets.

World Trade Institute. 'TTIP and the EU Member States', University of Bern, January 2016.

Wyplosz, Charles. 'European Monetary Union: The Dark Sides of a Major Success', *Economic Policy* 21 (2006): 207–261.

'The Impossible Hope of an End to Austerity', *CEPR's Policy Portal*, 14 May 2012, available at voxeu.org/article/impossible-hope-end-austerity.

Yalcin, Erdal, Felbermayr, Gabriel and Sandkamp, Alexander. 'New Trade Rules for China? Opportunities and Threats for the EU', 2016, available at www.europarl.europa.eu/RegData/etudes/STUD/2016/535021/EXPO_ STU(2016)535021_EN.pdf.

Yap, James. 'Beyond "Don't Be Evil": The European Union GSP+ Trade Preference Scheme and the Incentivisation of the Sri Lankan Garment Industry to Foster Human Rights', *European Law Journal* 19 (2013): 283–301.

Yerkes, Mara and van der Veen, Romke. 'Crisis and Welfare State in the Netherlands', *Social Policy & Administration* 45 (2011): 430–444.

Yiangou, Jonathan, O'Keeffe Mícheál and Glöckler, Gabriel. '"Tough Love": How the ECB's Monetary Financing Prohibition Pushes Deeper Euro Area Integration', *Journal of European Integration* 35 (2013): 223–237.

Zachmann, Georg. 'Making Low-Carbon Technology Support Smarter', *Bruegel Policy Brief* No. 2015/02, 18 August 2015, available bruegel.org/2015/08/ making-low-carbon-technology-support-smarter/.

Zahariadis, Nikolaos. 'Leading Reform Amidst Transboundary Crises: Lessons From Greece', *Public Administration* 91 (2013): 648–662.

'The Politics of Risk-sharing: Fiscal Federalism and the Greek Debt Crisis', *Journal of European Integration* 35 (2013): 277.

Zahn, Rebecca. 'The Regulation of Healthcare in the European Union: Member States' Discretion or a Widening of EU Law? Femarbel and Ottica New Line', *Common Market Law Review* 51 (2014): 1521–1538.

Zuleeg, Fabian. 'Can the Eurozone's Economic Governance Combine Political Accountability, Legitimacy and Effectiveness?', *EPC Discussion Paper*, 1 September 2015, available at www.epc.eu/pub_details.php?cat_id=17&pub_id=5870&year=2015.

Index